History —of— Seneca County

◇ OHIO ◇

FROM THE CLOSE OF THE
REVOLUTIONARY WAR
TO JULY, 1880

EMBRASSING MANY PERSONAL SKETCHES OF PIONEERS, ANECDOTES,
AND FAITHFUL DESCRIPTIONS OF EVENTS PERTAINING TO THE
ORGANIZATION OF THE COUNTY AND ITS PROGRESS

William Lang

HERITAGE BOOKS
2010

HERITAGE BOOKS
AN IMPRINT OF HERITAGE BOOKS, INC.

Books, CDs, and more—Worldwide

For our listing of thousands of titles see our website
at
www.HeritageBooks.com

A Facsimile Reprint
Published 2010 by
HERITAGE BOOKS, INC.
Publishing Division
100 Railroad Ave. #104
Westminster, Maryland 21157

Index Copyright © 1999 Heritage Books, Inc.

Entered according to an Act of Congress, 1880,
by William Lang, in the Office of the
Librarian of Congress, at Washington, D.C.

— Publisher's Notice —
In reprints such as this, it is often not possible to remove blemishes from the original. We feel the contents of this book warrant its reissue despite these blemishes and hope you will agree and read it with pleasure.

International Standard Book Numbers
Paperbound: 978-0-7884-1387-2
Clothbound: 978-0-7884-8332-5

Dedication:

TO THE YOUNG MEN AND YOUNG WOMEN OF SENECA COUNTY,
CHILDREN AND GRAND-CHILDREN
OF THE PIONEER FATHERS AND MOTHERS,

THIS BOOK IS KINDLY ASCRIBED,

WITH THE HOPE THAT THE PERUSAL OF ITS PAGES
MAY TEND TO INSPIRE NEW LOVE AND VENERATION
FOR THAT NOBLE OLD BAND OF MEN AND WOMEN,
NOW RAPIDLY PASSING AWAY,
AND TO APPRECIATE PROPERLY THE RICH LEGACY
THEIR VALOR HAS BEQUEATHED.

BY THE AUTHOR.

PREFACE.

SOME fifteen years ago I cherished a desire to write a history of Seneca county. Want of confidence in my ability to do justice to the subject, conflicted with this desire for many years, until finally, about one year ago, at the solicitation of friends, I commenced the work in earnest and prosecuted it with such ability and industry as I had at my command.

I had collected material for this purpose many years, without regard to order. My task required close application and patient labor, but I found consolation in the thought that I was engaged in a work of gratitude and paying a debt of friendship I owed to the memories of the generous and noble men and women who, nearly fifty years ago, stretched the hand of welcome to an exiled boy in a strange land and among strangers. Thus my work became a source of pleasure, and now, that I am about presenting it to the public, I wish to add that nothing has been set down in malice. Truth requires that the shady side shall accompany the light, else the picture be deficient.

I have faithfully endeavored to avoid errors, but have no doubt some may be found, therefore claim no perfection for the work.

Having lived in Seneca county from my boyhood, and taken an active part in public life, I became identified with many affairs in the progress of events; and since I found it necessary to connect my own name with some of the scenes I describe, the reader will please excuse the liberty I took, for if I know my own nature, there is very little egotism in its make-up.

I wrote in a conversational way, and with the same freedom with which I would talk to a friend.

My intention was to pass before the mind's eye of the reader, a true and faithful panorama of Seneca county, from the time she broke her bands of "forest wild" to July, 1880; and to do justice to the memory of the men and women who figured upon the stage of her progress during that time. This was the height of my ambition, and the reader is left to himself to judge whether I have succeeded. He will, I am sure, give me credit at least, for presenting to him a variety of subjects in a plain, comprehensible way, without resorting to etherial flights and stretching after high-sounding terms to express a generous thought.

Many biographical sketches are scattered through the work—pen pictures of men and women, as they appeared to me. These may also not be perfect, but some of them will seem natural to the reader that knew the persons.

It is a source of regret to me that some people in Seneca county, who had it in their power to furnish material for this enterprise, took no interest in it, and in consequence, many valuable points may have been overlooked; but I take great pleasure in expressing gratitude to all who were so friendly as to aid me in my researches.

My especial thanks are hereby tendered to Dr. C. G. Comegys, of Cincinnati, a son-in-law, and to Miss Diathea Madison Tiffin, of Chillicothe, a daughter, of Governor Tiffin, for valuable material found in the life of the illustrious Governor; and to the gentlemanly editors of the newspapers of Tiffin; to the several county officers, who have so willingly and courteously assisted me in searching records.

To Mrs. Sally Ingham, to the Rev. Joseph Bever, Mr. Charles W. Foster, Elder Lewis Seitz, Dr. B. Williams, Esquire Kelley, Dr. J. W. Crawford, Dr. J. C. Myers, Hon. James Purdy, of Mansfield, Mr. Luther A. Hall, Mr. N. L. Brewer, Mr. D. V. Flummerfelt, Mr. Mark A. Harris, Judge Hugh Welsh, Mrs. T. Stanley, Mrs. R. R. McMeens, J. H. Pittenger, Esq., Father Evrard, Father Healey, Rev. J. H. Good, D. D., Mrs. Geo. Strausbaugh, Dr. A. A. Rawson, of Iowa, Judge Pillars, Governor Charles Foster, and to many others, I tender my sincere thanks.

Proper credit has been given to the authorities I consulted, but if any omissions have occurred, I desire to make the proper apology here.

Conscious of having pursued and prosecuted this labor with none other than the best of motives, to preserve from the tooth of time, for a while, scenes and events that helped to make up the history of this good old county of ours; regretting that some abler pen did not take up the task; knowing full well also that my shortcomings will pass through the usual ordeal of criticism, I can only fall back upon my old motto that has guided my life, and I fear, may at times, have given unintentional offence:

> "Purity of motive and nobility of mind
> Shall rarely condescend
> To prove its rights and prate of wrongs to others;
> And it shall be small care
> To the high and happy conscience
> What jealous friends, and envious foes,
> Or common fools may judge."

TIFFIN, O., July 1, 1880.   W. LANG.

CONTENTS.

CHAPTER I.
BATTLE OF FORT STEPHENSON- HARRISON AND CROGHAN—FORT SENECA—WIPINGSTICK—PERRY'S VICTORY ON LAKE ERIE—BATTLE OF THE THAMES—DEATH OF TECUMSEH.

CHAPTER II.
FOURTH OF JULY CELEBRATION ON PUT-IN-BAY—MONUMENTAL ASSOCIATION LAYING OF THE CORNER STONE—SPEECHES OF EL. COOK AND DR. PARSONS.

CHAPTER III.
PEACE—TREATIES—RESERVATIONS—CESSIONS—EMIGRANTS ARRIVING—WARS BETWEEN THE WYANDOTS AND SENECAS—SPEECH OF LOGAN AND HIS DEATH.

CHAPTER IV.
HARRISON IN COUNCIL WITH THE INDIANS — CROGHAN'S DEFENSE OF HARRISON—BLUE JACKET AND BEAVER- BLUE JACKET'S DEATH—ARMY ROADS- THOMAS CORWIN—JAMES MONTGOMERY—JAMES T. WORTHINGTON.

CHAPTER V.
SPEECH OF ISAAC I. DUMOND—SAMUEL CROWELL'S CONTRIBUTION—THE DOG-DANCE-SOW-DOWS-KY.

CHAPTER VI.
EARLY SETTLERS - THE HARRIS FAMILY—ROBBERY OF SPICER—THE BRUSH-DAM—PETER PORK—JACOB KNISELY AND CROW—GOING TO MILL—KILLING WITCHES—THE FIRST HORSE-RACE.

CHAPTER VII.
THE SENECA CHIEF PRESENTS THE GOVERNOR OF CANADA WITH 954 AMERICAN SCALPS—TALL CHIEF—THE TUQUANIAS—KILLING THE SQUAW OF GEORGE WASHINGTON—JUDGE HULBURT—CALEB RICE—BENJ. CULVER—REV. JAMES FINLAY—CAPT. JOSEPH- MRS. INGHAM.

CHAPTER VIII.
DEATH OF COMSTOCK—SENECA STEEL—EXECUTION OF SENECA JOHN—TRIAL AND DISCHARGE OF COONSTICK — JUDGE HIGGIN'S DECISION — JUDGE BIRCHARD'S STATEMENT—BENJAMIN F. WARNER—HARD HICKORY AND HIS DEATH—IMMIGRATION OF THE SENECAS TO THE NEOSHA AND COW-SKIN RIVERS—CHARLIEU—THE GIRTYS—THE DEATH OF DRAKE.

8   CONTENTS.

CHAPTER IX.

ROCKY CREEK—FORT BALL—COL. BALL ATTACKED BY INDIANS—ERASTUS BOWE—OAKLEY—NEW FORT BALL—FIRST POST OFFICE — MILLS—ARMSTRONG AND McCULLOCH SECTIONS—EARLY SETTLERS IN FORT BALL—LOCATION OF THE COUNTY SEAT—HUNTER'S MILL—EARLY SETTLERS IN THOMPSON, ON HONEY CREEK AND ROCKY CREEK—MELMORE—COL. KILBOURNE—HARRY BLACKMAN'S CORNERS--ANCIENT FORTIFICATIONS—COL. RICHARD JACQUA.

CHAPTER X.

FIRST MERIDIAN—BASE LINE—TOWNSHIPS—RANGES--SECTIONS—GENERAL SURVEY—ORGANIZATION OF SENECA COUNTY—THE OLD COURT HOUSE—FIRST COURT—FIRST ELECTION—FIRST MEETING OF THE BOARD OF COUNTY COMMISSIONERS—APPOINTMENT OF OFFICERS—BUILDING THE FIRST JAIL—RUDOLPHUS DICKINSON—SALE OF THE RESERVATIONS.

CHAPTER XI.

JESSE SPENCER—COUNTY ROAD FROM FORT BALL TO TIFFIN—WOLF SCALPS—ORGANIZING TOWNSHIPS IN CRAWFORD COUNTY—BUILDING THE FIRST BRIDGE—FIRST KILN OF BRICKS—DAVID BISHOP—ORGANIZING ALL THE TOWNSHIPS—HISTORY OF THE BUILDING, THE BURNING AND THE REBUILDING OF THE COURT HOUSE—BUILDING THE STONE JAIL—THE NEW JAIL.

CHAPTER XII.

THE WOOD-CHOPPER—HOW TO BUILD A CABIN—THE DIFFERENCE BETWEEN THE SETTLERS—THEIR BENEVOLENCE AND HOSPITALITY — PIONEER GIRLS — RUSTIC FURNITURE — THE HOMINY BLOCK — THE HANDMILL—GOING TO MEETING-INDIAN VISITORS—NATURAL FANNING MILL—"THE LIFE IN THE WOODS FOR ME"—HOME-MADE CLOTH—YOUNG AMERICA.

CHAPTER XIII.

GOVERNOR EDWARD TIFFIN—A BIOGRAPHY.

CHAPTER XIV.

SPENCER vs. HEDGES—THE BRUSH-DAM CASE—THE FIRST JURY TRIAL—BROUSE—THE SUGAR CAMP-INDIAN WAY OF COOKING COON-FOREST CULTURE—SCARCITY OF MONEY—WORK ON THE CANAL-JIGGERS AND CHICHA—THE MIAMI, DAYTON AND MICHIGAN CANAL—CANAL TAX OF SENECA COUNTY.

CHAPTER XV.

SANDUSKY RIVER AND THE CREEKS IN SENECA COUNTY—TOPOGRAPHY AND GEOLOGY OF THE COUNTY.

CHAPTER XVI.

JOSIAH HEDGES—CHANGE—FIRST PLAT OF TIFFIN—THE SAW-MILL—MIASMA—FIRST FRAME HOUSES—FIRST STORES — FIRST BRICK HOUSES — THE DUG-OUT—FIRST HOTELS—BLACK-STRAP—HENRY GROSS, Sr.—BREDOON'S DEATH—CREEGER FAMILY—THE FAMILIES OF HENRY CRONISE, HENRY LANG AND DR. BOYER.

CHAPTER XVII.

ADDITIONS TO TIFFIN—THE BRIDGES—THE BURNING OF THE FREE BRIDGE —CHOLERA—MR. HOFFMAN—LITTLE CHARLOTTE—JONNY DALRYMPLE— RAILROADS—FIRST TRAIN TO TIFFIN—HEIDELBERG COLLEGE—LIVES OF REV. J. H. GOOD, D. D., REV. C. V. GERHART, D. D., AND REV. GEO. W. WILLARD, D. D.

CHAPTER XVIII.

THE CHURCHES.

CHAPTER XIX.

BIOGRAPHIES OF JOHN GOODIN, MRS. ANN SENEY, R. W. SHAWHAN, C. SNYDER, GEO. RUMMELL, DAVID E. OWEN, JUDGES LUGENBEEL AND PITTENGER, JOHN PITTINGER, JOHN AND LOUISA FIEGE, C. MUELLER— WYANDOT CHIEFS—MARK, 6TH CHAP., 2D VERSE, IN MOHAWK.

CHAPTER XX.

SURPLUS REVENUE—POLITICS—FIRST POLITICAL JOLLIFICATION—TIFFIN IN THE WOODS—TIFFIN INCORPORATED—FIRST TOWN ELECTION OF TIFFIN — INCORPORATION AND ONLY ELECTION OF FORT BALL— INCORPORATION OF THE CITY—FIRST CITY OFFICERS—PLANK ROADS— PIKES—TELEGRAPHS—THE SCHOOLS OF TIFFIN.

CHAPTER XXI.

THE BANKS OF TIFFIN—INSURANCE COMPANIES—SECRET AND BENEVOLENT SOCIETIES.

CHAPTER XXII.

THE BENCH AND BAR.

CHAPTER XXIII.

THE BENCH AND BAR CONTINUED.

CHAPTER XXIV.

DRS. DREISBACH, KUHN, FISHER, HOVEY, AND OTHERS—TIFFIN MEDICAL SOCIETY—THE AGRICULTURAL SOCIETY—THE PRESS: MESSRS. LOOMIS, NAYLOR, GROSS—THE COUNTY INFIRMARY—AGRICULTURAL WORKS— THE GAS LIGHT COMPANY—THE PIONEER ASSOCIATION—DER BRUDERBUND—THE PHILHARMONIC SOCIETY—MRS. HARRIET CRAWFORD—DR. JOHN D. O'CONNOR.

CHAPTER XXV.

THE TOLEDO WAR.

CHAPTER XXVI.

SENECA COUNTY IN THE GENERAL ASSEMBLY—SENECA COUNTY ON THE TAX DUPLICATE—SOLDIERS OF THE REVOLUTIONARY WAR—SOLDIERS OF THE WAR OF 1812—SOLDIERS IN THE WAR WITH MEXICO—INDEPENDENT COMPANIES—OHIO MILITIA.

CONTENTS.

CHAPTER XXVII.
SENECA COUNTY IN THE WAR OF THE REBELLION.

CHAPTER XXVIII.
DR. ROBERT R. McMEENS.

CHAPTER XXIX.
ADAMS TOWNSHIP.

CHAPTER XXX.
BIG SPRING TOWNSHIP.

CHAPTER XXXI.
BLOOM TOWNSHIP.

CHAPTER XXXII.
CLINTON TOWNSHIP.

CHAPTER XXXIII.
EDEN TOWNSHIP.

CHAPTER XXXIV.
HOPEWELL TOWNSHIP.

CHAPTER XXXV.
JACKSON TOWNSHIP.

CHAPTER XXXVI.
LIBERTY TOWNSHIP.

CHAPTER XXXVII.
LOUDON TOWNSHIP.

CHAPTER XXXVIII.
PLEASANT TOWNSHIP.

CHAPTER XXXIX.
REED TOWNSHIP.

CHAPTER XL.
SCIPIO TOWNSHIP.

CHAPTER XLI.
SENECA TOWNSHIP.

CHAPTER XLII.
THOMPSON TOWNSHIP.

VENICE TOWNSHIP.

CHAPTER XLIII.

CHAPTER XLIV.
COUNTY OFFICERS TO 1880 INCLUSIVE, AND CONCLUSION.

APPENDIX.

THE EARTHQUAKE –THE GREAT HURRICANE—THE JERKS—THE MORMONS— SALUTATORY OF THE VAN BURENITE—THE OLD STATE HOUSE AND DIRGE OF THE STATE HOUSE BELL—THE TIFFIN PAPERS.

CENTENNIAL ORATION. JULY 4, 1876, AND CELEBRATION IN TIFFIN.

INTRODUCTORY.

THE great and bloody struggle of the Colonies, through a long seven years' war, being over, the British Lion retreated growling to his den and, following the Revolutionary War at the Treaty of Paris in 1783, peace was made with England, in which the Independence of these Colonies was recognized.

For the first time in the history of the human race, the intelligent world saw a young government start on its career with the conscious knowledge and proud proclamation of man's capacity for self-government.

> Then the genius of Freedom
> Her banner unfurled,
> And inspired with hope
> The whole civilized world.

But as the waves of the ocean continue to lash the shore long after the storm has ceased, so the agitation of the frontier, between the settlers and the Indians, continued for many years.

The intense passions and mutual hatred engendered by the conflict were not allayed by the Treaty of Paris. When the British forces withdrew to the Canadas or across the Atlantic, the Indians, who, long before and during the Revolutionary struggle, were a source of constant annoyance to the frontier settlers, still remained.

While the settlers were determined to get possession of the lands of the Indians, the Indians were equally determined not to relinquish their ancient hunting grounds. The life and property of the frontiersman were constantly in danger, and often at the mercy of the savages—the general government having neither the means nor military to afford protection; thus the frontier settler was left to his fate as before. Since then a century has rolled off into the ocean of time, and while still "Westward the course of Empire takes its way," the Indian atrocities upon the frontier settlements continue as of yore, and the question calls into requisition the wisest of statesmanship and the best and most vigorous policy of the government to meet it. The indications now are that the Indians must either give up their nationality and savage life, and become citizens of the United States, or be exterminated.

During the Revolutionary War and for some time thereafter, the military post of the British at Detroit supplied the savages, throughout the Northwest. with munitions of war, and encouraged and supported them in their villainous depredations upon the frontier.

The hot-bed of the councils of the savages was the Wyandot towns along the banks of the Sandusky river, of which Upper Sandusky was the leading one. There was a constant intercommunication kept up between these Indian towns and Detroit. This state of things continued for a long time after the Treaty of Paris, and until the British evacuated Detroit, when the Indians were finally thrown upon their own resources and compelled to come to terms.

Even in the late war with Great Britain, after Hull's surrender and with the British in possession of Detroit, the same policy was inaugurated under General Bartoe, and the Indians were again made the allies of the British, as we shall hereafter see.

Expeditions were set on foot against the British at Detroit and the Indians on the Sandusky, during the war, by the Continental Congress and afterwards by the government of the States. Fort Pitt was a small garrison in the charge of General Irvine. Here all the early expeditions were organized. Congress being fully aware of the fact that all the terrible atrocities along the frontier were directed and supported from Detroit, and in order to bring peace to the border, ordered General Laughlin McIntosh, from the regular army, to move upon Detroit. He descended the Ohio river with a force of regulars and militia to the mouth of Beaver river in October, 1778, where he established the first military post of the United States beyond the frontier settlements. Congress, however, reluctantly suspended the expedition against Detroit for want of means to prosecute it, and ordered General McIntosh to proceed upon and destroy the Indian towns in the vicinity that, in his opinion, would most effectually tend to chastise the savages. He thereupon undertook to move upon Sandusky and destroy the Wyandot towns. He started with one thousand men, and on reaching the Muskingum in the present county of Tuscarawas, he built a fort and called it Fort Lawrence, in honor of the President of Congress. Leaving Colonel John Gibson in charge of this post with fifty men, he returned with the rest of his army to Fort Pitt. Fort Lawrence was the first military post established on Ohio soil. In August following, Fort Lawrence was evacuated. This ended the first expedition. Fort McIntosh was also abandoned.

An expedition for the same purpose, under Col. Broadhead, was also a failure.

Another expedition was organized under the command of Col. Crawford.

CRAWFORD'S EXPEDITION.

The lamentable expedition of Col. Crawford falling into this period and being a part of the Revolutionary struggle, occurring before the Treaty of Paris, and the sad, terrible conclusion of which took place so near the border of Seneca county, an abstract relation of the same will not be out of place in these pages.

The British had succeeded in enlisting into their service all the savage element northwest of the Ohio river, and provided them with all the requisite munitions of war.

Deserters from the army under Washington, runaway tories and desperadoes from the Colonies, united with the savages to make their continued attacks upon the frontier as expressed in the language of Lord Chatham: "Letting loose the horrible hell-hounds of savage war."

The British directed the operations against the frontier from their military post at Detroit, where Henry Hamilton, a vulgar ruffian, was in command.

The Wyandots, Senecas and Shawnees were the principal tribes enlisted in this murderous warfare. Nearly all the smaller tribes were made allies of these. The Delawares were the peaceable nation amongst them that had not joined in the war upon the frontier, and even these eventually became enemies.

These elements, thus combined—British, savages, tories and desperadoes, were turned loose upon peaceable settlers, upon unarmed men, upon helpless women and children. They extended their atrocities all along the western frontier of Pennsylvania and Virginia.

The effect upon the frontier people can better be imagined than described. Their patient endurance became exhausted. It became now a war to the knife. To kill an Indian was a source of pleasure, and at the same time a signal for attack upon the settlement.

In a letter from General Washington to General Irvine at Fort Pitt, instructions were given to the latter in these words: "Still continue to keep yourself informed as to the situation at Detroit, and the strength of the enemy at that place." The subject of another expedition against Sandusky became quite popular, but Irvine hesitated, and at first rather opposed the project, but finally yielded to the popular demand, and even assisted in the enterprise.

The people became so clamorous in urging on the organization as to demand of General Irvine that he should himself lead.

This he declined to do for want of authority to leave his post.

The expedition was thoroughly considered and supported by the best of men along the frontier. No one doubted its propriety. Everybody saw the necessity. Sandusky was the infernal den from whence came all their trouble. Volunteers flocked in from every side. Then the place for rendezvous was fixed at Logan-town-at-Mingo, (Mingo Bottom,) now in Steubenville township, Jefferson county, Ohio. On the 24th of May, 1782, they met. There were four hundred and eighty in all. William Crawford was elected Colonel, and David Williamson, David Gaddis, John McClelland and one Brinton were elected Field-Marshals.

Early in the morning of the 25th day of May, the army, under Crawford, began its march from Mingo Bottom, in four columns. It was to lead in the straightest direction through the woods to Sandusky, a distance of one hundred and fifty miles. The route lay through what now constitutes the counties of Jefferson, Harrison, Tuscarawas, Ashland, Holmes, Richland, Crawford and near to the center of Wyandot. The whole distance was through a dense, unbroken forest, except where they reached the plains.

Nothing of any particular interest occurred except that on the second day out two Indians were discovered. They were shot at, but being missed, escaped. Fearing that they were scouts, Crawford pressed forward with greater speed.

On the 2d of June they reached the Sandusky river at a point immediately East of where Leesville, in Crawford county, now stands, and near the mouth of a small creek called "Allen's run."

The Sandusky river rises in Springfield township, Richland county, at the

"Palmer Spring," so-called. Taking a southwesterly course, and receiving several small tributaries, it enters Wyandot county about two miles north of the southeast corner, and pursues that course generally through Wyandot, Seneca and Sandusky to the bay, a distance of eighty miles from its source, along the stream. Its principal tributaries from the right bank are the Broken Sword and Sycamore, and from the left the Little Sandusky and Tymochtee, in Crawford and Wyandot counties.

The army was now approaching the enemy's headquarters. Slover, the guide, who had been amongst the Wyandots, said to Crawford that they were near the plains. These they reached on the next day, near the mouth of a small stream entering the Olentangy, or Whetstone.

To most of the volunteers the sight of the prairie, or plains, was a novelty. The islands of timber, the tall, coarse grass, prairie hens, wild geese, ducks, prairie owls, etc., attracted their attention. Little they thought and less they knew of the sad fate that awaited them.

How happily has a kind Providence drawn a curtain between man and his future!

The Olentangy is on the eastern boundary of Wyandot county. The Tymochtee is on the west. On the south these prairies form the north part of Marion county. Their extreme length, east and west, is forty miles; their extreme breadth, twenty miles; the average elevation above lake Erie, three hundred feet.

These were the favored hunting grounds of the savages, and to which they clung with a tenacity that bordered on desperation. The army camped about ten miles from their place of destination.

The next morning, the 4th of June, they started on their march, with great precaution, in a northwesterly direction, and reached the mouth of the Little Sandusky, where they found Indian trails leading in every direction. They crossed the river and followed a trail, but discovered no Indians. Slover, the guide, told Crawford that a Wyandot town was close by. A little further on they came upon the town but found it deserted. Crawford ordered a halt for consultation. The soldiers dismounted and refreshed themselves and their horses at the spring.

This forsaken town was on the east bank of the Sandusky, and about three miles south of the present town of Upper Sandusky.

The Sandusky of the Wyandots, as known to Slover and Zane, the guides, was eight miles below, where the Kilbourn road crosses the river. Here was the residence of Pomoacan—Half-King—as he was called.

Of all the Indian allies of Great Britain, the Wyandots were the most powerful, because they were the most intelligent, caused by their association with the French and British. In their treatment of prisoners they seldom, if ever, resorted to torture, which was common with the other tribes.

Arentz De Peyster, the commander at Detroit, had sent Butler's rangers to assist the Indians. The night preceding the battle, these camped in the limits of Seneca county, near the river in Pleasant township. They were mounted troops, and had two field-pieces and a mortar.

The Indians who had watched the progress of Crawford from Mingo Bottom to the Sandusky, had marshaled their host and were ready for action. Their combined forces greatly outnumbered those of Crawford.

The squaws and children had been sent to a ravine on the Tymochtee. Simon Girty was with the Wyandots. He was an Irish tory and an adopted son of the Senecas, who had captured him when young, and is described as a fierce, cruel and beastly creature. His Indian name was Katepocomen, which, if it means anything, ought to mean *devil*. He had been liberated, and having returned to the settlements became the friend of Crawford, aspired to office in Westmoreland county, Pennsylvania, failed, voluntarily returned to savage life and became the most savage of the savages. His name was a terror along the Ohio river and throughout the northwest. Yet when Simon Kenton was brought to Mac-a-chack town as a captive, under sentence of death, Girty got him released, and Kenton being taken to Detroit as a prisoner made his escape. But to return. It was now one o'clock in the afternoon. Crawford determined to pursue the trail to the other town, where he expected to find the enemy. At a point about one mile south of the present Upper Sandusky, Crawford called a council of war. Rose, the Surgeon, whom General Irvine had sent along with the expedition, and Zane, advised and urged an immediate return, because they feared that the Indians had too many warriors for them. Crawford then acquiesced, but they finally determined to pursue their march that afternoon only and then return. Immediately scouts came hurrying up announcing the discovery of the enemy. This news was received with evident satisfaction, and rapidly everything was put in readiness, and an advance ordered to meet the enemy.

The Indians came on a run to meet the troops. The Americans drove the savages from a grove they had in possession, and from that sheltered position fired upon them until night-fall. This grove is known by the name of "Battle Island," situated three miles north and one-half mile east of the court house in Upper Sandusky. When, in the Summer of 1834, I visited the battle ground, the oak trees were still bearing the marks of the bullets and of the tomahawks the Indians had used to cut out the balls.

When night set in the army built their camp fires and collected as best they could their dead and wounded. There were five killed and nineteen wounded.

On the morning of the fifth the battle was renewed at long range and with but little effect. The Americans still occupied the island of timber. During this day the Americans lost but four wounded. Plans were now discussed as to the manner of attack on the next day, when suddenly the scene changed. The appearance of Butler's rangers in the rear of the Wyandots struck dismay into the hearts of the army. Crawford abandoned all ideas of an attack and prepared for defense, when about two hundred Shawnees were discovered supporting the Delawares on the south. "They kept pouring in from all sides" are the words of Rose. At nine o'clock that night a retreat was resolved upon. The killed were buried and fires burnt over their graves to prevent discovery. Stretchers were made to carry the wounded. Just as the army was about to start, an attack was made on the troops, which threw them into great confusion, and two wounded fell into the hands of the enemy. They did not pursue the troops very far, however, not knowing that a retreat had been resolved upon. McClelland was reported killed. Williamson took command. Crawford, his son and son-in-law Harris were amongst the missing. The retreating army was compelled to

INTRODUCTION.

cut its way through mounted Indians and British cavalry, but reached the edge of the prairie, at two o'clock of the afternoon on the second day, south of Bucyrus. They were brought to a stand near Olentangy creek, called "Keen-hong-she-con-se-pung" by the Delawares.

Here a vast number of the enemy overtook the retreating army, but after a short engagement they were repulsed.

A rain storm now swept the plains in great fury. The men were drenched to the skin. The air became chilly. The march was continued while the enemy, following, kept up a constant fire upon them. By night-fall the army reached Leesville, forty miles from the battle ground on Battle Island, where they encamped, leaving the enemy a mile in the rear. The army reached Mingo Bottom on the 13th of June, and were discharged on the next day. The total number of killed and missing did not exceed seventy.

We will now return to follow up the fate of poor Crawford and his fellow sufferers.

It is undoubtedly true, that in the night after the last day's battle near the grove, Crawford was amongst those whose horses got fast in the muck, and while trying to save them, were left behind by the retreating army. He was heard to call for his son John, and for his son-in-law Harris, in the darkness of the night. He also called for Major Rose, and his nephew, William Crawford, but nobody could come to help him. Dr. Knight, who now came up to Crawford, told him that he believed the others were all ahead of them; but Crawford thought otherwise, and begged of the doctor not to leave him. His horse was useless, and he complained of the troops for thus leaving him. At this time an old man and a boy came up to Crawford, and the doctor and all started on a southwesterly course, and arrived near the cranberry marsh where some of the volunteers were also struggling to get their swamped horses out of the oozy soil. Now Crawford and his party took a northerly course, and reaching a point about two miles north from the battle ground, they started on a course due east, guided by the North Star. At midnight they reached the Sandusky river near the mouth of Negro Run. The old man falling behind, several times called for the others to wait. An Indian was heard to halloo, and nothing further was seen of the old man. The party passed on. At two o'clock next afternoon Capt. Biggs overtook the party. After an hour's travel—some on horseback and others on foot, Lieutenant Ashley being wounded, and a drenching rain overtaking them, which made their progress very slow, they camped two miles north of Bucyrus. The next morning they started on a southeasterly course, and found a deer that had recently been killed, and a tomahawk lying close by it. They sliced the flesh from the bones, and wrapping the venison in the skin, took it along. A mile further on they saw a fire, and left the wounded officer in charge of the boy, with orders to remain behind. Upon examination they came to the conclusion that the fire had been made by their own men the previous day. A most fatal conclusion! They roasted their venison and were about to start on, when a volunteer came up to them and told them that he had killed the deer, and abandoned it when he heard them coming, fearing they were Indians. Now all passed on and soon reached the trail of the retreating army. Knight and Biggs proposed to leave the trail. Crawford opposed the plan. Crawford and Knight were afoot; the rest on horseback. When the party were just east of Leesville. three Indians jumped up, and Dr. Knight took aim at one, but Crawford called to him not to fire. One of the Indians ran up to Crawford and took him by the hand. The other walked up to Knight and called him doctor, took him by the hand and said he had seen him before. The party had fallen into an ambuscade of Delawares, whose chief was Wingenund, (pronounced Win-ge-noond) at camp only half-mile away. Capt. Biggs fired, but hit no one. An Indian told Knight to call his people up or they would all be killed, but the other four got away for that time. Crawford and Knight were captives. The warriors returned to camp with their prisoners and captured horses. There was great joy upon their coming into camp among the savages.

The Delawares lived among the Wyandots by mere permission. The burning of prisoners was kept up among the Delawares when the Wyandots had abandoned it. Their chiefs, "The Pipe" and "Wingenund," therefore were under the necessity of obtaining the consent of the Wyandot chief before they could burn a captive. This consent was secured by a stratagem.

It was now three o'clock Friday afternoon, June seventh. On Sunday following the savages brought in the scalps and horses of Ashley and Biggs. The others again escaped. The Delawares had nine other prisoners besides Crawford and Knight. Some of the converted Delawares, who had gone back to heathenism, also brought in scalps of borderers. The chiefs soon knew that Crawford was the "Big Captain." Several of the savages were known to both Crawford and Knight.

On Monday, the 10th of June, the prisoners were ordered to march to Sandusky, the "Half King's" town, thirty-three miles away. Crawford hoped for help by Girty. Meeting him at Sandusky, he offered him one thousand dollars if he would save his life. Girty promised, but without any intention to keep his word. Crawford saw that "The Pipe" was very much enraged against the prisoners.

On Tuesday, June 11, "The Pipe" painted all the faces of the prisoners black, and told Knight to go to the Shawnees town and see his friends. This chief knew Crawford before his tribe joined the enemy, and told him that he would have him shaved, i. e., adopted, but at the same time painted him black also. Then the whole party started for the Wyandot town, eight miles below. A short distance on their way they saw four of their comrades lying near the trail, scalped. At the spring where Upper Sandusky now stands, to their dismay, another trail was taken northwestward to the Delaware town on the Tymochtee.

All ideas of hope for life had now vanished. When they reached Little Tymochtee creek, in what is now Salem township, in Wyandot county, the Indians made the prisoners sit down. Knight was put in the charge of an Indian, to be taken to the Shawnees town.

The squaws and boys now tomahawked the other five prisoners. An old squaw cut off the head of McKinley and kicked it about on the ground. The young Indians then dashed the bloody scalps into the faces of Crawford and Knight several times.

Again they started, and were soon met by Simon Girty and red savages on horseback, who had come to enjoy the scene of torture.

INTRODUCTION.

Wingenund and The Pipe were the prime movers in alienating the Delawares from their frontier friends and in making them enemies. They were so bitter in their hatred of the Americans that their cruelties knew no bounds. Having now full authority over their prisoners, the only ground for hesitation to commence the process of torture seemed to be to resolve upon how to perform it in the most hellish manner. As the party moved along towards Tymochtee, every Indian they met struck the prisoners. Girty said: "Is that doctor Knight?" Knight said yes, and offered Girty his hand, which he refused, and said: "Begone; you are a damned rascal!" They now reached Tymochtee creek, and were about three-quarters of a mile from the village, which was further down the creek.

I am now about to record the manner of Crawford's death. The scenes the poor captives had to pass through so far, are of themselves sickening, and calculated to rouse the sympathies of a heart of stone. The task creates a chill, and the pen moves reluctantly to describe an act so fiendish, brutal and repulsive.

"Man's inhumanity to man," it should be remembered, is not an attribute that characterizes exclusively the North American savage. Has not Europe, has not Asia, has not America equal cause to blush when tracing histories of white races? Thousands upon thousands fell beneath the sword of Mohammed for refusing to take the Koran. Europe, dressed in Christian attire, with her churches, her domes, her institutions of learning and refinement, burnt her martyrs at the stake. Her inquisitions, her "bridges of sighs," her blocks and guillotines glotted the pages of her history with the blood of her religious and political victims, while our own dear America burnt her witches and hung Quakers on Boston Common. Is the difference amongst savages found only in color or race?

About four o'clock in the afternoon on the eleventh day of June, the savages planted a stake in the ground near the right bank of Tymochtee creek, to which Crawford was tied. The Indian men then shot powder into Crawford's naked body, from his heels to his head until he was black all over. Not less than seventy shots were fired upon him. They cut off both of his ears, and when occasionally the throng around Crawford would allow Dr. Knight to get sight of him, the blood was running down both sides of his head. They built a ring of fire around the stake and within six or seven yards of it. It was made of small hickory poles and when burnt quite through in the middle, leaving the ends about five feet long, three or four Indians at a time would each take one of these burning sticks and hold the burning part to the naked body of Crawford, already black with powder. They placed themselves on each side of him so that whichever way he would run around the post, they met him with these burning fagots. Some of the squaws took broad pieces of chips and bark, with which they threw quantities of hot coals and embers on him, so that in a short time he had to walk over a bed of coals and hot ashes.

In the midst of these extreme tortures Crawford called to Girty and begged of him to shoot him. Receiving no answer, he called again, when Girty tauntingly replied that he had no gun, and turning around to the Indians behind him laughed heartily and seemed delighted at the horrid scene.

Girty walked up to Dr. Knight and told him to prepare for death also; that he was not to die at that place, but was to be burnt at a Shawnees town.

With a most fearful oath he added that he (the doctor) need not expect to escape death, but that he would suffer it in all its extremities.

He asked Knight whether he had any hopes of escaping it, but the doctor was too much absorbed with the terrible agonies Colonel Crawford was undergoing before his eyes and his own immediate fate harrowing up his soul, that he made Girty no answer.

Crawford bore his torments with the most manly fortitude. Several times he was heard to call on the Almighty to have mercy on his soul. Thus he continued in all these extremities of pain for more than two hours, as near as Knight could judge, when he laid down on his stomach. The savages then scalped him and repeatedly threw the bloody scalp into poor Knight's face, telling him that was the "Big Captain."

An old squaw, who to Knight looked more like Satan than a human being, took a board and shoveled coals and ashes on Crawford's back and scalped head. The wretched man then raised himself on his feet again and began to walk around the post.

They next held burning sticks to his body as before, and Knight was taken away from the scene.

The Indians had a tradition amongst them that Crawford breathed his last as the sun was going down.

On the next morning when Knight was started off for the Shawnees town and while he was passing the fire place, he saw the remains of Crawford almost burnt to ashes. Then the Indians told Knight that was his fate and gave the "scalp halloo."

The tradition runs—that after Crawford died, the fagots were heaped together, his body placed upon them and that the savages danced around the remains for several hours longer.

The Shawnees had great rejoicing when the news reached them, and the poor frontier settlers were filled with gloom and dismay. Crawford was mourned by all who knew him. We will throw the mantle of forgetfulness over the lonely cabin that contained the widow of the Colonel when the sad news reached her ear.

The language used by General Washington on this occasion, shows the deep feeling of his noble heart.

"It is with the greatest sorrow and concern that I have learned the melancholy tidings of Col. Crawford's death. He was known to me as an officer of much care and prudence; brave, experienced and active. The manner of his death was shocking to me, and I have this day communicated to Congress such papers as I have regarding it."

On the 6th of August he writes to General Irvine, thus: "I lament the failure of the expedition against Sandusky and am particularly affected with the disastrous death of Colonel Crawford."

The various narratives of the place of execution and burning of Colonel Crawford were so conflicting, for a time after the white man began his settlements along the Tymochtee, that the best light tradition could throw on the subject fixed the place where now a monument is erected to the memory of Crawford and his sad fate.

INTRODUCTION.

The monument stands on the farm once owned by Daniel Hodge, in Crawford township, Wyandot county, near Crawfordsville, and a short distance from Carey on the Cincinnati, Sandusky & Cleveland railroad. Colonel William Crawford was born in the year 1732, in Orange county, Virginia, of Scotch-Irish parents.

When General Washington was employed by Lord Fairfax to survey the large tracts of lands he had in the west of Virginia, the young surveyor often stopped at the house of Crawford's parents, when he made the acquaintance of William Crawford.

They became warm friends and their attachment lasted through life. They were both about the same age.

Crawford learned from Washington the art of surveying. Both served under Braddock at Fort Du Quesne. They were then in the prime of life and vigor. Crawford was with Washington at the crossing of the Delaware, at Trenton, and Princeton in 1777. He was sent by Washington to take charge of Fort Pitt under instructions from Congress. From thence forward his services were devoted to the frontier, where he displayed the highest qualities of military genius. The expedition against Sandusky was a favorite scheme with him, and was to have been the crowning achievement of his life, after having served in the war of the revolution six full years.

We will close this part of our work by simply relating, in a short way, the wonderful escape of Slover, the guide, and of doctor Knight.

DOCTOR KNIGHT.

On the morning of the 12th of June, the doctor was again painted black, and put in the charge of a Delaware savage, a rough-looking cuss by the name of *Tutelu*. Then they started for the Shawnees town, some forty miles away, Tutelu on horseback driving the doctor before him. The doctor tried to make the Indian believe that he felt cheerful, and spoke of living with him in the same house, etc., which seemed to please the savage. They traveled about twenty-five miles that day and camped. In the morning Tutelu fixed up the fire. The doctor asked Tutelu to fix up a fire behind him to keep the mosquitos away. When the savage turned his back the doctor struck him with a stick on the head and the Indian fell forward with both hands into the fire. He soon recovered and ran off howling. Knight seized the Indian's gun, but pulling back the cock, broke the mainspring. This occurred near the Scioto in Hardin county, a short distance down the river from Kenton. Knight then took the Indian's blanket, a pair of new moccasins, powder horn and gun, and started in a northeasterly direction. Shortly before sundown he reached the plains. Here he hid himself until night-fall, when he proceeded on and reached the woods on the other side by daylight. He avoided the track taken by the army outward as much as possible. On the second day of his escape he reached a point in Richland county, where "Spring Mills" are situate, about noon. In the evening he began to be very faint. During the six days of his imprisonment he was nearly starved. He had thrown away the gun as useless, and was now compelled to live on green gooseberries and herbs. The blow he had received with the back of a tomahawk still hurt him very much. He crossed the Muskingum near the mouth of the Conotten, an eastern affluent, in

Tuscarawas county. He reached fort Pitt on the morning of the fourth day of July in safety. He afterwards became the surgeon of the Seventh Virginia regiment. He was married on the 14th day of October, 1784, and died on the 12th day of March, 1838, the father of ten children. Dr. Knight is entitled to the credit of furnishing to history the most truthful relation of this sad expedition.

SLOVER.

Slover and his two fellow captives were taken to a Shawnees town. The inhabitants came out and beat and abused the prisoners greatly. They seized the oldest one of Slover's companions, stripped him naked, and painted him black with coal and water.

They sent a messenger to Wapatomica to get ready for the frolic, as they were coming, and when they approached the town the savages came out with clubs, guns and tomahawks. They told the prisoners they must run to the Council House, about three hundred yards away. The man painted black was the principal object of their sport. They struck him and shot powder into his flesh; women and children all engaged in the frolic. shouting and beating their drums. Arriving at the door the man was cut very badly and the blood was streaming from the wounds inflicted by the tomahawks and rifle wads. He laid hold of the door, but was pulled back. Slover saw him carried away, and the Indians slowly killing him. He saw his dead body near the Council House, cruelly mangled. Then they cut off the head and limbs and stuck them on poles outside of town. The same evening he saw the bodies of three others mangled to about the same condition. One of these was William Harrison, the son-in-law, and the other William Crawford, the nephew, of the Colonel. The Indians also had their horses.

On the next day a large council was held. Slover was examined as to his knowledge of the frontier. He could speak the language of the Miamis. Delawares and Shawnees. Captain Elliott and James Girty also came and assured the savages that Slover had lied, that Cornwallis was not taken, etc. Hitherto Slover had been treated kindly. Now they began to abuse him also. This council lasted fifteen days. About one hundred warriors were present.

See the humanity of the British commander at Detroit, De Peyster! At the close of this council a dispatch was brought in from that dignitary by a warrior who had just arrived. It was in these words:

"My children, provisions are scarce. When prisoners are brought in we are obliged to maintain them, and some of them run away and carry tidings of our affairs. When any of your people fall into the hands of the rebels, they show no mercy; why, then, should you take prisoners? Take no more prisoners, my children, of any sort—man, woman, or child."

The Ottawas, Chippewas, Wyandots, Mingoes, Delawares, Shawnees, Monseys and Cherokees participated in this council. They laid plans for Louisville and Wheeling. All prisoners thereafter were to be put to death. They put a rope around Slover, stripped him naked and blacked him, took him five miles away, tied him to a tree near a hut and beat him. They then took him about two miles further to Mac-a-chack, near West Liberty, in Logan county. Slover was tied with a rope around his neck to a post and a fire built around him. A rain coming up put out the fire, and the burning was postponed until next day. They danced around him until late into the night, striking and wounding him. They then took him to a block house and tied him. Three Indians watched him. Near morning the Indians were all asleep, and Slover, succeeding in untying his rope, ran away into a corn field. He found a horse close by, used his rope for a halter and put off. On the third day out the horse gave out and was abandoned. Slover traveled on foot and in his naked condition reached the Ohio near Wheeling. He returned to Fort Pitt on the 11th of July. The last straggler had returned.

THE ORDINANCE OF 1788—SETTLEMENTS OF OHIO—PIANKESHAW'S SPEECH
—TERRITORIAL ORGANIZATION—CLARK'S CAMPAIGN.

Although the treaty of Paris was signed in September, 1783, the news did not reach the United States for more than one month later, and it was nearly two months later before it reached the western frontier. Meanwhile the conflict in the west was kept up with all its terror. Settlements were attacked along the Ohio river and abandoned. Expeditions were organized, prosecuted and abandoned, often in disaster. The struggle to conquer the Indians and possess the west seemed almost hopeless.

Now came the tidings of peace and a new life seemed to spread over the land like the dawn of day following a night of storm.

A Mr. Dalton was government agent on the Wabash. He called a council of the chiefs and announced to them the fact that peace was declared in the following words:

"My children! What I have often told you has now come to pass. This day I received news from my great chief at the falls of Ohio. Peace is made with the enemies of America. The tomahawk is buried. The Shawnees, the Delawares, the Chicasaws, and the Cherokees have taken the Long Knife by the hand. They have given up the captives they had taken. My children of the Wabash, open your ears, and let what I tell you sink deep into your hearts. You know me. Near twenty years I have been among you. The Long Knife is my nation; I know their hearts. Peace they carry in one hand and war in the other. Consider now which you will choose. We never beg peace of our enemies. If you love your women and children, receive the belt of wampum I present you. Return to me the captives you have in your villages, and the horses you stole from my people in Kentucky. Your corn fields were never disturbed by the Long Knife while your warriors were robbing my people."

Mr. Dalton presented the chief with a belt of blue and white wampum. There were several tribes represented on the occasion, but Piankeshaw was recognized as the head chief of the most powerful tribe. He accepted the emblem of peace, and then with much dignity of manner, replied:

"My Great Father, the Long Knife: You have been many years amongst us; you have suffered by us. We still hope you will have pity and compassion upon us, on our women and children; the sun shines on us, and the good news of peace appears in our faces. This is the day of joy to the Wabash Indians. With one torgue we now speak. We accept your peace belt.

We received the tomahawk from the English. Poverty forced us to it. We were followed by other tribes. We are sorry for it. To-day we collect the scattered bones of our friends and bury them in one grave. Here is the pipe that gives us joy: smoke of it. We have buried the tomahawk; have formed friendships never to be broken, and now we smoke out of your pipe.

We know that the Great Spirit was angry with us for stealing your horses and attacking your people. He has sent us so much snow and cold weather as to kill your horses with our own. We are a poor people. We hope that God will help us, and that the Long Knife will have compassion on our women and children. Your people who are with us are well. We shall collect them when they come in from hunting. We love them, and so do our young women. Some of your people mend our guns. Others tell us they can make rum out of corn. They are now the same as we. In one moon after this we will take them back to their friends in Kentucky.

My Father! This being the day of joy to the Wabash Indians, we beg a little drop of your milk (rum to let our warriors see that it came from your breast. We were born and raised in the woods. We could never learn to make rum. God has made the white man master of the world."

Having finished his speech, Piankeshaw presented Mr. Dalton with three strings of wampum as a pledge of peace. Every reader must be impressed with the tone of despondency that pervades this address and the melancholy spirit that asks for rum.

In all the various treaties and intercourses for peace with the Indians, the reader is frequently met by the term "Long Knife." By this expression, of course, is meant the "white man," or the "general government." The way the term came to be used, is said to have occurred in this wise: A Colonel Gibson, while stationed at Fort Pitt, in a certain attack with his troops upon a company of Indians, and getting into a hand to hand fight, cut off the head of an Indian with his sword, in one stroke. This struck terror into the hearts of the other Indians, who fled, and reported to their chiefs that a pale face had cut off the head of an Indian with a "Long Knife."

The British traders in Canada kept up their business with the Indians as before, and, in direct violation of the treaty, replenished the fuel that was still burning in the hearts of the savages throughout the northwest against the white people.

The vast territory lying north of the Ohio river and extending far west to the Mississippi, was claimed, by charters from the King of England, by Connecticut, Massachusetts and Virginia. Each of these states now consented to relinquish its claim to the general government with the exception of reservations by Connecticut and Virginia. These two states, embarrassed by the war, retained each a portion of the territory for the purpose of paying its debt to the revolutionary soldiers.

The region thus ceded to Connecticut, lying north of the 41st degree north latitude, and extending from the west line of Pennsylvania to the west line of what is now Huron county, was called the "Western Reserve" —"Firelands." It extends from the lake, south, to what is now known as the "base line," fifty miles wide and one hundred and twenty miles long from east to west.

Virginia retained the lands lying between the Scioto and the Little Miami, which was called the "Virginia Military District."

By these cessions the general government became possessed of the vast region of uninhabited territory extending to the lakes of the north and west to the Mississippi river, now forming the states of Ohio, Indiana, Illinois, Wisconsin and Michigan. By the celebrated ordinance of 1787, no less than three nor more than five states were to be organized in this vast realm as soon as the number of white inhabitants would warrant. The Federal Government now established a territorial government over the same.

Let us not forget before leaving this part of our subject one beautiful feature in that great ordinance, engrafted upon it by slave owners, and which teaches a lesson for meditation, when the passions of party strife will admit of sober reflection, and give the better part of our nature nobler impulses and a larger field:

"No man shall be arrested for his mode of worship or his religious sentiments. The utmost good faith shall be observed toward the Indians: that their lands shall never be taken from them without their consent, unless in just and lawful war.

"*There shall be neither slavery nor involuntary servitude in said territory, otherwise than in the punishment of crime whereof the party shall have been duly convicted,*" etc.

Now companies began to be organized in the Atlantic states for the purpose of establishing colonies in this territory. The Ohio Company, formed of officers of the army and soldiers of the revolution, located between the Muskingum and the Hockhocking rivers. The government owed many of these large sums of money and had nothing to pay them with but land. They took their lands at one dollar per acre, and paid for it in scrip or *other evidences of debt for revolutionary services*. The purchase included about one and a half millions of acres.

John Cleves Symmes, of New Jersey, purchased 54,000 acres between the Little Miami and the Great Miami for sixty cents an acre.

General Rufus Putnam, with his party, settled near the mouth of the Muskingum on the 7th day of April, 1788. One remarkable feature in all these early settlements is the fact that the colonists were generally men of culture, refinement and high moral worth. They framed simple codes of laws and published them by nailing them against trees.

The ordinance which organized the government was placed in the hands of a governor and three judges. General Arthur St. Clair was appointed governor, and immediately proceeded to organize his council. The whole country north of the Ohio river, between the Muskingum and Hockhocking, was designated as the county of Washington, with Marietta, of course, as the county seat. Marietta was named in honor of Marie Antoinette, the unhappy queen of Louis XVI., and in token of gratitude for the aid furnished by France in the revolution. Here the first civil court was held for the *northwestern territory*, on the 2d day of September, 1788.

Mathias Denman, of New Jersey, purchased a section of land and a fraction, for which he paid five shillings per acre. He laid out a town and called it Losanteville, which was afterwards changed into Cincinnati. How the price of land has increased in that section!

HER COMMERCE.

The commerce of Cincinnati for the year ending January 1, 1879, amounted, in value of goods imported and exported, to $409,446,803. For the present year, with the renewed activity in business of all kinds; the great production in agricultural and mining districts, the increase in manufactures and the higher values, it is easy to see that they will aggregate fully $500,000,000. Of the sum for last year, $185,000,000 were for exports, and $223,000,000 imports. Among the former may be mentioned pork and hog products at a value of over $10,000,000; groceries, $5,000,000; cotton $10,000,000; whisky, $18,000,000; malt liquors; $2,000,000; boots and shoes, $5,500,000; butter, $1,250,000; coffee, $5,000,000; furniture, $5,000,000; hardware, $5,000,000; oil, $3,000,000; tobacco, $15,000,000. In imports there were cattle valued at $8,000,000; coal, $3,000,-000; coffee, $5,500,000; cotton, $10,000,000; flour, $3,000,000; boots and shoes, $3,500,000; hardware, $5,500,000; hogs valued at $12,000,000; sugar, $6,500,000; tobacco, $10,000,000; whisky, $7,000,000; wheat $4,000,000.

Vincennes, near the western line of Indiana, was also made the county seat of another county, bounded on the south by the Ohio river, on the east by the Great Miami, and on the west by the Wabash, larger than several states of the Union. St. Clair proceeded to the Mississippi where a few huts on the left bank formed another settlement. Here he established the county of St. Clair, embracing nearly the whole of Illinois.

It would be a source of great pleasure to record here some of the very many incidents, of a most thrilling nature, connected with the early settlements along the Ohio river and along the mouths of the Miami and Muskingum.

But, admonished by the fact that too many of our pages are being taken possession of by these reminiscences, I will only describe a few of the expeditions that were organized from time to time to subdue the savages, because all or nearly all of these had a tendency to rescue the valley of the Sandusky and northwestern Ohio from the owners, who by force of circumstances and without paper title, were the monarchs of the soil. These expeditions are given in the abstract without regard to chronological nicety. For detail, the kind reader will of course peruse more general and extended history.

General Clark was a military leader of Kentucky, stationed at the falls. He was a man of great force of character and considerable military ability. When he heard of the disastrous battle at Blue Licks, he resolved to pursue and punish the Indians. He formed a junction with Colonels Floyd and Logan, which gave him a force of about one thousand men. Colonel Boon joined the army as a volunteer. They crossed the Ohio on the 30th of September, 1782, and commenced their march up the Little Miami. They reached the old town of Chillicothe, where they chastised the Indians terribly and destroyed their town, their goods and their crops, and returned victoriously.

Again, in the fall of 1786, General Logan organized another great campaign against the savages in Ohio, in which many prominent men from Kentucky took part. It was the intention of the General to make this expedition the finishing stroke in the war against the savages. Colonel Floyd and General Logan with their troops again marched on the Indian villages on the Scioto, and laid them waste, killing many savages. Simon Kenton accompanied this expedition. All the villages were burnt, and nearly all the inhabitants were slain or taken captives. A region of forty miles wide and one hundred miles in length, was laid utterly desolate. The company, under the command of Simon Kenton, took no prisoners. It was

INTRODUCTION. 27

their object to wreak such terrible vengeance upon the savages that they would never again make raids upon the settlements. The party with General Clark was less successful. His provisions became exhausted and a large number of his men deserted him to keep from starvation. Without accomplishing anything, he with his half-starved men, returned to the falls of Ohio, covered with shame and confusion at the unmerited disgrace of their arms. The unfortunate General never recovered from the blow. He sunk into profound melancholy, in which at length he died, aged and poor. The failure of Clark excited the vindictive Shawnees on the Wabash, and urged them on to further outrages. The winter following, the depredations of the savages were extended all along the frontier of Pennsylvania and Virginia, a distance of over three hundred miles.

It is estimated that between 1783 and 1790, the Indians killed, wounded and took captive, fifteen hundred men, women and children, and destroyed property worth fifty thousand dollars, which sum at that time was considered immense. There were no millionaires in those days. Fortunes were not made and lost in one stroke. Men were not made rich or ruined by the sale or purchase of railroad stocks, and there were no "bulls" nor "bears" in Wall street; hence there was no Black Friday in that struggle for life. Fortunes made and lost in a day, speculations in railroad, steamboat and mining stocks. Black Fridays in gold, and the making of millionaires in a day, are the things of a faster age. For better or for worse?

GENERAL HARMAR'S EXPEDITION.

In the fall of 1790, Gen. Harmar, at the head of three hundred regular troops, and about one thousand militia, was ordered to march upon the Indian towns along the lake and chastise them to such a degree as to arrest all future depredations.

On the 21st of September this expedition rendezvoused at Fort Washington, and on the following day commenced their march upon the Miami villages. It took them seventeen days' hard marching over a rough and swampy country before they came into the vicinity of the enemy. Meantime, provisions became scarce. The General found himself under the necessity of sweeping the forest with numerous small detachments, and as the woods swarmed with Indians, most of these parties were cut off.

At length the expedition, thus greatly reduced, came within a few miles of an Indian town. Here Captain Armstrong was ordered, at the head of thirty regulars, and Col. Hardin, of Kentucky, with one hundred and fifty militia, to advance and reconnoitre. In the execution of this order they suddenly found themselves in an ambuscade by a large body of Indians, who immediately opened fire upon them.

The militia gave way, and the regulars attempted a more orderly retreat. The Indians, with tomahawks held high in the air, rushed upon and completely surrounded the troops. The regulars attempted to open a passage with their bayonets, but they were all destroyed except their captain and one lieutenant, who made their escape. The loss of the militia was very trifling.

Notwithstanding this heavy blow. Gen. Harmar advanced upon the villages, which he found deserted and in flames, the Indians themselves having fired their houses. He also found here several hundred acres of corn, which he destroyed. Marching on to the other villages he found them destroyed in the same manner, and he also destroyed the corn near there. Then the army commenced its retreat from the Indian country, supposing the Indians to be sufficiently punished.

After a march of about ten miles on the homeward route, the General received news which led him to suppose that the Indians had returned to their burning villages, and he immediately detached eighty regular troops, with nearly all of the militia, the former under the command of Major Wyllys, and the latter under Col. Hardin, with orders to return to the villages and destroy such of the enemy as presented themselves. The detachment countermarched with all possible speed to the appointed spot, fearful only that the enemy might have noticed their return and escaped again before they could reach them. The militia, in loose order, took the advance. The regulars brought up the rear. Just as the troops were nearing the town, a number of Indians were observed, and a sharp action immediately ensued. Shortly the savages fled and were hotly pursued by the militia, who in the ardor of the chase were drawn into the woods, quite a distance from the regulars.

Suddenly several hundred Indians appeared from the opposite quarter, rushing with loud yells upon the regulars, thus unsupported by the militia. Major Wyllys, a brave and experienced officer, formed his men into a square and endeavored to gain a more favorable spot, but was prevented by the impetuous attack of the Indians. In spite of the heavy fire poured in upon them, they rushed upon the bayonets and hurled their tomahawks with fatal accuracy. Putting the bayonets aside with their hands, or clogging them with their bodies, they were quickly mingled with the troops, where they used their knives with such terrible effect, that in two minutes the bloody struggle was over. Major Wyllys fell, one lieutenant and seventy-three privates. One captain, one ensign and seven privates, three of whom were wounded, were the sole survivors of this short but desperate encounter. The loss of the Indians was about equal. The attack was as finely conceived as it was boldly executed. When the militia returned from the pursuit of the flying party it was too late for help. They soon effected their retreat to the main body, with a loss of one hundred and eight killed and twenty-eight wounded. This dreadful slaughter so reduced Gen. Harmar's army, that he was happy to return to Fort Washington with the fraction he had left, having utterly failed in his mission.

This disaster was followed by a loud demand for a greater force to form a new expedition, which was also accomplished, as we shall presently see.

ST. CLAIR'S EXPEDITION.

By an act of Congress of 1781, Arthur St. Clair, Governor of the northwestern territory, was also appointed Major-General and Commander-in-Chief of the military forces.

An army of two thousand men assembled at Fort Washington. An expedition was organized against the Indians on the Maumee. A blockhouse was erected twenty miles north of Cincinnati, and called Fort Hamilton.

INTRODUCTION.

Twenty miles further north they erected and garrisoned another fort and called it St. Clair. Still another further on was called Fort Jefferson. Five or six weeks were employed at these works. Provisions became scarce, and at a point about ninety miles from Fort Washington, sixty Kentuckians, disgusted with the proceedings, shouldered their muskets, and in defiance of all authority, commenced their march homeward. Gen. St. Clair was daily expecting fresh supplies, and fearing that the deserters might secure them, sent quite a force to protect the provisions. This left him only about 1,400 men. November had come with its storms and rains. They were compelled to cut their way through a dense forest, over wet soil, and the movement of their artillery was attended with great difficulty.

Gen. St. Clair was aged, infirm, and suffering greatly with gout. Somebody was certainly to blame for undertaking a campaign at this season under these circumstances, and the sequel will show that they were out-generaled by the Indian chiefs. On the third of November they reached a point one hundred and twenty-five miles north of Fort Washington, and still fifty miles south of the Indian towns on the Maumee, which they were on the march to destroy. It was a dismal day; the ground was covered with snow, and the feet of the soldiers were soaked with water. Cutting their way through the pathless forest they reached a creek, a confluent of the Wabash. Here they camped for the night. The militia were sent across the creek, and bivouacked in two parallel lines, with a space of about two hundred feet between them. Soon they had a roaring fire in this intermediate space, illuminating the forest far and wide. No scouts were sent out, for all were nearly perishing with cold and fatigue, and there were no signs of any foe. But the shrewd savages were watching every movement, and, having assembled around the camp in great numbers, each selected his position behind some tree where he could be protected and remain unseen. St. Clair's men were huddled closely together, without any protection, hovering around their fire. On the other side of the creek the regulars were stationed around their fires, also, fully revealed to the savages. The troops could not well have been put into a more exposed position. The night passed away quietly. Meanwhile, the savages were preparing for the slaughter. The day had dawned, and the militia were preparing their breakfast in thoughtless confusion, when the yell of a thousand savages and the discharge of musketry fell upon their ears. Every Indian had a soldier for a target; scarcely one missed his aim. The slaughter was terrible. The militia became panic stricken, and fled with utmost haste, many of them without their guns. They plunged pell-mell through the creek and through the first lines of the regulars, and stopped a tumultuous, helpless mass at the second.

All this was the work of fifteen minutes.

Now the little army of less than a thousand men were huddled together in terror-stricken confusion, and exposed to a deadly fire from every direction. No foe to be seen, except when a savage would make an exchange of trees. There was no room for bravery, except to meet death without a tremor. There was no room for heroism, because the enemy was invisible.

Col. Drake was in command of the second line of regulars, and stopped the flight of the militia. He formed his line and charged into the forest. The wary Indians retired before him, while the bullets from all around were rapidly striking down his men. As Drake drew back his position, the Indians closed in like the waves of the sea. It seems that a large body of sharp-shooters had been detailed especially to attack the artillerymen. In a short time every man at the guns was shot down. Within one hour from the commencement of the attack, one-half of St. Clair's men were either killed or wounded, and nearly every horse was shot. The Indians killed over nine hundred of St. Clair's army, took seven field-pieces, two hundred oxen, a great many horses, but no prisoners. The wounded were tomahawked and scalped on the spot. The Indians lost but sixty-six warriors. For the Governor's official account of this disaster, see Abb. History of Ohio. page 324.

The Governor was himself not wanting of bravery. He did all he could under the circumstances. Eight bullets passed through his clothes and hat. He had three horses killed under him. The men who tried to bring up the fourth horse fell dead with the animal, and the invalid Governor was compelled to retreat on foot, which he did with wonderful alacrity.

An old, worn-out horse was overtaken and the Governor put upon that, and but for that timely aid he would have been left upon the field to fall into the hands of the savages. Greatly would they have rejoiced at the opportunity to apply the torture of Crawford to another "Big Captain."

We are compelled, for want of space, to omit recording any of the very many thrilling scenes connected with this sad page of frontier history, and will only mention the remarkable fact that amongst the camp followers there were no less than two hundred and fifty women—they, with a great many of the men in the ranks, taking it for granted that there would be no fighting; that the Indians would sue for peace; that garrisons would be established, under whose protection they and their husbands might find new homes. Fifty-six of these were killed, and tortured even more brutally than the men. Some accounts state that even two hundred of these women fell victims to savage barbarity. Some time after this disaster an old squaw was heard to say that "her arm got very tired that day scalping white men." The troops never stopped in their retreat until Fort Jefferson was reached. thirty miles away.

On reaching the fort and finding the provisions exhausted there. it was thought best to proceed on and meet the wagons loaded with provisions that were expected every day, and could not be more than one or two days' marches away. So the army, exhausted and terrified as it was. pressed on at ten o'clock that night and met the wagons the next morning. A part of the flour was immediately distributed, and the balance sent on to the fort. The main body now proceeded to Cincinnati and reported at Fort Washington.

Three distinguished Indian chiefs led the battle—Blue Jacket, Buckongahelas and Little Turtle. These were men of remarkable ability. Little Turtle, especially, took great interest in bringing his tribe to adopt civilization. He inquired of Gen. Harrison respecting the organization of the national government. He met Kosciusko in Philadelphia, in 1812. and quite a warm friendship sprung up between them. Little Turtle lived several years after the late war, and was esteemed for his wisdom. courage and humanity. His grave is near Fort Wayne.

The most simple explanation of the defeat of St. Clair is, that he was out-generaled by chiefs who were his superiors in Indian warfare.

And shall we ask the question why such humane chiefs would allow these horrible atrocities to be perpetrated before their own eyes?

Let us take the Yankee way by asking a question to answer another. Were not the inquisitions, the crusades, the burnings at stake carried on under the preaching of the glorious gospel of Jesus Christ, pleading for love to God and your fellow-man, scenes of atrocity equal to these in all their horror?

GENERAL WAYNE'S CAMPAIGN.

St. Clair's defeat raised a fearful storm of indignation against him. He was a man greatly esteemed for many manly traits of character. He was sincerely devoted to the public welfare. He was born in 1734. He received a liberal education, studied medicine, joined the army and was with Gen. Wolf at the storming of Quebec, in 1763. In the revolutionary war he was appointed Major-General and stationed at Ticonderoga. Before he was appointed Governor of the northwestern territory, he was a member of the Continental Congress, and succeeded Hancock as chairman. He continued in office as Governor until he was removed in 1802, by Thomas Jefferson. He died on the 31st day of August, 1818, poor in means, at the age of eighty-four.

The sad fate of St. Clair's army spread grief and mourning amongst the frontier settlements.

Those in the Miami country were abandoned. Many of the pioneers went with the army across the Ohio river. The Indians crowded their ravages upon the settlements, and became so bold as to appear in the streets of Cincinnati to spy out a plan for an attack upon Fort Washington.

It was nearly a year before Congress took any action in the matter. Depredations on the frontier were constantly going on.

Gen. Scott, soon after the St. Clair disaster, achieved a complete victory over the Indians, near the river, but statistics of the same are not very accessible, and particulars are wanting.

New troops were gathered at the falls of the Ohio for another expedition, under the leadership of Anthony Wayne, whose impetuosity gave him the name of "Mad Anthony."

Wayne was born in Easton, Pennsylvania, on the 18th day of January, 1745. He was a surveyor at eighteen years of age. In 1775 he raised a regiment of volunteers, and became its Colonel. He became a Brigadier-General, and was at Brandywine. He led the capture of Stony Point. In 1792 Gen. Washington appointed him successor of St. Clair in command over the army of the northwest.

In September, of 1793, Gen. Wayne had so far organized his army as to be ready to move into the Indian country. He reached Fort Jefferson by rapid marches. This fort was situate about twenty-five miles southwest of Sidney, the county seat of Shelby county. He fortified the camp well, and called it Greenville, now the seat of justice of Darke county. Here he made winter quarters. Commissioners had been sent to the Indians, who failed to conclude a peace, inasmuch as the Indians demanded that all the white settlements should be removed across the Ohio river, and the northwest belong exclusively to the Indians. This meant resistance. Both sides prepared for war. On the 17th day of October, 1793, Lieutenant Lowry and ensign Boyd, with ninety men, while escorting to camp Greenville a train of twenty wagons loaded with grain and stores, were attacked by the Indians, under the leadership of Little Turtle. The Americans were totally routed, losing both officers, fifteen men, seventy horses and all their wagons.

On the 24th day of August, the Governor of Kentucky had furnished Wayne with sixteen hundred mounted volunteers, under the command of Gen. Scott. In December, Wayne moved upon the place where St. Clair was routed, built a fort and called it Fort Recovery. The place is now in Mercer county, and within one mile of the Indiana state line. It was on Christmas day when they pitched their tents on the old battle ground. Before the men could make their beds they had to carry away the bones, which they buried the next day. Amongst these were six hundred skulls. In many cases the sinews still held the bones together. Here one company of artillery and one of riflemen were left. The rest returned to Fort Greenville.

General Wayne then advanced up the Auglaize to the Maumee. Here in the very heart of the enemy's country, he constructed a fort and called it "Fort Defiance," a very appropriate name. He put up two block houses directly between the junction of the two great streams. Stout palisades enclosed nearly two acres of ground. A wall of earth outside of the pickets was faced with logs. Beyond that a ditch was dug fifteen feet wide, eight feet deep, filled by water from the Auglaize.

The Indians in this region were far advanced in civilization, by their intercourse with the French, and the country around was well cultivated. More than a thousand acres were in corn. Apple and peach orchards had been started. General Wayne returned to Greenville, leaving the fort garrisoned. The troops under his command now numbered about three thousand. As far as could well be ascertained, the Indians numbered about two thousand. Many British officers and Canadian troops were associated with them, still encouraging the savages to resistance.

General Wayne was under full instructions from General Washington as to the manner of procedure.

The Indians watched all these works closely and resolved to make a desperate effort to capture the forts. On the 30th of June, 1794, some fifteen hundred Indians with several companies of Canadians, with faces blackened and in Indian costumes, led by British officers in full uniform, made a furious attack on Fort Recovery. Major McMahon was encamped just outside of the works with one hundred and fifty troops. The enemy rushed upon the detachment and assailed the fort from every side, but were repulsed and compelled to abandon the field, where on the 4th day of November, 1791, they had gained so great a victory. Major McMahon, lieutenant Drake and twenty other officers were killed and thirty wounded. The loss of the enemy was very heavy; the exact number was never ascertained until it was disclosed at the treaty of Greenville.

Gen. Wayne obeyed very closely the instructions of General Washington even to the minute rules of laying off a camp. Fort Defiance was one hundred and three miles from Greenville. Now Wayne pressed forward

INTRODUCTION.   33

and down the Maumee to the rapids, some forty-five miles, and within seven miles of the old English Fort Miami, erected Fort Deposit. The army that assembled here numbered two thousand regulars and eleven hundred riflemen, commanded by Gen. Scott. Scouts now ranged through the forest, one of whom, William Wells, was captured, and who had been raised by the Indians and deserted them, joining his own people. He was the adopted son of Little Turtle.

On the 13th day of August, Gen. Wayne issued a very interesting proclamation to the Indian chiefs, requesting them to meet him in general council, for the purpose of agreeing upon terms of peace. His proposition was rejected in substance. They sent back to Wayne a message, saying: "If Gen. Wayne will remain where he is for ten days, and then send Miller to us, we will treat with him; but if he advances we will give him battle."

Gen. Wayne had already sent his army on the march and met the messengers on their return, near Fort Meigs. They stated that the Indians were dressed and painted for war.

At 6 o'clock of the morning of the 20th day of August, Wayne advanced from Fort Deposit and took position at Presque Isle. Here they met and routed the savages and British forces from Detroit. The victory was complete, and amongst the dead enemies were many whites, armed with British muskets and bayonets. The Americans encamped for three days within sight of the British fort. Messages were passed between Gen. Wayne and the commander of the fort, as to the right of the British to its occupation. Major Campbell refused to give up the fort, whereupon Gen. Wayne carefully inspected the works. The British had four hundred and fifty men and ten pieces of artillery. It was decided not to attack the fort. Gen. Harrison, afterwards President of the United States, was aid to Gen. Wayne in this campaign. Now Gen. Wayne sent out his cavalry, which laid waste the whole valley of the Maumee for fifty miles. Winter approached, and the Indians were destitute of homes and provisions. In September another fort, forty-seven miles from Fort Defiance, was erected, and named after the General, Fort Wayne. Leaving a garrison here, Gen. Wayne returned to Greenville on the 20th day of November.

The Indians, thus left in utter destitution, were also anxious for peace.

Accordingly, in July following, a general council was called to meet near Greenville, represented on the part of the Indians by the chiefs east of the Mississippi river. Negotiations continued for six weeks. On the 3d day of August the treaty was signed. Gen. Wayne signed in behalf of the United States. The following tribes were represented: Wyandots, Delawares, Shawnees, Ottawas, Chippewas, Potawatomies, Miamis, Eel Rivers, Weas, Kickapoos, Piankeshas and Kaskaskias.

The treaty of Greenville ended for a time the war with the savages east of the Mississippi. This was in reality the end of the war of the revolution.

Gen. Wayne never received the honors that were due him from his country for the great services he had rendered. At the close of the year 1796, returning from Detroit to the eastern states, he was taken sick in a log cabin at Presque Isle, now Erie, Pennsylvania, which at that time was a small hamlet in the wilderness. After a short illness he died, and at his request was buried under the flag of the fort.

According to the Treaty of Paris, in 1783, the British military post at Detroit, and all the other forts within the recognized boundaries of the United States, were to have been withdrawn "as soon as convenient." Yet for more than ten years they not only retained these posts, but supplied the savages with munitions of war, and urged them to, and helped them on, in their atrocities against the frontier settlers. John Jay was sent over to England, as a special minister, to urge the amicable evacuation of these forts, (Fort Meigs was one of them), and with much difficulty succeeded in obtaining a promise that his request should be complied with before the 1st day of June, 1796. The posts at Detroit and Maumee were accordingly delivered over to Gen. Wayne.

Thereupon the whole of the northwestern territory was organized into five counties. Washington county embraced all the territory between the Muskingum and the Little Miami, extending from the Ohio river forty miles north, with Marietta the seat of justice. All that portion between the Little and Great Miami, within forty miles of the Ohio river, was called Hamilton county, Cincinnati the county seat. Knox county embraced the land between the Great Miami and the Wabash, also bordering on the Ohio river, with Vincennes its county seat, and where Gen. Harrison, while Governor of the territory, built a two-story brick house for a residence, (which the writer saw in August, 1876, while stumping Indiana for Tilden). The county of St. Clair included the settlements on the Illinois and Kaskaskia rivers, as well as those on the upper Mississippi, with Kaskaskia for its seat of justice. Wayne county embraced all the Maumee, Raisin and Detroit rivers, with Detroit for its county seat, taking in the whole of Michigan and a part of Indiana.

This vast region, then embracing but very few and very small settlements of white people, reaching from Fort Pitt to the Mississippi river, over howling forests and oceans of prairies, is now teeming with millions of happy, prosperous and intelligent people. Where once the birch canoe was the only mode of travel over the still waters of the Ohio and Mississippi, the stately steamboat, with its comforts and luxuries, is "queen of all she surveys," while railroads and telegraph lines cut the country in every direction, furnishing means to interchange both thought and traffic.

We will not undertake a more extended description of the various settlements made in Ohio after the treaty of Greenville, and refer the kind reader to the more elaborate history of Ohio, confining ourselves more closely hereafter to events particularly tending to affect the subject of our task.

Early in the year 1796, arrangements were made to establish a colony in that part of Ohio known as the Western Reserve. A surveying party was sent out, which, coasting along the shores of Lake Erie, landed on the 4th of July at the mouth of a little stream called Conneaut. Here they celebrated their landing day and the anniversary of the birth-day of the republic at the same time. This company consisted of fifty-two persons, only two of whom were females, Mrs. Stiles and Mrs. Gunn. There was one child. The next morning they commenced the building of a large blockhouse, which was to be their dwelling place and store house at the same time, and called it "Stow Castle." This little colony suffered very much from exposure, want of food,

INTRODUCTION.   35

the inclemency of the following winter, and disease—incidents to frontier life.

Emigrants began to flock into the Reserve in considerable numbers, and commenced settlements in various places—some of these fifteen or twenty miles away from the nearest white neighbor. The hardships encountered by these isolated settlers are easier imagined than described. It required a full day's journey to find a neighbor to assist in sickness, or any other emergency.

As early as 1755 there was a French trading post on the banks of the Cuyahoga river, near the mouth of which the beautiful city of Cleveland now stands. Ten years after the landing of the pioneers at Conneaut, a Moravian missionary, Zeisberger by name, with several Indian converts, left Detroit in a vessel called the Mackinaw, and cast anchor at the mouth of the Cuyahoga. They then ascended the stream ten miles to the deserted village of the Ottawas, where they settled, and called the place "Pilgrim's Rest." In the fall of 1796, the surveyors, who landed at Conneaut, advanced to the mouth of the Cuyahoga and laid out the plan of a city which they named Cleveland, in honor of Gen. Moses Cleveland, the agent of the land company. He was a lawyer of Canterbury, Connecticut, a man of note and wealth.

During the year 1790, the Connecticut Land Company constructed the first road on the Reserve. It ran from the Pennsylvania line to Cleveland. From 1799 to 1800 there was but one white family in Cleveland—that of Major Carter. Emigrants soon flocked in and made quite a little colony in 1801. The Indians soon commenced coming to Cleveland to do their trading. They spent the winter in hunting, and in the spring flocked to Cleveland, traded off their furs, and returned to their homes on the Sandusky and Maumee. Other companies of emigrants followed from time to time.

The emigrants to Ohio from New England and the middle states usually traveled in wagons until they struck the Ohio, at Wheeling. They then took boats and floated down the river several hundred miles, locating here and there, wherever friends had advised them to go, or interest led. In the year 1796, the whole white population of the northwestern territory was estimated at 5,000 souls. They were generally scattered along the banks of the Muskingum, Scioto and Miami, and their affluents, to within fifty miles of the Ohio river.

Cincinnati then contained one hundred log cabins, about one dozen frame houses, and six hundred inhabitants.

Col. Massie, a Virginian, in 1795, having secured large bodies of excellent land west of the Scioto, upon the branches of Paint creek, erected a station near the mouth of the creek, and soon after laid out a town three miles above. This town the Indians called Chillicothe, which means town. The town increased very rapidly in proportions. Emigrants were constantly arriving. It was the first town west of the mountains which was built in peace and quietude, undisturbed by Indian atrocities. Other emigrants ascended the Muskingum to Zanesville.

The settlements on the Detroit and Maumee rivers were annexed to the county of Wayne. Detroit was the seat of justice. Two full regiments garrisoned these forts in 1798. Five counties comprised the whole northwestern territory. Forty miles above Chillicothe there were three or four cabins near the right bank of the Scioto, at Franklinton, now incorporated within the city of Columbus. A few vagabond whites, who had given up civilization for barbarism, were scattered amongst the Indians, and as the settlements of the pioneers were extended along the trails of the Indians, the savages, both white and red, retreated further into the interior. New counties began to be organized in proportion as new settlements sprang up in every direction.

For eight years Cincinnati had been the centre of military preparations, and the sounds of the bugle, the fife and drum reverberated through her streets and along the hills that fringed the beautiful stream.

Now all was peace and order, and the hum of busy life took the place of war and preparations for war. Cincinnati started on her great mission of commercial greatness.

The strongest tide of emigration flowed into the valley of the Scioto, so famous for its fertility, its level plains and rich bottom lands. The Governor organized a new county, called Ross, of which Chillicothe was the seat of justice. There were then but three cabins between this town and the Hockhocking river. The country about Lancaster belonged to the Wyandots, where they had a town of bark huts, containing a population of about five hundred, who gradually withdrew to their brethren at Upper Sandusky.

This year (1798), as shown by the census taken at this time, the population of the territory amounted to five thousand free white males. The people were therefore entitled, by the ordinance of 1787, to what was called a second grade of territorial government. Gov. St. Clair accordingly issued a proclamation ordering an election to be held in the several counties on the third Monday of December, following, to elect twenty representatives to serve as a Lower House of the Territorial Legislature.

The men elected were gentlemen of the first order of intelligence and patriotism, and were unsurpassed by any legislative body that has met in Ohio at any time hitherto. They met at Cincinnati on the first Monday in February, 1799. Edward Tiffin was one of them. He was afterwards elected Governor, as we shall presently see. This Territorial Legislature nominated ten men to the President of the United States to serve as a Legislative Council.

The first regular session of the Legislature was to be held at Cincinnati on the 16th, but did not organize until the 20th of September, and continued for nearly three months. It is said that the address of the Governor was remarkable for its polished diction. Capt. William H. Harrison, subsequently President of the United States, was elected first delegate to Congress.

Congress, in order to prevent large bodies of land from falling into the hands of speculators who would check emigration by greatly advancing the price, devised a mode of survey and sale, by which the public lands should be laid off into small tracts and held open for sale to any individual.

In 1800 Trumbull county was organized in the Western Reserve, and an immense population flowed in from Pennsylvania. In 1801 the state of Connecticut relinquished her claim of jurisdiction of the Western Reserve, and received a title in fee simple of the soil from the United States.

In the session of 1800, Congress divided the northwestern territory into

INTRODUCTION. 37

two parts. The eastern portion, which contained 80,000 square miles, embraced the regions of Ohio and Michigan. This was still called the northwestern territory. The balance, called the Indian territory, comprised all the country from the Great Miami to the Mississippi, and from the Ohio river on the south to Lake Superior, and the sources of the Mississippi on the north, containing 180,000 square miles, now embraced in the states of Illinois, Indiana and Wisconsin.

ORGANIZATION OF OHIO AS A STATE GOVERNMENT.

In consequence of his awful defeat, Gov. St. Clair became very unpopular, as shown by the first election of Governor. The census of 1800 showed a population over which he presided of 42,000, a number large enough to entitle the territory to admission into the Union as a state. Petitions were presented to congress for that purpose.

On the 30th day of April, 1802, an act was passed by Congress, authorizing the call of a convention to form a state constitution for a state to be called the State of Ohio.

The convention assembled at Chillicothe on the 1st day of November, and on the 20th of the same month a constitution was ratified and signed by the members. It became the fundamental law of the state without being left to a vote by the people, and remained such for nearly fifty years thereafter.

The constitution created three departments of government—executive, legislative and judicial. The legislature was composed of a senate and house of representatives. The judiciary department was vested in the supreme court, circuit courts, and justices of the peace. The judges were elected by joint ballot of both houses of the legislature, for a period of seven years. The justices of the peace were elected by the people of each township for three years, as now. St. Clair, as a candidate for Governor, received but few votes. Edward Tiffin was almost the unanimous choice. The boundaries of the state were fixed as they now are.

By act of congress the sixteenth section in each township was set apart for the use of schools. The salt springs were reserved to the state, and three per cent. of the proceeds of the sale of the public lands was to be used for the construction of roads.

The first legislature organized seven new counties. There were now fifteen. The whole northwestern part, being more than one-half of the state, was in the possession of Indians.

The first court in Greene county was held in a log cabin. Gen. Benjamin Whitman was the presiding judge. He had a friend by the name of Davis who had a mill near by. While the court was in session, Davis and another man, whom Davis had accused of stealing his hog, had a fight, and Davis whipped him. With his hair and clothes badly disheveled and bruises on his face, he came into court, and approaching the table where the judge sat, addressed his neighbor thus: "Ben., I have whipped that cussed hog thief. What's the damage? What's to pay? There's my purse. Take what's right." He put down his purse and shaking his clenched fist at the judge, continued: "Ben., if you'd steal my hog I'll be hanged if I wouldn't whip you too." Eight dollars paid fine and costs.

There is also a good story told that occurred some time afterwards while

Judge Tappan was on the bench in some county in the Miami valley. The court was held in a log cabin and a stable close by was used as a jail. A trial had just been closed and the judge was charging the jury. The defendant in the case was a man who had an enemy in the crowd. This man spoke out occasionally and approvingly of what the judge said. He was an old friend of Judge Tappan and felt perfectly at liberty in speaking to the judge at any time, as he pleased. Judge Tappan was near-sighted, and when this man in the crowd would repeat his interruptions by saying, "That's right! give it to him judge," "Give it to him old gimlet eye," etc., the judge stopped in his charge to the jury, and asked: "Who is that man making this disturbance?" The man spoke up and said: "It's this old horse, judge!" Judge Tappan then spoke up quickly and said: "Sheriff! take that old horse to the stable and feed him on bread and water twenty-four hours!" The order was promptly executed and the court proceeded.

There was neither a pleasure carriage nor a bridge in the state at this time. Men wore homespun and buckskin clothes. Women wore linsey woolsey; and flax, hemp and wool were all the materials from which clothing was constructed for Sunday wear, spun by the family and woven by the family or at the loom of some neighbor. Settlers were compelled to keep dogs for the protection of their calves, sheep, hogs and poultry.

As a general rule the rifle was used to keep the family in meat from the game in the forest.

Ohio was now a state and a member of the Federal Union, starting on her proud career.

The first legislature met at Chillicothe on the first day of March, 1803. The territorial laws were, so far as was thought practicable, embraced in the new state laws. Judges were elected, courts organized, the practice regulated and provisions made for the election of justices of the peace. A secretary, an auditor and a treasurer of state were appointed and their duties prescribed. Laws were passed for leasing school lands and salt reservations. Senators were elected to Congress and laws passed for the election of members to the House of Representatives.

While this legislature was in session the treaty for the purchase of Louisiana was concluded with France under President Jefferson.

The second General Assembly met in Chillicothe in December, 1803. At this session laws were passed enabling aliens to hold title to lands; to make appropriations of the three per cent. fund for roads, to improve the revenue system, to regulate the duties of justices and constables, to regulate the common law and chancery practice of the state. (In 1809-10 the laws were revised.) Gen. Lewis Cass was the first person admitted to practice law in the northwestern territory.

About this time the Indians, who had behaved well from the time of the treaty of Greenville, began to resist the tide of emigration setting in westward. The celebrated Tecumseh, aided and encouraged by British influence and supported by his brother, "The Prophet," soon made it evident that the west was again about to experience a repetition of savage warfare. In 1811 Gen. Harrison, Governor of the Indian Territory, residing at Vincennes, marched against the town of "The Prophet," upon the Wabash,

INTRODUCTION.   39

and arrived at Tippecanoe on the 6th of November. This was their principal town. Here he was met by Indian messengers with whom an agreement was made that hostilities should not take place before the next morning and that then an amicable conference should be held. Just before day-break, however, the savages, in violation of their engagement, made a sudden and furious attack upon the troops in their encampment. Nothing but the precaution of sleeping in order of battle, on their arms, saved the troops from a total defeat. Nineteen-twentieths of Gen. Harrison's men had never been in any battle, but they behaved in excellent manner, like veterans. Gen. Harrison had only about seven hundred men. The Indians were nearly a thousand strong. The Americans lost thirty-seven killed and one hundred and fifty wounded. The Indians lost forty killed. The number of wounded was unknown. The little town of The Prophet was laid in ashes. The Indians were left very much enraged against the government. Harrison returned to Vincennes.

An incident must be recorded here that occurred in that year which, in its bearing on the future of America, was worth more than a thousand battles. "A steamboat started from Pittsburgh down the Ohio River bound for New Orleans."

The Indian name of Tecumseh means "Crouching Panther." The name of "The Prophet" was "Olliuachica." They were twin brothers of the Shawnees tribe. "The Prophet" was an orator of great renown and a religious teacher. Tecumseh, from his abilities as a warrior and statesman, would have attained eminence in any nation of the globe. They were born near Chillicothe.

The result of the battle of Tippecanoe, no doubt, drove thousands of the Indians into the service of the British in the late war with the United States, the elements for which were then already gathering proportions.

In 1812 the second war with Great Britain commenced. A council of Indians and British met at Malden in Canada. A Wyandot Chief, Walk-in-the-Water, a great warrior and orator, was present. Round Head, another Wyandot Chief from Canada, and two other Wyandot Chiefs, together with Tecumseh and his brother, pledged their support to the British.

Black Hoof, another Wyandot Chief, was friendly to the Americans. He is spoken of as a noble, generous man, and a great orator. So was also Between-the-logs, another Wyandot Chief whom the author once saw at Tymochtee.

INCIDENTS IN THE WAR OF 1812—FORT MEIGS, FORT STEVENSON.

Return J. Meigs was Governor of Ohio. William Hull was Governor of the Territory of Michigan. Hull was ordered to raise troops and take charge of the post at Detroit. Ohio raised three regiments of volunteers for three months. They rendezvoused at Dayton and, when joined by a regiment of regulars, numbered 2,500 men. They reached the Maumee at Perrysburgh on the 30th of June, 15 days after leaving Dayton, with 160 wagons. The road had to be cut for nearly the whole distance, 120 miles, through swamps and dense forests. They crossed the Maumee in boats and reached Detroit on the 5th of July. The British erected a fort on the opposite side of the river, and on the 15th of August, Gen. Brock, the British commander, summoned Hull to surrender. This being refused, they commenced to bombard and storm the fort. The British force consisted of seven hundred regulars and six hundred savages.

The Americans, except their commander, were anxious and ready for battle. Their numbers exceeded that of the enemy by two to one. When every soldier in the fort was waiting for the order to fire, they were ordered to lay down their arms, which they reluctantly obeyed and a white flag was raised on the fort.

"Without shedding a drop of blood," says Atwater, without firing a single gun, the fort with all its cannons, taken with Burgoin at Saratoga from the British, with a vast amount of powder, lead, cannon balls and all munitions of war, all, all were unconditionally surrendered to the enemy. Let us see: 2,500 men with all their arms; 25 pieces of iron cannon, and 8 brass ones; 40 barrels of powder—all were surrendered to about 1,000 militia and a few Indians. Cass and McArthur were amongst the prisoners.

The whole of Michigan fell into the hands of the British.

Two years thereafter Gen. Hull was tried before a court martial and sentenced to be shot for cowardice, but President Madison remitted the sentence.

After the disaster of Gen. Winchester, Gen. Harrison withdrew his forces from the Maumee to the Sandusky. Early in February he returned to the Maumee, however, and established his extreme advance post at the left bank and built Fort Meigs.

He had a force of 2,000 men. In early spring Proctor moved upon this fort with 3,200 men, 1,800 of whom were Indians under Tecumseh. Proctor was certain of success and promised Tecumseh to deliver Gen. Harrison over to him as a captive. After four days' firing from his batteries, Proctor demanded the surrender of the fort. This was refused. Harrison having anticipated the attack had sent messengers to the Governors of Ohio and Kentucky for aid. The call was promptly responded to, and troops were sent forward immediately. By this time the Indians had completely invested the fort. Twelve hundred Kentuckians were now nearing the fort and received orders from Gen. Harrison to land on the opposite side of the river, and spike the guns of the British battery. Gen. Clay landed his Kentuckians as ordered. Col. Dudley led the attack on the batteries and drove the British from the guns and spiked them. Had Gen. Harrison's orders been promptly obeyed and had the Kentuckians returned to the fort as they were ordered, all would have been well; but the troops were so determined to finish the work, that instead of returning, they disobeyed and followed a band of Indians who led them into an ambush. Gen. Harrison and his officers shouted to them from the fort, to return, but they persisted in their pusuit when, on a sudden, twice their number of Indians rose up and cut off their retreat. They opened a severe fire upon the troops and those that were not slaughtered were taken captives, and made to run the gauntlet. As soon as Tecumseh heard of this butchery, he ran up and stopped the carnage.

In the night following, the savages were cooking their meal in a large kettle over the fire, close by their camp. They had strings tied to each ration. On some of these strings was the flesh of Americans they had slain.

INTRODUCTION.   41

Gen. Harrison kept up the fire from the fort for some time into the night. Before morning Proctor raised the seige and left.

From the command under Col. Dudley of eight hundred men, only one hundred and fifty escaped. All the rest were either killed or taken prisoners. The loss of the garrison during the seige was one hundred and eighty-nine.

Harrison repaired to the southern part of the state for re-enforcements, leaving Gen. Green Clay in command of the fort. On the 20th of July, scouts reported that Proctor was again ascending the river, with a force of 5,000 men, including Indians under the command of Tecumseh. The Indians alone numbered 4,000. There were but a few hundred men defending the fort and the situation looked hopeless. Tecumseh instituted a sham fight near the fort to draw the garrison out, and many of the men were of the opinion that the fight was between the Indians and the arriving troops from southern Ohio. It was almost impossible to restrain the men in the fort from making an attack upon the Indians. They were on the verge of a mutiny, and it required all the cool resolution that Gen. Clay was possessed of to keep order.

Proctor again raised the seige and withdrew to the mouth of the Sandusky. A vigorous attack upon the fort and in the absence of help from the outside, the surrender of it would by all human probability have been a question of a few hours. The ignorance of Proctor as to the condition of the fort, was the bliss of Gen. Clay.

The closing scenes of the late war in the west, and especially the battle of Fort Stevenson and Perry's victory on Lake Erie, being in the valley of the Sandusky river and near the mouth of the bay, seem to make a very proper commencement of the history of Seneca county, and at the same time close the Introduction, which gave the reader a bird's-eye view and a short history of the north-western territory.

CHAPTER I.

BATTLE OF FORT STEVENSON—HARRISON AND CROGHAN—FORT SENECA—DEFEAT OF THE BRITISH—WIPINGSTICK—PERRY'S VICTORY ON LAKE ERIE—BATTLE OF THE THAMES—DEATH OF TECUMSEH.

WHERE the beautiful little city of Fremont now stands, there was once a small Indian town, composed of wigwams on the high banks of the river, and some near the shore. This town was inhabited by Wyandots, who had several other towns along the banks of the Sandusky river. They distinguished between these Sandusky towns by calling one the "Little Sandusky," the other "Upper Sandusky" and this lower one "Lower Sandusky." The whites afterwards added another Sandusky at the mouth of the river and called it Sandusky City, which still bears that name.

At this Lower Sandusky, which retained that name for a long time, General Harrison had a fort erected and pickets put up enclosing about one acre of land, and called it Fort Stevenson. The pickets around the fort had old bayonets put into them near the top, to prevent scaling them with ease. It was both a garrison and a trading house. The works were not sufficient to hold more than two hundred men. The defense of this fort was entrusted to a heroic young man by the name of George Croghan, who was then major, and but twenty-one years old. The only piece of artillery in the fort was one iron six pounder, which, at this writing, is still mounted on its carriage, standing on the ground where the fort used to be, and is familiarly known amongst the people of Fremont by the name of "Old Betsy."

About twelve miles up the river, on the left bank, was another stockade called Fort Seneca, with one hundred and forty men, where Gen. Harrison had taken position to rendezvous his troops, and from which he could protect the large amount of property which was collected along the valley of the river. Gen. Harrison was informed of the approach of the British and the Indians, and sent Mr. Connor and two Indians (Senecas) to Major Croghan, with instructions to abandon the fort, burn it and all the stores he could not take away and report to Fort Seneca. But the messengers got lost in the woods, and did not reach Fort Stevenson until 11 o'clock next day.

Major Croghan, being of opinion that he could not retreat, sent back the following answer:

"SIR—I have just received yours of yesterday, 10 o'clock p. m., ordering me to destroy this place and make good my retreat. It came too late to be carried into execution. We have determined to maintain this place, and, by Heavens, we can!"

Gen. Harrison immediately sent Colonels Wells and Ball, supported by a corps of dragoons, with a very severe reprimand to Major Croghan, and relieving him of duty, putting Col. Wells in command. Major Croghan returned to Fort Seneca with the dragoons as a prisoner.

Gen. Harrison was fully satisfied with the major's explanation and immediately restored him to his command, with instructions. Soon the scouts reported the advance of the British, while the Indians began to show themselves on the opposite side of the river. The British gunboats came in sight and landed troops one mile below the fort. The Indians, four thousand strong, displayed themselves in all directions. The British placed in position a five and a half-inch howitzer to open fire upon the fort. Gen. Proctor sent Major Chambers with a flag to summon a surrender. Major Croghan dispatched ensign Shipp out of the gates to meet him. After the usual ceremonies, Major Chambers said:

"General Proctor demands the surrender of the fort, as he is anxious to spare the effusion of blood," etc.

To this, ensign Shipp replied that the commander would defend the fort to the last extremity, etc., and that if the fort should be taken there would be none left to massacre.

The enemy then opened fire with their six-pounders from the boats, and the howitzer on shore, which was continued through the night with very little effect. Maj. Croghan reserved his fire. He, however, occasionally fired his gun from different points to make it appear as if he had several pieces at his command.

The fort was surrounded by a dry ditch, nine feet wide and six feet deep. On the middle of the north line of the fort there was a block house from which this ditch could be raked in either direction, by artillery. Here the piece was placed, loaded with slugs and grape shot. Now, the artillery of the British was placed on the shore about two hundred and fifty yards from the fort.

BATTLE OF FORT STEVENSON.

From this battery and the howitzer they poured an intense fire upon the northwest corner of the fort. Late in the night Gen. Proctor ordered an assault. They came within twenty paces of the fort before they could be discovered. Then a galling fire was poured upon them from the fort; but the British pressed forward and leaped into the ditch, led by Col. Short.

The masked port hole was then quickly opened, and the six-pounder spit grape and slugs through the crashing bones and quivering nerves of more than three hundred men, at the very mouth of the gun. The carnage was terrible. Fifty fell at the first discharge. A tumultuous retreat ensued. Two other assaults were easily repelled by the riflemen. Col. Short had just ordered his men to leap the ditch, cut down the pickets and give the Americans no quarter, when he fell into the ditch, mortally wounded. He hoisted his white handkerchief on the end of his sword and begged for that mercy, which, a moment before, he had ordered to be denied to his enemy. The assault lasted about one-half hour. The loss of the enemy was not less than one hundred and fifty. The garrison reported one killed and seven slightly wounded.

In the gloom of the night the British hastened away with their boats, leaving, in their haste, one boat loaded with clothing and military stores. On the next morning seventy stand of arms and some pistols were picked up around the fort.

So far, general history. In connection with this, one of the most brilliant military achievements in the late war with Great Britain, we will relate an incident that, as far as my knowledge and research extends, has never been published.

The Reverend James Montgomery, who was appointed agent for the Seneca Indians under President Monroe, a sketch of whose life is found elsewhere in these pages, took charge of his agency in 1819. He here became intimately acquainted with all the chiefs of the Senecas. Amongst these was a man known by the name of Wipingstick. He was a very intelligent and trustworthy Indian, highly honorable and reliable. He often related to Mr. Montgomery the following narrative concerning the part he was ordered to take in the affair at Fort Stevenson. I am indebted to Mrs. Sally Ingham, the only surviving child of Mr. Montgomery, a sketch of whose life will also be given herein, for the narrative. She, too, often heard Wipingstick relate the affair to her father:

Gen. Harrison had learned enough of Wipingstick to trust him. On the day before the battle at Fort Stevenson, Gen. Harrison sent Wipingstick with a letter to Major Croghan, with instructions and a signal. When the Indian arrived near the fort, and to make himself agreeable to the British and the Indians, he cursed the Americans in the most approved style.

When he saw that the coast was clear and that he was himself unobserved, he approached the fort, peeped through the pickets, wrapped the paper, with his handkerchief, into a ball and threw it over the pickets into the yard. Lounging around under the bushes a little while, he observed his handkerchief, in the same form, fly over the pickets again, falling outside. It contained an answer from Major Croghan to Gen. Harrison. With this Wipingstick made his way through the forest to Fort Seneca, and reported to Gen. Harrison the same night. This was the evening before the battle, which was fought on the 2d day of August, 1813.

Wipingstick was a Seneca chief, then about thirty years old, and had a wife and one child. He was a man possessed of many noble traits of character, truthful, hospitable, friendly and honorable. He was five feet four inches high, squarely and compactly built, very muscular and active. He had a pleasant, open face, pleasing voice and was very talkative. At the war-dances he was the leader, and carried a war-club about eighteen inches long, with a ball at the end of the handle and a swell at the other end. This club was cut full of hieroglyphics and was painted red. He danced with the club in his hands, swinging it, yelling and whooping, which he kept up for a long time, and until the sweat would drop from his face.

He attended Mr. Montgomery's funeral, and seemed very much affected by the loss of his old friend. The families of Montgomery and Wipingstick were very intimate.

On the next day, after the battle of Fort Stevenson, Gen. Harrison came down, but the Indians had fled across the country in the direction of Fort Meigs, and the British down the river.

BATTLE OF LAKE ERIE—BATTLE OF THE THAMES—DEATH OF TECUMSEH.

Now both parties made vigorous preparations for a naval battle, to decide as to who should be master of the lake and its shores. Detroit was still in the hands of the British. In a few months the government had nine vessels ready for service, carrying fifty-four guns, and manned by about six hundred sailors and marines. The fleet anchored just off the mouth of Sandusky bay, and sailed from there to Put-in-Bay, a harbor on one of the islands of the lake, and about

BATTLE OF LAKE ERIE. 47

thirty miles from Malden, where the British fleet was riding at anchor. Commodore Barclay had six vessels, carrying sixty-four guns, manned by about eight hundred men.

On the morning of the 10th of September, 1813, at sunrise, the British fleet was discovered, in full sail, in the distant west. Commodore Perry immediately got under way and formed in line of battle, bearing down upon the enemy. He hoisted his flag with the motto: "Don't give up the ship!" which was greeted by the cheers of the crew. For two hours the hostile fleets approached each other with that dead silence that always characterizes the immediate attack at sea. Everything on the American fleet was order and discipline; no noise, no bustle. The men stood at their guns with lighted matches, watching the enemy, waiting for orders and occasionally glancing at the countenance of their young commander.

At fifteen minutes after eleven a bugle was sounded on the Detroit, the advance ship of the enemy. Loud cheers burst from all their crew, and a tremendous fire was opened upon the Commodore's flag-ship, the Lawrence, which she was compelled to sustain for forty minutes, on account of the shortness of her guns, without firing a shot. Now all the other vessels of the enemy were drawn around the Lawrence, with the determination to destroy her first. Perry's other vessels could not come to her aid for want of wind. For two hours the doomed vessel withstood this terrible bombardment, while but two of her guns could be used in her defense. Through all this, perfect discipline was observed among Perry's men. The Lawrence was reduced to a wreck. Mangled bodies were scattered all around. All the crew, except three or four, had been either killed or wounded. The last gun, fit for service, was worked by the Commodore himself, and his officers.

It was now 2 o'clock in the afternoon. Capt. Elliot, of the Niagara, brought his vessel into close action. Commodore Perry left the Lawrence in charge of Lieutenant Yarnell, and, taking a boat, went over to the Niagara, where again he hoisted his flag with the dying words of Lawrence. He brought all his vessels within pistol-shot of the boats of the enemy, and opened a murderous fire from all his boats, which was kept up until every ship of the enemy struck its colors.

The engagement lasted three hours. Never was a victory more decisive and complete. The American squadron took more prisoners than they themselves had men on board. The principal loss of the Americans was on the Lawrence, where, of her crew, twenty-two were killed and sixty wounded. The loss of all the other vessels was but five killed and thirty-six wounded. The British loss was more severe.

Commodore Barclay, who had lost an arm at Trafalgar, now lost the other also, and received a severe wound in the hip beside. The loss on the American ships in all, killed and wounded, was one hundred and twenty-four. The loss of the British was over two hundred, killed and wounded, and six hundred were taken prisoners. Every British vessel was taken. Commodore Perry sent word to Gen. Harrison, at Fort Meigs, saying: "We have met the enemy and they are ours." The next day the funeral obsequies of the fallen officers, on both sides, took place near the margin of the bay, in an appropriate manner. The crews from both fleets united in the ceremony. What a lesson! Yesterday both parties were engaged in deadly strife; to-day they join their sympathies, associate as brothers to pay the last tribute of respect to their fallen companions.

On the 29th of September Gen. Harrison took possession of Detroit, there being no force there to resist him, and again the whole peninsula was thus restored to the United States.

Gen. Proctor, with his army and disheartened Indians, was on a rapid retreat into the heart of Canada. The river Thames, which empties into lake St. Clair, then ran through a wild, unbroken forest. Proctor was pressing his retreat along its valley.

Gen. Harrison left Detroit on the 2d day of October, to pursue the foe, with a force of over 3,000 men. The mounted infantry were commanded by Col. Johnson, of Kentucky. Proctor was overtaken on the 5th, at a point where the Thames protected one flank of his army, and a great marsh the other. The Indians were stationed in the forest beyond the swamp. This spot was about eighty miles northeast of the mouth of the river. Proctor had under his command one thousand British regulars and eighteen hundred Indians, under the command of Tecumseh.

The British were routed and ran away. Gen. Harrison then turned upon the Indians, routing and killing them. Proctor's loss was sixty-nine, killed and wounded, and six hundred prisoners. The Indians left one hundred and fifty dead upon the battle-field, Tecumseh amongst them.

This Col. Johnson here mentioned was Col. Richard M. Johnson, of Kentucky, who afterwards, in 1836, was elected Vice-President of the United States. The reader, who remembers the wonderful presidential campaign of 1840, will also remember how hard the Democrats tried to prove that Col. Johnson himself killed Tecumseh, and how equally hard the Whigs tried to prove that it was not true. The question is still an unsettled one. Mr. Abbott, in his history of Ohio, proves the utter falsity of the assertion that Johnson killed Tecumseh, while Mr. Knapp, in his history of the Maumee valley, is so well convinced of the fact that he proves it, even by affidavits, beyond all question of doubt.

CHAPER II.

FOURTH OF JULY CELEBRATION ON PUT-IN-BAY—ORGANIZATION OF A MONUMENTAL ASSOCIATION — CELEBRATION OF PERRY'S VICTORY — LAYING OF THE CORNER-STONE — SPEECH OF ELUTHERUS COOK — SPEECH OF DR. PARSONS AND THE OTHER THREE SURVIVORS OF PERRY'S FLEET.

RECURRING again to the incidents of the battle of lake Erie, the author hopes that a description of subsequent events, inaugurated to erect a suitable monument to the memory of Commodore Perry and his braves, on Put-in-Bay, may not be considered out of place here. Fearing that the occurrences I am about to describe may become lost to history, and conscious of the fact that the reader will find, in the addresses of the Hon. Elutherus Cook and Dr. Parsons, the best description of that eventful scene, I have no apology for giving them a place in these pages, and especially because certain citizens from Seneca county took a very active part in the movement.

An effort was put on foot amongst very many distinguished and patriotic men, in a number of counties bordering on lake Erie, to erect a monument on Gibraltar rock, Put-in-Bay, to the memory of Commodore Perry.

In the year 1852, five companies of the Ohio volunteer militia decided to celebrate the anniversary of American Independence by holding a three days' encampment on the renowned and beautiful island of Put-in-Bay.

The following finely equipped and disciplined companies assembled on the island on the evening of July 3, 1852:

Bay City Guards, Capt. R. R. McMeens, of Sandusky.
Sandusky Yægers, Capt. Louis Traub, of Sandusky.
Sandusky Artillery, Capt. L. A. Silva, of Sandusky.
Washington Guards, Capt. William Lang, of Tiffin.
Tiffin Artillery, Capt. T. H. Bagley, of Tiffin.

Capt. McMeens was chosen commander for the occasion. The weather was delightful. The green and rocky fringe around the bay; the broad, blue lake; the presence of a host of happy men, women and children; the imposing martial appearance and strict discipline of the military; "the army" passing in grand review before Gen. Isaac A.

Mills, and his aid, Col. A. A. Camp, and the eloquent sermon delivered by the Rev. E. R. Jewett made that Fourth of July Sunday on Put-in-Bay a fixture in the memory of all who were there.

This was the first military celebration ever held on the island. In the evening of the third day, when the camp was about to break up, the tents being struck and everything packed to get on board, the artillery under Capt. Bagley, were firing their farewell gun. As the last shot was being fired, and Frederick Roller was "sending home" the last cartridge, it exploded and threw Mr. Roller a great distance. He fell near the edge of the water, being badly burnt in the face, losing one eye and having a crippled hand for life. He, however, gradually recovered, and is still amongst the living. This sad occurrence was the only circumstance that marred the pleasures of that ever-memorable Fourth of July celebration.

During the first trip of the steamer Arrow from Sandusky to the island, a preliminary meeting was held on board for the purpose of organizing a monumental association, and with a view of erecting, at some suitable place on the island, a monument to the memory of Commodore Perry.

The Rev. Dr. Bronson was chosen chairman, and Mr. Henry D. Cooke secretary. On motion of Pitt Cooke a committee of five was appointed to draft resolutions expressive of the sense of the meeting in reference to the erection of a "monument on Gibraltar rock, Put-in-Bay, commemorative of Perry's victory on lake Erie, and in honor of the dead who fell in that memorable engagement."

Messrs. J. A. Camp, W. F. Stone, Wm. S. Mills, H. D. Cooke and Rev. W. Pitkin, were appointed such committee. Mr. Stone was appointed to lay the proceedings of the meeting and the resolutions before the assembled crowd at Put-in-Bay.

When, on Monday afternoon, the masses assembled, the proceedings and resolutions of the preliminary meeting were approved, and a committee appointed to draft a constitution for the organization, Rev. Jewett in the chair. The committee having withdrawn, returned and reported a short constitution. It provided that any person paying one dollar to the treasurer should thereby become a member. A board of managers was appointed, and an executive committee.

Gen. Lewis Cass was chosen President.

Col. J. J. Abert, U. S. Topographical Engineer, Washington City; Hon. Elisha Whittlesey, Commodore R. F. Stockton, Gen. Cadwalader, Philadelphia; Hon. Reuben Wood, Ohio; Mayor John G. Camp, Sandusky; Capt. Stephen Chamberlain, Buffalo; J. A. Harris, Cleveland,

and Judge Burnett, of Cincinnati, were appointed vice-presidents. My lamented friend Dr. R. R. McMeens was secretary, and took a very active part in the movement. Some funds were collected, and so the matter rested until 1858, when the executive committee, consisting of E. Cook, Wm. S. Pierson, F. S. Thorpe, J. A. Camp and R. R. McMeens issued a card dated Sandusky, Ohio, September 1, 1858, calling a mass meeting for the 10th of September, 1858, to renew the proceedings instituted on the 4th of July, 1852. "This was the most glorious and thrilling spectacle witnessed on lake Erie since the day of Perry's victory. The cities and towns along the shores of the lake poured out large delegations of people. The bay itself presented a most grand and glorious pageant, crowded with a fleet of magnificent steamers, sail vessels and yachts, all decorated with gaily colored banners, streamers and pendants, while a battery of fourteen brass cannon waked the echoes of old Erie with a welcome that made the old rocks of Gibraltar tremble with their reverberation," says Dr. McMeens.

Some of Perry's old veterans were there, old men who had heard the firing during the battle, statesmen, soldiers, women, children—all animated and inspired with the soul-stirring scene.

Ten steamers, three yachts, and twenty other sailing vessels anchored in the bay.

Eight thousand people gathered in groups about the shore.

Governor Chase was chosen president of the day. A number of vice-presidents and secretaries were appointed; also, a committee on exercises. Gen. J. W. Fitch, of Cleveland, (now Lieutenant-Governor) was marshal of the day. Mr. Elutherus Cooke, of Sandusky, delivered the oration.

Four of the survivors of the battle were present: Captain Stephen Champlin, who fired the first and last gun in the conflict; William Blair, of Lexington, Richland county, Ohio; Thomas Brownell, of Newport, Rhode Island, who was second in command of the schooner Ariel, and Dr. Usher Parsons, of Providence, R. I., the surgeon of the flag-ship Lawrence at the time of the battle, were introduced to the vast assemblage in the order named, and were greeted with wild applause. They each made short speeches, expressing their gratitude for their kind reception, and Dr. Parsons gave a highly interesting description of the battle, the treatment of the wounded, and incidents of the surrender of the enemy. It is a pity that the odes, poems and songs that were read and sung can not find room here. One—only one of these gems —must not be overlooked, however. It is the production of my old, lamented friend, Dr. R. R. McMeens, the secretary of the monumental association, whose friendship is cherished still, though he has long since passed away. A short sketch of the life of the doctor will be found in Chap. XXVIII.

THE ISLANDS OF ERIE.

By R. R. McMeens, M. D.

The Islands of Erie arrayed in full dress,
Enrobe the lake scene with strange loveliness,
As gorgeously decked in bright verdure they lie,
In the soft mellow haze of the still autumn sky.
No more brilliant gems, though lauded they be,
Ever gleamed 'mid the groups of the old Grecian sea.
They circle the storm-brewing gates of the west
To soothe the "mad spirit" of Erie to rest,
And lend their slight forms to the rage of the sea
To shelter the storm-tossed in succoring lee ;
Or, like sentinels, seem to be pointing the way
To the harboring arms of bold "Put-in-Bay."

When the winds breathless sleep in their caverns of peace.
How sylph-like they sit on the lake's lucent face,
Or mirrored in beauty on crimson dyed wave
When the sun silent sinks in her gold-tinted grave.
And the purple horizon depends as a shroud,
Of a tapestried mantle, in folds of rich cloud,
Then deep'ning so gently upon the pale glow,
So sombre and sad, scarcely seeming to know
When the last flitting ray of fading twilight
Merges in darkness and death gloom of night.

Oh! Islands of Erie, how many a scene
Of shipwreck and battle around you have been !
How many a gallant young hero went down
When Perry and sailors won glorious renown !
You stand as proud monuments over the dead,
Who sleep at your feet in their coffinless bed,
While the winds shriek or whisper a requiem sigh,
And the waves join in murmuring a fond lullaby.
And the mariner, gliding along by your side,
Recounts all their deeds with emotions of pride.

Oh ! Islands of beauty, on Erie's broad breast
That smile in the sunshine like havens of rest ;
Or when the storm-god in his wrath wildly raves,
Like "sisters" of mercy hang over the waves.
E'er bloom in your freshness as lovely as now,
To enrapture the eye and make the heart glow.

Governor Chase, the chairman, opened the meeting with a few brief remarks of welcome. Thereupon, Mr. W. S. Pierson, chairman of the committee, reported the following list of permanent officers of the association, viz:

President—Hon. Lewis Cass, of Michigan.

Vice-Presidents—Hon. Isaac Toucey, of Connecticut; Dr. Usher Parsons, of Rhode Island; Sidney Brooks, of Rhode Island; Thomas Brownell, U. S. N.; Gov. Elisha Dyer, Rhode Island; Wm. Wetmore, Esq., Rhode Island: Hon. Edward Everett, Massachusetts; Hon. W. H. Seward, New York; August Belmont, Esq., New York; Hon. Millard Fillmore, New York; Capt. Stephen Champlin, New York; Gov. W. F. Packer, Pennsylvania; Wm. G. Moorehead, Esq., Pennsylvania; Gov. S. P. Chase, Ohio; S. Starkweather, Cleveland, Ohio; Elutherus Cook, Sandusky, Ohio; L. Collins, Toledo, Ohio; Ross Wilkins, Detroit, Michigan; John Owen, Detroit, Michigan; Col. Todd, Kentucky; Col. John O'Fallon, St. Louis, Mo.; J. Y. Scammer, Esq., Chicago, Illinois; Hon. John Wentworth, Chicago, Illinois; Capt. J. P. McKinstry, U. S. N.; Commodore Jos. Lanman, U. S. N.; Lieut.-Gen. Winfield Scott, U. S. A.

On motion, Wm. S. Pierson, of Sandusky, was chosen treasurer, and Dr. R. R. McMeens, of Sandusky, corresponding secretary.

A committee of management was then also appointed. The following letters were then read by Mr. Pierson:

WASHINGTON CITY, Sept. 6, 1858.

DEAR SIR:—Your invitation to me, to form one of the numerous assemblage which will meet at Put-in-Bay on the 10th inst., has just been received, and, while I thank you for remembering me in connection with that interesting occasion, I regret that it will be out of my power to avail myself of your kindness, as I shall be necessarily detained here by my public duties. But though absent, I shall not the less participate in the feelings of gratitude and exultation which the event, you propose to commemorate, is so well calculated to inspire in every American breast. The victory of Perry upon Lake Erie, not far from the place of your convocation, on the 10th of September, 1813, was one of the most glorious, as well as one of the most important achievements recorded in our military annals.

I was with the army, then encamped in your region of country during that hard-fought battle, where we were all awaiting, with anxious solicitude, the operations of the fleets, as the command of the lake was essential to our movements, and now, after the elapse of almost half a century, it would rejoice me to hear my fellow citizens to recall and recount the glories of that memorable day, 'mid the scenes where they were gained, and which they will ever illustrate. It is good for the American people to assemble together in the time of their strength to commemorate the deeds of patriotism and valor which, in the time of their weakness, enabled our country to pass safely through the trials to which she was exposed. Such a tribute of departed worth is the object of the proposed convocation, and I beg leave to express my deep sympathy with the feelings which have prompted it.

With much regard I am, dear sir,

Yours truly,
LEWIS CASS.

Dr. R. R. McMeens.

Navy Department, Sept. 6, 1858.

Dear Sir:—I have the honor to acknowledge the invitation through you, of the executive committee, to be present on the 10th inst., at the inauguration of laying of the corner stone of a monument to be erected on Gibraltar Rock, Put-in-Bay Island, in commemoration of Perry's victory.

I regret to state that my engagements will deprive me of the pleasure of participating with you on the interesting occasion.

I am with much respect

Your obedient servant,
ISAAC TOUCEY.

R. R. McMeens, M. D.

Portsmouth, Va., Sept. 3, 1858.

My Dear Sir:—I have received your esteemed favor of the 27th ult., requesting my presence and participation in the ceremonies at the contemplated inauguration of the monument on Gibraltar Rock, in commemoration of our glorious naval triumph under the gallant Perry on the 10th September, 1813.

As one of the five surviving officers whose fortune it was, together with our brave tars, to be present on that glorious occasion, I thank you for your kind remembrance of me.

I regret that present indisposition precludes the pleasure of being with you, to join you in doing honor to whom honor is due—the brave dead—and renders imprudent at this time an absence from home.

I am, sir, your obedient servant,
H. N. PAGE,
Captain U. S. Navy.

R. R. McMeens, M. D.

Cincinnati, O., Sept. 9, 1858.

Usher Parsons, M. D.:

My Dear Doctor:—Yours of the 1st inst. arrived before my return from the "Yellow Springs," which afforded me no little pleasure to hear you intend to be at the glorious celebration at Put-in-Bay. I am denied the pleasure of participating with you in consequence of sickness. I confidently flattered myself, twelve days ago, I would be enabled to be present and unite with the few survivors in celebrating the most brilliant achievement of the memorable battle of Lake Erie, on the 10th of September, 1813, in which battle I was. Shortly after Col. Croghan's victory where I was on the morning after the British made good their retreat, I volunteered at Camp Seneca, and was lead by Gen. Wm. Henry Harrison to Perry's fleet.

I pray the good people who have been instrumental in promoting the celebration may continue it annually for all time to come.

May the blessing of Heaven guide and preserve all who attend the celebration, truly and sincerely is my prayer.

Most sincerely your friend,
W. T. TALIOFERRO.

NEW YORK, August 28, 1858.

MR. F. T. BARNEY, SANDUSKY CITY, O.:

MY DEAR SIR:—In answer to your favor of the 21st ult., on the subject of the erection of a monument on the little Island of Gibraltar, I have to say: That if said monument be to the memory of Commodore Perry, as I suppose it is, I will be too happy to contribute to it, not only by the free gift of the land requisite, but by procuring subscriptions in New York and one or two other places, which I think I can do. I accordingly hereby confer upon you and my friend, Simon Fox, power to grant a sufficient part of said Island of Gibraltar, in perpetuity, for the erection of said monument, with such reservation as you may deem necessary to prevent any sort of injury to my property in the group of islands. It would please me if I and my successors after me were appointed keepers of the ground ceded, and of the monument.

Respectfully yours,
RIVERA ST. JAGO.

After the reading of these letters, Gov. Chase introduced Hon. E. Cooke, of Sandusky, who spoke as follows:

Ladies, Gentlemen, Fellow-Countrymen:

I rise as the organ of the executive committee to bid you welcome to these classic shores, immortalized by American valor and rich in the associations of a nation's glory. But how can I find language suitably to express my congratulations of the assembled thousands who surround me, and whose presence this day gives the lie to the reproach that "Republics know not how to be grateful?" If I could hope to be heard by an audience so immense. I would thank you in the name of our common country for having come up in such vast numbers from the beautiful cities of the lake and the interior, to this patriotic consecration. But with a voice impaired by the wasting power of many years, I hope to say but little else than to offer up my fervent thanksgiving to Almighty God for those evidences of enthusiastic gratitude and patriotic devotion which the occasion has inspired, and which your presence this day proclaims.

We have met to commemorate one of those rare and signal events, which, considering the vast interest it involved, the glory it achieved and the benefits conferred, has few parallels in history. We shall find it difficult, however, justly to appreciate the importance of Perry's victory, without calling to mind, for a moment, the peculiar condition of our country which preceded and followed its achievements. A sanguinary war had for more than a year been raging between Great Britain and the United States. How it was sustained on the land and on the ocean, history has recorded. It must be admitted, however, that its commencement on the Niagara and in the north-west was characterized by defeat, disaster and disgrace. Whether the inglorious surrender of the fortress of Detroit and the consequent uncontrolled possession of the vast north-western territory by the enemy, were chargeable to treachery or cowardice, it is not now necessary to inquire.

FOURTH OF JULY CELEBRATION—SPEECH OF HON. E. COOKE. 57

The event smote the heart of the nation with dismay and covered the whole land with conscious humiliation. Our whole vast frontier, from Buffalo to Arkansas, was at once thrown open to the stroke of the tomahawk, and exposed bare and defenseless to the merciless incursions of the savage foe. The authority and protection of the United States had ceased within its borders. The course of the enemy, leagued with their savage ally, was everywhere marked with rapine, massacre and devastation. The heart-rending and bloody tragedy of the river Rasin, and other doomed localities, followed in succession. Consternation and alarm everywhere prevailed. Thousands "without distinction of age or sex" were expelled from their peaceful abodes by the invading foe, and the face of Heaven was insulted by the murder of men, women and children, and by the wanton conflagration of defenceless cabins and villages. The flower and chivalry of the land were cut off in their glory, and their bones whitened the face of the wilderness. Deeds of cruelty and unutterable horror were enacted, which filled the whole land with lamentation and wrung drops of agony from the heart of the nation. A dark cloud hung over our devoted country, throwing down from its frowning armory the paleness of death upon her cheek, and its coldness upon her bosom. True the assaults upon the defences of Harrison and Croghan on the Maumee and Sandusky had been gallantly and gloriously expelled, but these exploits, brilliant as they were, availed little to the relief of the frontiers, while the entire possession of the lake, by a well-manned fleet of veterans, remained in the undisputed control of the foe, with power to descend at any moment with their combined forces upon any portion of our exposed frontier. The crisis demanded action, vigorous action, combined with valor and talent to direct it. The command of the lake had become to us indispensable. In view of this, the creation of an American fleet, the timber for which was then growing in the wilderness, was ordered by our government, as well for the purposes of protection as invasion. In March, 1813, the charge of its construction and command was assigned to Oliver H. Perry, of Rhode Island, who, in spite of almost superhuman obstacles and difficulties, in less than three months completed his work and launched his vessels at the harbor of Erie. But although he frequently sought to engage the enemy he was unable to bring them into action until the ever-memorable and ever-glorious day we meet to commemorate.

Of the battle and its thrilling incidents I have no time to speak. I am not here with a tongue of fire to relight and emblazon the splendors of the achievement. That office must be left for a more elaborate address, and to others better fitted for the task. And I rejoice to say that some of its touching details will be given you to-day, in burning words, from a living and honored actor in the scene. On this point, therefore, I need only add, that although between single ships on the ocean, the trial had been before signally glorious to our flag, yet this was the first American squadron that ever made battle with an enemy, and this "was the first English fleet, since England had a navy, that ever had been captured." And if any thing further were wanting to heighten the brilliancy and achievement, it may be found in the fact that our fleet was inadequately and unequally provided with men and cannon—manned mostly by raw recruits uninured to battle, and commanded by young men without experience in naval warfare. While on the other hand, that of the British was fully armed—furnished with men who had encountered many conflicts on the ocean, and commanded by the experienced and veteran Commander Barclay, who had won rich laurels under Nelson, at the immortal battle of Trafalgar.

Such was the tremendous contrast between the opposing forces. Shut now the volume that records the event, and tell me, thou man of naval and military science, upon what principle of human probability can the triumph of our arms, in a conflict so unequal, be predicted?

The contrast was great, but to the dauntless Perry by no means appalling. After the line of battle had been set and all was made ready, an hour—a silent hour—was occupied in advancing to the conflict; an hour in which the lives of the squadron, the fate of the north-west and the honor of the nation were suspended upon the talents and collected valor of one man. How appalling the responsibility! How terrible the probation! How vast the interest involved! How intense the gaze of millions upon the issue! At such a moment, men of the present generation, picture to yourselves the solemn spectacle, the sublime pageantry of two hostile armies watching the movements from the opposite shores of the lake; of defenceless thousands throughout the unprotected region of the north-west, whose lives and homes were at stake; yea, of millions of two great nations, whose final triumph hung upon the issue—all, all awaiting with breathless anxiety, the result of the conflict, and tell me if it was not an hour in which the stoutest heart of the hero, charged with such a battle, might have justly trembled. Yet the heroic Perry remained unagitated, unshaken and invincible. He had no fear but for the safety and honor of his country; no ambition but to conquer or die in her defence.

A quarter before 12 o'clock the solemn suspense was broken and the conflict began. At 3 o'clock the battle ended. Its thunders were hushed. Their echoes had died away upon the distant shore of the lake, and the deep "silence of nature" succeeded, broken only by the cries of the wounded and the dying. As the smoke of battle rolled away, it revealed a victory, which shed undying glory upon the Republic, and gave immortal renown to the victors; a victory which wiped from our escutcheon the disgrace of Hull's surrender, avenged the insulted honor of our flag, and dissolved forever the spell of boasted British maratine invincibility. THE PUPIL OF NELSON had struck to the youthful Perry, and the country rang with acclamations of joy.

In estimating the immediate and momentous results of this victory, it should not be forgotten that it at once opened a pathway for Gen. Harrison, to the subjugation of Malden, to the re-conquest of Detroit, to the restoration of peace and safety of our whole extended frontier, and to the crowning glory of his campaign, by the capture of the entire British army, at the battle of the Thames. It changed at once the entire theatre of the war in this region, and transferred it, with all its dread pageantry of death and devastation, from our own soil to that of the bewildered, astonished and panic-stricken foe. And, it is no exaggeration to assert, that from the moment of this victory, the ambitious schemes of the enemy upon our western borders were forever blasted, and that the last vestige of British domination in the north-west practically expired with the last expiring notes of the last cannon, whose thunder closed the battle of Lake Erie.

In view of these grand and glorious results—connected with the direct influence they exerted to revive the public spirit; to restore fresh vigor to the American arms; to awaken the national confidence; to sustain the national credit and to strengthen the arm of the government, at that gloomy period of the war, it is no wonder that the news of the victory flew on the wings of the wind, electrifying the whole nation with joy, and filling the heart of every patriot with gratitude and exultation. No wonder that the bells of every church throughout the Republic rang out their merry peals as the news traversed the interior, and that every city and hamlet in the land blazed forth with bonfires and illuminations and other manifestations of the high-wrought public rejoicings.

And shall we, who are now in the peaceful enjoyment of the full fruition of these results; shall we, standing here in sight of the spot where the great battle which secured them was fought and won; shall we, who have fixed our homes and set up our household gods in the midst of the territory thus rescued and defended, remain indifferent to an event which conferred such priceless blessings, which cost so much blood and peril to achieve it, which added so much wealth to the fame of the nation, and which still commands the applause and admiration of the world? No, never, never.

To these scenes, then, let us with each returning anniversary come up for our instruction. Let us here re-kindle the beacon-fires of patriotism, which Perry left, on yonder cliff, with a fervent prayer that they burn forever. Let us bring honors this day for the noble dead who perished in the fight; and let the laurel and the cypress be kept forever fresh and green upon the lonely graves where their ashes are enshrined. In a word, let us seek our great practical lesson of public duty and patriotic daring in the contemplation of the exploits and sacrifices of that dauntless band, who near this spot, periled their lives for their country. But above all, let us this day signalize our grateful appreciation of their glorious deeds by efficient measures for the erection of a monument on yonder "Gibraltar Rock," to the memory of Perry and his noble companious—there to stand forever, a perpetual memorial of our convictions of the unmeasured benefits conferred upon the western states by their patriotic and heroic valor.

At no distant day upon that consecrated spot, where sleep the ashes of the brave who fell in the conflict, "with solemnities suited to the occasion, with prayer to Almighty God for His blessing," and in the midst of a cloud of witnesses like these which surround me, let the corner stone of that monument be laid. There let it rise. There let it stand as long as the blue waters of Erie shall continue to dash against its rock-bound base, to mark the spot which must be forever dear to us, to our children and to our children's children, down to the last syllable of recorded time.

The lapse of forty-five years has laid down in the dust most of the brave men who participated in the victory. The illustrious chief himself, who on that proud day, amid the roar and smoke and storm of battle, inscribed his name upon the shield of immortality, has been compelled to yield to the only foe he could not conquer; but all, thank Heaven, are not yet gone. A little remnant of that immortal band still linger among the living, to reap the rich reward of their labor and perils, in the affections and benedictions of their countrymen; and four of these have kindly yielded to the earnest invitation of the committee, and are now present, to receive an expression of the gratitude of the country, for which they put their lives at hazard, and to which they devoted the flower of their youth.

Fortunate should we esteem ourselves that we have been permitted to behold this spectacle; a spectacle, the like of which in thrilling interest and imposing grandeur, was never before vouchsafed to the present generation. Happy indeed that God has granted us the sight of these veteran survivors under circumstances so novel and affecting. Soon, alas, too soon, shall we seek in vain for one survivor, and the last of the heroic band will be seen on earth no more forever. Let us then bring fresh honors, this day,Ito those who still remain to link the living with the dead, 'ere the grave shall have closed upon them forever.

Gallant and venerable men! with grateful hearts we bid you welcome. thrice welcome to these island shores, and to these bright scenes of your early glory. We thank the God of mercy for having prolonged your lives that we might thus greet you, and that you might behold this deeply earnest demonstration of your grateful countrymen.

On revisiting the memorable spot where you linked forever your own fame with the glory of your country, after the absence of nearly half a century, it is not strange that the stirring incidents of the victory in which you so honorably shared, should come down upon your memory like an avalanche from the past, and agitate you with conflicting emotions.

How changed the scene since last your eyes beheld these lovely shores! True, the same lake which you then saw wreathed in smoke of battle and encrimsoned with the blood of your companions, still continues its ceaseless funeral wail over the slumbers of the buried brave, or chants its loud anthems to the praise of your gallant deeds. The same sun. which then looked down from its mid-day throne and fired your young hearts to deeds of glorious daring, still smiles upon your return to this renowned theater of your youthful courage and patriotism. But in other respects how great the change! The haughty foe is gone—the din of war is hushed, and instead of the thunders of hostile cannon, and the shrieks of your dying comrades, you have heard to-day the shouts of a new generation, who have come out from all the borders of the lovely land you defended, to greet you with the loud acclaim of an overflowing and universal gratitude.

Forever, hereafter, the 10th of September, 1813, shall be sacred to our hearts, as it has long been glorious to our country. It was your good fortune, most honorably, to participate in the dangers of that day. Imminent were the perils you encountered; glorious the deeds you performed, and great the sacrifices you made for your country. I will not attempt their eulogy. They have already found their place with those of your departed compatriots, among the solemn archives of our country, where they can never die; and the history which records them is but an imperishable transcript of your claims upon our gratitude.

You have come to most of the thousands before you as from a distant age, to revive recollections and recount incidents around which the mists of tradition have begun to cluster, and you find yourselves to-day in the midst

FOURTH OF JULY CELEBRATION—SPEECH OF HON. E. COOKE. 61

of a generation now in the full vigor and meridian strength of manhood, who had not seen the light of heaven when you had nobly bared your breasts to the shafts of death in defense of the rights and honor of your country.

You are now where you stood forty-five years ago, with trailed banners, at the funeral of your valiant dead. Like myself, you belong to a former generation. You look around you in vain for your youthful companions-in-arms and brothers in peril. They have been gathered to their fathers. But you look around you not in vain for the evidences of your country's happiness, and for the rich rewards of your patriotic sacrifices and toils; you look around you not in vain for the joy and gratitude of the living thousands who surround you, and who have been made happy—most happy—to bid you welcome, thrice welcome, on this consecrated day.

We forbear further to betray our emotions, for eulogy belongs less to the living than to the dead, and there is not a heart throughout this vast assembly that does not frequently pray that we may long be spared the duty of granting to you our last and highest honors. Distant, far distant, be the day which shall mark your setting sun. May the same God who shielded you in battle, and guided and preserved you in after-life, still smile upon your declining years, and cover them with his richest and choicest blessings."

Thereupon Mr. Cooke introduced Capt. Stephen Champlin to the crowd. He was the last surviving commander of the Perry squadron, who led the Scorpion in the front line of battle, and who fired the first and last gun in the conflict. He was received with tremendous cheers. Thereupon Gov. Chase read the Captain's speech, as follows:

"MR. PRESIDENT:—Unaccustomed to speak in public, and having no confidence in my voice, I ask the favor of you to read the following reply to the flattering sentiments just offered:

Fellow-Citizens:—I cordially thank you for the distinguished honor paid to the memory of my old commander, Commodore O. H. Perry, and the gallant officers and men under his command in the battle on this lake, and also the flattering notice of my services on that occasion. You have amply rewarded me for the toil and exposure of life on that eventful day. Next to a consciousness that I performed my duty faithfully, is the approbation of so vast a multitude of my fellow-citizens. I renewedly thank you, and beg leave to offer the following sentiment: 'The thirty-six volunteers of Gen. Harrison's army, who came to us in our greatest need, to whom we were much indebted for their valuable services.'"

Six rousing cheers were given for Capt. Champlin.

Mr. Cooke next introduced the venerable William Blair, of Lexington, Richland county, Ohio, as one of the thirty-six volunteers of Gen. Harrison's army, just referred to, and exhibited to the audience, from the neck of the old veteran, a rich and massive silver medal, bearing the impress of Perry, with appropriate inscription, which had been voted to him, with the thanks of the commonwealth, by the state of Pennsylvania, of which he was then a citizen, in testimony of his patriotism and bravery at the battle of lake Erie. The old hero was too much affected to say one word, but amidst a storm of applause acknowledged the kindness shown him by a modest bow and a flow of tears.

Thomas Brownell, of Newport, R. I., was then next introduced. He commanded the schooner Ariel in the battle. He was greeted with rousing cheers, and responded by thanking the crowd for the flattering and cordial expression of feeling, and assured them that it was all gratefully appreciated by him.

Dr. Usher Parsons, of Providence, R. I., the surgeon of the flag-ship Lawrence at the time of the battle, was then introduced, and gave a detailed and thrilling account of the engagement. His address was listened to with the most intense interest, and was frequently interrupted with cheers that made the welkin ring. Dr. Parsons said:

MR. PRESIDENT, AND CITIZENS OF THE LAKE SHORE:

The survivors of the battle of Lake Erie here present have listened with intense interest to the eloquent address just delivered, and thank you most sincerely for the cordial reception you have given to its friendly and complimentary allusion to our services on the day we are now assembled to commemorate.

Forty-five years ago we were here as spectators and participants in the battle, and now, in advanced years, are invited to join a vast number of patriotic citizens, gathered from the beautiful and flourishing cities bordering this lake, to celebrate the victory then gained by our squadron.

We have come hither, my friends, to honor the memory of those who fell in that glorious conflict, and are sleeping under the soil near where we are now gathered. We have come, also, to pay a grateful tribute of respect to the memory of Commodore Perry, and his associates in the battle, who have since passed away in the ordinary course of human life. And you, citizens of the lake shore, have sought out and invited here a little remnant of survivors to bless our eyes with evidences of your prosperity and happiness, and to warm our hearts with tokens of assurance that our toil and peril of life on that eventful day are not forgotten. Would to God that more had been spared to participate with us in these generous demonstrations of gratitude and respect. But they have passed away, and in a very brief period of time no spectator will be left to tell the story of "Perry's Victory."

That victory derives a general interest from the fact that it was the first encounter of our infant navy, in fleet or squadron. In contests with single ships we had humbled the pride of Great Britain. The Guerrier, Java and Macedonia had surrendered to our stars and stripes. But here, on yonder waves, that nation was taught the unexpected lesson that we could conquer them in squadron. But this battle derives a particular interest from its bearing on the war of 1812, and from the relief it brought to your shores—in wrenching the tomahawk and scalping knife from savage hands; shielding a frontier of three hundred miles from the assaults and conflagrations of a combined British and savage foe; opening the gates of Malden to Gen.

FOURTH OF JULY CELEBRATION—SPEECH OF DR. PARSONS.   63

Harrison's army, that enabled it to pursue and capture the only army that was captured during the war, and in restoring to us Detroit and the free navigation of the upper lakes.

My friends, you have read, and your fathers have told you, the story of this victory. Yet from the interest you still manifest by coming here in thronging multitudes, as well as by the expressed will of some present, and of the press, it is apparent that you wish the story to be repeated, probably with the desire that you may hereafter relate it to your children as coming from a spectator of the scene. I will therefore give a brief sketch of the battle.

I shall not detain you with a description of the construction and equipment, but commence with our arrival here, twenty-five days before the action, and our cruising in that time between Malden and Sandusky, and receiving near the latter place a visit from Gen. Harrison and suite, preparatory to an attack on Malden.

Early in the morning of the 10th of September, 1813, while we lay at anchor in the bay, a cry came from the mast-head—"sail, ho!" All hands leaped from their berths, and in a few minutes the cry was repeated, until six sails were announced. Signal was made to the squadron: "Enemy in sight; get under way." And soon the hoarse sound of trumpets and shrill pipe of the boatswain resounded throughout our squadron, with "all hands up anchor, ahoy!"

In passing out of this bay it was desirable to go to the left of yonder islet, but on being notified by sailing-master Taylor that adverse winds would prevent, the Commodore replied: "Go, then, sir, to the right; for this day I am determined to meet and fight the enemy."

There were nine American vessels, carrying 54 guns and 400 men, and six British vessels, carrying 63 guns and 511 men.

At the head of our line were the Scorpion, Capt. Champlin, and Ariel, Lieut. Packet; next, the flag-ship Lawrence, of 20 guns, to engage the flagship Detroit, the Caledonia to fight the Hunter; the Niagara, of 20 guns, to engage the Queen Charlotte; and lastly, three small vessels to fight the Lady Provost, of 13 guns, and Little Belt, of 3 guns. Our fleet now moved on to attack the enemy, distant, at 10 o'clock, about five miles.

The Commodore now produced the *burgee*, or fighting flag, hitherto concealed in the ship. It was inscribed with large white letters, on a blue ground, legible throughout the squadron: "DON'T GIVE UP THE SHIP,"— the last words of the expiring Lawrence, and now to be hoisted at the mast head of the vessel bearing his name.

A spirited appeal was made to the crew, and up went the flag to the foreroyal, amid hearty cheers throughout the squadron, and the drums and fifes struck up the thrilling sound, "all hands to quarters."

The hatches, or passage-ways to the decks, were now closed, excepting a small aperture ten inches square, through which light was admitted to the surgeon's room, for receiving the wounded, the floor of which was on a level with the surface of the lake, and exposing them to cannon ball as much as if they were on deck.

Every preparation being made, and every man at his station, a profound silence reigned for more than an hour—the most trying part of the scene.

It was like the stillness that precedes the hurricane. The fleet moved on steadily till a quarter before twelve o'clock, when the awful suspense was relieved by a shot aimed at us from the Detroit, about one mile distant. Perry made more sail, and coming within canister distance, opened a rapid and destructive fire on the Detroit. The Caledonia, Capt. Turner, followed the Lawrence in gallant style; and the Ariel, Lieut. Packet, and the Scorpion, Capt. Champlin, fought nobly and effectively.

The Niagara failing to grapple with the Queen, the latter vessel shot ahead to fire upon the Lawrence, and with the Detroit aimed their broadsides exclusively upon her, hoping and intending to sink her. At last they made her a complete wreck; but, fortunately, the Commodore escaped without injury, and stepping into a boat with his fighting flag thrown over his shoulders, he pushed off for the Niagara amid a shower of cannon and musket balls, and reached that vessel unscathed.

He found her a fresh vessel, with only two, or at most three, persons injured, and immediately sent her commander to hasten up the small vessels. Perry boarded the Niagara when she was abreast of the Lawrence, and further from her than the Detroit was on her right. The Lawrence now dropped astern and hauled down her flag. Perry turned the Niagara's course towards the enemy, and crossing the bow of the Lawrence bore down headforemost upon the enemy's line, determined to break through it and take a raking position. The Detroit attempted to turn, so as to keep her broadside to the Niagara, and avoid being raked; but in doing this, she fell against the Queen, and got entangled in her rigging, which left the enemy no alternative but to strike both ships. Perry now shot further ahead, near the Lady Provost, which, from being crippled in her rudder, had drifted out out of her place to leeward, and was pressing forward towards the head of the British line to support the two ships. One broadside from the Niagara silenced her battery. The Hunter next struck, and the two smaller vessels, in attempting to escape, were overhauled by the Scorpion, Capt. Champlin, and the Trip, Mr. Holdup; and thus ended the action, after 3 o'clock.

Let us now advert for a moment to the scenes exhibited in the flag-ship Lawrence, of which I can speak as an eye-witness. The wounded began to come down before she opened her battery, and for one, I felt impatient of the delay. In proper time, however, as it proved, the dogs of war were let loose from their leash, and it seemed as though heaven and earth were at loggerheads. For more than two hours little could be heard but the deafening thunder of our broadsides, the crash of the balls dashing through our timbers, and the shrieks of the wounded. These were brought down faster than I could attend to them, farther than to stay the bleeding, or support a shattered limb with splints, and pass them forward upon the berth-deck.

When the battle had raged an hour and a half, I heard a call for me at the small sky-light, and stepping towards it, I saw the Commodore, whose countenance was as calm and placid as if on ordinary duty. "Doctor," said he, "send me one of your men," meaning one of the six stationed with me to assist in moving the wounded. In five minutes the call was repeated and obeyed, and at the seventh call I told him he had all my men. He asked if there were any sick or wounded who could pull a rope, when two or three crawled up on deck to lend a helping, but feeble, hand in pulling at the last

FOURTH OF JULY CELEBRATION—SPEECH OF DR. PARSONS. 65

guns. The hard fighting terminated about three o'clock. As the smoke cleared away, the two fleets were found mingled together, the small vessels having come up to the others. The shattered Lawrence, lying to the windward, was once more able to hoist her flag, which was cheered by a few feeble voices on board, making a melancholy sound compared with the boisterous cheers that preceded the battle.

The proud, though painful, duty of taking possession of the conquered ships was now performed. The Detroit was nearly dismantled, and the destruction and carnage had been dreadful. The Queen was, in condition, a little better. "Every Commander, and second in command," says Barclay, in his official report, "was either killed or wounded." The whole number killed in the British fleet was forty-one, and of wounded ninety-four. In the American fleet, twenty-seven were killed and ninety-six wounded. Of the twenty-seven killed, twenty-two were on board the Lawrence; and of the ninety-six wounded, sixty-one were on board this same ship—making eighty-three killed and wounded out of 101 reported fit for duty on the Lawrence on the morning of the battle. On board the Niagara were two killed and twenty-three wounded—making twenty-five; and of these, twenty-two were killed or wounded after Perry took command of her.

About 4 o'clock a boat was discovered approaching the Lawrence. Soon the Commodore was recognized in her, who was returning to resume command of his tattered ship, determined that the remnant of her crew should have the privilege of witnessing the formal surrender of the British officers. It was a time of conflicting emotions when he stepped upon the deck. The battle was won, and he was safe; but the deck was slippery with blood, and strewed with the bodies of twenty officers and men, some of whom sat at table with us at our last meal, and the ship resounded with the groans of the wounded. Those of us who were spared, and able to walk, met him at the gangway to welcome him on board, but the salutation was a silent one on both sides—not a word could find utterance. And now the British officers arrived—one from each vessel—to tender their submission, and with it their swords. When they approached, picking their way among the wreck and carnage of the deck, with their sword-hilts towards Perry, they tendered them to his acceptance. With a dignified and solemn air, and with a low tone of voice, he requested them to retain their side arms; inquired with deep concern for Commodore Barclay and the wounded officers, tendering to them every comfort his ship afforded, and expressing his regret that he had not a spare medical officer to send them; that he had only one on duty for the fleet, and that one had his hands full.

Among the ninety-six wounded, there occurred three deaths. A result so favorable was attributable to the plentiful supply of fresh provisions sent off to us from the Ohio shore; to fresh air—the wounded being ranged under an awning on the deck until we arrived at Erie, ten days after the action; and, also, to the devoted attention of Commodore Perry to every want.

Those who were killed in the battle were that evening committed to the deep, and over them was read the impressive Episcopal service.

On the following morning the two fleets sailed into this bay, where the slain officers of both were buried in an appropriate and affecting manner. They consisted of three Americans—Lieutenant Brooks, and midshipmen

Lynch and Clark; and three British officers—Captain Finis, and Lieutenant Stokes, of the Queen, and Lieutenant Garland, of the Detroit. Equal respect was shown to the slain of both nations, and the crews of both fleets united in the ceremony. The procession of boats, with two bands of music; the slow and regular motion of the oars, striking in exact time with the solemn notes of the dirge; the mournful waving of flags, and sound of minute guns from the ships, presented a striking contrast to the scenes of two days before, when both the living and the dead, now forming this solemn and fraternal train, were engaged in fierce and bloody strife, hurling at each other the thunderbolts of war.

On the eighth day after the action, the Lawrence was dispatched to Erie with the wounded, where we received a cordial welcome and kind hospitality.

The remainder of the vessels conveyed Harrison's army to Malden, where they found the public stores in flames, and Proctor, with his army, in hasty retreat. Perry joined Harrison as a volunteer aid, who, with our troops, chiefly from Ohio and Kentucky, overtook and captured the army. Perry then accompanied Harrison and Commodore Barclay to Erie, where they landed amid peals of cannon and shouts of the multitude, and from thence proceeded to Rhode Island.

Commodore Perry served two years as commander of the Java, taking with him most of the survivors of the Lawrence. He after this commanded a squadron in the West Indies, where he died, in 1819.

Possessed of high-toned morals, he was above the low dissipation and sensuality too prevalent with some officers of this day, and in his domestic character was a model of every domestic virtue and grace. His literary acquirements were respectable, and his taste refined. He united the graces of a manly beauty to a lion heart, a sound mind, a safe judgment, and a firmness of purpose which nothing could shake.

But this intelligent audience already know and appreciate his noble virtues and honor his glorious achievements. The maps of your shores and inland towns and counties are inscribed with his name; and the noble State of Ohio, and the United States are about to decorate the walls of their respective capitols with splendid representations of the battle we are this day commemorating.

My friends, in the name and behalf of the citizens of Rhode Island. I tender you their grateful acknowledgements for the honor done that little State on this interesting occasion. She sent hither the commander of the squadron, and a majority of the officers and men. She glories in the victory gained, and regards the name and fame of her gallant son as one of her choicest jewels, and will ever cherish grateful sentiments towards those who respect and honor his memory. You have come hither, my friends, for this holy purpose from all the cities of the lake shore, and are about to lay the corner stone of a monument to perpetuate his memory and fame. Though his name will outlive structures of marble, or of bronze, yet rest assured that the citizens of Rhode Island will hail with delight the report of this day's transactions, and in their future western pilgrimages will linger about this spot and invoke Heaven's choicest blessings on you in return for your generous magnanimity.

Old companions in the conflict. I rejoice to see you and once more take

FOURTH OF JULY CELEBRATION—CONCLUSION.

you by the hand, and a more fitting occasion than the present could hardly occur or be conceived of. In the days of our youth we came to the rescue of this lake, and to assist in restoring peace to the frontier. A kind Providence has lengthened out our days beyond man's allotted period of existence, and now, after a lapse of nearly half a century, permits us to revisit the place where important scenes transpired in our early years, and to unite in celebrating the victory achieved by our much-loved commander. We joyfully survey the wonderful changes and improvements that have occurred since the war of 1812. Buffalo was then a populous village, but soon after a heap of ashes; Erie contained but a score of dwellings; Cleveland was a cluster of log cabins; Sandusky, the same; Toledo was nowhere, and Detroit in possession of the enemy, and not a single American vessel was left on the lakes on which to hoist our stars and stripes.

And what do we now behold? A population increased an hundred fold; magnificent and prosperous cities; lofty spires and domes on temples of worship; colleges and seminaries of learning; extensive commerce; railroads diverging and intersecting in all directions; the white, outspread wings of commerce gliding to and fro, and freighted with the exhaustless products of the north and northwest—aye, and ploughing yon crystal waves, once shrouded in the smoke of our cannon, and crimsoned with the blood of our companions.

Old friends, we part to-day, probably to meet no more. Our memories of the past, and the happy experiences of this celebration, fill our hearts with grateful and tender emotions, and will serve to gild the evening twilight of our days. I bid you an affectionate farewell.

Mayor Starkweather, of Cleveland, then made a short speech. He was followed by Joshua R. Giddings. D. Bethune Duffield, Esq., of Detroit, delivered a poem of rare beauty, describing the battle. Judge Mason, of Toledo, also spoke.

ON BOARD THE STEAMER QUEEN CITY.

Dr. Usher Parsons pointed out from the steamer Queen City, on her trip homeward, with three other survivors on board, the locality where the fleet had come to anchor a few days before the engagement, and fired three guns, a signal previously agreed upon between Commodore Perry and Gen. Harrison. "The next day" (said the doctor) "Gen. Harrison, and his suite, among whom were the celebrated Governor McArthur and Hon. Lewis Cass, with a number of Indian chiefs, came on board, drenched with rain. Here we received the volunteer reinforcement from the army. A day or two after the reception of Gen. Harrison and suite, they were saluted with the usual number of guns. They stood, during the time, on the quarter-deck of the Lawrence, in full-dress uniform. I have never since looked upon a nobler and a more martial staff of officers. When the firing began the "Indian braves" dodged below in double-quick time, and remained in the cabin until it ceased. Their ears were not used to that kind of thunder."

The author took a very active part in this celebration, and must be excused for referring to it here, because it always seemed to him very wrong that the plan of the association was not carried out. After all these patriotic effusions of eloquence in prose and song, and these thousands of people, with one voice, agreeing to erect the monument on Gibraltar rock, as then and theretofore contemplated—that all this should be set at defiance, and the plan frustrated by a few selfish men, can not be successfully apologized for. There is certainly no more appropriate spot on earth for a monument to Perry and his braves than right at the spot where the corner stone was laid at Gibraltar rock in 1858. If the present generation should fail to carry out the plan then inaugurated in such glorious style, and with such high hopes of success, may not a Mr. Jay Cooke, with his acknowledged patriotism and his wonderful recuperative powers, yet erect such a monument upon that corner stone that shall be worthy of the day and deed? While in the zenith of his fame Mr. Cooke built a palatial mansion near the corner stone, where it was laid more than 21 years ago. In this mansion many ministers of the gospel throughout the land, for several years, found and enjoyed Mr. Cooke's hospitality, and made the acquaintance of the superintendent, Mrs. McMeens, the distinguished Tiffinite, the widow of my late and lamented friend, Dr. McMeens, the efficient secretary of that "monumental association," and who preserved the proceedings of the 10th day of September, 1858.

Whatever became of the funds, I do not know, and would not have anybody believe that improper use was ever made of them; but one thing I do know: That soon after that glorious inauguration, efforts were made to build a monument to Perry in the public square at Cleveland; that succeeded. I can never look at it, or think about it, but feelings of sadness pervade my whole being. If there is, in fact, no wrong connected with it, it is certainly away from home. Why did not the people of Sandusky, and of the islands, protest against the robbery? Why did Toledo and Detroit stand by and see this thing done? Such is life!

CHAPTER III.
PEACE—TREATIES—RESERVATIONS—CESSIONS—EMIGRANTS ARRIVING—WARS BETWEEN THE WYANDOTS AND SENECAS—SPEECH OF LOGAN—LOGAN'S DEATH.

PEACE.

And now smiling peace with her blessings and treasures
Did visit the plains of Columbia again.

THE annihilation of the British fleet on Lake Erie, the re-conquest of Detroit, and the utter overthrow and dispersion of the British army at the battle of the Thames, brought peace to the northwestern frontier. The population of Ohio was now three hundred thousand. At the conclusion of Wayne's expedition, only eighteen years previous, it was but five thousand. The battle of the Thames took place October 5, 1813. Peace was made at Ghent, in Switzerland, between the United States and Great Britain, December 24, 1814.

After the fall of Tecumseh the Indians abandoned all hopes of arresting the advance of civilization, and tribe after tribe exchanged its hunting grounds for rich annuities from the United States, and retired beyond the Mississippi.

There was no permanent state capital in Ohio before 1812. Chillicothe continued to be the capital *pro tem.* until 1810. Then the state legislature met at Zanesville. In 1812 the high bank on the Scioto, just opposite Franklinton, was selected by a committee of the legislature as a site for the future capital. This region was then an unbroken wilderness. In December, 1816, the legislature met there for the first time. The site is on the same parallel with Philadelphia, four hundred and fifty miles distant, and on the same longitude with Detroit, from which it is one hundred and seventy miles south. On the same day, when the first sale of town lots in Columbus took place, war was declared with Great Britain, June 18, 1812.

Great efforts were now made to extinguish the Indian titles in Ohio. Generals Lewis Cass and Duncan McArthur met a large delegation of Indian chiefs, warriors and sachems at the foot of the rapids of the Maumee, on the 29th day September, 1817. Gens. Cass and McArthur were the commissioners representing the United States. The Wyandots,

Senecas, Delawares, Shawnees, Potawatomies, Ottawas and Chippewas were represented in behalf of all the northwestern Indians. A treaty was then and there concluded by which all the lands of the Indians within the State of Ohio were ceded to the United States forever. At that time no white man had settled in Seneca county.

At this treaty the United States granted to the Senecas a tract of land containing thirty thousand acres, lying upon the east side of, and adjoining, the Sandusky river, mostly within the boundaries of what now constitutes Seneca county. The chiefs of the Senecas, to whom this cession was made, were Takawmadoaw, Captain Harris, Isahowmasaw, Joseph, Tawgyou, Captain Smith, Coffeehouse, Running-about and Wipingstick.

At another treaty, held about one year thereafter by the same commissioners in behalf of the United States and these Indians, at the same place, ten thousand acres more were added to the Seneca reservation, adjoining the other tract on the south, thus making the whole reserve to contain forty thousand acres.

To the Wyandots was ceded a tract twelve miles square, now in Wyandot county, and the southwest corner of Big Spring township, in Seneca county, about twelve square miles.

For further information concerning this Indian reservation on Big Spring, see the documents:

DEPARTMENT OF THE INTERIOR,
OFFICE OF INDIAN AFFAIRS,
WASHINGTON, MAY 11, 1880.

W. LANG, ESQ., Tiffin, Ohio—*Sir:*—I am in receipt, by reference from the Commissioner of the General Land Office, of your letter, dated 7th of January, last, in which you state that you have been informed that there was an Indian reservation of about twelve square miles in the southwest corner of Seneca county, Ohio; and, as you are writing a history of said county, you desire to be informed as to whom it was made. You expressed the opinion that it belonged to the Delawares.

In reply, I have to state that the second clause of the second article of the Wyandot treaty of September 17, 1818, (7 stat., p. 179), contains the following stipulation, to-wit:

"That there shall be reserved for the use of the Wyandots residing at Solomons-town, and on Blanchard's fork, in addition to the reservation before made, sixteen thousand acres of land, to be laid off in a square form on the head of Blanchard's fork, the center of which shall be at the Big Spring, on the trace leading from Upper Sandusky to Fort Findlay."

This reservation was known as the Big Spring Indian reservation, and was located in township 1 N. and 1 S., range 12; and 1 N. and 1 S., range 13, in Ohio.

It appears from an examination of a map that about two-thirds of this reservation was situated in the southwest corner of Seneca county, and the remainder south and west thereof.

By the provisions of the first article of the Wyandot treaty of January 19, 1832, (7 stat., p. 364), the reservation was ceded to the United States.

Very respectfully,

R. E. TROWBRIDGE, *Commissioner.*

Upon the receipt of the foregoing letter, the writer hunted up the law ceding this Big Spring reservation to the United States, and it is added here as a sort of relic. My old friend, Dr. G. W. Sampson, who is still living, was one of the witnesses.

ARTICLES OF AGREEMENT AND CONVENTION Made and concluded at McCutchenville, Crawford county, Ohio, on the nineteenth day of January, 1832, by and between James B. Gardiner, specially appointed Commissioner on the part of the United States, and the Chiefs, Headmen and Warriors of the band of Wyandots, residing at the Big Spring, in said county of Crawford, and owning a reservation of 16,000 acres at that place:

WHEREAS, The said band of Wyandots have become fully convinced that whilst they remain in their present situation in the state of Ohio, in the vicinity of a white population, which is continually increasing and crowding around them, they can not prosper and be happy, and the morals of many of their people will be daily becoming more and more vitiated; and understanding that the government of the United States is willing to purchase the reservation of land on which they reside, and for that purpose have deputed the said James B. Gardiner as special commissioner to treat for the cession of the same;

Therefore, To effect the aforesaid objects, the said Chiefs, Headmen and Warriors, and the said James B. Gardiner, have this day entered into and agreed upon the following articles of convention:

ARTICLE I. The band of Wyandots residing at the Big Spring, in the county of Crawford, and State of Ohio, do hereby forever cede and relinquish to the United States the reservation of 16,000 acres of land granted to them by the second article of the treaty made at St. Mary's on the 17th of September, 1818, which grant is in the following words, to-wit: "There shall be reserved for the use of the Wyandots residing at Solomon's-town, on Blanchard's fork, sixteen thousand acres of land, to be laid off in a square form, on the head of Blanchard's fork, the center of which shall be at the Big Spring, on the road leading from Upper Sandusky to Fort Findlay."

ARTICLE II. The United States stipulate with the said band of Wyandots, that as soon as practicable after the ratification of this treaty, the aforesaid tract of 16,000 acres shall be surveyed into sections and put into market and sold in the ordinary manner of selling the public lands of the United States; and when the same shall be sold, or as soon as any part thereof shall be disposed of, (be the price received therefor, more or less,) there shall be paid to the chiefs, headmen and warriors, signing this treaty, for the benefit of all the said band of Wyandots, the sum of one dollar and twenty-five cents per acre for each and every acre so sold, or for sale. The said price shall be paid in silver, and in current coin of the United States.

ARTICLE III. For the improvements now made upon said reservation, the United States agree to pay a fair valuation in money, according to the appraisement of Joseph McCutcheon, Esq., (or such person as the Secretary of War may depute for that purpose,) and an appraiser to be chosen by the band of Wyandots. And in case the said appraisers shall not be able to agree upon any of their valuations, they shall call to their assistance some competent citizen of the county of Crawford.

ARTICLE IV. There shall be reserved for Roe-nu-nas, one of the oldest chiefs of said band, one-half-section, to contain 320 acres, and to include the improvements where he now lives.

ARTICLE V. It is expressly understood between the present contracting parties, that the said band of Wyandots may, as they think proper, remove to Canada, or to the river Huron, in Michigan, where they own a reservation of land, or to any place they may obtain a right or privilege from other Indians to go.

ARTICLE VI. It was expressly agreed before the sitting of this treaty that that part of the fifth article relating to the granting to the said band of Wyandots' lands west of the Mississippi, and every other article in relation thereto is wholly null and void, and of no effect.

ARTICLE VII. Inasmuch as the band of Wyandots herein treating have separated themselves from the Wyandots at Upper Sandusky and on the Sandusky plains, they ask of the general government that there may be a special sub-agent and protector appointed for them while they remain in the State of Ohio, and they respectfully recommend Joseph McCutcheon, Esq., of the county of Crawford, as a fit and proper person to act in such capacity; and that he may have the power to employ such interpreter as he may think proper in his intercourse with said band.

The aforesaid articles of agreement shall be mutually binding upon the present contracting parties, when ratified by the President of the United States, by and with the consent of the Senate thereof.

              J. B. GARDINER.

    Roe-nu-nas,   Matthew Greyeyes,
    Bear-Skin,   Isaac Driver,
    { She-a-wah, or John D. Brown,
    { John Solomon,* Alexander Clarke,
    John McLean.

Done in the presence of C. Clarke; secretary of the Commission; Joseph McCutcheon, J. P. in the county of Crawford, Ohio; John C. Dewitt, Richard Reynolds, G. W. Sampson.

(To the Indian names are subjoined marks).

EXPLANATION.

In the first draft of this treaty provision was made for the removal of the band west of the Mississippi, but they refused to accept of a grant of land, or to remove there, and the articles having relation thereto were accordingly omitted. It was therefore necessary to omit the sixth article; and circumstances did not admit of time to remodel and copy the whole treaty. J. B. GARDINER,

            Special Commissioner.

The facts are that the Indians got drunk, and it was dangerous to remain any longer amongst them.

"The Wyandots," says Abbott, "were considered the bravest of all the Indian tribes." Several of their chiefs were men of high moral and religious character. In the early occupation of Canada by the French, the Catholics, with a spirit of devotion and self-sacrifice which has never been surpassed, established a mission there. The first Protestant who preached to them was John Stewart, a mulatto, of the Methodist church. The Rev. James B. Finley, one of nature's noblemen, established a Methodist mission here and organized a school. Between-the-logs, a Wyandot chief, became quite a celebrated preacher. They built a large mission house a short distance northeast of Upper Sandusky. It was of stone, and a very substantial structure. Pity the

---

*This John Solomon afterwards attached himself to the main tribe of Wyandots at Upper Sandusky, and moved to the west with them. He returned with his squaw to Wyandot a few years after, and remained there to the time of his death, which occurred in 1878. He was present at a pioneers' pic-nic in Shoch's woods, on Honey creek, in Eden township, on the first day of September, 1877, and being called upon for a speech, stepped on to the stand and related, in very broken English, an account of a bear hunt. He was a tall and noble looking man. His squaw is still living.

people of Upper Sandusky have not kept it in repair as a land-mark of the historic past! The roof has fallen in, and there is nothing left of it but the stone walls.

Sum-mun-de-wat, another christian chief, was brutally murdered by some miscreant white men, who enjoyed his hospitality. I speak of him, especially, because this chief was very well known and respected by the early settlers of Seneca county. He was a special friend of our lamented townsman, Dr. Kuhn.

At a treaty held at Washington City, on the 29th day of February, 1831, the United States were represented by Mr. James B. Gardiner, and the Senecas by Coonstick, Seneca Steel, Captain Good-hunter, Hard-hickory and Small-cloud-Spicer, their chiefs. George Herrin acted as interpreter. Gen. Henry C. Bresh was sub-agent. At this treaty the Senecas sold their whole reservation to the United States, with full authority to sell the same. The proceeds were to be placed in funded stock at five per cent. interest, which was to be paid to the Senecas as an annuity, after deducting the cost of building for the latter a saw mill and a grist mill near Green Springs. They were to have, also, 70,000 acres northwest of the State of Arkansas, on the Neosho and Cowskin rivers, and ninety miles from Fort Gibson.

The Wyandots ceded their reservation to the United States in 1842. At this cession the last foot of soil in Ohio passed away from the red man to the race that conquers the world—the Caucasian.

Emigrants who crossed the mountains and descended and settled in the Ohio valley, usually brought with them their household goods, and their flocks of sheep, their horses and cattle. They crossed the mountains in large wagons, and drove their flocks before them. On reaching the Ohio river they put all on board of flat-boats and descended the river to their places of destination. But when emigration began to set in for northwestern Ohio, the emigrants had to find their way through a dense forest, as best they could. There were no roads open, and no bridges across any of the numerous creeks and rivers with which this northwestern part of Ohio abounds. There were immense swamps on both sides of the Sandusky, and along all its tributaries. Farther west and north the country was almost one continuous, immense swamp as far north as the Maumee, and west to Indiana, and far into that state. The soil was very rich, it must be admitted, and the farmer well knew that as soon as the water and the forest were conquered, the soil would eventually reward him for his toil. But to subdue these and become master of the situation required almost super-human power, the most patient fortitude, heroic courage, untiring

EMIGRATION.

perseverance, great self-denial and hard labor, without reward, or hope of reward, for a long time to come. The British and Indian foes were subdued and conquered, but now there were other foes to conquer; not only the forests and the swamps and other tasks inevitable, but diseases incident to frontier life, and especially those that attended the life in the woods. Many of the settlers of, and emigrants to, the valley of the Sandusky, who came from the states of New York, Pennsylvania, Maryland, New Jersey and Virginia; and, also, some from Ireland, France and Germany, were in comfortable circumstances, and after having paid for their land, mostly entered, or bought at government prices, had some money left, and were somewhat prepared for emergencies; but by far the largest number of them expended their last dollar to pay for their land, and then trusted to Providence, their iron will and strong arms, for success. Those that came by the way of Lake Erie had to encounter the forest as soon as they touched the shore. Those that came over the mountains by way of Pittsburg, had to make their way through the forest almost from the time they crossed the Ohio river. It was the same way with those who came from the south. Nothing but forest as soon as they left the settlements on the Scioto, the Muskingum, or the Great Miami, except the Sandusky plains. The way through the woods was marked by cutting a piece of bark from a tree as big as a man's hand, about five or six feet from the ground, and on both sides of the tree. Then, by cutting away the underbrush and removing fallen timber, a wagon track was opened by winding around between the trees. One or two men, with their axes, would walk ahead of the team, blaze the trees and remove obstructions.

In the absence of a compass, on a cloudy day, the course east and west, as well as north and south, was found by observing the moss on the trees, which always grows most profusely on the north side. When the team came to a stream it was often very troublesome to cross. Fallen trees, brush and drift-wood had set the water back and dammed the stream. Then a crossing had to be found by driving up or down the stream, and cutting a road, as it became necessary. Finally, the land, or tract of land, that had been bought, or was soon to be purchased, was found, and a halt ordered. Those that were fortunate enough to have their own teams were rich; but emigrants from Europe, who had hired teams at Cleveland, Sandusky, Dayton or Pittsburg to bring them here, were left in the woods and the teams started back. Here was the emigrant, with his wife and children, with their clothing, bedding, a few cooking utensils, very little provision, an axe or two, cross-cut saw, iron wedges, some carpenter tools, a gun, some ammunition, and, best of all—a will. A few poles leaned against a large tree, and brushes thrown upon the poles, soon made a roof and a shelter. Two forks driven into the ground about five feet apart, and a pole laid upon the forks, would be sufficient to suspend a small iron kettle in which the meal could be cooked. Life in the woods had commenced.

Very few people had come as far as the Sandusky river before the land sales, as the sales of the government lands were called. The Senecas, as has already been stated, owned 40,000 acres, mostly in the present limits of Seneca county, and the Wyandots twelve miles square immediately south of the Senecas, which tracts, of course, were not in market. Some men left their families in the settlements and came to the Sandusky valley on foot or on horseback, on a sort of an exploring expedition, prospecting and looking up tracts that suited them, then return and bring the family, or go to Delaware, make an entry, and then return and start with the family. Before the land sales, however, and up to the year 1820, a very few families had located between these reservations. Those who settled along the banks of the Sandusky, will all be named, and as near as possible described in these pages.

The Wyandot Indians had a tradition as to the history of their tribe that located their ancestors north of the St. Lawrence, where their wigwams were spread along the Utiwas down to Coon lake, and to the mouth of the gulf. They were then known as the Hurons, and their country they called Cu-none-tat-tia. The Senecas, who were also a large tribe, occupied a large tract of country south of the St. Lawrence. How it came that the Hurons changed their name to Wyandot is not known—nor is it material.

Nor is it worth investigating why a Greek name—Seneca—was ever given to a tribe of American savages.

A legend about a war between these two tribes, preserved by tradition, of course, may not be out of place here, for the dwellers of the valley of Sandusky river occupy the last hunting grounds of these tribes east of the Mississippi river.

A man of the Hurons—as the story goes—wanted a certain squaw for his wife, but she objected, and said that her wooer had never taken any scalps—that he was no warrior. To remove this objection to his suit, he raised a small war-party, and in their hunt for scalps, fell upon a party of Senecas and killed and scalped some of them.

This caused a war between the two tribes that lasted more than a century, and which they supposed was fully a hundred winters before the French came to Quebec. Both tribes were greatly wasted in the contest. They often made peace, but the first opportunity the Senecas had to take advantage of the Hurons, they would destroy all they could—men, women and children.

The Wyandots, fearing the danger of being entirely exterminated, concluded to leave their homes on the St. Lawrence, and go to the vast west. They made their escape to the upper lakes in their canoes, and settled in several villages in the vicinity of Green Bay. After a few years the Senecas raised a war-party, followed the Wyandots to their new homes, destroyed one of their villages, killed a number of the Wyandots and returned. This was some time before the Indians had any knowledge of fire-arms or gun-powder. Their implements of war consisted of bows, arrows and the war-club; also, a war-axe, which was a stone cut to an edge on one side or end, a broad, flat ball at the other end, and near which a groove was made around the stone to receive the thin end of the handle, which was bent into the groove and fastened with a string cut out of a raw-hide.

Soon after this the French laid out and built Quebec, and opened trade with the Indians; supplied them with, and instructed them in the use of, fire-arms and various other instruments. The Senecas, feeling themselves proficient in the use of fire-arms, made up a war-party against the Wyandots at the upper lakes. They came upon them in the night, fired into their huts and terrified them exceedingly. The Wyandots thought it was lightning and thunder, but resisted the Senecas and drove them away. A few years later the Senecas made a third attack upon the Wyandot settlements, and took nearly all of them; but it so happened that at that time the young men were all engaged in a war with the Fox Indians along the Mississippi. The few that the Senecas had not killed agreed to give up resistance, return with their conquerors and become one people. It was agreed that the Senecas would wait two days to give the Wyandots time to get ready, collect their goods, get into their canoes and join them on the morning of the day at a point where the Senecas had gone to wait for them. They had a grand dance during the night.

Meantime, the Wyandots had sent word to other Wyandot villages, which the Senecas had not disturbed. They met, consulted together, and agreed to go down, and as near to the Senecas as possible without being observed, and listen to what they were doing. They equipped themselves, went down, and found the Senecas engaged in the dance, and feasting on two Wyandot men they had killed and roasted, as they said, for their beef; and as they danced, they shouted their victory, and spoke of how good their Wyandot beef was. They continued the dance until near the break of day, and being tired, laid down and soon fell asleep. Then the Wyandots fell upon their sleeping foes and killed all of them. Not one was left to tell the tale of destruction. This ended the war for many years.

Now the French supplied the Wyandots with guns, also. At length another war broke out between these tribes. Both parties met in their canoes, on lake Erie, and the Senecas lost every man engaged. The Wyandots themselves were so badly exhausted that they allowed the canoes of the Senecas to float on the water, while they hastened to the shore. Thus ended this war, and the last trouble between the two tribes.

After that the Wyandots came with their canoes to the mouth of the Sandusky river, and took possession of its entire valley. They built their towns along its banks and tributaries, and up into the plains. There is neither history nor tradition of any note about them until the outbreak of the revolutionary war, when they perpetrated their infamous depredations along the back counties of Pennsylvania and Virginia—particularly those of Washington, Yougiogheny and Westmoreland.

It was the depredations of the Wyandots that caused the various expeditions against western Indians, and especially that of Crawford. Nearly all these failed, and the savages were never properly chastised until Gen. Wayne came down upon them. From the peace at Greenville until the war of 1812, there was no trouble with the Indians on the frontier. During this war the Wyandots, Shawnees and Senecas remained friendly to the United States. The deaths of Tecumseh and his brother, The Prophet, and their defeat on the Thames destroyed their power in the northwest forever.

Lewis Cass and Duncan McArthur, as commissioners of the United States, on the one part, and the sachems, chiefs and warriors of the Wyandots, Senecas, Delawares, Shawnees, Potawatomies, Ottawas and Chippewas, on the other part, held at the foot of the rapids of the Miami, of lake Erie, on the 29th day of September, 1817, a treaty, wherein all the lands of these Indians in Ohio passed over to the United States. At this time there was not a single white settler within the present limits of Seneca county.

At this treaty the United States granted to Takawmadoaw, Captain Harris, Isahowmasaw, Joseph, Tawgyou, Captain Smith, Coffeehouse, Running-about and Wipingstick, chiefs of the Seneca tribe, 30,000 acres adjoining the Sandusky river, on the east side, mostly within the present limits of Seneca county. At a subsequent treaty, viz: September 17, 1818, 10,000 acres were added. These 40,000 acres were afterwards known as the Seneca Reservation.

Thereupon, this remnant of several tribes of Indians, and mixtures of others, such as Cayugas, Mohawks, Onondagas, Tuscarawas, Wyandots and Oneidas, settled upon this reservation. The Cayugas predominated in number. There was not one full blood Seneca amongst them. The Mingoes were originally Cayugas, and their chief was Logan. After the murder of Logan's family, the Mingoes scattered in bands all over the northwest.

Their hunting grounds were along the banks of the Scioto and the Olentangy, and some Seneca chief significantly remarked: "Their children were raised on their backs." They had no particular home. At the time of the treaty they had concentrated along the banks of the Sandusky, and the testimony of a Seneca chief, who knew Logan well, proves the fact that Logan spent his last days upon the banks of the Sandusky river.

The place where the celebrated speech of Logan was delivered, by an interpreter, sentence by sentence, was under a tree seven miles south of Circleville. Logan had refused to join a commission of peace. Here is the speech:

"I appeal to any white man to say if he ever entered Logan's cabin hungry, and he gave him not meat; if he came naked and cold, and I clothed him not. During the last long and bloody war Logan remained idle in his cabin, an advocate for peace. Such was my love for the whites, that my countrymen, as they passed me, said: Logan is the friend of the whites. I had thought of living among you, but for the injuries of one man. Col. Cresap, last spring, in cold blood and unprovoked, murdered all the relations of Logan, not sparing even my women and children. There runs not one drop of my blood in the veins of any living creature. This called on me for revenge. I have sought it; I have killed many; I have fully glutted my vengeance. For my country, I rejoice in the beams of peace. But do not harbor the thought that mine is the joy of fear. Logan never felt fear. He will not turn on his heel to save his life. Who is there to mourn for Logan?"

President Jefferson has written of this powerful address of Logan: "I may challenge the whole orations of Demosthenes and Cicero, and of any more eminent orator, if Europe has furnished more eminent, to produce a single passage superior to the speech of Logan."

The poet Campbell, in "Gertrude, of Wyoming," has thus beautifully versified its sentiments:

"He, left, of all my tribe,
Nor man, nor child, nor thing of living birth;
No, not the dog that watched my household hearth
Escaped that night of blood upon our plains.
All perished. I alone am left on earth!
To whom not relative nor blood remains—
No, not a kindred drop that runs in human veins."

The fate of Logan was a very sad one. His last years were melancholy in the extreme. Homeless, childless, friendless—he wandered about, from tribe to tribe, with never a smile, and apparently without a joy. His friends were all dead, his tribe dwindled away, and, in his great dejection, he resorted to the fatal stimulus of strong drink. He was at last murdered by an Indian. Logan was sitting by the camp fire, silently musing, with his blanket over his head, his elbows upon his knees and his head upon his hands. An Indian, influenced by some unknown motive of revenge, stealthily approached him from behind and buried his tomahawk in his brain. Thus fell this unfortunate chieftain—the last of his race.

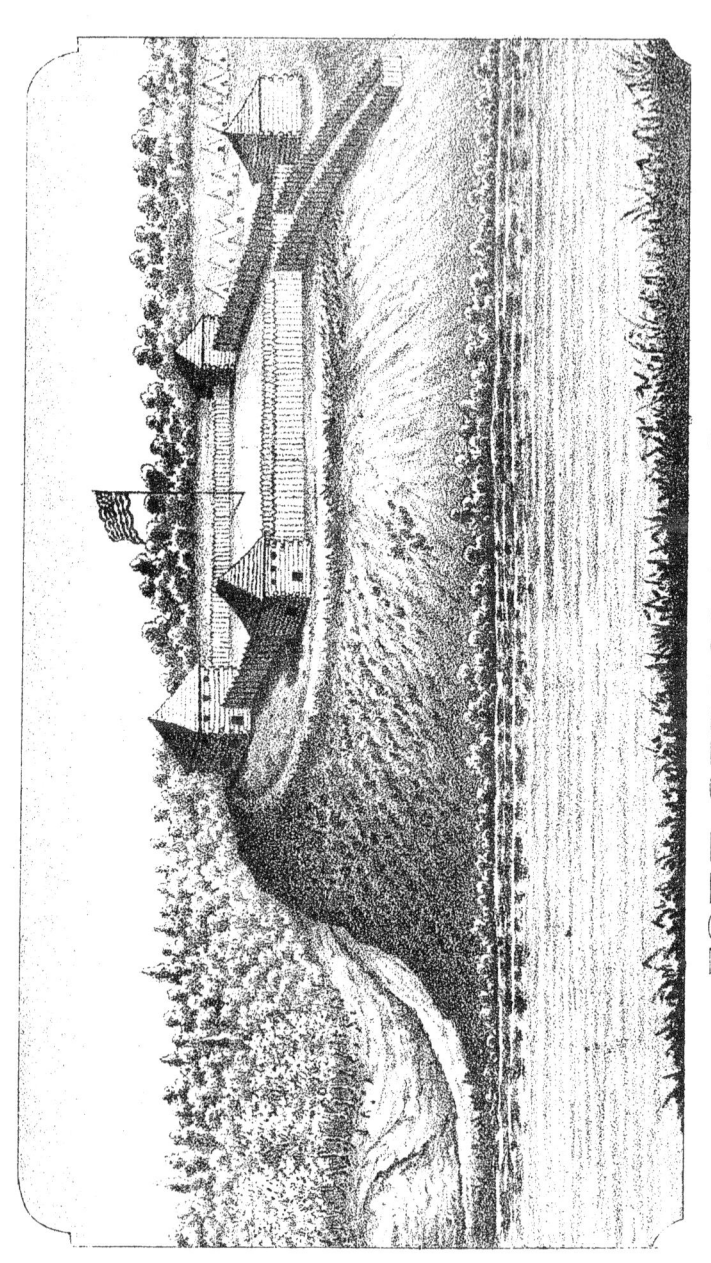

FORT SENECA IN 1813.

CHAPTER IV.

COUNCIL WITH INDIANS—HARRISON'S SPEECH—HARRISON AT FORT SENECA—CROGHAN'S DEFENSE OF HARRISON—BLUE JACKET'S PLAN TO ASSASSINATE HARRISON—BLUE JACKET'S DEATH—ARMY ROADS—THOMAS CORWIN—ANECDOTE OF CORWIN—SKETCHES OF JAMES MONTGOMERY AND JAMES T. WORTHINGTON.

ABOUT the first of July, 1813, a detachment of men, under the command of Gen. Harrison, erected a stockade upon the west bank of the Sandusky river, within the present limits of Pleasant township, in this county, to which was given the name of Camp Seneca.

It was situated upon a bank, about forty feet above the bed of the river, close to the old army road, and contained within its enclosure about one and one-half acres of ground. It was built nearly in the form of a square, surrounded by pickets of oak timber a foot in thickness and twelve feet high. Between this spot and the river are several springs of water, one of which was inside of the pickets.

On the east side were two rows of pickets, six feet apart, the space filled with earth. On the south was a single row of pickets. A little beyond this was a deep ravine, between which and the camp an embankment was thrown up, traces of which are still remaining. On the west was a single row of pickets, with a ditch about six feet deep, and twelve feet wide. On the north there was also a deep ditch, with an embankment, upon the top of which were placed the pickets.

A blockhouse was erected at the southwest corner, sixteen feet high, and about twenty-five feet square, which has long since passed away. It consisted of large logs, with port-holes for cannon and small arms, and was located in such a manner as to completely command the ditch. There was a projection at the northeast corner, strongly picketed, used, perhaps, as a magazine; and two small blockhouses at each of the other corners, with port holes. The spot is one mile south of the northern boundary of Pleasant township, the section line between sections 8 and 9 running through it. There is a deep ravine on the south of the spot.

Previous to the building of this camp, in June, 1813, Gen. Harrison held a council with the chiefs of the friendly Indians, at Franklinton, the Delawares, Wyandots, Shawnees and Senecas being represented. He urged upon them the necessity of taking a decided stand in the war with Great Britain, and say whether they were in favor of, or against, the United States; that the President wished no false friends; that the proposition of Proctor to exchange the Kentucky militia for the tribes friendly with us, indicated that he had received some hint of their willingness to take up the tomahawk against us; that to give the United States a proof of their good disposition, they must remove with their families into the interior, or the warriors must accompany him in the ensuing campaign, and fight for the United States. To the latter proposition the chiefs and warriors unanimously agreed, and said they had long been anxious for an invitation to fight for the Americans. Tarhee, the oldest Indian in the western country, who represented all the tribes, professed in their name the most indissoluble friendship for the United States. Gen. Harrison then told them that he would let them know when they would be wanted in the service, and said to them: "But you must conform to our mode of warfare. You are not to kill defenseless prisoners, old men, women or children." He added that by their conduct he would be able to tell whether the British would restrain the Indians from such horrible cruelty. For, if the Indians fighting with him would forbear such conduct, it would prove that the British could also restrain theirs if they wished to do so. He humorously told them that he had been informed of Gen. Proctor's promise to deliver him into the hands of Tecumseh, to be treated as that warrior might see fit, provided he, Proctor, succeeded at Fort Meigs. "Now, if I can succeed in taking Proctor, you shall have him for your prisoner, provided you will agree to treat him as a squaw, and only put petticoats upon him; for he must be a coward who would kill a defenseless prisoner."

There can be no doubt of that arrangement between Proctor and Tecumseh, for the latter sought for revenge since the battle of Tippecanoe. "Tecumseh insisted and Proctor agreed," says Dawson, "that Gen. Harrison and all who fought at Tippecanoe should be given up to the Indians to be burned." Major Ball ascertained the same facts from prisoners, deserters and Indians. And this, also, proves the other fact: That Tecumseh had intended to violate his promise made to Harrison at Vincennes.

In the same month, and while still at Franklinton, Gen. Harrison was informed of the movement of Proctor upon Fort Meigs. He started with re-enforcements, and having learned that it was a false alarm, returned to Lower Sandusky, on the first of July. On the following day he set out for Cleveland to see after public stores, and the building of boats to transport the army across the lake. When Gen. Harrison returned to Lower Sandusky, and being informed that a large body of Indians had been seen passing Fort Meigs, he concluded that it was only a feint, and that the real object of the enemy was to surprise Fort Stephenson or Cleveland. He immediately removed his headquarters to Fort Seneca, nine miles above Lower Sandusky. From this place he could fall back and protect Upper Sandusky, or pass by a secret route to the relief of Fort Meigs, if necessary—two points to be defended—Lower Sandusky being of comparatively little consequence. Major Croghan was left, as already stated, at Fort Stephenson, with one hundred and sixty men. There were then about six hundred troops at Fort Seneca, a force too small to assist Fort Meigs. Gen. Harrison's anticipations proved to be correct. The enemy moved upon Fort Stephenson.

Gen. Harrison, as early as the 21st of April, in a letter to the Secretary of War, speaking of the operations of the campaign, with his usual and wonderful sagacity, remarked: "I shall cause the movement of the enemy to be narrowly watched; but in the event of their landing at Lower Sandusky, that post can not be saved. I will direct it, in such an event, to be evacuated. The stores there are not of much consequence, excepting about five hundred stand of arms, which I shall cause to be removed as soon as the roads are practicable; at present, it is impossible." These arms were subsequently, and before the battle, taken away. Gen. Harrison was fully convinced that Fort Stephenson could not be defended against heavy artillery, and the fort must be abandoned and burned, provided a retreat could be effected with safety.

The orders left for Major Croghan, stated: "Should the British troops approach you in force, with cannon, and you can discover them in time to effect a retreat, you will do so immediately, destroying all the public stores. You must be aware that the attempt to retreat in the face of an Indian force, would be vain. Against such an enemy your garrison would be safe, however great the number."

To show that Gen. Harrison's opinion as to the safety of Fort Stephenson was proper, it should be remembered that at a council of war, composed of McArthur, Cass, Ball, Paul, Wood, Hukill, Holmes and Graham, it was the unanimous opinion that the fort could not be held against heavy artillery; that the post was relatively unimportant; that the garrison should not be re-enforced, but withdrawn, and the place destroyed. Thereupon, and immediately, the order was despatched to Croghan to leave, as already stated.

In addition to what has already been said of the battle of Fort Stephenson, and Gen. Harrison's relation thereto, it should be remembered that there were only about 800 troops at Fort Seneca. One-fifth of these were cavalry and the remainder raw militia. To have marched upon an enemy five times their number, with these troops, would, in all human probability, have resulted in disaster. There were then, also, one hundred and fifty-six soldiers at Fort Stephenson, and to leave these to the mercy of the tomahawks, was a responsibility that no military leader of the capacity of Gen. Harrison, would overlook. In addition to all this, Gen. Harrison had every reason to believe that Tecumseh, with his following, were making for Fort Stephenson. They were then lying in the swamp between that point and Fort Meigs, 2,000 strong, ready to strike upon either camp—Upper Sandusky or Fort Seneca—the moment it should be ascertained that Harrison had moved to the relief of Fort Stephenson. Under all these circumstances he was bound, by every military principle, to retain that position in which he could, with the greatest certainty, accomplish the best result. He therefore determined to wait for a time the progress of events, hoping that re-enforcements would arrive before the fort could be reduced. On the night of the second of August, he was informed of the retreat of the enemy, and re-enforcements having arrived before morning, he set out with 300 militia for the fort, attended by dragoons, and ordered the remainder of the disposable force, under Gens. Cass and McArthur, to follow. Upon reaching the fort, Harrison was informed that Tecumseh was in the swamp south of Fort Meigs, ready to make for Upper Sandusky on the first opportunity. He thereupon directed Gen. McArthur, who had not yet arrived, to return to Camp Seneca with all possible speed.

Gen. Harrison, in his official report, said: "It will not be among the least of Gen. Proctor's mortifications to find that he has been baffled by a youth who has just passed his twenty-first year. He is, however, a hero worthy of his gallant uncle, George R. Clark." President Madison immediately conferred the brevet rank of Lieutenant-Colonel on Major Croghan.

Shortly after an attack was made on Gen. Harrison in some public prints, as to his conduct in the defense of Fort Stephenson, to which Major Croghan promptly replied, by forwarding to a newspaper in Cincinnati a communication dated Lower Sandusky, August 27, 1813. in which he gives the true reasons for disobeying Gen. Harrison's orders to destroy the fort, etc., and says: "I have with much regret seen in some of the public prints such misrepresentations respecting my refusal to evacuate this post, as are calculated not only to injure me in the estimation of military men, but also to excite unfavorable impressions as to the propriety of Gen. Harrison's conduct relative to this affair. His character as a military man is too well established to need my approbation or support. But his public services entitle him at least to common justice. This affair does not furnish cause for reproach. If public opinion has been lately misled respecting his conduct, it will require but a moment's cool, dispassionate reflection, to convince them of its propriety. The measures recently adopted by him, so far from deserving censure, are the clear proofs of his keen penetration and able generalship."

The letter concludes with the following paragraph, alike honorable to the soldier and gentleman: "It would be insincere to say that I am not flattered by the many handsome things which have been said about the defense which was made by the troops under my command; but I desire no plaudits which are bestowed upon me at the expense of Gen. Harrison. I have, at all times, enjoyed his confidence so far as my rank in the army entitled me to it, and on proper occasions received his marked attention. I have felt the warmest attachment for him as a man, and my confidence in him as an able commander remains unshaken. I feel every assurance that he will at all times do me ample justice; and nothing could give me more pain than to see his enemies seize upon this occasion to deal out their unfriendly feelings and acrimonious dislike. And as long as he continues (as in my humble opinion he has hitherto done) to make the wisest arrangements, and most judicious disposition which the forces under his command will justify, I shall not hesitate to unite with the army in bestowing upon him that confidence which he so richly merits, and which has on no occasion been withheld."

Whoever now lives to remember the ever-memorable presidential campaign of 1840, with all its attending circumstances and displays, too tedious to enumerate, will also remember the heat of passion and excesses of party strife exhibited on both sides. Something of it may be recorded in other pages. I desire here only to express my great regret to know that in American politics the personal character of the opposing candidate, and his personal feelings, and his pride, seem to have nothing in them that his political enemies should regard as sacred. The candidate on the other side, for any office, high or low, is regarded as public property, and every political enemy has full license to assail him at his pleasure. For a proud and intelligent people, in the choice of men for officers, to resort to all manner of personal vituperation and abuse of opposing candidates, and to assail, blacken, traduce, and ruin, if possible, by all manner of means, characters that may be as fair and honorable as those of the best of men, and simply to win at the polls, is a crime against good breeding, against common justice, against good morals, and against ordinary decency.

The ladies of Chillicothe had a right to present Col. Croghan with a splendid sword if they saw fit so to do, and to make him a nice speech--certainly they had. But to have it said that they presented Gen. Harrison with a petticoat, and have that paraphernalia painted on transparencies and carried through the streets in democratic processions to turn to ridicule the valuable services of an able, high-minded and patriotic citizen and soldier like Gen. Harrison, seemed very wrong to me then, young as I was, and the impression sticks to me still. It seemed equally wicked to paint Martin VanBuren on transparencies with the sword in one hand and the purse in the other, to make people believe that the Little Fox of Lindenwald would usurp and destroy free government. And to cap the climax of this manner of political warfare, after a candidate has been abused and vilified to the hearts' content of his opponents, and is elected withal, nevertheless, then not only quietly submit to the administration of the duties of his office, but to shake hands with him and congratulate him upon his success ! Such things can be done only in America.

While Gen. Harrison was at Camp Seneca he narrowly escaped being murdered by an Indian. The reader will remember that the Delawares, Shawnees, Wyandots and Senecas had been invited to join the army under Harrison against the British and their Indian allies. Quite a number of them had accepted the invitation, and had reached Fort Seneca before the arrival of the Kentucky troops. Before the departure of these friendly Indians from their respective towns, an unfriendly Indian had insinuated himself into the good graces of the chiefs under pretense of friendship for the Americans, but with the intention of killing the commanding general. He was a Shawnees, and was known by the name of Blue Jacket, but was not the celebrated Blue Jacket who signed the treaty of Greenville with General Wayne. He had formerly lived at the Indian town of Wapakoneta. He had been absent from his tribe some time, and had returned but a few days before the warriors of that town had set out to join the American army.

He informed the chiefs that he had been hunting on the Wabash, and at his own request was permitted to join the party that was now getting ready to march to Fort Seneca. Upon their arrival at McArthur's blockhouse, they halted and encamped for the purpose of receiving provisions from the deputy Indian agent, Col. McPherson, who resided there.

Before their arrival at that place, Blue Jacket had communicated to a friend of his, a Shawnees warrior, his intention to kill the American general, and requested his assistance. This his friend declined, and endeavored to dissuade him from attempting it, assuring him that it could not be done without the certain loss of his own life, as he had been at the American camp, and knew that there was always a guard around the General's quarters, who were on duty day and night.

Blue Jacket replied that he was determined to execute his intention at any risk, and said: "I will kill the General, even if I was sure that the guard will cut me into pieces no bigger than my thumb-nail."

No people on earth are more faithful in keeping a secret than the Indians, but each warrior has a friend from whom he will conceal nothing. It was the good fortune of Gen. Harrison that the friend and confidant of Blue Jacket was a young Delaware chief by the name of Beaver, who was also bound to the General by ties of friendship. He was the son of a Delaware war-chief of the same name, who had, with others, been put to death by his own tribe, on the charge of practicing sorcery.

Gen. Harrison had been on terms of friendship with his father, and had patronized his orphan boy, at that time some ten or twelve years of age. He had now arrived at manhood, and was considered among the most promising warriors of his tribe. To this young chief the friend of Blue Jacket revealed the fatal secret. The Beaver was placed, by this communication, in an embarrassing situation; for, should he disclose what he had heard and been entrusted with, he betrayed his friend, than which nothing could be more repugnant to the principles of an Indian warrior. Should he not disclose it, consequences equal, or even more to be deprecated, were likely to ensue. The assassination of a friend—his father's friend—whose life he was bound to save and defend, or whose death to avenge, by the same principle of fidelity and honor which forbid the disclosure.

While in this state of meditation and hesitation, the young Delaware being undecided as to which of these conflicting duties was the strongest, Blue Jacket came up to the Delaware camp somewhat intoxicated, vociferating vengeance upon Col. McPherson, who had just turned him out of his house, and whom he declared he would kill for this insult. The sight of the traitor raised the indignation and resentment of the Beaver to the highest pitch. He seized his tomahawk, and advancing towards the villain, said to him: "You must be a great warrior; you will not only kill this white man for treating you as you deserve, but you will also murder our father, the American chief, and bring disgrace and mischief upon us all. But you shall do neither; I will serve you as I would a mad dog."

A furious blow from the tomahawk of the Beaver stretched the unfortunate Blue Jacket at his feet, and a second finished him.

"There," said Beaver, to some Shawnees, who were present, "take him to the camp of his tribe and tell them who has done the deed."

The Shawnees approved of the act, and were pleased to have escaped the ignominy which the villainy of Blue Jacket would have brought upon them.

It is impossible to say what was the motive of Blue Jacket to attempt the life of Gen. Harrison. He was not one of the Tippecanoe Shawnees, and therefore could have no personal resentment, or cause for malice, against the General. There is but little doubt that Blue Jacket came from Malden, under British influence, when he arrived at Wapakoneta, and that he came for the express purpose to assassinate Gen. Harrison; but whether he was instigated or hired by any person, or conceived the idea himself, has never been ascertained.

The country west of the Sandusky river was not only a dense forest, but also a vast swamp, in which the Indians themselves found no spots suitable to build their wigwams. This great swamp was the country of the Wolfcreeks—sluggish streams that come together near the mouth where Wolfcreek proper enters the Sandusky river in Ballville township, Sandusky county. There were no Indian trails through this swale. These followed the banks of the river on both sides, from the headwaters of the Sandusky to the mouth. Along these trails they built their towns, and the army road, made and opened in the late war, under the direction of Gen. Harrison, following the left bank of the river on high ground wherever practicable, and without any line of survey. There was another army road from Delaware to Fort Seneca, on the east side of the river. Along this road Fort Seneca and Fort Stephenson were supplied with provisions. And right here, before proceeding any further in this narrative, it may be asked:

"What in this world can possibly be said of the history of a part of our county that was once a dense forest and a dead swamp? What historic events can be connected with the hard work requisite to reduce both forest and swale, and enable the pioneer farmer to raise his bread and support his family?"

This question arises very naturally, and it must be admitted that, while no great battles were fought within the boundaries of Seneca; while it can not boast of a Lexington, a Bunker Hill or a Yorktown; while it was not the birth-place of any person whose name has adorned general history, yet it will be admitted that men of not only state, but of national notoriety, and whose names have adorned not only the history of our state, but also that of the general government, were identified with events that transpired within her borders, and a history of Seneca county without a relation of the movements of Gen. Harrison along this valley would be nothing but a fraction of what it should be. There was also another character identified with Fort Seneca. It was "Tom, the wagon-boy," as he was then familiarly called. Let us see who he was. Mathias Corwin, in 1798, settled in what is now Warren county, and which was then as complete a wilderness as Seneca in 1820; and the school houses and opportunities for education were also of a like character. He had a son by the name of Thomas, who, in 1812, when the war broke out, was about fifteen years of age. Our unnatural enemies were stimulating the savages all along our northern frontier to kill, burn and destroy. Gen. Hull had made his disastrous surrender at Detroit. All plans of the War Department in the northwest were thus deranged. Our soldiers, unsupplied with food, were in danger of starvation.

In this emergency, Judge Corwin determined to send a team to the extreme frontier, loaded with supplies for the suffering troops. His son Thomas drove the team. He came by the Delaware army road to Fort Seneca, with the load, while Gen. Harrison was there. This trip attached to him the name of "Tom, the wagon-boy," for life. He became highly popular with the people of Ohio in after years, and won honors at the bar, in the legislature of the state, in the council of the general government as Senator from Ohio. He was Governor of Ohio, and Secretary of the Treasury under the administration of Mr. Fillmore. In 1861, President Lincoln appointed Mr. Corwin Minister to Mexico. He died in the City of Washington, on the 18th day of December, 1865.

Mr. Corwin was a fine specimen of a self-made man. He was recognized by friend and foe as a man of strict notions of honor, an able lawyer, a great statesman, and an orator of the first order. He could hold a crowd as by magic, and his anecdotes, accompanied with his unsurpassable grimaces and applications, were irresistible in their effect.

Mr. Corwin was a man about five feet nine inches high, very compactly built, muscular and fleshy, with strong features, dark eyes, high forehead, black hair, short neck and of very dark complexion. He was gentle, social, kind.

The writer was present one time when a company of gentlemen met at the old American house, in Columbus, and heard Gov. Wood tell a good joke on Mr. Corwin in his presence. Gov. Wood said: "A few years ago, in the winter, while Mr. Corwin was in Columbus attending to business in the United States District Court, the mulattoes in Columbus had a dance, and had given notice that none but pure mulattoes would be admitted. One of Mr. Corwin's friends offered a small bet that he (Mr. Corwin) could not get in to see the dance because he was too dark for a mulatto. Mr. Corwin accepted the bet, and, dressing himself in the best manner he could to deceive the door keeper, put a hat with a very wide rim on his head, and the party started for the ball. Mr. Corwin presented his ticket, and the mulatto door keeper lifted up the rim of Mr. Corwin's hat, and said: 'Can't get in heah, Massa—one shade too dark;' and Mr. Corwin lost the bet."

The Senecas took possession of their lands soon after the treaty, and began to build cabins and open little clearings around them. By virtue of the treaty, the United States were obliged to establish an agency near the reservation, to provide for their wants, and in every way to assist in carrying into effect the conditions of the treaty. The Rev. James Montgomery was appointed agent for the Senecas. On the 19th day of November, 1819, he moved with his family into the old blockhouse of the fort, and immediately took charge of his office.

Mr. Montgomery was born in Westmoreland county, Pennsylvania, November 20, 1776. He finished his education in Pittsburgh, and when he was seventeen years old, moved with his widowed mother to the state of Kentucky. His father died in the revolutionary war in Johnstown, New Jersey, of camp fever. The widow and her children settled on one of those celebrated "tomahawk claims" in Kentucky, and which, as a matter of course, became involved in litigation, which was usual, and lost. Mr. Montgomery married a Miss Kaziah Rouse, and in 1806 moved into Champaign county, Ohio, and located eight miles east of Urbana. He preached through that county as a minister of the Methodist Episcopal Church. In the year 1812, he moved with his family to Springfield, Ohio, and while there he was appointed by Gov. Meigs commissary for the army. After the war he moved back to Champaign county, and while there, received his appointment from the president as agent for the Seneca Indians. The family lived in the old blockhouse seven years, when he built a large cabin close by, where he afterwards lived with his family to the time of his death, which occurred on the 1st day of June, 1830. During his residence here, whenever the duties of his office as Indian agent would admit of it, he attended to his ministerial duties, and became generally respected and beloved by all who had an opportunity to enjoy his acquaintance. He was possessed of a noble, manly character, kind, generous and hospitable. His house became the headquarters for traders. The latch string of his door was always out. Ministers, lawyers, surveyors, Indians and whites made Mr. Montgomery's house a stopping place. The Indians called him Kuckoo-wassa—new acorn. He was but fifty-four years old when he died. The Rev. Ezechiel Cooper, a Methodist Episcopal preacher, preached his funeral sermon from the text:— "Blessed are the dead who die in the Lord." All the chiefs and braves of the Senecas attended his funeral. He was buried in the old cemetery near the fort. He had eleven children—two sons and nine daughters. Mr. William Montgomery, who was afterwards extensively engaged in the mercantile business in Tiffin, was his oldest son. Mrs. Sally Ingham, who now resides in the city of Tiffin, is the only surviving member of that large family.

Mr. Montgomery was about five feet six inches high, strong and compactly built, without being corpulent. His carriage was straight and erect. He had black hair and eyebrows, dark eyes, prominent nose, smooth forehead, rather heavy lower jaw, clenched lips, a frank and open countenance, which, together, would mark him, not only as a man of great decision, but also as a leader in any capacity. He had a clear, strong voice, fine control of language, and was altogether practical in his orthodoxy. His conversation was cheerful, humorous and instructive. He was the kind neighbor, affectionate husband and father, an honest officer, and a blessing to all around him. Shortly before his removal to Fort Seneca, he was ordained by Bishop Asbury, in Lebanon, Warren county, Ohio, in 1819.

Among the many visitors at the old blockhouse was Mr. James T. Worthington, who was employed by the government to survey several of the townships in Seneca county into sections and quarter-sections. Mr. Worthington often stopped at Montgomery's for meals. He was then a young man, about twenty-three years old, about five feet eight inches high, slender built, with light brown hair, brushed back and over the left side, of fair complexion, grey eyes, expressive, intellectual countenance, pleasing in conversation, gentlemanly in his bearing, and very good looking. His grey linsey-woolsey Indian hunting shirt, with cape and fringe, became him very much. He was a son of Governor Worthington, of Ohio.

The early emigrants to the valley of the Sandusky were compelled to make their way through forest and swamp as best they could. They had to follow old army roads, or Indian trails, fording streams, and winding through the woods for hours and days by blazed trees. There was no bridge across any stream in the whole valley of the river—nor could a house or cabin be found to stop at. They had to camp out, and sleep in the wagon, or on the ground, with no roof but the trees, or the broad canopy of heaven. When Mr. Montgomery moved into the old fort, there was no bridge between Urbana and Lower Sandusky. When the writer came to Seneca, in 1833, there was no bridge in the county. Neighbors on opposite sides of streams, made a way to get across by falling a tree across and walking over the log.

In the years 1819 and 1820, there were but five families of white people living between Fort Seneca and Fort Ball. These were the Dumonds, William Harris, Abner Pike, (who had a cabin near the place where Ezra Baker afterwards built a frame house near the mill,) an old man by the name of McNutt, and widow Shippy. Benjamin Barney, Anson Gray and Joel Chapin also arrived about that time.

Anson Gray afterwards married one of the Harris girls—Jane. The farm, about one mile south of the present town of Fort Seneca, which was afterwards owned by the Rev. J. J. Beilhars, of the German Lutheran church, and where he died, was bought at the land sales, by Anson Gray. In after years Gray moved with his family to Illinois. In 1820, old Mr. McNutt lived in a log cabin at a place that afterwards became familiarly known as the "Wright farm." Here McNutt cleared some land. The cabin was built for a school house, and was the first school house built in the Sandusky valley.

"The Barney Boys," as they were familiarly called, afterwards lived with Joel Chapin, in the same house. Afterwards, Lorenzo Abbott and Joel Chapin and their families lived in the same house. They had rented the place, and had about thirty-five acres cleared and under fence.

The widow Shippy also lived on the Wright farm, in a cabin near the school house.

Three brothers: Willard, Francis and Ezra Sprague, lived in a cabin on the farm that is now known as the Gangwer place. Ezra afterwards lived with a family by the name of Downing. Most all of these first cabins were built in the woods, without regard to section lines, roads, or anything else, except to get to some neighbor, if possible, and with a view of buying the lands at the sales, or entering them at the land office after the sales. Several of these cabins were built by the Indians before they moved together on to their reservation to the east of the river. Other settlers that came on afterwards occupied the cabins on the west side of the river that the Senecas had abandoned. In these cabins the early settlers made themselves as comfortable as they could while they waited for the time of the land sales. There were no cabins any distance west and from the river, and but two more between the fort and Lower Sandusky.

A Mr. Wilson lived in a cabin at a place that afterwards became known as the Frank Abbott farm. Caleb Rice lived in a cabin on the farm now owned by Mr. William Montgomery. Daniel Rice, who married Ann Barney, was the first justice of the peace in that neighborhood. He was a brother of Caleb Rice, and his widow is still living with her son, north of Clyde, in Sandusky county.

CHAPTER V.

SPEECH OF ISAAC I. DUMOND BEFORE THE SENECA PIONEER ASSOCIATION —SAMUEL CROWELL'S CONTRIBUTION—THE DOG-DANCE-SOW-DOWS-KY.

ON THE 22d day of February, 1869, being the anniversary of the birth of George Washington, in conformity to a call previously issued, a large number of the pioneers of Seneca county met at the court house in Tiffin, to organize a Pioneer Association. At one of the subsequent meetings, February 22, 1871, Mr. Isaac I. Dumond, one of the first settlers near the west bank of the river, in Pleasant township, read a paper before the Association, which is given below in full. The further proceedings of the Association, of general interest, will be referred to hereafter. Mr. Dumond said:

LADIES AND GENTLEMEN:—My father moved with his family to what was then called "The New Purchase," on the Sandusky river, in 1821, at which time I was in my twentieth year.

We found the entire country a wilderness, with no other than the rude improvements made by the Indians.

There was but one public road known as a highway in all the region of the country designated as the new purchase, which was opened in the fall of 1820, and ran on the east side of the Sandusky river, north and south, then known and still continuing as the Marion State Road.

My father settled in what is now Pleasant township, in this county, where, for a time, we had to encounter many difficulties. During a part of the year the roads were almost impassable, by reason of the mud mixed with the branch roots. During the summer, mosquitoes and house-flies gave us a degree of trouble that none can realize, except from experience. The flies would gather on a horse in such quantities that a single grab would fill a man's hand. The Massasaugar, or prairie rattle-snake, was another unpleasant enemy, which appeared in great numbers. I killed five in cutting a small piece of oats; but to my knowledge, no one ever suffered from them.

At that time there were few families living along the entire route from Tymochtee (which name means, in the Indian language, "the stream around the plains") to Lower Sandusky.

We had few mechanics; but the one most needful was a blacksmith, which we found in Leroy Cresey, at Fort Ball.

Dr. Brainard was the only physician in the neighborhood, and his practice extended from Lower Sandusky, his place of residence, to Tymochtee.

Throughout the entire settlement there was not a lawyer to be found.

SPEECH OF ISAAC I. DUMOND.

The only minister we had was the Rev. James Montgomery, of the M. E. church.

Jesse and George Omsted had our only store between Delaware and Lower Sandusky.

There was considerable travel during the spring and early summer of 1821, by men in search of land, till August, when the land sale occurred.

Our greatest privation was want of mills. Our nearest mill was at Cold creek, about twenty-four miles distant, and without a direct road leading to it. The difficulties in some cases were very trying. For example: Mr. Barney and Daniel Rice arranged for a trip to mill, each with a team of oxen and wagon. As they had to cross the river, the grain was hauled there, unloaded and ferried across; then the wagon ferried over, and afterwards the team swam over, when they could reload, hitch and proceed. This was in April, 1821. After having their grain ground, and on their homeward route, they were overtaken by a snow storm. The snow was damp, and fell to the depth of a foot, rendering the road almost impassable, and so weighed the bushes down over them, that they were compelled to abandon their wagons, and with much difficulty succeeded in reaching home with their oxen.

Although the year 1821 was a trying one, it had secured to many a sufficient amount of land to afford a home for the future, and to encourage us. We had an abundant crop.

Many of the people had acted as squatters. The Indians, who had formerly lived on the west side of the river, had removed to their reservation on the east side, and abandoned their old homes and houses, which were appropriated by the white settlers, and held until they wished to go, or were displaced by a deed from Uncle Sam, conveying the same to somebody else. The settlement was weak in 1821, and to raise a log-cabin, the neighbors were often summoned from places five or six miles distant.

Of those who came previous to the land sales, some suffered from sickness, and, becoming discouraged, left, and others died; but immediately after the land sales the population steadily increased, and in 1823, Mr. Rumley built a mill on Green creek, and soon after, Mr. Moore built a mill on the Sandusky river, in order to supply the increased demand, which greatly diminished the inconvenience we had all experienced.

The early settlers were in the majority; rough, but generous, whole-souled and kind towards one another, and ever ready to lend a helping hand to the needy.

The use of intoxicating drinks was our greatest evil. Some would get on sprees, and after taking much whisky, would form a ring, and with bells, horns, tin pans, log chains, or any noisy instrument, engage in a hideous dance, sing, and give Indian war-whoops. Such a state of society was not the rule entirely, however, and was wholly displaced in a short time by the ingress of more refined people, who controlled the moral standard of the neighborhood. That enemy of civilization—whisky—was hard to subdue, however. This is always the case. I remember when farmers would trade a bushel of corn for five quarts of whisky, and this was as necessary for harvest as provisions.

In the fall of 1824, the first general muster of the militia took place at

Fort Seneca. The regiment numbered about 400 men, under Gen. Rumley and Col. J. B. Cooley, who gathered from over the country between Cold creek and Tymochtee, many having to camp out in order to reach the fort in time.

A considerable trade was carried on between the southern portion of the state, after the close of the war of 1812, and Lower Sandusky and Sandusky City. Teams came loaded with flour, bacon and whisky, and returned with fish or merchant goods, which were sold at Urbana, Springfield and Dayton.

The Indian tribes here at the time of the first settlement by the whites, were the Senecas, Cayugas, Mohawks and Oneidas. The Senecas—the most numerous—and Cayugas occupied the lower part, and the Oneidas and Mohawks the upper part of the reservation, which was nine miles north and south, and six miles east and west, on the east side of the Sandusky river. The land was held in joint stock, and each had the privilege of making improvements, as he wished.

They numbered several hundred, and were not bad in general character, but friendly and kind when well treated and not maddened by whisky, for which they had a strong passion. I have known them to offer two or three dollars' worth of goods for a quart of whisky; and, when intoxicated, would give anything they possessed for it.

They depended largely upon hunting for subsistence, in which, when children, they commenced by shooting fish and small game with the bow.

Most of the Indians and squaws cultivated each a small piece of land, varying from a half to two acres, which they formerly did with a hoe; but seeing us use the plow, and the amount of labor saved thereby, they concluded to abandon the custom of their fathers. Seeing two Indians plowing on the opposite side of the river one day, I crossed over and discovered them going the wrong way over the land, throwing the furrows in, and next time running inside of it, and then another, which they thought very well, until I turned them the other way, and gave a little instruction, which they thankfully received. They raised a soft corn, which they pounded into meal and used to thicken soup.

They had much idle time, which they all liked—the children spending it in shooting, the old people smoking from the pipes made in the heads of the tomahawks, with an adjustable handle for a stem. They smoked the sumac leaves, dried and pounded, which gave a pleasant odor.

The young Indians had a love for sports. Their chief summer game was ball—a game in which ten or twelve to a side engaged, the ground being marked off in a space of about sixty rods, the center of which was the starting point. Each player had a staff some five feet long, with a bow made of raw hide on one end, with which to handle the ball, as no one was allowed to touch it with his hands. At the commencement, the ball was taken to the center and placed between two of the staffs, each pulling toward his outpost. Then the strife began to get the ball beyond the outpost by every one, the success in which counted one for the victor, when the ball was taken to the center again and a new contest began. The squaws and older Indians constituted the witnesses to these sports, and added zest by their cheers.

The favorite winter sport was running upon skates. They would spread a blanket on the ice and jump over it with skates on, trying to excel in the distance made beyond.

Another favorite sport was to throw upon the snow, to run the greatest distance, snow snakes made of hickory wood, about five feet long, one and one-half inches wide, one inch thick, turned up at the point like a snake's head, and painted black.

The Mohawks and Oneidas had some very well educated people, and most of their tribes could read and write. They had religious services every Sabbath in the form of the Church of England, held by a minister of their own tribe. They were excellent singers, and often attracted the whites to their religious exercises, which pleased them very highly.

The Senecas and Cayugas were more inclined to adhere to the custom of their forefathers. They held in reverence many gatherings. The green corn dance was prominent among them, but that most worthy of note was, the dog dance. This was the great dance, which took place about midwinter, and lasted three days, at the close of which they burnt their dogs.

Great preparations were made for this festival. Provisions in great abundance were collected to constitute a common store. from which all were fed. The two dogs were selected, often, months in advance, well fed and made fat. They were as near alike as possible, and white, with yellow spots. When the time for the festival arrived, the dogs were killed—but in what way I never learned—washed clean as possible. trimmed with pink ribbons about the neck. each leg and foot, and about the tail. After the hairs over the entire body were carefully smoothed down, they were hung up by the neck to the arm of a post. similar to a sign post, where they remained through the services.

The dance was held at the council-house, which was built of logs, about twenty feet wide and seventy-five feet long, with three holes in the roof to allow the smoke to escape. At these places fires were kept burning during the season, over which were suspended brass kettles containing provisions.

At this time. strong as was their appetite for whisky. none was allowed on the premises. and any intoxicated person appearing was sent off at once.

All things being ready. their war dance began, which was participated in by none but those fit for the service of the warriors. Blue Jacket led the band. Each dancer carried a war-club in his right hand, and had tied to each leg a string of deer hoofs, which rattled at every step. The object was to assist in keeping time to the music, which consisted of an Indian sing-song. and the beating with a stick on a dry skin stretched over a hominy block.

When the music commenced. Blue Jacket would step out and walk around the fire, exerting himself to display some warriors' exploits. About the second round, others would fall in. and continue until the ring around the fire was full, all moving with their faces toward the fire, until they came to some change in the music, when they would turn their faces outward, and at another change trail in single file. all the while keeping time to the music.

While the Indians were thus engaged, the squaws formed another ring around another fire, but moved very slow. They would tip on their heels and toes, alternately, and endeavored to move with the music.

At meal time all were seated with wooden bowls and ladles, when they were served by those appointed, until all were satisfied. Then all were quietly awaiting the next scene. Soon a rumbling noise was heard at the door in one end of the house. This startled the squaws and children, who then ran to the other end of the house. Then the door flew open, and an Indian came in, dressed in bear skin, and skins of some other animals. He wore a false face, and carrying a dry turtle shell filled with stones, he would throw that about. This, added to his low, growling voice, and menacing ways with his head, made a frightful object. Almost immediately thereafter the door at the other end of the house would open and a similar character enter, and soon another drop from the roof, who, striking his hands, proceeded to throw live coals and embers in every direction among the rushing crowd. After this performance these demons, as they were represented to be, contested in a foot race. At the end of the third day they burnt the dogs.

Although much mirth was indulged in, there was a sort of solemnity maintained throughout the entire services.

So far, Mr. Dumond. Although Mr. Dumond had not the advantages of an education, having spent his boyhood days on a farm, and in the forest, it must be admitted that his recollections of early days are set forth in a clear and interesting style.

The people of Seneca county will, in all human probability, never have an opportunity to witness scenes of a like character, and the county being named after these savages, a further relation of incidents connected with their stay on the reservation will not be deemed out of place here. The following is taken from Butterfield's history, who copied from the *Sidney Aurora:*

More than half of the present township of Adams, and so much of Pleasant township as lies east of the Sandusky river, together with a portion of Clinton and Scipio townships, formerly belonged to the Seneca Indians. But as we have given a geographical description of most of what was their grant of land, we proceed to a more minute account of that nation, and we can not better introduce this subject than by giving the following, from the scrap-book of Samuel Crowell, of Lower Sandusky, which was published in the *Sidney Aurora*, in 1844, as it relates some interesting facts relative to this nation, but particularly, as it describes their famous chief, "Hard Hickory." Says the writer:

> The Senecas who roamed these wilds
> In ages long by gone,
> Are now rejoicing in the chase,
> Towards the setting sun.
>
> Their sacrifices offered up,
> And Deity appeased,
> Their Fatherland they left in peace,
> With their exchange well pleased.

SAMUEL CROWELL'S CONTRIBUTION.

On the first day of February, some fourteen years ago, I witnessed an interesting, and to me, a novel, religious ceremony of the Seneca tribes of Indians, then occupying the portion of territory now comprising a part of Seneca and Sandusky counties, Ohio, familiarly known to the inhabitants of this region as the Seneca Reservation.

The fact that this nation had recently ceded this reserve to the United States, and were about to commemorate, for the last time in this country, this annual festival, previous to their emigration to the Rocky mountains, contributed not a little to add to it an unusual degree of interest.

To those acquainted with the characteristics of the red men, it is unnecessary to remark that there is a reservedness attached to them, peculiarly their own; but especially, when about to celebrate this annual festival, they seem, so far, at least, as the pale-faces are concerned, to shroud their design in impenetrable secrecy.

And the festival of which I now speak might have been, as many others of a similar character were, observed by themselves with due solemnity, and without the knowledge or interference of their white neighbors, but that the general poverty and reckless improvidence of the Senecas were proverbial, and those were the causes which awakened the suspicions of the inquisitive Yankees.

In order, therefore, that the approaching festival, as it was intended to be the last of those observances here, should not lack in anything necessary to make it imposing, and impress a permanent recollection of Sandusky on the minds of their rising race, no effort was spared, and no fatigue regarded, that would tend to promote this object. Thus, for some time previous to the period of which I am now speaking, by the unerring aim of the Seneca rifle, the antlers, with the body of many a tall and stately buck, fell prostrate. And in crowds the Indians now came into Lower Sandusky, with their venison and their skins; and the squaws, with their painted baskets and moccasins, not, as heretofore, to barter for necessaries, but chiefly for ornaments.

* * * * * * * * * *

The principal headmen, or chiefs, were Good Hunter, Hard Hickory and Tall Chief. There were also some "sub," or half-chiefs: among those of the latter rank, Benjamin F. Warner, a white, or half-breed, had considerable influence.

This Warner was a white man, and had previously been a fireman on a steamboat that plied between Buffalo and Green Bay. On one of the downward trips he persuaded an Indian woman who was traveling to New York to elope with him. They came to the Seneca nation and were adopted by them.

In this, as in other nations, civilized as well as savage, though there may be several men of apparent equal rank, yet there is usually one, who, either by artificial or universally acknowledged talent, directs, in a great measure, the destinies of the nation, and such, among the Senecas, was Hard Hickory.

[And yet they killed him for robbing them, as we shall hereafter see.—AUTHOR.]

And, as in the mind of man there is something intuitive, better known than defined, by which instinctively, as it were, we find in the bosom of another a response to our own feelings. So, in the present case, this noble Indian soon discovered in the late Obed Dickinson, a merchant of Lower Sandusky, a generous, confiding and elevated mind, whose honorable vibrations beat in unison with his own.

[This Mr. Dickinson was the brother of the Hon. Rudolphus Dickinson, and uncle of the present Judge Dickinson, of Fremont.]

To Mr. Dickinson, therefore, he made known the time when they would celebrate their festival, by sacrificing their dogs, etc., and cordially invited him to attend as a guest, and, if so disposed, to bring a friend with him.

Correctly supposing that I never had an opportunity of witnessing this religious rite, Mr. D. kindly requested me to accompany him to their council house, on Green creek, in that part of this county included in the present township of Green Creek. On giving me the invitation, Mr. D. remarked that by taking a present in our hand, we should probably be made the more welcome; in accordance, therefore, with this suggestion, we took with us a quantity of loaf sugar and tobacco.

It was some time in the afternoon when we arrived, and immediately thereafter we were ushered into the council house, with demonstrations of public joy and marked respect.

As soon as seated, we gave our presents to Hard Hickory, who, rising, held one of them up, and pointing to Mr. D., addressed the Indians in an audible voice, in their own tongue; then holding up the other, he pointed to me, repeating to them what he had before said. This done, he turned to us and said: "You stay here as long as you want; nobody hurt you." Confiding in the assurance of this chief, I hung up my valise, in which were some important papers, for I was then on my way further east, attending to my official duties as Sheriff of this county, and felt perfectly at home.

To the inhabitants of this section of Ohio a minute description of the council house would be deemed unnecessary. Suffice it to say, that its dimensions were perhaps sixty by twenty-five feet; a fire-place in the center, and corresponding therewith, an aperture was left in the roof for the smoke to ascend.

Contiguous to the fire-place were two upright posts, to which a board fourteen or fifteen inches broad was firmly fastened, and over this board the skin of a deer was stretched very tight. On a seat near by this board sat a blind Indian with a gourd in his hand, in which were beans or corn. With this he beat time for the dancers. Such was the musician, and such the music.

The dancing had commenced previous to our arrival, and was continued, with little intermission, for several successive days and nights. An effort by me to describe their manner of dancing would be fruitless. I have witnessed dancing assemblies in populous cities of the east, among the refined classes of society, but having seen nothing like this, I must therefore pronounce it *sui generis*. I was strongly solicited by some of the chiefs to unite with them in the dance; I, however, declined the intended honor, but gave to one of them my cane, as a proxy, with which he seemed much delighted. Several of their white neighbors, both male and female, entered the ring.

There was, on this occasion, a splendid display of ornament. Those who have seen the members of a certain society, in their most prosperous days, march in procession in honor of their patron saint, decorated with the badges and insignia of their order, may have some conception of the dress and ornamental decoration of those head men while engaged in the dance.

I will select "*Unum E Pluribus.*" Their doctor, as he was called, wore very long hair, and from the nape of his neck to the termination of his *queue*, there was a continuous line of pieces of silver—the upper one being larger than a dollar, and the lower one less than a half-dime.

Some of the more inferior Indians were stuck over with baubles and hung round with strings. Many of them wore small bells tied around their ankles; and those who could not afford bells had deer-hoofs in place thereof. These made a jingling sound as they put down their feet in the dance.

The squaws, also, exhibited themselves to the best advantage. Several of them were splendidly attired and decorated. Their dresses were chiefly of silk, of various colors, and some were of good, old-fashioned queens-gray. These dresses were not "cut," as our fair belles would say, *a la mode*, but they were cut and made after their own fashion; that is, not so long as to conceal the scarlet hose, their ankles, their small feet, or their moccasins, which were so ingeniously beaded and manufactured by their own olive hands.

Nor must I omit saying that the propriety and correct demeanor of the Indians, and the modest deportment of the squaws, merited the highest commendation.

At the commencement of each dance, or, to borrow our own phraseology, each "set-dance," a chief first rose and began to sing the word "Yah-Ho-Wah!" with slow, sonorous and strong syllabic emphasis, keeping time with his feet, and advancing round the house; directly arose another, and then, in regular succession, one after another, rising and singing the same word, and falling in the rear, until all the Indians had joined in the dance. Next, the squaws, at a respectful distance in the rear, in the same manner, by seniority, rose and united in the song and dance.

Now the step was quicker and the pronunciation more rapid—all singing and all dancing, while Jim, the blind musician, struck harder and faster with his gourd on the undressed deer-skin; thus they continued, the same, for more than an hour, without cessation.

The Indian boys who did not join in the dance, amused themselves the meanwhile, discharging heavily loaded muskets through the aperture in the roof, the reverbetions of which were almost deafening. Taken together, to the eye and ear of a stranger, it seemed like a frantic festivity.

Tall Chief, who was confined to his bed by indisposition, felt it so much his duty to join in the dance with his people, that he actually left his bed, notwithstanding it was mid-winter, came to the council house, and took part in the dance as long as he was able to stand.

About the "noon of night," Hard Hickory invited Mr. D. to accept of a bed at his residence. To this proposition we readily assented. Here we were hospitably provided for, and entertained in a style which we little anticipated. Even among many of our white inhabitants, at this early day, a curtained bed was a luxury not often enjoyed. Such was the bed we occupied. Shortly after our arrival at the house of this chief, Mr. D. retired. Not so with our friendly host and myself. While sitting near a clean brick hearth, before a cheerful fire, Hard Hickory unbosomed himself to me unreservedly. Mr. D. was asleep, and the chief and I were then the only persons in the house.

Hard Hickory, among other things, told me it was owing chiefly to him that this feast was now celebrated; that it was in part to appease the anger of the Good Spirit, in consequence of a dream he lately had, and as an explanation, he gave me the following narration:

"He dreamed he was fleeing from an enemy; it was, he supposed, something supernatural—perhaps an evil spirit; that after it had pursued him a long time, and for a great distance, and every effort to escape from it seemed impossible, as it was now at his heels, and he almost exhausted. At this perilous time he saw a large water, to which he made with all his remaining strength, and at the very instant, when he expected every bound to be his last, he beheld, to his joy, a canoe near the shore; this appeared as his last hope; breathless, and faint, he threw himself into it, and that moment, of its own accord, quick as an arrow from the bow, it shot from the shore, leaving his pursuer behind."

While relating this circumstance to me, which he did with earnestness, trepidation and alarm strongly expressed in his countenance, he took from his bosom something neatly and carefully enclosed in several distinct folds of buckskin. This he began to unroll, laying each piece by itself, and on opening the last there was enclosed therein a miniature canoe.

On handing it to me to look at, he remarked that no other person, save myself and he, had ever seen it, and that as a memento, he would wear it in his bosom as long as he lived.

It was a piece of light wood, resembling cork, about six inches long; and, as it was intended, so it was, a perfect model of a canoe.   *   *   *

The night now being far advanced, he pointed to the bed and told me to sleep there—but that he must go to the council house to the dance, for his people would not like it if he would stay away—and wishing me good-night, he withdrew.

So far, Mr. Crowell. Another eye-witness of this last sacred ritual proceeds to relate the remainder of that night's proceedings at the council house, as follows:

The first object which arrested our attention was a pair of dogs, male and female, suspended on a cross—one on each side. These animals had been strangled—not a bone was broken—nor could a disarranged hair be seen. They were of a beautiful cream color, except a few dark spots on one— naturally—which same spots were put on the other, artificially, by the devotees. The Indians are very partial in the selection of dogs entirely white for this occasion, and for which they will give almost any price.

Now for part of the decorations, and a description of one will do for both: First, a scarlet ribbon was tastefully tied just above the nose, and near the eyes, another; next, around the neck was a white ribbon, to which were attached some bulbs, concealed in another white ribbon; this was placed directly under the right ear, and I suppose it was intended as an amulet, or charm. Then ribbons were bound around the fore-legs, at the knees, and near the feet. These were red and white, alternately. Around the body was a profuse decoration; then the hind-legs were decorated as the fore-legs. Thus were the victims prepared, and thus ornamented, for the burnt-offering.

While minutely making this examination, I was almost unconscious of the collection of a large number of Indians, who were then assembled to offer their sacrifices. Adjacent to the cross was a large fire built on a few logs; and, though the snow was several inches deep, they had prepared a sufficient quantity of wood, removed the snow from the logs and placed thereon their fire. I have often regretted that I did not see them light this pile. My opinion is, that they did not use ordinary fire, but struck fire with a steel, this being deemed sacred.

It was near morning, and the sun about rising, when the Indians simultaneously formed a semi-circle, enclosing the cross, each flank resting on the pile of logs.

Good Hunter, who officiated as high-priest, now appeared and approached the cross. Arrayed in his pontifical robes, he looked quite respectable.

The Indians being all assembled—I say Indians, for now there was not a squaw present—at a signal given by the high-priest, two young chiefs sprang upon the cross, and each taking off one of the dogs, brought it down and presented it on his arms to the high-priest, who, receiving it with great reverence, in like manner advanced to the fire, and with a very grave and solemn air, laid it thereon. This he also did with the other. He then retired to the cross.

In a devout manner, he now commenced an oration. The tone of his voice was audible, and somewhat chanting. At every pause in his discourse he took from a white cloth he held in his left hand a portion of dried, odoriferous herbs, which he threw on the fire. This was intended as incense. In the meanwhile, his auditory, their eyes on the ground, with grave aspect, and in solemn silence, stood motionless, listening to every word he uttered. Thus he proceeded, until the dogs were entirely consumed and the incense exhausted, when he concluded his service.

The oblation now made and the wrath of the Great Spirit, as they believed, appeased, they again assembled for the purpose of performing a part of their festival different from any I had yet witnessed. Each Indian, as he entered, seated himself on the floor, thus forming a large circle, when one of the old chiefs rose, and with that native dignity which some Indians possess in a great degree, recounted his exploits as a warrior; told in how many fights he had been the victor, the number of scalps he had taken from his enemies, and what, at the head of his braves, he yet intended to do at the Rocky mountains, accompanying his narration with energy, warmth, and strong gesticulation. When he ended, he received the unanimous applause of the assembled tribe.

This meed of praise was awarded to the chief by "three times three" articulations, which were properly neither nasal, oral, nor guttural, but rather abdominal.

Others followed in like manner. Among these was Good Hunter; but he

"Had laid his robes away,
His mitre and his vest."

His remarks were not filled with such bombast as some others, but brief, modest and appropriate; in short, they were such as became a priest of one of the lost ten tribes of Israel.

After all had spoken who wished to speak, the floor was cleared and the dance renewed, in which Indian and squaw united with their wonted hilarity and zeal. Just as the dance ended, an Indian boy ran to me, and with fear depicted on his countenance, caught me by the arm and drew me to the door, pointing with his other hand towards something which he wished me to observe.

I looked in that direction and saw the appearance of an Indian running at full speed to the council house; in an instant he was in it and literally in the fire, which he took in his hands and threw coals and ashes in various directions through the house, and apparently, all over himself. At his entrance, the young Indians, much alarmed, had all fled to the other end of the house, where they remained crowded together in great dread of his personification of the Evil Spirit. After diverting himself with the fire a few moments at the expense of the young ones, to their no small joy, he disappeared.

This was an Indian disguised with a hideous false-face, having horns on his head, and his hands and feet protected from the effects of the fire; and though not a professed "fire-king," he certainly performed his part to admiration.

During the continuance of the festival, the hospitality of the Indians was unbounded. In the council house and at the residence of the Tall Chief were a number of large, fat bucks, and fat hogs, hanging up and neatly dressed. Bread, also, of both corn and wheat, in great abundance.

Large kettles of soup, ready prepared, in which maple sugar, profusely added, made a prominent ingredient, thus forming a very agreeable saccharine coalescence. All were invited, and all were made welcome; indeed, a refusal to partake of their bounty was deemed disrespectful, if not unfriendly.

I left them in the afternoon enjoying themselves to the fullest extent; and so far as I could perceive, their pleasure was without alloy. They were eating and drinking—but on this occasion no ardent spirits were permitted —dancing and rejoicing, caring, and probably thinking not of, to-morrow.

The word Sandusky, that has given names to so many towns and other places, and especially to this river, seems to be buried in obscurity, as to its origin. Authors differ materially, and their researches seem to have led them into mists where it is easy to become associated with error. In fact, it requires a good, strong light in every direction of inquiry to discriminate between truth and error. History is not exempt rom the rule. Even in the popular sciences of the day, one thinker refutes and attacks the assertions and the theories of another; and heretics, critics and free-thinkers seem to think that they can find errors in the preaching of the glorious gospel of our holy religion, and the administration of the church of God on earth. So it is. Men will differ on almost everything. To avoid being denounced as a critic, the views of the several authors on the origin of the word Sandusky are recorded here without comment, except one instance, and this only.

Says Mr. Butterfield, p. 74: "As to the origin of the name of this river, there are two opinions. By some it is believed to be a word of French extraction, given to the bay and river by the Indians, in honor of the first French trader who visited the country. In Champaign county, Illinois, there is now living a man of this name, who claims that one of his ancestors, settling at an early period upon the Sandusky, and becoming a great favorite among the Indians, they, as a mark of respect, gave his name (Sow-dows-ky) to the river and bay."

Nobody will deny the fact that the Butterfields are a little prejudiced in favor of the French, and they have a right to be; but nobody will believe that "Sow-dows-ky" is a French name. If the origin in that direction had been traced to a Russian or a Pole, it would have been more excusable. The French have no *w* in their alphabet, nor in their names.

Of the old Indian tradition given by the warriors to Gen. Harrison, the following is the origin: After the naval fight between the Wyandots and Senecas, heretofore mentioned, the conquering band, having landed at Maumee, followed the lake shore towards the east, passing and giving names to bays, creeks and rivers, until they arrived at Cold creek, where it enters the Sandusky bay. Being charmed with the springs of clear, cold water in this vicinity, they pitched their tents and engaged in hunting and fishing. By them (the Wyandots) the bay and river were called Sandusky, meaning, in their language, "at the cold water."

Mr. John H. James, an old veteran pioneer of Urbana, Ohio, in a note to the *American Pioneer*, mentions a part of a conversation he had with William Walker, at Columbus, in 1835-6, when he was the principal chief of the Wyandots at Upper Sandusky, and says: "I asked of him the meaning of the word 'Sandusky.' He said it meant 'at the cold water,' and said it should be pronounced 'San-doos-tee.' He said it carried with it the force of a preposition." The Upper Cold Water and the Lower Cold Water, then, were descriptive Indian names, given long before the presence of the trader, Sow-dows-ky.

In the vocabulary of Wyandot words given by John Johnson, Esq., formerly Indian agent in Ohio, printed in Archæologia Americana. vol.

1, p. 295, the word "water" is given "Sa-un-dus-tee," or, "water within water pools."

The historians of Ohio seem to be satisfied with the meaning of the word as "at the cold water;" but Mr. Butterfield, in his Crawford, p. 147, says that Sandusky is the old "San-dus-quet" of the old French traders and voyagers; "Sah-un-dus-kee," "clear water," or, "San-doos-tee," "at the cold water." * * * * Or, it may have been derived from "Sa-un-dus-tee," "water within water pools."

They will stick in the Frenchman, any way. But no matter about the origin. It is not very likely that any better light will ever be thrown upon the origin of the word.

While on this subject, it should also be remembered that the terms, "Miami of the Lake," or "Miami of Lake Erie," wherever they occur, should not be confounded with the "Great" and "Little Miami," which are tributaries of the Ohio. The former terms simply mean and signify the Maumee river. "Mad Spirit" is the Indian signification of "Erie."

CHAPTER VI.

EARLY SETTLERS—STATEMENT OF MRS. STANLEY—THE HARRIS FAMILY—ROBBERY OF SPICER - THE BRUSH-DAM—PETER PORK—JACOB KNISELY AND CROW—GOING TO MILL—KILLING WITCHES—WOLVES—THE FIRST HORSE-RACE.

STATEMENT OF MRS. STANLEY.

TO WM. LANG, ESQ.—Being one of the oldest settlers of Seneca county now living, and remembering a great many incidents connected with the early settlement of the county along the Sandusky river, I will comply with your invitation and hereby send you a short statement, which you may use, if found appropriate. Respectfully,

TABITHA STANLEY.

"My grand-father came from England, a young man, and single. His name was Samuel Harris. My grand-mother's name was Betsey Boner, and she was a native of Ireland. They were married in Philadelphia, Pennsylvania, long before the revolutionary war, and settled in Harrisburgh, Pennsylvania, where my father, William Harris, was born in 1760.

After the war he married Mary Mead, whose father came from Wales. My father enlisted as a soldier in the revolutionary war when he was but a mere boy, only fourteen years old, as a private, and served during the war to the close. He never received a pension for his services in the war until after he moved to Seneca county, when Mr. Abel Rawson, one of the pioneer lawyers of Tiffin, procured it for him.

My parents raised ten children. Betsey, my oldest sister, was married to David Roberts; Hettie was married to Moses Hunt; brother Augustus was married to Aurelia Clark; Nancy was married to Chambers Mead; Polly married James Eaton; brother Samuel died in what is now Townsend township in Sandusky county, Ohio, in 1826, in the twenty-eighth year of his age, and unmarried; John married Betsey Hays: Minerva married Benjamin Barney; Tabitha, (myself,) married Benjamin Culver in 1828; and Jane, the youngest of our children, married Anson Gray. Minerva, Jane and myself were married in this county and were amongst the few first white girls that were married here at that time. Barney, Culver and Gray were amongst the few first settlers that located here.

My father moved from Harrisburgh into Livingston county, in the state of New York, where we lived until the year 1818, and in that year we moved back to Pennsylvania and settled near Meadville, in Crawford county. Here my sister Nancy was married to Chambers Mead. She died at Meadville. When we left Livingston county, New York, to move to Pennsylvania, some of my brothers and sisters were married, and stayed there. Father and mother, with the rest of us children that were not married—Nancy, Samuel, John, Minerva, Tabitha, Jane, and Marshal Harris—started together. When we got to Olean Point my father bought a boat, called a scow. On this he put our goods, wagon and all. John and myself took three horses and two cows, and drove them overland for Lawrenceburgh. On the way there a man overtook us, and at his request we let him ride one of the horses, and the rascal ran away with the horse. There was at that time no road down the valley of the Allegheny. When we all met at Lawrenceburgh we left the scow, and hitched the horses to the wagon and traveled together to Meadville. where we settled. Here we stayed about two years ; then my brother Samuel and a young man by the name of John Eaton, from the state of New York, started for Ohio on foot, for the purpose of prospecting and exploring the country. They came to the valley of the Sandusky, and wrote back to us to pack up and come out here : that they had found an excellent country, etc.

The following winter my father and brother John started for Ohio to meet the boys here, leaving the rest of us at Meadville. My father was a gunsmith by trade, and brought his tools with him. He put up a shop on the north east part of a piece of land that afterwards became the property of my husband, Benjamin Culver, and known as the Culver farm, near Fort Seneca.

In the following spring father and John came back to Meadville, and then we all started for the Sandusky valley, except my sister Nancy, who was then married. When we got here we found the country a dense wilderness. We put up with Barney's folks, and moved into the same cabin they occupied, which had been built by William Spicer, who then had moved upon his section in the Seneca reservation, east of the river. Spicer was an Indian captive, and had a family of half Indian children. Their names were John, James, Small Cloud, Little Town, and one daughter, who was married to another white captive by the name of Crow. Spicer was a great help to the new comers, for he had cattle, horses and hogs in large numbers. He used to let his land out on shares, and often furnished horses and oxen to farm with. He sold a great deal of corn to the immigrants ; also cattle and hogs, and often let cows out for pay. He was a good neighbor, ever ready and willing to help the needy. People often borrowed his horses and oxen to go to the mill. We had to go to Monroeville or to Cold Creek Mills, to get our grinding done—some thirty miles away, through forest and swamps, without any bridges across the streams, and no road or any other way to guide the traveler but blazed trees.

The Barney family consisted of West. who was the oldest, and Benjamin. both single, a widowed sister, Mrs. Polly Orr, who afterwards married John Eaton, who came out here with my brother Samuel in 1819, as already stated, and Ann, the youngest sister, who was afterwards married to David Rice, in the fall of 1820. Benjamin Barney married my sister Minerva in the winter of 1820. David Smith of Fort Ball, who was then a Justice of the Peace, solemnized the marriage, and played the violin that night at the wedding dance. Mr. Erastus Bowe came with Mr. Smith to the wedding. Mr. Bowe was the first settler in Fort Ball.

The wedding was a rural affair, indeed. The dancing was done on a pungeon floor. A pungeon is a plank about six inches thick, split out of a solid log, and then hewed on one side and "spotted" on the other so as to fit even on the sleepers. This made a very solid and substantial floor to dance on. Boards were very scarce and hard to get, on account of the great want of saw mills. We came here in the summer of 1820. That fall we all took sick, and became so reduced in strength that one was not able to help the other. There was no doctor nearer than Huron county, where doctor Stephenson lived. He came sometimes, and stayed a day or two to supply us with medicine. We were all fortunate enough to get well.

The following year my brother Augustus came. Soon after his arrival his wife took sick and died, leaving him with two children, both small.

We were all well and hearty the next year, except my mother, who was then very sick, but recovered. Benjamin Barney moved to Fort Seneca, close to the old fort built by General Harrison in 1812, and then occupied by Mr. James Montgomery, a Methodist preacher and agent for the Seneca Indians. He, (Mr. Montgomery,) was also afterwards elected Justice of the Peace, and solemnized the marriage ceremony when Mr. Culver and I were married. Mr. Montgomery was considered a very good man, and was highly respected. One of his sons died. I was the only white girl outside of the family who attended the funeral.

Mr. Benjamin Barney and Mr. Anson Gray both moved with their families to the state of Illinois, and both became wealthy. Gray and his wife are both dead. Barney's wife is also dead, but Barney is still living and is now about eighty-four years old. One year ago, when he was here on a visit, I saw him at Mr. Rice's, in Townsend township, Sandusky county, when he was very hearty and active.

Very few white people lived here when we came. Mr. Bowe, Mr. Risdon, Mr. David Smith and Mr. Levi Crissey lived in Fort Ball; Abner Pike, Ezra Sprague, Willard Sprague, Francis Sprague, widow Shippey, Nathan Shippey, Robert and Lorenzo Abbott, Dorcas and Polly Shippey, Joel Chapin, Mr. McNutt, who had two sons—Alexander and Daniel—Caleb Rice and Daniel Rice, Pardon Wilson, Phineas Frary, Sidney Barney—a cousin of Benjamin Barney—Samuel, Silas, Hiram, Asel and Phineas Pike, Louisa Emmerson, who taught school, Eliphalet Rogers, Henry Rogers, Ebenezer Mills, Daniel Mills, Jeremiah Chapman, Hannah Jackson, the Rollins family, and the Dumond, Duke and Montgomery families, constituted about all the white people that lived within ten miles of the fort, except the captives on the reservation.

They used to have their military trainings on the Culver farm, then known as the Spicer place. At one of these trainings I first saw Mr. Hugh Welsh. I think he was the fifer for the Company. Caleb Rice was Captain, my brother Samuel was Lieutenant, John Eaton was Orderly, and West Barney was Ensign. They used to meet there every year. The general muster was held near the stockade of the fort.

The reservation extended from a point opposite Baker's mill to a point opposite the mouth of Wolf Creek, in Sandusky county. The Mohawks lived on the farms now owned by the Frys. Flummerfelts and Claggetts. The Senecas lived opposite the old fort and below. Some of them lived near Green Springs, and up to what is now Watson's Station on the C. S. & C. R.

HISTORY OF SENECA COUNTY.

R. Crow lived further up, opposite my father's, joining the Spicer section on the north.

In 1821 a log cabin stood at a place near what is now Sandusky street in Tiffin, and where Captain Bagby built a very nice residence opposite the old residence of Luther A. Hall, Esq. This residence is now occupied by a family named Lewis. Into this cabin a gentleman from Auburn, New York, moved in that year. His name was Mr. Childs. There was but himself and his wife. They were well dressed, and both very handsome. Mr. Childs had been in the mercantile business in the state of New York. He was then about twenty-five years old, when he took sick and died in the cabin. Soon after his death Mrs. Childs was delivered of a child, and the neighbors took her and the babe to Judge Ingraham's, who then lived near neighbor to Mr. Bowe, where, after suffering about nine days, she also died. The widow Orr, a sister of the Barneys, took the child to raise and kept it one year, when a sister of Mrs. Childs came out here, and took it back to Auburn with her. Somebody had named the child Nancy. Childs and his wife were both buried in the old grave yard, near the B. & O. depot."

So far Mrs. Stanley. This William Spicer, who played so conspicuous a part in the history of the Seneca Indians while living in this valley, was a native of Pennsylvania, and was captured by the Indians when he was very young. When the white settlers first came into this valley Spicer had been on the Sandusky forty years, and during the revolutionary war. There is but little known of his history. The Wyandots took him to the banks of the Ohio, and used him as a decoy to bring boatmen to the shore. They tied him to a tree near the bank of the river and compelled him to call on the boatmen for help, and while the savages lay in ambush any person approaching Spicer became an easy prey. Many were thus made to suffer the cruelty of the Wyandots, but it is to be presumed that Spicer played his part merely by compulsion.

Mr. Mark A. Harris, whose observations were as close as his recollections are fresh and minute, says:

I came to Seneca county with my grandfather, William Harris. with whom I had always lived, and up to the time when my aunt Tabitha married Mr. Culver; then I lived with them. This was in 1828. My uncle, Benjamin Culver, bought eight hundred and four acres of land at the sales. His homestead consisted of three hundred acres. The Flummerfelt and Abbott farms are also parts of Culver's purchase. He also owned the land where the " Cronise saw-mill" used to be, in Liberty township. These lands he bought at the sales, in Delaware. Horton Howard was receiver, and Platt Brush was register of the land office. Mr. Brush lived near and south of Fremont. He married for his second wife a widow Green, from Maryland, formerly—the mother of the Honorable Frederick W. Green, who was Auditor of Seneca county for a long time, and afterwards represented this congressional district in Washington. This was during the ever memorable

THE HARRIS FAMILY.

trouble occasioned by the repeal of the eighth section of the "Missouri Compromise." After serving a term in Congress, Mr. Green was appointed Clerk of the U. S. District Court for the northern district of Ohio, when he moved to Cleveland, where he lived up to the time of his death, which occurred in the spring of 1879.

The Barneys came here from Massachusetts in 1818, and settled near the old fort. It seems that nearly all the settlers in that vicinity preferred to be near the fort, so as to have the benefit of its protection in time of danger. There were three brothers of these Barneys—West, Benjamin and Marshal: and two sisters—Polly Orr, whose husband and one child had died here, and Ann Barney, the youngest sister. Marshal also died here, and he, Mr. Orr and his child were buried at the Spicer place. Ann married Daniel Rice, who was afterwards elected justice of the peace—the first one in the township. His widow is still living in Sandusky county, north of Clyde.

Benjamin Barney was a very resolute and honorable man, and a great friend to William Spicer; and when Spicer was robbed Benjamin took great interest in having the robbers brought to justice, and securing the money. This was probably the first robbery in Seneca county, and it occurred in this wise, viz:—Spicer was well off, and took in a great deal of money from the sale of hogs, cattle, horses and corn. His money was all in gold and silver. Spicer lived on the top of the hill on the west bank of the river, opposite the north point of the island in the river, and about four miles south of the fort. One afternoon when Spicer was alone in his cabin, a man by the name of Rollins came in and demanded Spicer's money and the key of his chest. Spicer refused to deliver over, and Rollins struck him with a club on the head, which stunned him, and he fell. While in this condition he heard Rollins laugh, and also heard some others come in, but could not tell who they were. When Spicer recovered his consciousness, the men and his money were gone.

Spicer was a small man, and had no education; he could not count much, and did not know exactly how much money he did have, but it was generally believed that he had between six and seven thousand dollars.

This Rollins was a carpenter by trade, and at the time of this occurrence was employed to help a certain Paul D. Butler in building a saw mill on the left bank of the river, where Lafayette street, in Tiffin, comes down to the river. Some of the timbers of this mill were afterwards used by Mr. Josiah Hedges in the building of the saw mill standing on the left bank of the river, opposite Reuben Kedler's mill, so-called.

As soon as the news of the robbery became known, the neighbors turned out to assist the constable in the chase after the thieves and the recovery of the money. A man by the name of Downing lived on the top of the hill back and south of Baker's mill, some three miles north of Tiffin, in a cabin near the river. The constable, Mr. Papineau, in company with Benjamin Barney, came to Downing's house and sat down to talk awhile, when a little girl of the family said to these men, "My papa put something nice under there:" pointing to the hearth-stone. They arrested Downing, and raising the hearth-stone, found over five hundred dollars in silver under it. Afterwards some six hundred dollars more were found in the spring at the foot of the hill close by the cabin. These six hundred dollars were supposed to have been put into the spring by this William Rollins who struck Spicer, and who was also arrested soon after. Downing got away from the constable, and was never heard of afterwards. Judge Fitch, who lived near the river, below Elder Kating's, also found some money supposed to be Spicer's, in a ravine that runs across the north west corner of the Culver place, (as then known.) This sum was also over five hundred dollars. All this money was promptly restored to Spicer.

Butler, Case, and quite a number of others were arrested, and were all taken to Norwalk, in Huron county, for trial. Caleb Rice also assisted in making these arrests. Some of the prisoners escaped before trial; Case, Butler and some others were acquitted. Rollins was the only one that was convicted of the robbery, and was sentenced to the penitentiary for the term of eleven years. He was pardoned out before his term expired, Spicer himself signing the petition.

The saw mill near the old Fort Ball I spoke of, was a very rickety affair, and so was the dam that supplied the water. The dam was made of brush laid across the river with the points up stream. On the top of each layer of brush other brush were laid cross-wise, and then another layer on top of these like the first layer, and so on. The whole string of brush was held down by boulders and dirt put on top of the brush. The dam reached to the right bank of the river at a point where doctor McFarland's stable now stands. Mr. Jesse Spencer owning the saw mill and the land on that side of the river, and Mr. Josiah Hedges the land on this side, somehow, trouble arose between these men about the dam. It is possible that the water in the river was set back, and overflowed some of Mr. Hedges' land.

One night, however, Mr. Hedges procured a number of men with picks and shovels, and had a ditch dug in a half moon shape around the east end of the dam, and on the next morning the water of the river flowed through the ditch, leaving dam and saw mill high and dry.

This Judge Fitch, above mentioned, was a tall, slender man, very intelligent and communicative, and in every way an excellent citizen. Elisha Smith kept tavern where the Holt house, so-called, now stands on Sandusky street in Tiffin. That tavern used to be the place for July celebrations. On these occasions it was customary for Judge Fitch to come up and treat all the young men. Then he would say to them that before long they would have to take care of the government, etc. One time we had a Fourth of July dance there when fifteen couples attended, which took nearly all the people that were here.

Abner Pike lived on the Ezra Baker farm, near the old house on the hill. He came here with his family from New Jersey. His wife was a sister to this Butler that built Spencer's saw mill. Pike was a man of medium size, stout and compactly built, had dark hair and dark eyes, and a dull look; he was not very cleanly in his person, and as lazy as he was ignorant, but otherwise a harmless sort of a man.

Mr. Erastus Bowe had a tavern at the old Fort Ball. It was a double log house, one story high. It was built of rough logs, and had two rooms. Mr. Bowe was a pleasant, sociable gentleman, and highly esteemed.

My grandfather was a gunsmith by trade, and wherever he lived, in Pennsylvania, New York or Ohio, had Indians for customers, and in this way he became acquainted with the languages of several tribes. He had no difficulty to talk the Seneca when we came here. He carried on his gun shop until he died, in 1834.

Samuel and John Wright, in later years, became the owners of the farm that from thence bore their name. They were from Rochester, New York. John Wright and Daniel Bissell, also from New York, put up a distillery near the springs on the banks of the river, on this farm. I worked in, and conducted, the distillery for a long time. The business was done in the firm name of "Bissell & Wright." When the farmers brought their corn to be distilled on shares or to be exchanged, we gave them five quarts, and when the corn was cheap and plenty, we gave them six quarts of whisky for one bushel of corn.

About that time two young ladies came to my aunt, Mrs. Culver, from New York on a visit. They were sisters: Mariah Hunt, the oldest, and the younger, Sylvia Ann Hunt, daughters of her sister. While here, the two Mr. Wrights made their acquaintance and married them. John Wright married Mariah, and Samuel Wright married Sylvia Ann. Samuel and his wife did not live very happily; some young merchant from Tiffin became too intimate in the family, and in some way a divorce was brought about. Wright went away. Soon after this occurrence, Mr. Rufus W. Reid, from Tiffin, married Mrs. Wright. Reid was at that time engaged very largely in the mercantile business and the produce trade. He built a large warehouse near the depot of the Mad River & Lake Erie Railroad, then in Fort Ball. The building is now occupied by Mr. Solomon Koup, as a door, sash and blind factory.

Mr. Reid was the rival of Mr. R. W. Shawhan, not only in the mercantile business, but also in the various conflicts in the establishment of banks in Tiffin, each striving to become master of the situation. One succeeded, and the other went down. Reid failed in business, and giving himself up to his appetite for strong drink, lived a very hard life up to his death. Mrs. Reid is still living in Cincinnati.

Those that knew Mr. Reid well must acknowledge that with all his faults, and before he fell, he possessed business qualities of the highest order, combined with a wonderful degree of perseverance. He was gentlemanly and courteous, highly intelligent and accomplished, possessed of a rare memory, and as the presiding officer of a lodge of F. & A. M. he had scarcely his superior in any quality that properly belongs to that station—except virtue.

How truly the words of the poet may be applied to him:—
"Pity he loved an adventurer's life's variety!
He was so great a loss to good society."

But, to let Mr. Harris proceed.

When I was about eleven years old, I had to go with my uncle, John Harris, to the mill at Monroeville. This was the nearest mill to our home, and about thirty miles away. We could not get across the river with a team, so we hauled our corn to the shore of the river, and unloaded it there. Then we took our team home, and loading our corn into a dug-out—a canoe made out of a log—we hauled it across and unloaded it on the other shore. Then we borrowed a yoke of oxen from Mr. Spicer, and a cart from Crow, (we did not say "Mister" to an Indian,) and loaded up our corn and started. The next night we stopped with a man by the name of Nichols, near Bellevue, and in the evening of the second day we reached Monroeville. There were a great many customers ahead of us, and there was no prospect for us to get in for about a week ; so we started for Cold Creek mills, which were eleven miles northwest from here. They had just commenced dressing the millstones when we arrived, and after waiting two days at Cold Creek, we started home with our grist. At Cold Creek we bought a bushel of peaches, which were then, and especially with us in the woods, a great variety. Afterwards they grew almost spontaneously, and produced abundantly, until within about fifteen years ago. Now it is seldom that a crop of them can be raised in this county. The first night on the way home we reached Dr. Stephenson's. The next day our provisions gave out. We came to a fire in the woods where a man had been chopping, and being very hungry, we looked around amongst the logs for provisions that the wood-chopper might have hidden somewhere, and found raw pork and bread. We divided even with the man, and putting his half back where it was, made way with ours, and drove on. When we got home we were gone nearly a week.

The only place where we could get fruit at that time was at Whitecker's, below Fremont about two miles. Mrs. Whitecker was a widow and a captive of the Senecas, and she received this place by the treaty. One time her son James stalled with his wagon near our house, and he had to abandon it. When he left he told me to tell the Senecas that the wagon belonged to him, and then they would not touch it.

Some time after we arrived here, I went up the river with Hiram Pike, who wanted to get a pair of shoes he had up there to get mended. We came to a little clearing of about two acres, in the midst of which was a cabin. Here the shoemaker lived. His name was Johnson, and his cabin the only one on the right bank of the river from the reservation far up towards the town of McCutchenville. It was situated where Jefferson and Perry streets cross. The first log heap that was burnt on the Tiffin side, was where the Commercial Bank now is, next lot north of the court house.

Mr. Erastus Bowe lived near the old fort, on the west bank, and David Smith lived in a cabin, somewhere near or at the place where the Ohio stove works now are. Up the hill, near where McNeal's store now stands, there was an old Indian cabin, into which Mr. Agreen Ingraham soon after moved. Close by this cabin Mr. Milton McNeal soon after built his store, and he was the first merchant on that side of the river.

William D. Sherwood entered six hundred and forty acres of land, including the farms afterwards owned by the Rev. John Souder and the Stoners. Sherwood built a cabin at the Souder place. There was no other house on the army road between the Sherwood cabin and Fort Seneca. Sherwood's wife died in this cabin, and was buried in the graveyard that was situated between the depot of the B. & O. Railroad in Tiffin, and the late residence of Mrs. Joseph Walker on the hill, and where Mr. Francis Wagner now lives. All traces of the graveyard are gone. Mr. Sherwood's son was here a few years ago, looking for his mother's grave, but could find no trace of it. Phineas Frary, another old settler, married a Miss Cochran. A. M. Courtright married a sister of Mrs. Frary, and settled up the river somewhere south of Tiffin. Mrs. Harriet Segur was one of the Cochran girls. She is still living on her farm, on the reservation. The council-house used to stand on that place. This was made of three lengths of logs, cornered as usual, and where the logs came together at the ends, they were flattened and laid on top of each other. The roof was made of bark, with a hole left in the middle to let the smoke out.

I knew all the Indians on the reserve, and was well acquainted with Crow. He was stolen by the Wyandots on the Loyal Hannah in Pennsylvania, and given to the Senecas, who adopted him. Crow was about two or three years old when he was taken away. The parents were away from home at the time, and the other children out after berries. The savages got away with the child unobserved.

When Crow's father came to hunt him up, he stopped at Crow's and sent for my grandfather to come and interpret the conversation. Crow could not talk English. So I went along and heard all that was said. Mr. Jacob Knisely came on horseback to look for his son. He stated all about the manner of the stealing of his son, and said he had now visited all the lodges of the other tribes without success. My grandfather had been with the Senecas so much that he spoke their language quite fluently. He was one of the few who made their escape at the massacre of Wyoming.

They talked a long time. Crow did not want to talk: denied every recollection of his white ancestry, and often refused to give any answer. Finally Mr. Knisely said to him, "If you are my son, then your name is Jacob." With this, Crow jumped up and said, "That is my name, and I am your son; I recollect that, but I kept it all to myself for fear that somebody would claim me and take me away." Crow then sent up to the Wyandots and had his foster-mother come down, who corroborated Mr. Knisely's version of the stealing of his child. She was a very old squaw, and stayed several days, and as long as Mr. Knisely stayed, to satisfy herself that Crow would not go back with his father. Mr. Knisely tried every way to induce his son to go back with him to Pennsylvania; he said that his wife had been sick some time; that she had mourned for her lost child some fifty years, and would be willing to die if she could only once more see her dear boy. The scene was very affecting; but Crow was immovable. He said he had now a family of his own to look after and could not go, but promised to visit his parents some other time. He laughed heartily over the idea as to how he would look dressed up like a white man. Mr. Knisely left one morning, and Crow accompanied his father as far as Bellevue, where they stayed together all night. Crow returned next day, and when the Indians started for their new homes in the West he went with them. He never went to see his parents at all. Crow got his share in the treaties with the Wyandots, as well as with the Senecas, and became quite well off. Crow's first wife was a full blood Indian; his second wife was a daughter of William Spicer. White Crow was his oldest son, who came back here on a visit in 1852, and stayed with me one night. He had just then been at Dayton, Ohio, where he left his second son at school, and where his oldest son was also securing an education. Tears came into his eyes when he looked at the old reservation, and he regretted that he had ever left.

When the Senecas were paid off, Crow received for his improvements nine hundred and fifty dollars, and another Indian paid him fifty dollars on an old debt. Martin Lane was an interpreter for the Senecas, and went with them to the west, and returned here.

It is a most remarkable fact, that while it is very hard to make a civilized man out of a savage, the civilized man takes to savage life like a fish to water.

Col. McIlvain was the chief agent for the Senecas, and often stopped with Lane at the Spicer place. The Senecas were very slow getting ready to go. Finally they got their things on the wagons and started. Spicer was dead before they left here.

Crow died at his new home, of cholera. White Crow got rich, and adopted the name of his grandfather Knisely.

PETER PORK.

A man by the name of Benazah Parker lived on the west side of the street, near where Lorenzo Abbott had his store, in the village then called McNutt's Corners, afterwards Swope's Corners, and now Fort Seneca. Parker kept a whisky shop, and often sold whisky to the Indians in violation of law, and for which he was frequently arrested and fined. Yet he went on in his infamous business. In the night of the 4th of October, 1829, they were having a high time at Parker's. The whole gang was drunk, and Parker administered a mock sacrament to his drunken crowd. Seated about on benches, he passed corn-dodgers to them for bread, and whisky for wine, accompanied with blasphemous remarks. Pork was there. He was a mean, ill-tempered savage, had committed several murders, and had no redeeming trait about him. Pork asked for whisky, and Parker refusing, he became very angry and ugly. Parker ordered him out, and Pork refusing to go, Parker took a burning stick from the fireplace, and making with that towards Pork, was stabbed by Pork in his side. Pork dropped the knife and ran.

Says Mr. Harris:—

My uncle, Anson Gray, was at Parker's at the time this occurred. He used to drink to excess often at that time, but he afterwards reformed, became highly respectable and wealthy.

Pork got out and ran home, and when he went to bed he stuck his scalping knife into a crack in a log close by his bed, and within reaching distance. His squaw noticed that there was something wrong, and when Pork was sound asleep she took the knife away and put a wooden one in its place.

The neighbors became aroused, and getting a warrant for the arrest of Pork, Judge Jaques Hurlbut, one of the best and most influential of men in that vicinity, took with him Jonathan Abbott, Anson Gray, Stephen Ross, Jeremiah Hays, John Harris, Silas Pike and Henry Yeaky. When they got to Pork's house he jumped out of bed, took hold of the wooden knife, kicked out the lantern, and struck Judge Hurlbut with the wooden knife with such force that he cut his home-made cloth overcoat to the skin. The Judge called out, "Boys, he is stabbing me." They had a hard struggle with the villain, but finally subdued him. They put him on a horse, and tied his feet together under the horse, to prevent escape. On the way to Tiffin he said to his escort, "To-morrow me die;" thinking that he would be executed. They put him into the old hewed log jail that stood at the south-east corner of the court house yard in Tiffin. Pork was tried, Judge Lane presiding, and was sent to the penitentiary for a term of three years; but when the Senecas left he was pardoned and went with them. The sentence was made light from the fact that Parker had often violated the law, in selling whisky to the Indians. Abel Rawson was prosecuting attorney.

Parker lived some fifteen months after he was stabbed, and died from the effects of the wound, as it was supposed.

Some four years after the Senecas went away, Joseph Herrin, a half blood Mohawk, came here on a visit. While here he learned that Pork had killed Joseph Silas, a cousin of his. Herrin said: "This makes three cousins of mine that Pork has killed, and when I come home I kill Pork." He kept his word, and when in 1852 White Crow came here, he said that "Herrin knocked Pork down, and cut his throat clear off."

Butterfield says that Pork had committed no less than eight murders. He was a Cayuga, a stalwart, brutal monster, and the terror of the neighborhood. He had killed Strong Arm—Teguania—an Indian of his tribe, just before the fatal affray with Parker. Both had been at Lower Sandusky, and returning home drunk, got into a fight with axes. Tequania was badly mangled. Doctor Dresbach, of Tiffin, dressed his wounds, but he died in nine days. Pork also killed "Thomas Brandt's old wife," as she was called, who lived in a cabin by herself. He met her one day, killed her, and covered her remains with brush.

Pork was sentenced for "stabbing with intent to kill," in the Parker case, on the 28th of April, 1830.

Mr. Harris proceeds:

While Mr. Ingraham lived in the old cabin near McNeal's store, the whole family took sick, and no one was able to help the other. Mrs. Stanley went up and waited on them. One of the Ingraham girls married a Mr. McGee, who afterwards carried on a drug store at Fremont. Melissa married Frank Abbott, the youngest of the Abbott family, who is still living.

Old Mr. Andrew Dukes, also an old settler, had one son, John, and one daughter, Sophia, by his first wife. He married, for his second wife, Mrs. Gittie Swimm, who was a widow, and sister of Mr. Isaac I. Dumond. He lived near the Dukes' burying ground. Dumond married old Mr. Dukes' daughter, Sophia. John Dukes married another sister of Mr. Dumond. So father and son married two sisters, and Mr. Dumond was both brother-in-law and son-in-law to Mr. Dukes, and Mr. Dukes was both father-in-law and brother-in-law to Mr. Dumond.

HARD HICKORY

Was a large, noble looking man, and nearly half white, about six feet high, had little chin whiskers, was very straight and muscular, spoke English well, and was highly respected. He had a large nose, and was about fifty years old when they left.

GOOD HUNTER

Was of medium height, had a melancholy look, most always drooped his head, walking or sitting, but had a sharp eye, and was considered smart. He was a full-blood Seneca, a little gray, about fifty years old, and took the place of Seneca John after he was killed.

SENECA JOHN

Was a splendid looking Indian, strictly honest, as many of the Senecas were, was very straight, square-shouldered, and had a frank, open, noble look. He carried a silver ring in his nose, and one in each ear. He wore a fur hat and broadcloth coat, cut Indian fashion, with a belt, and a silver band three inches wide on each upper arm. He was a stylish man, and of commanding bearing. He lived near Green Springs when he was executed, then about thirty-eight years old.

SENECA STEEL

Was a small Indian, very active, but there was nothing otherwise uncommon about him. Seneca John, Comstock and Coonstick were his brothers.

Mr. Montgomery preached Spicer's funeral sermon. George Herrin, a half Mohawk, was interpreter, and gave the sermon in the Indian, sentence by sentence. (Slow preaching.)

One of Spicer's boys, Small Cloud, was a fine looking fellow, a half blood. He married Crow's daughter by his first wife. Little Town Spicer had three or four wives. Both these Spicer boys went west with the Senecas.

Whenever an Indian was buried they built a pen of poles about three feet high around the grave, and laid poles over the top. Before they left they carried these pens away and threw the poles over the bank.

Crow was a great deer hunter, and shot many a fine buck after night.

He would then carry a pole seven feet long, pointed at the end, with a fork at the upper end. A piece of bark, about fifteen inches wide and two feet long, was fastened to the fork so as to make the bottom level and the other end sticking up along the pole, like a letter L. A candle was put into the bottom part, and Crow holding this over his head, was in the shade, but could see objects far. off. The deer would look at the light, and not notice Crow in the dark. As soon as Crow saw a deer he would stick the pole in the soft ground, and make sure of his game. This was called "fire hunting," and Crow would always travel along the edge of the river, where the deer would come down to drink and find "salt licks,"

The Indians made their wax candles by using cotton rags for wicks, and pouring the melted wax into dry stocks of the wild parsnip, which they used as candle-moulds. They had another light for house use, made of strips of fat pork, which were dried in the chimneys, fastened to a stick so that they hung straight down. When dry and hard, these were stuck into a hole bored into a chip, for a candle stick, and then lit, making as good a light as a candle. The name for a candle was "gigh-di-tagua."

There was a great deal of sickness amongst the Senecas in 1822, and many died. They believed themselves bewitched, and holding a council on the subject, condemned four poor old squaws to be tomahawked for witchcraft. Next day, these squaws went to Lower Sandusky and bought whisky. When they came back they got drunk, and when in that condition they said they were ready, and told the executioner to "cut away." One Indian killed them all. His name was Jim Sky.

Says Mr. Harris:—

A few days after the execution some of the Indians brought the tomahawk to my grandfather's shop, to have it put into better shape. It was a "pipe tomahawk." Soon after a young Indian came in and saw the tomahawk laying on the bench, when he broke out in a horrible oath, and told me to lay it away, for that had killed his mamma. He then cried aloud a long time. His name was Good Spring.

Seneca Joseph had an old squaw living with him who was suspected of being a witch. She was very sick, and Mrs. Stanley used to go over to see her often. One day, when she came there the old squaw was dead, and all drawn up crooked; so they made a crooked grave to fit her. They laid bark on the bottom, wrapped her in a blanket, put her in and covered her with bark, and then filled up the grave with dirt.

One of the Shippey girls came to our house one day on horseback; having heard some wolves howl, she was afraid to go home alone, and some of our folks had to go with her. She afterwards married John Rickets, and Mr. Rezin Rickets, in Hopewell township, is a son of William Rickets, brother to John.

The wolves used to make a fearful howling noise, which they sometimes kept up all night. No one can now imagine what terrible feelings the howling of the wolves would create, on a dark, wintry night, when we were in bed ; the wolves howling on the one side, and the Indians keeping up their everlasting tum, tum, tum, on the other, dancing all night.

MOUND BUILDERS.

There were several mounds on the Culver place, and we often plowed up bones and ancient crockery. In 1850 we opened one of these mounds, and found a very large skeleton, with a well shaped skull, and a stone pitcher near the head. The pitcher seemed to have been made of sand and clay. Small vessels of the same material, filled with clam-shells, were placed inside of the elbows. Some of these pitchers would hold half a gallon. We gave them to Gen. Brish. These things were as wonderful to the Indians as to us.

HORSE-RACE.

Some time after Doctor Dresbach came to Tiffin, he and Mr. Josiah Hedges and their riders came to the Spicer place to have a horse-race. They had a straight track made through Spicer's corn fields. Dresbach had a small gray mare. Hedges' horse was a bay belonging to a friend of his by the name of Connell. McNeal's clerk rode the Dresbach mare, and Albert Hedges rode the Connell mare. Hedges' bay won.

The same day the Connell horse ran against some body's elese horse, on the same track. At the outcome the bay stopped short and threw Albert Hedges clear over the fence, and he had his ankle dislocated. They came down here to have the race, because they could find no other place so free from stumps. The track was straight from the bank of the river to the hill where Mr. Toomb's house now stands. This was the first horse-race in Seneca county.

CHAPTER VII.

THE SENECA CHIEF PRESENTS THE GOVERNOR OF CANADA WITH 954 AMERICAN SCALPS—TALL CHIEF—THE TUQUANIAS—KILLING THE SQUAW OF GEORGE WASHINGTON—JUDGE HULBURT—CALEB RICE—BENJ. CULVER—REV. JAMES B. FINLAY—CAPT. JOSEPH—MRS. INGHAM—CAPT. JOSEPH—CAPT. SHERWOOD—SKETCH OF MRS. INGHAM—EARLY MARRIAGES.

THE Senecas were, at one time in their history, a very powerful race, and about the time of the revolutionary war the most savage and cruel of any of these forest monsters. About the time they took possession of their reservation in Seneca county, there was scarcely anything left of them, and those that did settle here were a mixed rabble of several tribes, half-breeds and captives.

For more than a century this tribe had been in contact with the white race, in peace and in war; and instead of deriving the benefit which naturally ought to have followed, from this intimacy, they deteriorated to more abject barbarism still, and dwindled down to a handful of dirty, stupid, superstitious, worthless rabble. Had not this county once been their home, and been named after them, nobody would care to read or learn anything about them. As it is, the reader would scarce be satisfied, in perusing a history of this county, without having an opportunity to learn all there was of them, and what they were like when they roamed over the ground that contains so many happy homes as now enjoyed by the people here. All these sprung up by magic, as it were, since the last satanic yell of these hell-hounds of the woods died on the desert air.

The manner in which the British government carried on both her wars with the United States. by making these red fiends their allies, and supplying them with everything needful to perpetrate their cruelties upon the white people along the frontier, put that government in a worse light still, looked at from every stand-point that time may justify. For a high-toned, christian people, claiming the mastery of the seas, and upon whose territory the sun never ceases to shine, not only justifying midnight butcheries of her superior enemy by savage warfare, but helping it along and approving these atrocities, calls aloud for universal condemnation.

The relation of Great Britain with the western savages, and the power this red ally exercised on the western frontier, is clearly shown in a letter that Dr. Franklin furnished the *American Remembrancer*, an authority which nobody will dispute.

The British government had sent its agents to all the Indian tribes to enlist the savages against the colonists. The Americans sent Benjamin Franklin to Paris to secure, if possible, the aid of France in favor of his countrymen. Dr. Franklin wrote an article for the *American Remembrancer*, which, in that day, exerted a very powerful influence in both Europe and America. It purported to be a letter from a British officer to the Governor of Canada, accompanying a present of eight packages of scalps of the colonists, which he had received from the chief of the Senecas. As a very important part of the history of the times, the letter should be recorded. It was as follows:

"MAY IT PLEASE YOUR EXCELLENCY:

"At the request of the Seneca chief, I hereby send to your Excellency, under the care of James Hoyt, eight packages of scalps, cured, dried, hooped and painted with all the triumphal marks, of which the following is the invoice and explanation:

"No. 1—Containing forty-three scalps of Congress soldiers, killed in different skirmishes. These are stretched on black hoops, four inches in diameter. The inside of the skin is painted red, with a small black spot, to denote their being killed with bullets; the hoops painted red; the skin painted brown and marked with a hoe; a black circle all round, to denote their being surprised in the night; and a black hatchet in the middle, signifying their being killed with that weapon.

"No. 2—Containing the scalps of ninety-eight farmers, killed in their houses; hoops red, figure of a hoe, to mark their profession; great white circle and sun, to show they were surprised in day time; a little red foot, to show they stood upon their defense, and died fighting for their lives and families.

"No. 3—Containing ninety-seven, of farmers; hoops green, to show that they were killed in the fields; a large, white circle, with a little round mark on it, for a sun, to show it was in the day time; a black bullet mark on some, a hatchet mark on others.

"No. 4—Containing one hundred and two, farmers; mixture of several of the marks above; only eighteen marked with a little yellow flame, to denote their being of prisoners burnt alive, after being scalped; their nails pulled out by the roots, and other torments; one of these latter being supposed to be an American clergyman, his hand being fixed to the hook of his scalp. Most of the farmers appear, by the hair, to have been young or middle-aged men, there being but sixty-seven very gray heads among them all, which makes the service more essential.

"No. 5—Containing eighty-eight scalps of women; hair long, braided in the Indian fashion, to show they were mothers; hoops, blue; skin, yellow ground, with little red tad-poles, to represent, by way of triumph, the tears of grief occasioned to their relatives; a black scalping knife or hatchet at the bottom, to mark their being killed by those instruments. Seventeen others, being very gray; black hoops; plain brown color; no marks but the short club or *cassetete*, to show they were knocked down dead, or had their brains beaten out.

"No. 6—Containing one hundred and ninety-three boys' scalps, of various ages; small green hoops, with ground on the skin, with red tears in the middle, and black marks, knife, hatchet or club, as their death happened.

"No. 7—Containing two hundred and eleven girls' scalps, big and little; small yellow hoops; white ground tears, hatchet and scalping knife.

"No. 8—This package is a mixture of all the varieties above mentioned, to the number of one hundred and twenty-two, with a box of birch bark, containing twenty-nine little infants' scalps, of various sizes; small white hoops, white ground, to show that they were nipped out of their mothers' wombs.

"With these packs, the chiefs send to your Excellency the following speech, delivered by Conicogatchie, in council, interpreted by the elder Moore, the trader, and taken down by me in writing:

"*Father*—We send you herewith many scalps, that you may see we are not idle friends. We wish you to send these scalps to the Great King, that he may regard them, and be refreshed; and that he may see our faithfulness in destroying his enemies, and be convinced that his presents have not been made to an ungrateful people," etc.—Abb. Hist. of Ohio, p. 189.

Is the reader at a loss to determine which is the most lovely of the two — the American savage or the British savage — the giver or the receiver of these scalps?

Mrs. Sally Ingham, in her contribution, says:

My father was the Rev. James Montgomery who was appointed the first agent of the Seneca Indians. He took charge of his office in November, 1819, when we moved into the old blockhouse at Fort Seneca. I was then a little girl eight years old. Louis Tuquania was then the head chief of the tribe.

Tall Chief was a tall, noble looking specimen of an Indian, sober and honorable. Seneca John, Steel, Coonstick and Comstock were nephews of Tall Chief. Comstock died very suddenly when Coonstick was out west for some time, and when he returned an investigation was instituted to ascertain the manner of his death. John, his brother, was found guilty of the murder by having procured the services of a medicine woman who administered poison to Comstock. Coonstick, Shane and Steel were his executioners. I think the particulars given by Gen. Brish are, perhaps, the most correct version of the whole affair.

We lived in the old blockhouse seven years. The pickets were yet there when we came. Some of them had been broken down.

The Senecas were an exceedingly superstitious people, and notwithstanding all the influences brought to bear upon them to love and embrace the christian religion, they were very stubborn, and seemed to prefer their untutored notions about the Deity to the beauties of divine revelation.

The belief in witches was a part of their faith, and whenever anything occurred that troubled them, they were sure that some witch was at the bottom of the mischief. Their vengeance then generally fell upon some poor old squaw, who was then almost certain of being killed.

An old squaw, the wife of an Indian by the name of George Washington, an old chief during the revolutionary war, and then an old man, was charged with being a witch, and the whole tribe was prejudiced against her. She was soon condemned to die, and even her husband consented to her death.

The poor old squaw was at the hominy block, pounding hominy, when the Indians came into her hut. Without any further ceremony, and without asking any questions, Shane struck her on the head with a tomahawk, and she fell. Shane then called another Indian to come and finish her, which he did very promptly. The husband of the squaw stood by and permitted the outrage, without the least interference.

When my father heard of this, he sent for some of the chiefs and told them that if another circumstance like it was ever permitted to occur again, he would have the matter investigated, and the murderers punished under the laws of the white people. This seemed to have the desired effect, and for some time afterwards nothing further was heard of killing witches on the reserve.

The Senecas had their annual green-corn-dance, which was a sort of thanksgiving frolic, and differed very much from the performances of the dog-dance, which seemed to be a proceeding and ceremony of a more sacred character. The dog-dance was the grand dance, and generally lasted nine days. It always took place about the time of our Christmas. They would then dress in their best style, and observe every rule with great punctuality. The dance commenced by one Indian shooting off his gun through the smoke hole in the roof. The Indians then, all armed to the teeth, would one by one enter the dance, one chief leading, whooping and yelling, drums beating, chains rattling, etc. They danced up and down, and the old chiefs, in a guttural sound, which approximated a roaring, indicated the time with their "Yah-Ho-Wah!" The squaws never danced with the men, but formed a ring by themselves. The squaws danced to their own music, which was a sort of whine on a high note, and seemed to come from a great distance.

They feasted on the best that the forest and their little corn patches could afford.

At a certain part of the dance one Indian would appear, dressed in a bear skin, and another in a deer skin, with polished brass for the eyes of the animals, to make the figures look fearful. Thus fixed up, they ran around the ring of dancers. This was to scare away the evil spirits. They had one dance in the afternoon, and one after supper.

My father often went over to the council house where, and while, the dances were going on, to keep the white people from selling whisky to the Indians. Father often talked to them about their dances, to ascertain their meaning or origin, but never succeeded in getting any intelligent explanation from them, any further than this, viz: They said their ancestors were rich at one time, and used to sacrifice fat cattle and sheep; now their children were poor, and could only sacrifice the best they had, and that was their white dogs.

When the dogs were ready to be sacrificed, they held them up by the legs and said a long ceremony over them; then they laid them on the burning log-heap. During this part of the performance, the Indians stood around in perfect silence, almost motionless, and looked as solemn as the grave. Good Hunter officiated as priest. After the dogs were laid on the fire, Good Hunter laid a sprig of dried herbs on the dog, and then every other Indian and squaw did the same, in rotation, and in perfect order, without saying a word. Each dog was put through this ceremony separately. After that, an Indian came running in and scattered fire and ashes all around the council house and over the people.

In the burial of their dead, a hole was left in the box, near the head, to let the spirit come through, and the corpse was supplied with cakes of sugar and bread. After the box was let down into the grave, the Indians marched around it, and each dropped some green sprig upon it—very much like the burial ceremony of a member of some secret society in this respect, in these days. When the grave was filled up, the squaws pulled their blankets forward over their heads and as far out as their elbows would reach, and cried with a sort of howling voice, while the men stood motionless, and looked on without shedding a tear.

The chief, Tuquania, had a twin sister who was a medicine-woman. The twins were born with one eye each. One time my mother was very sick, and for want of a better doctor, we sent for this squaw. The snow was very deep, and yet she went out into the woods with a hoe and got some herbs. Then she came over to our house and made tea with these herbs and cured mother.

We loved the old squaw very much after that, and always made her feel welcome at our house. When father died, she attended his funeral, and seemed to be very much affected.

This Benazah Parker, who was stabbed by Peter Pork, was a man about five feet six inches high, of dark complexion, dark hair and eyes, and was about thirty-seven years old. There was nothing prepossessing in his appearance. He was stabbed in October, 1829, and died some time in the month of January, 1831.

Jaques Hulburt and Shepherd Patrick bought the land, with the old fort, at the sales.

Father had charge of the Indians some ten years, and up to the time of his death, when Gen. Henry C. Brish took charge of the agency, and it was not long after that when the Indians were taken away. I think it required only three or four wagons to take all their things.

Mr. Hulburt was one of the first associate-judges of the court of common pleas for Seneca county. He was about five feet eight inches high, lean of flesh, but well proportioned; had a dark complexion, dark hair and eyes, a high forehead, pleasant and gentlemanly in his intercourse with people. He was a man of exemplary character, fair education and excellent judgment. He enjoyed the confidence and esteem of all who knew him. He taught the first grammar school in this county. My sister Maria, Mrs. Keen and myself attended his school. He was a member of the Presbyterian church. When he sold his Fort Seneca farm, he bought the land where Fort Stephenson stood, and built a house there. So he was the owner of both forts. The house he built at Fort Stephenson was a one-story frame house, with a porch on the east side.

[At the first celebration of the battle of Fort Stephenson, on the 2d day of August, 1839, Mr. Elutherus Cook delivered his oration from that porch to the assembled thousands, when Mrs. Ingham sat by a window, inside of the house, and the writer stood near the porch, listening to the oration—more than forty years ago. Mrs. Ingham was an old Whig, and therefore enjoyed the speech, which was more of a political than historic character, and therefore out of place, while the writer did not like the very many bitter remarks hurled at the Democratic party, which he then thought were ill-timed, and thinks so still.]

Mr. Hulburt opened a store in Lower Sandusky. He was afterwards elected a member of the House of Representatives, in the legislature of Ohio, from Sandusky county. He died of consumption, December 25, 1836.

Caleb Rice was the nearest neighbor we had. He was a millwright by trade, an excellent mechanic, and a very intelligent man. He built the mill for the Senecas at Green creek, about one-half mile below the springs. He was constantly involved in law-suits, occasioned by his general disposition to evade his promises. He was a bad financier, and outside of his intelligence and mechanical skill, of very little account.

Benjamin Culver, another neighbor, was a Canadian by birth, and possessed of considerable wealth. He bought the best farms on the river bottom. He was about forty-eight years old when he was married to Miss Harris, who was then a beautiful young girl. Miss Harris was the only white girl at my brother's funeral, who died at the fort in 1820. Mr. Culver was a man of excellent heart, a true friend and a good neighbor. The only fault in his life was his love for strong drink. He died in 1840, when he was about sixty years old.

William Spicer was a white man, and was captured by the Indians when quite young. He spoke the language of the Cayugas and the Senecas fluently. He had accumulated a good deal of money at the time he was robbed. A man by the name of Rollins was sent to the penitentiary for the robbery, but it was generally believed that others got the money. Spicer was very filthy in his personal appearance—perhaps never washed himself; at least, he looked as if his face had never come in contact with the element called water. His house was the dirtiest on the reserve. His voice was rough and extremely offensive. He was respected by nobody.

Crow was a German boy, and was stolen by the Wyandots in Greenbriar county, Pennsylvania, when quite young. His father, Jacob Knisely, found him here fifty years after he was stolen. My father went with Mr. Knisely to look him up. Crow refused to go with his father. The meeting and parting of father and son was very affecting on the part of Mr. Knisely. Crow did not seem to care much. My father often spoke about this scene, with much feeling.

The father of Mr. Isaac I. Dumond came here with his family shortly before the land sales, and settled near the fort. He was a man about five feet eight inches high, compactly built, and slow of speech. He was kind and hospitable, and a good neighbor. His family consisted of wife and eight children—four sons and four daughters. Mr. Dumond was a member of the old school Baptist church. Elder Kating often preached in Mr. Dumont's cabin. He lived here some twelve years after he came, and died in a small frame house he had built near their cabin, and close to the road. I heard the Reverend Robert Finley preach often, and afterwards his son, James B. Finley, and still later the nephew of the latter. They were all great preachers, and men of high standing in the estimation of the people. James B. Finley was about fifty years of age when I saw him, a man of striking personal appearance, about five feet ten inches high, heavy built, very straight, with light complexion, light brown hair, and gray eyes; his features were regular and prominent, his countenance was expressive and earnest, and his manners were naturally kind and winning, yet there was great force and decision of character about his general make-up. His sermons were in conformity with his appearance and temperament—forcible and convincing. His voice was loud and clear; he was a good singer, and a great revival preacher. He belonged to the Urbana circuit, where his father preached before him, but his services were extended throughout northwestern Ohio.

It is scarcely necessary to add that there were neither melodeons nor organs to assist in the singing, and churches that cost from thirty to fifty thousand dollars, with organs that cost one thousand dollars or more, were not thought of in those days, in this region.

Seneca John used to get drunk occasionally, and it troubled my father very much to ascertain the way John got his whisky. He finally hit upon a plan to catch a man by the name of Broughton, whom he had suspected for some time. He took Mr. Isaac I. Dumond, Shane and John with him to Broughton's one evening. Father had dressed himself in Indian costume, and when the party were seated around on benches in Broughton's house, John called for whisky, and after drinking some, handed the glass over to father, who tasted it to be sure that it was whisky. Then father threw back his feathers and blanket, and when Broughton recognized him he almost sank into the ground.

After a severe reprimand from father, Broughton promised to sell no more whisky to Indians, and he was let go without punishment for the time being.

Steel and Gostick looked nearly alike, and both were about one quarter white. Comstock was a full blood Cayuga, well dressed, cutting great swells, a dashing, fine looking and sober Indian. He was not as large as the other chiefs, rather small on the contrary, but squarely built. With all his gayety he was modest and reserved, and highly esteemed by Indians and whites.

Tuquania, a half brother to head chief Tuquania, was at one time a captain in the French service. He and his sister were both of French mixture. While in the service of the French, Tuquania had acquired many French ways and manners. He was also converted by a French priest and had embraced the catholic religion; and he often said that he was sure of being a christian, because he was baptized "Joseph." Yet, for some reason or other, he would join in the dog dance. He was about sixty years of age in 1819, and lived to go west with his tribe. He was the most intelligent Indian on the reservation. He wore a red vest, buckskin leggings with a white ruffled shirt over the leggings, and a nice shawl over his head on Sunday. His hair was nicely braided. Very proud of his education and French training, he often put on great airs, and said, "This is the way the French officers do." His overbearing disposition often got him into trouble with other Indians, all of whom he regarded as vastly his inferiors, and very frequently father was called upon to settle his troubles for him.

A man by the name of Keeler lived near the river bank. He had a family of six children; he came from the state of New York, and bought forty acres of land. The family suffered greatly with sickness. I don't remember what became of them.

Alexander McNutt and his brother, Daniel McNutt, were also here in 1819. Daniel had a family, and Alexander married a sister of Isaac I. Dumond. My father solemnized their marriage.

William Montgomery started a store in 1833, in a log cabin, in the village that is now called Fort Seneca.

Eliphalet Rogers bought a farm near Wolf creek. He married Hannah Jackson, who had lived at Mr. Bowe's a long time. Rogers was an honest, home-spun sort of a man. His farm became afterwards known as the Snook farm.

Almon Rollins married Mary Sherwood, and Lorenzo Abbott married her sister Jeanette. The two couple were married at the same time. Jeanette was then only fourteen years old.

Old Mr. Sherwood was captain of a militia company, and very proud of his station. He was a great talker, and somewhat boastful. He did not live to be very old.

Mr. William Harris, the gunsmith, was a man about five feet ten inches high, stout and well built. He was poor, but a man of considerable refinement, and strictly honest. He drank some, but not to excess. He came here with his family after the Barneys, but before the Dumonds, and was amongst the first that settled near the fort.

The Pikes and the Chaneys lived on the Spicer place when we came to the fort.

There were three of these Tuguanias. One was the head chief, another was the Joseph, and the third was the Armstrong Tuguania, the son of the one eyed medicine woman.

MRS. SALLY INGHAM.

The subject of this sketch was born in Champaign county, Ohio, on the 4th day of February. 1811. She is the fifth child of the Rev. James Montgomery, and was but eight years old when the family moved into the blockhouse at Fort Seneca. She grew up from childhood into a blooming maiden, on the banks of the old Sandusky, among a few white settlers on one side, and the Senecas on the other side, of the river.

In these wild and rural scenes of her childhood, she lived under the droppings of the sanctuary, blessed with the love of christian parents, and a cheerful disposition, that lets the owner look upon the sunny side of life—a blessing that never forsook her in all her life-long pathway.

For want of other schools she received her primary education in the household, and afterwards took lessons in English grammar from Judge Hulburt. She also attended a grammar school taught by Edson B. Goit, Esq., in Lower Sandusky, Ohio. With this training she was enabled to teach school herself, and kept her first school near John Crum's, on the state road, three miles north of Tiffin; and after the death of her father, she taught two years longer.

When she was about getting ready to attend the grammar school at Fremont, she went to McNeil's store at Fort Ball, to buy a pair of shoes. Mr. Sardis Birchard sold them to her. He was then clerk in the store, and afterwards became familiarly known in Lower Sandusky by the name of Judge Birchard, the uncle of President Hayes.

On the 25th day of March, 1832, Mrs. Ingham was married to Mr. Milton Frary, a young farmer in Pleasant township, in this county, who died in 1852. After living in widowhood seventeen years, she married a Mr. Alexander Ingham, from Cleveland, Ohio, who also died in April, 1870.

Mrs. Ingham is still in the enjoyment of good health, and the same old happy disposition. She has a most remarkable memory of past events. The names of persons, places and incidents are at her tongue's end, and her ready delineation is easily discernible by reading her narrative. She has her father's temperament and appearance, strongly marked. Her conversation is both instructive and amusing, couched in splendid English, and sweetened by her christian training, which unconsciously crops out on every occasion.

If she ever had an enemy, he must have died long ago. She is beloved by all who know her, and welcome at every door.

For more than fifty-two years she has been a faithful member of the M. E. Church, in good standing; and while she enjoys her trust and confidence in God, she is not bowed down by the weight of the cross, but seems rather to bear her faith and increasing weight of years as an enjoyment.

She has now lived in Seneca county longer than any other person in it, and is the last and only remaining member of a once very large family.

Mrs. Ingham had four children: James R. Frary, who was married to Hattie F., daughter of the Rev. Andrews. He died in Tiffin, in March, 1862, well known among the merchants and business men of Tiffin; Emily, now the wife of Jacob Baker; Sarah, who was married to Ralph Gates, and died in 1877; Justin, who died in 1863, as a prisoner of war in a rebel hospital in Danville, Virginia.

The writer, in gratitude for her many narratives of men and things pertaining to early life in Seneca county, can only wish her many more years of life in the enjoyment of her happy nature, in health, comfort and contentment.

EXECUTION OF SENECA JOHN.

CHAPTER VIII.

DEATH OF COMSTOCK—SENECA STEEL—DEATH OF SENECA JOHN—COONSTICK—TRIAL AND DISCHARGE OF COONSTICK—JUDGE HIGGINS' DECISION—JUDGE BIRCHARD'S STATEMENT—BENJAMIN F. WARNER—HARD HICKORY AND HIS DEATH—IMMIGRATION OF THE SENECAS TO THE NEOSHO AND COWSKIN RIVERS—CHARLIEU—THE GIRTYS—THE DEATH OF DRAKE.

GENERAL Henry C. Brish, who succeeded Mr. Montgomery in the agency of the Senecas, relates the following incident as illustrative of the superstition of the Seneca Indians, and of the composure with which their warriors would meet death. The tribe had dwindled down to about four hundred souls:

About the year 1825, three of the prominent chiefs—Coonstick, Steel and Cracked Hoof, went on an excursion to seek a new home and fresh hunting grounds for their people. They returned after an absence of nearly three years. Coonstick and Steel were brothers. They had left behind them an older brother, Comstock, who was chief of the tribe, and a younger brother, John—Seneca John.

The two brothers who had gone west, finding on their return that their elder brother, Comstock, was dead, and that their younger brother, John, was chief in his stead, charged John with having caused the death of Comstock by witchcraft. He denied the charge, and said:

"I loved my brother Comstock more than I love the green earth I stand upon. I would give myself up, limb by limb, piecemeal by piecemeal—I would shed my blood, drop by drop, to restore him to life."

But all this protestation of innocence, and love for his brother, was of no avail. His brothers told him that he must die, and that it was their duty to be his executioners. John calmly replied:

"I am willing to die. I ask only that you will allow me to live until to-morrow morning, that I may see the sun rise once more. I will sleep to-night on the porch of Hard Hickory's lodge, which fronts the east. There you will find me at sun-rise."

They acceded to his request. Coonstick and Steel, awaiting the morning, when they were to kill their brother, passed the night in a lodge near by. In the morning, they proceeded to the hut of Hard Hickory, (who himself told this story to Gen. Brish). He said that just as the sun was rising, he heard the approaching footsteps of the brothers, and opened the door of his hut to peep out. There he saw John asleep, wrapped in his blanket. His brothers awoke him. He arose and took from his head a large handkerchief, which was wound around it. His hair, which was very long, fell upon his shoulders. The doomed chief looked calmly around for the last time upon the landscape, and upon the rising sun, taking, evidently, a farewell view, and then said to his brothers that he was ready to die.

The brothers had brought with them another Indian warrior by the name of Shane. Coonstick and Shane each took John by the arm, and led him along towards the place of his execution. Steel followed behind with his gleaming tomahawk in his hand. They had advanced about ten steps from the porch when Steel struck his brother a heavy blow with his tomahawk, upon the back of his head. He fell to the ground, as the blood gushed from the dreadful wound. Supposing him to be dead, they dragged him beneath a tree near by. There, perceiving signs of life, Steel drew his knife and cut his brother's throat from ear to ear. The next day the corpse was buried with the customary Indian ceremonies.

This horrible scene occurred in Seneca county in the year 1828. Steel was arrested and tried in Sandusky county, and was acquitted. So far, Abb.

Butterfield has this in addition, viz:

Supposing this blow sufficient to kill him, they dragged him under a peach tree near by. In a short time, however, he revived, the blow having been broken by the great mass of his hair. Knowing that it was Steel who had struck the blow, John, as he lay, turned his head towards Coonstick and said: "Now, brother, do you take your revenge."

This so operated upon the feelings of Coonstick, that he interfered to save him; but it enraged Steel to such an extent, that he drew his knife and cut John's throat from ear to ear.

Gen. Brish also said:

Three years thereafter, when I was preparing to remove them to the west, I saw Coonstick and Steel remove the fence and level the ground, so that no vestige of the grave remained. John chose the place for his execution near Hard Hickory's lodge because he did not wish to be killed in the presence of his wife, and because, also, he wanted Hard Hickory to witness that he "died like a man."

Judge Higgins, in a communication to Knapp's History of the Maumee Valley, says:

Upon the extinguishment of the Indian titles, there were several tribes that continued to occupy their former homes, and retained their titles to small reservations of land. Among these Indians was the tribe of Senecas, who held a reserve of ten miles square, on the Sandusky river, a few miles above Fremont. The political relations between these Indians and the United States government were peculiar. The United States claimed, and exercised, an ultimate sovereignty over all Indian reserves, and they conceded complete personal jurisdiction and independence to the Indians within the boundaries of their reservations. Questions requiring decision upon this relation were frequently occurring in the course of my judicial experience. Among others, was a case occurring in the Seneca tribe, of peculiar interest.

DEATH OF SENECA JOHN.

During the session of the Supreme Court in Fremont, in 1822, (It must have been in 1829 or 1830.—AUTH.) some person in Lower Sandusky entered a complaint before a justice of the peace against a head chief of the Senecas for murder, and he was arrested and brought before the justice, accompanied by a number of the principal men of his tribe. The incidents upon which this proceeding was founded are very interesting, as illustrating the Indian life and character. With this head chief—Coonstick—I was somewhat acquainted. He was a noble specimen of a man; of fine form, dignified in manner, and evincing much good sense in conversation and conduct.

The Judge then goes on to relate the killing of Seneca John, concerning which he differed some as to the facts, and proceeds:

These facts being presented to the Supreme Court, they decided that the execution of the criminal was an act completely within the jurisdiction of the chief, and that Coonstick was justified in the execution of a judicial sentence, which he was the proper person to carry it into effect. The case was dismissed, and Coonstick discharged.

Judge Sardis Birchard, of Fremont, the uncle of President Hayes, had a store in Lower Sandusky during the time the Senecas were on their reservation. He was called "Judge" from the fact that during the existence of the old constitution of Ohio, it required three associate Judges to sit with the Circuit Judge to hold what is now known as "Common Pleas Court." Mr. Birchard was one of them.

Tall Chief, Hard Hickory, Seneca John, Curly Eye, Good Hunter and others, traded with him. Mr. Birchard often attended their dances, and said that Rudolphus Dickinson, Judge Justice and Mr. Fifield often danced with the Indians. The Indians called Mr. Birchard "Ansequago," and they told him that it meant "the man who owns the most of the land."

Mr. Birchard, in his communication to Knapp's History, says:

I remember well the death of Seneca John. He was a tall, noble looking man, and was said to have looked very much like Henry Clay. He was always pleasant and cheerful. He was called the most eloquent speaker on the reserve. He could always restore harmony in their council when there was any ill-feeling. In the evening before the morning of his death, he was at my store. The whole tribe seemed to be in town. Steel and Coonstick were jealous of John, on account of his power and influence. John was a great favorite among the squaws. John bade me "good-bye." and stood by me on the porch before the store as the other Indians rode away. He looked at them as they moved off, with so much sadness in his face that it attracted my attention, and I wondered at John's letting them go off without him. John inquired the amount of his indebtedness at my store. We then went behind the counter to the desk. The amount was figured up and stated to John, who said something about paying it, and then went away without relating any of his trouble.

The principal head men or chiefs of the Senecas, were Good Hunter, Hard Hickory and Tall Chief; there were also some half-chiefs. Among those most noted was Benjamin F. Warner, a white man, who had previously been a fireman on a steamboat. He had eloped with an Indian woman and settled down among the Senecas.

Hard Hickory was the leading mind among them. He was a leader of no ordinary grade. He was possessed of polished manners, seldom seen in an Indian. He spoke the French language fluently, and the English intelligibly. Scrupulously adhering to the costume of his people, and retaining many of their habits, this chief was much endeared to them. His urbanity, his intelligence and ardent attachment to the whites, and, above all, his strict integrity in business transactions, obtained for him — and deservedly — the respect and confidence of all with whom he traded. The merchants of Lower Sandusky reposed such trust in him, that when some poor Indian came to ask for goods on credit, if Hard Hickory would say that he would see them paid for, no more was required. Thus his word passed current with, and for, the whole tribe. Mr. Obed Dickinson was a particular friend of Hard Hickory.

Hard Hickory fell from his high station as an honest man. Tempted by money, he became first a thief and then a liar. How many of our own people—some, even, in our own town of Tiffin—who, for a long time in their business life, were regarded and esteemed as men of profound integrity and honesty, who had stood aloof for a long time from all manner of crime, and had enjoyed the confidence and esteem of all who knew them, and while at the height of their glory, became dizzy and weak; and as they fell, took down with them, not only the money of the men whose confidence they had secured, but the general condemnation of all honest men in the community! How often we are deceived in our fellows! We often let men of tried and acknowledged honesty stand aside, and take obscure men who had no record for unflinching honor, put them in places of honor and trust, and about the time we begin to think they are fire-proof, they fall down deep and take our money with them. After the fall we compromise with some agent of the thief, and secure as much of the money that was stolen from us as we can, and let the gentlemanly thief go—perhaps to run for some office. The Indians don't understand etiquette in that way, it seems.

An annuity of $1,600 was due from the state of New York, for a limited number of years, to certain families of Cayugas, of one of which Hard Hickory was a member. This annuity was regularly paid, up to their removal, at their old home on the Sandusky. By an arrangement with the general government in their treaty at Washington, that annuity was to be forwarded to them at their new home on the Neosho, through the hands of the government agents.

In the year 1834, a draft for the sum due them from New York, was forwarded and received by them; and in order to make a distribution of the money among those entitled to receive it, it was necessary to have the draft cashed, for which purpose Hard Hickory, with George Herrin, the interpreter, were delegated to go to Fort Gibson. They went, sold the draft, and received the money.

Hard Hickory then proposed to Herrin a trip to Washington City to see after the business of the tribe, relative to their land sales in Ohio. Said he: "Let us go while we have this money; it will make no difference to our people, as our Great Father, the President, will pay us back all the money we spend in going there and returning home, as he did when we went to our treaty."

So off they started to Washington. For more than a month they reveled in all the luxury and dissipation of the city, until they were tired of them. Now they determined to go home, and requested the Commissioner of Indian Affairs to reimburse them, and furnish means to return with. This, of course, was refused.

On arriving home, their money was nearly gone. Hickory was then called before his people to give an account of himself. He stated that there was something wrong about the draft, and he had to go to Washington to arrange it; that the President said it should all be made right, and they would get the money soon, all in silver.

Doubting this statement, they sent a messenger to Fort Gibson to ascertain the truth. He reported, on his return, that Hickory had drawn the money on the draft, and consequently the chief's statement to the contrary was false. A solemn council was called, before which he was summoned to appear. He appeared; he plead guilty to the charge of falsehood, and made no attempt to palliate or justify the offense, but threw himself upon the mercy of his people, offering, at the same time, to surrender all his horses and other property as an indemnity for the money spent, which would have been sufficient, or nearly so, to have satisfied the amount. The council lasted several days. In the debate as to the punishment of Hickory, some of the chiefs made efforts to save his life. A majority, however, were against him. He had betrayed his trust, and dishonored his high station as a chief. At length the verdict came that *Hard Hickory must die.*

If Hickory had stood forth before his people and asserted at once the truth of the matter—in other words—had not lied about it, he would have saved his life and honor. "And from my knowledge of the tribe," says Gen. Brish, "that would have been the result."

In hopes that he would yet be spared, and that no one would attempt to kill him in the presence of his wife, who was much respected, he confined himself to his house, heavily armed. For several days and nights his house was surrounded. At length, the notorious Shane, who helped to murder Seneca John, volunteered to kill him in his house. Shane, having just returned from the Cherokee country, went to the house in the night and rapped at the door. Hickory recognized his voice, and naturally supposed that he had at least one friend who would try to save him. Hard Hickory was the uncle of Shane.

On being assured that Shane was alone, Hickory directed his wife to unbar the door and let him in, which she did. Shane wore a blanket, and approached Hickory in the middle of the room, holding out his left hand, while his right was under the blanket, holding the handle of a long knife. Hickory held out his right hand to Shane, and as soon as their hands were grasped, Shane drew his knife and stabbed Hickory through the body, and then dragged him out of doors, where several Indians stabbed and tomahawked him. Thus perished the renowned chief Hard Hickory, with the seal of falsehood stamped upon his hitherto fair character.

This Benjamin F. Warner had become entirely Indian in his habits, and associated with Hard Hickory and other chiefs. Those who described him as part Indian, were simply mistaken. He was a Yankee by birth, but became an Indian by choice. His wife's name was Kon-ke-pot; she was from Green Bay, and a Mohican. The Senecas adopted the family. Warner became a sort of major-domo of the tribe, and in common with them, drew a portion of their annuities from the government. He transacted a great deal of business for the Senecas. If a horse was missing, Warner would be sure to track and find him. He could stock a gun or a plow, build a house, tan a skin, and was always ready for either work or sport, but sober.

He emigrated with the Senecas to the west. His wife died on the journey, soon after crossing the Mississippi, and Ben, with his child, accompanied the tribe to the new reserve on the Neosho. Warner had a cow, which he gave to a poor family who had buried their father and husband near the door of their cabin, near the west line of Missouri.

"The family were in utter destitution, and we gave them all we could spare. On leaving them, the woman cried out: 'You have left a cow behind.' On looking back, I saw Warner's cow in a small picket enclosure, near the house, and called his attention to the fact. His reply was: 'I put her there myself; guess the woman'll want her worse than I shall.' Benjamin Franklin Warner proved that he carried a noble heart under a rough exterior."

There was an old Indian living on the Vanmeter tract, in this county —a Mohawk—whose name was Charliéu, and who was famous for his animosity to the Americans. At the age of about twenty-five, he fought, with the rest of the Canadian Indians, under Montcalm, upon the heights of Abraham, where the brave and generous Wolf was killed. At that time he was married, and had one child. He fought during the late war on the side of the British, and had a large number of scalps in his possession, which he had taken during the war. He joined the Senecas, with the rest of his tribe, in 1829, and with them, started for the distant west. At St. Louis he was taken sick, and died on the 26th day of April, 1832. As he wore several crosses suspended from his long hair, he was claimed by the Roman Catholics, and received a christian burial in the Catholic church-yard in that city. He was supposed to be over one hundred years old when he died. He spoke French fluently, and was well known to the first settlers of this county.

The removal of the Senecas to the west was agreed upon at Washington City, on the 28th day of February, 1831. This treaty was made between James Gardiner, Commissioner on the part of the United States, and Comstock, Seneca Steel, Captain Good Hunter, Hard Hickory and Small-Cloud Spicer, chiefs of the Seneca tribe. George Herrin acted as interpreter, and Gen. Henry C. Brish as sub-agent. The proceeds of the sale of the Seneca reservation were to be put into funded stock at five per cent. interest, which was to be paid to the Indians as an annuity, after deducting the cost of building for the Senecas a blacksmith shop and grist mill. The United States gave them seventy-six thousand acres of land, lying along the Neosho and Cowskin rivers, northwest of the state of Arkansas, and ninety miles above Fort Gibson. (See chapter 29.)

In the fall of the year 1831, the Senecas started for their home in the west, when there were just 510 of them, all told, the most mixed-up-mess of humanity imaginable. A portion of them traveled overland, and after experiencing numerous hardships and many accidents, finally succeeded in reaching Missouri in the following spring. The division in charge of Gen. Brish traveled by water, encountering but little difficulty. They reached the Ohio river at Cincinnati, where they took a boat.

Their new home is a beautiful country, and at this time probably owned by the whites. On the 26th day of April, they all met above St. Louis, and arrived on the Neosho on the 4th day of July, following. On the 26th day of August, 1845, they had been reduced down to the number of one hundred and forty-three. It is to be presumed that at this time there is nothing left of that once powerful tribe of savages but their name.

So mote it be.

Simon Girty, the most infamous of all the white savages amongst the red skins, was adopted by the Senecas, and became not only a great scout, but also an expert hunter. He was from Pennsylvania, to which state his father had emigrated from Ireland. The old man was beastly intemperate, and whisky was his great delight. "Grog was his song, and grog he would have." His sottishness turned his wife's affection. Her paramour knocked the old man on the head and won the price.

This couple left four sons—Thomas, Simon, George and James. The three latter were taken prisoners, in Braddock's war, by the Indians. George was adopted by the Delawares, became a ferocious monster, and died in a drunken fit. James was adopted by the Shawnees, and became as depraved as his brother. It is said that he often visited Kentucky, at the time of its first settlement, and inflicted most barbarous tortures upon all captive women who came within his reach. Very many acts of cruelty are charged to him, and yet Proctor and Elliott petted him. In Kentucky and Ohio, Simon sustained the character of a most brutal barbarian; everything cruel and fiend-like was associated with his name. Indian life and brutality suited his nature, and with all his cruelties, that stamped him as a hyena more than any other beast, it was said of him that he saved many prisoners from death. His influence was great, and whenever he chose to do so could save many poor captives.

In September, 1777, he led the attack on Fort Henry, on the site of Wheeling, and demanded the surrender of the fort in the name of his Brittanic majesty. He read the proclamation of Governor Hamilton, and promised the protection of the crown, if the garrison would lay down their arms and swear allegiance to the king. He warned them to submit peaceably, and said that he could not restrain his warriors, then very much excited. Col. Shepherd, the commander, rejected his propositions, and a shot from a thoughtless youth made Girty retire. He opened the siege, and failed. He was also repulsed from Baker's station.

In 1782 he led a powerful body of savages upon Bryant's station, in

Kentucky, about five miles from Lexington. The Kentuckians made such a gallant resistance that the Indians were anxious to retire, when Girty, thinking he could frighten the garrison into a surrender, mounted a stump and made a speech to them. He told them who he was, made all manner of promises of protection, etc. A young man by the name of Reynolds, fearing the officers would believe Girty, volunteered his remarks, and said to Girty : "You need not be so particular to tell us your name ; we know your name, and you too. I've had a villainous dog. He was an untrustworthy cuss. I named him Simon Girty, in compliment to you, he is so like you: just as ugly and just as wicked. As to the cannon ; let them come on. The country is aroused, and the scalps of your red cut-throats, and your own, too, will be drying on our cabins in twenty-four hours. We've a big score of rods laid in to scourge you out again." This response of Reynolds was effectual. The Indians withdrew, and were pursued to the Blue-licks, where they lay in ambush and defeated the Kentuckians with great slaughter.

Girty also led the attack on Colerain, in St. Clair's defeat. He died at Malden in 1815, blind and poor.

There seems to be something in a name, after all. Whether names give to the possessor certain traits of character, or whether beings of certain dispositions will naturally assume names, nobody can tell : but while these monster brothers became the terror from the Ohio to the lake, away out in the northwestern part of Illinois another monster by the same name— Michael Girty—became the terror of the prairies.

For similarity of name and character, let a few words suffice, which we take from Matson's History of Bureau County, Illinois. It may be true that Mike was a son of Simon; but nobody will care to know. I extract :—

Mike is said to have been a son of Simon Girty, a well known, notorious outlaw, who in 1780 escaped from justice in western Pennsylvania, and found refuge amongst the Indians of Ohio, where he exercised great influence. Mike Girty was born of a squaw, and spent his early life among the Indians of Ohio. He came to this country soon after 1821, and was employed as interpreter by the fur company. Here he married a squaw and raised a number of sons. Mike tried hard to gain the confidence of the Indians, but they did not trust the treacherous half breed.

On the 21st of June, 1827, Gen. Cass, as Indian agent, held a council in Bureau county, with the Indians. Girty acted as interpreter. Cass gave him a silver medal, as a token of friendship, which he carried to the day of his death.

After the close of the Black Hawk war, a numer of Indians returned to Bureau county. Among them were the squaw and pappooses of Girty ; but Girty himself was not among them. His fate at that time was unknown, but it was generally believed that he had been killed in battle. Some time after that, on a clear, bright day in the month of June, 1836, when the prairies were covered with wild flowers and the farmers busy with their work, Girty passed along the road to Princeton. Here he found a group of buildings, where a few years before not a house could be seen. He carried on his back all his camp equipage—blankets, gun, kettles and provisions. His once straight, manly form was now bent, not from age, but from disease and great fatigue. His head was without a covering, and coarse, black hair was hanging down to his shoulders in confused masses. They said that "he was undoubtedly the last of the Mohigans." He was not inclined to answer any questions, but passing up the street and looking at a painted building. he said: "That big wigwam; great chief live there, I speck." When he was told that it was a church he passed on, not knowing what that was. He said as he started on, "Big warrior; great brave." He directed his steps towards Indiantown. Here he found everything had changed. At the foot of the hill, near a spring outside of town, Girty camped for the night, being overcome by sickness and fatigue. Here he gave himself up to feelings of despair. The smoke of his camp fire, and his loud coughing, attracted the attention of Dr. Langworthy, who visited the camp and offered his assistance; but Girty appeared sullen, and would only shake his head. On the third day after his arrival at Indiantown, he started west. About one week thereafter, a man traveling on the old Sac and Fox trail, saw on the prairie north of Barren Grove, two wolves eating a carcass. Out of curiosity, he rode up to see what it was they were eating, and found it to be the carcass of an Indian partly devoured. Near the remains lay a gun, knife, tomahawk, blankets, a copper kettle and a pot. Around the neck was a buckskin cord, to which was attached a silver medal with this inscription: "A Token of Friendship. Lewis Cass. U. S. I. A." Thus ended that out-law.

Oakley was the first post-office in Seneca county. At the time this was established there was but one mail route in the county, and this led through the county, from Lower Sandusky to Columbus. Soon after the time the Senecas settled upon their reservation, or about that time, the mail was carried on horseback by a young man named Urich Drake, who was a son of Judge Drake, of Marion county. Young Drake was killed by an Indian, as it was supposed at that time. He was found, torn by the wolves, and marks of a knife were also discovered on his body.

In 1830 Judge Drake came to this county to find out, if possible, who it was that murdered his son; and if it should be ascertained that the murderer was an Indian, then also to find the tribe he belonged to. He called upon Mr. Brish, then agent of the Senecas, and in company with him proceeded to the residence of "The Crow." Martin Lane acted as interpreter. Crow said that the son of Judge Drake was killed by an Indian whose name was "Big Kittles." and that he had fled to Canada soon after the murder. The Judge returned home, fully satisfied that his son was murdered by a Canadian Indian. But such was not the fact. Mr. Brish, sometime subsequently, asked George Herrin what Indian was called Big Kittles. The reply was that it was Spicer, the white man who lived upon the banks of the Sandusky.

It appears that the young man had passed over to the east side of the river, and when near Spicer's house was met by him and accompanied to the place where he was to cross back to the west side of the river. Spicer mounted the horse behind Drake, and as soon as they had reached the opposite bank he drew his knife, and reaching around the young man, with one effort cut him nearly in twain.

He then dragged him behind a log, near the spring just below the dam of John Keeler on the Sandusky river, (about three miles north of Tiffin.) As soon as this was done he went to Crow's house, who, observing that he (Spicer) was covered with blood, inquired whether he had killed a deer. Spicer replied that he had killed a white man; whereupon Crow ordered him to be gone, as in all probability he would be pursued, and if traced to his (Crow's) residence, they might suspect him of being accessory to the murder. Spicer fled to Canada, but after awhile returned. These particulars were kept a profound secret until related to Mr. Brish.

The foregoing is taken from Butterfield's History of Seneca County, and is given here for whatever it is worth. The two stories don't agree, and the latter, upon which the greatest stress seems to be laid, is the least likely to be true. The reader will remember that Crow's wife was the daughter of Spicer, and that Crow and Spicer were on intimate terms. There is no evidence that Spicer had ever left the reserve. Herrin, the interpreter, probably lied to Mr. Brish.

This much of the story, however, is true; viz: That the young man was killed about that time, while carrying the mail to Lower Sandusky, and near Fort Seneca. The writer saw and conversed with a brother of the murdered mail-carrier on this subject, a few years ago in Marion. The family were not satisfied as to the manner of the death. It is also true that in front and on the east side of the residence of the Reverend Henry Lang, in Fremont, and about three rods from his door, up on the hill opposite and north of Fort Stephenson, an humble little slab marks the grave of poor Drake. The inscription, which is still legible, is, "U. Drake. 1811."

CHAPTER IX.

ROCKY CREEK—FORT BALL—COL. BALL ATTACKED BY INDIANS—ERASTUS BOWE—OAKLEY—NEW FORT BALL—FIRST POST OFFICE — MILLS—ARMSTRONG AND McCULLOCH SECTIONS—EARLY SETTLERS IN FORT BALL— LOCATION OF THE COUNTY SEAT—HUNTER'S MILL—EARLY SETTLERS IN THOMPSON, ON HONEY CREEK AND ROCKY CREEK—MELMORE—COL. KILBOURNE—HARRY BLACKMAN'S CORNERS--ANCIENT FORTIFICATIONS—COL. RICHARD JAQUA.

ROCKY CREEK has its source near the south line in section 33, Reed township. Running north about three miles, it takes a westerly direction through the center of Scipio township, entering Eden near the north-east corner, and sweeping through several sections, turns in a north-westerly direction and enters the Sandusky river at its right bank, in the city of Tiffin.

Nearly opposite, and west of the mouth of this stream, on the left bank of the river, where Lafayette street now strikes the same, is a large spring of excellent, cold water. This spring attracted the attention of Col. Jas. V. Ball, when in 1813 he was about to build a stockade near the army road on the bank of the river, under instructions from General Harrison. A detachment of men, under the command of the Colonel, built the stockade, and called it "Fort Ball."

In September, 1833, a company muster was held near the place where the old fort used to be. There was an open space between this point and where the stove works now are. The trees were cut, but very many stumps still remaining, interfered very much with the evolutions of the "army." My lamented friend, Christopher Snyder, (a sketch of whose life will be found elsewhere herein,) and myself attended this company muster. It was the first display of American military either of us ever saw. The sun shone very hot, and to get into some kind of shade we both sat down under a small sycamore bush that grew out from under an old log, bedded half way into the ground. This log was a part of the old fort, and the little sycamore bush grew up into a tree that stands close by the residence of Dr. Hovey at this writing. This camp was built as a temporary place of security in case of necessity, and as a magazine for supplies. It consisted of stakes a foot in thickness fixed in the ground, with old bayonets driven through

FORT BALL.

them horizontally, near the tops. Against these logs were piled upon the outside, and over the logs dirt was thrown from a ditch, which surrounded the whole. There was room in the interior for five hundred men.

After the battle of Tippecanoe, and while General Harrison was at Fort Seneca, he sent a detachment of men up the river to strengthen this camp. The soldiers were quartered here several days, during which time they were very short of provisions, and, being compelled to subsist on fish, a part stood guard while the rest were fishing, to protect them, if necessary, from the lurking savages. Before the battle of Fort Stephenson this detachment left for the Maumee, but the post was occupied occasionally until General Harrison left the country.

The remains of several soldiers that had been buried near the fort were afterwards found in digging in the vicinity. One was exhumed last summer when laying pipes for the water works in the street, about half way between the river and the stove works.

Col. Ball with his troops on their way to the Maumee, about a half mile south-west of Ballville in Sandusky county, and a day or two previous to the assault upon Fort Stephenson, had a skirmish with a number of Indians. The squadron was moving towards the fort, when suddenly they were fired upon by the Indians from the west side of the road, whereupon Col. Ball ordered a charge. He, with his suit and the right flank, came into the action immediately. The Colonel struck the first blow. He dashed in between two savages and cut down the one on the right; the other, being slightly in the rear, made a blow with a tomahawk at his back, when a spring of his horse to one side let the tomahawk cut deep into the cantel and pad of his saddle. Before the savage could repeat the blow he was shot by Corporal Ryan. Lieutenant—afterwards General James Hedges, of Mansfield, Ohio— the surveyor of Tiffin, and brother of Mr. Josiah Hedges, the proprietor of Tiffin, following in the rear mounted on a small horse, pursued a large Indian, and just as he came up to him his stirrup broke and Hedges fell from his horse, head first, knocking the Indian down. Both sprang to their feet, when Hedges struck the Indian across the head, and as he fell ran him through with his sword. It is said that many years thereafter, the stirrup was found and sent to the gallant Hedges, at Mansfield.

At this time Captain Hopkins was pursuing a powerful savage on the left. The savage turned and struck a blow at the captain with a tomahawk; the captain's horse sprang to one side, and the blow failed of execution. Cornet Hays and Sergeant Anderson ran up and soon dispatched the savage. The Indians were twenty in number, of whom seventeen were left dead on the ground.

On the 18th of November, 1817, Mr. Erastus Bowe, the first settler in Seneca county, arrived at Camp Ball, where some hired men had erected for him a double log house within the limits of the camp. Many of the stakes were then still standing. This was the first settlement in the county. Here Mr. Bowe kept tavern, which was the first in Seneca. Hotel bills must have been high in those days, because butter cost two shillings a pound, pork six dollars per hundred, and flour twelve dollars a barrel. The house of Mr. Bowe was the only one on the left bank of the river within the present limits of Tiffin, when the town of Oakley was surveyed and platted.

In 1819 Mr. Joseph Vanse surveyed a town upon land granted to one Robert Armstrong, known as the Armstrong section, and called it Oakley. This was the first town surveyed and platted in the county. Bowe's tavern was in that survey.

Mr. David Risdon, who took a very active part in opening up the county to civilization, and who became very popularly known as a surveyor and citizen, was appointed the first post-master in the county, the office being located here at Oakley. There was then but one mail route in or through the county, and that extended from Columbus to Lower Sandusky, along the army road.

It was said of Mr. Risdon, that while he was post-master he used to go fishing occasionally, and carry the mail matter with him in his hat. People that were anxious to get their mail, and could not wait for his return, would follow him up, along the river. Mr. Risdon would then take the post office from his head, and look for papers and letters.

In 1821 two brothers, Ezra and Case Brown, erected the first grist-mill in the county, upon Honey creek, near Melmore. A Mr. Free, from Bloom township had the first grist ground there. The event was hailed with great joy amongst the early settlers, who had hitherto been compelled to go to Monroeville, Cold Creek, Upper Sandusky or Mount Vernon, to get their grinding done. John Knitzer, an early settler from the state of Pennsylvania, also erected a grist-mill a short distance down the creek from Melmore, in 1827. Mr. Knitzer was esteemed by those who knew him, for his intelligence and manly qualities.

In 1819 Abner Pike settled in Oakley, and afterwards located on the farm of the late Ezra Baker, near where the mill by that name still stands on the Sandusky.

In 1824 the town of Fort Ball was surveyed by David Risdon. This included the whole of Oakley. Some people, who knew but little of the sagacity of Josiah Hedges, were of the opinion that if the lands on the west bank of the river had not belonged to Robert Armstrong, the county seat of Seneca would have been located there.

At the treaty of the Miami of lake Erie, the United States granted this tract to Robert Armstrong. It was a section of six hundred and forty acres, and known as the "Armstrong reservation."

Armstrong was taken captive by the Wyandots when a child three years old, in Pennsylvania. He married a half-blood, and was much respected. He spoke excellent English, and one could scarcely discover that he was raised amongst the savages. This land was granted to him by the United States for his services as interpreter. He died in 1825, in the Wyandot reserve, about two miles from Upper Sandusky. At the same treaty the United States also granted to the children of William McCulloch a section of six hundred and forty acres, lying just north of and adjoining the Armstrong reserve. McCulloch was killed by a cannon ball at the siege of Fort Meigs, while sitting in General Harrison's tent, and was at that time employed by the United States as interpreter.

Ely Dresbach, from Circleville, a graduate of the Ohio Medical College, also settled in Fort Ball, on the 17th of February, 1823.

Rodolphus Dickinson, from New York, the first lawyer in Seneca county, also settled in Fort Ball in 1824.

Abel Rawson, from Massachusetts, arrived on the 15th of February, 1826, and settled in Fort Ball.

A Mr. Jesse Spencer, the proprietor of Fort Ball, and Mr. Josiah Hedges, the proprietor of Tiffin, two towns adjoining on the river, were each striving to secure the location of the county seat in their respective towns. Other people became interested, and for a long time there was a very bitter conflict between these rival parties for success. They sometimes came to blows about it. The brush dam was also a bone of contention, and one time, even after the county seat was located in Tiffin and Mr. Hedges had the two story frame building put up, (which will be further described,) for a court house, he knocked Mr. Spencer down, for which Hedges was arrested and for a short time imprisoned in this court house. Finally Mr. Hedges bought out Jesse Spencer, and became the owner of Fort Ball. Thereupon Mr. Hedges had additions surveyed and platted by James Durbin, re-numbering the lots and extending the limits of Fort Ball, which from that time forward was known by the name of New Fort Ball, until it was finally merged into, and became a part of, the city of Tiffin.

The open square across the street, south of and opposite McNeal's store, was the place intended for the location of the court house. New Fort Ball was surveyed and platted in 1837. It is situated upon the eastern portion of the Armstrong section, and contained six hundred and twenty in-lots, together with several additions that had then already been made to Tiffin, "Pan Yan" among them, which was situated between the iron bridge and the tunnel.

In 1821 Josiah Hedges entered the land where the old town of Tiffin was afterwards located, at the Delaware land office. The town was surveyed and platted by the brother of the proprietor, General James Hedges, of Mansfield. The first stick was cut upon the town plat in March, 1822, and soon thereafter Henry Welch, of Eden township, John Mim and two other men, Wetz and Drennon, had each a lot given to them, with the condition that each should build a cabin on his lot and move into it with his family, which was done accordingly.

James Spink, of Wooster, came here in the same month, and brought with him a stock of goods. In the following winter his store was broken open and robbed of nearly all its contents. This so discouraged Mr. Spink that he left in disgust.

Simeon B. Howard, from the eastern part of Ohio, also located in Tiffin about that time.

Finally the day arrived when the great trouble about locating the county seat was to come to an end. The legislature, during the winter session of 1822, had appointed three commissioners to locate the county seat for Seneca county, viz: Messrs. Herford, Miner and Cyrus Spink. These gentlemen arrived here on the 25th of March, 1822, and located the seat of justice for Seneca county at Tiffin, where it has ever since remained. The Fort Ballites were very much chagrined and put out about it, but finally came down.

Very soon thereafter Mr. Hedges built a mill on the right bank of the river, immediately north of Tiffin, where the present brick mill now stands, the dam of which is still flowing back the water of the river throughout the whole extent of the city along the river. The mill was known by the name of the "Hunter mill," because Mr. Samuel Hunter, the oldest son-in-law of Mr. Hedges, had charge of it. To show how great a spite the principal inhabitants on the Fort Ball side of the river entertained against Mr. Hedges, they influenced Mr. Spencer to bring an action against Mr. Hedges, for flowing Spencer's land by the dam. They also decried the mill, and said all the hard things of Mr. Hedges and his mill they could. Soon the patronage of the mill fell off, and the enterprise seemed to fail, however necessary and scarce the mills were.

HEDGES' MILL—TIFFIN.

Then Mr. Hedges resorted to a stratagem, which soon proved to have the desired effect. Hedges sent out word to all his customers and the people far and near, that he would likely be compelled to take his mill away, and that if they wished their grinding done they must hurry up, etc. This notice raised such general indignation in the country against the enemies of Mr. Hedges that it turned the tide in his favor, and Hunter's mill became the most popular mill on the river. Mr. Hedges bought Spencer's Fort Ball, and peace was restored to the border. At the time the commissioners located the county seat at Tiffin, there were but six cabins in it. The greater number of the early settlers were on the Fort Ball side, and the lawyers, doctors, merchants and all, were in unison in their fight upon Mr. Hedges, but he outgeneraled them all.

Tiffin was named after Governor Edward Tiffin, the first governor of Ohio, who was a particular friend of Mr. Hedges. At this writing three daughters of Governor Tiffin are still living—two in the town of Chillicothe, Ross county, and Mrs. Dr. Comegys, in Cincinnati—the only surviving members of the governor's family.

The location of the county seat took place two years before Seneca county was really organized and clothed with judicial or municipal powers.

During the latter part of the year 1819, and during 1820, the beauty of the "oak openings" and the richness of the soil attracted quite a number of people to Thompson, and the Whitneys, Underhills, Purdys, Clarks, Demicks, Twisses and others became squatters, awaiting the land sales.

About the same time the towering oaks, soil and scenery along the banks of Honey creek and Rocky creek, made the immigrants say; with the disciples of old: "It is good for us to be here; let us make here three tabernacles: one for thee, one for Moses, and one for Elias."—

Here came the Welches, the Clarks, the Sponables, the Browns, the Bakers, the Searleses, the Pratts, the Craws, the Knapps, the Cornells, the Houghs, the Bretses, the Downses, the Jaquas, the Gibsons, the Bundages, the Kagys, the Penningtons, the Fleets, the Watsons, the Kollers, the Eastmans, the Omsteds, etc.

With the exception of a few early settlers in Fort Ball and near Fort Seneca, all the early settlements were made on the east side of the river, especially along Honey creek and Rocky creek. West of the river was nearly all forest and water, sometimes badly mixed, and there were no settlements at all.

Col. Kilbourn, also a pioneer surveyor in Seneca county, took a very active part in its organization. He surveyed the state road already described and known by his name; also the towns of Melmore and Caroline in this county.

Among my first acquaintances in America, was my friend James M. Stevens, of Melmore. He and I were apprentices and learned our trades at the same time, in the same shop, in Tiffin. James is a great singer—was at that time—and among the many songs he sang was the poem composed by Col. Kilbourn on Melmore. James used to sing it to the tune of "How tedious and tasteless the hours."

Friend Stevens—well, I don't like to say much of the living—but James is a very clever man. He lost an arm in the war of the rebellion, and is now familiarly known as Colonel Stevens. The poetry on Melmore is recorded here, not so much for its poetic excellence, but because James used to sing it.

MELMORE.

Where honey-dews from the mild heaven,
  Distil on the foliage below—
Where Honey creek's waters are given
  T' enrich the sweet vales as they flow;—
Where playful the heart-cheering breeze
  Sweeps o'er the sweet bosom of flowers—
There Melmore is seen through the trees,
  With fragrance and health in her bowers.

This country and village to prove,
  Of pleasure and health the abode.
Kind Nature has found in her, love,
  And on her good children bestowed.
The fees to her agents are small,
  For titles in form which they give;
Then come, men of enterprise—all
  Accept, and in happiness live.

Merchants and laborers come,
  A fortune is offered you near;
Here make it your permanent home,
  The country will cherish you here.
Come taste the Melmorian springs,
  Possess the Melmorian lands,
Wealth, honor and pleasure they'll bring,
  To strengthen your hearts and your hands.

EARLY SETTLERS.　　　　149

  So healthy the country is, 'round.
   That doctors have little to do ;
  So moral the people are found,
   They live without ministers, too ;
  So honest our neighbors we call,
   So peaceful and happy at home,
  They've need of no lawyers at all,
   And none are desired to come.

On the 5th of April, 1822, Noah Seits, from Fairfield county, settled upon the north-east quarter of section twenty, in what is now Bloom township. This was the first settlement within its limits. Thomas Boyd came with his sister, Mrs. Mary Donnel, in the spring of the same year, and also settled here. Mr. Boyd was a native of Pennsylvania, much esteemed among his neighbors.

In the same year, Joseph McClelland and James Boyd settled upon Honey Creek, in Bloom, and were soon followed by Abraham Kagg, Lowell Robinson and Nehemiah Hadley. The following year John Seitz, George Free and Jacob Bretz became citizens of this township. John Seitz passed through this county during the late war, in company with twenty others, with wagons loaded with clothing for the soldiers at Fort Stephenson, where they arrived three weeks after the battle.

Harry Blackman, from Genesee county, New York, settled here in Bloom, on a farm that became afterwards very familiarly known as "Blackman's Corners." After residing here sixteen years, he removed into Eden township, where his place was again called "Blackman's Corners." The town that was afterwards laid out here by Dr. James Fisher, and surveyed by James Durbin, in 1830, called Elizabethtown, (after the name of the doctor's wife, Elizabeth, who was a daughter of Dr. Boyer, of Tiffin), never flourished, and at this time there is no trace of it left. At one time it had a blacksmith shop, a wagon shop, some dwellings and a tavern.

William Anway, soon after the land sales at Delaware, in 1821, came from the town of Scipio, in Cayuga county, New York, and settled in what now constitutes Scipio township. This township was so named at the request of Mr. Anway. He was the first settler in this neighborhood. Mr. Timothy P. Roberts came in 1824, and erected the first frame dwelling house in the county, in which he resided to the time of his death.

William Anway built a log house at the corners where the South Tiffin road and the Marion State road cross each other. The spot where the house stood is now covered with a circle of evergreens that were planted there in memory of the Anway family.

Moses Smith put up a small frame building across the road from Anway's house, in which he kept a store for awhile. Robert Dutton was the first man that died in the township, and was buried on his farm, which is now owned by Frederick Fox. William Pierce, a colored man, put up and carried on the first blacksmith shop in the township. Mary, daughter of John Anway, was the first child that was born in the township. She is the wife of Mr. John Wilcox, of Republic. A Mr. Langley was also among the first settlers.

These names, with a few others, made up the white population of Seneca county to about the time of the land sales.

This Col. Kilbourn, the surveyor above spoken of, was a man about five feet eight inches high; he had a nose somewhat Roman shaped. In 1843, he was bald and gray; he had blue eyes, prominent features and expressive countenance. He was a great talker, and very interesting in conversation. He lived in Columbus, where he associated with the best society, and was highly esteemed. He was a great singer, and often produced his own poetry, adapted to some familiar tune. The widow of one of his sons became the wife of Mr. Reber, a lawyer in Sandusky City. This son was a phrenologist of some note, in Columbus.

Honey creek is the largest affluent of the Sandusky river at its right bank. It rises near New Haven, in Huron county, in the marshes, and near the point where Richland, Huron, Crawford and Seneca counties corner. It enters Venice township immediately after it leaves the marshes, and taking a northwesterly direction through Venice, it enters Bloom near its northeast corner. Then, taking a westerly direction through Bloom, it flows into Eden township, and making a large curve in Eden, it cuts across the southwest corner of Clinton and enters Hopewell in section thirty-six, and there the Sandusky river at the right bank.

To people who were born and raised along this stream, and to those who have lived here a long time, the present beauty and scenery, the splendid farms in high state of cultivation, the beautiful farm houses, large barns, and every improvement calculated to add to the comfort and enjoyment of life, may have very little attraction; but to people from abroad, strangers that visit this valley, there is not in all this northwestern Ohio anything equal to it.

There is an excellent spring near the left bank of Honey creek, about sixty rods below Koller's mill, in section nine, Bloom township. About one hundred and fifty yards from this spring, and in a direction west of south, the early settlers found ruins of ancient fortifications of very singular construction and workmanship. There was nothing about the works that would indicate the Indian, and the fort must have belonged to a people who preceded the Indians, and of whom the Indians themselves had no knowledge. The work was constructed of stone, some of which were dressed. The main buildings were in a circular form, about one hundred feet in diameter. At the side towards Honey creek there was attached to each of these circular walls a stone appendage of about twelve feet square, with an opening towards the spring. There was a space of about three hundred yards between these circular walls. Both buildings seemed to have been alike. As late as 1838, the walls were about five feet high, but crumbling down.

There was no sign of any mortar having been used in the erection of the buildings, and yet it seemed that the stones had once been held together by some cement, from the manner in which they rested upon each other. The stones had fallen down on both sides of the wall, and the piles on each side were as high as the wall itself.

RICHARD JAQUA.

The father of Richard Jaqua was a citizen of the state of Connecticut. Soon after the revolutionary war the family moved into Columbia county, in the state of New York, where, on the 9th day of April, 1787, Richard Jaqua was born. Some time thereafter the family moved to Canada West, and settled near Brockville.

On the 9th day of October, Richard Jaqua was married to Elizabeth Wilsee, a young *Canadienne*. When the war between England and the United States broke out, Jaqua was the owner of two hundred acres of land, and considerable personal property.

When he was drafted as a soldier to join the British army, his American pride was stronger than the laws of Canada, and he at once determined that he would not take up arms against his native land, and that he would make his escape to it at the first opportunity. Soon after the draft, and on the last day of the year 1812, he and nine others crossed the St. Lawrence, about forty miles below Kingston.

One of these others was his friend, Ezra Brown, who, also, afterwards became one of the first settlers of Seneca county. Jaqua carried a small feather-bed and bed-clothes, and Brown carried the clothing for both. When the party arrived on American soil, they traveled on foot through the snow, and reached an American picket-fort late in the night. The next morning the whole party of run-aways were sent, under guard, to Ogdensburgh, in the state of New York, where Major

Forsythe was in command. The Major examined each man separately, and being fully satisfied of the truth of their statements, gave each man a pass.

Jaqua then went over to his native county of Columbia, and on the 3d day of April, 1813, started back for Ogdensburgh. On his way he met his friend Brown at Morristown, New York. They were both experienced in the use of small boats, and intimately acquainted with the dangerous places in the channel of the St. Lawrence. Here they came to the conclusion that they would help other deserters to get over to the American side, and for that purpose procured a craft, by the means of which they helped a goodly number of the fugitives to get across the river to the American side.

This sort of employment was exceedingly dangerous, inasmuch as no crafts of any sort were allowed to touch the Canadian shore; yet these friends followed up this work during all the summer and fall of 1813. The Canadian authorities became fully informed of these operations, and sent a squad of men to a small island opposite Gibway Point, with instructions to capture both Jaqua and Brown as they were passing to and fro.

One night Jaqua, Brown, Patterson, and five others crossed over to Gibway Point and secreted themselves until morning. Patterson walked along the beach to attract the attention of the guard. Immediately three men were seen putting out from the island in a punt-boat, and landing on Gibway Point, pulled their boat on shore, and then made for Patterson. These men and Patterson, getting into sharp conversation, Patterson receded from the British and the shore, and when they were far enough away to be considered safe, Jaqua, Brown, and the other men, who were secreted with them, jumped up, and with cocked guns and the help of Patterson, took the men prisoners and handed them over to a militia captain at Rawsee. This captain detailed a guard, consisting of Sergeant Whipple, Jaqua, Brown, and several others, to take the prisoners to Sackett's Harbor, which they did.

In the fall of the same year, 1813, the American army, under Gen. Wilkerson, was in camp on the American side of the St. Lawrence, a short distance below Gravelly Point. Gen. Hamlin, with his troops, was also stationed at a point on the same side called French Mills. Hamlin was very anxious to have Wilkerson, with his men, join him, but to bring this about, it would require a long and tedious march by land, or to embark the whole force in boats and proceed down the St. Lawrence, through the Thousand Isles, which, all knew, was a dangerous undertaking.

RICHARD JAQUA.

Hamlin sent two messengers with his orders for Wilkerson, and when these arrived at Morristown, where Jaqua and Brown then were, one of the messengers was taken sick, and became unable to proceed further. The other messenger employed Jaqua and Brown to take him to Gen. Wilkerson's headquarters. They took the punt-boat, and, traveling by night only, they reached Gen. Wilkerson's camp in two weeks after they left Morristown. In a few days thereafter, Brown and Jaqua were engaged by Gen. Wilkerson to pilot him and his forces down the river to Gen. Hamlin, through the Thousand Isles. Jaqua and Brown, with their punt-boat and a flag, took the lead, and the fleet, with Gen. Wilkerson and his forces, passed safely through the Thousand Isles, and reached a point about four miles above Fort Prescott, called Hog Point, where they landed. Here the army remained a few days, and then crossed the river into Canada. For about four weeks thereafter, Jaqua and Brown were constantly busy piloting parties down the river. For fear of trouble from the Canadian authorities, Mr. Jaqua kept his name, and the fact that he was drafted in Canada, a profound secret during all the time he was associated with the movements of the American troops along the St. Lawrence.

On the 14th day of May, 1814, Mr. Jaqua enrolled his name as a private in a company of minute men under Capt. Ellis, at Houndsfield, about five miles above Sackett's Harbor. During his service in that company, one Wolsey was in charge of a fleet of small boats loaded with stores belonging to the United States, and vessels then in process of construction. When the company arrived at a point off Big Sandy creek, near Sackett's Harbor, they were noticed by the British fleet, and Wolsey, to save his fleet, ran it into the mouth of Big Sandy. The bar at the mouth of the creek prevented the British vessels from passing in. Thereupon the British immediately embarked in small boats, and followed Wolsey. The alarm was given to the minute men, who arrived very soon at the scene, and, joining with a company already there on duty, gave the British battle. After a sharp fight for a short time, the British retreated, leaving ninety-six of their men dead on the field. Mr. Jaqua succeeded in having his family brought across in the fall of 1813, and now joined them. In 1815 he was engaged in hauling timber and lumber to Sackett's Harbor, where some seventy-four vessels were being built.

He moved to the western part of the state of New York, where he lived six years, and then moved to this county, in 1822, and settled in Eden township, where he lived to the time of his death. His friend Brown had preceded him as a pioneer to this county.

Colonel Jaqua, as he was familiarly called, received neither compensation nor pension from the government for all his valuable services, until 1872. His property in Canada was all confiscated by the British authorities. Upon his petition to Congress, the Hon. C. Foster representing this district in Washington, Congress generously acknowledged and recognized Mr. Jaqua's merits, and granted him a pension, by special act, that tended very materially to gladden the few remaining years of the Colonel's life.

Col. Jaqua was a little more than six feet high, and well proportioned. He was blessed with an iron constitution, and great force of character. In his boyhood days his chances for education were not very good; but whatever he lacked in book-learning, he made up by his sound sense and clear judgment. In stature and personal appearance, in his movements and tone of voice, he resembled Josiah Hedges, the proprietor of Tiffin, very much. He had a noble bearing, an open, frank, but sincere countenance; heavy lower jaw, clenched lips, dark eyes, nose not very large and a little of the Roman shape, and a fine forehead. His very looks would say: "I'll do as I agree, sir." He took a very active part in public affairs in Seneca county, and contributed largely to the development of her resources, having lived here more than half a century. He was social in his nature, hospitable, generous, kind. He was a good neighbor, a good citizen, a good husband and father, and, above all, an honest man. He died, without a struggle, in peace with God and mankind, on the 26th of September, 1878, aged ninety-one years, five months and seventeen days. His wife had preceded him to the other world on the 7th of May, 1877, aged eighty-six years, seven months and four days. This venerable couple lived in happy wedlock nearly seventy years—more than two generations of time. The Colonel was buried with the plain, but impressive ritual of Masonry, having been an honored member of the order during the greater part of his life. *Requiesce in pace.*

CHAPTER X.

FIRST MERIDIAN—BASE LINE—TOWNSHIPS—RANGES—SECTIONS—QUARTER SECTIONS—GENERAL SURVEY—ORGANIZATION OF SENECA COUNTY—THE OLD COURT HOUSE—HOLDING THE FIRST COURT—FIRST ELECTION—FIRST MEETING OF THE BOARD OF COUNTY COMMISSIONERS—APPOINTMENT OF FIRST TREASURER—COLLECTOR OF TAXES—SURVEYOR—PROSECUTING ATTORNEY—ORGANIZATION OF BLOOM, SCIPIO, CLINTON, HOPEWELL, SENECA AND ADAMS TOWNSHIPS—BUILDING THE FIRST JAIL—RUDOLPHUS DICKINSON—REED TOWNSHIP—SALE OF THE RESERVATIONS.

HITHERTO, the cabins of the early settlers were near the forts of Seneca and Ball, with a few scattered along Rocky creek, Honey creek, Silver creek and in Thompson. The "Black Swamp" commenced immediately west of the river; in fact, the Sandusky river was the eastern boundary of the Black Swamp.

These settlers were mere squatters. They could buy no land, because there was none in market. Outside of the Indian reservation, the title to all the territory was in the United States; and this *new purchase* could not be offered for sale until after a survey thereof was made and reported, in order to enable the government to make proper descriptions of tracts, designating each in such manner and with such certainty as to avoid, if possible, all controversy as to boundary lines, etc.

During all this time the squatters explored and prospected, making selections of localities at or near which they intended to buy, as soon as the lands were offered for sale. They built their huts wherever they pleased; fished and hunted. Some made small openings to raise vegetables, taking their chances for the improvements falling into the hands of somebody else; others that lived near any of these reservations, farmed the lands of some of the Indians on shares. Thus the squatters were employed making themselves comfortable, raising stock and getting ready to open farms for themselves.

Let us now give some attention to the manner in which this new purchase was brought into market.

The survey of the Western Reserve was started at a point on the west line of Pennsylvania, where the forty-first degree of north latitude crosses the same. The surveyor then followed this parallel due west,

·measuring ranges of five miles each. At the end of the twenty-fourth range he reached the southwest corner of the Connecticut reserve, which is now also the southwest corner of Huron county. From this point a line was drawn north to the lake, and parallel with the west line of Pennsylvania, which formed the western boundary of the Western Reserve. So that all the territory north of this parallel to the lake, and all east of this north line to the state of Pennsylvania, constitutes the Western Reserve; sometimes called the "Connecticut Reserve," and sometimes "the Fire Lands." These lands were reserved by Connecticut for the purpose of paying with them debts the colony owed to revolutionary soldiers, to people who had their property burnt or otherwise destroyed by the British army, etc., war debts generally.

Let us remember now, that this parallel of forty-one degress north latitude is the southern boundary, and the *base line* of the Western Reserve ; that the ranges on that line are five miles ; that there are twenty-four ranges in all; and that the townships on the Western Reserve are five miles square.

Soon after the treaty of the Miami of the Lake, already mentioned, the general government ordered all the lands thereby secured to be surveyed. This was then "the new purchase."

Mr. Sylvanus Bourne, under instructions from the general land office of the United States, started a survey from the east line of the state of Indiana on the forty-first parallel N. L. This state line, which of course is also the west line of Ohio, he called the *first meridian.* Running his line on this parallel east, he planted a stake where the end of the sixth mile was reached. This made one range, and the first range in his survey. The end of the seventeenth range brought him within fifty-two chains and seven links of the southwest corner of the Western Reserve. A line drawn due north, by his compass, cut the west line of the Western Reserve exactly at the northeast corner of Seneca county. There is therefore a strip of land lying all along and east of the seventeenth range, that is not in any range, 52.07 long on the south end, running to a point just eighteen miles north. This tract is called "the gore." The ranges in the new purchase are six miles wide—17x6—102. The ranges on the Western Reserve being five miles wide—24x5—120 ; 102 plus 120—222. Therefore the distance from the state line of Pennsylvania to the state line of Indiana is two hundred and twenty-two miles and this gore 52.07.

From these six mile posts, lines were drawn due north to the north line of Ohio and to Lake Erie, and south to the Virginia military land districts. This line thus drawn along the forty-first parallel north latitude, being the base of operation for all future surveys, is called the *base line*. The territory between these six-mile posts is called a range, and runs north and south from the base line, as above indicated. Parallel with this base line, and six miles distant therefrom, other lines were surveyed, starting from this meridian north and south of the base line, and running east until other surveys were met. The north and south lines, or range lines, thus cut at right angles by the east and west lines, or township lines, formed tracts of territory, each six miles square, called townships. Each additional east and west, six mile line, from the base line, adds another township to the number. The townships, therefore, are numbered from the base line north and south; and townships one north or south means all the townships along the entire length of the base line, having the base line for the northern or southern boundary. The next townships north or south are numbered two, and so on, until Michigan or lake Erie on the north, or some other survey on the south is reached.

In describing a piece of land, therefore, we say, for example, "Township two (2) north, range fifteen (15) east"; because this is the second township north of the base line, lying north and in range fifteen, counting the ranges from the meridian as above.

A Mr. Holmes assisted Mr. Bourne in the survey of the range and township lines.

Four gentlemen were appointed by the Commissioner of the general land office, to survey and sub-divide Seneca county into sections, quarter and half quarter sections. They were J. Glasgow, Price F. Kellogg, James T. Worthington and Sylvanus Bourne.

Seneca county has five ranges, from the thirteenth to the seventeenth, both inclusive, and three townships north—one, two and three. There are therefore fifteen townships in the county, the Sandusky river cutting it from the south to the north into two parts nearly equal; and the county seat being near the center of the county, makes Seneca county almost unequalled in shape and beauty by any other county in the state.

Mr. Glasgow surveyed the townships north of range thirteen—Big Spring, Loudon and Jackson.

Mr. Worthington surveyed the townships north of range fourteen, viz: Seneca, Hopewell and Liberty; also, those north of range fifteen, viz: Eden, Clinton and Pleasant. Mr. Bourne surveyed those north of range sixteen, viz: Bloom, Scipio and Adams. Mr. Kellogg surveyed those north of range seventeen, viz: Venice, Reed and Thompson, and the gore. It is to be understood here, that the townships as here named are the same as they are now known, and not as established from time to time by county commissioners. The geographical lines of the townships were established by these surveys. It is also to be understood that the Indian reservations were not included in these surveys.

Each township being six miles square, makes just thirty-six sections, each one mile square, and containing six hundred and forty acres each. The sections are numbered by commencing at the northeast corner of the township; running west, brings section six into the northwest corner; the next section south of this is section seven, and running east, brings section twelve immediately south of section one; then calling the section south of twelve number thirteen, running west and so on, brings section thirty-one into the southwest corner, and section thirty-six into the southeast corner of the township.

The sections were again sub-divided into quarters and half quarters, with lines at right angles, making it very easy to describe the quarter of a quarter.

It is scarcely possible to conceive of a plan for the description of land for the purposes of purchase, sale or taxation, more beautiful, geographically, or for business more convenient.

In the survey of the entire northwest, this order was strictly adhered to.

We must also remember that in all these surveys, the Sandusky river having been, by act of Congress, declared a navigable stream, is not included. The surveys run only to low water mark of the stream, and therefore necessarily and unavoidably create many fractional sections. These surveyors finished their work in 1820.

There were then, also, several other Indian reservations, aside from the Seneca reservation, viz: The Armstrong reservation; the McCulloch reservation; the Van Meter reservation; the Walker reservations, and a reservation of about twelve square miles occupying the southwest corner of the county, belonging to the Wyandots. These reserves were not surveyed, and not offered for sale until after the last Indian had gone, when, in 1832, a Mr. J. W. Christmas surveyed them all. Thereupon these reserve lands were brought into market also.

The field notes in the General Land Office at Washington show the time when these surveys were made and the persons who made them, as above given. How Mr. Butterfield, in his history of Seneca, can lay the time in 1819, and say that Alex. Holmes ran off the sections, etc., is not very clear.

This new purchase thereupon was laid off and divided into two land districts—the Delaware and the Piqua land districts, by a line drawn north and south through and near the center of the new purchase. This placed Seneca county in the Delaware land district.

On the 3d day of August, 1821, the lands in the Delaware land district north of the base line, were first offered for sale at Delaware at a minimum price of one dollar and twenty-five cents per acre. Large quantities of land in this county were purchased at these first sales, but very little of it above the minimum price.

Before the subject is dismissed, it may be well to state another fact in connection with these surveys, that should be generally understood: "The boundaries of the general surveys can not be changed."

Congress, as early as the year 1805, laid down certain general principles in regard to the unchangeableness of the lines and corners established by government surveyors, which have been continued operative down to the present time, and are still in full force. These principles are contained in the second section of an act entitled "An act concerning the mode of surveying the public lands of the United States," approved February 11, 1805, and are as follows, to-wit:

1st. All the corners marked in the surveys returned by Surveyor-Generals, shall be established as the proper corners of sections or sub-divisions of sections which they were intended to designate ; and the corners of half and quarter sections, not marked on said surveys, shall be placed as nearly as possible, equally distant from those two corners which stand on the same line.

The Boundary Lines actually run and marked in the surveys returned by the Surveyor-General, shall be established as the proper boundary lines of the sections or sub-divisions for which they were intended ; and the length of such lines as returned by the Surveyor-General aforesaid, shall be held and considered as the true length thereof.

Experience has demonstrated the wisdom of this enactment. No law ever passed by Congress has contributed so much to prevent disputes in regard to boundaries of the public lands. Considering the extent of the territory over which the public surveys have been extended, embracing whole states, now thickly settled with people, and affecting interests involving many thousands of dollars, cases of litigation growing out of disputed boundaries, are surprisingly rare. "System of Rectangular Surveying," by J. H. Haws, p. 119.

Although this law may in some instances work a hardship to individuals, giving to one party more land than to another, yet it is one of the conditions under which the land was acquired, and the evil in these cases is measurably small compared with the great benefit derived from these fixed and unchangeable lines and corners of the public lands.

Whenever, therefore, questions should arise as to the correct corners and lines of lands, with this knowledge of the law before us, and proper examination of the field notes, where the same are established, great annoyance, heartaches and money may be saved.

If any of the old land-marks of early life in Seneca county shall be omitted or overlooked in this book, it will not be because the writer has not been sufficiently industrious in his efforts to look them up for record. Indeed, sometimes I fear that my persistent inquiries about affairs of former days among my old pioneer friends, have been burdensome to many of them, and I have no other apology to offer but my earnest purpose to preserve, for the use of their children, a full and faithful record of Seneca county's past.

Very many people in Seneca county perhaps never knew, and others have forgotten, the fact that there was an Indian reservation, containing about twelve square miles, belonging to the Wyandots, in the southwest corner of Big Spring township. This reservation, and another piece of the same lying south of the same and adjoining it, was procured by the United States and brought into market with the Seneca reservation, long before the Wyandots sold their large reservation to the general government. (See chap. III.)

To preserve the time of the sales of these reservations in Seneca county, the proclamation of Gen. Jackson, then President of the United States, is here added, because the fact itself, as well as the time, are both important and historic. And it is also to be remembered, that these sales took place some ten years after the land sales spoken of in a former chapter.

Mr. George W. Gist, a very able surveyor, had located in Tiffin a short time before these Indian lands came into market, and to enable the purchasers of these lands to make the proper selections, published a notice in the *Seneca Patriot*, the only newspaper then published in the county, (and of which further notice will be taken hereafter) in these words:

LAND PURCHASERS, LOOK HERE!

The subscriber has on hand a quantity of plats, and descriptions of the sections and lines of the Seneca and Big Spring reservations. Persons going on either of the said reserves, will find them of much advantage. They are made from the original field notes of C. W. Christmas, Esq., District Surveyor.   GEO. W. GIST, Surveyor.

The President's proclamation ordering these sales, is in the words following, viz:

BY THE PRESIDENT OF THE UNITED STATES.

In pursuance of law, I Andrew Jackson, President of the United States of America, do hereby declare and make known, that public sales will be held at the Land Office of Piqua and Bucyrus, in the *State of Ohio*, at the period herein designated, for the disposal of certain lands heretofore reserved for the benefit of certain tribes of Indians in said State, and which have been by them relinquished and surrendered unto the United States, to-wit:

At the Land Office at Piqua, on the fourth Monday in December next, for the sale of the late Shawnee reservation on Hog Creek, situate in townships three and four, south of range six, east, containing twenty-five square miles; also for the sale of the late Shawnee reservation at Wapochkonuetta, situate in townships four, five and six, south of ranges five, six and seven, east, containing one hundred and twenty square miles; also for the sale of the late Seneca and Shawnee reservation at Lewistown, situate in townships six and seven, south of range seven and eight, east, and in township seven, south, range nine, east, containing sixty-two square miles.

At the Land Office in Bucyrus, on the second Monday in December next, for the sale of the late Wyandot reservation at the Big Spring, situate in townships one, north, and one, south, of ranges twelve and thirteen, east, containing twenty-five square miles; also for the sale of the late Seneca reservation on the Sandusky River, situate in townships two, three and four, north of ranges fifteen and sixteen, containing forty thousand acres.

The lands reserved by law for the use of schools, or for other purposes, will be excluded from sale.

The sales will be kept open for a period not exceeding two weeks, and no longer than necessary to offer the whole of the lands.

Given under my hand at the City of Washington this thirteenth day of November, A. D. 1832.

ANDREW JACKSON.

By the President.

ELIJAH HAYWARD, Commissioner of the General Land Office.

These sales took place eight years and nine months after the organization of Seneca county.

A. M. Stewart, who published the atlas of Seneca county some six years ago, took ·Mr. Butterfield's history for data; and speaking of early roads, copies the story of the Bell road. They say that "Gen. Bell, from Wooster, surveyed a road in 1812, which took his name." There is no trace of any survey of Bell's road to be found anywhere, and all there was of it, is this:

Gen. Bell was ordered by Gen. Harrison to pick out—not survey—a suitable track for a road on the west bank of the Sandusky river, to Lower Sandusky from Upper Sandusky, over which military stores, troops and provisions could be carried. Gen. Bell and his men followed along the left bank of the river on the highest ground, without paying any attention to courses or distances; and this Mr. Meeker they speak of, with his men, cut and carried to one side, underbrush and was other obstructions, and blazed the trees as they worked along. This the surveying they did on this road. A similar road was opened along and near the right bank of the river, leading from Delaware to Lower Sandusky. These army roads answered all practical purposes for several years; first for military movements, and then for emigrants and settlers. Nor is it true that Mr. Risdon afterwards surveyed these army roads into state roads; but Mr. Risdon did survey a state road from Upper Sandusky to Lower Sandusky, in 1821, without paying any attention to any army road. His survey ran as nearly straight as possible, and scarcely ever touched the army road.

In 1820, Israel Harrington surveyed the Morrison state road, still known by that name, leading from Croghansville (Fremont) to Delaware. This was the first road surveyed and opened in Seneca county, east of the river, while the road surveyed by Risdon was the first one west of the river—both state roads. The Morrison road was named after one of the commissioners, who located the road.

Colonel James Kilbourn, a pioneer surveyor, already introduced, surveyed a road leading from Portland, (now Sandusky City) to Upper Sandusky, to which he gave his own name, in 1822. It is said that Thomas Baker and Ezra Brown, two distinguished pioneers, both from the state of New York, were the first settlers in Seneca county who came on that road.

A history of the surveying and opening of the principal roads of the county might be made interesting enough to some people, but would not warrant the space it would necessarily require.

The legislature divided this new purchase into fourteen counties, by an act passed on the 12th day of February, 1820. Of these, Seneca county was the ninth in the order named in the act. It was to consist of townships, one, two and three, north of ranges thirteen to seventeen, both inclusive, and to remain a part of Sandusky county, until organized into a county with municipal powers, by a future act of the legislature.

The commissioners of Sandusky county organized four townships in this county, from time to time, outside of the reservations, as follows:

Thompson was organized on the 25th day of April, 1820, with the following boundaries, viz:

Beginning at the northeast corner of the Seneca reservation, in Sandusky county, running thence north to the (then) present trailed road from Croghansville to Strong's settlement, (not very definite); thence east until it shall intersect the fire-lands; thence south with said line to the base line; thence west along said line until a line due north will strike the place of beginning. This territory comprised the

ORGANIZATION OF TOWNSHIPS.

present townships of Thompson, Reed, Venice, and two and one-half sections along the east sides of Bloom, Scipio and Adams, and a part of Sandusky county.

On the 8th day of May, 1820, the said commissioners organized Seneca township, which was the second township in the county, and included all the balance of the county not embraced in the boundaries of Thompson; so that two townships contained the whole county.

On the first Monday in June, 1820, the said commissioners organized Clinton township, fixing the boundaries as now established, except that part west of the river, viz:

Commencing where the township line, between two and three, strikes the river on the east bank thereof; running thence with said line to the northeast corner of township two, in range fifteen; thence south with the range line between ranges fifteen and sixteen, to the southeast corner of the aforesaid township; thence west to the township line between townships one and two; thence northerly with the meanders of the river to the place of beginning.

It was named after DeWitt Clinton, Governor of New York.

Eden, the last township organized by the commissioners of Sandusky county, was fixed with its present boundaries in 1821, viz: T. 1., N. R. 15, E.

This still left Seneca township embracing all west of the river to the west line of the county.

To preserve a record of what part of the Seneca reservation was within Seneca county, let us commence, for a starting point, on the right bank of the Sandusky river, about one-quarter of a mile south of the south line of section seven, in Clinton township, running due east on a line parallel with the south section lines of sections seven to thirteen, inclusive, in Clinton, and extending the same line to a point a short distance south of the center of section ten, in Scipio; thence running due north through Adams to the north line of Seneca county; thence west on said north line to the right bank of the Sandusky river; thence south along the meanderings of said right bank to the place of beginning.

Under the organization of these townships, elections were held as follows: In Thompson, at the house of Joseph Parmenter, on the 6th day of May, 1820; in Seneca, on the 1st day of June, 1820; in Clinton, on the 15th day of June, 1822, and in Eden, on the 4th day of June, 1820, at the house of John Searles, who lived near Rocky creek, and a short distance south of the Rocky creek meeting house. The successful ticket at this election in Eden, was: David Clark, township clerk; John

Welch, James Mathers and Henry Craw, trustees; Ira Holmes and John Searles, fence-viewers; John Searles, treasurer; Hugh Welch and Ira Holmes, appraisers; Samuel Knapp and John Welch, supervisors; Thomas Welch, constable.

Seneca township, at its first election, elected the following ticket, viz: West Barney, John Lay, David Risdon, trustees; John Keller and David Rice, overseers of the poor; James Montgomery, Erastus Bowe and Joel Chapin, supervisors; P. Wilson, lister; Asa Pike, appraiser; Thomas Nicholson and Abner Pike, fence-viewers; John Boughton and Joel Lee, constables.

A lister was an officer whose duty it was to report to the trustees, and afterwards to the county auditor, a list of the able-bodied white male inhabitants liable to perform military duty. For this work he was by law entitled to seventy-five cents per day.

At the state election in this year, the whole county polled twenty-six votes, all told.

It will be noticed that in these elections no justice of the peace was elected. Sandusky county exercised judicial power over the whole of Seneca county, until Seneca became established as a county by law.

ORGANIZATION OF SENECA COUNTY.

On the 22d day of January, A. D. 1824, the legislature of Ohio passed the following act for the organization of Seneca county, in the words and figures following, viz:

AN ACT
To Organize the County of Seneca.

SECTION 1. *Be it enacted by the General Assembly of the State of Ohio,* That the county of Seneca be and the same is hereby organized into a separate and distinct county.

SEC. 2. That all justices of the peace, and other officers residing in the county of Seneca, shall continue to discharge the duties of their respective offices until their successors are chosen and qualified according to law.

SEC. 3. That the qualified electors residing in the county of Seneca, shall meet in their respective townships on the first Monday of April next, and elect their several county officers, who shall hold their respective offices until the next annual election, and until others are chosen and qualified according to law.

SEC. 4. That all suits and actions, whether of civil or criminal nature, which shall have been commenced, shall be prosecuted to final judgment and execution, and all taxes, fines and penalties, which shall have become due, shall be collected in the same manner as if this act had not been passed.

This act to take effect and be in force from and after the first day of April next.
JOSEPH RICHARDSON,
Speaker of the House of Representatives.
ALLEN TRIMBLE, Speaker of the Senate.
January 22, 1824.

ELECTION OF OFFICERS. 165

In conformity with the foregoing act, notice in writing was posted up in the several (four) townships in the county, for the holding of the election. The only officers to be chosen at this election were a sheriff, three commissioners and a coroner. For sheriff, Agreen Ingraham received one hundred and ninety votes; and for coroner, Leverett Bradley received two hundred and six votes. Both were elected.

At the same time the following named persons were also elected as county commissioners, to serve until the next annual election in October, viz: William Clark, Jesse S. Olmstead, Benjamin Wetmore.

On the 7th day of June, 1824, the board of commissioners organized and held their first session. The first business in order was the hearing of a petition presented by Rollin Moller, praying for the location of a road. The petitions for four other roads were heard at the same session.

The petition of Thomas Boyd and others, viz: the qualified voters of Eden township, "predicated upon the following reasonable ground" —the petition says—to-wit: "laboring under great inconvenience, from the distance, of attending public elections, and having a sufficient number of qualified electors in the township, we pray your honorable board to set off said townships, Nos. 1 and 2, in range 16, and constitute them a legal township, to be known by the name of Bloom."

The board granted the petition, and ordered that townships 1 and 2, in range 16, (Bloom and Scipio) which were organized with Eden township, and townships 1 and 2, in the 17th range, (Venice and Reed) and fractional townships Nos. 1 and 2, in range 18, be set off and declared by the board of commissioners a legal township, to be known by the name of Bloom.

On the same day, June 7th, 1824, the board of commissioners also appointed Milton McNeal treasurer, and David Risdon collector of taxes for Seneca county.

Nathan Whitney was allowed two dollars and twenty-five cents for three days' services in listing Thompson township; Joseph Osborn was allowed three dollars and seventy-five cents for listing Eden; George Park was allowed one dollar and eighty-seven and a half cents for listing Clinton; and Joseph Keeler was allowed two dollars and twenty-five cents for listing Ft. Seneca township.

David Smith, for his services as clerk for the commissioners, was allowed three dollars for three days.

At the next session of the board of county commissioners, (who were elected in October previous) on the 7th day of December, 1824, the petition of William Anway was presented to the board for the organization of Scipio township. The reason for such organization claimed in the petition is the fact that there were *sixteen legal voters* residing in the territory composed of Scipio and Reed, and the board granted the petition accordingly.

At the same session, Neal McGaffey presented a petition for the opening of a county road from the public square in Fort Ball to the public square in Tiffin, across the river by the most suitable ground. On the same day the township of Hopewell was organized, including Loudon, and an election ordered to be held. The trustees to be elected were authorized to take charge of the school lands. Seneca township was then reduced to what now constitutes Seneca and Big Spring.

On the 8th day of December, 1824, the county commissioners cast lots to ascertain how long each was to serve; whereupon it was found that Thomas Boyd was to serve for one year, Benj. Whitmore for two years and Doctor Dunn for three years. Ever since that time Seneca county has elected but one commissioner each year, except when by death or resignation the election of another became a necessity.

The same day the board rented from George Park his north chamber for a county clerk and auditor's office, and agreed to pay him one dollar per month for the use of the same. The chamber was a part of Eli Norris' old tavern. The ground where it stood is now covered by the National Hall block. At the same time Clinton was fixed to its present status, and an election ordered.

William Cornell was appointed keeper of the standard measure, the device of the seal to be a circle with the letters therein, "SEN. CO., OHIO."

On the sixth day of June, 1825, commissioners were appointed to locate a road in Crawford township, T. 1, S. R. 13 E., and for that purpose met at the house of Jas. Whiticker, on the 6th day of July following.

Wm. Harpster was allowed two dollars for listing Sycamore township; Jesse Gale the same amount for listing Crawfordt township. It would therefore appear from this, that the commissioners of Seneca county exercised jurisdiction over Crawford county until it was organized.

At the same session the commissioners settled with the auditor and treasurer, and found a balance in favor of the latter of $13.46.

Mr. Hedges had built a two story frame house on the lot immediately north of the court house square, on the place now occupied by the east end of the Commercial bank and the office of the *Seneca Advertiser*. The second story was used as a court room and the lower three rooms for offices. The first court in Seneca county was held in this frame house, and that was the court house of Seneca county until the brick court house was built in 1836.

ELECTION OF OFFICERS.

Judge Ebenezer Lane, of Norwalk, who was the circuit judge of the judicial district of which Seneca county formed a part, held the first court in Seneca county, on the 12th day of April, 1824. Under the old constitution of Ohio, the circuit judges were appointed by the Legislature for the term of seven years. There were also appointed by the Legislature three associate judges in each county for the term of seven years. These associate judges were not lawyers, but were selected from the business men of the county, generally from the party that had a majority in the Legislature for the time being. These associate judges, with the presiding or circuit judge, formed the court, a majority of whom was necessary for the transaction of business.

The first associate judges appointed for this county were William Cornell, Jaques Hulburd and Matthew Clark. This court, at its first session, appointed for the clerk of the court, *pro tem*, Neal McGaffey, and for county surveyor David Risdon.

The court lasted about thirty minutes, and then adjourned for want of other business.

On the 12th day of October, in the same year, the first annual election was held in the county, when the following officers were elected, viz: sheriff, Agreen Ingraham; coroner, Christopher Stone; auditor, David Smith; commissioners, Benjamin Whitmore, Thomas Boyd and Doctor Dunn.

The court in this year appointed Rudolphus Dickinson prosecuting attorney, and the county commissioners appointed Milton McNeal county treasurer.

With this small commencement old Seneca started on her proud career to future greatness.

Mr. Dickinson, being the first lawyer who settled in Seneca county, and who took a very active part in the organization of the county and public affairs generally, was appointed by the court the first prosecuting attorney of the county.

He was born at Whateley, Massachusetts, on the 28th day of December, 1797, and was a graduate of Williams College in that state. Immediately after he left college he came to Columbus, Ohio, where he taught school and read law in the office of Gustavus Swan, in that city. After his admission to the bar he located in Tiffin, Ohio, in the year 1824, on the Fort Ball side, where he joined the opposition of the few settlers against Mr. Hedges in his efforts to build up Tiffin. Mr. Dickinson was appointed by the court the first prosecuting attorney of the county. His name is identified with the first cases tried in the early sessions of the courts of Seneca county. He was the attorney for Jesse

Spencer in the suit against Mr. Hedges about the brush dam, the most celebrated among the early cases tried in the county. In May, 1826, Mr. Dickinson resigned his office of prosecuting attorney, and Abel Rawson was appointed his successor. In the same month Mr. Dickinson removed to Lower Sandusky, and in 1827 he married the daughter of John Beaugrand, one of the oldest settlers of Lower Sandusky and who at an early day was a partner of General John E. Hunt, of Maumee City. Mr. D. took great interest in schemes for starting the public works of the state, in which he occupied a high prominence among his cotemporaries. Among these public enterprises were the Wabash and Erie Canal and the Western Reserve and Maumee Road. He was a member of the Board of Public Works from 1836 to 1845. During this period the state of Ohio suffered great financial embarrassment, and her credit ran down to fifty per cent. below par, her bonds selling for fifty cents on the dollar. Mr. Dickinson's influence with the leading men of the state and the Legislature, contributed largely in saving the credit of the state and preventing the entire suspension of public improvements.

Mr. Dickinson was elected to Congress in 1846, and re-elected in 1848. He died soon after the commencement of the second term of his service at the city of Washington in 1849, on the 20th day of March, at the age of fifty-one years, two months and twenty-two days.

On the fourth day of July, 1825, the commissioners of Seneca county held an extra session of the board to receive proposals and bids for the building of a jail in Tiffin. Benjamin Whitmore and Doctor Dunn were present. The bids were opened and the contract awarded to Elijah Fargurson, he being the lowest bidder, for the sum of four hundred and fifty dollars, payable when the work was completed. Josiah Hedges was surety on the bond of Mr. Fargurson for the promp compliance with his agreement to perform the same.

The early settlers will remember this, the first public building put up in Seneca county. It stood at the southeast corner of the present court house square, and was made of hewed logs fitted tightly on the top of each other, with hewed logs for the ceiling and heavy oak plank for the floor. The doors were made of double planks with wagon tires bolted across them for hinges, and a large padlock on the door. There were two rooms in this log jail—one on the east side and the other on the west side. The windows were cross barred with heavy tire iron. To the south end of the jail was attached a frame building as wide as the jail, (about twenty feet), with a narrow stairway to the garret, and two small rooms below. This frame part was intended as a residence for the sheriff, but was never occupied for that purpose. The jailor lived there occasionally; and finally, and until the old log jail was torn down in 1840-41, my old friend, John Fiege occupied this frame part of the jail for a cabinet shop, and Marquis Y. Groff lived immediately across the street from the same, on the south side of Market street.

In the December session of the county commissioners, Christopher Stone was allowed one dollar as appraiser of Clinton towwhship.

At the same time, December 5th, 1825, and upon the application of Agreen Ingraham, the commissioners passed an order by which all that part of Clinton township lying west of the river was attached to Hopewell, for the reason, undoubtedly, that there were no bridges over the river and it was therefore more convenient for the people on the west side to get together and hold their elections, etc.

The log jail being finished and the work done to the satisfaction of the county commissioners, it was accepted on the 31st day of March, 1826. John Mim presented his account for rent of room for the use of the county clerk and auditor for nine months, at fifty cents a month, $4.50, which was allowed on the 5th day of June, 1826. On the same day Josiah Hedges was paid $25.85, expenses incurred by him in the location of the county seat.

Milton McNeal was re-appointed county treasurer, and William Patterson collector of taxes for the ensuing year.

Adams township was organized on the 5th day of December, 1825, but it consisted only of the sections not included in the reserve. The electors were ordered to meet at the house of Samuel Whiteman to hold the election, on the 25th day of December, 1826. To make the township of any reasonable size the commissioners attached to Adams a tier of sections from and along the west side of Thompson.

On the fifth day of December, 1825, Reed township was also organized with its present boundary, and the electors ordered to meet at the house of Seth Reed on the first day of January, 1827, to hold their election. Dec. 5, 1826, the commissioners ordered the auditor " to cut a diamond in the jail door five inches square."

CHAPTER XI.

JESSE SPENCER—COUNTY ROAD FROM FORT BALL TO TIFFIN—WOLF SCALPS—ORGANIZING TOWNSHIPS IN CRAWFORD COUNTY—BUILDING THE FIRST BRIDGE—FIRST KILN OF BRICKS—DAVID BISHOP—FINAL ORGANIZATION OF ALL THE TOWNSHIPS—HISTORY OF THE BUILDING, THE BURNING AND THE RE-BUILDING OF THE COURT HOUSE—BUILDING THE STONE JAIL—THE NEW JAIL.

IN A former chapter it was said that the Indian reservations were not surveyed into sections until after the Senecas had left the country; but this statement should be qualified so as to except the Armstrong, the McCulloch and VanMeter sections.

Robert Armstrong and the heirs of McCulloch had full power to dispose of their respective reservations in any manner they saw fit, after the patent from the United States had been issued to them. The transfer required only the approval of the President of the United States endorsed thereon.

The patent from the United States to Robert Armstrong was issued under the treaty aleady mentioned, and bears date of October 12, 1823.

On the 29th day of the same month Armstrong sold and deeded four hundred and four acres of his reservation to Jesse Spencer, for three thousand dollars. The deed from Armstrong to Spencer was approved by President Monroe, and signed by him in his own hand writing. The part of the Armstrong reserve sold to Spencer extended from the Sandusky river westwardly. Mr. Spencer laid out and platted the village of Oakley, including the old stockade, (Fort Ball,) and extending down the river to the railroad bridges, and west to somewhere near the B. & O. depot. It was not much of a town, even on paper. No trace of it can anywhere be found, and Mr. Spencer never caused any record to be made of this, his first town in Seneca county. The only buildings the town of Oakley ever contained were the log cabin hotel of Mr. Bowe and the cabin of Mr. David Smith, near where the stove works now are. The cabin of Mr. Agreen Ingraham was up on the hill where the aristocracy afterwards settled, around about McNeal's store, after Mr. Spencer laid out Fort Ball.

Mr. Gilford Bowe says his father's hotel stood near the bank of the river, and right in Washington street, close by the north end of the iron bridge. The old army road passed close by it. The hotel was pulled down when Spencer opened a street that way in his Fort Ball.

In less than two years from the time Mr. Spencer bought the part of the Armstrong section, as above stated, he laid out Oakley, then Fort Ball, built the brush dam and the saw mill, became involved in about two dozen law suits, had a half dozen knock-downs, sold his town, brush dam and saw mill to Mr. Hedges, and quit. The deed from Spencer to Hedges for Fort Ball is dated June 16, 1825. In this deed Spencer reserved to himself some in-lots and out-lots of his town of Fort Ball.

Mr. Spencer came here from Perry county, Ohio, where he formerly lived. It seems that the locality and the people here failed to meet the approbation of Mr. Spencer, and he withdrew his company and his interest from the county soon after his sale to Mr. Hedges.

The viewers appointed on the county road petitioned for leading from the public square of Fort Ball to the public square in Tiffin, and those on another petition for a county road leading from the public square in Tiffin to the public square in Fort Ball—two distinct sets of viewers, and two distinct lines of roads—reported unfavorably on both. Mr. Neal McGaffey thereupon, on the 8th day of June, 1825, gave notice of his intention to appeal the case to the Court of Common Pleas. There is no record to show the fate of the roads in the court. The streets of Fort Ball, as laid out by Spencer, seem to have supplied the great want of a county road running from McNeal's store to the court house square in Tiffin, and the appeal was never prosecuted.

On the 19th day of March, 1827, the commissioners passed a resolution authorizing the auditor to draw an order on the treasurer for the sum of two dollars extra, and in addition to the sum of four dollars paid by the state, for the scalp of every wolf killed in Seneca county. These beasts were very numerous here at that time, and a very great annoyance to the pioneers. It was almost impossible to keep any poultry, hogs or sheep. They would even attack and kill young calves.

One would naturally suppose that the wolves would flee from the approach of the settlers, but wild and shy as they naturally are, and however hard as it may be to get a shot at one in day-time, yet they made themselves sociable about the cabins at night. Their howling at night, hideous as it sounds by itself, seemed to echo through the forest in long vibrations, especially in a dark, cold night of winter.

When the cold lasted any length of time, it was dangerous to be out after night without a torch, and domestic animals, unprotected, were sure to be killed. Wolves are afraid of fire.

They seemed to be more numerous in Seneca than in any adjoining county, and were found most plenty along the Sandusky river, and along the several branches of Wolf creek, which was very appropriately named after them.

By the law of the state, four dollars were paid for wolf-scalps, and every county was authorized to add such additional sum to the four dollars as the commissioners would order. The counties adjoining Seneca refused to add any further sum to the state premium on scalps, and the two dollars added in Seneca became a great inducement to kill wolves in Seneca county. Money was exceedingly scarce in those days, and hard to get. The idea of raising six dollars in money for one wolf's-scalp, excited the skill and avarice of many a pioneer. Men would work on farms, at trades, at anything, a whole month for that much money and board—yes, and then very often take their pay in store goods, or other barter, at that.

The greater number of wolves that were killed were caught in traps made expressly for wolves. Those that were shot were comparatively few. The ingenious trapper was the most successful man to get the premiums on scalps. Some of these trappers in Hancock, Wood, Sandusky, Huron and Crawford, living near the county line—yes, and some of those that lived a considerable distance away—when they found a wolf in the trap, in making the morning rounds, would strike the wolf over the head with a club and thus stun and disable, but not kill him. Then they would hitch a horse or an ox to a sled, and haul wolf and trap into Seneca county, and there finish killing the wolf; so that the trapper could make an affidavit that the wolf was killed in Seneca. This county paid for many a scalp of a wolf that was caught in some other county. There was money in it. The result was, that in the course of a few years the wolves became very scarce. Along towards the year 1840, scarcely any scalps were presented for premium.

After the organization of Seneca, and before Crawford county was organized, the commissioners of Seneca county, upon petition for that purpose, organized three townships in Crawford, as follows, viz:

On the 7th day of December, 1824, upon the petition of Joseph Chaeffee, Crawford township was ordered to organize, and to hold an election on the 25th day of December, 1824, at the house of said Chaeffee, then and there to elect three trustees and a treasurer, to take charge and dispose of the school lands belonging to said township.

On the 7th day of March, 1825, the said commissioners ordered that the original surveyed townships: No. 1 in the 15th range, No. 1 in the 16th range and No. 1 in the 17th range, south of the base line, be set off and organized into one township, and to be known by the name of Sycamore township, and that a similar election be held therein on the 25th day of March next ensuing.

On the same day, said commissioners also ordered that the inhabitants and qualified electors in the original surveyed township one, south, range thirteen, be notified to meet at the house of Jesse Gale, on the last Saturday of March, 1825, and elect trustees, etc. This township is now in Wyandot county.

On the 7th day of March, 1826, said commissioners also ordered that the original surveyed township one, south, range fourteen, be set off from the township of Crawford and organized into a legal township, to be known by the name of Tymochtee, and that the qualified electors therein meet on the first Monday in April next, at the house of Joseph Chaeffee, in Crawford township, and those in Tymochtee to meet at the house of Jesse Gale, and then and there to elect trustees, etc.

The first effort to build a bridge in Seneca county by the public authorities, was made by the commissioners on the 2d day of August, 1827, when they met for the purpose of taking into consideration the propriety of building a bridge across Rocky creek, at the east end of Market street, in Tiffin. That was the end of this effort, and no other step was taken to build this bridge until the 6th March, 1834, when the board appropriated $50, and appointed Marquis Y. Graff to superintend the work. Reuben Williams did the work. It was made of very heavy oak timber, and lasted until it became dangerous to cross it, when the trustees of Clinton township erected the present stone bridge in its place.

On the 5th day of June, 1827, Mr. Agreen Ingraham, having been elected treasurer of the county, was required by the board to give bond in the sum of $3,000.

At the December session of the same year, the commissioners allowed Wm. Toll, who was deputy sheriff and jailor, $3.46 for boarding prisoners.

Thomas Chadwick burnt the first kiln of brick during the summer of this year, and furnished brick to build a chimney in the jail, for which he was allowed the sum of $22.50.

Joseph Pool was paid $14.00 for laying the floor, and William Toll was paid $23.50 for building the chimney.

The votes cast in Seneca county for state senator were ordered to be returned to Delaware county, which was then a part of this senatorial district, and the county that cast the largest number of votes in the district.

At the same session, Benjamin Pettinger was paid $9.00 for nails used in building the jail. Nails were then a rarity, and just coming into use. There were no nails used in building cabins, as we shall see hereafter. If a man were to be compelled to build a house now-a-days without nails, he would scarcely know how it could be done. It was no trick, at all, for a pioneer.

David Bishop, who had come to Tiffin about one year before this time, was appointed keeper of weights and measures, by the board at this session.

Bishop was a sort of character by himself. He was a carpenter by trade, and a rival of Reuben Williams in that line. He was a large, powerful, muscular man. Francis Bernard was a stone and brick mason. He and Bishop had a great many fights, and when Bernard was sober, he would almost invariably whip Bishop; and Bernard's friends charged Bishop with cowardice, because he would never whip Bernard except when he (Bernard) was drunk. Bishop was the auctioneer for a long time, and a wonderful man to talk and boast. He was friendly to everybody—kind and hospitable—and was afterwards elected sheriff of the county. He was a good officer, and faithful to duty.

On the 1st day of June, 1829, Reed township was organized to its present limits.

Dr. Williams, a sketch of whose life will be found elsewhere herein, insists that the township was named for Seth Read, and by him. Read was an early settler there, and a singular, original sort of a character. The doctor says: "The name of the township ought to be spelled as it was first intended—R-e-a-d".

In the early records of the court of common pleas, and in the pleadings of the lawyers, the name of Eden township was spelled E-a-t-o-n.

Pleasant township was organized with its present boundaries, June 6, 1831; Loudon township was organized with its present boundaries, but no election was ordered until upon the application of Charles W. Foster, who says in his petition, that there were twenty electors in Loudon, and asks for an order to hold the first election, to have the school lands taken care of. So ordered on the 4th of March, 1834. At the March term, 1833, the auditor of the county for the first time became *ex-officio* clerk of the board of commissioners. At this session, the bond of the county treasurer, having theretofore been fixed at $15,000, was reduced to $8,000.

Thompson was organized within its present limits, March 5, 1833.

At the December session, 1833, on the 3d day of said month, the following other townships were organized as now known, viz: Scipio, Adams, Clinton, Pleasant, Loudon, Big Spring.

ORGANIZATION OF TOWNSHIPS. 175

Liberty township was organized on the 5th day of June 1832, within its present limits, upon the petition of John L. Fleck, and an election ordered.

Jackson township was organized within its present limits on the 4th day of December, 1832, and an election ordered.

Thus every township in the county was organized, the election of township officers ordered, and the government of the county completed.

In organizing Clinton township as originally surveyed, adding to it the portion lying west of the river, which, for the sake of convenience, and for want of a bridge across the Sandusky river, had for a time been attached to Hopewell, the proposition met with a strong opposition. Nearly everybody on the west side of the river signed a remonstrance. The spirit of opposition to Tiffin had spread from Fort Ball clear to and all along the east line of Hopewell, and it seemed to be a sort of luxury when an opportunity offered itself to fight Tiffin and the east side. But the board fixed the boundary as it now is, and the feeling of resentment gradually abated.

For want of a court house, the several county officers furnished their own rooms and presented their accounts for the rent to the board of commissioners for allowance. Mr. Rawson, the county recorder, was allowed office rent for the year ending December 6, 1832, ten dollars. The other officers—clerk, auditor, sheriff, etc., received about the same amount.

When the old frame building above described, in which the courts were held for awhile, became too small—for it was very inconvenient—the county commissioners made arrangements with the officers of the M. E. church to have the courts held in their church, for which they paid $9 to $12 a session, as rent. The grand jury and the petit juries were furnished rooms in the hotels.

This Methodist church was the largest public building in town. It stood on the lot now occupied by Joseph Harter as a marble shop, with the gable end to the street, one story high, built of brick. The supreme court and the circuit courts were held there up to the time when the new court house was finished, and after the old frame building was abandoned.

For several years the question as to the propriety of building a court house was agitated by the people and by the board of commissioners, and finally, on the 4th day of March, 1828, the board resolved to meet again on the 24th day of the same month, at the present place of holding the court.

March 24, 1828—At this meeting the board ordered that notice be given for the reception of proposals to build a court house, and that the commissioners will meet for that purpose on the 14th day of April then next following.

April 14, 1828—Board met, etc., and say in their entry, "not sold." Nothing further was done towards building a court house until in the session of the commissioners on the 5th day of December, 1833, when they appointed John Baugher and Calvin Bradley a committee to proceed to the county seats of Loraine, Portage and Richland, and take a correct description, together with the cost, etc., of each court house in the said counties, and report the same to the board at their meeting, on Friday, the 27th day of December, 1833.

This was the first step towards building a court house that looked like business.

John Seitz, M. Y. Graff and John Crum were then the commissioners.

December 27, 1833—Board met and adjourned to January 3, 1834, when they again met and received the reports of Baugher and Bradley. The expense of the trip, $93.80, was allowed. Adjourned to Friday, January 17, 1834. At this meeting it was ordered that a court house be built of brick, and that notice be published for proposals, etc., up to February 13, 1834.

February 13, 1834—Board met and adjourned to next day.

February 14, 1834—The board contracted with John Baugher to build the court house for $9,500.00.

March 4, 1834—David Campbell was paid $2.00, printer's account for publishing notice for proposals.

March 5, 1834—Calvin Bradley was paid $15.00 for draft and specifications. Brown & Magill's printers' account of $3.25, was also paid. Jacob Stem was appointed as agent to negotiate a loan of $6,000.00 to pay for the court house, and a bond was issued to him for that purpose.

March 15, 1834—Mr. Stem reported that the amount, $6,000.00, was deposited in the Baltimore Savings Institution, Maryland. Thereupon the board loaned this amount to Mr. Stem until the interest should compensate him for his trouble.

June 3, 1834—The board allowed Mr. Stem $8.55 for postage by him expended in procuring the loan.

June 7, 1834—The board advanced to John Baugher $250.00 on his contract to build the court house.

On the first day of August, 1834, the Commissioners caused the following entry to be made in their journal, viz:

The commissioners—John Seitz, John Crum and Nicholas Gœtchins, present—paid John Baugher two thousand dollars, and took his receipt on

COURT HOUSE COMPLETED.

his bond (being the first payment towards the court house in Tiffin.) Also, received Jacob Stem's note for twenty-five dollars, being the interest on his note (which was given him by his paying the two thousand dollars which John Baugher receipted to the commissioners.) The commissioners fixed the spot and staked out the ground for the court house, and adjourned.

March 8, 1836—The board of commissioners made this further entry on their journal, viz:

Paid John Baugher seven hundred and eighty-two dollars; also, a county order amounting to two hundred and eighteen dollars, the whole amounting to one thousand dollars.

August 19, 1836, the further entry was made on the commissioners' journal, viz:

Settled with John Baugher and accepted the court house, and paid him the balance of three thousand, two hundred and seventy-nine dollars and seventy-six cents in orders on the county treasurer, and an order on Jacob Stem for the balance of said Stem's note of seven hundred and sixty-eight dollars—making the sum of $4,047.76, which, with the moneys heretofore paid, makes the sum of $9,500.00, the full payment.

They then, also, paid Uriah P. Coonrad, for notifying James Gray, $1.50; and James Gray $1.00 for inspecting the court house.

On the same day the board made an agreement with John Baugher to furnish the court house with benches, tables, etc.; with Frederick Kridler to furnish chairs and settees, and with Luther A. Hall to furnish the stoves.

On the same day David E. Owen resigned his office of county auditor, and the commissioners appointed Levi Davis to fill the vacancy, who entered into bond, and took the oath of office.

The history of the building of the first court house in Tiffin, is recorded here for the benefit of those who may be interested in, or desire to know, the steps that were taken from time to time, from the beginning to its completion, and the names of the persons that figured in the work. Of all the men that were engaged in the work, from the commissioners down to the hod-carriers, there are only three still living, viz: Mr. Adam Wilhelm, now living in Seneca township; Mr. Peter Simonis, now living in Carey, Wyandot county, Ohio; and Mr. Engelman, a carpenter, living in Findlay, Ohio. The others have all gone to their long homes.

On the 11th day of January, 1836, the following entry was made on the journal of the commissioners, viz:

The board proceeded to fill a vacancy occasioned by the expiration of the term for which Abel Rawson was appointed recorder for Seneca county, to-wit: On the 10th day of January, 1829, by the court of common pleas, for

seven years thence next following, which time having expired, the board appoints the said Abel Rawson recorder, as aforesaid, and until the next annual October election. JOHN SEITZ,
LORENZO ABBOTT,
Commissioners.

The county recorder was first elected by the people in October, A. D., 1836.

A very curious entry was made on the journal of the commissioners on the 6th day of December, 1838, in the following words and figures, to-wit.

Josiah Hedges presented a petition from sundry inhabitants of Adams and Pleasant townships, praying for a new township to be made out of the above named townships, to be called "Sulphur Springs." After taking said petition into consideration, they protest the same, and petitioners go hence from whence they came.

The first step taken for the purchase of a farm, and the erection of a county infirmary for Seneca county, was the entry on the journal of the county commissioners, on the 7th day of June, 1841, upon the petition presented by Jacob W. Miller and others, on the 3d day of March, 1841. The petition was read at this session, and postponed for further consideration.

While writing on the subject of this court house, it may be well to state here, in connection with the subject, the circumstances of the burning of the court house, and the rebuilding of the same.

The reader must not look for any chronological arrangement in this work, as there is no effort made towards order in time in the relation of subjects. This is not intended as a reference book. Its object is to preserve descriptions of early times and scenes; the memories of men and women who first built homes in this forest, then called Seneca county; recollections of their manner of living; their trials and hardships; their pleasures and their griefs; their virtues and their vices; to please, and, if possible, to instruct. The data were so carefully collected that they may be relied upon with confidence.

The spring term of the court of common pleas was appointed to commence its session on the morning of Tuesday, the 24th day of May, 1841. The sheriff, on the Saturday previous, the 22d, cleaned out the court room, and, dusting off the seats, left the windows open to let the dust escape. They were found in that condition when the people came together after the alarm of fire. The window in the little room of the northeast corner, up stairs, however, was shut. The men who bursted in the door to this room were repulsed by the fire and smoke, and could save nothing of its contents. The *Tiffin Gazette,* of May 29, 1841, says in its editorial on that subject:

Our village, which has hitherto been exempt from calamity by fire, has at last been robbed of its most splendid ornament by this destructive agent.

Our late beautiful court house is now a heap of ruins. It was discovered to be on fire between two and three o'clock, Sunday morning last, by which time the flames had made such progress that it was impossible to arrest them by any means the citizens had at command. The result was the total destruction of the building. Total, we say, for, although a large portion of the walls are yet standing, it will not, we think, be found expedient to allow them to remain as part of the new edifice. The court house contained the offices of the recorder, treasurer, auditor, sheriff, clerk of court, and grand jury room, which was occupied by Messrs. Cowdery and Wilson.

The recorder's office was then in the southwest corner, and the records were easily secured, being the farthest away from the fire. The greater part of, and all the important records in, the clerk's office, were saved. Very little injury was done to the books in the auditor's office. The sheriff, also, saved most of his important papers; but all the papers in the treasurer's office were destroyed. A strong current of wind carried the flames in that direction, and drove the people away. Richard Williams had his law office in the treasurer's room, and lost his entire library.

Cowdery and Wilson got out of their office everything of value, as they thought; but when the back stair-case and wooden partition wall attached thereto, took fire and threw a brilliant light into their room, which was also on the ground floor, Mr. Cowdery came to the writer, while I was helping to save the records in the clerk's office, and said: "William, there is a case of pigeon holes containing valuable papers in our office, yet. I wish you would jump in and save them for us; you are single, and if you get killed, there is neither wife nor child to cry after you." I thought the proposition a very reasonable one, and jumped through the window and saved the papers. The pigeon hole case was just commencing to blaze.

The court house was considered fire-proof. Oak logs, hewed one foot square, were laid close together over the whole lower story. These were covered with sand eighteen inches deep. The idea was this: That if the upper story should ever burn, the sand on these logs would arrest the further progress of the fire, and save the records and papers below.

It seemed, however, that when the back stairway caught fire, it communicated with the logs very rapidly. A slight current of wind carried the flames all along the ceiling of the offices; and the office of Cowdery and Wilson, being close to the stair case, had the logs burnt nearly through at this time, and the sand had commenced pouring down. One jump brought me into the south window of the office, when three logs, with about twenty loads of sand on top, fell down into the office. Another jump out, landed me on my hands and feet on the ground, with the cheers of the crowd on that side; but before I could get up, the whole cornice on the south side fell and nearly covered me; but, as good fortune would have it, a piece of the cornice that fell close by, end-ways, operated as a prop to the balance, and I was pulled from under the rubbish without injury.

After the first alarm of fire, a few bucketfuls of water would have been sufficient to put it out. It was then just breaking through the cornice and roof, at the northeast corner of the house. There was no way to reach the fire. There was no fire-engine, no hooks, no ladders, no fire company. The people were as helpless as children, and doomed to stand by and see their new and beautiful court house burn down. They did all they could do. They saved the records, some of the furniture, and the neighboring buildings.

There was a great difference of opinion as to the cause of the fire. Some laid it to incendiarism; others laid it to Mr. John Elder, who was deputy clerk, for leaving his candle burning in his room in the upper story, immediately below where the fire first broke through. John was seen, late in the evening, coming down stairs, dressed up, and some time after the roof was all ablaze, came back, being dressed for Sunday. He had a bed, his clothing, books, and some furniture in the room, and slept there. Be this as it may, Sunday morning, May 23, found the court house in ashes within its walls. The gable ends had fallen in, and all the chimneys but one.

On the Monday following, Mr. David Bishop, a most daring, reckless man, in some way got up on to the north wall and walked eastward towards the only chimney yet standing, and just as he stretched out his hand to touch it, it fell outside to the ground. How Mr. Bishop avoided falling after it, is simply a miracle.

The commissioners, at their June session thereafter, paid Mr. Joseph Walker, as trustee of the Methodist Protestant church, $25 for the use of their church in holding the May term of the court for that year.

On the 10th day of June, 1841, the county commissioners ordered as follows:

That the auditor be required to give public notice by advertisement in the *Van Burenite* and *Tiffin Gazette*, of Tiffin; the *Ohio Statesman* and *Ohio State Journal*, of Columbus; the *Norwalk Experiment*, of Norwalk; the

REBUILDING THE COURT HOUSE.

Sandusky Democrat, of Lower Sandusky; and the *Findlay Courier*, of Findlay, until the 22d day of July next, for rebuilding and completing the court house without delay.

On the 23d day of July, 1841, the board contracted with John Baugher to build a new house, using the walls of the old house, which were considered all-sufficient, and have ever since so proved to be— *i. e.*, the carpenter and joiner work and painting, for $3,080. Jacob Emich contracted for the brick work, furnishing all necessary material, for $800. Allison Phillips contracted for the plastering work, with the material, for $450.

At the January session, 1843, of the board of commissioners, the new court house was accepted and occupied.

In 1866, an addition was made on the east end of the court house, with a vault and safe for the treasurer, and vaults made to preserve the records and papers in the other offices. The addition constitutes the office of the recorder and treasurer, with grand and petit jury rooms above.

On the 9th day of June, 1843, the county commissioners contracted with Ephraim Riker to build the jail and sheriff's residence, on Madison street, for $3,487.

In 1877, the new jail on Market street was built.

CHAPTER XII.

THE WOOD-CHOPPER—HOW TO BUILD A CABIN—THE DIFFERENCE BETWEEN THE SETTLERS — THEIR BENEVOLENCE AND HOSPITALITY — PIONEER GIRLS — RUSTIC FURNITURE — THE HOMINY BLOCK — THE HANDMILL— GOING TO MEETING—INDIAN VISITORS—NATURAL FANNING MILL—"THE LIFE IN THE WOODS FOR ME"—HOME-MADE CLOTH—YOUNG AMERICA.

"Some love to roam
O'er the white sea foam,
Where the wild winds whistle free;
But a chosen band
In a forest land
And a life in the woods for me."

THE ENEMIES of the country, red and white, had been subdued and driven away by victories and treaties, and the frontier made safe and protected against their atrocities. Now the forest was to be conquered; diseases incident to frontier life to be met and endured; swamps to be drained; roads to be opened and bridges to be built; lands to be cleared and fenced; life to be sustained for several years without any income—without having anything to sell; and, first of all, a cabin to be built—a home to be secured.

Money was very scarce. Every dollar the immigrants had was invested in land, as a general thing. Among those who afterwards were considered the most wealthy were men who cleared lands for others at fifty cents per day, boarding themselves, or for eight to ten dollars per acre, to raise money for indispensable necessaries of life, or to pay taxes. Many pioneers were compelled to work on the canals, to get a little money, leaving their families alone in the woods for months at a time. (See chapter on "Canal System.")

The "oak openings" in Thompson township, undulating and "fair to look upon," covered with beautiful wild flowers from early spring to late in the fall, attracted the attention of men from Pennsylvania, and of some from New York, who were seeking for places to build homes in the west.

DIFFERENCE BETWEEN SETTLERS.

The settlers along Silver creek, Honey creek, Rocky creek and the river were from Maryland, Pennsylvania, New York, Virginia, Kentucky, and from southern Ohio. The German, Irish and French immigrants, a vast majority of whom located west of the river, began the life in the woods here about the year 1829, and continued their coming until about 1850. The larger part of them came hither between 1830 and 1840. The settlers east of the river were principally native Americans, and familiar with the customs, habits, manner of living, laws and language of the people—could buy and sell without an interpreter, and transact all kinds of business in their own American way. Not so with the emigrant from a foreign land. Everything was new and strange to him; the language of the people, their laws, manner of living, even the tools they worked with—all, all was new and strange.

There never was a people in the world that could beat the Americans in the use of the axe, and as a wood chopper the American frontiersman never had his equal.

Perhaps it did look awkward to see a man raise his axe over his head to chop down a tree, hacking into it all around in some fashion to get it down. But this was no laughing matter; the thing had to be learned by experience. The foreigner had no wood to chop in the land of his birth. A crooked axe-handle, and such an axe, were not in use in his country at that time. An American coming upon a German chopping in the woods, would often stop and show him how to *swing*, and not *raise* the axe perpendicularly, etc. The teacher was kind enough in his gratuitous lesson, and while his talk was all "lost upon the desert air," the foreigner saw the utility in the swing, and soon became an apt scholar. The manner in which the tall timbers along Wolf creek came down to let the sun shine in upon the ground, was one of the very many testimonials that proved how rapidly the man from western Europe became Americanized, and especially the German.

There was another distinguishing feature between the American and foreign frontiersman. The American, familiar with his language and the habits of his people and having a knowledge of what he was to meet in the west, accustomed to the use of tools, etc., had no ocean to cross to come here. He found his neighbors to be his own countrymen. He could pack his household goods, with his family, into a wagon, drive his cattle before him, and when the spot was selected where he would build his home it did not take him very long to make himself and his loved ones comfortable—at least comparatively so. The settler from a foreign land was compelled to reduce his household goods to the smallest possible quantity, on account of the vast distance he had to travel from his native hills and valleys to find a place to locate, in the the woods of Seneca county.

And hither he came without a domestic animal, without any knowledge of the country or the people here, without any preparation to meet the task that his new life demanded of him, often without tools and generally without the knowledge how to use them. Those of you, American neighbors, who were at home here, and had means to help yourselves with, may perhaps imagine, but you never could realize, the heart-aches and hardships this difference created, and what the man who had paid his last dollar for the piece of land upon which he now came, with his wife and several small children, to build a cabin—destitute of almost everything except his iron will and industry—had to undergo. When he met his American neighbor he could not tell him what he wanted. Under such circumstances, it was indeed very hard to fight the battle of life in the forest.

But in these trying times there was one great virtue almost universal among all classes of people, without distinction as to nativity, race or religious affiliations—a virtue that towered above their mighty oaks, brighter than a beacon light, as warming in its effects as the rays of a summer sun, cheering as a mother's smile, and soothing, like a calm from the gardens above. It was that generous, broad, innate, heaven-born hospitality that characterized the settler in the woods. As misery loves company, the man who had himself realized the same scene, was quick to furnish the necessary relief. It was not considered a hardship at all, when several of the neighbors came with their axes, a yoke of oxen and a log chain, cross-cut saw, froe, maul, etc., and often in one day put up a log cabin and covered it with clap boards before night. Another day or two, and the owner had put up a fire-place at one end and a door in the side. If the new comer could re-pay by working back, all right; if not, it was all the same. And so with everything else. A favor was not asked in vain; for it was granted, if possible, as a matter of course. The latch-string was always out, night and day.

There were neither castes nor classes in society then. Some, it is very true, were in much better circumstances than others, even then; but their work, their deprivations, their hardships, their sufferings and mutual dependence upon each other in the hours of distress and need, together with their social gatherings, brought all down to a common level, or elevated all to a higher plane of neighborly love—as you please to have it—thus forming a society that the outside world, away from the frontier, never knew. There was no night so dark or stormy, no swale so deep, no distance so great, but that a call in case of sickness, distress or death, would be promptly responded to. To feed the hungry, to furnish relief in cases of distress and need, and to help each other was the mission of the society. It was only necessary to have one's wants made known; help came of itself. And even in after years, if, by reason of sickness, accident or mishap of any kind, a neighbor could not take care of his harvest or make his hay, neighbors volunteered their services and did the work, without asking or expecting pay.

Viewing pioneer life from this standpoint, is it to be wondered at that neighbors would thus share and sympathize with each other? All this mutual help came spontaneously, without reward or expectation thereof. Woman then, more than ever, proved to be that sweet angel of charity at the bed-side of the sick and dying, ministering to the suffering, and smoothing the pillow of the departing.

In a case of distress it was no uncommon occurrence for a man and his wife to get out of a warm bed in the dark hours of a cold, winter's night, light a torch made of the bark of shell hickory, and leaving their children alone in the cabin, wind their way through the forest, through snow and water for miles, to tender their kind offices to a suffering neighbor.

How well the beautiful words of the poet apply to this noble pioneer neighborhood:—

> "No precious gem that crested fortune wears,
> Nor priceless pearl that hangs from beauty's ears,
> Shine with such lustre as the tear that breaks
> For others' woes down virtue's manly cheeks."

To go three, four or five miles and help a man raise a cabin, was in the order of things. The work had to be done, and the man could not do it alone. That was enough; and there was no dodge or disposition to get away from it, or make an apology. To *help*, was as imperative as the laws of the Medes and Persians. If a man was notified to help at a "raising," and did not put in an appearance, it was regarded as a failure to perform a binding obligation, and a repetition of the same had a tendency to injure the man's character in the esteem of his neighbors. To avoid this, a man would often neglect his own affairs and go, rather than be talked about and blamed for dodging a duty. Nothing would excuse him but sickness or accident.

If boulders or other stones could be found handy, they were rolled together and put on top of each other, to form the back and sides of a fire-place. A clay bank would answer as a substitute. The sides and back of a fire-place thus made secure, the next thing was to top out and up, a chimney. This was done with sticks split out of an oak log, laid over each other in a square form on the top of the back and sides of the fire-place until a heighth of one or two feet above the comb of the roof was reached, and then it was well plastered on both sides with soft clay. If flag stones could be found for a hearth, very good; if not, a clay hearth answered nearly as well, and the latter was the most fashionable hearth in all that part of the country where stones were scarce.

In building a cabin, an accomplished "corner man" could carry up a corner in less than one-half the time it would take an ordinary chopper. To make the notches fit the saddles neatly, required both skill and practice; and by looking at the corners of a cabin it was very easy to tell whether the corner man understood his business or not. The porch, or "stoop," as the Yankees used to call it, was made at the side of the cabin where the road was expected to be made thereafter.

On the first or second logs above the door the end logs on that side were allowed to run as far out and over the side, as the porch was to be wide. Upon the ends of these projecting logs a straight log was laid length-wise, and formed the plate of the roof. As the gable end logs were now cut shorter to form the roof, poles were laid on these length wise also, and in line with the plate. These were called "ribs," and answered the purpose of rafters. The clap-boards were laid on these. A clap-board was from six to eight inches wide, split out of a white oak block about four feet long, from one-half to one inch in thickness, and was laid on these ribs without being shaved. These clap-boards were now laid down, projecting over the plate about six inches. At each end of the plate a wooden pin held up a long straight pole, which was laid on the top of the clap-boards to hold them down. Then another layer of clap-boards was put down, and another long, straight pole placed on these, and so on. To prevent these poles from slipping down, sticks, called "knees," were put from the lower pole to the next one, end-wise. These long poles were very appropriately called "weight poles," for they held the clap-boards down and kept them straight. Thus the roof was made.

Now the logs were cut off in the side of the cabin where the doors were wanted, down to the lower log. The doors in the sides were generally put opposite each other, for several reasons, viz: for ventilation, to get out at the back way, and very often to let the horse or the ox, that had just hauled in a back-log, walk out at the other door, without being put to the necessity of turning around.

For want of a sawed plank, a straight piece of puncheon was used to

BUILDING A LOG HOUSE.

hold up the ends of the logs thus sawed off for the door, and was pinned against these ends very firmly, forming at the same time the door jamb. A sheet or an old quilt was made to answer for a door until some boards could be procured for that purpose. These were hard to find. Saw mills were scarce, and often far a way; but when the necessary boards were procured, they were pinned to two cross pieces split out of a straight block, the larger end of which projected about six inches, and having an inch hole through it. This cross piece was called a batten, and while it served that purpose it was also a hinge. The inch hole in the projecting end of the batten fitted over a wooden pin put into the door jamb, standing upright, and supplied the hook. Next, a wooden latch and catch was fixed to the other edge of the door, with the string by which the latch was raised running through a small hole and hanging down outside, and the door was done. There was no glass to be had for the window, and for the want of it a piece of paper pasted over the hole let light enough through to see by, especially when the paper was greased.

It required considerable mechanical skill to make a good puncheon floor. The puncheons were split out of straight oak logs and hewed with a broad-axe on one side, then spotted on the other to fit level on the sleepers below. All this required a knowledge of the use of the broad-axe, and some help. For want of either of these, a clay floor was made by filling up the bottom, as high as the lower log, with clay; and to make a good one the clay was mixed with water and an ox or a horse led through it for hours at a time, to tramp the clay into a paste, and when thus prepared it was pounded with a piece of plank and leveled up to suit. The clay floor was thus even with the lower log, and the door swung nicely over it, and close to it. This kind of floor kept the wind from blowing under the cabin, added to its warmth, and was easily repaired. For want of boards or slabs the loft was useless until these could be procured; then a ladder, placed in a corner of the cabin, generally near the fire-place, led "up stairs." The spaces between the logs were filled up with short blocks, called "chinking," which were wedged together in such a manner as to prevent their falling out. The chinking was then covered with a coating of wet clay, inside and out.

Now the cabin was completed, and formed a human habitation as good and as comfortable as surrounding circumstances would admit of. There was not a nail in the whole structure. Two wooden hooks pinned against one of the joists held the familiar rifle in its place, ready for use at a moment's warning, and always in reach, for the ceiling of the cabin was never very high.

The furniture of the cabin was of the same rustic character. There were no large warehouses of ready made cabinet-ware in those days. Pieces of puncheon furnished with legs made good stools, and supplied the want of chairs. A similar piece, only larger and with longer legs, made a very good, substantial table. Bedsteads were often made with but one post. "How can that be done?" you ask. A two inch augur hole was bored into a log as high as the bedstead was to be from the floor, and as far from the corner as the width of the bed; then a similar hole was bored in another log as far from the same corner as the length of the bed. Poles were then driven into these holes, and at the point where these crossed each other they were cut off, and the ends driven into two holes, which were bored in a post at the same heighth from the floor as the holes in the logs. The bottom of the bed was made of basswood bark twisted and run over the poles and logs, the straps crossing each other at right angles. This was not a patent spring bottom, but answered the same purpose. Small pins driven into the joists held up the bed curtain which had been brought from home. Thus the cabin, with its large fire-place and crackling fire, began to assume an air of rural comfort and coziness that could only be realized in the cabin age.

The table furniture was generally of tin or pewter. Queens-ware or china-ware were not only expensive, but heavy and unsafe to take along on the journey. The cooking utensils were equally as simple and practicable. A tea kettle, Dutch oven, coffee pot and skillet; sometimes, a reflector to bake in, constituted the most essential articles. The handle of the skillet had to be very long to enable the cook to use it without getting too close to the fire. Very often, the end of the handle was held up by a string suspended from a log in the ceiling, which was very convenient. Pins driven into the logs, with boards laid on top, formed convenient shelves, and everything was made as handy and convenient as could be.

The trees near the cabin were now brought down and burnt up, to start a clearing and open a patch for corn and vegetables. The patch was enclosed with a rail or brush fence, and those who knew the use of roasting ears, lived in clover when they were fit for use. A very excellent cake was made from corn that was a little too hard for roasting ears, in about this manner: A piece of tin, perforated from one side, made a grater. The corn in the ear was rubbed over that, and a soft meal secured, which, mixed with an egg and a little salt, made a very good cake. It was baked in a skillet, generally, but often on the back of a shovel, washed clean, and set up before the fire at an angle of about 45 degrees. "Johnny-cake" was baked that way, and made a very good substitute for bread. A piece of fat venison or bear's meat, with corn cake and a glass of milk, made a feast "fit for a king to eat." No conquests celebrated by royalty, no festive night, with royal pomp and circumstance, furnished a meal so free from heart-ache and wrong, so full of true happiness and real enjoyment, as that of the pioneer frontiersman.

Afterwards, when people could afford the expense, they built houses of logs hewed on two sides—often one and one-half—sometimes two stories high. When whitewashed on the outside, they looked very cleanly and comfortable.

It was no uncommon occurrence with people who lived near the trails of Indians, to have a number of these red men come into the cabin and lay around the fire all night. They would come in at most any hour of the night, without making any noise, and in the morning, when the inmates of the house awoke, they found the Indians sound asleep on the floor, with their feet towards the fire. The cabin door was scarcely ever locked, and the Indians never learned the custom of knocking at a door to be allowed admittance. Parents would often leave their cabin of evenings in the care of their children, to sit up with a sick neighbor some miles away, when Indians would come in for a night's lodging, stay all night, and go away without molesting or disturbing anything.

Flouring mills were scarce, and often far off. Gradually, some of these useful structures sprung into existence along the river and on Honey creek; but even then, when a man had no team, he continued to experience the trouble of reducing his corn into meal as theretofore. The corn did not get as hard then as it does now. The corn patches were in the woods, in spots here and there around the scattered cabins, and the air was filled with moisture, which kept the corn wet and soft. To prepare it for the hominy block, or the mill, it had to be dried before the fire, for it would not shell without this preparation.

The hominy block was a piece of a log about two feet long, set up on end, with a hole burnt into the upper end, forming a mortar. The end of a hand-spike was split to receive the sharp end of an iron wedge, which was held to the handle by an iron ring driven down tightly upon it. The head of the wedge crushed the corn in the hominy block, and thus they had a mortar and pestel. The corn often required a great deal of pounding before it would become fine enough for meal. The meal was then sifted, and the finer portion used for cakes, while the coarser part was the hominy. Fanning the hominy a little while in a tin pan, drove all the shells out of it.

A very good hominy was also made without pounding it, by soaking the corn a day or two in strong lye made of wood ashes. This loosened the shell, and softened the hard part of the grain. The lye being poured off and the corn soaked again in fresh water for awhile, would swell very large, and lose the taste of the lye, and when boiled soft made very good hominy.

Some of the settlers who had ingenuity enough, and could find flagstones that answered the purpose, constructed instruments they called "hand mills." Let me describe one of these, for they answered not only the purpose of the family that owned one, but also that of the neighbors round about, who brought their corn already shelled to grind it. When two or three of the neighbors met at the hand mill the same evening, one had to wait until the other was done, and it often took steady work until away beyond midnight, to grind corn enough for bread to last during the next day:

It was a very simple affair. Two stones, about twenty inches in diameter, dressed round, formed the real mill. The mill was erected near the chimney corner. The lower stone was made stationary on a block; the upper stone, called the runner, was turned by hand in this wise: A pole was firmly fixed into a square hole on the top, near the edge. The upper end of the pole entered a hole in a board, or a log, over head, loosely. A broad hoop, made of a clap-board shaved thin, was fixed around the stones to keep them to their places and keep in the corn. One person would then turn the stone, while the other fed the mill through a hole in the side called "the eye." It was hard and slow work, and the men took "turn about." While this work would take two men two hours to grind meal enough for the family for the next day, yet it was an improvement on the hominy block, after all.

The old saying that "necessity is the mother of invention," never was applied any where with greater force than in the life of the pioneer. As soon as ground enough was cleared, and wheat could be raised, no time was lost to try it. It was very difficult to stir up loose ground enough between the roots and stumps to receive the seed. Wheat drills would have been of no value then. But small crops were raised in the start. The threshing was done with flails or thin poles, sometimes on the ground, cleared up for that purpose. Now, to get the chaff away from the wheat was another difficulty. When the wind would blow, a sheet was spread on the ground, and a handful of wheat, held high up over the sheet, was allowed to run through the hand,

INCONVENIENCES OF PIONEER LIFE.

while the wind blew the chaff to one side—a natural fanning mill. They had another way to clean wheat when the wind did not blow. Two men took hold of the four corners of a sheet, and wafted it, with a strong sweep, towards another man, thus creating a current of air in his direction, which separated the chaff from the wheat as it fell from his hands on to a second sheet provided to catch the clean grain. This was cleaning wheat in a calm.

A description of the difficulties in getting grinding done at the mills, is given in a former chapter, and it is only necessary to add here, that that inconvenience was a very general one.

Excepting cases of sickness, the hardest part of pioneer life was the commencement of it, and more so, especially, with those that came here without a good preparation for the task such scenes would necessarily require. If a man had money enough to go into the older settlements and buy for himself a yoke of oxen, he was considered a "made man." Those that had no team at all, were doomed to depend upon those that had, to get their logging done, their milling, their plowing, and other team work. This was attended with great delay, frequent disappointments, and many other inconveniences, as may well be supposed, and necessarily made progress exceedingly slow. Horses were also a rarity. Oxen did nearly all the work a team had to do, and were, in fact, better adapted for such use then than horses. People that had oxen and a wagon attended church in style; others had to walk.

For want of churches, religious services took place at the cabin of some settler, and it made very little difference what christian denomination the preacher belonged to, for the people would attend service any way. The same mutuality of feeling was well sustained when, afterwards, funds were raised to build churches. People would subscribe and pay liberally with labor, material and money to the erection of churches they did not belong to or affiliate with. It was expected of every man that he should patronize religion, and not stand aloof when a call was made upon him for such a purpose. A family was naturally supposed to belong to some church. Atheists, infidels, materialists and deists were not known, or did not care to be so designated. This religious feeling, so general, allied with the broad benevolence so usual and common among the pioneers, had a wonderful effect upon society at large, and directly or indirectly compelled men to be sober, honorable, honest, industrious and frugal, in order to be entitled to attention or respect from anybody. It is to be regretted that that element in frontier society did not live to reach this age and generation.

It should not be forgotten that there were no bridges across the streams in those days, and people found their way out to some open road, or to a neighbor, by following blazed trees; that it was then necessary to wade through swamps, climb over, or walk along on logs. Men did not wear polished boots, and with such as they had, could well make their way to meeting on Sunday. But ladies without horses to ride, and no team of any kind, had to get to church as best they could—for go, they would. And it was also regarded as perfectly in order to see girls carry their shoes and stockings in their hands, wade through the water, and after walking several miles through the woods, when near the meeting house, sit down in a fence corner, or behind a big tree, and put on their shoes and stockings.

After the meeting was over, they took them off again, and walked home barefooted, in the way they came. Sometimes a beau was polite enough to carry the shoes and stockings to the house, and thus embrace the opportunity to see "the old man."

The girls were as pretty, in their log cabins, as ours are now in their drawing-rooms, and equally as virtuous, and possessed of as much true womanhood as now, to say the least. The trails of their dresses were not as long as they are worn now, and perhaps the texture was not so fine, but they looked the very picture of health and beauty in their linsey-woolsey, and other home-made flannels; and if you married one of these girls, you had a wife in the fullest sense of the term, and a companion for life that would stand by you, come what would. It was not necessary, then, to hire a German or Irish chamber-maid to fan your frontier bride while she, seated in a rocking-chair, played her guitar, or hold up her trail as she stepped into her carriage. And there was no need of a French cook, chamber-maid, and a laundry-girl—making three—to wait upon the bride. These hangers-on were all dispensed with. The kitchen, the parlor, the wash-room and the drawing-room were all in the same room, and the fire in the big fire place warmed them all.

Courtships among young people had their inconveniences, very true, but daughters were scarcely ever out of their mothers' sight, and at their social gatherings old and young commingled together.

While pioneer life had its rough sides, and its deprivations, it must not be supposed, for a moment, that it was a dark and gloomy life, and destitute of joys and pleasures. There is a certain peculiar pleasure attached to it that is almost indescribable. Chopping in the woods, burning brush and log heaps, wife and children joining in the work; the quiet and solitude of the forest; fishing and hunting; the relief from the restraints and conventionalities of refined society; the hope for future prosperity; of nearer neighbors; of better roads and markets; of bridges, stock-growing, fields enlarging, sons and daughters growing into usefulness—these and a thousand and one other incidents made "the life in the woods" wonderfully fascinating, and created around it a halo of most peculiar happiness and loveliness. Any survivor of that generation of men, will now exclaim, when recurring to those days: "The life in the woods for me!"

There was no terror in the howling of the wintry blast when the little clearing had grown large enough to prevent the trees from falling on the cabin. The family, snugly tucked away in their warm beds, in the little cabin, lit up from the big fire-place, were not annoyed by the howling, whistling and whining of the winds in the tree-tops, nor by the crashing of breaking limbs, and the thundering of a big, falling tree. It is very true, that some of us who had to sleep aloft, often found our shoes, stockings, and, in fact, all our clothes, even our bed-clothes, covered by a bed of snow, when we waked up in the morning; for these clap-board roofs would let the snow into the cabin with wonderful facility, especially when the wind blew with it. But it was the work of a moment to shake the snow from our clothes, and get down the ladder to the fire-place, where they soon dried.

These fire places were generally very spacious, occupying nearly the whole end of the cabin, leaving just room enough for a ladder to go aloft on one side, and for a cupboard on the other. The back-log, about six feet long, and two or three feet in diameter, if green, lasted longer than a dry stick, of course, but it always disorganized the house to put a back-log to its place. It was handled and rolled over with hand-spikes, and when in its place, it was an easy matter to build a good fire in front of it, thus throwing the heat forward into the room.

For want of help to get the back-log to its place, it often became necessary to hitch a horse or an ox to it, and thus "snake" it into the house lengthwise. The log-chain was then unhitched, and the "critter" led out of the opposite door.

The wolves passed away gradually, and no longer did their wretched howling, long drawn out, make the nights hideous about the lonely cabin. Sheep could now be raised with greater safety, and wool and mutton were both highly valued. Then came into use the large spinning wheel, with its "boy," and peculiar hum. Woolen socks became a luxury. Men and women wore homespun clothing. Weaving looms became plenty, and those who had no loom could get their cloth woven by a neighbor, very cheap. The hemp and flax were spun on small wheels. Linen warp and woolen filling made linsey-woolsey. This made dresses for women and children, and wampuses for the men to work in. People now dressed more comfortably. An overcoat of home-made cloth, with a double cape, was very becoming to the backwoodsman in his wolf-skin cap. Many of the long winter evenings were spent in spinning wool and flax, some using the reel, some the swift, while the men made hickory brooms or axe-handles. Every one was employed until bed-time. The little cabin looked like a bee-hive on a large scale.

These pages are not intended as a criticism on anybody, or anything. Their object is merely to preserve, from oblivion, scenes and incidents that accompanied the time and the circumstances in and under which this beatiful patch of country, we love to call "Old Seneca," commenced to be opened to civilization, and the memory of that noble, heroic class of men and women who devoted their lives to the task, and who are fast passing away.

It is questionable, however, whether the present generation is possessed of the gratitude, love and veneration properly due to its pioneer friends, for what they did and endured to make Seneca county what it is. Perhaps there is not as much of that filial love, affection, veneration and esteem due from the child to the parent, shed abroad throughout society as there should be. Boys talk of the time when they shall be twenty-one years old and then be their own masters—independent, free to do for themselves, under obligation to nobody. They call the father "the old man," the mother "the old woman."

It sounds so cold and so hard, so distant and so void of love, and seems to ignore everything the honored parents did to make "Young America" to be a man. There is no duty that love enjoins upon the human heart, more sacred, next to the love of God, than the filial love and affection a child owes its parents.

If this is a world of cause and effect, it can scarcely be presumed that a violation of this law is not followed by the penalty.

A good story is told of a man who had an old father living with him who was nervous, and trembling with age. His wife was a very cleanly and tidy woman. The old father often spilled his food on the table cloth, and they made him sit at a small table in a corner, by himself. Even there he occasionally broke a dish, being unable to control his nerves.

One day the son took an axe and chopped at a block, making a little trough. His little boy, by his side, asked him what he was making, and the man told the child that he was "making a trough for grand-pap to eat out of." This answer put the little fellow into a deep study, and after awhile he looked up and said to his father: "Pa, when you be an old man, I will make a trough for you, won't I?" The man dropped his axe, took the little fellow by the hand, and walked into the house.

When I see Young America driving his fine horses, hitched to a splendid buggy, with silver-plated harness, nice whip with a blue ribbon tied half-way up, holding the lines in his kid-gloved hands, going "two-forty on the plank" over roads that his old father made through a dense forest, chopping down the trees, cutting them into logs, and hauling them away with a yoke of oxen, to enable him to drive between the stumps; then wait a long time before the stumps decayed, so that a furrow could be drawn to grade the road and let the water run away,—I would like to tell the young man to sometimes think of these things. When I see "Young America" standing at the corners of streets, with boots nicely polished, fine broadcloth suit, fine silk hat sitting on one ear, walking-cane of the latest style, with a cigar stuck in his face at an angle of forty-five degrees,—though all this may be very nice—I would most kindly whisper into the ear of my young friend to remember, also, his honored father, who, in his honest home-spun, with his pants in his boots, worked hard all his life, struggling against poverty and want, and all other hardships that belonged to pioneer life.

The reading of the history of one's country should tend to create patriotic pride. Why should it not also stimulate a renewed and a higher veneration for the fathers and mothers that made the history?

Pioneer tales and reminiscences may have a charm in them for some, but others do not care to read them—regard them as they would a fish story, and remain undecided whether they shall believe them at all, or not.

Well! It is for only the better part of human nature that this book is written, any way.

So mote it be.

CHAPTER XIII.

GOVERNOR EDWARD TIFFIN—A BIOGRAPHY.

IT IS SAID that Governor Tiffin, of Chillicothe, was a particular friend of Mr. Josiah Hedges, at the time the latter laid out and platted Tiffin, and for that reason named his town after his friend.

There are so many incidents and historic events interwoven with the life and public services of Governor Tiffin, and there is so much beauty in his private life and character, that to withhold them from the reader seemed wrong to the writer, especially after so much research and unexpected success in securing the material. Some may be glad to preserve a memoir of the distinguished and illustrious pioneer after whom the capital of our county is named.

The peculiar traits of character of Doctor Tiffin, as a leading man in his day, associated, as he was in his public life, with men of strong minds and remarkable ability, tended largely in starting our noble state on her proud career. The old "Buckeye state" was especially favored in being led into the constellation of this union of states by the hands of such distinguished patriots and statesmen as met in the territorial legislature in Cincinnati, and in the first constitutional convention, in Chillicothe, from 1798 to 1805, and after. They stamped their own individuality upon their time, directed the first, infantile steps and determined the destiny, of the young and growing state.

There are three daughters of Governor Tiffin still living—two in Chillicothe and one in Cincinnati, as the following documents will show. The letters annexed prove the kindness that the family of Tiffin seem to have inherited from their honored father, and their readiness to assist in the work of giving to the readers of these pages a faithful memoir of the person and character of Governor Tiffin.

Upon the suggestion of Mrs. L. R. Dresbach, of Tiffin, and being informed that a Doctor Comegys, living in Cincinnati, was a distant relative of the Governor, the writer addressed a letter to him. Upon this, answers were received, and the material furnished from which the sketch of Governor Tiffin is written:

BIOGRAPHY OF GOVERNOR TIFFIN.   197

CINCINNATI, January 21, 1880.
MY DEAR SIR:—
Yours of the 17th inst. received. I enclose a memoir of Governor Tiffin written in 1869. The preface explains it. I had intended writing a fuller account of his distinguished career, but seem never to find the time.

The Governor was a man of medium stature, dark chestnut hair, deep blue eyes, a pure type of English features and rather florid complexion, very active in movements and quick in his mental actions.

I shall be glad to answer any further questions. I am pleased to see your effort to do justice to the noble pioneer race.

Very Respectfully,
W. LANG, ESQ.   C. G. COMEGYS.

CINCINNATI, January 24, 1880.
DEAR SIR:—
Yours of the 22d inst. is received. Gov. Tiffin had no children by his first wife; by the second five—one son and four daughters. Three of the latter are living, viz: Mrs. M. Scott Cook, (Mr. Cook is the uncle of Mrs. President Hayes), Miss Diathea Madison Tiffin, both residing in Chillicothe, and Mrs. Comegys, wife of Dr. Comegys, of Cincinnati. The oldest daughter is dead. She was the wife of Joseph Reynolds, Esq., of Urbana, Ohio. His only son, Edward, was killed in 1853 by an accident on the Erie Railroad at Yonkers, N. Y. He was a young physician and returning from Paris, where he had been residing for two years for medical observation.

I will write to Miss Tiffin, who, I hope, can furnish you with a steel engraving of her father's face. I hope, also, that she will be able to furnish you with a copy of General Washington's letter, introducing young Tiffin to Governor St. Clair.   Yours, Respectfully,
W. LANG, ESQ.   C. G. COMEGYS.

CHILLICOTHE, OHIO, February 2, 1880.
DEAR SIR:—
At the request of my brother-in-law, Dr. Comegys, of Cincinnati, I send you a copy of General Washington's letter to Gov. St. Clair. Also by express a copy of Johnson's engraved portrait of my father.

Yours, Respectfully,
WM. LANG, ESQ.   DIATHEA M. TIFFIN.

Attached to the foregoing letter of Miss Tiffin is the letter of General Washington, introducing young Tiffin to Governor St. Clair, who at the time of the writing was governor of the Northwestern Territory. The reader will notice the modesty and delicacy of General Washington, that characterize all his writings. This letter was recently found among old papers in the possession of Dr. St. Clair, and was never published before:

SIR:—
Mr. Edward Tiffin solicits an appointment in the territory northwest of the Ohio. The fairness of his character in private and public life, together

with a knowledge of law resulting from close application for a considerable time, will, I hope, justify the liberty I now take in recommending him to your attention; regarding with due attention the delicacy as well as importance of the character in which I act. I am sure you will do me the justice to believe that nothing but a knowledge of the gentleman's merits, founded upon a long acquaintance, could have induced me to trouble you on this occasion.

With sincere wishes for your happiness and welfare,
I am, etc.,
GEORGE WASHINGTON.
Gov. St Clair.   January 4, 1798.

There is no doubt but that a knowledge of the fundamental principles of law was a powerful factor in placing young Tiffin among the first statesmen of his time, and the wonderful sagacity of Gen. Washington comprehended the man and the place where he might be utilized.

CINCINNATI, February 6, 1880.
DEAR SIR:—

Since I wrote you I have found a letter addressed to me by the late Col. Allen Latham, of Chillicothe, written at a time when I thought I would enlarge my memoir of the old Governor. I sent the Colonel a copy of my memoir, and asked him to write me what he could of his recollections. It harmonized with my statement, as you will see, and you will get a better description of his person and his gentlemanly manners. He belonged to the old *regime* of highly cultured men.

I have a copy of his first message to the Legislature; also his message in regard to the capture of the Blennerhasset-Burr expedition, and President Jefferson's laudation of the Governor's activity, etc., etc. If you desire to use them in your narrative, I will send them to you.

One of the most flourishing towns in the state bears Tiffin's name, and as you are about writing a history of the pioneer era, I feel that you can make your work more attractive by such details, as well as honor a distinguished man of his time.   Very Respectfully,
W. Lang, Esq.   C. G. COMEGYS.
[See Appendix.]

Edward Tiffin was born in the city of Carlisle, England, June 19, 1766. His parents were in but moderate circumstances, and his uncle, Edward Parker, after whom he was named, assumed the care of his education. He was fitted for the study of medicine, upon which he entered at an early age; but before he had completed the course he embarked for this country with his parents and family, when barely eighteen years of age, and landed in New York. He proceeded to Philadelphia, where he followed the course of medical lectures in the University of Pennsylvania. He then rejoined his father's family, who

BIOGRAPHY OF GOVERNOR TIFFIN.

had settled in Charlestown, Berkely county, Virginia, and began the practice of medicine when but twenty years of age.

His thorough training brought him speedily into notice, and his success soon gave him a fine reputation and a lucrative practice. He is described by one who knew him well, as "possessed of such buoyancy of spirit and sprightliness of temperament, pleasing manners and fine conversational powers, as made him the favorite in the gay and fashionable circles of Berkely."

In 1789 he married Mary, daughter of Robert Worthington, and sister of Governor Worthington. She was a woman of fine culture, and is described by an eminent minister as 'one of the most conscientious and heavenly-minded women he had ever met.' With her he lived happily for nearly twenty years.

The manuscript minutes of Mrs. Peters, the venerable mother of the Hon. Rufus King, of Cincinnati, throw much light on the subject of dates concerning Gov. Tiffin's settlement in Ohio.

The issue of land warrants by the state of Virginia to her revolutionary soldiers, to be located in Ohio, or the Northwest Territory, which Virginia had ceded to the general government, drew largely the attention of Virginians to that region. Thomas Worthington, with other owners of scrip and a party of surveyors, left Virginia in 1797, and arrived at Chillicothe the same month. The town was then called "Massieville," having been laid out by Gen. Massie a year before. It contained about one hundred cabins, and there were about fifty more scattered about the surrounding country. An encampment of one hundred Indians was near at hand. Worthington selected lots of large size for himself and his brother-in-law, Edward Tiffin, and after constructing two comfortable dwellings—the first that had shingle roofs and glass windows in the settlement—he returned to Virginia. Both Worthington and Tiffin were men of marked piety, and being in possession of slaves, and not being able to manumit them under the laws of Virginia, they determined to take them to the new free soil of Ohio and the northwest.

In the latter part of March Tiffin, Thomas and Robert Worthington, with their wives and children, and their negroes, left Berkeley county, Virginia, for their new homes. The ladies and children were in carriages, the gentlemen on horses; the male negroes were on foot, and their women and children on horseback. These, with pack-horses laden with household goods, even mirrors and domestic fowls in cages, made a long train, exciting great local interest on their departure, and attracting unusual attention in all the settlements and hamlets in the wilderness through which they moved. In about two weeks they reached Pittsburgh, without any accident by the way. There they embarked in "broad horns" on a full river, and floated peacefully and swiftly on its broad bosom, swaying from shore, amidst all the strangeness, and granduer and deep silence of the wilderness. They landed at the mouth of the Scioto, where Portsmouth now stands, and thence took their slow and tedious march through the unbroken and thick forest of the valley of the Scioto, guided only by the blazed path of earlier pioneers.

On the 27th day of April, 1798, they at last reached their destination, having been more than thirty days on the way. The whole community came out to welcome them, and to assist in the unloading of their train and the care of their wonderful stores. Such a cavalcade had never before been seen; so much refinement, intelligence and abundant possessions of useful and ornamental household goods had never before been found on the frontier. Worthington and Tiffin were both elected to the territorial legislature that met in Cincinnati in 1799.

The country was a vast forest, roamed over by savages and wild beasts. The settlements were few but rapidly increasing.

"Upon the banks of the Scioto there was a small hamlet of log houses, beautifully situated, which was called Chillicothe," says another writer.

Edward Tiffin would have made an accession of value to any settlement in the west. Here he selected his residence. He was a man of well cultivated mind, gentlemanly manners, a friendly spirit, and his conduct was guided, not only by high morality, but by true christian principles. He immediately identified himself with his new home and its enterprising people. He rapidly acquired a reputation, not only as a physician, but also for his virtues as a man.

An old friend says of him that "In his medical career he answered day and night, to the utmost of his ability, all professional calls, often enduring severe suffering from the inclemency of the weather, in long and fatiguing rides over wretched roads or by blazed paths, crossing swollen streams at dangerous fords, and with the full knowledge, often, that the patient was too poor to make him any remuneration."

As a surgeon and physician he stood in the front rank of the men of his time, and several instances are remembered that show how ready he was to employ the highest resources of the profession under sudden emergencies. On one occasion, while distant from home, a terrible accident made it necessary that an amputation of the leg should be

BIOGRAPHY OF GOVERNOR TIFFIN.

made. The Doctor was without instruments, yet he quickly contrived all that was necessary, performed the operation and saved the man's life.

Thus he was busily engaged until the fall of 1799. But it is very evident that his active mind was taking a wide range in public affairs; for the people, recognizing in him abilities other than professional, called upon him to serve them as a representative in the territorial legislature, which started him on his career in the political world.

That body met in Cincinnati on the 18th day of September, 1799, when that great city was but a collection of log cabins and a few small frame houses, "basking in the sun," under the protection of the guns of Fort Washington.

Judge Burnet, in his letters to the Ohio Historical Society, says of the Ross county delegation, that "They were not excelled in talent and energy by any other in the territory. She selected her strongest men; Worthington, Tiffin, Findley and Langham were qualified to exert an influence in any deliberate body, and they did not fail to employ it. They were natives of Virginia, except Tiffin, who was born in England and, it was said, came to this country as surgeon's mate in the army of Burgoyne." This latter statement, though generally believed, is not true, however. Tiffin was but eleven years old when Burgoyne surrendered.

The best proof of Dr. Tiffin's appreciation, is shown in the fact that he was unanimously elected speaker of that important and august body, and retained that position to the end of the territorial government.

He frequently took part in the debates, and more especially encountered Judge Sibley, of Detroit, whom Judge Burnet describes as a well educated and able lawyer, and possessed of large powers of mind. Tiffin was an impassioned debater, while Sibley was very cool and deliberate in his arguments. Many years afterwards Mr. Sibley visited Gov. Tiffin, and Mr. Samuel Williams, who was often present while they talked over the exciting scenes of their legislative career, says that Dr. Tiffin remarked at one time, "In our debates, Mr. Sibley, I wished a thousand times that I could have the same calm, philosophic and imperturbable spirit which you possessed; I saw and felt the advantage it gave you in debate." "And I," laughingly replied the Judge, "well remember, Doctor, how often I wished that I could infuse into my remarks the same ardor of feeling which you displayed in your speeches."

In the autumn of 1802, at the election of delegates to a convention to form a constitution for the new state to be called Ohio, Tiffin, Worthington and Massie were elected from Ross county.

The convention met in Chillicothe in November following, and Edward Tiffin was chosen president. Here his intelligence, fairness and readiness in decision, united to most courteous manners, elevated him so much in the estimation of that body of able men, that he was brought forward, at the conclusion of the business before the convention, as the candidate for governor. He was elected in January, 1803, without opposition, receiving 4565 votes. In October, 1805, he was re-elected unanimously, receiving 4783 votes. He declined to be a candidate for a third term.

His state papers are brief, but clear in their suggestions for the enactment of all those measures that would open roads, develop agricultural and mineral resources, advance education, protect the frontier and favor immigration. The highest proof of his qualifications and executive abilities, are his repeated unanimous elections.

The most notable feature of his gubernatorial career was the arrest of the Burr-Blennerhasset expedition. In the latter part of 1806, Aaron Burr collected numerous boats and quantities of stores in the neighborhood of Blennerhasset Island, below Marietta. Governor Tiffin, learning that the expedition was ready to sail, dispatched a courier to the commandant at Marietta, and directed him to occupy a position below the island, where with a field battery they could command the channel. Burr, seeing that his plans were discovered and knowing the impossibility of running the blockade, abandoned the expedition and fled.

The press of the eastern states lauded Gov. Tiffin for his prompt and successful destruction of the nefarious scheme, and President Jefferson, in his letter to the Ohio legislature, February 2, 1807, commends the Governor for his promptness and energy in destroying the expedition. [SEE APPENDIX.]

At the expiration of his term of office, in 1807, Governor Tiffin was elected United States Senator and took his seat in December, his credentials being presented by John Adams.

The annals of Congress show that he was constantly in his place, and a member of important committees; indeed, by a special vote of the Senate he was added to the committee on fortifications and public defences. The war feeling was rising every day, stimulated by the aggressions of England, whose men-of-war lay in Hampton Roads, and in fact patrolled the lower Chesapeake, searching our merchantmen for their seamen.

His career as governor of Ohio was characterized by wise statesmanship and great efforts in developing the vast resources of the young state. So were his efforts in the Senate of the United States marked by his tireless energy and wonderful perseverance. In this enlarged sphere of power he did very much to promote the interests of Ohio. Public lands were surveyed, new measures for the transportation of the mails were organized, and the navigation of the Ohio river was much improved.

The death of his wife, in 1808, so overwhelmed Gov. Tiffin that he determined to abandon public life, and therefore, at the close of the session in March, 1809, he resigned.

On his return to Ohio he settled on his farm and devoted himself to agriculture. But he was not allowed by his fellow citizens to give up his public career entirely, for at the fall election he was elected to the legislature; he was unanimously chosen speaker of the House, and so he continued to act for several sessions following. A former citizen of Chillicothe writes of him, that he gave great satisfaction as speaker, by his perfect familiarity with its duties, and the promptness and correctness of his decisions.

In the meanwhile Gov. Tiffin had resumed his practice and married again; his second wife being Miss Mary Porter, from Delaware, whose family had recently settled in Ross county. She was a lady of rare personal beauty, quiet manners and exemplary piety.

During the first term of Mr. Madison's administration, Congress passed the act creating the office of Commissioner of the General Land Office, and Mr. Madison selected Gov. Tiffin to take charge of this important department. The appointment was wholly unsolicited and unexpected by him or any of his friends. The first intimation of his appointment was the receipt by mail of his commission, with a friendly letter from the President, and letters from Mr. Worthington and several old colleagues, urging him to accept the position. The gratifying manner in which it was tendered determined him to do so, and in a few days he started on horseback for Washington, a journey that then required two weeks.

The land affairs of the nation were in much confusion; the books, documents, maps, etc., were scattered in various bureaus of the State War and Treasury departments, and it required a great amount of perplexing labor to organize, methodically, the new department. But by the next meeting of congress all was arranged, and Commissioner Tiffin made the first comprehensive and statistical report to congress on the public lands—their quantity, location, and probable future value to the government. His labors, in part, are exhibited in the state papers. When the British army approached Washington, in 1814, and orders were given to hurry off the public papers, Mr. Tiffin was the only one who, by prompt action, carried all his department to a place of safety. The other departments lost many valuable papers in the conflagration ordered by the British general.

Nothing could wean Governor Tiffin from his Ohio home, and Mr. Madison gratified the wish of his heart by ordering an exchange of office with Josiah Meigs, who was then surveyor-general of the west, with his office in Cincinnati. Mr. Meigs was appointed commissioner of the general land office, and Gov. Tiffin was made surveyor-general, with the privilege of locating the office in Chillicothe. There he located, and continued at the head of this office of surveyor-general, during the remainder of the term of Mr. Madison, and through the succeeding administrations of Mr. Monroe and Mr. J. Q. Adams, and into that of General Jackson, up to within a few weeks of his death, when General Jackson appointed General Lytle, of Cincinnati, to supercede him. He received his successor on his death-bed, transferred to him his office, and died a few days thereafter.

There were several thousand dollars in his hands belonging to the United States, which were promptly handed over; and so were his books and papers, in the best of condition. This office had control over the vast realm known as the northwest, and the beautiful arrangement of the surveys of the public lands is greatly due to the sagacity and order that marked Gov. Tiffin's life.

Gov. Tiffin was reared in the pale of the Church of England, and after his removal to this country, he continued his relations to the same organization, which still existed almost as the state church of Virginia —for the American hierarchy had not yet been established. But the Tory character of many ministers during the revolution, and the almost abandoned state of so many churches, before the establishment of the Protestant Episcopal church, had so alienated the people from its communion, that a greater opportunity was offered for the propagation of the Methodist doctrines and usages. The unusual zeal and fervid manner of the new preachers, excited universal attention, and great religious excitement and inquiry prevailed. The great Missionary Bishop, Francis Asbury, traveled far and wide in the states and territories, to the remotest settlements, preaching with great eloquence and power— organizing societies and consecrating ministers.

Dr. Tiffin and his wife united with the society that was organized at Charlestown, Virginia, in 1790. There the Doctor was consecrated by

Asbury as a lay preacher, and during all his subsequent political life, he continued, to some extent, to exercise the functions of that office. Upon his removal to Ohio, he regularly performed ministerial duties in the new settlements. He did this intelligently, and without ostentation, and his catholic sentiments won for him the respect of all parties. Whenever the Episcopal church in Chillicothe was without a rector, he was called to read the service and a sermon from some established collection.

In the infancy of society, men of ability have often been called upon to perform very varied functions in civil and moral affairs. The statesman, the warrior, the philosopher, have all acted the part of priests to the edification of communities and states. In the wild state of the frontier at the beginning of this century, the preservation of the religious sentiments of the people was as much the duty of the leading men of the day, as any other work they could perform, whilst laying the foundations of the state, and this man, so distinguished in position and place in those times, was not ashamed to celebrate high religious services.

The last years of the Governor's life were but little diversified by incidents. He withdrew from the regular practice of medicine upon his appointment as commissioner in 1812; but after his return to Chillicothe, in 1814, he dispensed advice and medicine from his residence, gratuitously to the poor, and to many of his former patients, who still insisted upon consulting him. But his own health began to give way about 1820, and he suffered from a most distressing complaint.

On Sabbath evening, August 9, 1829, in his old home in Chillicothe, he died. His faithful old friend, Williams, says that: "He had long been sensible of his approaching end, and contemplated the solemn event, not only with calm complacency, but with a joyful anticipation of heavenly rest. He retained his full reason to the last, and gently sank away."

In stature, Doctor Tiffin was about five feet six inches high. His head was large; his face, English in type, was full and florid, with regular, prominent features. His countenance was expressive, especially when in animated conversation. He was particularly remarkable for the activity and quickness of his movements, and the prompt manner in which he discharged his duties. Dr. Monnet used to say that what Dr. Tiffin could not do quickly, he could not do at all. Nothing was put off for to-morrow that could be done to-day.

As a public officer, his accounts were always kept ready for settlement. Every dollar that came to his hands was promptly accounted for. His integrity was never questioned. While he managed his own affairs with prudence, he did not accumulate great wealth, as he might have done, but yet he never suffered any worldly embarrassment. He lived well, and in harmony with his position in society, but always within his income. He was hospitable, and in the days of his health, many of the most distinguished personages of the country enjoyed the hospitality of his board. His beautiful home was embellished by his refined taste. His earnest piety was an important element in promoting the best interest of his adopted town and country.

Gov. Tiffin left his widow and children in independent circumstances. Mrs. Tiffin died in 1827. They left five children, already mentioned.

Politically, Governor Tiffin was of the Jeffersonian school—the old Republican party; but for many years preceding his death, was not conspicuous as a politician. He was an intimate friend of Mr. Madison, and named one of his daughters after him.

Devoting all his time and his talents to the interest of the state, he very much neglected his own private affairs. But for this, he would unquestionably have accumulated a large fortune. His patriotism, however, was of a kind with that of the great men and statesmen of his day. "Everything for country—nothing for self." What a change has come over the minds of the leading men of these degenerate days! A reverse element seems to have set in upon the ebb and flow of American politics. "Everything for self, nothing for the country," seems to be the watchword of the hour. The men who pledged their lives, their property, and their sacred honors for country and freedom, are dead, but their sons and grand-children are here, and have not these inherited a part of the unselfish love of country that made their fathers great in the eyes of the world?

Col. Allen Latham, of Ross county, an intimate friend of Gov. Tiffin, furnished Dr. Comegys with the following items about the Governor, which the Doctor was so kind as to place at my disposal:

NINE MILE FARM, May 23, 1869.

DEAR SIR:—

At our last meeting you expressed a desire that I would write out my testimony in regard to that good old gentleman, your wife's father.

This I have done with pleasure, but very hastily, having very few papers to refer to and never seen any biographical notice of him.

His life is so completely identified with the early history of our state, that by proper industry a very interesting book might be written of him. The old journals and newspapers of that date are very hard to obtain, and I know of no perfect set at Columbus or elsewhere.

I have, perhaps, as many as any other individual, but they are in a great confusion. Yours, Truly,

DR. C. G. COMEGYS, Cincinnati, O. ALLEN LATHAM.

BIOGRAPHY OF GOVERNOR TIFFIN.

Doctor Edward Tiffin was Speaker of the House of Representatives of the first territorial Legislature northwest of the Ohio river, in the year 1801 and 1802. Robert Oliver was President of the Council, and General Arthur St. Clair was Governor of the Territory. Charles Willing Bird was Secretary of State.

He was president of the state convention that formed the constitution of the state of Ohio, which was adopted at Chillicothe Nov. 29, 1802. Thomas Scott was secretary of the convention.

He was elected the first Governor of Ohio, after the adoption of the constitution, and sworn in on the 3d day of March, 1803, and continued Governor until he was made Senator.

He was Senator from Ohio, in the Senate of the United States, from 1807 to 1809.

He was Speaker of the House of Representatives of Ohio in 1809-10, and in 1810-11. Thomas A. Hind and Ralph Osborn were Clerks.

He was appointed Commissioner of the General Land Office of the United States about 1812.

He was appointed Surveyor General of the United States public lands northwest of the Ohio river, when he returned to Chillicothe and held that office until 1829, in which year the office was removed to Cincinnati and General William Lytle was appointed by General Jackson, the Doctor being a friend of Mr. Adams.

Samuel Williams, Esq., a native of Pennsylvania, was the Doctor's chief clerk, and continued in that position to Robert C. Lytle and to Gen. Ezekiel S. Haynes, who are now all dead. Mr. Williams was an able clerk and an accomplished gentleman.

Joseph Tiffin, the Doctor's brother, Peter Patterson, Esq., Eleazer P. Kendrick, Esq., and W. Reynolds, the Doctor's son-in-law, were also clerks in the Doctor's office.

Mr. Kendrick is still living in Chillicothe, aged seventy-eight years on the 17th day of September last.

The Doctor was of medium height, say five feet eight or nine inches, rather portly, full faced, light hair, florid complexion and mild expression of countenance. His gestures were graceful, and he had a very musical voice.

The then young ladies and gentlemen on Sundays went to hear him read his selected sermons and the Episcopal service at the Masonic hall, after he had become quite infirm, and all regarded him as one of the best of men. He was one of the most accomplished gentlemen I had ever seen.

Notwithstanding his great suffering from a local complaint, which finally caused his death, he was very attentive to his public duties; and when most of our public men and early settlers were ruined by the revulsions consequent upon the war with England, he had the sagacity to convert his bank stock into real estate, although then at the highest prices, and thus saved an independence to his surviving family—a wife, a son and several daughters. If he had an enemy, I never knew him. He was a man of great learning, and an honor to his profession.

CHAPTER XIV.

SPENCER vs. HEDGES—THE BRUSH-DAM CASE—THE FIRST JURY TRIAL—BROUSE—THE SUGAR CAMP-INDIAN WAY OF COOKING COON-FOREST CULTURE—SCARCITY OF MONEY—WORK ON THE CANAL—JIGGERS AND CHICHA—THE MIAMI, DAYTON AND MICHIGAN, AND WABASH AND ERIE CANALS—CANAL TAX OF SENECA COUNTY.

SPENCER'S brush-dam, across the river, mentioned heretofore, is deserving of notice here for several reasons, viz: It was the first dam ever erected by man across this river, and of course was very crude. The water raised by it ran the first saw-mill on this river; it was located within the limits and near the center of the present city of Tiffin. It caused numerous contentions between Mr. Hedges and Mr. Spencer, the two rival proprietors of the two adjoining towns, that resulted in several knock-downs; its destruction became the cause of action in the first law-suit and the occasion for the first jury trial in the court of common pleas of this county, and finally it brought about the purchase of Fort Ball by Mr. Hedges, and the union of the two towns, forming the present young city of Tiffin. "Great oaks from little acorns grow."

Since the adoption of the present constitution of Ohio, and the consequent new code of practice, nearly thirty years ago, the young lawyers, as a general thing, have paid but little attention to the old common law pleadings and practice in vogue in former times, and old lawyers are gradually forgetting "the old way." The present age is the age of the "almighty dollar," and of "the reason why;" and the bar now seems to care as little about the former differences between debt, assumpsit, detinue, case, trespass, trespass on the case, trover, replevin, ejectment, etc., as does Young America generally about the times gone by. Extracts from the pleadings in this "brush dam case" are here added to refresh the memory of the reader concerning the mode of procedure at that time in like cases.

Jesse Spencer, the plaintiff, filed his præcipe for a summons to be issued against Josiah Hedges on the 22d day of September A. D. 1824.

THE BRUSH-DAM CASE.

The summons was served by A. Ingraham, sheriff, on the same day, by reading. Rudolphus Dickinson, the first lawyer that settled in this county, and who had located in Fort Ball, was the attorney for Mr. Spencer, and for want of any other lawyer here, Mr. Hedges was defended by Messrs. Parish, Parker and Coffinberry. Upon this summons there was a declaration filed by the plaintiff. The caption was in the usual form, and after stating that the said Hedges had been duly summoned to answer unto the said Jesse Spencer, in a plea of trespass, went on to charge as follows:

That the said Hedges, on the 1st day of May, A. D. 1823, and at divers other days and times between that day and before the commencement of this action, with force and arms, etc., broke and entered a certain close of the said Jesse Spencer, situate, lying and being in the township of Seneca, in the county of Seneca, aforesaid, and then and there pulled down, prosecuted and destroyed a great part, to-wit: forty perches of a certain mill-dam of the said Jesse Spencer, of great value, to-wit: of the value of two hundred dollars; and, also, then and there, tore down and dug up great quantities, to-wit: one thousand wagon loads of stone, from off the said close and dam of the said Jesse Spencer, to-wit: to the further value of three hundred dollars, and then and there took and carried away, and converted the same to his, the said Josiah Hedges', own use.

The second count ran thus, and is of interest to show where the dam was once located:

And, also, that the said Josiah Hedges, on the day and year last aforesaid, and on divers other days and times, etc., broke and entered another close of the said plaintiff. etc., situate and being, etc., abutting towards the west on that part of the Armstrong Reservation, so-called, which lies between a place forty poles north of the place called Camp Ball, and the south line of the said Armstrong Reservation, and abutting towards the east on the eastern bank of the Sandusky river, opposite the saw mill on said reservation. and then and there broke down, tore up, etc.

In the fourth count, the dam is located in these words:

Abutting on the western bank of the Sandusky river that lies between the southern section line of the said Armstrong Reservation and a place commonly called Camp Ball, and abutting towards the east, etc.

The fifth count charges the taking away of the stones, and the converting of them to Hedges' own use, and concludes by saying:

And other wrongs to the said Jesse Spencer then and there done, to the great damage of the said Jesse Spencer, and against the peace and dignity of the state of Ohio; whereupon the said Jesse Spencer says that he is injured, and has sustained damage to the amount of five hundred dollars, and thereupon he brings this suit.

Mr. Hedges in his answer denied "all and singular the premises," and defended the "wrongs and injuries," etc., and said that he was not guilty of the supposed trespass laid to his charge, etc., "and of this he puts himself upon the country, and the said plaintiff doth the like;" which means simply that he will submit this case to a jury. To this answer a written notice was attached "that the close in question was the property of the said Hedges, and that he had a legal right to do what he did."

The case was continued until the April term, 1825, when it was tried to the following jury, viz: James Mathers, Jesse Gale, John C. Donnel, William Foncannon, Smith Kentfield, Peter Yeaky, Ezekiel Sampson, Samuel Scothorn, James Cutright, Ezra Brown, Jacob S. Jennings, Elisha Clark, "who upon their oaths do say that the said defendant is guilty in manner and form, etc., and we do assess the plaintiff's damages by reason thereof, at $8.00. The court entered up judgment for that sum. The costs were $26.75. This ended the first law-suit and jury trial in Seneca common pleas.

The point upon which Mr. Hedges was found guilty, was the fact that, at the time the dam was erected, the land along the right bank of the river belonged to the United States; had not then been surveyed nor offered for sale, and Mr. Hedges was not then the owner of the same.

Mr. Ingraham, who had been appointed sheriff, gave bond in the sum of $5,000, and Rollin Moler, Michael Schaul, Joseph Pool and John A Rosenberger were his sureties.

At this court, William Doyle, from Ireland, was the first person naturalized in this county.

Mr. Spencer became so badly involved in numerous lawsuits that the executions against him seem to have swallowed up all his means.

Whenever the weather in winter would permit of out-door work, there was always enough of it to do. Great trouble was often experienced by those that had cattle to take care of. When the winters were open and mild, as was very usual then, the cattle could find grass in the woods and along the banks of the streams; but in very cold winters, with much snow, and no hay on hand, the poor animals suffered very much, and were compelled to subsist on "browse," which was the tender ends of tree-tops. The trees had to be cut down for that purpose, and while this labor had to be repeated every day during the frozen season, it was still very hard living for the cattle. Many died from exhaustion before spring.

Now was also the time to prepare for "sugar making." For want of buckets, or other vessels to catch the sugar-water, troughs were made of various lengths and widths, from poplar, ash, sugar, elm, or other wood, by chopping the blocks of the required length, and splitting them once in two. A dish was then chopped into the flat side. Some of the largest of these troughs would hold from one to two gallons. A hole was bored into the sugar-tree some three feet above the ground, and a "spile," made of a one-year's growth from an elder bush, and with the pith taken out, was driven into the hole, in the tree, to conduct the sap into the trough. The sap was boiled down in big iron kettles suspended on a pole, held up by two forks fixed in the ground at a convenient place in the sugar-camp. The time for this work generally commenced in February, when the frost began to come out of the ground and the sap to ascend. It often lasted away towards the latter part of March, when the ground froze hard during the night and thawed out the following day. This freezing and thawing time was considered good sugar weather. As the sap was boiling down, the impurities were nicely skimmed off, and when the sirup became so thick as to commence granulating, it was stirred with a paddle while the fire was allowed to go down. Those that preferred the sugar in cake form poured the thick sirup into tin pans, when it became hard in a short time.

The first few weeks of the sugar season made the best sugar. Towards the last of the run the sirup refused to granulate, and was preserved in that form and answered the purpose of molasses. It is decidedly the richest sweet that nature produces. Reader! Did you ever eat corn-pone with maple molasses? If you did, there is no use in saying anything further to you about it. Pone could only be baked in a Dutch oven, which was an iron kettle, flat at the bottom, with a flat, heavy iron lid. The oven was placed on coals and the lid covered with coals. It was of great use, and never had an equal.

The Indians learned the art of making sugar from the white people, but how to be cleanly about it, they never would learn. It required a very strong appetite to eat their sugar. Those who never saw them make it got along with it much easier.

Whenever their sirup was about ready to granulate they would have a raccoon ready to cook, which they would put into the sirup, hair, skin, entrails and all. The coon would get "done" in a short time, when he was taken out and allowed to cool off enough to be handled. A crust of sugar came away with the hair and skin. The flesh seemed nicely done, but the sugar—well!

Settlers that had large sugar-camps built little cabins in the woods, to put their troughs into in order to preserve them. Others set up the troughs on end and leaned them against the tree, dish side inward.

The writer has seen good use made of some of these sugar-troughs in seasons of the year when sugar-water did not run. They were rocked in the cabin of the settler with a sugar lump, in the shape of a young "Buckeye," in them. The little fellow was thus not "rocked in the cradle of the deep," but in a substitute much safer. Many noble men and women, now living in Ohio, were raised and rocked in these sugar-trough cradles; and the mother's lullaby, in the cabin, sounded as sweet as it ever did in the palatial mansion, with plate-glass windows and gilded door-knobs.

It was among the "rural felicities" to see a whole family employed in the sugar-camp on a pleasant day, some carrying sugar-water, some skimming the sirup, others preparing wood, each employed at something; and when night came on, the work was so reduced as to require but little, if any, attention before the next morning. Some of the neighbors would visit the camp, spend the evening and have a good chat. Neighbors seemed to think more of each other then than they do now; at least they visited each other oftener when the distance, the work and the weather would permit.

The time is fast approaching when sugar-making will be considered as a thing of the past, and the coming generation will not know what a sugar trough looked like. Our forests are passing away rapidly, and soon there will not be timber enough left to fence the fields or supply the demand for building and manufacturing purposes. On many farms in Seneca county, the little patches of woodland that are left, are already more valuable than the cleared land. Nobody makes calculations when there will not be wood enough in this county to answer the purposes of the family for cooking and heating, to say nothing about the timber with which to build houses and barns. Why not commence now to start a young forest? Take, say five or ten acres at a time, well fenced to keep out stock, on that part of a farm where the wood lot may be wanted, and plant with acorns, beech nuts, maple seed, or such other variety as may be desired. It will require no further care, and in a few years a young forest will gladden the heart of the owner. The one that plants the patch will not live to see large trees grow there himself, but ere long the purchaser will pay more for a farm that has a young wood lot growing up on it, than he will for one without it.

No attempt will be made to picture to the mind of anybody, the vexations and troubles inflicted upon the frontier by the then great scarcity of money. There was very little to be had for any purpose.

SCARCITY OF MONEY.

Barter and trade was the order of the day, and while this exchange was all right in some respects, it would not answer for others. Taxes could not be paid in that way, and the merchant, after waiting a long time, had to have cash with which to meet his bills in New York or Philadelphia. When some pioneer merchant brought on articles that were indispensable for the household, or for farming purposes, there was no money to buy them with. Often, long credits furnished no relief. When a man had anything to sell, it found no market for money. He could trade it away for something he wanted from his neighbor. If a man wanted an article from another, and had nothing to exchange for it, he paid in work by the day, or agreed to clear so many acres of land for the article. Men bought their cows, their horses or hogs, in that way. Corn and wheat were hauled by ox teams, generally to Mansfield or Portland, now Sandusky City, to be sold for money. Wheat raised under the difficulties described in a former chapter, hauled to a market, from forty to sixty miles away, where it could be sold for only thirty cents a bushel in cash, or for three shillings in trade, was not an article on which farmers became rich very fast. Portland was the principal market for wheat, and many a load of wheat was exchanged there, at three shillings a bushel, for salt at five dollars a barrel, when it took about one week to make the trip.

Getting grinding done at the few mills there were then in the country, was attended with equally great hardship. After the City Mill, now in the first ward of Tiffin, was put up, farmers from Crawford, Hancock and Marion counties came here to get their grists ground, and at times, fifteen, twenty, or more teams waited their turn and camped out a whole week, with the family at home on small allowance, or probably with no bread at all.

To relate all the troubles and inconveniences that pioneer life was subject to, would require volumes, and some of them, only, are here alluded to. The rest must be left to inference, which to most any mind should be easy.

The hardest of all the hardships that the frontier settler had to contend with, was the malarious diseases everybody was subject to. The ground was covered with water and decaying vegetable matter; the river and the creeks were clogged with drift-wood and fallen timbers; beaver dams set the water back, thereby covering large tracts of land, while cat-swamps (as they were then called) were very numerous. There were terrible thickets and jungles of brush-bushes of various kinds growing on rich, boggy soil.

The forest held the moist air with a wonderful tenacity, and the miasma, produced by the heat of a summer's sun, and thus held in the humid air and breathed constantly, tended to corrupt the blood and derange the functions of the liver. Fever and ague, and bilious fevers were very common, and men were often seen standing on the street on a hot summer day, pale as death, with overcoats on, buttoned up to the chin, their hands in their pockets and shaking so that their voices trembled. The chill was always followed by a fever, and when that was passed, the patient was all right again until next day, or day after. The chills returned again at regular intervals, either next day, or every other day. · People seemed to get used to them, and some were not reduced much by the chills, while others, and especially people from Europe, suffered very much more from these diseases. In general, those of European suffered more than those of American birth. Many a stout, robust man was reduced to a walking skeleton in a short time. Yet this fever and ague was not considered dangerous to life. It was exceedingly troublesome, nevertheless, especially when whole families were taken with it at the same time. It was a sad scene to come, or be called, into a house and see a large family, young and old, in their beds, some shaking, and others burning with fever, and not one of them able to help the other to a cup of water. The only case where death ensued from these chills that ever came to the notice of the writer, was that of an old German who lived on South Jefferson street, in Tiffin, and who died shaking in his chair.

The most serious aspect of these malarious diseases, however, was the various bilious fevers that often defied the skill and care of the physicians, and frequently proved fatal. The terrible heat in fever, the parched tongue, the delirium, followed by extreme prostration; and then the remedies, such as calomel, ipecac, jalap, Peruvian bark, quinine, castor oil, etc., etc., all—diseases and remedies—were simply horrible. Some summers were more sickly than others, but for many years, and until the country became partially cleared up, there was no summer without this terrible visitation.

Oh! how the people waited and prayed for the coming of fall, and for the first sharp frost. A good black frost, that killed the leaves and made the grass crash under your feet, generally put a stop to this monster phantom. The air became purer and more bracing, and it was very encouraging to see, in the faces of all, returning hope and cheer.

Whether the practice of medicine, as a science, has made the progress that its devotees claim for it, will not be argued here; but one thing must certainly be admitted, viz: that a great change has come over the dreams of the practitioner. The poor patient is now allowed the free use of water. This the practice, forty or fifty years ago, absolutely refused. It was simply cruel to let the poor sufferer burn up with fever, calling for water to relieve him, and have it refused because the doctor would not allow it. It would not do; it might hurt him, might salivate him, and all that sort of nonsense. But they would blister, bleed and cup him, while his physical powers gradually broke down. What a change a few years have brought about! By the art of preserving ice for use in summer, the article has found its way into the sick chamber, where it has proven both a luxury and a blessing. Patients are now allowed all the fresh water they want, and fresh air, also, without fear of being salivated.

One feature in cases of shaking ague, which was not very common, however, and which seems now like a strange phenomenon, should be mentioned here. It was called the "hungry shakes" by some. As soon as the chills began to creep down the back, the bones to ache and the shivering to commence, the patient was taken with a ravenous appetite, and could eat with a wonderful rapacity, while he often shook so hard that the victuals fell from his knife, fork or spoon as he tried to pass them to his mouth. It made bad worse, however, for the fever that followed such a shake, after eating, seemed to be more severe and the headache more distressing.

Thompson township, on account of the openings and purer atmosphere, suffered less with this plague than any other township in the county. In all the other portions of Seneca county the situation in this regard was about the same.

It was in these trying times that thousands of men were compelled, not by avarice, but by absolute, stern necessity, to find employment on the canals, the only public works then in the state, and the only places where money could be had for labor. It was a sad parting, when the father left his little ones in the care and charge of the pioneer mother, to go sixty miles or more from home and be gone for months at a time, to work on the canal and himself become subject to these malarious diseases. They were even more prevalent along the canals than elsewhere, because they were constructed through dense forests, along the most sluggish streams, and on the most level ground, in order to avoid the expenditure which locks would require and the delay they would naturally cause in the moving of traffic.

Log huts were built on the highest ground near the line of the survey, which were occupied as a headquarters for lodging, cooking, etc. They were as rough as they were temporary, and the contractor or the sub-contractor would spend no more money for the comfort of his men than was absolutely necessary. Beds and bedding were of the same character. With a temporary change of clothing, the men brought their blankets with them. A woolen blanket was a better protection against the mosquitoes at night than any other covering. These pests in warm weather formed into a sort of a cloud around their victims, day and night.

It is scarcely possible to find a place anywhere in the world better fitted to produce malarious diseases, than was the country at that time along the line of the Dayton and Michigan canal, and especially along the Auglaize, the Maumee and the Wabash in Indiana.

As the work progressed and the distance to and from the cabins increased, they were abandoned and new ones constructed near the works, in the same crude way. Whisky was cheap in those days, and in very common use. They had no temperance societies then, and every man was constituted a committee of one to mind his own business; nor had chemistry discovered the art of stretching or adulterating the article with poisonous drugs. Men who could afford the expense kept whisky by the barrel in their houses, and it was simply in conformity with the general idea of hospitality, then in vogue, to have the bottle and glass set before one when visiting a neighbor. There were then less drunkards, in proportion to the number of inhabitants, than there are now, and the pimpled cheek bones and rum-blossomed nose, so prevalent now among those who drink whisky habitually, were not seen then.

Very often men had to work standing in water all day. There were no rubber boots to be had then, and to avoid getting sick and to keep away the "shakes," it was thought necessary, by both employer and employes, that men should drink whisky so many times a day. In conformity with this generally conceded necessity, it was made a part of the contract with the laborer that, in addition to his pay, he should receive his glass of whisky so many times a day—three times, generally. The "boss" kept a barrel of it on hand, and if a man wanted more than his usual allowance he could have it by paying for it—twenty cents a gallon.

These whisky rations were called "jiggers," a very familiar term along the canals. I am not aware, however, that the whisky secured the object intended; I doubt it very much, for those that drank whisky became sick as well as those that did not. At times there were so many of the workmen sick in their cabins that less than half of them answered at roll-call.

It is a most wonderful fact, that at all times, among all races of men,

CHICHA—HOW MADE.

and in all countries, since the time of Noah, who "planted the first vine," people have had their beverages of some sort, liquors or other things that stupefied or intoxicated. For want of liquors they resorted to gums, opium or hasheesh, a gum produced from the exudations of the leaves and stocks of hemp, the smoking of which not only creates a deadly stupor, but fills the bewildered mind with visions of brilliant and supernatural scenes, while it breaks down and prostrates the nervous system of the poor victim, and gradually destroys life. [See Bayard Taylor's Travels in India.]

Along the river systems of South America, along the Orinoco, the Rio Negro, the Itenez, the Madeira, the Rio Beni, the Magdalena, the Matre de Dios and other tributaries of the Amazon; and up the mountains from Parma, through Ayacucho, Cazco, Cochabamba, along the lakes Titticaca and Ohuro, throughout the districts of Yungas, Yuracares and Magos, along the foot of the Illimani and Sorata, the Indians inhabiting these regions, nearly all in abject poverty and ignorance, and so degraded that their type is scarcely traceable, yet all claiming to have been descended from the once noble Incas, make a beverage of their own that beats them all. Of late years, the mongrel whites —Peruvians, Brazillians, Spaniards and Portuguese—that mingled and inter-married with them, have also adopted this revolting South American vice.

Along these rivers and mountains, to a certain degree of altitude, is found a bush with very thick, fleshy leaves, resembling in size and color the laurel. These leaves are gathered when they are most juicy and carried to the hut, where the family, young and old, chew them fine and spit them into some vat or vessel fixed for that purpose; when it is full another is filled in like manner, and so on, until the crop runs out or the requisite quantity is secured. These vats are allowed to stand undisturbed for several weeks, for the fermentation to proceed, and when that ceases and some of the elements have been precipitated and others have accumulated on top, the liquor becomes clear and is then drawn off into jugs of earthen ware. In addition to the home consumption of this liquor, a certain quantity is required for tithe in kind, or for taxes from the sale of it, so that each family will know how much to produce. This liquor is called "chicha," (pronounced "chicka,") and the bush that furnishes the leaf is called the "chicha bush." Whether the bush gives the name to the liquor, or the liquor to the bush, does not appear, nor is it very material.

When chicha making is over, the Indians of certain tribes are not allowed to touch a drop of it until the chief has his drink of it first.

On a certain day each family brings a certain quantity of the liquor to the council-house, where, after a short ceremony over it, the chief takes his fill; then the next in authority, then the next, and so on, until the officers are all supplied. Then the common rabble fall in, and a general drunk ends the festivities.

Of late years, since maize came into use in South America, a chicha is made by masticating the grains in the same way as the leaf, but the liquor made from corn is said to be inferior to that made from the chicha bush; both, however, make people most beastly drunk. Think of it— a lot of old squaws, with decayed teeth, chewing leaves or corn and spitting them into a tub to make liquor of! The saliva produces the sugar that foments into alcohol and assists the work of fermentation. [See Humboldt's Travels in South America, and Herndon and Gibbons' Explorations of the Sources of the Amazon. The writer's mind recurred to this circumstance when he thought as to the probable origin of the word "jiggers," and reflected whether or not the word "chicha" might possibly have become vulgarized or Americanized into this "jigger."]

The work on the canals commenced as early in the spring as the weather would permit and the frost was out of the ground, and was prosecuted with a will until along in July, when the laborers broke down with bilious diseases, and the work had to be abandoned in consequence, until after the few first early frosts in the fall, when it was again resumed and pushed forward into the winter.

During the time the father was at work on the canal and the mother with her little ones alone in the cabin, miles away from neighbors, no doctor to call to assistance in case of sickness, no one to counsel or help in time of need, the trials and incidents of such a life lead the contemplative mind to sad and serious meditation. Let us try to forget scenes like these, for they will never occur again.

A short history of the Ohio canal system might be made interesting here, would space only permit; but to give the reader a bird's-eye view of it, its origin, rise and progress, its final triumph, the excitement it produced in the political world, the success and defeat of men aspiring to office depending upon the way they stood on the canal question, the railroads finally driving the canals into the back ground, etc., would make a small volume by itself. A short synopsis, and extracts from reports and papers pertaining to the history of the Ohio canals, must here suffice.

"In any true history of the early settlements and material progress of the Maumee valley, the two important canals—the Wabash and Erie, and the

CANAL SYSTEM.

Miami and Erie—which unite near Defiance, and thence reach the Maumee bay by a common trunk, must fill an important page," says Knapp. "However valuable may be the railroads built long afterwards, it is still true that the canals have prepared the way, settled the country, and laid the foundation of its cities, of which Toledo at the mouth, and Fort Wayne at the source of the river, are the chief."

In 1816, Hon. Ethan Allen Brown, of Cincinnati, had a correspondence with DeWitt Clinton, who was then the head of the board of canal commissioners of the state of New York, upon the subject of the proposed canal to connect the waters of lake Erie with those of the Hudson river.

The legislature of Ohio, in February, 1820, passed an act under which three commissioners were appointed to locate a route for a navigable canal between lake Erie and the Ohio river. The act also proposed to ask of Congress a grant of one or two millions of acres of land for the purpose, but nothing was accomplished under this act.

In his inaugural address, December 14, 1818, Gov. Brown says:

If we would raise the character of our state by increasing industry, and our resources, it seems necessary to improve the internal communications and open a cheaper way to market for the surplus produce of a large portion of our fertile country.

During the next three succeeding sessions attention was called to the subject of canals.

In 1822, Micajah T. Williams, of Cincinnati, a representative from Hamilton county, in his report as chairman of a committee, to whom the matter had been referred, discussed elaborately the propriety of connecting lake Erie with the Ohio river. A short extract from that report will show the condition of the state and its industries at that period:

It is a well established fact, that man has not yet devised a mode of conveyance so safe, easy and cheap, as canal navigation; and although the advantage of easy and expeditious transportation is not likely to be perceived when prices are high and trade most profitable, yet the truth is familiar to every person of observation, that the enormous expense of land carriage has frequently consumed nearly, and sometimes quite, the whole price of provisions at the place of embarkation for a distant market. This is essentially the case in relation to all commodities of a cheap and bulky nature, most of which will not bear a land transportation many miles and consequently are rendered of no value to the farmer, and are suffered to waste on his hands. The merchant who engages in the exportation of the produce of the country, finding it a losing commerce, abandons it or is ruined; and crops in the finest and most productive part of the state are left to waste on the fields that produced them, or to be distilled to poison and brutalize society.

On the 31st day of January, 1822, a bill was passed appointing Benj. Tappan, Alfred Kelley, Thomas Worthington, Jeremiah Morrow, Isaac Miner and Ebenezer Buckingham, Jr. commissioners, "Whose duty it shall be to cause such examinations, surveys and estimates to be made by engineers, etc., to ascertain the practicability of connecting lake Erie with the Ohio river, from the Ohio river to the Maumee river by a canal through the following routes, viz :—from Sandusky bay to the Ohio river, from the Ohio river to the Maumee river, from the lake to the river aforesaid by the sources of the Cuyahoga and Black rivers and the Muskingum river, and from the lake to the sources of Grand and Mahoning rivers to the Ohio river."

On the 27th day of January, 1823, a supplementary act was passed with a view of connecting the lake with the Ohio river, and also of ascertaining whether a loan could be secured for that purpose, thus making in fact the canal commissioners also the fund commissioners.

DeWitt Clinton, in a letter to Williams, says :

The state of Ohio, from the fertility of its soil, the benignity of its climate and its geographical position, must always contain a dense population, and the products and consumptions of its inhabitants must forever form a lucrative and extensive inland trade, exciting the powers of productive industry and communicating aliment and energy to extend commerce. But when we consider that this canal will open a way to the great rivers that fall into the Mississippi; that it will be felt, not only in the immense valley of that river, but as far west as the Rocky mountains and the borders of Mexico; and that it will communicate with our great inland seas, and their tributary rivers : with the ocean in various routes; and with the most productive regions of America, there can be no question respecting the blessings that it will produce, the riches it will create, and the energies it will call into activity.

In 1824, a survey was made for a canal from Cincinnati along the Miami valley to the Maumee river at Defiance, thence along the left bank of the same to the bay, and an estimate thereof reported to the legislature. Mr. Williams directed the survey and for ten years thereafter was the leading spirit of the enterprise. Samuel Forrer was the head of the corps of engineers. More than one-half of this route was through a dense forest ; there was not one house between St. Marys and the mouth of the Auglaize.

On the 28th day of May, 1828, the President of the United States approved an act of Congress, granting to Ohio a quantity of land equal to one-half of five sections in width on each side of the canal, from Dayton to the Maumee river at the mouth of the Auglaize, reserving each alternate section to the United States, and the lands thus reserved were not to be sold for less than two dollars and fifty cents per acre.

The summit division was put under contract in 1831-2, and a loan of $200,000 authorized on the credit of the state. Jeremiah Sullivan, Nicholas McCarty and William C. Linton were appointed the first board of fund commissioners of the state.

Just in time to save the land grant from dying under the limitation by Congress, the first ground was broken with great ceremonies on the 1st day of March, 1832, at Fort Wayne, then a little town of about four hundred inhabitants. At the close of that year only $4,180.00 worth of work had been done. The division uniting the waters of the Wabash with those of lake Erie was completed in 1835, and on the 4th day of July in that year the first boat passed through it. This was the beginning of canal navigation in all that vast region lying north of Dayton and west of Cleveland. Its cost was $7,177 per mile.

Canals in other parts of the state were agitated and prosecuted during this time, but all these works suffered from the same two great causes, viz: sickness and want of funds. The Ohio portion of the Wabash and Erie canal was finally finished in 1843, and at the celebration of the event, on the Fouth of July of that year, at Fort Wayne, Lewis Cass delivered the oration. The Miami canal extension, now called "Miami and Erie," was opened for business in 1845. This completed the continuous line between Maumee bay and the Ohio river at Cincinnati.

For the history of other canals the curious reader is referred to the proceedings pertaining to the Hocking canal, the Walhonding canal, the Muskingum improvement, the Ohio and Pennsylvania canal, the Mohickon branch, etc.

Seneca county commenced paying taxes in 1826, and among her first assessments was a canal tax, which was continued and increased for many years. This chapter will close with a statement of the amount of taxes Seneca county paid to the treasurer of the state, as canal tax, from 1826 to 1835, both inclusive:

In 1826, $14.97.7; 1827, $147.49.6; 1828, $191.65.2; 1829, $310.88.1; 1830, $400.83.6; 1831, $470.92.3; 1832, $553.64.6; 1833, $466.14.0; 1834, $282.88.7; 1835, $167.77.8.

CHAPTER XV.

SANDUSKY RIVER—THE WOLF CREEKS—SILVER CREEK—HONEY CREEK—ROCKY CREEK—SPICER CREEK—MORRISON CREEK—SUGAR CREEK—GENERAL DRAINAGE—TOPOGRAPHY AND GEOLOGY OF THE COUNTY.

A HISTORY of Seneca county would be an utter failure without a record of the nature of its soils, its sub-stratum, its drainage, etc. It requires a mind learned in the science of geology to enable a person to speak intelligently on the subject. Fully conscious of his inability in that respect, the writer has drawn largely upon the "Report of the Geological Survey of Ohio," made under a law passed by the General Assembly of Ohio, in March, 1869, by which the Governor of Ohio was authorized, by and with the advice of the Senate, to appoint a chief geologist, and one or more assistants, not exceeding three in number, who were to constitute a geological corps, and whose duty was to make a complete and thorough geological, agricultural and mineralogical survey of each and every county in the state. The second section of said act defines the object of said survey, viz: To ascertain the geological structure of the state, including the dip, magnitude, number, order and relative position of the several strata, their richness in coals, clays, ores, mineral waters and manures, building stone and other useful material. To secure accurate chemical analyses of the soils, etc. To ascertain the local causes that produce variations of climate in the different sections of the state. To collect specimens of rocks, ores, soils, fossils, organic remains, etc., and to make report of same, etc.

The expenses were paid by the state, and considerable sums must yet be appropriated to finish the work, and to pay for the printing and binding of the unfinished reports.

The survey was to commence about the first of June, following. J. S. Newberry was appointed chief geologist, and E. B. Andrews, Edward Orton, and J. H. Klippart assistant geologists. Some ten other persons were appointed as local assistants.

These reports are, and will be, published in limited numbers only,

LATITUDE—LONGITUDE—DRAINAGE. 223.

and but few of the readers of these pages will be the owners of them. They will be very large and bulky, and require a considerable research to find the material desired for our purpose. The friendly reader will long since have been called to his fathers, before the state of Ohio will again appoint a corps of geological engineers to make a survey of Ohio at an expense of hundreds of thousands of dollars. That part of these reports referring to the agricultural department, has not been distributed as yet.

In view of all these facts, the larger portion of this chapter is devoted to this interesting subject. Let us look at Seneca county from this standpoint.

It is stated in a former chapter (Chap. X.) that the base line forming the south line of Seneca county is the forty-first degree north latitude. Find on the map section thirty-one in Eden township, and run your finger up to section nineteen in Clinton, due north, which is seven miles from the base line, and you have the latitude of Tiffin, 40°, 7' N. of the equator, and longitude 6°, 8' W. of Washington. Tiffin is therefore 86 miles north of Columbus, and 34 miles southwest of Sandusky. There are just twelve ranges between the west line of Seneca and the State of Indiana, being 6x12=72 miles.

Seneca county is bounded on the south by the counties of Crawford and Wyandot; on the west by Hancock and Wood; on the north by Sandusky, and on the east by Huron. Its length and width are described in Chap. X. Its shape is a rectangular parallelogram, containing fifteen townships.

NATURAL DRAINAGE.

The Sandusky river, running through the county from the south to the north, divides it into two nearly equal parts, and is the principal stream in the county. The left bank of the river, in its general bearing, is higher ground than the east, or right bank, and the country west of the river descends almost immediately as it recedes from the river, shedding the waters from near the river bank into the east branch of Wolf creek. The result is, that there is not a single stream or creek that enters the left bank of the Sandusky river in Seneca county. A little brooklet that runs a short time after a rain, called Bell's run, enters at the Spooner farm, a short distance south of Lugenbeel's dam (formerly so called). Tymochtee and Wolf creeks are tributaries of the Sandusky at its left bank, but the former enters the river in Wyandot, and the latter in Sandusky county.

The river, in its northward course, enters section 36 in Seneca township, and immediately turns into section 31 in Eden, and returns again into Seneca, where it keeps on its course along the eastern tier of sections in Seneca township, and enters section 36 in Hopewell; taking a straight northward direction, it turns northeastwardly and enters section 19 in Clinton, passes through Tiffin, runs through sections 17, 9 and 5 in Clinton, enters section 32 in Pleasant, where it makes many turns in all directions, and finally leaves the county in the northeast corner of section 5 in Pleasant.

The various branches of Wolf creek start near the southern line of the county, west of the river, the eastern branch running almost paralel with the river throughout the county. A short distance north of the north line of Seneca county the several branches of Wolf creek unite, and, taking a short turn eastwardly, immediately enter the river.

There seems to be a water shed all along the east line of the county of Seneca that sends its waters westward into the Sandusky. Honey creek and Rocky creek both run in a westerly direction about twelve miles, without taking into account their meanderings, when they run southwest about six miles, then turn northwest, and in that direction enter the river. Honey creek takes up Silver creek near the northeast corner of section 24 in Eden, from an easterly direction, and enters the Sandusky in section 36 in Hopewell. Rocky creek enters the river at Tiffin in section 19, in Clinton; Willow creek and Morrison creek flow into the Sandusky in section 17, in Clinton; Spicer creek mouths into the Sandusky in section 28 in Pleasant, and Sugar creek in section 22 of the same township. In this township two small brooks—rain water creeks—each about one mile long, enter the river from the left bank. Six creeks enter the river from the east, within fifteen miles from the base line. Thus it is seen that Seneca county is well watered.

This peculiarity in the southern bends of both Honey creek and Rocky creek is not confined to this county, and may be due to the halting retreat of the glacier, when throwing down the unmodified drift with which that portion of the country is covered. The divides between these creeks, along their upper waters, would in that case be the moraine accumulations, which further west and at lower levels, were not sufficient to divert the drainage from the general course of the main valley. They may be compared to the extended moraine which shut off the St. Marys and the Wabash rivers from their most direct course to lake Erie, along their upper waters.

SURFACE FEATURES.

The county presents more diversity of surface than Sandusky. The northwestern part, including the townships of Jackson, Liberty and

Pleasant, the northern half of Hopewell, and a small part of Loudon, present the peculiar features of the lacustrine region.

The Niagara limestone rises, in wide undulations, above the surface of the drift, and is as frequently supplied with sandy accumulations and bowlders as in counties further north. The surface of these townships, otherwise, is very flat. The remainder of the county, west of the Sandusky river, as well as the townships of Clinton and Eden on the east, is entirely without such limestone exposures, and the surface, when not broken by drainage valleys, is gently undulating. The eastern part of the county is considerably more elevated than the middle and western, and the surface is characterized at once by longer and more considerable undulations, which have the form, very often, of ridges, evenly covered by drift, running about northeast and southwest. This greater elevation is due to the greater resistance of the Corniferous limestone to the forces of the glacial epoch, not to upheaval, as many fancy; while the original inequalities in the drift surface have been increased by the erosion of streams. There are still, even in the eastern portion of the county, flat tracts where the drainage is so slow, that the washings from the hill sides have leveled up the lower grounds with alluvial and marshy accumulations. In such cases the elevated drift-knolls are gravelly, and show occasional boulders; but in the level tract which has been filled, no boulders, or even stones of any kind, can be seen.

The streams are bounded by a flood plain and a single terrace. The latter, in case of the smaller streams, is not well defined, especially where the general surface is not flat. The following heights of this terrace, above the summer stage of the river, were ascertained by Locke's level:

Sugar creek, N. W. ¼ Sec. 27, Pleasant township, 42 ft. 2 in.
Honey creek, Sec. 20, Eden township, 58 ft.
Sandusky river, Sec. 24, Seneca township, 63 ft. 3 in.

SOIL AND TIMBER.

The soil, consisting principally of the old drift surface, is what may be termed a gravelly clay, with various local modifications. The principal exceptions are the alluvial flats, bordering the streams, where the soil consists largely of sandy marl, with varying proportions of vegetable matter, the depressions in the old drift surface, which have been slowly filled by peaty soil, and the sandy and stony ridges, in the townships of Jackson, Liberty and Hopewell. With the exception of the marsh known as Big Spring Prairie, in the southwestern part of

Big Spring township, the whole country is in a tillable condition. Hence, it is settled with a class of intelligent and prosperous farmers, who keep the land generally under constant cultivation. The original forest, which is now to a great extent removed, embraced the usual variety of oak, hickory, beech, maple, elm, ash, poplar and walnut.

GEOLOGICAL STRUCTURE.

The rocks that underlie the county have a general dip towards the east. Hence, the Niagara limestone, in the western portion of the county, is succeeded by the higher formations in regular order in traveling east. They are the water limestone, the Oriskany sandstone, the Lower Corniferous, the Upper Corniferous, the Hamilton shale, and the Huron shale, or black slade. The eastern boundary of the Niagara enters the county a little east of Green Spring, in a southwesterly direction, and crossing the Sandusky river at Tiffin, it turns westward nearly to the center of Hopewell township, where it again turns southwest, and leaves the county at Adrian. All west of this line is underlain by the Niagara, which is not divided into two belts, as in Sandusky and Ottawa counties. The strip of the waterlime which separates it in those counties, probably just indents the northern line of the county in Pleasant township. The out-cropping edge of the Upper Corniferous is the only other geological boundary that can be definitely located. Those on either side are so obscured by the drift, that their located positions on the map must be regarded as conjectured. In general, however, the waterlime underlies a strip along the eastern side of the Niagara area, about five miles in width on the north, but widening to nine miles on the south. The Lower Corniferous underlies the western part of Bloom and Scipio townships, and the eastern part of Adams. The Upper Corniferous occupies the most of Thompson and Reed townships, the western portion of Venice, and the eastern portion of Bloom and Scipio. The Hamilton and the Black shale have not been seen in out-crop in the county, but are believed to underlie a small area in the southeastern portion of the county. The Black shale may be seen in the valley of Slate Run, Norwich township, in Huron county.

The Niagara shows the following exposures:

IN JACKSON TOWNSHIP,

S. W. ¼ of section 36, in a little creek. No dip discoverable. In section 22, a prominent ridge is crossed, and slightly excavated by the railroad. The ascent is so gentle the grade rises over it. N. W. ¼ of section

31, of the Guelph aspect, shows numerous fossils, used for making roads, and for lime.

IN LIBERTY TOWNSHIP,

S. W. ¼ of section 4, in west branch of Wolf creek; dip 6 or 8 degrees west of the S. E. ¼ of section 5.

Section 3, half a mile west of Bettsville; frequent exposures along the west branch of Wolf creek. When observable, the dip is to the west.

Section 10—Along the east line of the section, in the form of ridges. N. E. ¼ of section 28, N. W. ¼ of section 2, horizontal; in the west branch of Wolf creek, setting back the water nearly a mile. N. W. ¼ of section 24, considerably quarried for foundations and abutments of bridges. S. W. ¼ of section 30, by the roadside. N. E. ¼ of section 36, in Wolf creek. S. W. ¼ of section 34, S. W. ¼ of section 31, in thick beds, used by Mr. George King in the construction of his house; dip 5° N. E. N. W. ¼ section 29.

IN PLEASANT TOWNSHIP,

Northwest quarter of section 10, in the bed of Wolf creek, dip northeast, glacial scratches, south 56° west, northwest quarter of section 20. In the bed of the river at Fort Seneca, just below the dam, a fine grained, bluish limestone has been a little quarried for use on roads. But owing to its hardness and the unfavorable location, it was not regarded suitable. It probably belongs to the Niagara, although the opportunities for examination were too meager to determine exactly. Center and southeast quarter of section 28, in thick beds, in Spicer creek.

IN HOPEWELL TOWNSHIP,

Northeast quarter of section 22. Has the aspect of the Guelph on the land of Henry W. Creeger; surface exposure, section 16, where the road crosses Wolf creek.

In these surface exposures very little opportunity is offered for ascertaining the lithological characters, or the mineralogical and fossil contents of the formation. The chief exposure of the Niagara within the county is in the Sandusky river, between Tiffin and Fort Seneca.

From Tiffin, descending the Sandusky river, rocks show constantly to within half a mile of the line between Clinton and Pleasant townships. Throughout the most of this distance, the dip of the formation (Niagara) is from five to ten degrees toward the southwest, but with various flexures and undulations in all directions. The thickness of bedding exposed is between fifty and sixty feet. The following minutes on this exposure will show the undulations in the dip of the beds, and the manner of the occurrence of the fossiliferous beds, which have by some been regarded as a distinct member of the Upper Silurian above the Niagara. They make, here, a sudden appearance within the formation, having horizontal continuity with the more usual hard, gray, and thick-bedded Niagara, which contains fewer fossil remains.

Ascending the river from section 29, in Pleasant township, glacial furrows, S. 44° W., the dips of the Niagara were observed, together with the water lime formations to some distance southwest of Tiffin, varying from three to eighteen feet in all directions, and resulted thus:

Total southwest dip... 87 ft. 10 in.
Total northeast dip... 33 ft.
Actual southwest dip of the formation............ 54 ft. 10 in.

From this it appears that the Niagara limestone, especially the uppermost, fifty-five feet, is, in general, a gray crystalline, rather fine-grained, compact, or slightly visicular and unfossiliferous mass; and that the fossiliferous parts are rough and visicular, of a light buff color, apt to crumble under the weather, and not horizontally continuous.

The green shale, which in Sandusky county represents the Salina, has nowhere been seen in Seneca county. The only place within the county where the junction of the Niagara and waterlime has been observed, is in the quarries at Tiffin, within the corporate limits. A few rods above the iron bridge on Washington street, a quarry has been opened in the left bank of the Sandusky which may be designated as quarry No. 1. The Niagara shows in a broad surface exposure, over which the river spreads, except in its lowest stage. The quarry has not penetrated it, but the overlying water lime beds have been stripped off, showing a section of 12 feet in their beds, belonging to phase No. 3. This lies conformably on the Niagara, so far as can be seen, the separating surface presenting no unusual flexures or irregularities. The only trace of the Salina is in the tendency of the color and texture of the Niagara towards those of the water lime, visible through its last three or four inches. It is bluish-drab, porous, crystalline, with some indistinct greenish lines and spots. It contains much calcite, and some galena. From this character it passes immediately into a bluish-gray crystalline rock, in thick, firm beds, with spots of purple, heavy and slightly porous, the cavities being nearly all filled with calcite.

The principal exposures of the waterlime are in the quarries at Tiffin.

Quarry No. 2 is located a quarter of a mile above the last, on the

GEOLOGICAL FORMATION.

right bank of the river, and is known as the city quarry. The dip here is southwest, six or eight degrees. Supposing the dip is uniform between quarries Nos. 1 and 2, there must be an unseen interval of twenty-five or thirty feet of the formation separating them. Total exposed, 17 ft. 9 in.

The characteristic fossil, liperditia alta, may be seen in nearly all parts of this section, but it was especially noted in Nos. 3 and 7. This rock is all hard and crystalline, but with a fine grain. No. 3, without careful examination, might be taken for Niagara, if seen alone. When broken into fragments for roads, the color of the pile, weathered a few months, is a pleasant bluish gray. Yet on close examination, the blue tints vanish, and the stone shows a drab, a dark or brownish drab, a black and a bluish gray, (the last two only on the lines of the bedding) depending on the fracture or surface examined.

The river, just in the southern limits of the city, is flowing east. The rock can be followed along the same bank of the river eighteen or twenty rods from the foregoing quarry, and has an irregular surface exposure throughout that distance, with a continuous dip southwest. The rock then follows the bluff, which strikes across a path of river bottom, and is not seen again until a mile further up the river. It is here quarried and burnt into lime. The dip is in the opposite direction—that is, towards the north. This is quarry No. 3. Total, 27 ft. 9 in.

This rock is quite different in most of its external aspects from that described in the last two sections, and it probably overlies them. It is much more loose-grained and porous, and is almost without bituminous films. The beds are generally six to twelve inches, but sometimes three feet in thickness. It has more constantly the typical drab color of the waterlime, and it shows, besides the liperditia alta, another bivalve like atrypa sulcata, and a handsome species of orthis; also, a coarse favositoid coral, all of which are often seen in the water lime.

In the S. E. ¼ of section 22, Hopewell township, Mr. Henry W. Creeger quarries water-lime in the bed of Wolf creek; dip south six or eight degrees.

The waterlime appears in thin, drab beds at the bridge over the Sandusky in N. E. ¼ of section 23, Seneca township, with undulating dip.

In S. E. ¼ of section 29, Clinton township, where the road crosses Rocky creek, the waterlime is exposed, having the feature of No. 8, of quarry No. 3 at Tiffin. [See Vol. I, Geology p. 618.]

The Oriskany sandstone is nowhere exposed in this county, but its line of outcrop probably passes through Adams, Clinton and Eden townships.

The Lower Corniferous has been observed in the following places:

S. W. ¼ of section 1, Eden township. Along the bed of a little creek, tributary to Rocky creek, a magnesian, buff, granular limestone is exposed. It has no fossils, so far as can be seen in the meager outcrops. It is also seen in the banks along the creek, on the farm of Mr. Ferguson. It was formerly quarried, to a limited extent, and used for rough walls. It is rather soft at first, but is said to become harder when the water is dried out. There is no dip discoverable.

N. W. ¼ of section 20, Bloom township. In the right bank of Silver creek there is an exposure of higher beds of the Lower Corniferous, as follows, from above:

No. 1—In beds of two to six inches; buff and dark buff, magnesian; very slightly fossiliferous; some hard and crystalline, some soft and spongy. These edges do not appear to be slaty. They have been long weathered and lie loose. This is near the junction of the Lower and Upper Corniferous. 10 ft.

No. 2—Magnesian; rather hard; crystalline; non-fossiliferous; buff when dry; fine grained; banded with darker buff, or with brown when in thicker beds. Beds ¼ inch to 2 inches. These edges appear slaty. 2 ft.

Total .... 12 ft.

Lying nearly horizontal five or six rods, at the east end of the bluff the beds dip east and disappear. A little west of this exposure the magnesian, non-fossiliferous, thick-bedded characters of the Lower Corniferous may be seen in the bed of the creek. Eighteen or twenty rods to the east, the features and fossils of the Upper Corniferous appear in an old quarry by the roadside, where the dip is E. N. E.

S. W. ¼ of section 3, Scipio township. Along the channel of Sugar creek, on the land of Enoch Fry, a stone is exposed which appears like Lower Corniferous. It is soft, coarse grained, and without visible fossils. A pond located near this place, which has precipitous banks and sometimes becomes dry, is probably caused by subterranean disturbances and erosion.

The quarry of Mr. David Wyatt, N. W. ¼ of section 1, Scipio township, is in a thin-bedded, bluff stone, which has no tendency to blue, without fossils, and included within the Lower Corniferous.

The Lower Corniferous is also exposed S. E. ¼ of section 34, Adams township, along the public road.

N. E. ¼ of section 26, Eden township. A fine-grained, argillacious, gray rock, weathering buff, without visible fossils, appears in the road. It seems apt to break into angular pieces, three or four inches across. It is rather hard. It is probably included within the Lower Corniferous.

The opportunities for observing the lower portion of the Corniferous within the county are not sufficient to warrant a general section and description.

The Upper Corniferous, owing to its greater hardness and toughness, was not so generally destroyed by the ice and water of the glacial epoch, and now may be more frequently seen, thinly covered with coarse drift, occupying the highest parts of the county and forming the main water shed. The coarseness of the drift on these higher tracts is owing to the washings by rains and freshets since the close of the glacial epoch. It is an unassorted hardpan, and sometimes covers glacial striæ in the rock below.

This part of the Corniferous is exposed in the following places within the county. It furnishes a very useful building stone, and is extensively used for all walls, foundations, and some buildings.

IN THOMPSON TOWNSHIP,

N. W. ¼ of section 20. It closely underlies most of the section. The drift being thin, the soil sometimes shows fragments. A quarry is owned by Mr John W. Paine.

S. W. ¼ of section 16. Mr. George Good's quarry; beds horizontal, in the midst of a field in fine cultivation, with a surface gently undulating; drift at the quarry eight inches, but rapidly thickening further away. Same ¼ section. Samuel Royers' quarry exposes about eight feet perpendicular; beds about horizontal.

S. W. ¼ of section 14. Reuben Hartman's quarry exposes about eight feet of blue, thin beds, which seem to have been shattered, falling towards the west, the firm beds having a slight dip towards the northeast. Large, handsome flagging is obtained at this quarry.

N. E. ¼ of section 2; Benjamin Bunn's quarry. There are here about three feet of drift over the rock. The beds are exposed about six feet perpendicularly; dip not observed, although there is a falling away by fracture towards the west.

S. W. ¼ of section 1. Charles Smith's quarry faces the west; indeed, the same is true of Hartman's and Bunn's. Mr. Royers' quarry is an irregular opening, facing mostly north and west. Mr. Good's faces north and east.

S. E. ¼ of section 1. In the edge of Huron county, Mr. George Sheffield has a quarry in horizontal beds; gravelly soil eighteen inches.

S. E. ¼ of setion 1. Quarry of William Clemens.

N. E. ¼ of section 21. Quarry of Joseph Shirk. This consists of a mass of shattered and dislodged beds, from which, however, good stone is taken. In one place, a mass showing a perpendicular thickness of five feet is twisted away from its original position, the planes of jointing indicating where it ought to be. It is removed two feet from its natural place. The projection beyond the face of the other beds tapers, in the distance of about fifteen feet, to a few inches, and is hid by debris.

Northeast quarter of section 15, quarry of John M. Krauss.
Northeast quarter of section 29, quarry of Mrs. Joseph Hoover.
Northeast quarter of section 10, quarry of Isaac Karn.
Northwest quarter of section 11, quarry of Tunis Wygart.
Northwest quarter of section 2, quarry of Grimes heirs.

Many others also have small openings in the rocks in this township. They are nearly all in the midst of cultivated fields, and there is a remarkable absence of boulders, although the rock is sometimes seen projecting above the surface. There are a few boulders, but they are such as belong to the drift, and have been dug out by the erosion of streams, or by man. They are not thick about rocky outcrops, as in the lacustrine region.

IN BLOOM TOWNSHIP.

Northwest quarter of section 11. Lewis Fisher has an extensive quarry in the Upper Corniferous, in the valley of a little tributary to Honey creek. About fifteen feet of bedding are exposed, lying nearly horizontal. The lowest beds are about eighteen inches in thickness, and softer, yet of a blue color like the rest. In working Mr. Fisher's quarry, it has become necessary to remove about ten feet of hardpan drift.

Northeast quarter of section 10. Jacob Detwiller's quarry is also an extensive opening, and exposes beds a few feet lower than Mr. Fisher's. The lowest seems to be of a lighter color, and must be near the bottom of the Upper Corniferous. A stream disappears in this quarry, in time of freshet.

Southwest quarter of section 2. Henry Detterman's quarry is located in the valley of Honey creek.

Northeast quarter of section 20. Along the banks of Silver creek there is considerable exposure of the Upper Corniferous, and it is extensively wrought by Abraham Kagy. The beds here have a continuous dip, E. S. E., affording opportunities for the following sections:

No. 1—Fossiliferous beds with chert, which weathers white; thin-bedded, of bluish-gray color. 7 ft.

No. 2—Thin, flaggy, lenticular beds; fossiliferous; drab-buff color; hard, brittle, and sometimes with vermicular impressions. 4 ft.

[NOTE.—No. 2 would probably be thicker-bedded if freshly exposed.]

No. 3—The same as No. 2, but in more even beds. 28 ft.

Upper Corniferous exposed ....39 ft.

Northwest quarter of section 29. Noah Einsel has a handsome quarry, in beds which dip E. N. E.

Northwest quarter of section 20, Reed township. The Upper Corniferous is quarried by Mr. Armstrong.

THE DRIFT.

Throughout this county, this deposit lies as it was left by the glacier. The mass of it is an unassorted hardpan, but it shows locally the glacial stratification incident to streams of water arising from the dissolution of the ice. Such cases of stratification are most common in the great valleys where the waters necessarily accumulated. They are by no means common, nor uniform in their location in the drift vertically. In some cases the stratification arises nearly or quite to the surface, or prevails to the depth of thirty or forty feet; in others it embraces one or more beds of hardpan, which have irregular outlines. In section 20, Eden township, the banks of Honey creek were particularly noted, and may be described as follows:

No. 1—This is imperfectly exposed, but wherever seen is in unassorted hardpan with considerable gravel. It forms the soil of the county, and is of a brownish yellow color. 25 ft.

No. 2—Is blue, and composed of alternating beds of compacted hardpan, containing water-worn and scratched pebbles of all kinds and sizes, apparently unassorted and unstratified, and beds of coarse sand, extremely fine sand and coarse gravel. From the sand and gravel layers issue springs of ferriferous water. The sand layers sometimes graduate into impervious, clay-like beds, and can hardly be called sand. The lowest seen in No. 2 is a layer of eighteen inches, at least, of clear sand. 30 ft.

No. 3—Talus of round pebbles and stones, mostly limestone, and frequently stained with iron oxide. 3 ft.

The thickness of the drift cannot be stated with certainty. At Attica, in the township of Venice, wells penetrate it to the depth of sixty feet without striking the rock. This is the highest point within the county, and the general surface is rolling.

MATERIAL RESOURCES—BUILDING STONE.

Next to the products of the soil, the most important resources of Seneca county consist in the products of the quarries. Throughout most of the county there is no difficulty in obtaining good building stone, although the best quarries are situated a little unfavorably for the townships of Loudon, Big Spring, Seneca, Eden, Pleasant, Venice and Reed. The quarries at Tiffin furnish stone throughout a radius of many miles, while those in Bloom township supply a great tract of country south and east. The quarries in Thompson township, although located in the Upper Corniferous, are affording one of the best qualities of stone in northwestern Ohio; they are favorably exposed for working, but less developed than similar openings in Bloom township. This is doubtless due to the superior advantages of quarries further north, and at Bellevue, in Sandusky county, for reaching market and for shipment by railroad.

LIME.

For lime, the Niagara and waterlime formations are chiefly used. They are more easily quarried and more cheaply burned than the Upper Corniferous. Both are burned at Tiffin, but the kilns are rude and the expense of burning is greater than where the improved kilns are employed.

CLAY.

Clay for brick and red pottery is found in suitable quantities in all parts of the county. Many establishments for the manufacture of brick employ the surface of the ordinary hardpan, including even the soil; others reject the immediate surface, which contains roots and turf, and burn the hardpan from the depth of a foot or two. This material, although liable to contain pebbles of limestone, which injure the manufactured article, generally has it in such small quantity and in so comminuted a state, as to require no other flux for the silica. The tile, brick and pottery made in this way are suitable for all purposes where no great degree of heat is required. Mr. J. M. Zahm, of Tiffin, after many careful experiments, has succeeded in making a good quality of hydraulic cement by mixing the finest of the drift clay, in proper parts, with ordinary carbonate of lime or tufa. He has also produced from the drift clay near Tiffin, by making proper selections, a very fine pottery, some of which cannot be distinguished from the terra cotta ware used for ornaments and statues. It has a very vitreous fracture, a smooth surface, and a dark red or amber color. From the drift clay near Tiffin, Mr. H. W. Creeger also obtained a fine material for pottery and for glazing with salt.

BOG-IRON ORE.

Before the development of the lake Superior and Missouri iron mines, one of the principal sources of iron in the northwest was the bog ore deposits, which are scattered over much of the country. In northwestern Ohio the numerous furnaces which were employed on these deposits along the south shore of lake Erie, and in counties further south and west, rendered bog ore an important item of mineral wealth. It produces an iron known as "cold short" owing to the presence of phosphorus, which cannot be used for wire or for sheet iron, but is valuable for castings. On the contrary, iron from the ores which contain sulphur as an impurity, or silicon, is friable or brittle when hot, and is distinguished as "red short." When these two qualities occur in close proximity, or in circumstances favorable for transportation, they may be mixed in the process of smelting, and the resulting iron is greatly improved. The lake Superior ores, which are the only ones smelted in the furnaces of northwestern Ohio, are quite free from sulphur, and hence at the present time the bog ores possess but little commercial value. It will be only in connection with the sulphur ores of the coal measures in the southeastern part of the state, that the bog ores can be made of any mineral value.

In Seneca county bog ore occurs in a number of places. It is not in sufficient quantities, usually, to invite expenditure of capital, and in the absence of abundant fuel, it will probably never be of any economical value. It was met with on the farm of W. B. Stanley, about two miles southeast of Tiffin, where it underlies a peat bog, covering irregularly perhaps fifteen or twenty acres.

It also occurs on the land of Mr. Foght, southeast quarter of section 27, Seneca township. It has been taken out here in large blocks, roughly cut while wet, and set up for back walls in rude fire places. On being exposed to the air, or especially to fire, it becomes cemented and very hard. There is also a deposit in section 11, in Clinton township, exactly on the south line of the Seneca Indian reservation.

CHAPTER XV.

LIFE OF JOSIAH HEDGES—CHANGE—FIRST PLAT OF TIFFIN—THE SAW-MILL MIASMA—FIRST FRAME HOUSES—FIRST STORES—FIRST BRICK HOUSES—THE FERRY—THE DUG-OUT—FIRST HOTELS—BLACK-STRAP—HENRY GROSS—MR. BREDOON'S DEATH—THE CREEGER FAMILY—HENRY LANG—HENRY CRONISE--DR. BOYER'S FAMILY—PHILIP SEEWALD.

JOSIAH HEDGES.

AMONG the most remarkable of the leading pioneers of Seneca county, was Josiah Hedges, the founder of Tiffin. He was born April 9, 1778, near West Liberty, Berkley county, Va., and throughout his whole life preserved the characteristics of the true Virginian. He left his father's home at an early age, with a determination to carve out his own fortune. The first enterprise which he undertook on his own account, was a trading excursion to New Orleans on a flatboat, laden with fruit, which he floated down the Ohio river from Wheeling to New Orleans. The voyage lasted six weeks. He finally settled in Ohio in 1801, one year before it was admitted as a state, and located in Belmont county, where, for a number of years, he was one of the most active and prominent citizens. He was the first sheriff of that county, and for a number of years clerk of the court. He next engaged in the mercantile business at St. Clairsville. His capital was limited, but was slowly and surely increasing by prudence and sagacity—firm traits in his character that never forsook him through life.

In those days, merchants in the west were wont to purchase their goods in Philadelphia, journeying across the Alleghany mountains on horseback, and carrying their specie in their saddle bags. In 1819, he opened a branch store in Mansfield, having as a partner his brother, Gen. James Hedges. Soon thereafter he removed from St. Clairsville to Mansfield. In 1820, he made a journey to Fort Ball, in this county.

His natural foresight very soon suggested to him the possibility of a speculation, and he immediately decided to enter the land opposite to Fort Ball, on the right bank of the Sandusky river. Here the county seat was located soon thereafter, in the heart of the town that Mr. Hedges caused to be platted immediately after his purchase of the land at the Delaware land office. In 1822 the first stick was cut on the plat of Tiffin, at a place near the Commercial bank, in the first ward. In the same year Mr. Hedges built a saw mill on Rocky creek, a short distance east of the court house, and a frame building on the lot north of the court house, which was afterwards used for very many purposes —for a court house, Masonic hall, offices and shops, etc. The same building is still in existence, and stands near the mouth and on the left bank of Rocky creek and also on the bank of the Sandusky river, and is now used as a paper box factory. In the same year he also built the flouring mill on the Sandusky river, which was afterwards known as the "Hunter mill." By a prudent and liberal course in disposing of his town lots, he saw the place increase steadily, and in 1828 he secured the removal of the land office from Delaware to Tiffin, thus giving the town a new impetus. In 1825, and again in 1830, he was elected a member of the House of Representatives from this district, in which capacity he served to the satisfaction of the people. In 1837 he disposed of his interest in the store to a son, and from that time to the close of his life, devoted all his time to the interest of Tiffin and his growing wealth.

In his younger days Mr. Hedges was an athletic and vigorous man, and well up to nearly four score years he retained a large portion of his mental and physical vigor, and was always able to attend to his own affairs. He was generous and just in his dealings with his fellow men; benevolent and kind. He assisted all the christian denominations in Tiffin, and granted lots for the erection of churches, in addition to his liberal subscriptions. He was the originator of many, and the supporter of all, public improvements. He was possessed of that large and unselfish hospitality that characterized all the early settlers. He was generous to the poor, and always willing to lend a helping hand. When a man bought a lot from him on which to build himself a home, and could not pay as he had agreed to do, Mr. Hedges would never trouble him, as long as the purchaser showed a desire and willingness to pay. Yet he looked after his interest, and expected men to come up to their promises. While he had no love for drones and loafers, the man of work and industry always found in him a friend. Those that sought his advice in business, never called on him in vain; and when he knew the man to be true and faithful, was ready to help him, if necessary, with *material advice*. He was as sincere in all his intercourse with his fellow men as he was just and generous; and while he was the good neighbor and citizen, the safe counsellor and faithful friend, he was also an indulgent and affectionate father and devoted husband.

His kindred, both old and young, will ever gratefully remember him. To him they could always go with loving confidence; his heart was ever open to them.

Although not a member of any church, Mr. Hedges was a good and true man; and upon his dying couch he expressed a willingness to go, and assured his friends around him of his unfaltering trust in that Savior "who has promised to save all who may turn towards Him in faith and penitence." He sank away quietly, as if but entering upon a sleep. Without a groan or a struggle, the good old man took his departure, and passed away "like one that draws the drapery of his couch around him and lays down to pleasant dreams."

Mr. Hedges was first married September 29, 1807, to Rebecca Russell, in Belmont county, Ohio. He had by this union six children, two of whom are still living—Mrs. Clarinda Hunter, widow of William Hunter, and Mrs. Rebecca Walker, widow of Joseph Walker. His first wife died July 8, 1816, aged thirty-one years. After living a widower about one year, he was again married on the 10th day of July, 1817, to Eliza Hammerly, of Martinsburgh, Virginia. This union was blessed with nine children, of whom Cynthia A. wife of Luther A. Hall, Esq., of Tiffin, Ohio, Mary Jane, wife of A. C. Baldwin, of Tiffin, Ohio, Minerva, wife of Harrison Noble, Esq., the present mayor of the city of Tiffin, Elizabeth, wife of John G. Gross, for many years a prominent merchant of Tiffin, and Sarah, wife of the Hon. W. W. Armstrong, late secretary of state, and now of the *Cleveland Plaindealer*, of Cleveland, Ohio, the faithful and esteemed friend of the writer, are still living. His second wife died on the 10th day of November, 1837. He was married again October 29, 1844, to Harriet, daughter of Henry Snook, of Seneca county, who is still among the living, highly respected. Mr. Hedges died in Tiffin, on the 15th day of July, 1858, aged eighty years, three months and six days.

While it is very true, and it might well be said, that Mr. Hedges died greatly beloved by his large family and all his neighbors and friends, yet he was "not without sin;" he was mortal and human. While he was endowed with very many manly traits of character, his social nature, and the allurements of friends, at times led him to excesses that he afterwards openly regretted. While he was governed by strict principles of honor, living faithfully up to his promises, and while he would never voluntarily offer an insult to, or hurt the feelings of, any person, it was exceedingly unsafe for any man to offer an insult to him within three feet of his shoulders.

Up to about his seventy-fifth year his step was permanent and regular, and his carriage wonderfully straight for one of his age. From that time onward the increasing years wrought their mark upon his powerful frame. On a pleasant day he would walk with short steps about town, in his double gown, with a stick in his hand, dragging his shoes, tramped down at the heels, often with his smoking cap on and smoking his familiar short pipe—the very picture of a comfortable sunset after a long, summer day.

In stature Mr. Hedges was a little over six feet high, and well proportioned. His carriage was very straight, his movements and gestures, as well as his conversation, very decided. He had nothing of suavity or "blarney" about him. He was very economical with his words in business transactions, and would say no more than was necessary to accomplish the work in hand. His intercourse with men, while it was pleasant enough in business, and utterly void of offense, yet bore that peculiar, almost indescribable, natural aristocracy that so much characterizes the true Virginia gentleman of the olden school. His voice was clear, a little metalic, and on a rather high note for so large a person. He had a fine forehead, a sharp, small, black eye, a prominent nose, not very large, clenched lips, high cheek bones, heavy lower jaw, and in his *tout ensemble* was the very image of firmness and decision.

CHANGE.

"O'er us, we scarce know whence or when
A change begins to steal,
Which teaches that we ne'er again
As once we felt, shall feel.
A curtain, slowly drawn aside,
Reveals a shadowed scene
Wherein the future differs wide
From what the past has been."

The law of change is stamped and deeply imprinted upon all earthly things. The bud that opens its leaves into a flower, to greet the first rays of the rising sun, gives up its glory to the gentle zephyr at noon, and is gone. The towering oak, that defied the storms and wintry blasts for centuries, finally yields to the demands of nature and crumbles its substance to the earth from whence it sprung. The rocks and hills submit to the wear and tear of the seasons, and change form, under the law of disintegration. Seneca county no longer wears the beauty of her pristine grandeur. Its noble forest is broken and gone, and with it the wild aborigines and still wilder beasts. The drift-wood

CHANGE.   241

is removed from the river and the creeks, the streams are gradually becoming more nearly straight, and the great swales are nearly all laid dry by judicious ditching. Rich crops reward the labors of the husbandman, and the shouts and songs of happy children have taken the place of the hideous howling of the wolf and the roaring of the ravenous panther. The echo of the woodman's axe has made way for the shrill whistle of the steam-factory and the locomotive, and thousands of happy, prosperous and intelligent people worship God in splendid meeting houses, erected where the blue smoke of the council fires of the Indians rose in curling clouds over the tree tops. The trail of the Indian is wiped away by public roads that bring market to every door.

And so has Tiffin yielded to the law of change. There is no trace left of the few cabins that first marked the place called Tiffin. They have passed away like the stakes the surveyor drove into the ground among the trees to show the width of the streets and alleys that were to be.

Many reasons may be assigned for the fact that Seneca county settled up more rapidly than any other county in northwestern Ohio; and among these may be enumerated the rich soil and splendid timber; its water-privileges and water supply; its excellent drainage and accessibility to market; its inexhaustible quantity of building stone, its climate, etc., etc.

And shall we not give the pioneers of Seneca county great credit for their sagacity, at least, in selecting this spot for their new homes, when, in the lifetime of many of us who are still here, and before our own eyes, this county threw off its mantle of forest wild, and became the first wheat-growing county of the great state of Ohio, both in acreage and number of bushels produced to the acre? What a change!

In the preceding chapters, the attention of the interested reader was directed to things of a general nature, affecting nearly all parts of the county alike. Hereafter, local affairs will enlist the services of the old goose-quill, and an effort will be made to describe men and things in their individual localities.

Let us commence with Tiffin, and starting with her in the woods, on the banks of the turbid Sandusky, trace her to the spring-time of 1880. Then let us take up the further progress of each township, without any particular attempt at order, locating and naming the old settlers, and describing some of them as their neighbors knew them—thus, if possible, obtaining a bird's-eye view of Seneca county generally, with its happy thousands and its various industries.

16

The first plat of Tiffin contained 118 lots—each block of 12 lots facing four streets, with a cross alley through the center. It had three streets running east and west, viz: Perry, Market and Madison, starting near Rocky creek and ending near the river; and three streets running north and south, viz: Jefferson, Washington and Monroe, starting near the river, and ending at an alley 180 feet south of Madison street. The east end of this alley is now Tiffin street, and leads from Jefferson to the old cemetery.

This was Tiffin, with a little opening and a cabin where the gas works now are. Another was built soon thereafter, near where the Commercial bank now is, and another a little south of Naylor's hardware store.

This survey was made and the town platted before Seneca county was organized, as was before stated, and therefore the plat had to be recorded in the recorder's office of Sandusky county, which was done on the 28th day of November, A. D. 1821.

No change was made in the plat of Tiffin until 1831, on the 27th day of May, when Mr. Hedges had his southern addition to Tiffin surveyed and platted. This contained in-lots from 119 to 146, both inclusive, and out-lots from 1 to 12, both inclusive. The public cemetery was laid just north of out-lot No. 7. This addition was a string of lots, one on each side of Washington street, running south to the first alley now north of the German Catholic church and the junction of the roads. The lots from both sides run endwise to the street. Not a single cross street intersects them to this day. Jefferson street and Monroe street were also extended south, the same distance through these out-lots.

The wonderful energy of Mr. Hedges, and his untiring industry, produced a saw mill, near Rocky creek, already mentioned. It stood near the mill race, and some thirty rods southeast of the point where Circular street intersects East Market. The dam was close by the saw mill—in fact, the water ran from the dam directly into the mill, without a head-race, and, after passing through the wheel, emptied into the creek again, so that the mill had neither head nor tail-race. A race, however, was constructed from this dam to the City Mill, still standing. This saw mill was built in 1826, and was run night and day to supply the great demand that was made upon it for lumber with which to build frame houses, and for other purposes. It became the center of attraction, and looked like a bee-hive on a large scale while it lasted. Everybody was in need of boards, and had to have them.

Mr. Hedges, having so many irons in the fire, could give the saw mill no personal attention, and rented it to one Joseph Janey, and afterwards to my dear old friends, U. P. Coonrad and Christopher Y. Pierson. It was then a paying institution, and these two young carpenter partners made the saw mill count. They published a notice in the *Seneca Patriot*, in 1832, that one of the partners could be found at the hotel of Calvin Bradley. Bradley then kept the Center House, which will be noticed hereafter.

The saw mill burned away in the spring of 1833, and this ended the partnership with the mill. Neither was ever rebuilt, but the dam remained to supply the City Mill. The dam set the water back, far up Rocky creek, to the lands of Mrs. Nolan, and in summer time the water was covered with a green scum. The people, suffering so much from malarious diseases, concluded that the dam injured the health of the town, and importuned Mr. Hedges to remove it. He refused, however, and finally suit was brought against him to compel him to move the dam.

At the trial, all the physicians in the town were witnesses, and testified both for and against the dam. They had some trouble to satisfy the defendant's counsel and the court upon the material qualities of the malarious poison. One of the doctors, (who also did a little preaching with his practice, at times,) seemed to be very positive in his testimony. He said that miasma could be noticed in the air when it was quiet, early in the morning, by sunrise, in the form of a fine, blue streak interwoven with the fog. The writer did not know how it was, but heard both Drs. Dresbach and Kuhn say that they did not believe it. Mr. Hedges then put up a saw mill on the left bank of the river, opposite Hunter's mill. This also was kept in constant operation, and frame houses and shops sprang up in every direction, as by magic, for awhile.

Mr. Milton McNeal put up the first frame buildings on the Fort Ball side, which were his store and dwelling house. Mr. Hedges built the Masonic Hall and his frame residence. Mr. Richard Sneath put up his hotel on the ground now covered by the Grumund block. John and Benjamin Pettinger had a small stock of goods in a one and one-half story frame building that stood on the southwest corner of Washington and Market, about twenty feet from Market, and about sixty feet from Washington, with the gable end eastward. Judge Pettinger lived in the west end with his family. Mr. Henry Cronise had a very handsome stock of goods in his two-story frame, hereafter described, on lot 68, now in the fourth ward, and where he lived with his family some time after he retired from public life, and when he moved to his beautiful home on south Washington street, where he died.

Brick yards were now started; one in Fort Ball, and the other, by John Strong, at the south side of Tiffin street, near the east end, and which was kept in operation for many years thereafter.

In 1831, Patrick Kinney, Philip Hennessey and another Irishman whose name has escaped me, entered into a contract with Mr. Strong for the making of brick sufficient to build the first Catholic church in Tiffin, and became personally responsible for the payment.

The church was erected in the fall of that year, near the south side and east end of Madison street, opposite the old stone jail, and on the present old Catholic cemetery. It stood with the gable end towards the street, with a cupola at the north end of the roof. Its little bell was the first church bell in the county, and while its note was on a high key, it was pleasant to hear its cheerful echo through the woods.

The remainder of the brick from this kiln Mr. Strong sold to Mr. John Goodin, who built with them the first brick hotel in town, on lot No. 86, now owned by Mr. John Lœsser, in the fifth ward. This hotel was then considered a grand affair. The large fire-place in the bar room is there yet, but closed up. The porch of the second story, which extended clear over the pavement, and had a heavy roof over it, has passed away. The town council had it removed because it obstructed the view of the street; but it was the most conspicuous part of the hotel.

The M. E. Church on Market street; the store buildings of Henry Ebert (who is now lying a corpse at this writing, and will be buried to-day, April 2, 1880); John Park's store; a small, one-story brick immediately south of Sneath's hotel, where Mr. Andrew Glenn kept store, and the one-story, small brick school house, nearly opposite the old M. E. Church, were about all the brick buildings in Tiffin and Fort Ball, excepting the dwelling house of Dr. Kuhn, and the little 12x14 yellow brick on Sandusky street, which was Mr. Rawson's law office, and afterwards became the office of Drs. Dresbach and Carey.

There were no fractional lots in the first platting of Tiffin, and the spaces left between the lots and the river and Rocky creek, were laid off afterwards in numerous additions, named and numbered.

There was no bridge across the river, and none across Rocky creek. The streets were full of stumps and logs, and after the erection of the saw mills, the pavements in front of the houses were designated by slabs laid lengthwise. These answered a good purpose enough in the mud, but when the weather was dry, the slabs curled up and became great nuisances to fast walkers. Then would have been very appropriate the adoption of a rule that was introduced and put in force at an early day in the town of Lancaster, in Fairfield county. The town was troubled with much drunkenness, and every effort to arrest the evil seemed to be of no avail. Finally, an ordinance was adopted to make every man who was found drunk in town dig a stump out of the street in lieu of a fine. This plan worked well. It removed both stumps and drunkenness. Why not meet this evil of habitual drunkenness in a similar manner now, and make the vice a crime and punish it as such, instead of sympathizing with the drunkard, and keep firing away all the time at the retail dealer in liquors? Had Tiffin adopted the Lancaster rule, her streets would soon have made a better appearance.

The only way to get across the river at high tide, was to go down to the river bank, where, near the place now occupied by the barn of Dr. McFarland, there was a landing place for the ferry boat of Mr. George Park. The boat was an original dug-out, and the fare was two cents a trip. The Tiffin people had to go to Fort Ball to get their mail matter, and one man would fetch all the letters and papers for a whole neighborhood to some store on this side. As late as 1829, a thick woods back of the old fort, and extending up towards McNeil's store, prevented the view of the rival settlements from one to the other.

Mr. Park sold his ferry and the dug-out to Samuel Hoagland, who opened a little quarry on the left bank of the river, near the spring, to burn lime, and while he was thus engaged, he watched his chances for passengers. The sale of the lime, and the ferry, furnished him a comfortable livelihood.

Down by the river bank, on the ground now covered by the foundry buildings of Messrs. Loomis & Nyman, a Mr. Allen started a brewery, the first enterprise of this kind in the county, and produced a very palatable, light beverage. His beautiful wife officiated as clerk at the bar table. By some mishap or other, Mr. Allen and the brewery both vanished.

A Mr. Andrew Fruitchey had a tannery on the lot where the city hall now stands; and Messrs. John and Benjamin Pittinger had another where the gas works now are. Mr. Fruitchey died of cholera in 1834, one among the first cases in town.

Mr. Jacob Stem had a small store of goods in a small frame building near Mr. Ebert's, and soon thereafter formed a co-partnership with Mr. A. Lugenbeel, and the new firm opened up in a one-story frame building on the northwest corner of Washington and Market, where Simon Strycker's clothing store now is. Mr. R. W. Shawhan opened his first store in Tiffin on the south side of Market street, opposite the court house. The Commercial Row was built in the summer of 1835, and the Walkers and Masons opened up in it on a large scale. John Staub and Eli Norris were rival hotel keepers with Richard Sneath. George Park had a round-log-cabin hotel on Perry street, the first tavern in Tiffin. He afterwards put a two-story frame hotel on the lot now covered by the National Hall Block. Sometimes it was kept by Staub, and sometimes by Norris. Later on, Dr. James Fisher built the frame house on the northwest corner of Market and Monroe, where Staub kept tavern awhile. The building is now owned and occupied by Mr. Upton Flenner, who is also an old pioneer here.

Mr. Calvin Bradley built the Central House, in which he kept tavern himself, opposite the west part of the court house. Of all the older hotels in Tiffin, this is the only one remaining, and is now, and for a long time passed, has been, known as Remele's butcher shop.

This man Bradley was a wonderful man for energy and enterprise. He engaged in very many speculations, and while he kept hotel he also carried on the butchering business, selling meat twice a week. In 1832 he changed the name of his hotel to that of the Washington House. It had a high post in front, with a swinging sign on which was a golden lamb.

Edar and Bowe had a butcher shop in Fort Ball. They advertised fresh Meat for sale every Tuesday and Saturday. The market opened at the sound of the trumpet.

Where the Commercial House now stands, there was a two-story frame building occupied by Mr. James Mercer with his family, and in which he, in company with Mr. Henry Ebert, carried on the hatting business, manufacturing and selling hats. My brother Henry, the beloved pastor of the German Evangelical Lutheran Church of Fremont, learned the trade of hatter there, as the apprentice of Mr. Mercer.

Mr. Cronise's store contained a large stock of goods for that time, and like all other stores, was composed of all varieties of goods, such as dry goods, hardware, queensware and groceries.

One druggist advertised for sale at his stand, medicines, paints, oils, patent medicines, cross-cut saws, mill irons and tooth-ache drops.

In 1832, Mr. Cronise advertised that he would pay sixty-eight cents for flax-seed, in goods.

It was then, and for some time afterwards, very customary in Tiffin to keep molasses and whisky for sale at the stores. These articles were generally kept in the cellars. When farmers came in to trade, they were taken by the proprietor, or some clerk, into the cellar and treated to a glass of black-strap. This compound consisted of molasses and whisky—"'alf'-an'-'alf," as a Yorkshire man would say. Trading then went on as if nothing had happened. Sometimes a glassful was brought up with which to treat the ladies.

When, about 1836, Mr. Bradley put up the Western Exchange in the southern addition to Tiffin, on Washington street, it was considered a very hazardous enterprise. But he finished it, and kept hotel there. It is now occupied by Gray and Stevenson, as a tin-shop. Mr. Bradley kept the stage-office there, also. Standing at the crossing of Washington and Madison, you had to look through the woods to see the hotel. There was great difficulty to get to it from the north by team, when the roads were muddy. It was south of the deep hollow, so called, washed out by the ravine that crosses Washington and enters the fourth ward sewer. Many a time the stage driver, with four horses, was compelled to stop two or three times on his way up the hill before he reached the Exchange. Henry Gross put up a two-story hewed log house on the north side of Perry street, where he lived with his family and carried on the gunsmith business, together with the repairing of clocks and watches, the first enterprise of the kind in town. Mr. Gross was the first man the writer saw in Tiffin. Coming along Perry street from the east, on the 18th day of August, 1833, in the afternoon, ahead of the wagon, I saw a man standing in front of a log house, dressed in a long, homespun, brown cloth overcoat, buttoned up to his chin, a cloth cap, with a ring of fur around it, on his head, and both hands in his pockets. His hair was already turning gray. He had a prominent nose, regular, manly features, large, blue eyes, and an expressive, but pale countenance. The afternoon was very hot, and this man, attired in that way, so riveted the attention of the writer that it was hard to turn his eyes from him. Approaching, and saluting him, (he spoke German) the writer enjoyed the first conversation he had in Tiffin. This was Mr. Henry Gross, the father of Samuel Gross, of Bloomville, and Bovard and Henry Gross, of Tiffin—the latter one of the most celebrated mechanical geniuses in the United States, and of whom some notice will be taken hereafter. The old gentleman was shaking with the ague while we talked—the first case I ever saw. The following year, however, sad experience taught me more about ague and fever.

Mr. Gross was from Juniata county, Pennsylvania, where he was married to Miss Jane Hunter, on the 7th day of February, 1809. From there he moved to Tiffin, and arrived here in 1831. He was born July 21, 1783, and died here in 1834. Mrs. Gross survived him a long time. She was born in February, 1781, and died here, January 16, 1866, aged eighty-four years and ten months.

Jacob Plane was justice of the peace and postmaster on the Tiffin side, and lived in a two-story frame house that stood immediately south of where Marquart's drug store now stands.

Mr. Rawson had moved his law office to this side of the river. It was a small frame building that stood close by or about the place where Mr. H. Brohl now lives. Dr. Dresbach's office was a small, low brick building that stood on the alley immediately north of Fiege's cabinet warehouse.

The public square was full of logs and stumps. After Mr. Plane, Mr. Cronise had the post office in his building. Levi Keller had a blacksmith shop a little north of Goodin's hotel, where Loomis' stone front now stands. Valentine and Philip Seewald put up a double hewed log house, away out of town, near the southern extremity of the southern addition to Tiffin. There Valentine carried on the gunsmithing and lockmaking business, and Philip the watch repairing and jewelry trade. They lived there for a long time, and until they bought the lot where the Rust block now is, and moved upon that, where they both lived until they died.

Mr. Andrew Lugenbul lived in a small brick house now embraced in the house of Mr. John Remele, on Madison street. Joseph Howard lived in a large frame house on the northwest corner of Washington and Madison. Esq. Keen lived, in 1833, where he does now. David E. Owen, the auditor, lived in a part of the house with Esq. Plane. Mr. Joshua Seney lived near neighbor to, and east of, Mr. Hedges, on the south side of Perry, where Mr. and Mrs. Seney both died. Dr. Kuhn lived on the lot where the new jail now stands. His old office is still in existence, and stands close by, unoccupied.

Immediately north of Mr. Rawson's old law office, in the brick house still standing, lived widow Creeger, who had one son and quite a number of beautiful, intelligent daughters. They were from Maryland. Theresa, the oldest daughter, was married to Judge Benjamin Pittinger, in Maryland, and they moved to Tiffin for a wedding tour. All the other girls were married here. Eleanor to Frederick Kridler, the chairmaker. They lived on the southwest corner of Jefferson and Market. Anna Margaret married J. W. Miller, the tailor. Uriah was next. The next in age was Louisa, who married Gen. John G. Breslin, the founder of the *Seneca Advertiser.* Josephine married Mr. B. Pennington, the photograph artist, and Martha, the youngest, is the wife of Gen. Wm. H. Gibson. Mrs. Pennington and Mrs. Gibson are all that are now living of the Creeger family.

William Campbell had a cabinet shop on Madison street, some where near Esq. Bloom's residence. He married a Mrs. Staley, a widowed sister of Dr. Kuhn, who had several children, of whom the late Mrs. McFarland, formerly the wife of my venerable and distinguished friend, Dr. McFarland, was the oldest. She was a beautiful woman, highly accomplished, and much esteemed.

It is a most remarkable fact that Tiffin, in former days—yes, and all along until quite recently—had more beautiful women to the number of population, than any other town in Ohio, and the fact was generally conceded all over the country. The town became famous on that account.

Mrs. Thomas Ourand is also a daughter of Mr. Campbell. The family first lived in a log house on the lot where Mr. Charles Leiner, the hatter, now lives, on Market street. There was only one more cabinet shop in town, and that was built by Daniel H. Phillips, a brother of Mrs. H. Ebert. They were from Uniontown, Pennsylvania. The shop stood at the northwest corner of Jefferson and Market, where the Episcopal church now stands. On the 21st day of August, 1833, three days after my arrival in Tiffin, I entered that shop as an apprentice to Mr. Phillips, and there I found and made the acquaintance of my old friend, Col. J. M. Stevens, of Melmore, a former apprentice. Mr. Phillips lived in a log house east of the shop on the lot now owned by the Adams family. They had a young lady living in the family by the name of Mary Hendel, a daughter of Michael Hendel, who lived on Perry street. The family were Pennsylvania Germans, but Mary talked good English, also. In my great anxiety to learn English, I sometimes troubled people with numerous questions. Hearing the word "fact" used very often, and not being able to comprehend it, I asked Mary once at the dinner table what the word meant. She looked at me for a little while very sternly, thinking for an explanation, and then said: "Why! a fact is a fact, *du esel!*"

Mary is now, and for a long time has been, the happy wife of Mr. Jonas Neikirk, of Republic.

Next west of Mr. Kridler, lived Jacob Huss, the saddler, and next west to him, David Bishop. William D. Searles bought out Bishop, and started a tin-shop at that place.

Guy Stevens carried on the mercantile business close by, and south of Ebert's. He afterwards took, as a partner, Daniel Dildine, Esq., the present venerable justice of the peace, of Tiffin. They also started the first foundry in the county. It was located at the end of Monroe street, close by the river, and occupied the north end of the lot where Esq. Dildine now resides.

In 1837, a man by the name of Louis Bredoon, a hotel keeper in McCutchenville, had a short cannon cast at this foundry to be used at the coming Fourth of July celebration. He came after it with a wagon on the 24th day of June, and all hands concluded to try it first. They put the piece on the running gear of a wagon and loaded it very strong. It exploded, and played havoc all around. A piece of the iron struck Mr. Burdoon on the forehead and crushed in the skull from his left eye brow up to the hair. He was picked up unconscious, and carried to Goodin's hotel, then kept by Michael Hendel, where he soon after died. Dildine had several ribs broken; one Watson had a leg broken; other men were injured more or less. The wagon and the front door of the foundry were demolished, and pieces of the cannon were found great distances away. There has been no cannon foundry in Tiffin since. We buy all our guns of Krupp.

William H. Kessler carried on the tailoring trade in Fort Ball, and Moses D. Cadwallader and Jefferson Freese were rivals in Tiffin. Mr. Freese married a young lady that Dr. Fisher raised and brought with him here from Maryland. She was very pretty, and highly esteemed. Dr. Boyer lived in a stone house that stood where Emick's boot store is. This and the mill house were the only stone houses in Tiffin. Both are gone. One of Dr. Boyer's daughters married Lloyd Norris, who became the owner of the Van Meter section, and lived there. He had means they said, but very little polish. He was the father of the detective, John T. Norris. Another daughter of Dr. Boyer, Elizabeth, married Dr. James Fisher, one of Tiffin's early practitioners. Both were very polite and accomplished people. The Doctor is still living somewhere in Missouri. Our Richard Boyer, the broker, is the youngest of the sons, and Frances Hannah was the youngest daughter. She became the wife of John J. Steiner, one of the early lawyers of Tiffin. Both are now dead.

It is impossible to remember all the old settlers here, and the names of those that occur are only jotted down. Many of those on the Fort Ball side have already been named. There, also, lived Gen. H. C. Brish, Valentine and George Knupp, Andrew Love, William Johnson, George Ragan, Curtis Sisty, Levi Davis and Nicholas Leibe. Mr. Sting, the father of C. H. Sting, also built and carried on a little brewery, on Sandusky street. Leibe, Coonrad and Baugher married three sisters. Of these six, Mrs. Coonrad, alone, is living. They were the daughters of a widow lady, Mrs. Staub, and sisters of the once popular John Staub and Dr. Staub.

Among the early settlers of Tiffin were a few families from Germany, and being so few, are easily described. The first one of these the writer can call to mind is that of Mr. Andrew Albrecht, from Baden. He was a stone mason and brick layer by trade; had a wife and several children when he came here. His father-in-law, Christopher Zeis, lived with him. Mr. Zeis was with Napoleon the First in the Spanish campaign, and was fond of telling his exploits. With this family, also, came John Snyder and Christopher Snyder, shoemakers by trade, and who were nephews by a sister of the old soldier. John married Barbara Albert, step-daughter of a Mr. Hohmann, and carried on a shoe-shop in Tiffin until he died. He was decidedly the best boot maker Tiffin then had. These people came here in the fall of 1832. In August, of 1833, the Lang and Seewald families arrived here; also, the Vollmers, Julius Fellnagel, Joseph Ranker, Valentine and Louis Taumpler, Jacob Ernst, Henry Brass, the Blasius family, Francis Gilbert, Andrew Bloom, and a family by the name of Meyers, who lived in a two-story frame house where Ulrich's drug store now stands, and where Meyers tried the experiment of a brewery on a small scale. These institutions then required but small capital.

Two brothers from Marion, by the name of Kolb, built another brewery, up on the hill, near the crossing of Sandusky and Market. John and Francis Souder, Jacob Ernst, Adam Schickel, the musician, Frederick Hoffman, the Faulhaver family, and many others, then, also, made Tiffin their home.

Henry Lang, (whose baptismal name was George Ludwig Henry,) was the oldest son of Wilhelm, and Louisa Christina, daughter of a rope manufacturer by the name of Matzenburg, in Kochendorf, a small village near the city of Heilbroun, in North Wurtemburg. His father was an officer in the Forest Department, and was transferred to a station west of the Rhine in the Palatinate, the western province of Bavaria. Grandfather was born in 1739, and died at his new station in 1789, when but fifty years old. This was at Neu-Hemsbach, in the Canton of Winweiler. At the death of his father, Henry was but 19 years old, and the only help his widowed mother had; but young as he was, the forest authorities took notice of him, and appointed him the successor of his father in office. His deportment towards the people and the government, changeable as both were during the turmoil following the French Revolution, and scenes incident to the war, was such that he was retained in his place. Faithful and diligent in the discharge of every duty, he became beloved by all except wood thieves and poachers. His small salary supported him, his widowed mother, and an invalid step-brother on his father's side—Uncle Christian.

We Americans understand a "forester" to be a man that lives in the woods. The word is understood otherwise in Europe. There it means an officer of the "forest department;" one who superintends and takes care of the king's forest, and prosecutes offenders against the forest laws, etc.

On the 25th day of January, 1801, father was married to Catharine, the daughter of the school teacher Schuetz, in Vorder-Weidenthal, an old Alsacian family. This union was blessed with nine children—seven daughters and two sons. Two of the girls died in childhood. Louisa, the oldest daughter, married Philip Seewald, the jeweler, in September, 1828. Elizabeth, the second daughter, married John Gross, a cabinet-maker, in March, 1831; the other girls were all married here. Philipina was married to Valentine Seewald, in Tiffin, September, 1833, soon after we arrived here. Henrietta married Mr. J. M. Zahm, late county treasurer, May 2, 1836, and Hannah married Michael Schoch, who died here within a few months after their marriage. Hannah some time after married Mr. Edward Swander, well known in Seneca county as an intelligent and successful farmer. Mrs. Zahm is the only living daughter. Both sons, the Rev. Henry Lang in Fremont, and the writer, yet remain.

The very fact that father held his office from his nineteenth to his sixty-fourth year, when he resigned it to come to the United States, proves how much he was appreciated as a man and an officer, being in the possession of his office some forty-three years.

We came by wagon across France. There were no steamboats on the Rhine, and no railroads on the Continent. We left Havre de Grace, at the mouth of the Seine, on the 24th day of April, 1833, and after combatting many a storm on the ocean, landed at Baltimore on the 27th day of the following June. The family was on the way from April 3d to August 18th, when we reached Tiffin, after making a journey, by water and by land, of over 4000 miles. The name of the old three-masted sailing vessel which brought us over was "Jefferson," and she belonged to Boston.

The few of the early settlers yet living remember father Lang in his dark-green, broadcloth dress, bearing the style and color of his former office, and a cloth cap of the same color on his head. He was five feet ten inches high, very straight, with soldier-like bearing, had large blue eyes, an aquiline nose, a mild countenance, and was calm and self-possessed. He was never known to swear, or express a word in anger. He had a masterly control of his passions and appetites. He was not only moral, but a devoted christian. He never left his home in the morning without saying his prayer, and his evening prayers were full of warmth, and rich in poetic thought. He never used tobacco in any way; was never seen under the influence of wine; never played at any games; never used an unkind word towards mother or any of us children; and when he whipped us sometimes, we thought it could not be possible, for he was not angry at all.

Mother was the very embodiment of christian graces and tender love. It was she who caused our emigration to America, being influenced to that end largely on my account, for I was then just about old enough to be drafted into the army in time of need, and she wanted to secure me against the draft. Even when we did go, I was compelled to remain behind, because I was then seventeen years old. They bound me out to a relative of father's by the name of Wittich, who was a chair and spinning wheel manufacturer, as an apprentice, where I was to stay until the draft of my class. This satisfied the authorities. The contract was written on stamped paper, with a crown in the seal, (I have liked crowns and stamped paper ever since—but to no great extent.) The rest of the family started, and I went to my boss, where I was soon initiated into the arts and mysteries of splitting out sticks for the turning lathe. On the morning of the tenth day I was found missing; about one week afterwards I waited at the city of Metz for our folks to come. Let me add this: I walked from home to Havre de Grace, and from Baltimore to Tiffin. Father died here in August, 1838, in his sixty-ninth year, and mother died in June, 1849, in her seventieth year.

Reader, will you be kind enough to excuse this reference to my own family? It is hard to resist speaking of things and events that lie so near to one's heart. Let us proceed.

Mr. Fellnagel kept a tavern in the frame building where Mr. Jacob Boyer now lives, corner of Sandusky and Market streets. Andrew Bloom was a traveling tailor. He came here and got married, and is in the tailoring business still. He is familiarly known as Esq. Bloom.

Joseph Gibson was a shoemaker by trade. He was born in Frederick county, Maryland, in November, 1811, and married there Elizabeth Ott, on the 13th day of September, 1831; he located here in 1832, where his family have lived ever since. He died in July, 1857, two years after his return from California.

My old, esteemed friend, the Hon. Henry Cronise, was also a native of Frederick county, Maryland, a county that contributed more largely to the settlement of Seneca county, and supplied it with more means, muscle, and brains, than any other county in the world. He was born there on the 15th day of May 1789. His youthful days were spent in

Norfolk, Virginia. Upon his return to Maryland he engaged in the mercantile business, which occupation he pursued as long as he was in active life. In 1816 he was married at Fredericktown, Maryland, to Susanna Fundenburg, a young lady well known for her beauty and sweetness of disposition, which made her attractive and lovable through the whole of her life, and especially in her latter days, binding to her, with the closest ties of affection, children, grand-children and a host of friends. With all her personal attractions and her warm nature, mother Cronise preferred her home above all the allurements of society, where she would have been a queen in any circle.

In 1826 Mr. Cronise came to Ohio in company with several other gentlemen, and being very much pleased with Seneca county, located several sections in different parts of it, and purchased a house for his home, which remained such for nearly thirty years, during which time it was a sort of open house for neighbors and friends at home, and distinguished strangers from abroad.

After his purchase he returned to Maryland, and in the following year sent out a number of wagons loaded with dry goods; himself and family, then consisting of a wife and five children, followed in a short time, coming across the country in carriages and on horseback, and being four weeks on the road. On reaching Tiffin, the family moved into the house thus provided; it was located opposite Naylor's hardware store. Four other children were born here, making nine in all.

In 1840 Mr. Cronise established the *Van Burenite*, and operated it as its editor against the election of General Harrison, with great force. Mr. Cronise was elected to the legislature twice: once as a member of the House, and in 1846 as a member of the Senate.

He died on the 14th day of February, 1867. Mother Cronise survived her husband some years, and died in August, 1875. Thus passed away two of Tiffin's most distinguished pioneers, who had made and left their mark on the town. Mr. Cronise was a decided and firm Democrat, and as such, a leader in the county from the time he came here until he died. He was a shrewd and safe political counselor, and possessed of great political sagacity and influence. He was a stout, muscular man, square shouldered, well built, and of clear German type. He had dark brown hair, dark, hazel eyes, small, clenched lips, a fine forehead, strong lower jaw, nose ordinary, nervous-bilious temperament, which often causes the possessor trouble when unaccompanied by refinement and an iron will. It is apt to lead to impulsiveness. A high strung nature like this generally acts before it thinks, but it troubled father Cronise only at times of high political excitement. In his private life it was scarcely ever observable. He was much beloved by the Democrats, and hated in the same ratio by the Whigs. He had no charity for a political enemy; he knew he was right, and that was enough.

The Democrats in the county never had such leaders as Cronise, Seney and Goodin, either before or since their day. Firm, sagacious, earnest, active, untiring, unselfish—they sought the success of the party above personal ambition.

Aside from politics, Mr. Cronise was very kind, gentlemanly and courteous. He was like a father to the new comer and stranger, and especially to the Germans, whose language he spoke. His intercourse with others was very strongly marked by the peculiar genteel, polite, hospitable, yet dignified demeanor that marked the Maryland and Virginia gentleman of that day. Marquis Y Graff, Joseph Graff, Jacob Souder, the Pittengers, Dr. Boyer, the Holtz's, Dr. Kuhn, and others came under that rule, if rule it was. These are all dead except Mrs. John Pittenger and Judge Benjamin Pittenger, who are still living.

The writer always found in father Cronise a true friend, and records these lines with mixed feelings of pleasure and sadness, as a token of the high esteem in which his memory is cherished. Of pleasure, because of the opportunity to register my testimony to a tried friend ; of sadness, because those of us who enjoyed the company and counsel of Henry Cronise are getting less very rapidly, and are already but few in number.

PHILIP SEEWALD

Was born on the 26th day of September, 1799, in Sippersfeld, in the Bavarian Palatinate, Germany. He was the oldest son of Ludwig and Sophia Seewald. His father was a man who resembled Henry Clay of Kentucky very much. Both gentlemen happened to be in Tffiin on a visit at the same time, and it was a common remark how much they resembled each other. The mother of Philip was a Correll, and descended from a long line of school teachers in this village. Louis (Ludwig) Seewald was a wagon maker by trade, and Philip worked in the shop of his father as soon as he was old enough, and learned the trade. He was a natural genius, and when he was drafted into the Bavarian army he applied all his leisure hours to the study of the watch and the natural sciences. When he returned from the army he was a good watch maker, and very handy at any curious workmanship in iron. He married the oldest daughter of Henry Lang, above named, and a few years thereafter emigrated, with his family, to the United

States and settled in Philadelphia, Pennsylvania, where he opened a jewelry shop. When the Lang family came, in 1833, they stopped at Pittsburgh until Seewald and his family united with them, and then both families came to Tiffin together, where they arrived on the 18th day of August, 1833.

The early settlers will remember the jewelry store of Seewald, in the large, hewed log house, on south Washington street, in Tiffin. The front end was devoted to jewelry, and the back part to gunsmithing. Here he lived until about 1843, when he bought from John Goodin the lot where the Rust block now is, and where he lived the rest of his days.

He never made the English language a study, and spoke it very brokenly; but he built up a good trade with his skill and general reputation for honesty. By close application to his books he became well versed in general history and the popular sciences of the day. He was naturally a thinker and investigator; he took nothing for granted, and discarded everything that lacked a cause. He was firm in his judgment, and able to defend any position he took. His mind naturally lead him to the bottom of things. While he never obtruded his conclusions on anybody, he was strong in the defense of them when once formed.

His wife died on the 8th day of February, 1843. Three of their children were born in Germany, and the rest of them in this country. They had eight in all, of whom three sons and two daughters are still living. Louis Seewald, the jeweler, is the oldest son; William lives in New Mexico, and Philip, the youngest, in Hudson, Michigan. The boys were all jewelers. The oldest daughter is Mrs. Oster, and the youngest Mrs. Spindler, both residing in Tiffin.

Mr. Seewald was married again to Elizabeth Staib. This union was blessed with but one child, Sophia, who was married in the spring of this year to a Mr. Roll, of Cleveland, where they reside.

Philip Seewald was a short, robust, compactly built man, very strong and muscular. He had a very large head, that became bald early; well proportioned: large, fleshy nose; deep-set blue eyes; strong, manly features. His head was so large that he could find no hat large enough in the stores, and had to send his measure to Cincinnati. He was about five feet six inches high, and weighed, when in his best days, near 200 pounds. As years began to make him restless, he left his business in the hands of his son Louis, and made up a lot of instruments with which he built tower clocks. The clock in the tower of the court house is one of them.

Thus he spent the afternoon and evening of his life, ever busy, reading or making something useful or ingenious. He was widely known as the principal watchmaker in Tiffin, and as a man of strict, unflinching integrity, highly esteemed by everybody. He died on the 30th day of October, 1878, aged seventy-nine years, one month and four days.

CHAPTER XVII.

ADDITIONS TO TIFFIN—THE FERRY—THE BRIDGES—THE TOLL BRIDGE—THE FREE BRIDGE—THE BURNING OF THE FREE BRIDGE—THE CHOLERA—FREDERICK HOFFMAN—LITTLE CHARLOTTE—JOHNNY DALRYMPLE—THE RAILROADS—FIRST TRAIN TO TIFFIN—HEIDELBERG COLLEGE—REV. E. V. GERHART, D. D.—REV. J. H. GOOD, D. D.—REV. GEO. W. WILLARD, D. D.

IT WOULD require a book by itself to give a full description of the numerous additions that were made to Tiffin and to Fort Ball, and finally to Tiffin proper as a city of the second class, from time to time. The reader must be content with a mere reference to the same. At the commencement of this work, fear for want of material to write a book was uppermost in the mind of the writer, but now, and as he is about commencing this chapter, he is troubled to know what best to leave out, to prevent the book from becoming too bulky.

The desire to write personal sketches of many more of the old pioneers is very strong, and should be indulged would space only permit. Being conscious of the fact, that in the great stream of time generations after generations appear upon the stage of action, and are swept away in their order into the vast ocean of the past; and of this other fact, that we are forgotten by the few that ever knew us, to love or to hate us, about as fast as we go—I am strongly reminded of what my dear old friend, Frederick Fieser, Esq., the able and illustrious editor of the *Westbote*, in Columbus, once said to me, speaking on the subject of ambition, viz: that about all you can say of man is "he was born, took a wife, and died."

Yet, as this narrative progresses notices will be taken of a character here and there, that shall be deemed proper in its place.

The following are the additions made to Tiffin, from the time of the first platting, viz: New Fort Ball; Hedges' northern and southern additions to Tiffin; Norris and Gist's addition, June 15, 1832; Rawson's addition, May 30, 1833; Sneath and Graff's, January 29, 1834; Keller and Gist's, same date; Jennings', November 13, 1834; Williams', April 22, 1835; Waggoner's, January 13, 1836; Sheldon's, September 11, 1838; Hedges' second addition, July 26, 1851; Davis', May 16,

ADDITIONS TO TIFFIN. 259

1854; Springdale, May, 1854; Deuzer's, November 13, 1855; Allbright's March, 1856; Seney's, December, 1856; Avery, Butler & Cecil's, July 27, 1857; Heilman's, July 14, 1858; Hedges' second southern, February 26, 1859; Sub-division of lots 1 and 2 in block D; Bunn's W. pt; lot 2; block S; Noble's; Noble's second; Frost's; Schouhart's; Hunter's sub-division of out-lots Nos. 6 and 7 ; Jacob Heilman's; Scheiber's; Brewer's; Mrs. Walker's; Mrs. Walker's second; Goodsell's; Mrs. Hunter's; Tomb's; Gross'; Souder's sub-division; Stoner's; Mrs. Allen's; Bunn's second; J. T. Huss'; Davis Estate's ; Gray's; Lewis'; McCollum & Snyder's; Mechanicsburgh; Weirick's; Blair's; Remmele's; Fishbaugh's; Gibson's; Gwinn's; Shawhan's; Hall's; Cottage Park; Bartell's; Huddle's; Schubert's; Kaull & Glenn's; Houck's; Myers'; Ph. Wentz's; G. D. Loomis'; J. Bour's; Hayward's; Huber's; Fishbaugh's second; W. C. Hedges'; Zeigler's; Louisa Smith's; Harter & Sloman's; John Heilman's sub-division; Maria P. Kuhn's; J. Heilman's; Sullivan's sub-division ; Noble's re-sub-division. There were some seventy-two in all. The lots were re-numbered in March, 1854.

These additions and the several annexations the city council has made from time to time, with very questionable propriety, but under the severe law of the state that gives landed proprietors, in the territory to be annexed, no voice in the measure, have extended the limits of the city to embrace all of section 19, all of section 30 (except about one hundred and forty acres), about one hundred and forty acres in section 29, more than one-half of section 20, and about one hundred and sixty acres of section 18, in Clinton township—about 1760 acres in all.

In the fall of 1833 Mr. Hedges contracted with Reuben Williams, one of the leading carpenters at that time, to build a wooden bridge across the river on Washington street. Some of the work was done that fall, but during the following spring and summer the work progressed very slowly. It was finally completed far enough to have a few plank laid over it lengthwise, for the accommodation of foot passengers. During the spring and summer of 1834, another foot bridge was constructed a little distance further down the river, by boring holes into slabs and putting long sticks into them to raise the slabs above the water. Both of these conveniences together nearly ruined Mr. Hoagland's ferry.

A big freshet, in the fall of 1834, brought immense quantities of drift down the river—whole trees, straw stacks, fence rails, saw logs, etc.,—and made a lodgement at the bents of the bridge. Several men ventured to get on the top of the drift pile with their axes, and commenced chopping the long trees into pieces, in order to start them on their way. They made considerable headway; but when they saw large pieces of the Tymochtee bridge approaching, they got away just in time to save their lives. When these pieces of the Tymochtee bridge struck the gathered drift the whole mass went together, taking the new bridge along.

In the summer following Mr. Hedges built a better bridge at the same place, and when it was done he employed a colored man to collect toll. This was the first and only toll bridge that Tiffin ever had. Early in the spring of 1836, James W. Hill published a notice to the effect that he had rented the toll bridge from Mr. Hedges for the term of three months, commencing on the 1st day of April, 1836, and called upon those who had bargains with Mr. Hedges to cross the bridge, to call on him, in order to renew their contracts, etc.

The bridge was a great convenience, but the idea of paying toll became annoying to farmers, as well as to the merchants in Tiffin, and a plan was put on foot to have a free bridge constructed over the river at the west end of Market street. A subscription list was circulated, and when the requisite amount was subscribed the contract was let. It was a wooden, truss bridge with a roof over it. Guy Stevens, Benjamin Biggs, John Park and Dr. James Fisher were the building committee; Andrew Lugenbeel was treasurer.

There was great rejoicing in Tiffin when, on the 18th day of February, 1837, it was announced that the free bridge was opened to the public. It cost $2,200.00. Hedges' toll bridge became a free bridge also, as a matter of course.

This covered, free bridge was a fearfully dark place after night, and the women on either side of the river refused to cross it without protection, after dark. Some time after, lanterns were put up at each end during dark nights. Peter Vaness established a large carriage shop where Loomis & Nyman's foundry now is, near the bridge, and when the carriage factory burned down, the bridge caught fire and burned.

The old toll bridge lasted for ten years after that, when, on New Year's night of 1847, it was swept away by a freshet. Then the county commissioners put up in its place one of the most wonderful contrivances for a bridge that was ever seen. The plan of it was simple enough, but the great quantity of material used in its construction surprised everybody but the commissioners. The stringers that were laid from one bent to the other, and on which the plank were laid cross-wise, were of such ponderous size and weight that they absolutely broke the whole fabric down, very soon after it was finished.

When the people saw the danger of an accident, some one nailed boards across the ends of the bridge to keep teams from going on it, and in less than a week from that time, down it went. Then was constructed the wire suspension bridge, in 1853, which answered a good purpose for some time, and which also in its order gave way to the present beautiful iron structure, being the fifth bridge built at that place since 1833.

The free bridge on Market street burned away in the night following the 26th day of January, 1854, and was succeeded by the present bridge, which was built by the county commissioners. The fire in Vaness' carriage factory was discovered at two o'clock in the morning, and the roof of the bridge took fire from it within twenty minutes thereafter.

The morning of the 24th day of April, 1833, was cool and bracing; the sun shone brightly while the ebb of the Atlantic ocean set into the mouth of the Seine at Havre de Grace, France. To take advantage of the tide, several American packets in the harbor were making ready to leave the port. Sailors were running to and fro; some up in the rigging, others hoisting the anchor; some speaking English, some German, some French, some Spanish; some were singing, some swearing, and all were busy. Passengers crowding onto the boats with their goods, had their passes examined and their berths assigned to them. The ebb was up to high water mark, and the time had come to "let go." The few sails that were stretched swelled westward by the gentle breeze; the rudder groaned, and the old "Jefferson" began to move.

Two sailors pulled up a bunting at the foot of the rear mast, and when it got high enough to catch the breeze, it unfolded the "Stars and Stripes" of the United States of America for the first time to the eyes of the writer. The emotions that filled my heart at the sight I will not undertake to describe, for fear my kind readers might think me foolish. But think of a boy with a warm, hopeful nature, running away from his native land to escape its oppressions and military tyranny, leaving his native shore for the land of his hopes and desires, for the first time in his life standing under the "flag of the free," under which his future destiny is to be wrought out—and you can have an idea how the writer felt when leaving Havre de Grace.

On board of the Jefferson were one hundred and thirty-seven passengers, mostly from Bavaria and Baden. Of these, strange as it may seem, three families came to Tiffin without the least consort of action or understanding. When we landed at Baltimore every family had its own point of destination, and all scattered. The Lang family came here that same year, in August; the Hoffman family in the fall after, and the family of John G. Osteen came in 1840, I think.

This Hoffman family was from Meisenheim, in the Palatinate, and consisted of Frederick Hoffman, his wife and three children, John, Fritz and Charlotte. Charlotte was a little blue-eyed beauty, with fair skin, cheerful face, and flaxen locks falling upon her shoulders. Her friendly, sweet nature, attracted the attention of the people on board, and she became one of the pets. Charlotte was then about three years old, and had for a playmate another little girl that looked very much like her. She was the youngest daughter of a Mr. Maurer, on board, and afterwards became the wife of the Hon. Charles Bœsel, late senator from the Auglaize district, living in New Bremen.

Frederick Hoffman was then about forty years of age. He was a potter by trade; had traveled some; was very social and talkative— really attractive in conversation. He was a man of striking personal appearance. His carriage was very straight; he was about five feet nine inches high; not fleshy, but muscular. He had very black hair, black eyes, and very long, black eye-lashes; a large nose, and rather large, but well proportioned mouth; and deep, sonorous voice. His manners were easy and gentlemanly. The writer has but faint recollection of Mrs. Hoffman.

When the family came here in the fall of 1833, though late, Mr. Hoffman bought the lot now owned by the Henz family, next south to Dr. McFarland, and immediately erected a two-story hewed log house thereon. As soon as the house was done, the family occupied it and opened the first German tavern in Tiffin. The first German dance in Tiffin was held there about Christmas that year, 1833. The oldest son, John, and the writer were comrades on board the Jefferson, and we renewed our friendship with great pleasure after we came together again here. In the spring of 1834 Mr. Hoffman put up a potter's-shop and an oven on his lot, and burnt several kilns of good pottery, the first in the county.

In 1832 the Asiatic cholera broke out in Canada, and, sweeping along the Hudson and the St. Lawrence, visited the large cities along the seacoast. It raged with greater or less severity from Newfoundland to New Orleans in 1833. In 1834 cases occurred in many inland towns and cities. About the fore part of August in this year, news reached Tiffin that several cases had proved fatal in Sandusky City. People in Tiffin began to be apprehensive and expressed much concern on the subject. A constable, by the name of John Hubble, lived on Monroe street. His wife died on the 19th of August. The doctors refused to say much about the cause of her death, and it was rumored about that she had eaten green cucumbers that had caused her death. On the next day a small child of a German family that lived in the second story of Mr.

Hoffman's house, died. In the afternoon of that day the writer took the coffin to the house and put the little corpse into it. The father was absent from home, and the mother wished to wait for his return before she would have the child buried. Coming down stairs, I found Mr. Hoffman at the front door, and after talking awhile we parted. He had just recovered from an attack of billious fever and looked very pale. His pale face, white shirt and white pants, forming a violent contrast with his very black eyes and hair, made his appearance more impressive than ever. This was about four o'clock P. M. The following night about three o'clock his son John called me out of bed and requested that I should come down to the house and said his father was dying. When I reached the house, Dr. Dresbach came out and told me Hoffman had died of cholera. Now consternation and alarm spread like wild-fire over the town and country, and Tiffin changed its appearance very rapidly. Business stopped; people stood about the streets in groups. Some prepared to get away already. Several other cases occurred in the next twenty-four hours, and at the end of one week from the death of Mr. Hoffman there were only about seven families left in the place. Boss Phillips, and all the shop hands, were among the runaways, except a young man from Maryland, Mr. Wilson and myself. Mr. Campbell's cabinet shop was also shut up. Stores and all other public houses, except Sneath's hotel, were closed. Some movers, German, Scotch and Irish families, had stopped here on their way west. The Cronise family, the Seewalds, and the Lang families and part of Boyers staid. Father thought it was wrong to run away from each other in time of distress. Wilson and myself had the shop to ourselves, and made the coffins as fast as we could. Very often we made rough boxes answer. One Sunday we made seven. The town was very still and quiet during the day. Scarcely a man could be seen except the doctors running hither and thither. Boards were nailed across the doors of many houses. The nights were made hideous by the bawling of the cows and the howling of the dogs that had lost their masters and owners. When the disease began to abate Mr. Phillips called to see us once in a while. We made eighty-six coffins in our shop in five weeks from the time Mr. Hoffman died. One Sunday morning an ox-team came along Market street from the west, with a water-trough made out of a log, on the wagon, and a slab nailed over the top, going to the cemetery. Two men with pick and shovel followed. They buried a man that had died west of Fort Ball.

In a log house at the southeast corner of Perry and Jefferson, lived a Scotch family by the name of Dalrymple. They had a boy, Johnny, about thirteen years old, who, a few days before, was a picture of health as well as a picture of beauty. I loved him for his friendly nature. One day the mother came to the shop and requested me to come to the house and take his measure. He laid on his bed with a sheet over him, but looked as beautiful as ever. I ran to Dr. Dresbach and told him that I did not believe the boy was dead. The Doctor thought otherwise, but gave me a bottle of brandy, with orders to make it hot and rub it all over him with a flannel cloth. The mother assisted me, and in less than one half hour the poor fellow began to move and opened his eyes. Dr. Dresbach was called in and was much rejoiced at our success. He took him in charge and in about two weeks the boy was on the street again. The cases were getting less and people began to return. The weather was growing cooler and slight frosts were observable some mornings. People began to take courage with a hope that the cholera had left us. One morning Mrs. Dalrymple came to the shop crying and told us that her son was dead. His was the last case in Tiffin.

Towards the latter part of October all the stragglers had returned.

It is not true, as Mr. Butterfield would have it, that the disease was confined to the German and Irish emigrants exclusively. 'Squire Plane, David Bretz, Andrew Fruitchy, Mr. Brookover, and many others that died, were citizens here and natives.

The cholera returned again to Tiffin in 1849, in 1852, and again in 1854, with less severity, however, except for a short time in 1854, when on one Sunday, sixteen corpses were counted on the Fort Ball side, where it raged with the greatest fury. On that day Dr. Hovey, with the assistance of Joe Smith, George W. Zigler, William Holt, Thomas W. Boyce, Mrs. Flahaff, Miss Julia Gear, laid out eleven dead at the hospital alone. It took some moral courage to stare death in the face in times like these, and the names of these heroes and heroines are recorded here as worthy to be remembered. All the doctors did their duty, no doubt, but Dr. Hovey was, perhaps, the most active and industrious. For five weeks he was amongst his patients day and night without changing his clothes. The Rev. Mr. Sullivan, of St. Mary's Church, was amongst the fearless, and Dr. McCollum, until he himself was taken down. "There were giants in those days."

Strange as it may seem, the greatest mortality was on that side of the river, which may be partially accounted for from the fact that the pest-house was built there; but with all that there were fewer cases on the Tiffin side.

One thing more on this subject should be mentioned here. Mrs.

Hoffman died within one week after her husband, leaving the children strangers in a strange land. The boys were more able to help themselves. Little Charlotte found a good home in the family of Judge Ebert, who had no children. The good and kind Mrs. Ebert adopted Charlotte and raised and educated her with the love and tender care of a good mother. A young lawyer in Tiffin succeeded in winning her heart after she had grown up into womanhood, and little Charlotte is the happy wife of Governor Lee, of Toledo.

THE RAILROADS.

It is said that great events sometimes throw their shadows before. The subject of a railroad to Tiffin from some place was talked about nearly ten years before a locomotive was seen in town. When the subject of the Mad River and Lake Erie railroad began to be agitated, meetings were held in Tiffin from time to time, committees appointed to raise subscriptions, etc. In August, 1832, the *Sandusky Clarion* published an editorial in which it was said that the prospects of a road were good, and that $50,000 had already been subscribed.

In September, 1832, the following notice was published in the *Seneca Patriot:*

RAILROAD NOTICE.

The undersigned. Commissioners of Seneca county, for the Mad River and Erie R. R., will open books for subscription of stock for said road in Tiffin, Seneca county, on the fourth day of October. 1832, at the residence of Eli Norris.

HENRY CRONISE.
JOSIAH HEDGES.

The first sod for this road was cut at the end of Water street, Sandusky, Ohio, on the 7th day of September, A. D., 1835, by General Harrison, of Cincinnati, assisted by Governor Vance. The occasion was one of rejoicing; banners were hoisted to the breeze, while music and song filled the air.

The track was laid along Water street to the west end of the city. James Bell was the civil engineer for its construction, and W. Durlein his assistant. The first locomotive, called the "Sandusky," arrived there in 1838, and was used in the construction of the road. In the fall of 1838, the line was completed to Bellevue, fifteen miles, and the first train run there. Thomas Hogg, who afterwards moved to the island, was the engineer; John Paull, now dead, was fireman, and Charles Higgins, also dead, was conductor. The train consisted of the locomotive "Sandusky," a small passenger car, and a still smaller freight car, not exceeding twenty feet in length, which latter car remained for some time the only accommodation for carrying merchandise. It is said this locomotive was the first one in America that had a steam whistle. In 1839 work was done from Bellevue to Republic. The first locomotive reached Tiffin in 1841. Conrad Poppenburg was the engineer when the first passenger train ran to Tiffin; Earnest Kirrian was the fireman—both still living. Paul Klauer died in Urbana of cholera. He was also a hand on the train.

Since then, another route had been opened through Clyde and the old route entirely abandoned and taken up. The old charter bears date January 5, 1832. The company is now known by the name of Cincinnati, Sandusky and Cleveland railroad, and runs over one hundred and ninety miles of rails. Its main line is from Sandusky to Springfield, a distance of one hundred and thirty miles.

The Columbus division extends from Columbus to Springfield, forty-five miles, and the Findlay branch extends from Carey to Findlay, a distance of sixteen miles. This line of road is proverbial for its steady and safe traveling facilities, and is one of the best conducted roads in the country.

The Tiffin, Toledo and Eastern railroad.—On the first day of May, 1873, the first regular passenger train was run on this road. It traverses the county in a northwesterly direction. This road is now consolidated with the Mansfield, Coldwater and Lake Michigan, and is completed from Mansfield to Toledo, now under the control of the Pennsylvania company. Its depot in Tiffin is near the "tunnel," where the road crosses Washington street. The road is doing a large business.

The Baltimore, Pittsburg and Chicago railroad was completed to Tiffin in the early part of 1874. It is under the general management of the Baltimore and Ohio company, and crosses Seneca county nearly east and west. The bridge of this company across the Sandusky river is of iron, and decidedly the best railroad bridge in the county. The company is doing a very extensive business, but their present depot in Tiffin is a little board shanty, unworthy alike of the road and of Tiffin.

The Lake Erie and Louisville railroad runs through the northwestern part of the county to Fostoria, and the Columbus and Toledo railroad, running through Big Spring and Loudon townships, also touching at Fostoria, are in full operation.

The Pomeroy road (so-called), and hereafter to be known as the Atlantic and Lake Erie road, has been graded for some time, and is to be put into operation during the coming summer. It runs through Seneca and Loudon townships; also touching at Fostoria.

Thus Seneca county is cut by five railroads, in constant operation, with another in immediate prospect, and still another east and west road in embryo.

HEIDELBERG COLLEGE.

The Tiffin and Fort Wayne road was surveyed and graded about twenty-five years ago. It is almost forgotten, together with its own sad history.

The Clinton Line Extension, that was to run from Tiffin eastward, and towards the construction of which Tiffin and the people along the line contributed so largely, was another of the many gigantic frauds and robberies that have contributed so largely to make people, who are not in the railroad ring, and belong not to the large fish, so extremely cautious and reluctant when they are now asked to subscribe towards the building of another railroad. The numerous subscribers of the Mansfield, Coldwater and Lake Michigan, who have been sued to pay their subscription the second time, have some experience in the premises.

HISTORY OF HEIDELBERG COLLEGE AT TIFFIN.

The establishment of this college grew out of the desire of the "Reformed Church of Ohio" to found institutions (namely, a college and a theological seminary) where its candidates for the ministry might obtain a full and complete classical and scientific education; and where also all others fitting for the different professions, might have the benefit of that educational training so necessary for success in other ways.

In the year 1850, Rev. Hiram Shaull, the pastor of the First Reformed Church in Tiffin, by prompt and energetic action, succeeded in obtaining subscriptions to the amount of $11,030 from the citizens of Tiffin and vicinity, to be donated to the proposed college, on the condition that it be located at Tiffin. The proposition was accepted by the synod, at Navarre, Ohio, in September, 1850, and two professors were at once elected to open the school. These two professors have been in connection with these institutions from the start, a period now of thirty years. They were Rev. J. H. Good, A. M., of Columbus, Ohio, elected as professor of mathematics, and Rev. Reuben Good, A. M., of Darke county, Ohio, elected as rector of the preparatory department. These gentlemen promptly removed to Tiffin, and by November of the same year, opened the school, in the third story of a business block called "Commercial Row." Joel W. Wilson, Esq., and one of the professors, canvassed the city for scholars, and on the 18th of November, the college was opened with seven pupils. By the 15th of December the number had increased to eighty-two. During the first year one hundred and forty-nine (of whom twenty-five were in the classical department) were enrolled. The college campus, valued at $2,000, and containing five acres, was a donation from Josiah Hedges, Esq., the founder of Tiffin. The college was named "Heidelberg College," after the celebrated University of that name in Germany, and in honor of the only symbolical book of the Reformed church, namely, the "Heidelberg Catechism." The basement story of the college building was put up in the autumn of 1851. The corner stone (donated by Dr. Elias Heiner, of Baltimore, Maryland,) was laid on Thursday, the 13th of May, 1852, by Major Lewis Baltzell, President of the Board of Trustees; on which occasion an address on the "Dignity of Labor" was delivered by General S. F. Carey, of Cincinnati, Ohio, in the presence of a large audience. The campus was subsequently enlarged by the purchase of four acres from Hon. W. W. Armstrong, of Cleveland, Ohio. The college building was completed in the year 1852, at an expense of $15,000, and occupied for the first time in the autumn of that year. In 1871 a large house for the residence of the President was erected, at an expense of about $4,000. In 1873 a large three-story boarding hall was erected at an expense of about $8,000.

The following is a list of the professors and teachers who have been connected with the college since its establishment:

Rev. R. Good, A. M.
Rev. J. H. Good, D. D.
Rev. E. V. Gerhart, D. D., Pres.
Rev. H. Rust, A. M.
Rev. M. Kieffer, D. D., Pres.
Rev. J. H. Rutenick, D. D.
Rev. E. E. Higbee, D. D.
J. B. Kieffer, A. M.
Rev. G.W. Aughinbaugh, D. D., Pres.
Rev. G. W. Willard, D. D., Pres.
Rev. Joseph A. Keiller, A. M.
Charles Hornung, A. M.
Rev. P. Greding, D. D.
Rev. C. H. G. Von Lutenan.
Rev. H. Zimmerman.
C. S. A. Hursh, A. M.
Rev. A. S. Zerbee, A. M. Ph. D.
Rev. C. C. Knepper, A. M.
Mrs. A. M. Lee.
Miss Sarah J. Thayer.
Mrs. Elizabeth Gerhart.
Miss O. U. Rutenick.
Miss M. A. Moritz.
Miss Jane Hartsock.
N. L. Brewer, Esq.
Rev. J. J. Esher.
Rev. J. B. Kniest.
Rev. W. H. Fumeman.
Rev. J. V. Lerch, A. M.
Frederick Mayer, A. B.
Rev. Edwin R Willard, A. M.
Rev. Louis Grosenbaugh, A. M.
Rev. J. P. Moore, A M.
Wm. P. Cope, A. M.
Rev Eph. Epstein, M. D.

The following table will give a list of the students that have been in attendance:

COLLEGE YEAR.	IN COLLEGE.	IN PREPARATORY.	TOTAL.
1850-51	0	149	149
1851-52	26	148	174
1852-53	29	177	206
1853-54	47	175	226
1854-55	43	134	187
1855-56	22	125	147
1856-57	32	138	160
1857-58	29	104	133
1858-59	28	104	132
1859-60	21	84	105
1860-62	29	98	127
1862-64	23	192	215
1864-67	41	137	178
1867-68	71	156	227
1868-69	72	110	182
1869-70	85	96	181
1870-71	65	117	182
1871-72	61	83	149
1872-73	61	78	139
1873-74	72	124	196
1874-75	102	106	221
1875-76	90	75	165
1876-77	88	70	158
1877-78	84	85	169
1878-79	80	88	168

The financial agents of the College have been Rev. M. Shaull, and Elder Henry Leonard, of Basil, Ohio. The invested funds of the College now amount to over $100,000. The total number of students who have received their education in whole or in part in Heidelberg College, is about 3,300. Probably a majority of the families of Seneca county have been represented here. These students are found in all the professions and ranks of life. Nearly two hundred ministers of the gospel have gone forth from these institutions, and are scattered over the northern states, from the Atlantic to the Pacific.

Closely connected with Heidelberg College is

HEIDELBERG THEOLOGICAL SEMINARY.

This is strictly and exclusively a Theological school, held in the College building, but separate and distinct as a corporation, and having separate endowments and professors. It was commenced at

Tiffin about six months later than the College. The professors in this Seminary have been the following, the two last being still in office:
Rev. E. V. Gerhart, D. D., Professor of Theology.
Rev. M. Kieffer, D. D.,   "   "   "
Rev. H. Rust, A. M.; Professor of exegetical and historical Theology.
Rev. J. H. Good, D. D., Prof. of dogmatic and practical Theology.

The invested funds of the Seminary amount to about $35,000. It has a large library, donated by various persons. The largest donation was made by Rev. H. Helffenstein, of Pennsylvania. The number of students in the Seminary has been as follows, for the different years since it has been in operation:

SEMINARY YEAR.	NO. STUDENTS.	SEMINARY YEAR.	NO. STUDENTS.
1851-52	2	1868	9
1852	10	1870	21
1853	14	1872	22
1854	17	1873	22
1855	18	1874	21
1856-57	15	1875	13
1858	13	1876	24
1859	7	1877	19
1860	9	1878	11
1860-62	12	1879	9
1862-64	13	1880	11
1864-67	4		

Dr. Gerhart was sole professor in the Seminary (acting at the same time as president of the College,) from 1851 to 1855, when he resigned to accept the presidency of Franklin and Marshall College, at Lancaster, Pennsylvania. From November 1st, 1855, to 1861, Dr. Kieffer was sole professor, (also being president of the College.) From 1861 to 1869 the Seminary was conducted by two professors, Dr. Kieffer and Professor Rust. In 1869 Dr. Kieffer resigned, and Dr. Good, then professor of mathematics in the College, was elected his successor. From 1869 to 1880, the seminary has been in charge of these two professors.

REV. E. V. GERHART, D. D.—FIRST PRESIDENT OF HEIDELBERG COLLEGE.

Emanuel Vogel Gerhart is the eldest son of the Rev. Isaac Gerhart, inter-married with Sarah Vogel. He was born at Freeburg, (then Warren, now) Snyder county, Pennsylvania, June 13, 1817. In his second year his father became pastor of congregations in Lykens valley; his youth was passed in Millersburg, Dauphin county, where he enjoyed the advantage of such elementary schools as were then in existence. He began Latin at the age of eleven. In May, 1831, his father sent him to the high school organized by the Reformed Church, at York, Pennsylvania, then under the principalship of Rev. F. A. Rauch, Ph. D. When, in 1835, that school was removed to Mercersburgh, Pennsylvania, and erected into Marshall College, he was one of eighteen students who went with the institution. His classical course he completed in September, 1838, being one of six who composed the second graduating class of Marshall College. Immediately thereafter he became a teacher in the female seminary at Mercersburgh, conducted by Mrs. Sarah A. Young, and continued in that capacity for four years.

In September, 1839, he was appointed tutor in the Academy connected with the College, a position which he held for three years. He entered the Theological Seminary in September, 1838, and graduated in 1841, his theological studies being carried forward simultaneously with his teaching in the academy and female seminary. His theological teachers were the Rev. Louis Mayer, D. D., under whom he studied one year, and who resigned in the fall of 1839; the Rev. F. A. Rauch, Ph. D., for two years and a half, who died in March, 1841; and the Rev. John W. Nevin, D. D., for one year, he having been called to succeed Dr. Mayer in 1840.

Dr. Gerhart was licensed to preach the gospel by the Synod of the Reformed Church in the United States, at Reading, Pennsylvania, October, 1841. In May, 1842, he received and accepted a call to four churches in Franklin county, called the "Grindstone Hill" charge, and was ordained to the holy ministry by a committee of Mercersburgh classes, in the Union church at Grindstone Hill, August, 1842. As his engagement with the academy was still in force, during the summer of 1842 he taught at Mercersburgh during the week, and on Sunday served his pastoral charge. During September of this year he transferred his residence to Fayetteville. The following spring, at the instance of the Rev. Samuel Gutelius, he received, and was induced to accept, a call to Gettysburgh, Pennsylvania. This pastoral charge he served for more than six years, from May, 1843, to July, 1849. Then by the Board of Domestic Missions he was appointed missionary among the foreign Germans at Cincinnati, Ohio. He took charge of a small church on Bett's street, composed entirely of poor foreign Germans, which he served exclusively in the German language, for one year, living in a little shanty attached to the rear of the frame structure built in a sand bank. Here he labored for two years. During this time the church doubled its membership, a corner lot was bought on Elm street, and funds were subscribed and collected for the erection of the First Reformed Church, which still occupies the old site.

In the month of December, 1850, the Synod of Ohio and adjacent states elected him Professor of Theology in its Theological Seminary, and President of Heidelberg College, institutions of the Reformed Church, which, during the previous year, had been located at Tiffin, Ohio. Accepting this call, he removed to Tiffin in May, 1851. During the summer he undertook an agency in behalf of the seminary library, the seminary until then, having had no books. He visited Philadelphia and New York, where he collected funds and many volumes. The books presented and purchased constitute the nucleus of the library of this institution. A full report of his operations will be found in the minutes of the Synod of Ohio of 1852. The offices of Professor and President he filled for the term of four years; teaching and lecturing partly in the English and partly in the German language. At the same time he served several organized churches; during the first two years, three or four congregations in the vicinity of Tiffin. During the last two years he was pastor of the Second Reformed church (German) in that city.

The Board of Trustees of Franklin and Marshall College, Lancaster, Pennsylvania, elected him President of that institution at its annual meeting, held in 1854. He accepted the call and moved to Lancaster, in April, 1855. His connection with this college continued until July, 1868, a period of thirteen years. In 1858 he received his honorary title of Doctor of Divinity from Jefferson college. Through the death of the Rev. Henry Harbaugh, D. D., the professorship of systematic theology in the Theological Seminary at Mercersburg became vacant in December, 1867. At a special meeting of the synod of the Reformed church, held at Harrisburg, he was chosen Dr. Harbaugh's successor. This call he accepted and removed to Mercersburg in August, 1868. When, in 1871, the seminary was removed from Mercersburg to Lancaster, he continued in the service of the institution. The chair of Professor of Theology he has occupied up to the present time, March, 1880.

In the fall of 1864, St. Stephen's church was organized in the chapel of F. and M. college, composed of professors, families and students. Of this church he was made the pastor, and served as such until he ceased to be president of the college. When the Rev Dr. Nevin retired from the presidency, the associate pastors appointed Dr. Gerhart presiding pastor of St. Stephen's church, and up to the present time he has been fulfilling the duties of this office.

REV. JEREMIAH H. GOOD, D. D., PROFESSOR OF THE THEOLOGICAL SEMINARY AT TIFFIN, OHIO.

Near the Blue Mountains, in Berks county, Pa., in the village of Rehrersburg, Dr. Good was born on the 22d day of November, 1822. He is the son of Philip Augustus and Elizabeth Good. At the age of nine years (in 1831) he removed to the county seat, the city of Reading, where he received his preparatory education in the public schools and the academy. At the age of fourteen (September, 1836) he started for college, namely, Marshall college, then located in Mercersburg, Franklin county, Pennsylvania. It was at this time under the presidency of Dr. F. A. Rauch, a celebrated scholar from Germany. Spending two years in the preparatory department, and four years in the college, he graduated with the highest honors of the class on the last Wednesday of September, 1842. The class numbered nine, of whom four have been professors in colleges and seminaries, and one a member of Congress. From 1842 to 1845 he was sub-rector of the preparatory department of Marshall college, and at the same time student in the Theological Seminary under Dr. J. W. Nevin. In the autumn of 1845 he was licensed to preach by the Mercersburg classis, and in a few weeks thereafter followed a call to Lancaster, Ohio. From October, 1845, until October, 1847, he labored as pastor of the Lancaster and St. Matthew's Reformed Congregation, being at the same time principal of a select school. Elected by the Ohio Synod to edit its proposed religious paper, he removed to Columbus, Ohio, in October, 1847, and started the *Western Missionary* (now known as the *Christian World*, and published in Dayton, Ohio). Elected by the Reformed Synod, of Navarre, 1849, as Professor of Mathematics, in its projected college, he removed in October, 1849, (together with his brother, Professor Reuben Good,) to Tiffin, Seneca county, Ohio, and opened the new institution. At the same time he continued to edit the *Western Missionary* for three years longer, when it was removed to Dayton. From November, 1849, until September, 1869, (a period of twenty years,) he was Professor of Mathematics in Heidelberg College. He was then elected (by the Synod of Shelby, in May, 1869) to the chair of Dogmatic and Practical Theology, in the Theological Seminary at Tiffin, which situation he has occupied for ten years.

REV. GEORGE W. WILLIARD, D. D.,

was called to the Presidency of Heidelberg College in 1866. He was born in Frederick county, Maryland, June 10th, 1817, and graduated at Marshall College, Mercersburg, Pennsylvania, in 1840; served several important pastoral charges in the Reformed Church, and was the editor of the *Western Missionary*, the organ of the Synod of Ohio of the Reformed Church, thirteen years. He is still presiding over the college, which has enjoyed a good degree of prosperity under his administration.

CHAPTER XVIII.
THE CHURCHES.

IT WOULD have been a pleasure to the writer to prepare a history of the churches in Tiffin and in Seneca county, had not two causes prevented it: one the entire absence of any record of the organization, date, officers, ministers or members in many of them; the other, the cool indifference in regard to the matter with which my requests were answered. Such historic data as could be procured, however, are given here in detail, while those of the others, whose records are wanting, are described from recollection.

The little, brick Catholic chapel on Madison street has already been described. There are only to be added these additional facts: That the German and the Irish Catholics attended worship in it together for some time, as one congregation, and until the separation took place, when the Irish formed a separate congregation and built their brick church in Fort Ball, (as then called), and the Germans bought about two acres of Mr. Hedges, in the woods at the south end of Tiffin: Father Healy is the pastor of the Irish church, and Father Evrard the pastor of the German church, now standing on the two acres, between Washington and Melmore streets. [Further details will be given hereafter.]

It is also said that the little brick chapel was the fourth Catholic church erected in Ohio. After the separation of the two nationalities, the Irish people used the chapel as a school house, and employed one John Crowley as teacher. Through some carelessness about the stove the building took fire and burned down.

THE METHODIST EPISCOPAL CHURCH.

The Methodist Episcopal Church in Tiffin has already been alluded to, as one of the first brick buildings in Tiffin. The first church of this denomination that was erected in the county, was built on the bank of Honey creek, in Eden township, in 1828, and on the land now known as the Henry Schoch farm. This structure did not compare very favorably with the grand edifice this denomination now owns on Madison street, but it was a good, large, substantial, hewed-log building, and answered very well for the time. Their second church was built in Reed, in 1829; it was also made of logs, and was located on the Raymond farm, one mile east of the pike. Rev. James Montgomery used to preach in these churches occasionally, and also the venerable Thomas Thompson, still living, and who was one of the most popular and most generally beloved Methodist divines among the early ministers in this part of the country. The celebrated Finleys also preached in these log churches, as well as in private houses. The house of John Gibson, Esq., in Eden, was a meeting house almost every Sunday for a long time. The first presiding elder was James McMahon, who came to Tiffin in 1823, and preached in the old brick church. Luther A. Hall, Esq. bought the old church, when the congregation had put up the new one, now over the post office, used as a club room, and made a theatre of it. The Germans in Tiffin had organized a very good Thesbian Society about that time, and produced good pieces for amateurs—"Feldkimmel," for instance. The Methodists finally sold their church on the corner of Monroe and Market streets, and built a large edifice on Madison street. When finished it will be one of the grandest and most spacious church edifices in the county. Services are now held in the basement. The membership is nearly three hundred; the Sunday school numbers about two hundred scholars. Rev. J. W. Mendenhall is the present pastor. This congregation was admitted to the North Ohio Conference in August, 1848, Rev. Thomas Barkdall, presiding elder; and Rev. E. S. Gurley, pastor.

THE PROTESTANT EPISCOPAL CHURCH,

At the northwest corner of Jefferson and Market streets, is a neat, commodious structure; has regular services now, but the membership is not very large. The Rev. Williams is the pastor.

THE FIRST BAPTIST CHURCH

In Tiffin was organized on the 20th day of October, 1857, by the following named persons: Rev. Lyman J. Fisher, William J. Crawford, Elizabeth Crawford, Harriet Crawford, William Gallup, F. Brownell and Benjamin Tomb. The first public sermon was preached by the Rev. D. F. Carnahan. Their church was built on Perry street, and dedicated on the 2d day of December, 1860. Rev. L. J. Fisher preached the dedicatory sermon on the 1st day of July, 1868. The church has a membership of about one hundred and fifty. Its present pastor is the Rev. G. G. Harriman.

THE CHURCHES.

THE PRESBYTERIAN CHURCH

In Tiffin is one of the largest and most important religious associations in the city, as it is also one of the earliest. It numbers among its members many distinguished citizens. Their splendid church, at the southwest corner of Market and Monroe streets, was built in 1870. Its present membership is about one hundred and fifty; Rev. D. D. Bigger is its pastor at this time. The following historical items are taken from an anniversary discourse pronounced by Rev. D. D. Bigger, pastor of the First Presbyterian Church:

The First Presbyterian Church of Tiffin, Ohio, was organized about the first of July, A. D. 1831, and was formed by the withdrawal of members from the Melmore church who lived nearer Fort Ball than Melmore. In 1834 this society in Tiffin was formally chartered by the General Assembly of the state of Ohio, as the First Presbyterian Church of Tiffin, Ohio. The charter members were Milton Jennings, Peter Marsh, James W. G. McCluer, Allen Campbell, William Hunter, John Young, Ezekiel McFerren, "and their associates." The board of trustees named in the charter, were Milton Jennings, Peter Marsh and Allen Campbell, devout men.

In the year 1830 Rev. John Robinson came to the wilds of Seneca county, preaching the gospel and gathering the early settlers of Presbyterian predilection into local churches. In the summer of 1831, a local church was organized at Tiffin, the Rev. John Robinson officiating as their spiritual leader until the charter was secured, in 1834. Father Robinson is known as a thorough pioneer preacher, and many rich incidents are related of his pioneer experience.

The Rev. John McCutchen, the successor of the first pastor, was considered a revivalist of rare tact and talent, accomplishing much good. During the interim from 1837 to 1852 the church was supplied by the Rev. A. S. Dunton and Rev. John Whipple, in connection with Melmore. Rev. James Pelon occupied the pulpit from June, 1852, to March 21, 1858. The Rev. John McLain supplied the pulpit in Tiffin, in conjunction with that of the church at McCutchensville, from May 6, 1858, until his death, which occurred June 6, 1862. During the Rev. McLain's ministry the church edifice at McCutchensville was built. Rev. D. S. Logan served the church as stated supply for one year, from the month of December, 1862. In the winter of 1863, the Rev. J. E. Lapsley ministered to the church, resigning in the fall of 1866. In the spring of 1867, the Rev. R. B. Moore was called to the pastorate, and accepting, became the first installed pastor of this congregation.

Up to the pastorate of Rev. Moore, the congregation had worshipped in a sanctuary built in 1835, on the west side. Measures were taken to build a more commodious structure, and more centrally located. The efforts were successful, and the present handsome edifice, at the corner of Market and Monroe streets, was occupied for the first time in the winter of 1871. When completed, it is estimated that the entire outlay for constructing the building, purchase of lot, and furnishing, will not exceed $21,000, but will fully reach that sum.

278   HISTORY OF SENECA COUNTY.

Rev J. F. Pollock succeeded Rev. Moore, and was installed as pastor in 1873, during the month of September. After five years of faithful service, he resigned in March, 1878, accepting an invitation to South Toledo, Ohio. The present encumbent, the Rev. D. D. Bigger, being a duly installed pastor, has entered the third year of his ministry with the church. The society is in a most prosperous condition. The report for the year closing July 1st shows an addition of thirty to the membership, and over $3,000 raised for ecclesiastical and benevolent purposes, collected from the different departments of the church work. The following are the officers of the church:

SESSION.

David Smythe,   William Davidson,
John Kerr,   Robert Lysle,
Francis Frederici,   Nathaniel Beck, Clerk.

BOARD OF TRUSTEES:

David Laird, President,   James T. Knott, Secretary.
Henry C. Baltzell, Treasurer.   C. D. Sprague.
George H. Borney.   J. S. Bott,
William H. Kempher.

This denomination has churches located in this county at Fostoria, Melmore, Bloomville, McCutchensville and Republic. At the latter place a new church is under process of building, and will be ready to occupy this fall.

PLACE.	CHURCH.	PASTOR.
Tiffin,	First Presbyterian,	Rev. D. D. Bigger.
Fostoria,	" "	Rev. J. Hughes.
McCutchensville,	Presbyterian,	Rev. R. B. Moore.
Republic,	"	" " "
Bloomville,	"	Rev. J. S. Boyd.
Melmore,	"	" " "

THE GERMAN EVANGELICAL ST. JOHN'S CONGREGATION.

This is the only religious organization in Tiffin constituted after the manner of the union of the Lutheran and Reformed churches in Germany, a religious event that was celebrated among the Protestants of southern Germany on the 18th day of November, 1818.

This congregation in Tiffin was organized under a charter passed by the general assembly of Ohio on the 15th day of March, 1836, under the name of "The United German Evangelical Lutheran and German Evangelical Reformed St. John's Congregation of Tiffin, Seneca county." Andrew Albrecht, Philip Wentz, Valentine Seewald, Francis Souder, Andreas Bloom, Andrew Denzer, Philip Seewald, John Ditto, Jacob Boyer and William Lang were the charter members. Of all these, Andrew Bloom, Jacob Boyer and the writer are all that survive. The first constitution was adopted in 1838. Rev. Adam Adolph Conrad, one of the most pure minded of christian gentlemen, was its first pastor, and served the congregation for five years. In addition to this, Rev. Conrad served nine other congregations, including one in Lower Sandusky. He was a man of brilliant intellect and splendid oratorical powers, which, combined with his pleasing manners, won for him hosts of friends among all people. He had a frail body, and his labors were too severe for his physical strength. He died, after five years of constant service, in the thirty-fifth year of his age. His death was lamented by all classes of people. Rev. J. J. Beilharz, from Fayette, New York, took charge of the congregation in 1841. In 1849 the constitution was revised. Father Beilharz served the congregation twelve years, and was succeeded by a Mr. Wander, who had recently emigrated here from Silesia, Germany. His sermons were characterized by forcible and poetic thought, and true devotion. Mr. Wander died ten months after he preached his first sermon. Rev. J. J. Esher thereupon served the congregation up to 1855. Rev. Ruetenick served during an interim. Rev. J. G. Neuschmidt was the pastor from 1859 to 1870. Revs. Rein and Weisgerber served to 1873, when Rev. G. von Luternau became the minister and served until 1875, when the Rev. C. Zimmerman, the present incumbent, succeeded him.

By the frequent changes of ministers, and other causes, the congregation suffered much, and became much reduced in numbers; but by the indefatigable labors and the loveable disposition of this able and accomplished divine, the church has increased to more than one hundred and twenty members.

The first meeting house of this congregation was a hewed log building, and stood on the same spot where their beautiful, but modest brick church now stands, on south Jefferson street. It was built in 1836, and gave way to the present brick church in 1857. The pastor lives in a commodious parsonage on the same lot. A ladies' mite society, connected with the church, numbers forty members. The interest now awakened in the German Protestant element promises a constant increase of the congregation, and contributes largely to the preservation of the German language and the German mode of worship.

So much for a church that keeps a record.

THE FIRST REFORMED CHURCH OF TIFFIN, OHIO—ORGANIZATION.

The members of the German Reformed Church, mostly from the states of Pennsylvania and Maryland, living in and around Tiffin, desirous of worshipping God in accordance with the customs and doctrines of their fathers, determined to organize a congregation in Tiffin, in order that their wishes in this particular might be realized. They invited the Rev. John L. Sanders, of Frederick county, Maryland, to visit them, with the view of becoming their pastor. The invitation was accepted by this young minister, and on the 8th day of June, 1833, he commenced his labors among his new parishoners. On the 30th of the same month, a meeting of all who were desirous of going into the new enterprise, was called, at which time a constitution was adopted, and all who wished to unite with the proposed organization subscribed their names thereto. As well as can be ascertained, they were: Thomas Derr, Joseph Ogle, George Stoner, Jacob Kroh, Jonathan Foltz, Frederick Cramer, Joseph Foncannon, John Kime, John Martin, Ezra Derr, Christian Ramsburg, Frederick W. Shriver, George Schroyer, John Leydey, William Baugher, Christian Stoner, Elizabeth Ogle, Susanna Ramsburg, Rosanna Derr, Catharine Cramer, Susanna Foltz, Elizabeth Baugher, Margaret Kime, Sarah Kroh, and Mary Leydey. The next step taken was to elect a consistory, the members of which were to constitute the board of trustees also. A meeting of the members was held for this purpose, on the 21st of July, 1833, when six elders and six deacons were elected, who were ordained and installed according to the provisions of the Reformed church, on the same day of their election.

BUILDING OF THE CHURCH.

At the meeting aforesaid, the consistory was authorized to purchase a lot for the purpose of erecting on it a church edifice, to be built of brick. The lot upon which the present building stands was purchased from Josiah Hedges, for the sum of two hundred and fifty dollars, and was deeded to the trustees of the congregation, known then by the name of the German Evangelical Reformed Church, on the 16th day of August, 1834; the following persons constituting the board at that time: Jacob Kroh, Joseph Foncannon, Jonathan Foltz, Joseph Ogle, Frederick Cramer, David Rickenbaugh, John Ditto, John Kime, William Baugher, John Martin, Ezra Derr, and Peter Schlosser. Immediate steps were taken to build the proposed church. For various reasons the work progressed slowly, and the building was not ready for occupancy until the summer of 1835.

PASTORS.

The Rev. J. L. Sanders, who was licensed and ordained to the gospel ministry on the 7th of May, 1833, by the Maryland Classes of the German Reformed Church, was the first minister of the congregation. He served it from the time of its organization until the 7th of November, 1835, making the time of his pastorate two and a half years.

THE CHURCHES. 281

His successor was the Rev. Frederick Rahauser, who preached in both the German and English languages. He served the congregation about four and one-half years, when he resigned, and was followed by the Rev. Daniel Kroh, who had just been ordained to the gospel ministry.

The Rev. Kroh commenced his labors as pastor on the 18th of September, 1840, and was regularly installed over the congregation as such on the 12th of April, 1841. The church being without pews up to this time, the members sitting on slab benches, was furnished with pews, which made it a more comfortable place of worship than formerly. The Rev. Kroh continued as pastor until the 12th of May, 1846, when he resigned.

The Rev. Hiram Shaull became his immediate successor. During his pastorate the church building, which had not been plastered or painted, was finished, and was dedicated about the 1st of January, 1847. The Rev. Shaull, having been appointed by the boards of trustees of the Theological Seminary and Heidelberg College, located in Tiffin, to a joint agency for the purpose of endowing these institutions of learning, and feeling it to be his duty to accept this appointment, resigned the pastorate of the congregation, which took effect on the 1st of January, 1852.

The Rev. George D. Wolff then served the congregation as pastor for one year, after which he resigned. His resignation went into effect in July, 1853.

After a vacancy of one year, the Rev. William K. Zieber became the pastor. He commenced his labors here in the month of August, 1854. He labored with acceptance until the 1st of August, 1857, when he resigned, for the purpose of entering upon the duties of the office of general superintendent of Home Missions, under the direction of the different boards of Home Missions of the Reformed Church.

A vacancy again occurred for over one year, after which the Rev. E. E. Higbee became the pastor. He commenced his duties on the 1st of October, 1858. During his pastorate the present church edifice was erected, the old one being unfit any longer for use. It was commenced in the summer of 1860, and was completed the following spring. The Rev. Higbee continued to be the pastor until the 10th of March, 1861, when his resignation, which had been previously offered, went into effect.

The congregation was then served by the Rev. M. Kieffer, D. D., as a supply, until the 1st of July, 1863, when the Rev. L. H. Kefauver became its pastor, and has continued in this position to the present time.

The congregation is in a prosperous condition, with a communicant membership of 230, and a flourishing Sunday School of 250 scholars.

THE REFORMED CHURCHES IN SENECA COUNTY.

There are now fourteen churches in Seneca county belonging to the denomination known as the Reformed Church in the United States, descended from the Reformed Confession in Germany and Switzerland, whose best known representatives in the reformation age were Ulric Zwingle, John Calvin, Henry Bullinger, Zacharias Ursinus, and Casper Olevianus. The settlers in Seneca county who founded these churches were mainly of three kinds: first, those from Maryland (mostly from Frederick and Washington counties); second, those from Pennsylvania (Lehigh, Berks, Union, Northampton and other counties); third, those from Germany and Switzerland (mostly from the Palatinate, or Rhenish Bavaria, Westphalia, Nassau, Hessia, etc). The following table will show the location, founding and strength of these churches, together with such illustrative notes as it was in my power to gather, which, I hope, will have a historical value:

TABLE OF REFORMED CHURCHES IN SENECA COUNTY.

NAME.	WHERE LOCATED.	WHEN FOUNDED.	NO. OF MEMBERS.	SITTINGS.
First Church Tiffin,	Tiffin City,	1833	227	600
Zion's Church,	Thompson T'w'p,	1830	140	500
Salem Church,	Scipo, T'w'p,	1837	80	400
St. Jacob's,	Adams T'w'p,	1834	54	200
Bloomville,	Bloomville,	1850	90	300
Bascom,	Bascom,	1852	53	150
Salem,	Seneca T'w'p,	1853	50	300
Berwick,	Berwick,	1850	25	150
Olive Chapel,	Jackson T'w'p,	1852	57	250
Ft. Seneca,	Pleasant T'w'p,	1855	80	300
Caroline,	Venice T'w'p,		100	300
Second Tiffin,	Tiffin,	1850	240	400
Glade Union,	Pleasant T'w'p,	1875	40	250
Fostoria,	Fostoria,	1879	44	300

REMARKS AND NOTES.

It will be noticed that there is a Reformed Church in each of the fifteen townships of the county, with the exception, as yet, of Liberty, Reed, Eden and Big Spring. The following notes will rescue some facts from oblivion:

A special history of this church will be found in another place.

The Thompson church was organized in 1830 by Rev. Stauch,

THE CHURCHES.

the land being donated by John Heeter. It has had three church edifices, on the same ground; the first built in 1832, the second in 1843, and the third, one of the finest edifices in Seneca county, of brick, with a tall steeple, in 1873. The size is forty by fifty-five feet. The names of the ministers, in succession, are as follows:

1. Rev. Marchup.
2. " Frederick Rahauser.
3. " Frederick Wahl.
4. " J. C. Klar.
5. " David Kelley.
6. Rev. Eli Keller.
7. " Joseph A. Keller.
8. " Wm. H. Sandel.
9. " Wm. J. Peters.

The principal families at the start were: John Royer, Sr., John Wollenslagel, Adam Good, Jacob Bunn, Sr., John Bunn, Jr., John Bunn, Sr., Isaac Lewis, Henry Bowman, Rudolph Bowman, Henry Stetter, and Henry Bunn. Other families since, represented by Isaac Royer, Samuel Royer, John Royer, Manam Royer, Jared Royer, Emanuel Good, George Good, Adam Good, Jr., George Wollenslagel, Conrad Wollenslagel, John Wollenslagel, Jr., Christian Wollenslagel, Wm. Good, Wm. Bennehoff, John Matz, Neri Matz, Samuel Maury, Gottlieb Maury, Malachi Loeseber, Fred. Bowman, and Augustus Steinmetz. The value of the present church property is about $6,000.

Salem Reformed. church was first organized in Adams township (a union church, Reformed and Lutheran) by Rev. F. Rahauser. The original land in Adams township was donated by John German. The land on which the church now stands was purchased from David Wyant. There have been four church edifices, the first built in 1837. The present neat brick church was erected in 1868. The following have been the ministers:

1. Rev. F. Rahauser.
2. " Fred. Wahl.
3. " D. W. Kelley.
4. " J. C. Klahr.
5. Rev. Eli Keller.
6. " Joseph A. Keller.
7. " W. B. Sandel.
8. " W. J. Peters.

The original families were represented by John Hensinger, Andrew Mitower, Eli Karshner, Eli Dought, Joseph Kunes, and Jacob Britten; to which we may add as later ones: George Schoch, Ephraim Close, Anthony Harpster, Henry Bacher, Stephen Strauss, Adam Harkey, Monroe Kistler, C. Hensinger, John Hensinger, Jr., and Robert Close. The church nas a parsonage, and a church property worth about $4,000.

The St. Jacob's church, in Adams township, was originally gathered by Rev. Conrad, and organized as a Lutheran and Reformed Church. It was served for many years by Rev. J. J. Beilharz. In the year 1851, Rev. Prof. J. H. Good laid the basis, and subsequently organized the Reformed congregation of that name, and has been pastor until the present time. The church is built on land donated by Jacob Gruber. The following are the representative heads of the principal families: Herman Detterman, Jacob Gruber, Joseph Hilsinger, Paul Hobbes, George Detterman, Samuel Detterman, Henry Cook, Daniel Reiter, Daniel Gruber, Henry Detterman, H. Brinkman, F. Berlekamp, R. Berlekamp, Thomas Mohr, and others.

The original name of the Bloomville church was Mt. Pisgah; organized the 25th of August, 1850, by Rev. H. K. Baines, with George Swigart and Philip Heilman as elders, and Adam Baker and F. Zimmerman as deacons. The church is built on an acre of land donated by Simon Koler. The property is worth about $2,500. The ministers and supplies have been:

1. Rev. H. K. Baines.
2. " J. C. Klahr.
3. " David Kelley.
4. " M. Keiffer, D. D.
5. " J. H. Good.
6. " W. W. James.
7. Rev. Joseph A. Keller.
8. " L. Grosenbaugh.
9. " J. A. Steplar.
10. " J. D. Gehring.
11. " Samuel Shaw, since Aug., [1876.

The principal families are the Heilmans, Krilleys, Kolbers, Bakers, Geigers, Klahrs, Samsels, Frankenfields, etc.

The Bascom church was originally gathered by Rev. J. J. Beilharz, as a Lutheran and Reformed church, and a neat little church erected in the village of Bascom. On the 1st of January, 1852, it was organized by Rev. Prof. E. V. Gerhart as a German Reformed church. The first officers were, Benjamin Fried, elder, and Christian Deubel, deacon. The heads of the principal families have been: Dr. Henry Werz, John George Werz, Michael Walter, Michael Strong, Jacob Schmid, Nicholas Dewald, Peter Dewald, Philip Dewald, Jacob Kissabeth, Philip Kissabeth, Jacob Brendle, John Nau, George Shattner, John Kinkerter, Philip Stucky, Jacob Sherer, Conrad Bohn, Jacob Heisserman. The ministers have been:

1. Rev. E. V. Gerhart.
2. " M. Mueller.
3. " H. J. Rutenick.
4. " J. J. Escher.
5. " J. Matzinger.
6. " F. Strassner.
7. Rev. Jacob Kuhn.
8. " W. H. Fenneman.
9. " L. Richter.
10. " C. F. Krithe.
11. " J. H. Good.

Salem church, in Seneca township, was organized by Rev. Prof. E. V. Gerhart, on November 12th, 1853. The male members present at the organization were: Casper Bachman, Isaac Miller, Ludwig

Emich, Lambert Martin, John Houck, Jacob Schaub, Andrew Burgdoerffer, Frederick Baker and William Rex. Most of these had previously belonged to a Lutheran and Reformed congregation, originally organized by Rev. Conrad, in the year 1834. The first church was built in 1837, about one and one-half miles east of the present village of New Riegel, of hewn logs, fitted with split and hewn plank for its floor and seats. The building was eighteen by twenty-two, and about eleven feet high The Salem church, after its organization, built a neat and handsome frame church, still standing, on land purchased from Philip Nibergal. The heads of the principal families, in addition to those previously named, have been, John Miller, J. J. Buser, Jacob Shubach, N. Feindel, Wm. Wenner, Robert Burne, Esq., Fred. Shamacher, N. Enrich, W. Deis, Silas Hoffert, T. Wagner, J. Scherer, George Robb, John Rothfuchs, and others. The successive ministers have been:

1. Rev. E. V. Gerhart.
2. " M. Mueller.
3. " J. J. Escher.
4. " F. Strassner.
5. Rev. Jacob Kuhn
6. " W. H. Fenneman.
7. " L. Richter.
8. " J. H. Good.

The Berwick congregation was first gathered, so far as I can learn, by Rev. Frederick Wahl. The principal families were the Schumachers, Blooms, Millers, Longs, Spraus and others It has generally been supplied by the same pastors as have preached at Salem, which is only two miles distant. For a number of years now services have been suspended at this place, the members attending regularly at Salem.

The congregation at Olive Chapel, in Jackson township, was organized by Rev. Prof. R. Good, of Tiffin. The church was built in 1862, on land donated by Jacob Stahl. The successive ministers have been:

1. Rev. R. Good.
2. " M. Mueller.
3. " S. Shaw.
4. " H. Baer.
5. " T. F. Staufer.
6. " George Rettig.
7. Rev. D. Kroh.
8. " H. Daniels.
9. " T. J. Baeber.
10. " L. Richter.
11. " A. Casselman.

The original families were those of George and Jacob Stahl, F. Febles, C. Myers and some others. The value of the church property is about $1,000.

The Second Reformed Church, of Tiffin, grew from small beginnings, and was first organized by Rev. Frederick Wahl. Its ministers since have been, Rev. E. V. Gerhart, Rev. J. H. Good, and Rev. H.

Rust. The principal families, at its organization, consisted of the Swanders, Reifs, Emichs, Fieges, Blooms, Bachers, Seipels, Von Blons, Honsbergers, Knauses, Sohns, Kremers, Schneiders and many others. It possesses a property worth about $5,000 The "Frauenverein" numbers sixty members.

The Reformed Church, of Fostoria, was organized by Rev. A. Casselman, on the 23d of March, 1879, with twenty-five members, and incorporated on the 20th of April of the same year. The lot on which the church is built was purchased of James Fritcher for $300. The corner stone was laid on the 20th of May, and the building dedicated September 28th, 1879. The value of the church property is about $2,100. The officers of the church at its organization were:

Elders—Rev. M. Mueller and H. W. Kunkle.

Deacons—Samuel Stewart and Jacob Hofmaster.

The Fort Seneca congregation of the Reformed church was organized about the year 1857, by the Rev. M. Kieffer, D. D. who served it about four years. The following were the first officers elected:

Elders—Simon Shuman, Jacob Hale, Barney Zimmerman.

Deacons—Felix Beck, Henry Stoner, Daniel C. Richard.

Trustees—Barney Zimmerman, Henry Stoner, John Zeigler.

The church was erected shortly after the organization, at a cost of about $1,200, the lot having been donated by John Zeigler. Rev. S. Shaw, a student of the Theological Seminary at Tiffin, succeeded Dr. Kieffer in the pastorate in April, 1861, and was succeeded by Revs. H. Bair, W. James and G. Ficks, each of them serving only a short time. In the year 1866 Rev. G. W. Williard, D. D., President of Heidelberg College, took charge of the congregation, at which time it numbered only about thirty members. Things soon began to assume a more hopeful aspect, and encouraging accessions were made from time to time, until the congregation now, (April, 1880,) has a membership of eighty-five active communicants. The church building has been repaired several times, and is now in good condition. The congregation has a good Sunday school, with an average attendance of about sixty, and property worth about $2,000. The officers of the congregation now are:

Pastor—Rev. G. W. Williard.

Elders—Ph. Frey, Samuel Bair, Henry Stoner.

Deacons—Ch. Gangwer, Fred. Hade, Charles Zeis.

The Glade Union Reformed congregation was organized by Rev. Geo. W. Williard, D. D., December 17th, 1871. The following persons united in the organization: William Steckel, Clara Steckel, Francisca

Steckel, Jacob Bowersox, Susan Bowersox, Jacob Lowrie, Sarah Lowrie, William Shriver, Ann Marie Shriver, Elizabeth Shriver, Sophia McMeen, Leicester M. Koons, Susan Smith, A. L. Shaffer, Rachael Shaffer, and Oliver Watson. William Steckel and Jacob Bowersox were elected elders; A. L. Shaffer and Oliver Watson deacons. Their church was built in 1871, and dedicated July 2d, 1871. It was erected at an expense of about $1,000. Rev. George W. Williard, D. D., Jacob Bowersox and William Shriver were the building committee. Jacob Bowersox donated the lot.

Dr. Williard has served the congregation to the present time (1880) as its pastor, preaching every two weeks. The congregation has gradually increased and now numbers thirty-six members. The church will seat 200 persons. The property is worth about $1,500; much of the work in its erection was done gratuitously.

CHURCH OF THE UNITED BRETHREN IN CHRIST.

Through the kindness of the Rev. Joseph Beaver, the following facts have been secured, viz.:

The first organization was effected in the year 1831, at the house of Philip Bretz, one half mile east of Melmore. There are now sixteen church houses of this denomination in Seneca county.

THE ENGLISH LUTHERAN CHURCH.

In the absence of a record showing the organization of the first English Lutheran church in Tiffin, the writer is indebted to the kindness of Dr. J. Crouse, and the Rev. J. Livengood, of Butler, Illinois, who speak from memory only.

The first meeting was held in the brick school house on West Market street, in Tiffin, in the summer of 1843, where a congregation was organized by Mr. Lioengood. Afterwards they held their meetings in the German Reformed church, for a short time. This seemed to prove unpleasant on both sides, and an effort was made to build a small church. A part of a lot was purchased on the east side of Jefferson street, where the present church now stands, and a contract let to build a plain frame house thirty by forty feet. This was in the spring of 1844. The house was dedicated in the same year, Rev. J. Crouse, D. D. preaching the dedicatory sermon. The Wittenberg Synod held its next session in this church. Among the first members were David Rickenbaugh, Samuel Rule, Jacob Bowser, John Bowser, John Sechrist, George Ritsman, Simon Snyder, Mr. Rosenberg and the wives of these gentlemen. The whole number was about twenty-five. At the first organization Mr. Rickenbaugh and Mr. Bowser were elected elders, and Mr. Ritsman and Mr. Sechrist, deacons.

In 1865 the old frame church was moved away, and the present beautiful, brick edifice erected in its place. Dr. Crouse is now serving as pastor of the congregation in his fourth year. There are two hundred members enrolled, and two hundred scholars in the Sunday school.

REV. JOSHUA CROUSE, D. D

There are self-made men in the pulpit, as well as in other walks of life, and the subject of this sketch is one of these. This sketch is in its proper place here, because Dr. Crouse dedicated the first English Lutheran church here (the frame building,) afterwards the present brick edifice, and is now serving the congregation in the fourth year of his pastorate.

He is the son of Jacob and Eliza Crouse, (the maiden name of the latter being Wildisin,) and was born in Columbiana county, Ohio, on the 29th day of August, 1812. His parents came to Columbiana county in 1805, from Emmittsburg, Maryland. Young Crouse's education was the best the common schools in that country afforded at that time. He married when only twenty-two years of age, and taught school several terms for a livelihood, both English and German at the same time.

When he arrived at man's estate, and during the time and after he taught school, he felt very keenly the want of a thorough education, and applied himself to books with the iron will and persevering industry that always lead to success, in every walk of life.

From his boyhood up, he cherished a desire to become a preacher of the gospel, and when the time arrived for the choice of a life-work, no one employment suited his nature so well as that of the ministry of the gospel Many circumstances combined to prevent his engagement in the work, among which was his diffidence and fear of personal unfitness for the calling.

After he had passed his thirtieth year, a providential way seemed to open to him for the work. He still had his troubles, and doubts of being able to enter upon it; and there was a struggle between a keen sense of duty to preach and want of confidence in himself to meet the duty, which made him mentally wretched for some time. After passing months in this unhappy state of mind, he finally threw himself into the hands of God, leaving results to Him.

With that confiding trust, he preached about two years, by the common consent of the neighboring ministers, delivering his first sermon in

February, 1842. In September, 1844, he was examined by a committee of the Evangelical Lutheran Synod of Ohio and adjacent states, and was licensed at the same time. Preaching about three years longer, he was ordained in 1847. He has been in the service now a little over thirty-eight years; seven years of this time he was the financial secretary of Wittenberg College, at Springfield, Ohio.

Dr. Crouse is a fine specimen of a christian teacher; mild and friendly in his intercourse with others, broad and liberal in his views, a thorough theologian, a forcible and eloquent pulpit orator. His labors in the vineyard of the Lord during so many years have given ample proof that his conception of the mission of his life was well grounded.

METHODIST PROTESTANT CHURCH.

Soon after the secession in the old M. E. Church, a society of sixteen members was organized in March, 1829, under the conventional articles, by Rev. James Montgomery, at Fort Seneca. Mr. Montgomery was entirely alone as a reformer, there being no society nearer than one hundred miles; but he was "all in all" to his little flock up to his death. The little society was then left without a shepherd, but they resolved to stand fast. John Souder, then a layman, was elected class-leader. They kept up their meetings, and in 1832 Adget McGuire made them a missionary visit of four or five Sabbaths, during which he organized two other small classes. Daniel Gibbons, a young man, was then sent to them, who, in the next conference, reported one hundred and thirty-five members. After him, David Howell was appointed, who also made progress. Brother Souder, the veteran pioneer, long since known as a local minister, has lived to see the little flock grow into large proportions.

The congregation that was organized in Tiffin put up a brick church on Monroe street, which was dedicated on the 8th and 9th days of July, 1837.

John Souder, William Campbell, Joseph Walker and Daniel H. Phillips were the building committee. Here the congregation attended worship until their present large and beautiful church, on Market street, was built in 1872. Rev. Chandler is the minister.

ST. MARY'S CATHOLIC CHURCH.

The little brick chapel, near East Madison street, has already been described. It was not dedicated until the 7th day of January, 1837. Services were held in it, however, from the time it was finished. The bishops have made it a rule not to dedicate a church while it is in debt; a very good rule. It makes delinquent subscribers pay up.

The organization of the congregation dates back to September, 1829, when Bishop Fenwick, of Cincinnati; bought of Josiah Hedges the site. The building was postponed for want of means, and until Mr. Kinney and others contracted for the brick as before stated. Father Edmund Quinn took charge of the congregation in 1833. He was a venerable and noble looking priest, highly esteemed by all our citizens. He had his mother here with him. This brick church was finished in the spring of 1833. Father Quinn remained in charge of it until his death here, in the fall of 1835. Thereupon Bishop Purcell appointed the Rev. Father Schoenhenz, who continued to officiate until the fall of 1839, and was succeeded by Father McNamee and the Rev. J. P. Machebeouf, at present bishop of Colorado and New Mexico. Father Machebeout, in 1842, went to Sandusky City, and Father McNamee remained until 1847, late in the fall, when Bishop Rappe appointed the Rev. Father M. Howard, who remained until April, 1850, in September, when the Rev. M. Molon succeeded. him, and remained until 1852. He was succeeded by the Rev. M. O'Sullivan, who, in the summer of 1856, built the present St. Mary's church, and remained in charge until February, 1859, when its present pastor, the Rev. Father M. Healy, took charge of the church, and who has officiated now twenty-one years. There are 950 members belonging to this church. Father Healy organized three schools, in 1864, numbering now 160 scholars, and in 1870 built the present parsonage. Their present cemetery was purchased in 1878, containing five acres, east of the city, on the North Greenfield road, and was blessed by Father Healy, assisted by Fathers Evrard and Ahern, October 13, 1878.

SALEM CHURCH. EVANGELICAL ASSOCIATION.

About the year 1848, Jacob Snyder came to Tiffin with his family, and in the years 1854-55 the families of the Rev. J. G. Zinser, Ludwig Schubert, William C. Negile and M. Huber settled in the city; these organized a class and were served by the regular circuit preachers, in the following order, viz: Revs. F. Frech, John Erb, R. J. J. Kanaga and J. G. Theurer. Their services, both preaching and prayer meetings, were held in the houses of these families.

At the annual conference of 1856 this society was constituted a mission station, with fifty members. The Rev. L. F. Sheurerman became its first missionary, in 1857, and served until the spring of 1859, and since that time the church has been served by the following pastors, viz:—J. G. Theurer, up to 1860; J. G. Zinser, to 1861; C. Gramer, to 1863; G. Harenpflug, to 1865; J. Frankhauser, to 1867; E. B. Crouse, to 1868; F. Frech, to 1869; J. G. Theurer, to 1871; C. F. Negile, to 1874; E. B. Crouse, to 1876; C. G. Koch, to 1879; and N. Schupp since spring, 1879.

In 1858 the church and parsonage were erected, at a cost of $2,500 under the pastorate of L. F. Scheurerman and J. G. Zinser, John Loos and Jacob Snyder serving as trustees and building committee. Both church and parsonage have undergone repairs, at an expense of about $1,000. On the 21st day of April, 1858, the first Sunday school was organized, with thirty scholars, and has increased to eighty scholars, the present number. William C. Negile has been the superintendent from the organization to the present time—twenty-two years.

The Ohio annual conference held two of its sessions in this church, in 1865 and 1875. In 1871 the society became self supporting, and was changed from a mission to a station. In 1873, by an act of the society the Sunday evening preaching services were held in the English language, and shortly after an English class was formed, which was the origin of the Ebenezer church, now worshipping in their new edifice on North Washington street. However, the German and English classes worshipped together until 1876, when they became two separate organizations by common consent. Rev. J. Lerch served the English congregation, and C. H. Koch the German. This society enjoyed a special revival under the present pastorate, with a net increase, and it now numbers one hundred and twenty-five members.

EBENEZER CHURCH.

In the spring of 1876, the Ohio conference of the Evangelical Association established an English mission in Tiffin, called "Tiffin Washington street mission." The steps that led to this result were the following: An English class was formed in the German (Salem) church in 1873, for the benefit of the English speaking people. The pastor, the Rev. C. F. Ingle, of the Salem church, began English preaching service on Sabbath evenings.

Rev. Jesse Lerch was appointed the first missionary, the mission then numbering forty members. During the first year the church on North Washington street was built, at an expense, including the lot, of $7,100. Mr. Lerch served for three years, and in the spring of 1879 he was supported by the Rev. J. A. Hensel.

The mission at present numbers eighty-five members, and is in a flourishing condition, both financially and spiritually. Its Sunday school numbers eighty scholars; Mr. E. Nicolai is the superintendent

ST. JOSEPH'S CHURCH.

In 1845 the German Catholics of Tiffin, who for a number of years had been members of St. Mary's English church, solicited and obtained from the Right Rev. J. B. Purcell, Bishop of Cincinnati, the permission to organize a separate congregation. They numbered at that time from thirty to forty families. They went to work with energy and liberality, and selected near the city a beautiful site of two acres.

From 1845 until January, 1852, the new German organization was attended by priests of the Sanguinnist congregation, who came from Thompson or New Riegel (then called Wolf Creek), the Revs. F. Salesius Brunner, John Wittmer, J. B. Jacomet, Yacob Ringeli, M. Anton Meyer, P. Anton Capeder, F. X. Obermiller, Maximillian Hamburger, John Von den Broeck and Mathias Kreusch. The last named resided for a few months in the city, with a catholic family. In January, 1852, Rev L. Molon, pastor of St. Mary's church, was also appointed pastor of the German congregation, and had a separate service in each church every Sunday until September of the same year, when Rev. J. B. Uhlmann arrived from Germany and was appointed pastor of the young and flourishing congregation. The present parsonage was then built. Rev. Uhlmann remained in Tiffin until May, 1856, when he was sent to Canton, Stark county, Ohio.

His successor was the Rev. Joseph L. Bihn, who was removed in September, 1873, at his own request, after a pastoral ministration of more than seventeen years. In August, 1870, Rev. N. Schnitz became his assistant, and remained until August, 1872. In September, 1872, Rev. A. M. Meile was appointed assistant, and remained until July, 1873. Another assistant, Rev. J. A. Michenfelder, was appointed, but remained only eighteen days and was removed after the resignation of the pastor.

In punishment of the disorders which had compelled Rev. J. L. Bihn to give up his charge, the congregation was left without a pastor and the church closed for more than two months, after which time the Right Rev. Bishop, moved by the repeated petitions of the people, appointed the present pastor, Rev. Charles Evrard, under whose administration peace was at once restored and has since remained undisturbed. In August, 1877, the Rev. J. B. Heiland became his assistant, but was compelled by his failing health to leave Tiffin, in March, 1878.

At the time of the organization of the new congregation the leading men were Joseph Kuebler, Dr. Joseph Boehler, Michael Kirchner, Frank

Greulich, Joseph Vollmer, Michael Theissen, John Houck and John Bormuth.

The present church building was commenced in 1860, and consecrated September 14, 1862, by the Right Rev. J. M. Young, Bishop of Erie, in the presence and with the assistance of Right Rev. A. Rappe, Bishop of the diocese. The beautiful gothic edifice, under the able management of Rev. J. L. Bihn, did not cost more than $25,000, and is a standing monument of the zeal of the pastor and the liberality of the people.

When the congregation was organized, in 1845, a plain, brick church, 40x90 feet, was at once built for their use, on the lot where the present church now stands; but the continual increase of families, from forty to nearly three hundred, made the building of a new and larger church absolutely necessary. The old church was torn down in 1861, and the new one built on the same spot. A temporary building was erected to be used for divine service until the completion of the new church.

The records do not mention the existence of any parochial school before the appointment of Rev. J. B. Uhlmann, in 1852. A school was established by him in the spring of 1853, and was maintained and enlarged by his successor. A new school house was built by Rev. J. L. Bihn in 1858, which contained two large rooms. In 1862, after the completion of the new church, the temporary building used for divine service was divided for school purposes; it received a second story, and four large rooms were again furnished for the increasing youth of the congregation. In 1875 another room became necessary, and a building was erected in the rear of the old school house. The congregation has now seven classses of children, taught by one male teacher and six Ursaline sisters.

In connection with the history of St. Joseph's congregation must be mentioned the establishhment of two religious communities in Tiffin.

In 1865 the Ursaline sisters came from Cleveland to Tiffin. They formed a new convent, established an academy for young ladies, and took charge of the parochial schools of both congregations in the city. In order to secure their services, St. Mary's congregation paid $1,000, and St. Joseph's paid $2,000, for the purchase of the lots upon which the Ursaline convent and the academy were afterwards built.

In 1868, Rev. J. L. Bihn established another community near the limits of the city, under the name of "Citizens' Hospital and Orphan Asylum." It is under the care of the Franciscan Sisters of the Third Order, and has increased admirably since its creation. A new and large chapel was erected in 1878. The institution contains at present thirty-four sisters and novices, eighteen aged persons, and seventy-five orphans. Rev. J. L. Bihn, founder and superior of this community, resides there, and manages all the affairs of the Home with prudence and success.

CHURCH DIRECTORY OF TIFFIN FOR 1880.

METHODIST EPISCOPAL.—Madison street, west of Washington. Services morning and evening. Rev. J. W. Mendenhall, minister.

FIRST METHODIST.—Market street, east of Washington street. Services morning and evening. Rev. Chandler, minister.

PRESBYTERIAN.—Corner of Market and Monroe streets. Services morning and evening. D. D. Bigger, pastor.

BAPTIST.—Perry street, east of Washington. Services morning and evening. Rev. Rupe, minister.

CATHOLIC (German)—Head of Washington street. Mass at 8 and 10 A. M. Vespers, 3 P. M. Rev. Father Evrard, pastor; Rev. Father Heiland, assistant.

CATHOLIC (English)—Corner of Miami and Franklin streets. Mass at 8 and 10 A. M. Vespers, 3 P. M. Rev. Father Healey, pastor.

LUTHERAN (English)—Corner of Jefferson and Madison streets. Services morning and evening. Rev. Crouse, minister.

LUTHERAN (German).—Jefferson street, opposite Main. Services morning and evening. Rev. Zimmerman, minister.

REFORMED (German).—Jefferson street, south of Madison. Services morning and evening. Rev. Rust, minister.

FIRST REFORMED.—Corner Monroe and Madison streets. Services morning and evening. Rev. Kefauver, minister.

EVANGELICAL (English).—North Washington street. Services morning and evening. Rev. J. A. Hensel, minister.

EVANGELICAL (German).—Sandusky street, north of Perry street. Services morning and evening. Rev. Schupp, minister.

EPISCOPAL.—Corner Market and Jefferson streets. Services morning and evening. Rev. Williams, minister.

In the above the services are all understood for Sunday.

CHAPTER XIX.

JOHN GOODIN—MRS. ANN SENEY—REZIN W. SHAWHAN—CHRISTOPHER SNYDER—GEORGE RUMMELL—DAVID E. OWEN—WYANDOT CHIEFS AND FAMILIES—MARK, CHAPTER VI., II VERSE IN MOHAWK—ANDREW LUGENBEEL—JUDGE PITTENGER—JOHN AND LOUISE FIEGE—CHRISTIAN MUELLER—THE GREAT FIRE OF APRIL, 1872.

JOHN GOODIN.

AMONG the many distinguished pioneers of Seneca county was John Goodin, beloved and esteemed alike for his honorable course in life, and for his intelligence and friendly nature. He was born in November, 1800, in Somerset county, Pennsylvania, and when about six years old moved with his father and the family to Perry county, Ohio, near Somerset, where he was raised to manhood. When about twenty-two years of age he married Elizabeth Kishler, and six years thereafter, in 1828, they moved to Tiffin. There were six children born to them, four daughters and two sons, who are all married and living in the western country. Joel K. Goodin is the oldest son, and a lawyer of eminence in Kansas, and John R. Goodin was judge of the court in Kansas, a member of the legislature in Kansas, and a member of congress from that state, and lately also the Democratic candidate for governor. Joel was also a member of the legislature of Kansas.

In Tiffin John Goodin took a very active part in the development of the town and county. He built the brick hotel on Washington street, already mentioned, and kept it for awhile, when he rented it to T. J. McCleary, and moved to the lot now covered by the Rust block. There he lived until he sold the lot, with the frame house thereon, to the Seewalds, shortly before he moved to Kenton.

In 1840 he was elected to the senate of Ohio from the district composed of the counties of Seneca, Wood, Ottawa, Sandusky and Hancock, for two years. He was treasurer of Seneca county from 1835 to 1839 inclusive. In 1843 he moved to Kenton, Hardin county, Ohio, where he entered into the mercantile business with his brother, and engaged extensively in buying and selling real estate. His wife died in 1857.

On the 13th of January, 1859, he married again. By this union he had three children. In 1850, and shortly before the adoption of the new constitution of Ohio, he was appointed one of the associate judges of the county of Hardin. He then retired from public life and lived quietly and happily on his farm, close by Kenton. Three years before his death he had an attack of paralysis. He died on the 20th of February, 1876, seventy-five years of age. Mr. Goodin was a tall, slender man, of a well proportioned physique; very active and sociable. He had a kind word for every one, and was personally very popular. He was a very active and shrewd politician; a man of strict morality and honesty, faithful to his word and duty. He was highly esteemed wherever he was known.

MRS. ANN SENEY.

William Wood came from Holland to Philadelphia with a stock of goods, and took into his employ a young man from Maryland, by the name of George Ebert, who some time after married Mr. Wood's daughter. The young people moved to Uniontown, Pennsylvania, where Mr. Ebert became a prominent citizen and was greatly respected. He was there engaged in mercantile life for forty years. They had a numerous family, and their youngest daughter, Ann, was a beautiful girl, and received a very liberal education at the Brownsville female seminary.

Albert Gallatin, the illustrious secretary of the treasury of the United States, under Jefferson, and some other distinguished gentlemen from Washington, paid a visit to Uniontown. Mr. Joshua Seney was then the private secretary to Mr. Gallatin. The people of Uniontown prepared and had a very brilliant ball in honor of their distinguished guests. At this ball Mr. Seney and Miss Ebert met for the first time. This short acquaintance ripened into a love affair between these young people, which culminated in their marriage. They lived in Uniontown ten years after that time, and then moved to Tiffin, in company with Judge Ebert, in the summer of 1831. They had three children when they came to Tiffin, and there were five more born to them here, making eight in all, five daughters and three sons, who are all still living, but two.

Mrs. Seney became a member of the M. E. Church when eighteen years of age, and up to her death continued to be a faithful, devoted and highly esteemed member thereof. She was one of the mothers in Israel, and will be remembered for her christian virtues and her gentle nature as long as one person may live that ever knew her.

During the sickly seasons, and whenever Mrs. Seney could leave her own family, she would go from house to house among the sick, assist in caring for them, fetch them some palatable nourishment, cheer up the distressed with her always pleasant smile and christian consolation. She was born on the 13th of September, 1803, and died on the 5th of May, 1879. She was beloved by all who knew her. The entire community mourned her loss when she died.

MERCANTILE LIFE.

Among the many thousands of men who engage in mercantile pursuits there is but a very small per cent. that make a success of it. The vast majority of them die poor. According to the commercial reports for many years, only about five per cent. have made money and become rich, and of this small number those that are still in business, and are considered rich, take their chances in the ups and downs of life. There is a certain fascination in mercantile life that induces men to invest their all, and young men without means are anxious to become clerks in stores, where they often remain, working for their employers until they grow gray with age.

The substantial mechanics and, above all, the farmers are far more happy. Of all human pursuits there is no situation in life so well calculated to fill the measure of our joy and contentment as that of a farmer. The American farmer out of debt occupies the top round in the ladder of human happiness. Those farmers who, by long, hard work and economy, accumulated a little fortune, then sold out, took the money and put it into a store, made clerks of their sons, who ought to have been left on the farms, and after trying the experiment for a year or two, failed, are generally the most pitiable subjects in the commercial world. These will appreciate what has been said above.

REZIN W. SHAWHAN.

The father of the subject of this sketch was Frederick Shawhan, a native of Kent county, Maryland, but had settled in Virginia after the revolutionary war, in which he was an active participant, having enlisted when but seventeen years of age. He served under Generals Wayne, Green, Lafayette and Washington. He was at the capture of Stoney Point by Wayne, at the battle of Monmouth, at the crossing of the Delaware, and at the subsequent capture of the Hessians, at Trenton. In 1812 he moved to Ohio, and first located in Fairfield county. In 1820 he removed to Wayne county, and afterwards settled in Seneca county, and died near Tiffin, August 26, 1840, in the eightieth year of his age.

Rezin W. was born October 19th, 1811, in Berkely county, Virginia. He worked on a farm until he was about fifteen years old. His chances for education were very limited, comprising only a common district school education of eight months. In the year 1826, he entered the store of William McComb, in Wooster, Ohio, as clerk. When eighteen years of age he was employed as clerk in the store of Zopher T. Moore, with whom he remained about three years. In 1833 he visited Seneca county, where his father had settled, and in the fall of the same year accompanied his employer, Mr. Moore, to New York, where Mr. Shawhan purchased a stock of goods, getting credit on Mr. Moore's recommendation. With this stock he opened a store in Tiffin, which was then a very new town, with a population of about five hundred. His capital, to begin with, was small, but in spite of his limited school privileges, it seemed he had a wonderful facility in working addition and multiplication, which, together with his industry, close application to business, his unflinching fidelity to every promise, his sagacity, frugality and good management, tended to make his business increase very rapidly, and in the race for success he distanced every rival. He continued in the mercantile business for eighteen years, buying and selling goods, grain and provisions of all kinds. Up to 1840 the only way to obtain goods or ship produce was by wagon to and from Sandusky City. In 1840, Tiffin became the terminus of the Mad River and Lake Erie railroad, and so remained for several years. This improved trade in Tiffin very much.

In 1851, feeling the need of relaxation, he closed up his business in Tiffin and transferred the stock to a branch house he had at Carey. He devoted the three years then next following to the study of geography, history and the natural sciences. His love for books soon procured for him an excellent library, and he pursued his studies with the same zeal, close application and perseverance that characterized him as a merchant. He now added the benefit of travel to his scientific attainments. He visited the western states, where he purchased large tracts of land. In December, in company with his wife, he visited Cuba, where he passed the winter following, returning by way of New Orleans. In 1858 he attended the sales of the public lands in Omaha, Nebraska, and Leavenworth, Kansas, where he purchased some thirty thousand acres. In the same year, in company with A. G. Sneath, he started a bank in Tiffin, which, after the war, was merged into the National Exchange Bank of Tiffin, and in which he has ever since been a large stockholder. In 1866 he built the Empire block in Tiffin, and, in company with others, was again largely engaged in the mercantile business. In 1871 Mr. Shawhan took a trip to London, and passed two months in England. He is still in the full vigor of his health and manages his immense estate with the same tact and attention as in times of yore he controlled a small stock of goods on Market street.

In 1839, on the first day of April, he was married to Elvira Tuller, of Washington, Ohio, who is also still living.* Mr. Shawhan still enjoys excellent health, and, were it not for his white hair and beard, would promise fair to outlive many a young man not half his age. While the great number of buildings Mr. Shawhan has erected in Tiffin have undoubtedly added largely to his wealth, they have also, at the same time, added greatly to the wealth and improvement of the city and county, and with his various other operations in this county, for nearly fifty years, he has in a large measure contributed to the development of the resources of the county. Of the fourteen children which his father had, he and his brother Josiah, at Cary, and Mrs. Anderson, at Fostoria, are the only survivors.

CHRISTOPHER SNYDER.

A duty I owe to the memory of a dear old friend prompts the writer to record a short personal sketch of one of Tiffin's early merchants, whose name, for more than twenty years, was associated with mercantile life in Tiffin, and whose "German store" was a regular bee-hive of a place.

Christopher Snyder was born in the city of Eppingen, Grand Duchy of Baden, Germany, March 22d, 1810. He learned the trade of a shoemaker in his native town when a boy, and in the spring of 1832, he, together with his brother John, several years his senior, left their home for the United States. They came directly to Tiffin, with the family of Andrew Albright, already mentioned, when Christopher soon found employment in the family of Henry Cronise, whose hospitality and kindness to strangers were equal to the popularity of his name.

Richard Sneath kept the principal hotel in Tiffin, being located opposite the court house, on Washington street. Here Snyder found employment as clerk and steward, and soon had charge of the whole establishment. Mr. Sneath was an enterprising man, and in 1835 he built a store (one story frame, immediately south of Cronise's) with a little porch in front, painted green. Mr. Sneath bought a very good stock of goods, and a short time after he had opened up he took Mr. Snyder as a partner. This was in 1836. All the capital the young

---

*Since the foregoing was written, Mrs. Shawhan and Josiah Shawhan have both died; the former on the 20th of May, 1880, and Josiah at Upper Sandusky the day following.

German had was his honesty and his business qualifications. The German store soon became popular under the management of Christopher, who soon made hosts of friends by his straightforward, honest dealing, and his polished, polite behavior towards everybody. Meantime, Mr. George Rummell (hereafter mentioned) married Jane, the beautiful daughter of Mr. Sneath, and soon after Mr. Sneath sold his interest in the store to this new son-in-law, and to his old clerk, Christopher. The new firm started April 1st, 1837, and conducted the business at the same place, under the name of the "German store," for seventeen years, when, on account of ill-health, Mr. Rummell withdrew from the firm. From this time forward Mr. Snyder conducted the business alone, as he did up to the time of his death. In April, 1847, Mr. Snyder was married to Philipena, daughter of Philip J. Augspurger, of the village of Albig in Hesse-Darmstadt, Germany, who arrived with her sister, Miss Eva, in Tiffin, in the year 1844. Miss Eva is a twin sister of Mrs. Snyder, and was clerk in Mr. Snyder's store during the last few years of his life, where she acquired a general knowledge of mercantile business. Naturally talented, gifted with a lively, pleasant nature and good health, she has herself been in the mercantile business for more than twenty years, and built up a nice trade in the line of woolen yarns, zephyrs, general needle-work and fancy articles. At present she is in company with her widowed sister, Mrs. Snyder, in their store on Market street.

On the 22d of March, 1857, Mr. Snyder died, after a short illness, leaving his widow and three small children in good circumstances. Mrs. Snyder raised her children well, and gave them a good education. There were two daughters and one son: O. P. Snyder, well and favorably known among the business men of Tiffin; Augusta, who was married to Mr. Alf. D. Flen, and who died in Davenport, Iowa, about one year ago, and Philipena, the wife of Mr. Russel Knapp, of the *Tiffin Tribune*.

Christopher Snyder's short life was a most excellent specimen of "manhood turned to utility"; ever ready for business, open hearted, and strictly honest, friendly, yet dignified, he was one of the most popular merchants of Tiffin.

The family occupies a respectable position amongst the best families of the city.

Christopher and the writer became friends when first we met in Tiffin, in August, 1833. Our friendship grew stronger as years rolled on. Many a Sunday afternoon we spent in pleasant conversation under the old sycamore tree on the bank of the Sandusky river, talking about our native hills and our future prospects in this ' Yankee Land." In the year 1850 it became the duty of the writer to prepare a bill for the incorporation of the town of Tiffin with Fort Ball, into a city of the second class, and in drawing the boundary of the young city, I did not neglect the old sycamore tree, which now forms a point in the act of the legislature incorporating the city. Snyder and the old tree have passed away, and the writer is left in the evening of his life to record their memory. (See act incorporating the city of Tiffin.)

GEORGE RUMMELL.

The subject of this sketch was born in Columbiana county, Ohio, on the 12th day of March, A. D., 1804. His parents were from Pennsylvania. The ancestors came from Germany. George was born and raised on a farm, and received only a common school education, and before he arrived at manhood he learned the trade of a bricklayer. He came to Tiffin in the fall of 1834, and worked at his trade for about two years, and boarded at Sneath's hotel. Here he made the acquaintance of Jane, the beautiful daughter of Mr. Sneath, and married her on the 8th of November, 1835. Mrs. Rummell died March 27th, 1839. On the first day of April, 1837, Mr. Rummell and Mr. Snyder formed a copartnership in the mercantile business in Tiffin, and opened, and for seventeen years, conducted the well-known store on Washington street known as the " German store."

On the 1st of December, 1840, Mr. Rummell married Mrs. Mary Ann Lookingland, eldest daughter of Jacob Copenhaver. Of this union two sons and two daughters are still living. Towards the year 1850 the health of Mr. Rummell failed, and he was scarcely ever about the store. The whole responsibility rested upon Snyder, who was equal to the demand of the labor and responsibility the situation required. In the spring of 1854, Mr. Rummell sold his interest in the store to Mr. Snyder, and moved with his family onto a little twenty-acre lot just east of Tiffin, where his health improved very materially. He bought more land and became quite a farmer; began to look robust, attended market in Tiffin, and for many years looked like a new man. When the firm of Rummell and Snyder started their store in Tiffin, they had not five hundred dollars between them. In taking the store they also took Sneath's debts belonging to the store. One time the sheriff came with an execution, and gave the new firm notice that if the amount of the execution was not raised by ten o'clock next morning, the store would have to be closed. This was agreed to, and things looked blue for the young merchants. Next morning they met at the store and determined to deliver over to the sheriff not only the goods, but also the accounts, notes and cash on hand. Each partner was to take only stuff for one pair of pantaloons, and let the sheriff see it when he came for the key.

About nine o'clock, just one hour before the time fixed for the sheriff to come, Judge Lugenbeel came into the store, white all over with flour and mill dust. He had just come from his mill and had in his hand a shot-bag full of gold and silver. The judge was a great friend of the young merchants, and walking up to them, said: "Boys, I have some $1,700 in specie here, and have no use for it. If you will take it you can use it as long as you please." They then told the judge the strait they were in. Judge Lugenbeel hunted up Levi Keller, the sheriff, paid him the amount of the execution, and all went merry as a marriage bell. Their paper never went to protest. No one ever obtained a judgment against them. Their credit was as good in New York as anybody's. They made no large fortunes, but when they separated were worth about $10,000 each and out of debt. Mr. Rummell retired to his farm, and Mr. Snyder continued in business; both self-made men who left behind them a clear record; and having been amongst the early merchants in Tiffin, and amongst the few that made no failure of the business, their record is certainly not out of place here.

About the year 1871 Mr. Rummell's old troubles returned, and his health failed very rapidly. He died at one o'clock on the night following Thursday, December 12th, 1872, esteemed and beloved by all who knew him. The Rev. Mr. Collier, in preaching his funeral sermon, commended his many manly traits of character. For thirty-eight long years the writer enjoyed the friendship of Mr. Rummell, which was never disturbed, for a single moment, through all the chequered scenes of busy turmoil.

There are many merchants in Tiffin now doing flourishing business, controlling a great deal of property, and the writer hopes they may each and all form exceptions to the general rule—grow rich and die happy.

DAVID EVAN OWEN

Was not only an early settler and pioneer, but also a man of considerable notoriety and moral and public worth. He was the oldest son of Evan Owen, who came to Philadelphia from Wales. They were Quakers and very wealthy. The old gentleman owned a great deal of land near the town, which is now covered by the city of Philadelphia. The writer has in his possession the commission issued by Governor Thomas Mifflin to Evan Owen, appointing him justice of the peace for

Fishing Creek township, Northumberland county, Pennsylvania, dated September 1st, A. D., 1791, to hold the same from that date until (it goes on to say) "so long as you shall behave yourself well."

David Evan Owen, the subject of this sketch, was born on the 8th day of May, A. D., 1775, and was raised in the lap of wealth and luxury. He was sent to the college in Philadelphia, and received a very liberal education. He had grown to man's estate before his father failed, when young Owen was compelled to seek some livelihood for himself. He learned the trade of a house carpenter, and worked at this occupation several years.

On the 26th day of October, 1805, he was married in Berwick, Columbia county, Pennsylvania, to Jerusha Smith, of that place, and some time thereafter became the owner and editor of the *Berwick American*, a Democratic weekly newspaper. On the 20th day of November, 1820, he was appointed by President James Monroe, postmaster at Berwick; the commission is signed by Return J. Meigs, Jr., who was then postmaster general.

In 1813, September 7th, Simon Snyder, governor of Pennsylvania, appointed him justice of the peace for the townships of Bloom and Briar Creek, in Columbia county, Pennsylvania, "so long as you shall behave yourself well."

Mr. Owen published the first paper, in the English language, in Allentown, Lehigh county, Pennsylvania, called the *Allentown Star*. This paper was not a success, and he moved to North Whitehall, in the same county, where he taught school for a time. Before he moved to Allentown he was elected to the senate of Pennsylvania from the Columbia district, where he served two terms, and during which time James Buchanan was also a member. There was an air of aristocracy about Mr. Buchanan that Mr. Owen never admired.

Early in the spring of 1829 he moved, with his family, to Seneca county, where he arrived and settled on Rocky creek, on what is now called the "Huber farm," on the 9th day of May, that year. He put up a little cabin and cleared a few acres for corn, in that spring. Here Mr. Owen lived with his family in the dense forest in a most obscure way, known only by a few of his Pennsylvania relatives and neighbors. The Whigs had the county and everything their own way. In the fall of 1831, a few Democrats in town consulted together upon the propriety of putting a Democratic county ticket in the field. They having no suitable candidate for auditor, Mr. Daniel Dildine, Sr., said there was a man living up Rocky creek who would make a good candidate, whose name was D. E. Owen, and that he was a smart man and a great Democrat. They nominated him and elected him; the first Democrat elected to any office in Seneca county. He was the second auditor of the county. In 1833 he was re-elected, and while he served in this capacity, on the 27th day of August, 1833, Robert Lucas appointed him receiver of the "Ohio Canal Land office, at Tiffin, Ohio." Moses H. Kirby, the present senator from the district composed of the counties of Seneca, Crawford and Wyandot, was the secretary of state and signed Mr. Owen's commission.

In 1836 Mr. Owen was elected to the senate of Ohio from the senatorial district composed of the counties of Huron, Sandusky and Seneca. Joseph Howard was the Whig candidate, and one of the most popular men in that party.

On the 27th day of June, 1838, President Van Buren appointed Mr. Owen "Receiver of the public money for the district of lands subject to sale by the treaty with the Wyandot Indians dated April 26, 1836, to serve for four years, from June 25, 1838." Levi Woodbury was then Secretary of the Treasury. Land sales in Crawford county were ordered to take place, under the proclamation of the President, on Monday, the 6th day of August, 1838. On the 28th day of November, 1838, the President ordered another land sale, to take place at Marion, on the 28th day of January following. This last sale was for only two sections, both south of the base line—section 35, cranberry swamp on Broken Sword creek, T. 1, S. R. 1, and N. E. ¼ of section 2, T. 2, S. R. 2.

In conformity with the treaty, a certain per cent. of the proceeds of these sales was to be paid to the Wyandots, and the receipts for these dividends, in my possession, have the names of the following chiefs attached:

Ron-ton-dee or Warpole; Dou-wan-tout; Tay-on-dot-to-hach, Punch; Hon-don-yon-wan or Mathias; Day-on-quot or Half King; Manoncue or Thomas; Tay-arron-tooyea, or Between the Logs; Widow Harrahaat; Widow Big Sinew; Tay-qua-way; Hays; Black Sheep; Charloe; Summondewat; Tsooshia; Droosrousch; Coon Hawk; Gray Eyes; Bearskin; Touromee; Squeendehtee; Monture; Old Shawnee; Big Spoon; Cross the Lake; Ronuneay; Big River; Ground Squirrel; Young Cherokee; Tahautohs; Septemess; Gayamee; Little Chief; Fighter; Tall Charles; Solomon; Taress; Big Arms; Nooshutoomohs; Shreaeohhs; Tauranyehtee; Peacock; Curreesaquoh; Porcupine; Bob Cherokee; Satrahass; Kay-roo-hoo; White Wing; Half John; St. Peter; Ree-wandee-nun-toohk; Hisson; Snakehead; Split-the-logs; Daenundee; John Hicks; Mudeatoe; Soocuhquess; Wasp; Tondee; Vandeenoo; Summenturoo; John Baptiste; Soorontooroo; Racer; Big Kittle Child; White Crow, and many others.

One pay roll shows paid to these and others $22,212.

At the first land sales in Marion $57,106.50 were received.

When Mr. Owen resigned the United States Land Office, J. R. Poinsett, Secretary of War, under date of May 16, 1840, ordered Mr. Owen to deliver over his books, papers and moneys to John Goodin, who was appointed his successor as receiver, and who receipted in full.

The following table will show the amounts paid into the treasury of the United States from the sale of lands for seven years, viz:

YEAR.	AMOUNT.	YEAR.	AMOUNT.
1832	$ 2,623,781	1836	$34,877,179
1833	$ 3,967,781	1837	$ 6,776,236
1834	$ 4,857,600	1838	$ 3,081,939
1835	$14,757,600		

After Mr. Owen resigned his office as receiver of the Land Office, he kept a provision store in Tiffin, and was elected justice of the peace several times, which office he held as long as he was able to do public business, and until old age disqualified him for public life. He was a thorough politician, and perfectly at home in an office. He held office nearly all his life, and discharged every duty and trust with marked ability and fidelity; but he had very little idea of practical life outside of an office, and, like most politicians that do not know how to steal, died poor. He knew simply nothing about speculations, or the value of money. He provided and lived well while he had plenty, and when his money was gone he economized from the force of circumstances. He was a popular officer, a generous, liberal man; was strictly moral and scrupulously honest in all his intercourse with his fellow men, and was highly respected. Mrs. Owen died in Tiffin January 7, 1849, aged sixty-two years, nine months and sixteen days. Mr. Owen died September 9, 1857, aged eighty-two years, four months and one day. One son and three daughters are still living.

When Mr. Owen resigned the office of receiver of the canal lands Governor Lucas appointed Mr. Timothy Griffith, of Columbus, his successor.

Mr. Owen was a short man, being only about five feet and two inches high; he had a heavy head of dark brown hair, strongly marked features, light blue eyes; was stoutly built, fleshy, and withall active. He was a great reader, and very interesting in political conversations. He was well acquainted with nearly all the leading politicians of his time.

While Mr. Owen held the office of receiver of the canal lands, at

Tiffin, great quantities of land were sold, and the money paid was all gold and silver. The state had furnished Mr. Owen an iron chest to put his money into; it looked like a block of iron two feet square. When it was full he hired a team to haul it to Columbus.

One time Daniel Dildine, Sr., with his team, and Mr. Owen, on their way to Columbus with the chest, stopped at a hotel in Marion for the night. The hotel was crowded with all sorts of customers, and there was a great deal of carousal going on. What to do with the iron chest they did not know, but were of the opinion that it would not do to take it into the tavern, for it took four men to put it into the wagon Finally they concluded to leave it in the open yard in the open wagon, simply covering it with a little straw. The next morning everything was found all right. Nobody suspected that the two old farmers had $80,000 in gold in that old wagon.

For those who have a curiosity to read the Mohawk Indian, and further, to preserve a specimen of it from utter oblivion, there is attached hereto the 2d verse of the 6th chapter of St. Mark, followed by a translation of the same into Mohawk :

"And when the Sabbath day was come, he began to teach in the synagogue; and many hearing him were astonished, saying: From whence hath this man these things? and what wisdom is this which is given unto him, that even such mighty works are wrought by his hands?"

TRANSLATION.

"Neoni ne onea Wa-aweandadogeaghdane, tahhadaghsawer waghsakorihhonnyea et-hone synagogue; neoni yawetowanea yakott, hoende na-ah, wa-akorighcoaneghragoh, wairough: Kah oughdenoe tahhawe nekea—ea Tñinikarihhodease? neoni oghna Kamikoughrodea oughte ne roewawyh, ne kinongkeah n'agwagh Kayodeaghferas-hatsde yoyo'dch ne Rasno'nke?

ANDREW LUGENBEEL

Was born in Frederick county, Maryland, in 1806. On the 11th of September, 1832, he was married to Elizabeth Baltzell, of that county, who was a sister of Thomas Baltzell, formerly living in Seneca township, and of Dr. Kuhn's first wife. Soon after his marriage Mr. Lugenbeel moved to Seneca county, where he resided up to the time of his death. When the writer first got acquainted with Mr. Lugenbeel he was a partner in the mercantile business with Jacob Stern, in Tiffin. About 1834 he bought the land of Joseph Janay, where, in 1836, he built a grist mill on the river bank, a short distance south of town, that has ever since, and until very recently, been known by the familiar name of "Lugenbeel's mill." Mr. Lugenbeel took charge of the mill himself, and soon made it the most popular mill on the river.

After his appointment as one of the associate judges of the Seneca common pleas, he was familiarly called "Judge Lugenbeel," which title he retained to the time of his death. He took a very active part in public affairs, and was very successful in all his undertakings. He became one of the most popular, as he was certainly one of the most eminent, men in Seneca county. He was a man of clear views, naturally philosophic in his thoughts, of strong, clear, sound judgment, of polished manners without the least ostentation; a safe counselor, a true friend, kind, benevolent; a man of enlarged views, broad-gauged and generous. He was beloved by his intimate friends and esteemed by all. He was one of the originators of the Seneca county infirmary, and one of its first directors. He held a number of township offices also, and filled the bill wherever he was placed. The writer heard Judge Bowen say, at one time, that amongst all the associate judges in his very large circuit, there was not one the equal of Judge Lugenbeel for sound judgment and capacity.

About 1843 Mrs. Lugenbeel died, and the judge married Miss Jemimah Souder, December 11, 1845. The judge died December 10, 1863, in the fifty-eighth year of his age, without a child, leaving his estate, which was regarded as one of the best accumulations in the county, to his widow, who still survives him, but who seems to be either very indifferent or else knows but little about the judge, or both.

Judge Lugenbeel was about five feet nine inches high; had a fair complexion, very florid face, high forehead, blue, deep-set eyes, clenched lips; his face was always shaved smooth, and he never wore a beard. He was slow and dignified in his conversation, but whatever he said was solid. He never indulged in frivolous talk, and enjoyed conversation that required deep, sound thinking. He died while the country was in her throes of war, and his memory is fast becoming obliterated; but while he lived he was a true man and a most excellent citizen.

JOHN PITTENGER

Was born in Frederick county, Maryland, on the 16th day of January, 1778; was the oldest son among twelve children, two sisters being older. He was married to Julia Ann Gibson, at Graceham, in the same county, June 22d, 1817. Mrs. Pittenger was born April 12th, 1801, and is still living, now residing with her eldest living daughter, Mrs. R. R. McMeens, at Sandusky City, Ohio. There were nine children as the fruit of this marriage, five sons and four daughters, five of whom are still living, viz: Mrs. R. R. McMeens, at Sandusky City; J. H. Pittenger, attorney-at-law, at Tiffin, Ohio; Mrs. M. E. Stem, at Sandusky City; Mrs. H. S. Kendig, at Tiffin, Ohio, and Charles W. Pittenger, at West Liberty, Ohio.

John Pittenger worked on his father's farm, where he was born, until he was over thirty years of age, and when losing his health he moved to Graceham, a small Moravian village, in Frederick county, where he entered into the mercantile business, and which he continued until he removed to Tiffin with his family, in 1829

He came to Ohio first in 1823 or 1824, passed down to Cincinnati. Sitting on his horse on a hill overlooking the embryo city, he came to the conclusion that there was nothing there to make a city, and rode on down to North Bend, where he thought the prospect was better. From there he passed north through Indiana, crossed the Black Swamp into Seneca county. Here he was pleased with the fine timber and the streams, and concluded to locate here. In the fall of 1825, he sent a stock of goods by wagons from Baltimore, Maryland, and opened the same in the name of J. and B. Pittenger. Benjamin Pittenger is a younger brother, still living, and familiarly known by the name of Judge Pittenger. Leaving his brother Benjamin in charge of the store, he returned to Maryland. The store and building have already been described. The business was thus carried on until 1834. In 1837 Mr. John Pettinger carried on the business in his own name, until 1844 or 1845. In 1832 the two brothers started the tannery on Perry street, already mentioned, and conducted the same until they sold it to Fleming and Schock, about the year 1839. Mr. Pittenger was an active and industrious man. He carried on a farm on lands he entered in this county. He was constantly employed at something, and when he quit public life he started a nursery on the south side of Market street, on the lot now occupied by the "Turners' Hall" and Mr. John Nuser's residence. Here he busied himself with budding and grafting trees for a number of years.

He became a member of the Methodist church at an early age, and remained a consistent member all his life. His home in Graceham was a general stopping place for ministers of all denominations. Father Purcell, now arch-bishop of Cincinnati, frequently accepted his hospitality when he was at Emmitsburgh. Even after he moved to Tiffin he often entertained Methodist ministers at his house. He crossed the mountains on horseback nine times, between Frederick county, Maryland, and Seneca county, Ohio, upon the same horse—old Major—averaging fifty miles per day. The old horse, which lived till its twenty-sixth year, was a fine racker, but refused to work in harness.

While Mr. Pittenger was a man full of energy and business, he was quiet and unobtrusive. He was not very talkative; there was no flattery or blarney about him. He was sincere and earnest in his dealings with men. He was a large, muscular and bony man, not fleshy, but well built. He had a large head, clear blue eyes, an expressive face, and as the weight of years made their mark upon him his head became bald, his hair and beard white, and his once powerful frame broken down, so that towards the evening of his life he was quite stoop shouldered. He was a decided Whig, but never a leader in politics. He died on the 20th day of October, 1857, at the ripe age of seventy-nine years, nine months and four days.

BENJAMIN PITTENGER

Was a younger brother of John Pittenger. He was born in Frederick county, Maryland, on the 29th day of January, 1798, on a farm, where he was raised. On the 9th day of September, 1825, he was married to Theresa Creeger (already mentioned), and located in Tiffin in December of the same year. His wife died here December 8, 1847, at the age of forty-two years, leaving five children. Mr. Pittenger was married again on the 13th day of December, 1849, to Miss Mary Ann Hunter, who also died August 15, 1877.

Mr. Pittenger was one of the first associate judges of Seneca county, holding that position two terms (fourteen years), and was therefore familiarly known by the name of Judge Pittenger. He never was very fond of work, and therefore unlike his brother John, who was always busy. The judge was one of the early leaders of the Whig party in the county, and continued thus until that party fought its last battle under General Scott, in 1852; and when, in 1856, the Republican party was organized and John C. Fremont nominated for President, he attached himself to that party, and has voted with it ever since. The judge and his brother John were in partnership in Tiffin, in the mercantile trade, and in the tannery already described. They sold the tannery to Fleming and Schoch, in 1839.

Some twenty years ago the judge moved to his farm, about two miles from the city on the Melmore road, where he still resides. He has two sons, both married, and three daughters—Mrs. J. M. Naylor, Mrs. Ed. Naylor and Mrs. Al Buskirk.

Judge Pittenger, in the full vigor of his life, had a very straight carriage, was about six feet two inches high, had a full head of hair, bushy eye-brows, a long face and rather large nose He resembled General Jackson very much. But the eighty-two years of life that have passed over his head, have left it very white, and broken down his physical powers very materially.

The judge was not a man of great force of character, but honorable, dignified, kind and sociable.

JOHN AND LOUISA FIEGE.

There were also many mechanics in Tiffin who failed to make a success. This is a world of cause and effect, and, to a great extent, just as we make it. John Fiege came to Tiffin from Germany in 1834, a cabinet maker by trade. He was a good mechanic, a kind, clever man, and strictly honest in his dealings. He built up a large trade, and accumulated property rapidly. In 1836 he was married to Mary Louisa, oldest daughter of Philip von Blou, who located in Tiffin about that time and soon moved onto a farm in Eden township, where he lived a long time.

Mrs. Fiege was born in Waldmohr in the Bavarian Palatinate, on the 8th day of December, 1813. John Fiege was born in Oedelsheim, in the Electorate of Hesse, July 3, 1811. They had ten children in all, of whom three sons are still living, now familiarly and favorably known as the "Fiege Brothers," carrying on the most extensive furniture and undertaking business in the city. John Fiege was drowned in a mill-race March 31st, 1869. Mrs. Fiege died December 29th, 1874. Both were among the most highly esteemed people in Tiffin.

CHRISTIAN MUELLER AND VALENTINE SCHMIDT

Were brewers and coopers by trade. They came to Tiffin in 1847, from Bavaria. They produced lager beer in 1848, which is thought to have been the first in Ohio. In 1854 they erected a new brewery on River street, and conducted the business together until 1860, when Mr. Mueller bought Mr. Schmidt's interest, and carried on a very extensive business. He turned Schmidt's brewery into a malt house in 1872. Mueller's beer is celebrated all over Ohio and the west.

Mr. Mueller had promised to write out a little history of the breweries in Tiffin, but, like so many of our good intentions, it was left undone.

"Christ. Mueller," as he is familiarly called, is a very clever and congenial gentleman, of excellent social nature, and a fine conversationalist. He is a great lover of music, and was one of the most active among the founders of the "Bruderbund," a German singing association that was organized in 1854, and is still in existence. He has a large family, and with the great industry and energy necessary to

THE GREAT FIRE. 311

conduct his very extensive operations, he still preserves his youthful appearance; nor has he lost any of his innate jocular and friendly disposition. Valentine Schmidt died some fifteen years ago.

THE GREAT FIRE OF 1872.

The greatest losses by fire that Tiffin ever suffered, at any one time, occurred on the 13th of April, 1872. A very full description of it is found in the *Tiffin Tribune* of the 18th of April, 1872, from which I copy:

TERRIBLE FIRE!
TWO SQUARES BURNED OVER!
70 BUILDINGS DESTROYED!
$90,000 IN PROPERTY BURNT UP!
FIRE AN UNRELENTING MASTER!

FULL DETAILS OF THE FIRE OF SATURDAY.

Saturday, April 13, 1872, marks an epoch in the fire history of Tiffin that will never be forgotten by those who witnessed the terrible conflagration. About two o'clock and forty minutes, the alarm of fire was given in the second ward, and in a moment the fire bells of the city were ringing out the loud clamor of danger. During the day the wind had been blowing a gale, from a northwesterly direction, and when the alarm was given it was seemingly at its height. The different fire companies hastened to the second ward, together with the citizens generally; nearly everybody started immediately in the direction where the fire was supposed to be, with a seeming intuition that there was work to be done that would require the assistance of all.

Upon reaching the ground it was discovered that fire was burning on the roof of Mrs. A. Rawson's house, on Miami street, and the roof of the store occupied by A. McNeal, on Sandusky street, all connected with each other.

The engines were immediately put to work, one at a cistern near the engine house, and the other nearly opposite McNeal's store. In a few minutes the engine in front of the store had to move from the cistern, after working hard, as the heat was unendurable. The other engine got to work immediately, and was doing good execution, when the water in the cistern gave out. This necessitated a change in these two engines, with their hose, and gave the fire a free field, with but one engine to work on it. The wind seemed to gain in fierceness, and the building was one mass of flames. In the meantime, a large number of citizens had been carrying out and saving all that was possible of the furniture in the house, and goods from the store.

On the opposite side of Sandusky street, right directly in the face of the wind and fire, the hook and ladder companies and citizens were on the roof of Ogle's store and the dwellings in the rear, busy with buckets of water to save them. The fire raged higher and fiercer, and these buildings had to be deserted, as the heat was too intense to be endured.

Just at this time, about fifteen minutes after the fire was discovered, the word went around like magic that four barns were in flames, and a few rods in the rear and a little north of Ogle's store; so intently was the attention of every one directed to the first building on fire, and saving those near, that these barns were not discovered until every part of them was on fire and the flames were shooting up nearly one hundred feet. This changed the whole face of everything. It was found that the buildings first on fire and those near had to be left to their fate, and attention turned to the saving of property ahead of the fire. All became dire confusion among those most likely to suffer immediately from the flames. Attempts were made to save the buildings with buckets of water, and removal of furniture began. Women and children were crying with fright, and the owners of property, with pale faces and compressed lips, saw the impossibility of saving their houses.

Scarcely had the fire in the barns above mentioned been discovered, when flames were seen leaping up from Le Baron's stave factory, sixty rods or more distant. This burned fiercely, and the wind from a gale became almost a hurricane. Burning shingles, boards, coals and sparks flew in every direction, and ignited everything they touched. Fires were kindled in every direction; at this time, twenty-five minutes after the first alarm, upwards of fifty buildings were blazing furiously. The flames leaped from building to building; dense volumes of smoke covered the doomed ground, and it seemed that nothing but an interposition of Providence could stay the destruction. In thirty-eight minutes after the fire started, the roof of the house of Mr. Singer, on the east side of Washington street, was nearly burnt off, while everything inflammable between that and McNeal's corner was in flames. It was impossible to keep track of the buildings as they caught fire, for the fire seemed to start in every direction, with the regularity of the ticking of the clock.

Earnest, terrible fighting was done, but the heat was intense and showers of fire so great that the people were helpless in what is now called "the burnt district."

A DESPERATE FIGHT.

We arrived at Sneath's warehouse, Kaup's planing factory and depot. Here the desperate fight of the day was made. The fire was making fearful ravages and rapidly approaching these buildings which are divided from the burnt district by the railroad. Had the fire got into these large buildings, the Ohio Stove works, over forty residences, and Cunningham's mill would have been burnt, and the fire would have crossed the river and the business portion of the town would have been doomed. The two steamers were put to work at this point, and a large number of citizens took hold and worked with the firemen. Benner's house and barn and Bartell's saloon, directly opposite Sneath's warehouse, were burning fiercely. The water house and sheds of the railroad, with large piles of wood opposite the planing factory and the depot, were burning terribly.

THE GREAT FIRE.   313

In the warehouse, Smoyer & Bro. had 50,000 bushels of wheat, and 20,000 bushels of oats. The oats were in the upper story under the roof, and the precaution of bringing in pails there, had been taken. Six men were on the oats to watch the sparks which were blown under the shingles. As these sparks fell, they would throw water on them and extinguish them.

On the outside, men were on the roof with pails, and the fire company threw water onto the front, together with fighting the Benner and Bartell fire. The same work was done on the planing factory and depot, both of which were on fire inside and out several times. At one time the depot was in flames, and it was thought that it was doomed; the freight was partially removed. However, hose was got onto the roof, and the building was deluged and saved.

No conception of this can be pictured on paper. It was a dead fight between seething flames on one side and desperate men intent on saving hundreds of thousands of dollars' worth of property on the other. The latter prevailed.

Another very important key to the safety of the city was the saving of the house of Mrs. Glick, at the corner of Miami and Monroe. That, with the Holt house, was the only property saved on that square. A number of young men took hold there, and, with buckets of water, kept the fire away from it, or rather extinguished it whenever it burst out. The heat was so intense that those working had to cover their faces with wet cloths. It was saved after a determined fight, and after it was on fire several times.

We say this was another key to the safety of other property from the fact that directly opposite was an old dwelling that would have gone; next to that a frame, and so on, building after building, until the Cunningham warehouse was reached; all of which would have burnt, and the end would have been the destruction of all the factories and business portion of Tiffin.

It was a fearful time, and one we do not wish to witness but once in a life time.   *   *   *   *   *   *

The fire companies, as companies, and individually, did all it was possible for them to do. They were promptly on hand, and when the labor of the citizens was done, they kept at work, worn out as they were, till late on Sunday. They hung to their work faithfully and well.

About forty-five minutes after the fire started the entire property destroyed was in flames. The fire from Singer's house passed intervening buildings and ignited the pump-shop of Fishbingh and two houses, all of which were burnt. In the meantime fighting fire was done on all the buildings in that section.

The fire crossed the river and started Smith's brewery to burning, and the woods, trees and fences beyond for one and-one-half miles from the starting place of the conflagration, but no damage was done.

On the square first burnt, the furniture, bedding, etc., in many cases were removed to streets adjoining and left, as was supposed, in safety, but when looked for were found burnt up or on fire.   *   *   *

The city council telegraphed to Sandusky for help, but receiving no answer, did so again, and finally informed Sandusky that the fire was approaching the railroad bridge. Then the track was cleared by telegraph, and the engine reached Tiffin in forty minutes from the time she started, and threw water in less than one hour from the time she left Sandusky. After working one half hour she collapsed a flue. She was well handled up to that time, and Sandusky deserved Tiffin's compliments.

THE SUFFERERS AND THEIR LOSSES.

The larger portion of these losses are sustained by men in moderate circumstances, who cannot well bear the blow. Some are laboring men who have secured a home by hard knocks, and were thus left homeless.

Sandusky street—West side:
McNeal, goods in store	$ 2,000
Mrs. Rawson's buildings	3,500

Sandusky street—East side:
A. & F. Ogle, two-story brick building, and dwelling adjoining, one and one-half story, and two one-story frames	9,000
T. Collins, loss on goods	1,900
D. C. Baughman, two-story brick and frame barn, etc.	2,000
A. Meehan, two-story frame	2,000

Miami street—North side:
A. & F. Ogle, two frames, one brick and two barns	3,000
A. McNeal, two-story frame house, barn and wood	3,000
Mrs. Glick, frame barn and smoke-house	500

Franklin street—West side:
John Knott, house and barn	600
W. Shugan, two-story frame house	1,500
P. Hartner, frame barn	200

Adams street—South side:
P. Hartner, double house and two-story brick	3,800
N. Nubel, large barn	500

Franklin street—East side:
Mrs. Bresnin, frame house	800

Adams street—South side:
D. Arndt, brick house and barn	4,000
D. Bartell's brick, etc.	4,000
George Benner's house and barn	1,000

Adams street—North side:
Jacob Kuhn's frame house	1,000
B. Troxell's house and barn	1,800
Railroad company, two-story frame, etc.	2,000
Railroad company, loss on freight removed and whisky destroyed	500

Franklin street—East side:
M. Kuhn, two dwellings and one barn	2,500
Mr. Quinn, dwelling house	600
L. A. Baron, stave factory	15,000
T., T. & E. railroad company, ties burnt	500

Washington street—West side:
E. Umsted, house and barn	2,500
F. J. Wagner, house and barn	3,000
H. L. Kendall, brick house and barn	3,500
A. Brandebury, brick house	3,000

THE GREAT FIRE. 315

Washington street—East side:
Samuel Shade, barn, etc.. 1,000
F. Singer, brick house and barn..................................... 3,200
Minerva street:
George Fishbaugh, pump factory and barn, etc...................... 1,500
Paul Miller, house and barn.. 1,500
L. Bang, house.. 1,000

There were also a number of smaller losses, amounting to several thousand in the aggregate. The total loss reached $95,000.

CHAPTER XX.

SURPLUS REVENUE—POLITICS—FIRST POLITICAL JOLLIFICATION—TIFFIN IN THE WOODS—TIFFIN INCORPORATED—FIRST ELECTION—INCORPORATION OF FORT BALL—ITS FIRST ELECTION—INCORPORATION OF THE CITY— FIRST CORPS OF CITY OFFICERS—HARRISON NOBLE—PLANK ROADS— PIKES—TELEGRAPHS—THE SCHOOLS OF TIFFIN.

WHEN the revolutionary war ended the general government and the colonies were badly in debt; the former was compelled to repudiate, and those of the colonies that were lucky enough to have surplus lands under their old charters, were enabled to pay a large part of their debts by land scrips. Virginia and Connecticut, owning the entire northwestern territory, paid nearly all their colonial debts by these scrips, which secured the first titles to land northwest of the Ohio river. The general government struggled along with an empty treasury for many years, until finally the duties on imports and the proceeds from the sale of the public lands made her exchequer flush, and the statesmen of those days were troubled with the surplus revenue. There was no national debt, and the money accumulated in the United States treasury until it became a burden. The recommendation of General Jackson, to distribute it among the states, was approved by some and opposed by others. Some of the eastern states had no particular use for their shares, but it was a God-send to some of the states in the west, where the people suffered greatly for want of money, which was especially true of Ohio. The gross amount to be distributed was $20,000,000. The portion to Ohio was $1,423,000; and the amount that came to Seneca county was $31,756.73.03. The act passed congress and was approved by the President on the 26th day of March, 1837.

By an act of the general assembly of the state of Ohio, the county commissioners of each county were made fund commissioners of this surplus revenue for their respective counties. On the 2d day of May, 1837, these commissioners distributed the sum of $15,877.62.5, being the remainder of the amount coming to this county, to one hundred and fifty-eight persons, in sums of $100.00 each, secured by bond and mortgage on unencumbered real estate.

This was a great relief to Seneca county, as well as to Ohio generally. Mr. Read, the editor of the *Tiffin Gazette*, in concluding an editorial on this subject, May 13, 1837, said:

The amount thus loaned we hope may relieve, to some extent, the pressure felt in our community, and enable many to meet their little responsibilities under which they have been laboring. The loan has had a salutary influence in establishing confidence in our institutions and relieving the pressure, which, though perhaps not as bad as it might be, is sufficiently disastrous.

This testimony is here added to show the great want of money spoken of heretofore, when writing on the Ohio canals.

The general government is not troubled with a surplus of revenues in her treasury now. The interest on the national debt runs high up into the millions. Generations unborn will come and pass away, and this humble little book will be lost and forgotten, before the treasurer of the United States shall again be put to the inconvenience of distributing, among the states, moneys that have accumulated, and for which the general government has no use.

POLITICS.

A historian has no right to be partial, either in religion or in politics. When he has stated facts and events truthfully and honestly, as they occurred, he is done, and should leave others to form conclusions for themselves. Conscious of this rule, men and parties are spoken of, and the histories of churches given without favoritism or prejudice. Tolerant in all things, it is a very easy matter for a man to concede to another his right to judge for himself what is best for him in both politics and religion. Men often differ, and very honestly too, on almost every subject.

Few and scattered as the settlers were in Seneca county in the fall of 1828, and removed far away from the real theatre of action, one would scarcely have supposed that then and here, under the then surroundings, party spirit would run up to fever-heat; but it did. It took a newspaper two and three weeks to reach Tiffin from the Atlantic coast. But when they came and developed new steps taken by the parties, they were discussed, and sides taken by our people, with as much vehemence as anywhere, and the Adams men, the Clay men, the Jackson men and the Crawford men, in 1828, were no more decided in their respective choice of candidates and their attachment to party, in New York or Baltimore, than they were in Seneca county. Jackson was elected president, and the fight on the United States bank culminated in the removal of deposits, the vetoes of the re-charters, which agitated the whole country. Party spirit ran high in 1832, when Jackson was the Democratic candidate for re-election. Clay was the candidate and the embodiment of the Whig party. Clay and Jackson were both Masons. Great prejudices were entertained against both, and the Morgan affair was in everybody's mouth. The Masons were very much abused, and a new party was called into existence, called "anti-Mason," under the leadership of William Wirt, of Maryland, who was the candidate for president, and Amos Ellmaker, of Pennsylvania, for vice-president. The ides of November came on and Jackson was re-elected. Now the Democrats had to have a jubilee, and the first political jollification in Seneca county came off at the house of Colonel John Goodin, in Tiffin, on Thursday, the 6th day of December, 1832. Hon. David E. Owen was appointed president, and Andrew Lugenbeel vice-president.

In writing up the proceedings of this meeting, Mr. E. Brown, the editor of the *Patriot*, the pioneer newspaper of the county, and whose columns were open to the three parties alike (for he published "Clay politics," "Jackson politics," and "Wirt politics,") said:

Although many of our friends were unavoidably absent, viewing the lands in the "Seneca Reservation," previous to the sale of them, which commences on Monday next, yet the concourse was unusually large.

Thirteen regular toasts (one for each of the original states,) were offered, besides a number of volunteer toasts—some witty, some less so. Amongst those who participated were Henry Cronise, George Flack, Nathan L. Wright, Joseph Graff, Colonel R. Jaqua, Uriah P. Coonrad, Gabriel J. Keen, E. Brown, Jacob Kroh, Colonel John Goodin, A. Eaton, Samuel S. Martin, J. H. Brown, E. Locke, Frederick Kishler, P. J. Price, William Anderson, John Campbell, William H. Kessler, Joshua Seney, Andrew Mainz.

The *Seneca Patriot* will be noticed in the chapter on the "Press."

The following will show how Seneca county voted for fourteen years of its early history:

In 1828—Adams, (Whig,) received one hundred and eleven majority.
In 1830—Lucas, (Democrat,) received three majority.
In 1832—Clay, (Whig,) received twenty-nine majority.
In 1834—Lucas, (Democrat,) received five majority.
In 1836—Van Buren, (Democrat,) received one hundred and eighty-one majority.
In 1838—Shannon, (Democrat,) received one hundred and thirteen majority.
In 1840—Shannon, (Democrat,) received one hundred and sixty-one majority.

In 1842—Shannon, (Democrat,) received five hundred and sixty-three majority.

As a general thing the county remained Democratic ever since, with the success of an occasional opposition candidate, except in 1854 and 1855, when the Know.Nothings swept the county in a storm, electing their candidates by majorities over 1,400.

The following table shows the vote of Ohio, from the years of 1828 to 1842, both inclusive:

1828—Jackson,	67,597	Adams,	63,396	Maj. for Jackson,	4,201
1830—Lucas,	49,186	McArthur,	49,668	" " McArthur,	482
1832—Jackson,	81,246	Clay,	77,539	" " Jackson,	4,707
1834—Lucas,	70,738	Findley,	67,414	" " Lucas,	3,324
1836—Van Buren,	96,948	Harrison,	105,405	" " Harrison,	8,457
1838—Shannon,	107,884	Vance,	102,156	" " Shannon,	5,738
1840—Shannon,	129,312	Corwin,	145,442	" " Corwin,	16,130
1842—Shannon,	129,064	Corwin,	125,621	" " Shannon,	3,443

TIFFIN AND FORT BALL.

There is very little about Tiffin that attracted the attention of people and answered as an inducement for new-comers to settle down here. There was nothing inviting to the immigrant. Mr. Hedges offered his lots very cheap, indeed; caused the county seat to be located here, secured the removal of the land offices here, invested money to improve the town, built houses and mills and bridges, assisted in securing the post-office on this side, and all that, but the thing dragged and exhibited very little vitality for a long time. Simeon B. Howard bought in-lots, numbers 19, 20 and 21, for $60 on credit. Lots could be bought on almost any terms.

After the few first cabins were put up in the woods, and a few trees cut away to let the sun shine down upon them, the principal streets were opened, and thus the little settlement lingered along for many years, struggling against numerous adversities. The locality was sickly. Mechanics found no employment. The few settlers already here had no money to build with. Those that brought money with them preferred to invest in land, and there was no chance for speculation with a view of immediate profit. Fort Ball seemed to have the best of it for a great while. The *elite* and the rich gathered there and looked down upon a Tiffinite in contempt. They had the best store over there and the post-office, and McNeil's corner was the hub of civilization.

It seemed as if they would never forgive Mr. Hedges and those that acted with him, for the location of the county seat on this side. They called the commissioners, that located the county seat, very hard names; charged them with having been bribed, and predicted that all sorts of evils would follow. Even the purchase of Fort Ball by Mr. Hedges, failed, for a time, to allay this bitter feeling. It grew into fever-heat when the post-office was removed from Fort Ball to Tiffin, and Jacob Plane was appointed postmaster on this side, in the spring of 1829, under Jackson. Even Mr. Hoagland, the ferryman, became so incensed against Mr. Hedges that at every session of the court he would come into the court house on the second or third day of the term, take off his big stove-pipe hat at the door, walk up to the judges' desk with measured step, in his long brown overcoat reaching down to his shoes, holding in his hand a large role of manuscript, which he would lay before one of the judges, turn round and walk out again with an air of triumph, snapping one eye at the bystanders. In this manuscript he complained of Mr. Hedges for refusing to let Hoagland take stones out of the river, and many other things.

But the little town, thus languishing, did live (as the lawyers say); slowly and gradually increasing in numbers, until about the year 1833 it numbered probably 400 souls. For fourteen years, from the time of its platting, it was under the government of Clinton township, having no government of its own until the 7th day of March, 1835, the legislature of Ohio passed an act incorporating the town of Tiffin. The act contained twenty-one long sections. It provided, amongst other things, for the limit of taxation; for the use by the town of the county jail; for the election and appointment of officers; for building of sidewalks and improving the streets; for providing fire apparatus; for punishing the sale of intoxicating liquors, etc. The town embraced the first plat and first southern addition.

There was no election held under the law in April, 1835, nor in April, 1836. Nobody seemed to care for a town government, but in June. 1836, the following notice was published in the *Tiffin Gazette*, viz:

CORPORATION ELECTION.

Notice is hereby given that an election will be held at the house of Eli Norris, on Wednesday. the 29th inst., for the purpose of electing officers in conformity to the provisions of the act incorporating the town of Tiffin.

GEORGE W. GIST.
NICHOLAS GEOTHIUS.
M. M. MASON.
CHARLES LEWIS.
JOHN BAUGHER.
June 18. 1836.

GEORGE PARK.
M. D. CADWALLADER.
JOEL STONE.
J. W. MILLER.
DAVID BECK.

At this election Dr. H. Kuhn was elected the first mayor of the town.

TIFFIN AND FORT BALL.

The population of Tiffin proper, in 1840, was 728; 1850, 2,718; 1860, 3,992; 1870, 5,648, and in 1880, 7,882.

Tiffin outstripped Fort Ball in population and improvements. Business clustered around the public square and along Washington street, where it is yet holding sway with a most wonderful tenacity. Tiffin is unlike many other towns in the west in this respect, where business extends into various streets; but here it must be confined in a square or two and stick there.

No reason can be given for this singular freak, because there is no reason nor sense in it.

Fort Ball had no organization as a municipal corporation until the legislature, on the 13th day of March, 1849, passed an act authorizing an election for town officers to be held, fixing the boundary, giving corporate powers to the new town, etc.

Jacob Flaugher was elected the first mayor, James P. Pillars recorder, and J. H. Kisinger was appointed the first marshal. It was a short-lived affair, and no other election was ever held under the charter, for the organization of Tiffin, as a city of the second class, embraced both towns and allayed the old rival jealousy that had annoyed both sides so many years, and both had a right to say with Shakespeare:

> "Now shall the winter of
> our discontent
> Become glorious summer, etc."

The act, incorporating the city of Tiffin as a city of the second class, was passed March 23d, 1850. It took effect from and after its passage.

The first section provides for the boundary line of the new city, embracing both towns—Tiffin and Fort Ball—and additional territory. In the description of this boundary line is that "big sycamore tree" (mentioned before) and the little brook—both now passed away.

Section two provides for the election of not less than three nor more than five councilmen, from each ward, who, together with the mayor, constituted the "city council."

Section three provides for the division of the city into two wards; all east of the river to be the first ward, and all west to be the second ward.

Section four fixes the term of the officers to be one year, etc.

Section twenty-four provides for an election to be held in the month of April, 1850, and the place of voting to be designated by the mayors and council of Fort Ball and Tiffin jointly, and the returns to be delivered to the mayor of Tiffin.

Section twenty-five repeals the acts of incorporation of Tiffin and Fort Ball.

The act contains twenty-six sections; was prepared by the writer at the request of the councils of both towns, and was passed by the legislature without any change.

The first election was held on the 20th of April, 1850, and the following named persons were elected, viz:

Mayor—William Lang.

Treasurer—Robert Crum.

Marshal—Samuel H. Kisinger.

Councilmen, First Ward—William H. Gibson, William H. Keilhotz, Andrew Denzer.

Councilmen, Second Ward—Jacob Flaugher, W. M. Johnson, George C. Small.

J. W. Patterson, the last mayor of the town of Tiffin, certified the election returns.

On the 16th day of January, 1871, the city council, by ordinance, divided the city into five wards, as now. They are as follows:

First ward is all north of Market street, to the river; extending from Market street east to Circular; thence south to Rebecca; thence east along Rebecca to an alley lying east of lot 647; thence south along said alley to Main; thence east to the corporation line.

Second ward—All north of Miami to corporation line, on the left bank of the river.

Third ward—All south of Miami to corporation line, on the left bank of the river.

Fourth ward—All south of Market and west of Washington, and west of Melmore streets to the corporation line.

Fifth ward—All east of Washington and Melmore, and south of Market and the south and west line of the first ward.

The valuation of the taxable property in the city proper for 1879 was $2,403,593. The city tax for the same year was $83,087.83. For a number of years past the annual tax of the city has averaged three per cent. on the dollar valuation.

The following is a list of the

OFFICERS OF THE CITY

at this time (1880):

Mayor—Harrison Noble.

President of Council—Dr. J. F. E. Fanning.

Vice-President of Council—Dr. J. P. Kinnaman.

Clerk—C. J. M. Sullivan.

Harrison Noble

The treasurer of Seneca county is the treasurer of the city *ex officio*.
City Solicitor—Perry M. Adams.
Marshal—James F. George.
Street Commissioner—Scudder Chamberlain.

COUNCILMEN.

First ward—James Love, J. P. Kinnaman.
Second ward—John Marsony, Josiah P. Baker.
Third ward—J. F. E. Fanning, Charles Sting.
Fourth ward—John B. Ehrenfried, Ronaldo A. Gray.
Fifth ward—Peter Grammes, Benjamin Shinners.

HARRISON NOBLE.

The subject of this sketch was born in Salt Creek township, Wayne county, Ohio, where his father's family lived on a farm, on the 28th day of January, 1826. When the family moved to Seneca county he was about ten years old. He attended the first school at a log school house that his father and the neighbors put up on the northeast corner of section 19, in Jackson township. It was a school house of the kind they had in those days; a clap-board roof, pungeon floor, pungeon seats and pungeon desks. Bass-wood logs were split and hewed as smooth as possible, holes bored into the logs in the sides of the house, sticks driven tightly into the holes and the hewed pungeon, laid on the sticks, made a writing desk. Holes bored into another piece of pungeon and legs, about eighteen inches long, driven into them, made benches. An older brother of Harrison, Washington Noble, the oldest son of the family, taught the first school here. He had forty scholars the first winter. The house was warmed from a large fire-place put into one end of the school house that took a four foot back log. The end of the cabin was cut out and a sort of pen built on the outside. On the inside of this pen, having three sides, stones and clay were put up some five feet high for the back and sides of the fire-place. Upon this bank the chimney was raised with sticks and clay mortar. The wet clay was mixed with straw to keep it in its place and hold it together. Some of the children had to come three miles to school through the woods by paths and trails. It was a great hardship for some of the smaller ones when the snow was deep and the underbrush full of icicles. Water under the snow was often knee-deep. This may well be called getting an education under difficulties. Children attending the beautiful school houses in Seneca county now, can scarcely appreciate the condition of the first schools here. The large airy rooms in your high schools now-a-days, heated by hot-air furnaces, and supplied with beautiful and convenient patent desks, were not to be thought of then.

When Harrison grew up to be large enough to work, he helped his father clear land, and in a few years seventy acres were cleared on the homestead farm. The boys had their sports also in those days. It was not always hard work and no play.

He was a very good coon hunter, and kept a couple of blooded coon dogs with which he would scour the country around for coon; the Crossley boys, the young Bostons, and Hollopeters, often joining him. One night Harrison got out his Indian pony, took his dogs with him and went to Mud creek, where he caught seven coons. Boys often got their " spending money " in that way.

The wolves were still very troublesome then, and people that kept sheep or pigs had to stable them for protection.

The squirrels, chip-monks and crows were so numerous and troublesome that the people were compelled to make war upon them. Harrison often collected a lot of boys with guns and ammunition for a squirrel hunt. They appointed two captains, who picked their men one at a time, " turn about;" then they started in all directions. They were to meet at a certain place, and the party that had the least number of squirrel-tails, lost the price, which was two bushels of corn which the losing party had to furnish. The plumes of the left wings of crows, hawks or buzzards were also counted for so many squirrel-tails.

The boys also organized debating societies and spelling schools, which were held often at private houses, and which were a source of pleasure and mutual improvement.

The winters of 1844-5 young Noble spent at the college in Oberlin, and in 1846 he attended the Seneca county academy in Republic. In the winter of 1846-7 he taught a school in Tiffin, occupying one of the upper rooms in the two-story brick school house, still standing, on the north side of Market street, near the corner of Monroe and Market. Mrs. Gibbs, a Mr. Collins, and the writer were all the other teachers then employed in Tiffin. Collins was a tall, slender man, had a wife and child, was a preacher, and made terrible war on the Masons and Odd Fellows. He was going to break down their lodges and build the church of God upon their ruins. He returned to Wooster, where he formerly lived, and did not behave very well after his return. He left no ruins but his own.

In the following year Noble entered the office of his brother, Warren P., to read law. During his studies he taught a school in Liberty township four months, and boarded at the house of Mr. Eden Lease, who was then sheriff of Seneca county. Mr. Lease very often had more writs to serve than he could well attend to alone, and employed Mr. Noble to assist him. By these services and taking his wages as school teacher, he succeeded in paying his boarding until 1849, when he was admitted to practice law. He then immediately became a partner of his brother, Warren P., in the practice, under the firm name of W. P. and H. Noble.

This firm continued in business until the 1st of May, 1874, when Harrison Noble formed a new firm with Mr. Nelson B. Lutes, in the practice of law. This association continued until the 1st of May, 1880, six years, when it was dissolved by mutual consent.

In 1853 Mr. Noble was elected city solicitor of Tiffin, and served two terms, receiving $50 per year as his salary. In 1859 he was elected a member of the city council, and served twelve years, his term expiring about the time of the great fire, April 13th, 1872.

In 1863, while the militia of Ohio was being re-organized and regiments formed, Seneca county had two regiments. Mr. Noble was elected colonel of the Second Regiment.

In 1864, Mr. George S. Christlip was nominated by the Democratic county convention as their candidate for director of the Seneca county infirmary, and a few days before the election, his health failing him very rapidly, Mr. Christlip informed the Democratic central committee that he would not live to serve, and declined to have his name put upon the ticket. The committee, without the knowledge of Mr. Noble, had his name printed upon the tickets, in place of Mr. Christlip's. He was thereupon elected to that office, and served until 1870. It was customary with the directors of the infirmary to keep their own treasury, receive and pay out money, keeping their own accounts. Upon the urgent request of Mr. Noble, it was made a rule of the board to pay all the moneys received by the board into the treasury of the county, to be drawn out upon the order of the county auditor, after having been passed upon by the board. The rule is in vogue still, and works very well.

Mr. Noble is the present mayor of Tiffin, to which office he was elected in 1879. On the 3d day of June, 1858, he was married to Mrs. Minerva, the sixth daughter of Josiah Hedges, and two sons are all the children of this union. Harry H., the oldest, is now a student at Notre Dame University, at South Bend, Indiana, and Birdie M. is attending the union schools of Tiffin. Mr. Noble has an extensive practice, and takes a lively interest in the growth, the progress and the development of the material resources of the city and county.

Soon after their marriage the young couple commenced housekeeping in their pleasant home on the corner of Jefferson and Market, where they still reside.

PLANK ROADS.

In this year (1849), on the 22d day of March, the general assembly of Ohio also passed an act incorporating the Lower Sandusky, Tiffin and Fort Ball plank road company. Ralph P. Buckland, John R. Peas, John L. Green, James Justice, and John Bell, of Sandusky county; Lorenzo Abbott, Calvin Clark, Benjamin Tomb, Cyrus Pool, Vincent Bell, John W. Patterson, Warren P. Noble, and Rezin W. Shawhan, of Seneca county; Chester R. Mott, Joseph McCutchen, Robert McKelley, and Andrew McElvain, of Wyandot county, and all others associated with them, by subscribing stock, were made a body corporate and politic.

Another company, called the Tiffin and Osceola plank road company, was also chartered, and both roads put in operation A branch road from Fostoria to intersect the former, north of the mouth of Wolf creek, was also laid. Toll-gates were erected and tolls collected. These answered the purpose for awhile, and were very popular until they began to give way by the rotting of the plank. The tolls collected proved insufficient to keep up the necessary repairs and other expenses. Subscribers were assessed to pay a second time, a work that always has a tendency to injure the popularity of any joint stock company. Meanwhile the roads became worthless and were abandoned; toll-gates broke down, and the supervisors of common highways removed the plank by putting them on piles and burning them up. The stockholders lost every dollar they invested; never realized anything, and thus ended another wild, impracticable, foolish experiment.

For many years past, some of our citizens agitated the propriety of building pikes in Seneca county. The great inexhaustible quantity of stone in the county suitable for that purpose, the bad condition of the roads every winter and spring, together with the landed wealth and general enterprise of our citizens, seemed to warrant such a measure as wise and necessary. During the past winter (1879–80), meetings were held in several townships, and in Tiffin, in which the subject was discussed, and finally the county commissioners were prevailed upon to publish a notice in the Tiffin papers, calling upon the voters at the election on the first Monday in April, 1880, to vote on the subject, yes or no. If a majority of the votes cast had been in favor of pikes, the commissioners would have commenced the work under the law. The subject is still very fresh in the minds of all, and no attempt will be made to give the various reasons assigned by those opposed, why the measure should be defeated, and so large a portion of our people voted against pikes. Suffice it to say, that when the votes were counted, it was found that only 1,578 voted for pikes, while 5,156 votes were cast against the proposition. It is to be regretted, that an improvement so highly needed in our county, should find so few friends. Tiffin alone gave a majority in favor, some 500. All other election precincts in the county gave large majorities against the measure. In Big Spring, a township that needs good roads as badly as any other locality in the county, in a vote of 521, there was only one vote in favor of pikes.

The far or the near future must solve this question. The present generation prefers to stick in the mud.

THE TELEGRAPH.

About 1849, the first line of telegraph was constructed through Tiffin, along the Mad River and Lake Erie (now C. S. & C.) Railroad. A joke in connection with this enterprise is almost too good to be lost. Mr. Christopher Snyder, the merchant, was a good deal of a wag, and whenever he had a chance to get a "rig" on anyone, would spare neither friend nor foe.

Mr. Balthasar Ries was a German barber, and lived on East Market street. For many years he was in the habit of calling upon his customers at their houses, stores or shops, to shave them or cut their hair. He had a frame with two hooks to hang over the back of a chair, with a perpendicular piece that slid up and down and having a cushion on top to lay the head upon. He would carry this frame with him on his left arm, on which were also suspended a few clean towels. He was also supplied with a large tin cup, full of hot water, some soap, a brush, a few razors and a pair of scissors. Thus fitted out, he started on his beat—a traveling barber shop.

Mr. Ries was a small man, very active and nervous, with black hair and black eyes, pale face, polite and cleanly in his habits, but very credulous. Anything Mr. Snyder said was as good as gospel to him. One time, while he had Snyder down in a chair in his store, with lather all over his face, Reis wanted Snyder to tell him what those high poles along the railroad on the other side of the river were for. He said he had seen men climb up on them and fasten a wire from one to another, etc. Snyder was in a hurry to get done, and was not inclined to talk much; but Reis insisted on knowing all about it, and kept on quizzing and asking questions. Finally Snyder told Reis that that was a new way to go to California. (The gold fever was then at high tide). This remark made bad worse with Mr. Ries, and he was bound to have a full description of the thing. Finally Snyder told him that travel by steamer around Cape Horn was very expensive and dangerous, and to avoid both, this plan had been adopted; that when the work was completed clear to San Francisco an iron saddle would be placed across the wires to hold the traveler and his baggage, and when all was ready the thing would be touched off behind him, and that would send him across the country to San Francisco, where he would be received on a pile of straw, and from whence he could go to the mines when he was ready.

All this seemed very reasonable to Ries, but he said we lived in a most wonderful age, when improvements were made in all departments of life; and finishing dressing Snyder's hair, he went away. He was gone about an hour, when he returned very much excited, and setting his tin cup on the counter with such violence that the water flew in all directions, and shaking his fist at Snyder, threatened that he would never again believe anything he said: that people down street had laughed at him when he told them of the new way of going to California, etc. Snyder said that Joe Rauker had told him the same story, and he did not know any better himself, etc.; but Ries went away in a very nervous, angry mood.

Among the early pioneers in Fort Ball was also Andrew Love, who lived on the bluff on the McCutchenville road, where the river comes up close to the road.

Another pioneer, on the Tiffin side, was Alexander Mason. He built and opened the "Eagle Hotel," on the corner of Washington and Perry streets. It was a two story brick building, and received a third story when Mr. R. W. Shawhan became the owner, who fitted up and enlarged the hotel, when it was christened the "Shawhan House," J. W. Patterson, proprietor. Mason kept there in 1834 and 1835; Patterson opened the Shawhan House in 1850. The hotel has retained its name ever since, under several proprietors, among whom P. P. Myers, who really built up the reputation of the house and kept it the longest, was the most popular.

THE TIFFIN SCHOOLS.

There were but few children among the early settlers in Tiffin, and yet to secure a site and build a school house was one of the first public cares and enlisted the support of everybody. Application was made to Mr. Hedges for a lot to build a school house upon, and on the first day of February, 1828, Mr. Hedges executed a deed to George Donaldson, Jacob Plane, and Richard Sneath, school directors of school district number four, Clinton township, for in-lot numbered forty-two (42). It is situate on the north side of Market street, next west of the northwest corner of Market and Monroe. The deed has a whereas to it and commences in these words: "Whereas, heretofore Josiah Hedges has laid out and established a town by the name of the town of Tiffin, situate upon fractional section 19, T. 2 R. 15, and whereas a patent has been issued to said Hedges, etc. Now, therefore," etc.

A little one-story brick school house was built by these directors upon this lot close by the pavement, lengthwise with the street. It had room for about 60 scholars. The door was near its south east corner. There was one window at the east end, back of the teacher's desk, and two windows in each of the other sides. Here the various denominations held their meetings until they had churches of their own. The Protestant Methodists especially occupied the school house very often on Sunday and held their quarterly meetings there when the little school house was crowded to overflowing.

After the school house was finished and a new set of directors had been elected a notice was published in the *Seneca Patriot* for a teacher in the following form:

A TEACHER WANTED.

A gentleman who is well versed in arithmetic, English grammar and geography, and can give satisfactory reference for good moral conduct and steady habits, is wanted to teach the district school in Tiffin. It is desirable that application should be made before the first of November next, as the school will be vacant.   HENRY CRONISE,   } School Directors.
                                MILTON JENNINGS, }

September 28, 1832.

Under this notice Mr. Benjamin Crockett made application and was employed, and he continued to teach here for several years thereafter. The writer made his acquaintance in the winter following the fall of 1833. By my contract to learn the trade of a cabinet maker with Boss Phillips, I was entitled to four months' night school at the boss' expense. Apprentices were compelled to work every night at the bench until 9 o'clock, except on Saturday night, so that the loss of time and the payment of the teacher were to be taken in consideration. For want of a teacher of a night school, I traded my four months' night school for 30 days' day school in the fore part of the summer of 1834 and to go to Mr. Crockett. His school this summer was attended by a few flaxen-headed children and the writer was one of a few larger boys that attended. All the time Mr. Crockett and the writer could spend together was equally divided between us. While Mr. C. would take much pains to instruct me in English grammar and pronouncing words correctly in reading the history of the United States, he took the other half of my time to receive instructions in mathematics and in the geography of Europe. Thus my thirty days passed away and I became a graduate of Mr. Crockett's first school in Tiffin. This constituted the sum total of my schooling in America, and it was not long after, that the school examiners of Tiffin, Joshua Seney, Oliver Cowdry and Frederick Singer, gave me a certificate of qualification to teach school, when I became one of the first teachers in the two-story brick, still standing on the same lot, now occupied for a shop.

The little old, one-story school house was torn away in about 1844 and the two-story brick put up a little further from the street, with four rooms.

Here all the schools in Tiffin were accommodated until the young city organized under the union school system and preparations were made to build the beautiful school house on South Monroe street, now known as the high school building.

Simultaneously with the organization of the city of Tiffin, the question of inaugurating the union school system under the law, agitated the minds of some of our people also. Opinions as to its propriety differed very widely. The proud position that Ohio occupies in her educational department, when she taxes her wealth to educate her youth—in other words—when she makes the owners of property pay taxes to educate the children of those who do not pay taxes for want of property—was not appreciated by all our citizens. The friends of the measure were the taxpayers, the wealthy men of the city, one of the most active of whom was Mr. R. W. Shawan, who had no child to educate and paid the largest amount of taxes of any man in the county. To his honor be it said—the success of the measure depended largely on the part he took in its favor. Remarkable as it may seem, the enemies of the proposition were the poorer classes, who generally have the most children to educate. Nineteen of these, who worked hard, electioneering for votes against the measure all day, were the heads of families averaging five children to each, and whose taxes on the duplicate added together for all purposes did not reach the sum of thirty dollars.

The vote was taken in September, 1850, and a handsome majority secured in its favor. In October following, at the election for members of the school board, the following were elected, viz.:

William Lang, William D. Searles, George Knupp, A. C. Baldwin, W. H. Keilholts, W. H. Gibson.

THE SCHOOLS OF TIFFIN.

At the first meeting of the board, held on the first day of November, 1850, William Lang was elected president, W. H. Gibson, secretary, and A. C. Baldwin treasurer. The board then also appointed Messrs. J. H. Pittenger, R. G. Pennington and R. R. Bement as a board of examiners. Thus the new system was set on foot, and thousands of children have enjoyed the benefit of these union schools during these thirty years last past.

The following is a list of the first corps of teachers employed by the board, viz.:

Miss E. Augspurger—German school—she furnishing her own room, $20 per month; Mrs. Sarah Sands, also furnishing her own room, $20 per month; Miss Elizabeth Cronise and Miss C. Coffin, each $15 per month; William Fitzgeralds, $24 per month; Samuel Nolan, $22 per month; Miss Maria Andrew, $15 per month; Thomas J. Cronise, $24 per month.

The small amount of the school fund was equally divided among the three terms, and for want of sufficient means to pay the teachers, a tax of from one cent to one and one-half cents a day (according to class) was assessed on each scholar in attendance for that term. This mode of taxation lasted only one year and was dropped.

Rev. R. R. Bement was employed to superintend the schools during this winter only, for which the board paid him $12, on the 1st of May, 1851. On the same day the board offered Mr. S. S. Rickley, of Columbus, $400 salary as superintendent of the union schools, with the privilege of allowing him time also to teach a class in Heidelberg College. The offer was accepted, and Mr. Rickley was the first superintendent of the Tiffin union schools.

In 1852 the board purchased in-lots numbers 279 and 280, in the (then) second ward, where they erected the first union school house in the city, the same year, at an expense (including $900 paid for the lots) of $6,000. This is the school house immediately west of St. Mary's church.

In 1854 the board bought of Mr. Hedges the large lot upon which the present high school building now stands, and on the 28th of March, 1855, they resolved that when they should build a school house there, it should be put away from the street 125 feet.

On the 11th of April, 1855, a meeting of the voters in the city was held, in compliance with notice, and a resolution was unanimously adopted to build another school house in the city, and the board were authorized to levy a tax of two mills on the dollar of all the taxable property in the city for the year 1855, and three mills for 1856, 1857, 1858, and 1859, for that purpose.

On the 22d day of November, 1855, at a public meeting, the board was authorized to borrow a sum of money not to exceed the sum of $6,000, to be used in the building of the new school house, and interest not to exceed ten per cent.

On the 10th of June, 1856, the board passed a resolution to lay the corner-stone of the new school house with appropriate ceremonies, and to invite the Rev. L. Andrew to deliver the address.

On the 20th of January, 1857, another public meeting, held at the mayor's office, resolved to instruct the school board to proceed and finish the new school building, and to levy additional taxes on all the taxable property in Tiffin, for that purpose, as follows:

For the year 1857, one and one-half mills additional; for the year 1858, one and one-half mills additional; for the year 1859, one and one-half mills additional; for the year 1860, three and seven-tenths mills on the dollar; for the year 1861, three and seven-tenths mills on the dollar; for the year 1862, three and six-tenths mills on the dollar; for the year 1863, three and seven-tenths mills on the dollar, and to borrow another sum of money for that purpose, not exceeding $8,000; to issue bonds, etc.

In 1859 the third story was finished inside, and the first high school organized that fall.

The building, with the site, cost at least $45,000.

By a special vote of the citizens, January 30, 1871, the board was authorized to build two additional school houses; one in the first ward (college hill), and one in the second ward (as now). On the 17th of February, 1871, the board contracted for both of these structures, and had them put up at an expense of $7,500 each, sites included.

In 1878 the board built the large school house in the (now) third ward, in Fishbaugh's addition, at a cost, including site, of $5,800, making a total of about $72,000 invested in school houses and lots.

There are at this time about 2,700 youths in Tiffin entitled to public instruction. The school fund for the year 1879 was $19,315.34.

The board employs one superintendent and twenty-nine teachers, of whom the following is a list, including their respective salaries:

J. W. Knott, sup't	$1,200	Hallie Leavitt	$375
B. F. Myers, principal 2d dis.	800	Celesta Stoner	350
Susie R. Platt, prin. high school	700	Amelia Sauer	350
Lissette Herbig, prin. Ger. "	600	Venie Metz	350
Mrs. Mary Zartman	475	Lenora Mitchell	375
Mattie McLain	475	Jessie Poorman	350
Samuel McKitrick	450	Emma Merkelbach	300
Celia Williams	400	Laura Freyman	300

Minnie Holt	$400	Mary Hartman	$300
Kate Sughro	375	Warren E. Brinkerhoof	300
Frankie Van Pelt	375	Romanus R. Bour	300
Cora Pew	375	Martha Gwynn	250
Victoria Sawyer	375	Belle Byrne	250
Rosa Myers	375	Flora Barnes	250
Flora Poorman	375		

There are three German schools.

The following named gentlemen constitute the present board of education of Tiffin, viz:

President—Dr. E. B. Hubbard.
Secretary—Henry Brohl.
Treasurer—Warren P. Noble.
Prof. C. O. Knepper, Jacob F. Bunn, William Lang.

DR. E. B. HUBBARD

Was born December 28, 1840, at Chester, Hamden county, Massachusetts, where his father was a prominent business man. He graduated at Hinsdale academy, Massachusetts, and prepared to enter Williams college, but his father failing in heavy western land speculations, prevented it. In 1857 he came west with his brother, Dwight, and stopped at Bellevue, Ohio, where both engaged in teaching, Dwight being appointed superintendent of the schools there. Dr. Hubbard remained here three years, and is mentioned in the history of Huron and Erie counties as having been a very successful teacher. In 1860 he was called east to become supervisor of the state primary schools at Monson, Massachusetts, where he remained two years and pursued his medical studies in the large hospital connected with that institution; being, however, more interested in the preparation of drugs and medicines than in the medical practice, he chose that branch of the profession. On severing his connection with this, one of Massachusetts' noblest state institutions, he entered the pharmacy of Dr. Hutchins, in Springfield, Massachusetts, and applied himself to the thorough mastery of every detail of the drug business. He began business life as a junior partner in the drug store of Barrows and Hubbard, at Amherst, Massachusetts. His partner was a physician widely known, a disciple of the old school, devoting his time to his extensive practice, leaving Dr. Hubbard in the entire control of the store. With an intention of locating in Chicago, he sold out his business at Amherst, and came as far west as Bellevue, Ohio, where he stopped to visit old friends, and was persuaded to buy an interest in a drug store there. The firm was known by the name of Goodson and Hubbard. In January, 1874, he came to Tiffin and entered into partnership with Dr. H. K. Hershiser, in the well known corner drug store on Market and Washington. At the close of the first year he bought his partner's interest, and has remained in successful business there ever since. Ever since his location here Dr. Hubbard has taken a very lively interest in every measure calculated to promote the growth and welfare of Tiffin, his adopted city, especially in her educational interests. He has been twice elected a member of the school board; first in 1877, and again in 1880, and has been president of the board since 1878. He was married to Miss Helen M., daughter of Judge Sawyer, of Nashua, New Hampshire, on the 27th day of August, 1873, and Clara S. and Sheldon B. Hubbard help to make the household lively.

C. O. KNEPPER

was born in Somerset county, Pennsylvania, on the 20th of October, 1836, the oldest son of Jonathan and Margaret Knepper. He graduated from Heidelberg college in the class of 1862, and from the seminary in Mercersburg, Pennsylvania, in 1864. He was superintendent of the schools of Waterloo, Iowa, and of Waverly, in the same state. On the 24th day of June, 1868, he was married to S. Grace Dunnell, daughter of David Dunnell, of Massachusetts, the bride then living in Waterloo. This union was blessed with three children, one son and two daughters. In 1871 he was elected professor of the Alumni of Heidelberg and took charge of his position in 1872. In the spring of 1879 he was elected a member of the school board of Tiffin.

HENRY BROHL

was born in the city of Bonn, on the Rhine, on the 10th day of November, 1831. He attended the academy and university at Bonn, and before he had time to graduate he left his native city and country; he came to America and settled in Sandusky City in the spring of 1851. Mr. Brohl had also applied himself to the mercantile business while he lived in his native city, and when he removed from Sandusky City to Tiffin in 1855 he entered into copartnership with E. T. Abbott in the business of wholesale grocers. He continued in this firm until in 1857 he entered into partnership with Robert Crum in Tiffin in the sale of groceries and liquors. The business was conducted by this firm until 1865, when Mr. Brohl opened a saloon, which he has conducted successfully ever since. In 1856 Mr. Brohl was married to Miss Catharine Krautz, of Sandusky City. This union was blessed with seven children, who are all living. He was elected to the school board in 1877.

The reader who desires to see short biographical sketches of the other present living members of the school board of Tiffin, will find them in chapter 23, under the heads of Warren P. Noble, Jacob Bunn, and William Lang.

CHAPTER XXI.

THE BANKS OF TIFFIN—INSURANCE COMPANIES—SECRET AND BENEVOLENT SOCIETIES.

IN the spring of 1847 the question of establishing a bank in Tiffin was agitated by some of the monied men in the place, and it became apparent very soon that rival interests were growing into conflicting proportions. One wing followed the leadership of R. W. Shawhan, and the other, that of Rufus W. Reid, the leading rival merchants of Tiffin at that time. To the outside world it seemed at times that one party would succeed, and then the other, but finally Mr. Reid, who never was very scrupulous in any thing, succeeded in securing a charter.

On the 12th day of July, 1847, Benjamin Tomb, William H. Gibson, Samuel Waggoner, R. G. Pennington, Alfred Johnson, R. W. Reid, Daniel Smith, William Fleet, William M. Buel, and Daniel Brown, made the proper application for the organization of an independent bank. "Pending the granting of the application, they became convinced that the amount already subscribed was insufficient," (says Stewart, but they really became alarmed at the rival element showing greater force,) so they, in conjunction with others, enlarged the capital stock to one hundred thousand dollars. On the 2d of August, of the same year, they filed their amended application, which was speedily acted upon by the board of commissioners, and a charter for an independent bank, to be located in Tiffin, with a capital stock of $100,000, was granted them on the 9th of the same month.

Perhaps it would have been better for all parties concerned, as well as the community at large, if the other faction had succeeded. Who can tell?

The bank was organized by the election of Benjamin Tomb president, and Waggoner, Buel, Reid and Pennington, directors. Mr. Tomb resigned his position as president in 1848, and Abel Rawson was appointed in his place. Mr. Pennington was appointed cashier *pro tem.*, and afterwards William E. Chittenden, the regular cashier. They commenced business on the 13th of November, 1847. It was called the "Seneca County Bank." It flourished for a season, but the young craft carried too much Reid on board, and ran ashore. After the bank had suspended awhile, Charles L. Johnson, who was before that time a popular young merchant in Tiffin, bought the charter of the collapsed institution, kindled up its dying embers for a short season, and started afresh, in 1851. The old creditors crowded their claims without rest or mercy, and somebody obtained a judgment on cognovit in the court of common pleas of Franklin county, in Columbus, Ohio. A. P. Stone was treasurer of state. James T. Claypoole who was his particular friend, made application to be appointed receiver of the bank, assisted by some of the creditors, and finally succeeded, but at that time, as the agent of a creditor, he procured an execution on the judgment and came to Tiffin with it, where he placed the execution in the hands of sheriff Weirick, and hurried him down to the bank as quick as possible. , Mr. Johnson, when he found that he had a bigger load than he could carry, and as troubles began to thicken around him very rapidly, perpetrated the same folly that so many men are guilty of, by resorting to strong drink to drown his troubles. What a weakness! Just at a time when a man should bring all the powers of his manhood into requisition to bear him up under mental pressure, he drowns the man in the cup and retains the debauched substitute.

Weirick, the sheriff, and Mr. Claypoole hurried down to the bank before time of closing. They found Charley alone, holding on to a chair. The vault was open and a few old books scattered over the counter; everything seemed demoralized. They stated their business to Mr. Johnson, who said: " All r-r-right genl'men, c'm-n take all th'r-is."

The sheriff could find nothing that Mr. Claypoole would have him make a levy upon. Mr. Claypoole said some unpleasant things, but Charley laughed and asked Claypoole whether he would take something. They gave it up, and Mr. Claypoole, somewhat out of humor and very much excited, walked up to the telegraph office and hastily sent the following dispatch to treasurer Stone, at Columbus:

" Seneca county bank gone to hell; will be there to-night.
JAMES T. CLAYPOOLE."

This was on the 25th of April, 1857.

There were at that time some $63,000 of the Seneca county bank bills in circulation. Mr. Claypoole was appointed receiver, and proceeded to collect the bills, issuing his certificates in their stead.

On the 19th of February, 1861, Claypoole reported his proceedings to the legislature, and said, amongst other things, that the bank had bonds deposited with the treasurer of state for the security of the holders of its notes in the sum of $209,648; that all said bonds had been abstracted or paid out in violation of law, and that the holders of $57,000 of outstanding circulation were deprived of their pro rata share of said bank. He claimed that the state held securities for this circulation, in the sum of $50,000, and asked that the same be used for the redemption of the bills.

Nothing was done upon this report. War broke out and the Seneca county bank was lost sight of. The bills were hawked about the country, and sold for whatever they would fetch. In the session of the general assembly of 1864, the writer introduced a bill directing the treasurer of state to redeem the certificates so issued by the receiver, and the outstanding bills of said bank, which passed both houses and became a law on the 31st of March, 1864. The state lost nothing by the act. On the contrary, there were less bills and certificates outstanding than the securities in the hands of the treasurer of state, leaving a respectable balance in favor of the state. This balance was made up undoubtedly by bills that were lost or destroyed, and having never been presented, the state had the benefit of the loss.

In 1852, Arnold and Tomb (Sylvanus Arnold and Benjamin Tomb), established a private banking house, which lasted two years, when it changed into the name of Tomb, Huss & Co. The business was conducted in this name until 1865, when the company organized as the "First National Bank of Tiffin," with Benjamin Tomb for president, and John T. Huss cashier. For eleven years this bank did an immense business, but during the last year some people, who had a chance to know, questioned its soundness, and looked upon the institution with misgivings. Mr. Huss, the cashier, was a native of Tiffin, and a young man of excellent business qualifications. He was highly esteemed, and enjoyed the general confidence for honor and integrity. Nobody was willing to believe him guilty of any wrong. The state election of 1875 was over, and both parties quieted down to business.

It was the afternoon of the 15th of October, 1875. Several depositors from the city withdrew their deposits. The money in the bank had run down to a few thousand dollars. The clerks in the bank felt gloomy. Some of the directors consulted together as to the propriety of borrowing some money for a few days. Huss was at his house, where he had been for several days, feeling unwell, as he said. A gentleman from Cincinnati came that afternoon and stopped at the Shawhan house, with a view of seeing Mr. Huss the next morning about a large draft that was not just as it should have been. It was half-past four o'clock in the afternoon. The bank had closed, and for the last time. Mr. Huss was in bed. The family had gone into the dining-room to supper. A light shot was heard in the direction of Mr. Huss' room. A ball had passed through his heart from a revolver Mr. Huss had still in his hand. He was dead.

It will benefit nobody to describe the condition of things that was soon made manifest, and it had better not be recorded here Suffice it to say, that Warren P. Noble, Esq., was appointed receiver and paid the creditors sixty per cent. on their claims.

THE NATIONAL EXCHANGE BANK OF TIFFIN

Was organized in 1865. The following named gentlemen were the incorporators, viz: John D. Loomis, R. W. Shawhan, A. G. Sneath, J. M. Naylor, S. B. Sneath, W. W. Naylor, H. A. Buskirk, S. M. Ogden, Abel Rawson, A. B. Hovey, J. H. Good, Levi Davis, John Swigart, J. H. Pittenger, Robert Smith, E. T. Stickney, and J. A. McFarland. The capital stock was then $125,000, which has been greatly augmented since. The bank enjoys the general confidence of the community, and the only severe misfortune that befel the institution was the robbery of the bank by its former cashier, O. C. Zeller, who left the bank for Canada one night in the spring of 1878, and on the next morning the bank was short some $50,000.

The business of the bank proceeded right on as if nothing had happened, and while the community were shocked over the act, the confidence the people had placed in the institution was not shaken in the least.

The present officers of the bank are: J. D. Loomis, president; J. W. Chamberlain, cashier. Mr. Loomis has been its president all the time.

THE TIFFIN SAVINGS BANK

Was incorporated March 3d, 1873, under an act entitled "An act to incorporate savings and loan associations," passed February 26th, 1873. John G. Gross was the president, D. D. Dildine cashier. The institution was kept up about four years, and after the death of Mr. Huss it closed its business, and a majority of the stockholders joined in the

COMMERCIAL BANK,

Which purchased the First National bank building, and opened for business on the 23d day of June, 1876. The bank organized under their charter of May 18th, 1876, with a capital of $100,000. It has a constant surplus of over $7,000. W. P. Noble, president; J. A. McFarland vice-president; S. B. Sneath, cashier; J. A. Blair, assistant cashier.

THE BANK OF TIFFIN

Was organized in the fall of 1858, by Evan Dorsey and A. G. Sneath. In the fall of 1859, R. W. Shawhan bought the interest of Mr. Dorsey, and the bank was continued by the same name until it merged into the organization of the National Exchange bank in 1865. The Bank of Tiffin was kept during its whole existence in the room now occupied by John Neligh as a clothing store. Mr. Shawhan was then, as now, the owner of the building.

Mr. A. G. Sneath was cashier of the old Bank of Tiffin during the whole time of its existence, and of the National Exchange bank for about three years from the time of its organization.

INSURANCE COMPANIES.

The Seneca County Mutual Fire Insurance company was organized under a charter by the legislature of Ohio, passed March 19th, 1850.

The first meeting of the incorporators was held in the sheriff's office in Tiffin, in pursuance of notices published in the *Seneca Advertiser* and the *Seneca Whig*, when the Hon. A. Lugenbeel was appointed chairman and Hon. J. W. Wilson secretary.

On motion of Eden Lease, the by-laws of the Stark County Mutual Insurance company were adopted for the by-laws of this company.

William Lang was elected president for the ensuing year, J. W. Wilson secretary, and George Knupp treasurer. The secretary was authorized to act as general agent of the company; and thus the company started on its career with a good board of directors and officers, and with one of the most favorable charters for a mutual fire insurance company ever passed by an Ohio legislature.

On the 29th day of October, 1850, the first policy was issued and the last one on the 31st day of July, 1860, being number 1,502.

Immediately upon the organization of the company Mr. Wilson took charge of all its business and appointed very many agents in various counties in northern Ohio, the larger number of whom had no experience in insurance matters, and whatever they lacked in knowledge they made up in impudence and avarice.

They recommended all manner of risks, and would have insured powder mills if they had found any. In addition to all this, many of the applicants were worthless and irresponsible, and when assessments were made upon them, they could not be collected. The premium note was a lien upon the real estate of the insured, but very often prior encumbrances swallowed up the whole value. The agents themselves gave no bonds or other security for moneys that came into their hands, and when assessments were collected but small returns were made, for want of means to pay the losses, the officers borrowed money upon their own credit, as individual citizens, from the banks in Tiffin for that purpose, with a hope of being re-embursed from future collections.

The assessments were made very light to make a good showing, but were insufficient to pay losses and expenses. For several years the larger amounts of the losses were paid by money thus furnished, and when, later on, assessments were made larger, to cover back indebtedness, members complained and many surrendered their policies.

In this condition of things the directors found the affairs of the company when, in the fall of 1856, Mr. Wilson died, and William Lang was appointed secretary in his stead.

The company had then already run into evil report. Some of the agents were dismissed, and all brought to an account, but there was not vitality enough in the concern to recuperate. It dragged along with all its old troubles on hand, and new ones accumulating, until it was compelled to wind up. Mr. John McCauley was appointed the attorney of the company to collect the assessments and pay the liabilities. Many members had to be sued, but finally enough was collected to pay all, or nearly all, the indebtedness of the company.

The mutual plan is undoubtedly the best and most equitable system of insurance, but the officers and agents must be the owners of two great and indispensable requisites, viz: business qualifications and integrity.

THE FARMERS' MUTUAL RELIEF INSURANCE COMPANY OF SENECA COUNTY

Is not a Tiffin institution, but it holds its meetings here. It was organized in 1858 and reorganized and incorporated April 12, 1878. It has insured farm property to the amount of $2,500,000, paid all its losses, and is out of debt, with funds on hand.

The present officers are:
President—R. R. Titus.
Vice-President—J. W. Lawhead.
Secretary—D. M. Neikirk.
Treasurer—Peter Hoefling.

All of whom are also Trustees, together with the following, viz.:

Ed. H. Swander, Clinton,
D. J. Neikirk, Venice,
James Lott, Liberty,
Madison Finch, Bloom,
John Neikirk, Adams,

Benoni Rohrer, Hopewell,
Levi Keiller, Jr., Reed,
Joseph Rhodes, Eden,
Thomas J. Whalen, London,
Amos Decker, Thompson.

Its operations are confined to Seneca county alone.

TIFFIN MUTUAL AID LIFE INSURANCE COMPANY

Was organized on the 23d of January, 1878.

President—W. P. Noble.
Vice-President—John Houck.
Treasurer—Ed. Jones.
Secretary and General Manager—A. L. Flack.
Counselor—Andrew J. Brickner.
Medical Examiner—Dr. E. J. McCollum.

The association has issued over one thousand policies, is in a flourishing condition and is very carefully conducted.

INDEPENDENT ORDER OF ODD FELLOWS.

Seneca lodge No. 35 was instituted under its charter February 20th, 1845, by District Deputy Grand Master Joel Searles. of Columbus lodge No. 9, assisted by S. H. Bradley, P. G., of Morning Star lodge No. 26, Medina, Ohio. Applicants for the charter present were: H. G. W. Cronise, R. R. McMeens, James Sivils, B. D. Chapman, T. H. Sheldon, J. Oyler, who proceeded to elect the following officers, viz:

N. G.—T. H. Sheldon.
V. G.—B. D. Chapman.
Secretary—H. G. W. Cronise.
Treasurer—James Sivils.

Thereupon the officers were installed, and the following named persons were initiated, viz: John E. McCormack, N. Redd, W. P. Noble, Rolla Johnson. Two hundred and eighty-nine persons have been initiated in this lodge.

Its present officers are:

N. G.—H. J. Weller.
V. G.—P. G. Greis.
P. Secretary—Sharon C. Lamberson.
Treasurer—Samuel Stricker.
Trustees—Levi Weirick, D. C. Tunison, Sharon C. Lamberson.
Meets Monday nights.

OAKLEY LODGE NUMBER 317.

Date of its charter, June 10, 1857.

The following were the charter members: F. Don Benham, John T. Huss, J. W. Miller, L. M. Loomis, T. H. Bagley, T. W. Ourand, B. Pennington, E. G. Bowe, John Poorman, John E. McCormack.

The first officers of the lodge were:

N. G.—J. T. Huss.
V. G.—J. W. Miller.
Secretary—B. Pennington.
Treasurer—T. H. Bagley.

The present officers are:
N. G.—S. A. Fast.
V. G.—Charles Ernst.
Secretary—B. Pennington.
Treasurer—S. Chamberlain.

Present number of members, ninety-eight; number of dormants, seventy-eight.

Messrs. E. G. Bowe, B. Pennington, and S. Chamberlain have been delegates to the grand lodge.

One remarkable circumstance connected with this lodge is the fact that Mr. B. Pennington has been its secretary from the beginning now nearly twenty-three years.

Meets on Saturday evening.

HOBAH ENCAMPMENT NUMBER 19

Was instituted by Mark Taylor, Grand Patriarch, November 18, 1846. The charter members were: H. G. W. Cronise, George Knupp, F. Don Benham, L. M. Loomis, W. P. Noble, Richard Williams, Rolla Johnson, John G. Breslin.

The first officers elected and installed the same evening were:

Chief Patriarch—H. G. W. Cronise.
High Priest—F. Don Benham.
Senior Warden—George Knupp.
Junior Warden—John G. Breslin.
Scribe—Richard Williams.
Treasurer—Rolla Johnson.

The present officers are:

Grand Rep.—Scudder Chamberlain.
District Deputy Grand Patriarch—J. W. Love.
Chief Patriarch—John Ernst.
High Priest—S. Chamberlain.
Senior Warden—Samuel Stricker.
Junior Warden—P. H. Greis.
Scribe—J. W. Love.
Treasurer—H. C. Spindler.
First Watch—Joseph Seechrist.
Second Watch—W. Cupp.
Third Watch—J. W. Gordon.
Fourth Watch—H. Guggenheim.
O. S:—H. J. Stolzenbach.
I. S.—William Fleming.
First G. of. T.—B. Zuit.
Second G. of. T.—Aaron Kreader.

Present number of contributing members, forty-eight.

Meets Friday night.

KNIGHTS OF PYTHIAS.

Tiffin lodge No. 80, was organized January 12th, 1874, when the following officers were installed by Mr. James A. Swoope, Grand Chancellor, viz:

Past Chancellor—C. J. Yingling.
Chancellor Commander—H. L. Steckel.
Vice Chancellor—James Smith.
Prelate—A. M. Campbell.
Master of Exchequer—Ph. Emich.
Master of Finance—Harry Lutz.
Keeper of Record and Seal—C. J. Yingling.
Master of Arms—John Sohn.
Inner Guard—J. A. Flack.
Outer Guard—J. W. Love.

The lodge numbers now sixty active members, and is in a flourishing condition.

The present officers are:

Past Chancellor—O. P. Snyder.
Chancellor Commander—E. W. Stevenson.
Vice Chancellor—U. Clary.
Prelate—A. M. Hart.
Master of Exchequer—O. P. Frees.
Master of Finance—James W. Love.
Master of Arms—W. S. Wineland.
Inner Guard—Ed. Fry.
Outer Guard—Oscar Fraley.

Meetings Tuesday night.

Grand lodge Knights of Pythias meets at Dayton May 24th, 25th and 26th, 1880.

KNIGHTS OF HONOR.

Tiffin lodge No. 82 was chartered February 15th, 1875.

Its first officers were:

Dictator—Charles Martin.
Vice Dictator—Fred. K. Halderman.
Assistant Dictator—B. G. Atkins.
Reporter—G. K. Brown.
Treasurer—P. Scheib.
Chaplain———— ————.
Guide—D. Y. Chapman.
Guardian———— ————.
Sentinel—C. C. Parks.

Present officers for 1880.

Dictator—J. A. Hall.
Vice Dictator—P. J. Wilson

THE SOCIETIES OF TIFFIN. 345

Assistant Dictator—Fred. Nicolai.
Reporter—J. W. Chamberlain.
Treasurer—C. C. Parks.
Chaplain—J. W. Mendenhall.
Guide—B. G. Atkins.
Guardian—P. Scheib.
Sentinel—Thomas Grandon.

Number of members, twenty-five; number of past dictators, five, viz: J. W. Chamberlain, Charles Martin, Fred. K. Holderman, B. G. Atkins, W. H. Hall.

Meets at Druid Hall first and third Monday nights in each month.

ST. PATRICK'S TOTAL ABSTINENCE AND BENEVOLENT ASSOCIATION

Was organized February 1st, 1874, by Fr. Angelo, of the Passionist Order of Missionaries, and has eighty-four members.

Its first officers were:
Spiritual Director—Rev. M. Healy.
President—C. J. M. Sullivan.
Vice-President—Ph. B. King.
Recording Secretary—J. A. Coonrod.
Corresponding Secretary—J. M. Arndt.
Treasurer—T. F. Walsh.
Marshal—William King.

The present officers are:
Spiritual Director—Rev. M. Healy.
President—J. A. Coonrod.
Vice-President—Thomas Fitz Morris.
Recording Secretary—F. F. Keller.
Corresponding Secretary—C. J. M. Sullivan.
Treasurer—T. F. Walsh.
Marshal—John T. King.

The state convention was held in Tiffin July 19, 1879, when some thirty societies were represented. The national union, including the above, numbers six hundred societies, with twenty thousand members.

Meets at Riverside hall first and third Sundays in each month.

F. AND A. MASONS—SANDUSKY LODGE NUMBER 77

Was organized at Tiffin October 19, 1842, with the following charter members, viz: Rufus W. Reid, Charles F. Dresbach, Uriah P. Coonrad, Joseph Walker, E. Dresbach, Robert Crum, Agreen Ingraham, Israel Bentley, Samuel Mitchell, John Baugher, Henry Kuhn, Evan Dorsey, Thadeus Wilson, Vincent Bell.

TIFFIN LODGE NUMBER 320

Was organized April 5th, 1858, with the following charter members, viz: F. Don Benham, William Gallup, James Pelan, John G. Kennedy,

E. B. Searles, Robert Crum, H. C. Spindler, W. P. Noble, L. A. Hall, E. W. Reeme, Leander Stern, and continued to exist as Tiffin lodge until October 16th, 1866, when the two lodges were consolidated under the name of Tiffin lodge No. 77.

The following brethren served as officers in Sandusky lodge No. 77 from the date of its charter until the present writing (April 20, 1880), as follows:

W. M.:

R. W. Reid, from 1842 to 1849 inclusive.
Robert Crum, from 1850 to 1853 inclusive.
J. E. McCormack, from 1858 to 1861 inclusive.
Henry Kuhn, from 1862 to 1863 inclusive.
C. C. Park, from 1864 to 1868 inclusive.
A. H. Byers, from 1869 to 1871 inclusive.
G. K. Brown, from 1872 to 1873 inclusive.
J. P. Kuniaman, from 1874 to 1876 inclusive.
J. W. Chamberlain, from 1877 to 1878 inclusive.
D. Y. Chapman, from 1879 to 1880 inclusive.

Secretaries:

Joseph Walker, 1842.
F. W. Green, from 1843 to 1847 inclusive.
G. J. Keen, 1848.
H. W. Owen, 1849.
J. P. Pillars, 1850.
T. C. Tunison, 1851.
R. Williams, 1852.
G. E. Seney, 1853.
James Pelan, 1854.
J. G. Kennedy, 1855.
George H. Heming, 1856.
J. M. Stevens, 1857.
M. H. Church, 1858.
J. D. Arndt, 1859.
L. M. Loomis, from 1860 to 1863 inclusive.
J. G. Gross, from 1864 to 1867 inclusive.
Charles Martin, from 1868 to 1870 inclusive.
J. H. Frost, 1869.
B. G. Atkins, from 1871 to 1875 inclusive, and 1878.
N. N. Speilman, from 1876 to 1877 inclusive.
J. E. McCormack, from 1879 to 1880 inclusive.

TIFFIN LODGE NUMBER 320.

W. M.:

Robert Crum, from 1858 to 1860 inclusive.
D. F. DeWolf, from 1861 to 1863 inclusive.
A. T. Barnes, from 1864 to 1865 inclusive.
F. E. Franklin, 1866.

THE SOCIETIES OF TIFFIN. 347

Secretaries:
F. D. Benham, 1858.
J. G. Kennedy, 1859.
E. W. Reeme, 1860.
L. Adams, 1861.
A. T. Barnes, 1862.
C. Cronise, 1865.
R. Lysle, 1864 and 1865.
G. F. Hertzer, 1866.

SENECA CHAPTER NUMBER 42, R. A. M,

Was organized February 7th, 1849, by Jacob Groff, M. E. G. H. P., with the following charter members, viz: John J. Steiner, R. W. Reid, Alexander Smith, Joseph McCutchen, Agreen Ingraham, Abner Root, Henry Kuhn, Robert Crum, Peter Vannest.

High Priests:
R. W. Reid, 1849.
F. W. Green, 1850 and 1851.
C. K. Watson, from 1852 to 1854, and from 1866 to 1869 inclusive.
H. Kuhn, 1855, 1857, 1859, 1860, 1861, 1862, and 1863.
Robert Crum, 1856.
J. E. McCormack, 1859.
G. W. Sampson, 1865.
C. C. Park, 1870, 1871, and 1872.
J. W. Chamberlain, 1873, 1874, and 1875.
C. D. Davis, 1876 and 1877.
J. P. Kinnaman, 1878 and 1879.
Charles Martin, 1880.

Secretaries:
J. S. Barber, 1850.
H. D. Crum, 1851.
H. W. Owen, 1852.
T. W. Boyce, 1853 and 1854.
N. R. Kuntz, 1855.
H. Noble, 1856.
J. E. McCormack, 1860.
G. W. Sampson, 1862 and 1863.
J. G. Gross, 1865, 1866, and 1867.
Charles Martin, 1868, 1869, and 1870.
J. H. Frost, 1871 and 1872.
J. M. Stevens, 1873, 1874, and 1875.
James Smith, 1876, 1877, 1878, and 1879.
R. Lysle, 1880.

CLINTON COUNCIL NUMBER 47, ROYAL AND SELECT MASONS,

Was organized April 9th, 1867, with the following charter members, viz: C. K. Watson, C. C. Park, G. K. Brown, Charles Martin, J. F.

Marquardt, A. H. Byers, J. G. Gross, Jonathan Smith, Peter Vannest, Evan Dorsey, H. H. Souder.

T. I. Masons:
C. K. Watson, 1867 and 1868.
C. C. Park, 1869 and 1880.
A. H. Byers, 1870 and 1871.
Charles Martin, from 1872 to 1879 inclusive.

Recorders:
G. K. Brown, from 1867 to 1872, and from 1875 to 1876 inclusive.
J. M. Stevens, 1873 and 1874.
J. W. Chamberlain, 1877, 1878, 1779, and 1880.

DE MOLAY COMMANDERY NUMBER 9, KNIGHTS TEMPLARS,

Was organized at Republic August 10th, 1848, with the following charter members, viz: Josiah Roop, John P. Worstell, H. Benton, Platt Benedict, Daniel Watersons, Daniel Brown, Hiram Humphrey, M. V. Bogart, Edward Winthrop, H. L. Harris.

It remained at Republic until February 24th, 1869, when the first meeting was held at Tiffin, where it has remained ever since.

Eminent Commanders:

Edward Winthrop, from 1848 to 1851 inclusive.
Platt Benedict, from 1853 to 1857 inclusive.
M. V. Bogart, from 1858 to 1864 inclusive.
H. Bromley, from 1865 to 1870 inclusive.
J. W. Chamberlain, 1871, 1872, 1876, 1877, 1878, and 1880.
C. C. Park, 1873, 1874, 1875, and 1879.

Recorders:
H. P. Benton, 1848 and 1849.
E. T. Stickney, from 1850 to 1854, and from 1866 to 1867.
J. S. Smith, 1855.
H. Bromley, from 1856 to 1864 inclusive.
D. M. Neikirk, from 1868 to 1872 inclusive.
J. M. Stevens, from 1873 to 1875.
R. Lysle, 1879 and 1880.

All these Masonic bodies meet at Masonic hall, in the third story of Gross's block, corner Perry and Washington.

Stated meetings are held as follows:

Tiffin Lodge No. 77—First and third Tuesday evenings of each month.
Seneca Chapter No. 42—First Friday of each month.
Clinton Council No. 47—Second Monday evening of each month.
De Molay Commandery No. 9—Fourth Wednesday evening of each month.

ST. JOHN'S BENEVOLENT SOCIETY

Was organized March 28th, 1868, by Michael Kirchner, John Houck

THE SOCIETIES OF TIFFIN. 349

and Paul Vallmer, who called the first meeting. The first officers were:

President (from 1868 to 1878)—M. Kirchner.
Vice-President—A. J. Brickner.
Secretary—George Spies.
Treasurer—Anton Knebler.

The present officers are:

President—Francis Wagner.
Vice-President—John Ehrenfried.
Corresponding Secretary—W. Steltzer.
Financial Secretary—Philbert Houck.
Treasurer—Louis Ulrich.
Directors—A. J. Brickner, John Ewald, Peter Bonnuth.

ANCIENT ORDER OF HIBERNIANS, NUMBER 1.

Organized June 10th, 1876, with the following named gentlemen, who were the first officers, viz:

County Delegate—John K. Bresnin.
President—John Lyons.
Vice-President—T. T. Collins.
Recording Secretary—William Burke.
Financial Secretary—James Blake.
Treasurer—William Colthurst.

Present officers:

County Delegate—James Blake.
President—T. T. Collins.
Vice-President—James Whalen.
Recording Secretary—William Burke.
Financial Secretary—John Dore.
Treasurer—Michael Coughlin.

UNITED ANCIENT ORDER OF DRUIDS.

This is a German institution exclusively. It was organized on the 29th of April, 1859. The charter members were: Jacob Zimmer, Leopold Rose, J. C. Spindler, William Wolf, Philip Scheib, G. A. Lautermilch, Guenther Herzer, Benjamin Schimmes.

These eight men met with much difficulty in getting a lodge on foot, and conquering the prejudices so common against secret benevolent societies. Soon after the organization Jacob Zimmer, one of the best members, died, and the institution decreased to but five members, and seemed to approach dissolution. But by perseverance and patient endurance, the order here increased to sixty members. Of this number some have died and others moved away, so that there are now but forty active members left. Much has been done, however, during the twenty-one years last past to dry human tears and afford relief in time of need.

The present officers are:

Grand Officers—George A. Lautermilch, D. D. G. A.
Representative—Joseph Meyer.

Officers of Humbolt Grove No. 15, U. A. O. D.:
N. A.—Christ. Trothe.
W. A.—Frederick Schrikel.
Secretary—Charles Yung.
Treasurer—J. U. Mœshinger.
Inner Guard—August Dressel.
Outer Guard—Mathias Pfeifer.
Trustees—Balthasar Waelfling, Henry Lemp, John Reif.

CHAPTER XXII.

THE BENCH AND BAR.

WHEN the Hon. Ebenezer Lane was president judge and lived in Norwalk, his circuit embraced the entire northwestern portion of Ohio, including Huron, which extended north to Lake Erie, The first court was held in Tiffin, on the 12th day of April, 1824.

Present: E. Lane, President Judge; William Cornell, Jacques Hulburt, Matthew Clark, Associate Judges; Neal McGaffey, Clerk; Agreen Ingraham, Sheriff.

Under the old constitution of Ohio clerks of the supreme and circuit court were appointed by the judges thereof. The judges themselves were elected by the legislature for seven years.

The first lawyer who settled in Fort Ball was Mr. R. Dickinson, a sketch of whose life appears elsewhere. Mr. A. Rawson was the second lawyer who made his home here. Mr. Dickinson remained but a short time in Tiffin, from whence he moved to Lower Sandusky. Mr. Rawson remained here the rest of his life.

The first session of the supreme court began here on the 28th day of July, 1826, before Jacob Burnett and Charles R. Sherman, supreme judges. The next term was held by Judges Calvin Pease and Charles R. Sherman.

The judges holding these courts generally traveled their circuits on horseback, and the pioneer lawyers traveled with them in the same manner; all with large saddle-bags on their saddles, with law books and briefs, etc., in one end and refreshments in the other. Among the foreign lawyers who attended court here at that time were many distinguished gentlemen of marked character. Andrew Coffinberry, John C. Spink, John M. May, O. Parish, Frank Parish, James Purdy, were all able and distinguished lawyers. There was also Charles Olcott, and later came Charles L. Bolt, Ezra Stone, Mr. Beecher and others. My venerable old friend, Mr. James Purdy, of Mansfield, is the only survivor of all these foreign lawyers. He has promised to send a sketch of his early recollections of frontier practice, but said in a note of the 10th of February, 1880, to the writer: "At the age of 87 my memory is not retentive, but I will comply with your request as best I can in due time; at present my whole time is occupied with business.

· J. PURDY."

The record of the lives of these gentlemen, their practice, and incidents connected therewith, the scenes they participated in, and the events that transpired in their time would make a highly interesting book, and the writer had intended to write out sketches of some of them, but to keep this book within the limits marked out for it, he must abstain. I will say, however, that Mr. Coffinberry (Count Coffinberry as he was familiarly called) was the most remarkable figure of them all. In appearance he was the very image of Oliver Goldsmith. He had large features and a very striking appearance; he shaved smooth and his face carried a smile mixed with sarcasm. He was learned and witty, a good historian and exceedingly entertaining n conversation. He was a natural poet and published one of his poems called "The Forest Ranger" in book form. Selah Chapin settled here in the law practice at an early day; also Mr. Curtis Bates and Mr. Joshua Seney, Sidney Smith, William W. Culver, John J. Steiner and others. John K. Gibson, a promising young man, and older brother of General Gibson, was the first law student in Mr. Rawson's office in Tiffin. He died before he was admitted to practice.

The writer became associated with the profession when he commenced reading law in Tiffin, in 1840, and having, for forty years, been in daily intercourse with legal gentlemen, and amongst whom he counts his warmest and best friends, it would be a very great pleasure to remember them all and make a pen-picture of each one; but for the reasons already assigned a few only are sketched to any length.

During a number of years, when Judge Lane and Judge Reuben Wood were on the supreme bench together, they took for their part of the work the northwestern part of Ohio. They formed a wonderful contrast on the bench. Judge Lane was a very short, compactly built man; was near-sighted, had small black eyes, wore spectacles, had black hair, which he brushed straight down over his forehead, and when he read he held the book or paper close to his nose. He was a rapid talker and exceedingly active. Judge Wood was a six footer; very straight; had large forehead, light brown hair, brushed over to the right side; had large blue eyes, a large fleshy nose, clenched lips, deep and sonorous voice; spoke slowly and very impressively; thus they formed a striking contrast in their personal appearance on the bench.

THE BENCH AND BAR. 353

They were both on the bench in Lower Sandusky, on the 25th of July, 1842, when Judge Lane administered the oath to the writer, admitting him to practice law. These two judges seemed to have their work divided by the decisions they delivered. Judge Wood decided all or nearly all the criminal matters, while Judge Lane decided chancery cases, as a general thing. There was a certain degree of awe, importance and dignity attached to the bench in those days, that has vanished, to a very great extent, since the judges are elected by the people, and the office has become, at least, quasi-political.

The Hon. David Higgins succeeded Judge Lane on the common pleas bench and his jurisdiction at first extended all over the northwest of Ohio. He was succeeded by the Hon. Ozias Bowen, of Marion, who held his first court in Tiffin, on the 2d of April, 1838. His judicial district was then composed of the counties of Marion, Crawford, Huron, Seneca, Sandusky, Erie, and later, Wyandot.

Judge Bowen's time expired with the old constitution.

The first legislature under the new and present constitution, which divided the state into judicial districts, fixed upon nine as the number and designated them. These were then divided into five judicial circuits, the following counties constituting the first circuit, viz: Butler, Preble, Darke, Montgomery, Miami, Champaign, Warren, Clinton, Greene, Clark, Shelby, Auglaize, Allen, Hardin, Logan, Union, Marion, Mercer, Van Wert, Putnam, Paulding, Defiance, Williams, Henry, Fulton, Wood, Seneca, Hancock, Wyandot and Crawford. The five circuits made one for each supreme judge. Some fourteen years thereafter the supreme judges were by law excused from attending upon the circuits.

In 1853 the nine judicial districts were again changed and Seneca was put into the third sub-division of the third judicial district. This third sub-division was composed of the counties of Wood, Seneca, Hancock, Wyandot and Crawford. L. W. Hall was the first judge elected under the new constitution in this sub-division. The regular succession of judges hitherto is as follows: Hall, Whitely, Mott, Jackson, Beer. The following are the additional judges elected in the following order, viz: Plants, Seney, Pillars, Dodge, McCauley. The legislature changed the sub-district and the succession of the judges as follows:

On the 17th day of April, 1857, an act was passed providing for an election of an additional judge for the third sub-division of the third judicial district, composed of the counties of Seneca, Crawford, Wyandot, Hancock and Wood, and in the fall of the same year George E.

23

Seney was elected judge, and about the time his term expired, the legislature changed the district.

On the 8th of April, 1858, an act was passed creating the tenth judicial district and changing the sub-division, of which Seneca was a part. By this act the tenth judicial district was composed of the counties of Lucas, Wood, Seneca, Crawford, Hancock, Wyandot and Putnam. The counties of Seneca, Crawford and Wyandot were made the third division. Four days thereafter another act was passed attaching Lucas to the fourth district and making Seneca county the first sub-division of the tenth district, Wyandot and Crawford the second and Hancock, Wood and Putnam the third sub-division, leaving Judge Seney in this county, Seneca being then a sub-division.

Judge Whitely's time expired in 1861 and he was re-elected in the then third sub-division. Josiah S. Plants was elected in the second sub-division in the fall of 1858. In the fall of 1863, Judge Plants, while out in Indiana hunting prairie chickens, was mortally wounded by the accidental discharge of a gun. He was brought home to die; and Ohio lost one of her brightest, best and most promising young men.

Judge Plant's term had nearly expired when he died. Nobody was appointed to fill his place.

In the fall of 1862, and shortly before the expiration of his term of office, Judge Seney went to war with the 101st regiment O. V. I. as its quartermaster.

On the 1st day of May, 1862, another act was passed abolishing the tenth district and re-organizing the third district thus, viz: first sub-division, Logan, Union, Marion; second sub-division, Auglaize, Allen, Mercer, Van Wert, Putnam; third sub-division, Paulding, Defiance, Williams, Fulton, Henry and Wood; fourth sub-division, Seneca, Hancock, Wyandot, Crawford.

Under this act Whitely remained in this fourth sub-division, and Plants also, up to his death; so that now, and under this act, Whitely, Metcalf, Latta, Lawrence and Plants were the judges in 1863, Whitely serving in the second term.

This last named act provides for an election to be held in this fourth sub-division for a judge in 1866. At this time Judge Whitely's term expired, and Chester R. Mott was elected. He was succeeded by A. M. Jackson, who resigned his office, and Thomas Beer was appointed by the Governor to fill the unexpired term of Jackson, and at the expiration of that time (1876) was elected and is on the bench now. So far we have traced the time of the election of the judges in regular succession.

Eng'd by Geo E Perine N.Y

"Let us always seek and abide the right leaving consequences to the dispensations of Providence."

Yours truly,
A. Rawson

ÆTAT 72

On the 21st of February, 1868, another act was passed adding the county of Marion to this fourth sub-division and authorizing the election of an additional judge therein at the April election, 1868. James Pillars was elected judge under this act; re-elected in 1873, and was succeeded by Judge H. H. Dodge in 1877.

To recapitulate in short: Hall was elected in 1851, Whitely in 1856; re-elected in 1861; Seney in 1857 and Plants in 1858; Mott in 1866; Jackson in 1871; Beer in 1876; Pillars in 1868, re-elected in 1873; Dodge in 1877; McCauley in 1879.

On the 7th day of June, 1879, the "combined wisdom of Ohio" passed an act establishing a new district, number ten, again, and to be composed of the counties of Wood, Hancock, Seneca and Hardin, to be the first sub-division; Crawford, Marion and Wyandot to be the second sub-division, and Union and Logan to be the third sub-division of the tenth district. The act authorized an election of a judge in the first sub-division, and in October, 1879, John McCauley, of Tiffin, was elected under this act the first judge of the new sub-division.

INTRODUCTORY NOTE.

An individual of low extraction, without notable excellence or ancestral distinction, may, by rashness or the caprice of fortune, gain magnificent achievements and temporarily acquire an eminent position in society. His success, like the transit of a comet, may dazzle the vision by the rapidity and intensity of its brilliancy; and yet, leave little or no durable impress for the gratification of his descendants or the social advancement of mankind. Such history is generally exceptional, and constitutes no reliable basis for progressive imitation. But when an individual of humble origin, and perhaps the subject of some permanent bodily infirmity, without the prestige of wealth or influential relatives, by patient toil against long continued adversity, secures the esteem and confidence of the community around him, it is quite natural to seek the co-operatives which have produced these auspicious results. In whatever sphere he may have moved, or whatever may have been his vocation, whether elevated or lowly and unpretentious, it will generally appear that he has been true to its requirements. At all events, the example will be impressive and instructive.

Again, where under the influence of free institutions, like those of the United States, inducements for success and social progress are open to all, the hopeful expectation of future respectability, if not of eminence, will naturally invite every considerate, ambitious young man to prepare himself for and seek some honorable occupation and commendable position in society and the attainment of moral, intellectual, and religious habits. He early appreciates the necessity of self-reliance and self-exertion, assured that a praiseworthy notoriety and an approving conscience can be acquired and perpetuated only by securing the respect and confidence of the good. Therefore, stimulated by a laudable ambition, and hopeful of success, he cheerfully combats adversity, and ultimately acquires and retains the good opinion of the community, the basis of his usefulness and goal of his ambition. Influenced by the tenacity of his purposes and stimulated by his example, others, and especially his descendants, will be naturally, and yet, perhaps, unconsciously, induced to eschew the illusions of evil on the one hand, and cultivate, on the other, with patient assiduity, the love and practice of virtue as the only thornless pathway to happiness, distinction and success.

LIFE OF ABEL RAWSON.

[Abridged from notes written by himself.]

Abel Rawson was born at Warwick, Massachusetts, May 11, 1798: the third son of Lemuel Rawson and Sarah Barrus, who were married September 8, 1791. Abel was a lineal descendant of the sixth generation from Edward Rawson, who emigrated from England as early as 1637, and acted as secretary of the colony of Massachusetts Bay from May, 1650 to 1686.

When less than four years old he was seized with fever followed by disease of the tibia of the left leg, which, after years of intense suffering, resulted in the loss of the bone and deformity of the ankle and foot which ever afterwards remained.

At the age of sixteen, the crippled son was advised to secure sufficient education to prepare himself for a teacher. The parents could give their children a common school education, but, as Abel inclined to the legal profession, they agreed to furnish him with such clothing as could be manufactured in the family, while he must earn the expense required for tuition and board at the academy or at college and to obtain his profession.

The offer made by his parents was accepted by Abel, and he resumed his place in New Salem Academy, and during two or more ensuing years taught school in the winters for educational support.

Thereupon he was admitted to the Dartmouth University, at Hanover, New Hampshire, and remained until the middle of his junior year, when the decision of the "Dartmouth College case," by the United States supreme court, in February, 1819, closed the institution.

In view of these adverse circumstances, Mr. Rawson decided to enter upon his legal studies, and during two years remained with Messrs. Gregg and Smith, at New Salem, Massachusetts, but completed his course with S. C. Allen and John Nevers, of Northfield, in 1822. He was examined in May, 1823, and admitted to the bar at the term of court in August following, and during the fall and winter of 1823-4 opened an office at New Salem.

March 24, 1824, Mr. Rawson took the stage coach for Albany and thence to Buffalo, New York, being six days and nights on the road. He came to

Newberry, Geauga county, Ohio, and soon after went to Steubenville, but met with disappointment and returned to Newberry. He taught school for several months in Dover, Wayne county, Ohio, and in November, 1824, removed to Norwalk, in Huron county, where he taught school during the ensuing winter, and in March, 1825, obtained employment in the clerk's office.

At the August term of the supreme court, in 1825, he was admitted to the bar, the Hon. Elisha Whittlesey being chairman of the examining committee.

In June, 1825, Mr. Rawson visited Tiffin, Seneca county, Ohio, for the first time.

He passed through Bellevue, where stood but a single cabin. and thence through a dense forest to Tiffin. The territory was then occupied by the Seneca tribe of Indians.

Tiffin consisted of about a dozen families dwelling in rude cabins. The timber had been mostly removed on Washington street, south from the Sandusky river to Market street. There was no hotel in Tiffin, so Mr. Rawson forded the river and stopped at a tavern kept by one Elisha Smith, at Fort Ball, where he remained over one day.

Seneca county could give then but 300 votes. Tiffin had abundant water power, unimproved except by a primitive grist and saw mill, erected by Josiah Hedges, and everything appeared prospective and disheartening to aspirations for even the current expenses of Mr. Rawson.

He returned to Norwalk unassured, and finally went to a brother in Richfield, now in Summit county, in September, 1825.

After a crisis of mental anxiety, he started again for Seneca county, in February, 1826, and on the 15th he arrived in Fort Ball with less than ten dollars in money and a law library of the first volume of Swift's Digest and of Chitty's Pleading.

He opened an office in a small brick building, 14x16 feet and one story high, and still (1880) standing on the west side of Sandusky street, in the second ward of Tiffin, being the first brick building erected in the county, and also occupied by Dr. Eli Dresbach.

At the May term of the court of common pleas, May 5th, 1826, Mr. Rawson was appointed prosecuting attorney, to succeed Rodolphus Dickinson, in which position he was retained until October, 1833. During eight or ten years after Mr. Rawson opened his office, the president judge and members of the bar were entertained at Fort Ball for want of accommodations at Tiffin, and twenty-four to twenty-five attorneys from Columbus, Marion, Delaware, Mansfield, Norwalk, Sandusky City and Lower Sandusky (now Fremont) made frequent excursions in attendance upon court at Tiffin, attended by privation and exposure which now appears incredible.

About this time Fort Ball and Tiffin were bitterly contesting the question of the county seat, and many law suits were brought against Josiah Hedges, the proprietor of Tiffin, in regard to the extent of his right to the bed of the Sandusky river. Mr. Rawson was urged to take part in this litigation but declined, and finally the suits died away.

During 1828 Mr. Hedges retained Mr. Rawson to manage his legal business, which agreement continued nearly twenty years.

In March, 1828, Mr. Rawson was appointed by Platt Brush his deputy to take charge of the United States land office for the Delaware district about to be removed to Tiffin. There was no bridge across the Sandusky river, and in April, 1828, Mr. Rawson left Fort Ball and opened his law office in Tiffin. Mr. Rawson was then postmaster at Fort Ball, and Milton McNeal his deputy. During a temporary absence of Mr. Rawson, one Neal McGaffey made an attempt to have him removed for the reason that Mr. Rawson's office was in Tiffin, which place was supplied from Fort Ball, and the highway and mail route from Columbus to Lower Sandusky (Fremont) was on the west side of the river. After many shameless expedients made by McGaffey, John McLean, then postmaster-general, informed Mr. Rawson that he should be no more annoyed. Soon after McGaffey was dismissed from the offices of clerk and of recorder by the court of common pleas, and Joseph Howard was appointed their clerk, and Mr. Rawson recorder.

September 28, 1828, Mr. Rawson was married to Miss Sarah Ann Clark, at Royalton, Cuyahoga county, Ohio, and they returned to Tiffin about the middle of October following. Miss Clark was born February 14, 1806, at Hancock, in Addison county, Vermont. She had been well educated, but was mainly dependent upon her own exertions for support. This union contributed largely to the assistance and happiness of Mr. Rawson.

Governor McArthur issued his commission to Mr. Rawson, dated June 12, 1832, as notary public for three years, but he declined to qualify. At that period he rose at or before 5 o'clock in the morning, chopped his own wood before breakfast, which was at 6 o'clock, and also prepared fuel for his office. Amid other cares, Mr. Rawson acted as school examiner for more than ten years, without compensation.

In the spring of 1834 Joseph Howard resigned his offices of clerk of the supreme court and court of common pleas, and a certificate for those offices was issued to Mr. Rawson from Judges Wright, Lane and Collett, of the supreme court, dated April 24th, 1834, with that of the court of common pleas, but he declined, and in union with others recommended Luther A. Hall, a young man well qualified, who succeeded to the office and held it with credit during the ensuing seven years.

March 4th, 1828, congress granted 500,000 acres of land in Ohio to aid in the construction of her canals. February 12th, 1829, one land office was located at Tiffin, and on December 19th, 1830, Mr. Rawson was appointed register by joint resolution of the legislature, which position he retained more than six years.

The office was removed to Maumee City in the spring of 1837, and John Brough (since governor) was elected receiver. Mr. Rawson was reappointed register by Governor Vance, and commissioned April 15th, 1837, but declined.

January 5th, 1832, the Mad River and Lake Erie railroad company was incorporated by the legislature of Ohio, and in the following spring the company was organized and Josiah Hedges elected one of its directors. The road was constructed to Bellevue prior to 1836, but then suspended until 1839. Meantime the depot was established in Fort Ball, which aroused severe vituperation against Mr. Hedges, a director, and Mr. Rawson, the attorney for the road, and led to several suits at law before the excitement abated.

January 11th, 1836, Mr. Rawson was re-appointed recorder until the next annual election. Contrary to his wishes, he permitted the announcement of his name as an independent candidate for recorder, but which he had cause to regret, since it was the means adopted by Joseph Howard for his own election to the state senate. The election was held October 11th, 1836, wherein Mr. Howard was defeated; Mr. Rawson received 684 votes; Marcus Y. Groff, the Whig nominee, received 236 votes; Daniel Dildine, Jr., the Democratic nominee, received 592 votes, and Gabriel Keen, a Democrat, but independent candidate, received 150 votes, leaving Mr. Rawson elected by a plurality of ninety-two votes.

In the spring of 1834, Mr. Rawson purchased the *Seneca Patriot*, an old printing establishment, in aid of his brother Alonzo, who, for the ensuing two years, published the *Independent Chronicle*, of which the first number was issued April 26th, 1834.

The autumn of 1836 and the year 1837 witnessed an unprecedented monetary pressure and crisis which prevailed through several years. The reputation of Mr. Rawson insured him an immense amount of business, which extended to almost every Atlantic city from Bangor to New Orleans, and convinced him of the necessity of a partner. Early in 1838 he took Manly Chapin into partnership, which lasted two years. Robert G. Pennington succeeded Mr. Chapin, and continued as partner until Mr. Rawson retired from business.

Prior to 1842 several young men had studied law under the tuition of Mr. Rawson; John P. Connell, R. G. Pennington, W. H. Gibson, Warren P. Noble, and afterwards, Edson Goit, Frederick Lord, Luther A. Hall, John K. Gibson with others.

In the spring of 1844 Mr. Rawson felt the necessity of relaxation, and, at the Whig convention held at Baltimore May 4th, 1844, which nominated Henry Clay and Mr. Frelinghuysen, was delegate from the 9th district of Ohio; and in the same year was nominated for congress, but after an excited contest was defeated.

April 19th, 1847, Samuel Waggoner, Alfred Johnson, Benjamin Tomb, R. G. Pennington, with others, prepared their certificate for the Seneca county branch of the State Bank of Ohio, to be located at Tiffin, with a capital of $100,000, and recorded May 4th, 1847, in Seneca county records.

June 26th, 1847, Rezin W. Shawhan, A. Tuller, W. N. Montgomery, Jesse Stern, R. M. Shoemaker, and others, prepared their certificate for the Bank of Tiffin as a branch of the State Bank of Ohio, and recorded June 28th, 1847. These proceedings led to an unenvious strife, in which Mr. Rawson was unwittingly implicated.

July 12th, 1847, the application for the Seneca county branch was withdrawn, and a certificate recorded July 15th, 1847, for the Seneca County Bank of Tiffin, with a capital of $50,000, as an independent bank.

This was followed July 20th, 1847, by similar action on the part of the Bank of Tiffin, as an independent bank, with a capital of $100,000.

August 2d, 1847, the stock of the Seneca County Bank of Tiffin was increased to $100,000, which was followed August 7th by an increase in the stock of the Bank of Tiffin to $120,000.

Mr. Rawson was substituted for Hon. E. Lane as bank examiner, July

16th, 1847, without his knowledge, which led to violent opposition and an attempt was made to impeach his report by the Bank of Tiffin.

The final result fully sustained Mr. Rawson, and the Seneca County Bank of Tiffin was chartered August 9th, 1847.

February 8th, 1848, B. Tomb resigned as president and Mr. Rawson was appointed to fill the vacancy, but on May 25th, 1848, he also resigned.

The death of an only daughter, Aurinia H., February 10th, 1848, was a severe blow to an invalid mother, and on June 6th, 1849, Mrs. Rawson suddenly expired.

Thereupon Mr. Rawson abandoned his profession, and for several years devoted himself to out-door pursuits and the improvement of real estate.

In 1850 Mr. Rawson consented to become a candidate as a member for Seneca county of the convention to revise the state constitution, the election being on the first day of April. Excepting a printed address, Mr. Rawson took little interest in the canvass, and was defeated by E. T. Stickney with a majority of eighty-two votes.

In October, 1851, his name was used in the canvass for state senate during his absence in Iowa, of which, with his defeat, he was ignorant until his return; and also, in 1858, he was urged to accept the nomination for judge of common pleas, and in 1860 that for state senate, both of which he declined.

During this period Mr. Rawson devoted much of his time to closing professional business, and also to the education of his two sons, Allen A. and Homer C. Rawson, both of whom graduated at Rush Medical College, in Chicago, Illinois, in the spring of 1855, and in the following autumn and spring, settled in Adams county, Iowa, where they still reside (1880).

September 25th, 1856, Mr. Rawson married Mrs. Maria McNeal widow of Milton McNeal, who had died in September, 1834, with whom he afterwards enjoyed domestic quiet in declining years.

Especially during the last three or four years of his life did Mr. Rawson feel that his physical nature was yielding to the infirmities of age. This did not interfere with his cheerful recollections of the past, and regard for the friendly ties of the present, nor with his bright view of futurity. Conscious of a life of integrity and of honor, he said: "Let us always seek and abide the right, leaving consequences to the dispensations of Providence."

As the evening of Thursday, August 24th, 1871, was drawing a life of seventy-three years to a close, peacefully and gently the soul of Abel Rawson departed to the endless visions of eternity.

JOSHUA SENEY.

James Nicholson was a commodore of the United States navy in 1775, when he had command of the Trumbull, a frigate of thirty guns, and fought in her an action with the British man-of-war Wyatt, which, next to that of Paul Jones, with the Serapis, was the most desperate of the war. Eighteen members of the Nicholson family served in the navy of the United States. Commodore Nicholson had four daughters, who were all famous for their beauty and their accomplishments in both Washington and New York societies. Mr. Albert Gallatin, while a member of congress, married one of the girls; the second daughter became the wife of Colonel Few, the first senator from Georgia; the third married John Montgomery, a member of Congress from Maryland and mayor of Baltimore. Frances married Joshua Seney, a member of congress from Maryland also. This Seney family had two sons: Joshua was born November 20, 1793, in New York city, where he was raised and educated. He was a graduate of Columbia College and the University Law School. Before he entered upon the practice of law he was the private secretary of his uncle, Albert Gallatin (who in his day filled so conspicuous a place in the public esteem), for more than one year in Washington, where he mingled with the first men of the country who frequented the house of his uncle, and grandfather, Nicholson.

At a visit to Uniontown, Pennsylvania, he made the acquaintance of his wife, as noticed in a sketch of her life. He then practiced law in Uniontown ten years, when in 1831 he moved with his family to Tiffin, where he spent the rest of his days, and raised a large and highly respectable family.

Mr. Seney was one of the pioneer lawyers of Tiffin, and if his industry had been equal to his capacity, he would have been very successful as a practitioner. He had a natural aversion to anything that looked like labor. He was all politician, however, and a more shrewd, more calculating and far-seeing politician than Mr. Seney, Seneca county never had in any party. He was not selfish, nor sought office for himself. When he liked a person that aspired to office, he would do all in his power to aid him. He was severe on a political opponent. He enjoyed political agitations. Raised in the lap of wealth and luxury, he knew nothing about labor nor the value of money. He had very little taste for or appreciation of the practical part of life. His language was chaste and polished; but his manners were peculiarly his own. He often would pass his best friends on the street without noticing them; when at other times he was affable and friendly to everybody. He was perfectly at home in an office, however, and discharged every trust with ability and fidelity. He was clerk of the supreme court and treasurer of Seneca county. In 1840 he was one of the electors on the Democratic ticket of Ohio.

He wrote the finest hand of any lawyer that ever lived in Tiffin, and his records shame every clerk that has succeeded him. Mr. Seney was of medium height, but somewhat corpulent and compactly built. He had a large, well developed head, an expressive countenance, a piercing black eye, and a pleasant voice. He had the smallest hand of any man of his size that ever was known, and it was noticed by everybody that saw him

During the last few years of his life he had several attacks of heart disease that troubled him for a short time. One night he got out of bed, walked to the window and opened it, to let fresh air into the room, and, returning towards the bed, fell dead on the floor.

This was on the night following the 10th day of February, 1854. Mr. Seney was fifty-nine years, two months and ten days old when he died.

His three sons are lawyers of note: George E. Seney and Joshua Seney, the former in Tiffin and the other in Toledo, and both common pleas judges, and Henry Seney is in the practice at Kenton, Ohio, and when Judge McCauley was nominated for judge, Henry Seney gave him a very close chase for the nomination.

LUTHER A. HALL

Was born August 30th, 1813, in the township of Spafford, in Onondaga county, state of New York. He is the son of Luther Hall, who was a farmer by occupation, a native of Berkshire county, state of Massachusetts, and who died in 1849, at Freeport, Illinois.

Luther A. Hall was raised on a farm, working during the summer and attending district school during the winter until he was fourteen years old, when he became a pupil in a select school kept by Mr. Thomas W. Allis, at Skaneateles, where he remained two years. He then engaged as a clerk in a store and served in that capacity some three years. In the spring of 1833 he started on a trip to Ohio with a small stock of goods in a one horse wagon, from the sale of which he paid his expenses as he went along. He arrived in Tiffin on the 5th day of May, in the same year, and was first employed as clerk in the recorder's office at fifty cents per day, boarding himself. Soon after he entered the store of John Park as clerk, where he received ten dollars per month and boarding. The old settlers will remember the two-story brick building, fronting west, that stood on the corner of Washington and Market streets, where the National Exchange bank now stands; that was Park's store. During the time Mr. Hall was clerk for Mr. Park, he was appointed clerk of the supreme court of Seneca county and of the court of common pleas *pro tem.*, to which position he was appointed first as deputy in 1833, and permanently in 1834, May 5th. In 1835 he, in company with Josiah Hedges, engaged in the mercantile business, which was carried on until 1837, when the financial storm induced them to discontinue the business. The stock was closed out, the good debts collected, and liabilities paid. There were many losses from bad debts, but something was left when the final settlement was made. While Mr. Hall was clerk of the courts he read law with Mr. Rawson, when in the fall of 1840 he entered the Cincinnati Law college and graduated in 1841. In the same year he resigned the office of clerk of the courts, and entered upon the practice of his profession, and in which he is still engaged. In 1856 he was elected prosecuting attorney of Seneca county. In 1858, at the expiration of his office, he formed a copartnership with Mr. John H. Pittenger, of Tiffin. The firm of Hall and Pittenger is still doing business, and is the oldest law firm in the county.

In 1862 Mr. Hall was appointed assessor of the revenues, by Mr. Lincoln, for the ninth district of Ohio. This office he held until he was removed by President Johnson in 1865. In 1868 he was the presidential elector for the ninth district of Ohio, and cast his vote in the electoral college for Grant and Colfax. In 1867 he was one of the incorporators of the Toledo, Tiffin and Eastern railroad, and was elected president of the company, and served in that capacity until the road was completed, contributing largely to the success of the enterprise.

Mr. Hall was married to Miss Cynthia A., daughter of Josiah Hedges, on the 7th day of April, 1835. He is the father of four sons, who are all still living.

Mr. Hall is a little below medium size in stature, weighs about 135 pounds; he has a heavy head of sandy hair and sandy beard, now beginning to show the effects of many frosts; prominent nose, large blue eye, regular features, and a clear melodious voice. He is a careful pleader and a close reasoner. A lawyer of the old school, and loves the code, because—because it is the code.

[NOTE.—June 16, 1880—Mr. Hall died this afternoon at two o'clock, aged sixty-six years, ten months and sixteen days.

When the foregoing sketch of his life was written, Mr. Hall was in the full enjoyment of his health, as usual. He was never a very stout, robust man, but always was well enough to be about his business. During the last winter and spring especially, he seemed to enjoy better health than for many years. He attended court, which is now in session, every day, until last Saturday, and but very few members of the bar knew that he was complaining. When the news of his death reached the court room, there was a silence in court, a sadness imprinted on every countenance, a scene the like of which the writer had never experienced in the court room, where for forty years he attended every session.

Friend Hall took great interest in the production of this book, and assisted me very much with his clear recollection of past events, and his fluent and forcible way of relating them. He is gone, and another tie of friendship that has lasted forty-seven years is broken; an old heart left to mourn.]

OLIVER COWDERY.

Near the end of the Mormon Bible is added the testimony of Oliver Cowdery as to the "Golden Plates."

He was one of the brightest minds amongst the leaders of the Mormons, and the history of the order would have been a better one had his counsel and advice prevailed.

Mr. Cowdery was born in the state of Vermont, on the 3d day of October, 1804. After he had acquired a good common school education, he applied himself with great industry to the study of the dead languages and became very proficient in the Greek and Chaldee. He came to Ohio when he was a young man and entered the law office of Judge Bissel, a very distinguished lawyer in Painesville, Lake county, as a student, and was admitted to practice after having read the requisite length of time and passed an examination. His unfortunate association with the Mormons blasted the high hopes and bright prospects of an otherwise promising career, and planted a thousand thorns along the wayside of a life that was as pure and undefiled as that of the best of men. Cowdery had more to do with the production of the Mormon Bible than its history had ever given him credit for. He was the best scholar among the leaders. While others advocated the doctrine of polygamy, Cowdery opposed it, not only on moral grounds, but also, and principally because it was contrary to the great principles of christianity, and above all, because it was opposed not only to the great demands of civilization but to the spirit of the free institutions of our country. This opposition to polygamy brought Cowdery into conflict with the other leaders, and especially with Joe Smith; and while Cowdery gathered around himself the better and most intellectual element among the Mormons, Joe Smith became the leader of the coarser forces, with whom his great force of character soon made him very popular. The conflict came and Cowdery had to flee for his life, leaving his wife and two children behind him. Mrs. Cowdery's maiden name was Whitmer, and a sister of one of the Whitmer's who figured as a leader. She was a beautiful woman, whose quiet nature, sweet temper and kind disposition won her friends wherever she was known.

Mr. Cowdery came back to Kirtland. In the spring of 1840, on the 12th day of May, he addressed a large Democratic gathering in the street, between the German Reformed church of Tiffin and the present residence of Hez. Graff. He was then on a tour of exploration for a location to pursue his profession as a lawyer, having entirely abandoned and broken away from all his connections with the Mormons. In the fall of the same year he moved with his family to Tiffin and opened a law office on Market street.

Mr. Cowdery was an able lawyer and a great advocate. His manners were easy and gentlemanly; he was polite, dignified, yet courteous. He had an open countenance, high forehead, dark brown eye, Roman nose, clenched lips and prominent lower jaw. He shaved smooth and was neat and cleanly in his person. He was of light stature, about five feet, five inches high, and had a loose, easy walk. With all his kind and friendly disposition, there was a certain degree of sadness that seemed to pervade his whole being. His association with others was marked by the great amount of information his conversation conveyed and the beauty of his musical voice. His addresses to the court and jury were characterized by a high order of oratory, with brilliant and forensic force. He was modest and reserved, never spoke ill of any one, never complained.

He left Tiffin with his family for Elkhorn, in Wisconsin, in 1847, where he remained but a short time, and then moved to Missouri, where he died in 1848.

The writer read law with Mr. Cowdery in Tiffin, and was intimately acquainted with him, from the time he came here until he left, which afforded me every opportunity to study and love his noble and true manhood.

CHAPTER XXIII.

THE BENCH AND BAR CONTINUED.

SIDNEY SEA.

THE subject of this sketch was the most remarkable character that was ever associated with the Tiffin bar. He was unlike other lawyers in almost every thing, and seemed to avoid assimilation on purpose. In 1833 he had his office in the frame building on the south side of Market street, on in-lot No. 71, now occupied as a saloon. When the writer became acquainted with him he was known by the name of Sidney Smith. It is said that he was a graduate of the New Haven Law school, and that formerly he was a shoemaker by trade. He was married when he moved from Portage county to Tiffin, in 1832, and very soon secured a very good practice. He bought a farm in Scipio township, and laid out the larger portion of Republic. In June, 1836, he published a notice in the *Tiffin Gazette*, that he would sell his lots in Republic, a valuable farm close by, another farm six miles from Tiffin, and one and one-half lots between the court house and the free bridge, because he wanted to go to some southern latitude.

Two years thereafter he gave notice that he had left his property in the hands of Mr. Chapin to sell for him, and moved to Cincinnati, where he opened a law office. It is said that he there wore his pants in his boots. The boots had large red tops, on which were painted in gilt letters, "Sidney Smith, attorney-at-law."

About the latter part of 1840 he came back to Republic and opened a law office again in the name of Smith. He took a very active part in the presidential campaign, and made the first speech when the Whigs raised their log cabin on the lot where the Commercial bank now stands. In his political harangue on that day he was exceedingly personal and bitter. This was on the 3d day of June, 1840. He made many more speeches throughout Seneca county that summer and fall, but became so boisterous and abusive that the Whig central committee finally refused to make any further appointments for him.

The Whigs carried the day, as is well known, and whatever may have been the moving cause, other than that expressed in the petition itself, when the legislature met in Columbus, the following December, Mr Smith sent a petition to that body, praying for the passage of a law to change his name from Sidney Smith to Sidney Sea. The petition was all poetry, of his own manufacture, and being so utterly void of all reason, it was defeated in the senate, and on the 15th of January, 1841, on motion of Senator Hasletine, it was reconsidered, laid on the table, and finally passed on the 16th day of March, 1841.

The reason assigned in this poetic petition by Mr. Smith was: "That when Adam stood up in Paradise in obedience with the command of the Creator, to name all things, and all the living things had passed before Him receiving names in order, it got to be late in the afternoon, and poor Adam's vocabulary failed to hold out. Then Adam held his hands up to shade his eyes, and saw in a corner of the garden an infamously looking mob of humanity. He called them up, looked at them awhile, and being half angry and half provoked, called them all Smith." He wanted to get away from that crowd, he said, and the general assembly let him out.

About two years thereafter he was made brigadier general of this brigade, and when in uniform and on a fine horse, he was in his true element. The writer has seen large portions of the army of Bavaria and France, and many soldiers in this country, but never a man that looked more furious and brave on a horse than General Sea (as we shall now call him). He was indeed valliant as long as he was not opposed by anybody, but "caved in" when confronted; his acts often bordering on cowardice.

About this time an independent company, called Osceolas, had been organized in Tiffin, and by the kindness of General Nighswander, O. M. General of Ohio, had procured flint-lock rifles, with which they appeared on parade from time to time. It seems that General Sea and others had made efforts to procure arms for the several militia companies in this county and failed. Now to see these Osceolas parade the streets in Tiffin with their clean guns, and General Sea's men attend muster without arms, was too much for the General, and his poetic genius again took possession of him. One morning a lot of posters were stuck up all over Tiffin and copies sent all over the county calling a meeting of the " Grand Militaire" of the county at Tiffin, as follows:

ATTENTION
MILITARY MEN OF SENECA COUNTY!
INJUSTICE IN THE CAMP!
EVERY MAN TO HIS POST!

Blow ye the trumpet, blow, and sound the drum,
Send round the hand-bills, let the freemen come;
For equal rights the standard let us raise,
And let the Tiffin Junto foam and gaze.
Eight companies have we, old, faithful and true,
Whose rights are trampled on to bless the new.
Your old and patient prayers thrown in your face,
And Oceolas born to partial grace.
The quartermaster deals you pelting storms,
But takes the Oceolas to his arms;
He gives them guns, the brightest and the best,
Let's your old beards petition and be cursed.
Here, you can see, the Tiffin Junto reigns,
While you submit to penalties and pains.
Shall Oceolas flaunt their glittering steel,
And can the older brothers fail to feel?
Behold their sheen displaying to the sun,
And trudge your sober face and wooden gun.
Hear ye, brave spirits of our fathers gone,
And let your children put their reason on.
High soars the eagle out of mortal sight,
But why should justice tower a greater height?
The eagle sometimes stoops to mortal kin,
Then why not justice sometimes dwell with man.

If you arise and meet in Tiffin, on Saturday, the 14th inst., at 10 o'clock precisely, and peaceably, with united voice, proclaim your wrongs to the legislature, I think you may procure your rights, and arms enough of different description to make our brigade respectable, and I promise my feeble aid on the side of impartial justice. Why should a miserable faction rule the whole county? I hope and trust that our well-beloved brethren, the Oceolas, when they find that their older brothers are men, too, will be more anxious to give justice than to take wrong.

You've set me as a watchman on the wall. I see the poison hissing in the camp. I blow the horn. Let's peaceably extract the venomous teeth and let the reptiles live. SIDNEY SEA,
Brigadier General.

Let us all come up to the meeting and investigate the whole affair.
                    ASA WAY, Colonel.
                    G. M. OGDEN, Lieutenant Colonel,
                    HENRY METZGER, Adjutant,
                    JOSIAH ROOP, Quartermaster,
                    E. T. STICKNEY, Captain,
                    D. METZGER, Captain,
                    J. S. SPARKS, Captain,
                    PAUL DEWITT, 1st Lieutenant,
                    W. BURROWS, 2d Lieutenant.
REPUBLIC, January 3, 1843.

These indorsers all lived in Republic, or near by, and were easily induced to sign anything against Tiffin. After the burning of the court house, great efforts were made to remove the county seat to Republic, and build a new court house there, but they failed, and the grudge had not died away yet. The Tiffin Junto was nothing but the little independent military company, the most of whom lived in the country. These "reptiles" wronged nobody when they secured guns for themselves.

The meeting came off in the little old school house on Market street. The Osceolas were there in full force, and but few of the militia. General Sea came in, and taking the chair, called the meeting to order, and administered one of his usual reprimands to the Osceolas for not taking their turbans off. Colonel Gibson, who was invited to attend by Captain Poorman, of the Osceolas, being present, and the writer, who procured the guns, having explained to the meeting the manner of our organization, and the mode of procuring our guns, the meeting adjourned and

"The Duke of Brunswick, with his mighty men,
Marched up the hill and—then marched down again."

It is probable that the quartermaster-general of Ohio demanded security for arms that were distributed among the militia.

On one of the September muster-days, the "grand army" was drawn up in line from the river to Madison street, on Washington street, facing to the east. General Sea was on his high horse, in full uniform, and in his glory. George W. Black had a bakery and small beer-shop, nearly opposite the National hall. While the General was up street, a man slipped out of the ranks into Black's, and, securing a section of ginger cake, stepped into line again. Now came the General in full gallop, with his feathers flying in air and the yellow cuffs of his gloves up to his elbow, and noticing the man with his big ginger cake, stopped short, wheeled his horse facing the men, and shouted, "Attention! Great God! Look at this! A free born American citizen soldier, in the service of his country, eating ginger bread in the ranks!" The man wilted.

About the year 1843 General Sea left Republic and moved to Tiffin again, when he and Mr. L. A. Hall became partners in the law firm of Hall & Sea. They soon had a large practice, and while Sea was the better advocate, Hall was the better pleader. Mr. Sea's striking appearance and forcible address gave him great influence with a jury. He was quick and ready to catch a point, and unsparing in pressing it. This partnership lasted only about two years, and both continued in the practice in Tiffin.

General Sea was ambitious and used all the means at his command to get General John Bell, of Lower Sandusky, who was major-general of the 17th division O. M., out of office, with a view of filling it himself. General Bell was a most estimable gentleman and highly esteemed citizen, but he sometimes appeared on parade with a straw hat on his head; put on no style, and in 1838, while the Canadian or patriot war was raging, a lot of arms were stolen out of General Bell's warehouse, in Lower Sandusky. These two circumstances served General Sea's purpose, and he drew up charges against General Bell for the purpose of having him tried and court-martialed. He had his law partner, Mr. Hall, to copy the charges, and they were sent to Governor Shannon. Governor Shannon thereupon caused the following order to be issued, which convened the most distinguished, august and talented military men that ever formed a court-martial in Ohio, viz:

ADJUTANT GENERAL'S OFFICE.
COLUMBUS, OHIO, February 3, 1844.

A court-martial, to consist of seven persons, will assemble at the city of Columbus, state of Ohio, on Monday, the 19th inst., at 10 o'clock A. M., for the hearing and determining of charges preferred against Major-General John Bell, of the 17th division of Ohio militia.

The court will consist of:
Major-General John Snider, of the 1st division, president.
Major-General C. B. Goddard, of the 15th division, judge advocate.
Major-General George Rowe, of the 13th division.
Brigadier-General M. S. Wade, of the 3d brigade, 1st division.
Brigadier-General George Gephart, of the 7th division.
Brigadier-General Thomas Stockton; of the 2d brigade, 7th division.
Brigadier-General Sidney Sea, of the 17th division.
General W. F. Sanderson, provost marshal.
William Lang, Esq., assistant marshal.

By order of
E. GALE,
Adjutant-General.

WILSON SHANNON,
Commander-in-Chief Ohio Militia.

At the trial, which was held in the old United States court room, the Hon. Gustavus Swan, as counsel for General Bell, objected to General

Sea, and alleged that Sea himself had drawn up the charges and was therefore disqualified to sit and try the case. Witnesses were examined and the facts clearly established. Mr. L. A. Hall testified that General Sea had drawn the charges, and he (Hall) had copied them. The court, upon deliberation without Sea, decided that he could not sit. On the meeting of the court after dinner, this fact was made known to General Sea by the president, and he was politely requested to withdraw, but there he sat and allowed himself to be invited to leave the second time. He still refused to go, when General Goddard ordered the writer to take General Sea out of the room instanter. The order was obeyed slowly and reluctantly by both of us.

No matter what became of the case. It is referred to here only to show the shrewdness and head-strong, stubborn character of General Sea.

Suffice it to say that General Bell had to pay a fine for allowing the arms to be stolen from him.

Now General Sea was alone in the practice, and Mr. Jeremiah Carpenter, of Venice township, having an estate coming to him in Kentucky, employed the General to collect it for him. The General went to Kentucky, and after an absence of several months, returned with a beautiful horse he called Mazeppa. Mr. Carpenter claimed that he did not get all of the estate that was coming to him, and brought suit against General Sea. A long, sad, costly and angry litigation followed. Carpenter obtained judgment against Sea, and for want of goods and chattels, a writ of *ne exeat* was sued out, and under which General Sea refused to give security, simply that he would not leave the county, and preferred to go to jail. Whether the proceedings were right or wrong will not be discussed; but the case excited general notice and was the theme of gossip a long time.

While here in jail, General Sea, who always was a very voluminous pleader, prepared a petition against Judge Bowen and the associate judges for false imprisonment. It covered about two reams of paper, written on both sides. Judge Bowen offered $100 to any person that would make for him a copy of it. The case was never tried.

After he had lain in the stone jail some three months or more, Messrs. R. G. Pennington and Oliver Cowdery, as the attorneys of General Sea, applied to Judge Reuben Wood, of the supreme court, for a writ of *habeas corpus* to get the General out of jail. The writ was issued and Judge Wood came from Cleveland to Tiffin to hear the case on the 5th day of February, 1847. General Sea was discharged. This was the last official act of Judge Wood, for his term expired on the next day. The court house was crowded to overflowing during the trial, and on the following night the brass band, with a large crowd of citizens, gave General Sea a serenade. Much sympathy was enlisted in his favor by this time.

In 1848 General Sea, with his family, moved to Milwaukee, Wisconsin, since which time the writer has heard but little of him.

He was a most wonderful combination of mental force; shrewd, cunning, able, reckless, daring, crouching, vindictive, ambitious. An able orator, a forcible advocate, but unsocial and cold. He was reckless in his adventures, as well as in the abandonment of a good purpose.

"Pity he loved an adventurous life's variety,
He was so great a loss to good society."

COOPER K. WATSON.

In the fall of 1879, while Judge Watson was visiting his daughter, Mrs. John D. Loomis, at Tiffin, he promised to write a short sketch of his life for publication in this book, but being very closely occupied on the bench and his health failing, the promise was never complied with. The following is from the *Tiffin Tribune* of May 27th, 1880, and while it is very incomplete, it is perhaps the best that can now be obtained as a substitute for a sketch of his life:

Cooper K. Watson died in Sandusky, Ohio, Thursday, May 20th, 1880, aged about seventy years, after an illness of several weeks. We take from the *Sandusky Register* the following obituary, and desire to add, that after he moved to Norwalk, he was elected a member of the constitutional convention:

"The deceased jurist was born in Jefferson county, Kentucky, on the 18th day of June, 1810, and was therefore a month of reaching the full allotted measure of man's life. In boyhood he was apprenticed to a merchant tailor, and worked at his trade a short time.

He turned his attention, however, to the law, soon after reaching manhood. He began his study at Newark, and was admitted to the bar at Columbus. He practiced at Newark for two years, then moved to Delaware, where he remained four years; then went to Marion, where he lived five years, four of which he served as prosecutor of the county. He then moved to Fremont, where he lived eight years. While a resident of Fremont he became an intimate friend of the late Sardis Berchard, an uncle and patron of President R. B. Hayes.

About 1850 he took up his residence at Tiffin, and in 1854 was the Free Soil (K. N.) candidate for Congress, and was elected. He entered the house of representatives with John Sherman, and soon took rank as an ardent friend of liberty, and an uncompromising foe of the slave power. He was not re-elected, and at the close of his term returned to the practice of the law.

In 1870 he moved to Norwalk, where he remained until he made this city his home in 1874.

Although he changed his place of residence several times, he always took the front rank at the bar, and secured not only an extensive acquaintance in the central part of the state, but a wide reputation as an able and successful lawyer, his practice extending throughout central and western Ohio and into the district and supreme courts.

Before a jury he was clear, positive and convincing, and in the examination of witnesses, more especially in criminal cases, he was singularly successful; to cross-examine medical experts was his special delight, and few of them but left his hands with the disagreeable conviction that the lawyer knew more than the doctor.

In the practice of the law he was rigidly honest, far above the small tricks of the profession, and free from the vices by which lawyers gain a cheap notoriety and pile up money. Personally he was warm in his friendship, sociable and companionable with his friends, and tolerant of honest differences of opinion in religion or politics. He was sincere himself, and admired sincerity in others, and his earnestness in this regard led him to abhor shams and despise humbugs.

When in the full vigor of his mental powers he was a strong man on the bench, and had he been elevated to the bench twenty-five years ago instead of being sent to congress, he would unquestionably have attained the highest judicial honors.

In one aspect his career was a happy example to young members of the bar. While he had great natural abilities, the real secret of his success was his devotion to his books. He read constantly, patiently and understandly, and his law library is by far the largest and most complete in this section of the state.

He was greatly admired by such men as Judge Raney, Judge White and Judge Welch, and had a very warm personal friend in General Hayes, who, as governor of the state, appointed him judge to fill the vacancy caused by the death of Judge Lane.

In 1830 he married Miss Caroline S. Durkee, of Zanesville, who survives him. He leaves four children: Mrs. Eleanor Loomis, of Tiffin; Mrs. Caroline Willard, of Monroe, Michigan; Mrs. Nettie Gilbert, and Charles B. Watson."

JOSEPH HOWARD

Was one of the pioneer lawyers of Tiffin. He was a fair pleader, but no advocate; more politician than lawyer. He was a very gentlemanly man and always dressed neatly. There was a great deal of what was then called "aristocracy" about his house. When, in 1830, the judges of the court appointed him clerk, Mr. Neil McGaffey, his predecessor, was so much surprised at the change that he sued out a writ of *quo warranto* against Mr. Howard, but the case was never tried, and Mr. Howard officiated as clerk some four years. Under the administration of President Taylor he secured a clerkship in some department in Washington city, where he died.

ROBERT G. PENNINGTON,

One of the oldest lawyers in Tiffin, was born in Delaware county, Pennsylvania, in December, 1816, of Quaker parents, Joseph and Sarah Pennington, who were also natives of the same state. He was a descendant of Isaac Pennington, of Chalfort, England, who, with George Fox, Thomas Elwood, Robert Barclay and William Penn founded the Society of Friends, in England, about the middle of the sixteenth century.

One of Isaac's daughters, Gulielma, was the wife of William Penn, and his son, Edward Pennington, came with him to America and married the daughter of Samuel Jennings, the then governor of New Jersey, and from whom the Penningtons, of Pennsylvania and New Jersey, were descended.

In 1825 Joseph Pennington and family removed to Cayuga county, New York, where they lived until the spring of 1834, when they started for the west, expecting to purchase land and settle in the reservation in this county. They came to Buffalo by the New York and Erie canal and then up the lake in the old steamboat Enterprise, landing at Huron, thence by wagons to Tiffin, arriving on the 24th of May. The cholera breaking out in town, the people chiefly scattered to the country, and the Pennington family took up quarters in the southeast corner of Clinton township, where Joseph Pennington soon after bought a new farm, but subsequently purchased other lands and settled in Bloom township, where the family resided many years.

In 1837 Robert G. Pennington entered the Huron Institute, at Milan, Ohio, and after completing an academic course there, in the fall of 1839 began the study of law with Abel Rawson, Esq., then the principal lawyer in the county, having for a room-mate and fellow-student, John K. Gibson, a brilliant, noble young man, who died in 1841, before admission to the bar.

Mr. R. G. Pennington was admitted to the bar in the spring of 1842, at Columbus, Ohio, in a class with Jesse Stem, Edward Smith, Homer Everett and Geo. W. Thompson, and commenced and continued the partnership with Mr. Rawson until the latter retired from active business.

In February, 1842, Mr. Pennington married Caroline C. Kuhn, daughter of Captain Joseph L. Kuhn, late of the United States navy, and grand daughter of Lewis Chadwick Hargrace, British consul general of the Balearic island, belonging to Spain, and who was born at Port Mahon, on the island Menerca, one of the group, in 1821.

Three daughters are the fruit of this union: Eugenia Hargrace, wife of Almon Hall, Esq., of Toledo, Ohio; Caroline C., wife of Hon. W. R. Steele, of Wyoming territory, and Louisa Annette, the youngest.

Mr. Pennington has resided in Tiffin for forty years, and has directed his time and energies chiefly to his profession, yet, in the meantime, has given much of his means and attention to enterprises useful to the growth and prosperity of Tiffin. Amongst these are railroads, banks, and manufacturing interests, in which he was largely interested as stockholder. In 1847, with Benjamin Tomb and others, he organized the Seneca county bank, the first bank in the county, and was its first cashier. He also, with Edward Gywn, organized and put into operation the Gas Light Company of Tiffin, and for seven years was its president.

In 1856 he was the presidential elector for this congressional district, and took an active part on the stump in the canvass and cast his vote for J. C. Fremont for president.

He was from time to time candidate of his party for several places of trust and honor, amongst which were those of representative for the state legislature and member of the late constitutional convention. In all these cases he was unable to overcome the large Democratic majorities in the county and district.

In 1861, at the breaking out of the war, he took a deep and active interest in the perils that threatened the life of the nation, and with Colonel Lee, Major Dewalt, organized the 55th regiment O. V. I., and accompanied the regiment to the field as its quartermaster. In 1862 he was made adjutant general on the staff of General McLean, and after a service of two years, resigned on account of lameness and ill health. He returned to his profession, banking and manufacturing, suffering very severely in his finances by the revulsions during the last few years.

As a lawyer he is a better pleader than advocate. He is industrious, gentlemanly and polite, courteous and friendly. Aside from his legal and business qualifications, he is a great student of the popular sciences of the day, a clear thinker and profound reasoner on every subject he ever investigated. His friendship is warm and lasting, and the great beauty of his "make up" is the fact that he is always the same, to himself as well as to others.

GEORGE E. SENEY

Was born in Uniontown, Fayette county, Pennsylvania, May 29, 1831. He is the oldest son of Joshua Seney, a short sketch of whose life elsewhere. He graduated at the Norwalk seminary, read law in the office of L. A. Hall, and was admitted to practice in 1852. In 1857 he was elected judge of the court of common pleas. In 1858 the office of district attorney of the United States was tendered him, which he declined. He was the quartermaster of the 101st regiment O. V. I., and after serving two years returned to his profession. In 1874 he was the Democratic candidate for congress in this district and was beaten by only 139 votes. He was a delegate to the Democratic national convention at St. Louis. He is the author of "Seney's Code," and is a successful practitioner and an able and forcible advocate.

My venerable and distinguished old friend, the Hon. James Purdy, the veteran lawyer of Mansfield, Ohio, who is the only survivor of that pioneer band of lawyers that attended the sittings of the first courts in Seneca county, was kind enough to furnish the writer a few anecdotes and descriptions of a few scenes in connection with the practice in those early days, but it took some urging to induce Major Purdy (as he is familiarly called) to do so. Finally he penned, for the use of the writer, the following:

MANSFIELD, May 1. 1880.
W. Lang, Esq.:

DEAR SIR—At the age of 87 I retain vividly in my memory amusing anecdotes of the bar in those early days, a few specimens of which I give, that you may, if you desire, incorporate in proper language in your history of Seneca county.

In those days each circuit had a president judge—a lawyer—and in each county there were three associate judges—country gentlemen. The lawyers called this the "Demarara team." A sailor was fined, and as he stepped up to the clerk to pay, said he hoped the Demarara team was now satisfied. He was asked to explain, when he said: "In the Island of Demarara a team is composed of three mules and a jackass."

Some of the members of the bar traveled the circuit with the judge. This, the second circuit, was composed of the counties of Richland, Huron, Sandusky, Seneca, Crawford, Marion and Wood, the latter being organized in the winter of 1823-4. The members of the bar that traveled with Judge Lane were: Parish, of Columbus, Purdy, Parker, May and Coffinberry, of Mansfield, and Bolt, of Norwalk. All these practiced in Seneca county. The two first named handled the whole circuit, except Wood county, which was then inaccessible on horseback a great portion of the year. That county was reached by the members of the bar of Norwalk by sail-boats from Sandusky City. These circuitizers were called "Judge Lane's gang." They traveled on horseback, and in the spring term had muddy roads and deep streams to ford, sometimes nearly covering their horses, often affording amusing incidents. Coffinberry, May, Parker and myself left Tiffin for New Haven one day on the then traveled road. Two well-to-do farmers on that road had a suit tried at that term, Purdy for plaintiff and Coffinberry for the defendant. Contrary to his usual practice, Coffinberry abused the plaintiff personally. Six miles out they found a branch of Rocky creek more than mid-side deep to their horses and overflowing its banks. Coffinberry having been a sailor in his day, deemed it prudent to head up stream, and making allowance for lee-way, got out of the road and ran his horse against a tissue which was covered with water; his horse, "Old Tom," fell, the girt broke, rider, saddle and saddle-bags went over his head into the water. He got out as best he could and the journey was resumed. We reached the main stream, which was considered too deep to venture across that day. Here the plaintiff resided. In sight on the other side was the residence of the defendant. The gang determined to ask the hospitality of the plaintiff, but Coffinberry vehemently protested. Judge Clark, the plaintiff, most cheerfully received us, took Coffinberry into a room and gave him a suit of dry clothes, treating him more kindly than the rest of us, and would not permit him to apologize.

They left Tiffin for Norwalk on Sunday morning with Judge Lane, and reached "Strong's ridge" and "Strong's tavern," tired, hungry and thirsty. The family was absent, and the house closed. They went to the barn, where they found oats and fed their horses. Then they got into the house and into Aunt Molly's cupboard, where they found plenty of good, fresh-baked bread, biscuits, pies and all necessary accompaniments for a good dinner, of which they heartily partook. The bar was locked also, but the contents of a bottle that had the appearance of brandy attracted their attention. With the tongs, through a hole in the window, they caught the decanter by the nozzle and pulled it to the opening, where the thirsty customers were accommodated. It was emptied. Leaving in the bar double the amount of the usual charge, they closed the house. mounted and left. They soon met Mr. Strong and lady coming from church with quite a number of friends to partake of Aunt Molly's nice dinner, which they had just consumed. They left the Judge to apologize as best he could and went on their way.

Fort Ball, on the west side of the river, had been an applicant for the county seat and failed ; consequently there were frequent controversies between citizens of the two places. Mr. Hedges bought Fort Ball and combined their interests. A log jail was built in Tiffin, in which was left a very heavy piece of timber, hewed. The proprietor of Fort Ball was a tall, handsome man, and full of mettle. Parish had been his attorney. One day during a term of court, Parish commenced a suit against him for fees, and had him imprisoned. He raised the heavy timber, smashed the door to pieces, and made his way down street. Parish saw him and asked him how he got out of prison. He answered. "I took myself out on a writ of *habeas corpus.*" Parish, learning the facts, dismissed the suit and forgave the debt.

Members of the bar played cards at night for small sums of money, and sometimes were indicted for the same. One morning in court a jury was sworn to try a case in which Parish was of counsel. The prosecuting attorney, Mr. Sea, interrupted business and asked leave to arraign a person then in court, against whom an indictment had just been found. Leave was granted. He called Mr. Parish to stand up, and read to him an indictment containing two counts for gambling with cards. Parish promptly responded to one count, which he said was a gentleman's game, and plead guilty. To the other he plead "not guilty," and said, "that d—d shoemaker's game, I never play." (Sea formerly was a shoemaker by trade.)

J. Boyd, a farmer and early pioneer on Honey creek, boxed a young fellow's ears at a log rolling, for which he was indicted. William Clark, also an early pioneer and a farmer, had an old fashioned fisticuff with a neighbor, for which he was indicted also. Their trials came on at the same term; each determined to defend himself. Mr. Boyd's case was first heard. The witnesses were examined and the prosecuting attorney addressed the jury. Uncle Jimmy, although a very intelligent man, found himself very much embarrassed in examining the witnesses, and his speech in defence was a failure. He sat down discomfited. O. Parish volunteered to reply on behalf of the state, and scared him severely. He was found guilty and fined $5.00, the ordinary charge in such cases at that time.

Uncle Billy was intelligent and had practiced in justice's courts, besides he was naturally shrewd. His case came on. In examining the witnesses he did well. The prosecuting attorney made a short speech intending to give Parish full space to reply to Uncle Billy. The judge said, " Mr. Clark, do you wish to address the jury?" Having the fear of Parish before his eyes, he answered: "No, your Honor, that little speech is not worthy of an answer." Parish was disappointed, being cut off in this manner.

A large portion of the early pioneers of Seneca county emigrated from New York. In that state grand jurors receive no pay. The sheriff selected them from the most independent free-holders, who could afford to spend their time and money. They organized and adopted certain rules for their government. For absence at roll call they were fined a bottle of brandy. The Seneca county grand jury adopted the same rule, and the full bottle was always on the table. Judge Lane was notified of the rule, gave the grand jury a blowing up, ordered its repeal, and the practice discontinued.

Now these things were quite amusing to us, but whether the present generation will take any interest in them is for you to judge.

Very respectfully yours, etc..

J. PURDY.

Another case, in fact, one of the first jury cases in our common pleas court, should also be remembered. It was the case of Bennett against Knight for false imprisonment. The plaintiff had been arraigned before Knight as a justice of the peace, for stealing calves, and was by him sent to prison. Parish for plaintiff, Purdy for defendant. In his argument, Parish regretted that he had claimed in his declaration but $500. The small room in which court was held was densely crowded. A wag called out, " If the Bennetts can make $500 stealing calves they had better quit the hog business." The judge could not find the disturber in the crowd, and the contempt of court was necessarily left unpunished.

About two months before the death of Mr. Rawson, he visited the writer and requested him to insert in the history of Seneca county— if he should ever write one—the writer's response to a toast at a bar meeting, held in the Shawhan House, on the evening of the 30th of November, 1855. The meeting was an exceedingly pleasant affair. There is no merit in the poetry, and nothing but my respect for Mr. Rawson's request can apologize for the room it takes here.

[From the Tiffin Tribune of December 28, 1855.]

"THE TIFFIN BAR."

The above toast, read at the lawyer's festival, on the evening of the 30th, and assigned to Judge William Lang, called out the following poetical *jeu d'esprit* from the Judge:

When vulgar minds with epithets have done,
And spent on us their last of common fun;
When poets, statesmen, warriors, one and all,
Have run their course on this terrestrial ball,
The fame of Tiffin's green bag knights shall stand,
Comparing well with any in the land.
There's John J. Steiner, and our brother Scott,
The former now enjoys a farmer's lot,
The latter, charmed by Kate and Cupid's tune,
Has left the earth and moved to honeymoon,
Because, for law he never cared a feather,
So off he went with love, shoes, boots and leather.
Whenever ye in business counsel need,
Or need another in your cause to plead,
And ye in custody, and charged with crime,
And ye whose creditors no prose or rhyme
Can soothe;—and ye whose debtors stubborn be,
(Provided you always come with a fee,)
Here Rawson lives, and Watson, Pillars, too,
Johnson and Stem, Hall, Seney, Lamareaux;
Noble, Cronise, Dildine, Griffith, Ike,
Say nothing of the self-made lawyer Pike;
Here's Wilson, who once prosecutor, late,
Was chosen our own senator of state;
And he who much abounds in words and fun,
Of ready action, T. C. Tunison;
Here's Johnny Payne, the man who, by-the-by—
Was representative—near six feet high;
And Landon, Lee, who always for a song
Will make wrong right, and change right into wrong;
Omnipotent John Smith, and Stickney, Way,
Pittenger, Martin, Hedges, who, they say,
Has left the law—the higher, nobler rank,
And gone astray, with money—into bank.
Patterson, Birnside, at last, not least,
There's no such man as Welch, from west to east!
While on the bench of people's probate court,

Sits our esteemed and worthy John K. Hord;
Robert G. Pennington, poor fellow, gone
To see the railroad matters all alone;
And Gibson—so agreed among the gods,
Is treasurer of state by many odds.

Let satire scoff, and wicked critics frown,
There's no such galaxy from congress down!
Represented well in every station,
Look first to the counsel of the nation,
Then to the officers of state—then see
The senate's chairman—one of us was he;
And in the lower house, our Noble sat,
While we at home supplied the bench at that;
Made school directors, and encouraged science,
Turned stumpers and set statesmen at defiance;
Practiced philanthropy in christian meekness,
Made money, too, from other people's weakness,
Attended fairs and studied agriculture,
In short, watched everything from pink to vulture.

So onward, brethren, let us stand together,
In fortune's rays; in adverse, stormy weather;
Now push about the social flowing bowl,
Drink lusty draughts, fraternal flow of soul,
And may he now, and ever be a beast,
Who feels no joy in this fraternal feast.
And one and all, take counsel, be advised,
By no temptation let us be enticed
To lose the secret of this earthly life,
So full of blessings, full of peace and strife;
May each and every noble, honest heart
Be truly man, and bravely act his part;
And when we've finished every case below,
When nature's law shall bid us hence to go,
To meet the Judge of nations at the bar
Of His tribunal in the world afar;
May each in peace, prepared to close the race,
Make out himself a good, conclusive case.

The name of every lawyer then in Seneca county is here given, except the writer's.

WARREN PERRY NOBLE

Was born in Luzerne county, Pennsylvania, June 14, 1820. His father's name was William Noble, and his mother's maiden name Rebecca Lytle. The parents moved to Wayne county, Ohio, when they had three little children, and located in Salt Creek township, some ten miles east of Wooster. In 1834 the family moved to Medina county, where father Noble had bought a farm. He lived there years, when he sold the farm, and taking with him his oldest son, came to Jackson township, where he had previously entered 120 acres, and built a small cabin upon it. Then he returned for the family and brought them here in 1836. The cabin proved to be too small for so large a family, and some of the boys had to sleep in the wagons until another adjoining cabin could be constructed. By this time they had nine sons and one daughter. The daughter, Mary, is the wife of Mr. Histe, one of the present county commissioners. Of the sons but four are still living: the subject of this sketch, Warren Perry Noble, Harrison Noble, the present mayor of Tiffin, Captain Montgomery Noble, and John Noble, clerk of the court in Clay county, Kansas.

Warren P. lived with his father on the farm, and as he grew up to boyhood, received such school education as the country afforded ; but nature had endowed him with a good physique, with a more than average amount of brain, and above all, with a spirit of industry and perseverance that knew no tiring. He applied himself to his books, and was soon enabled to teach school in the neighborhood of his home, embracing Fostoria. Mr. John Lawrence, Hon. Charles Foster, Rev. Jacob Caples, Junius V. Jones, were among his scholars, and others who have also become eminent in life. In February, 1842, he entered the law office of Rawson and Pennington, in Tiffin, and in 1844 was admitted to the bar. From that time to this day he has faithfully applied himself to the practice.

In 1847, on the 17th day of August, he married Mary E., oldest daughter of Mr. F. Singer, of Tiffin. Mrs. Noble died on the 9th of March, 1853, leaving Mr. Noble with three little children; two little girls and a baby boy but a few days old. He raised and educated his children, and the girls are both married. Belle is Mrs. William L. Bates, of Dayton, Ohio; Mary Ellen is Mrs. Silas W. Graff, residing at Tiffin, Ohio; Warren Frederick, the son, is a graduate of the Ohio State university, of the class of 1879, and is now reading law in his father's office.

After living the life of a widower more than seventeen years, and raising his children until they were able to take care of themselves, Mr. Noble was married to Miss Alice M. Campbell, of Tiffin, Ohio, on the 27th day of September, 1870, and two most interesting little girls are the fruit of this marriage.

In 1846 Mr. Noble was elected a member of the house of representatives of the general assembly of Ohio, and re-elected in 1847. In the fall of 1848 he was elected prosecuting attorney for Seneca county, and re-elected in 1850, serving four years, except a short time before the expiration of his term, when he resigned. In 1860 he was elected to the thirty-seventh congress over Judge Carey, the Whig candidate for his second term, and was re-elected to the thirty-eighth congress over Judge Wooster, of Norwalk, who was his colleague in the previous term, having been thrown into this district by the change of districts prior to the election. Mr. Noble was a war Democrat, and served as such during the war to March 4th, 1865.

He was one of the trustees of the Ohio state university for ten years, having been first appointed by Governor Hayes. After the death of John T. Huss and the failure of the First National bank in Tiffin, Mr. Noble was appointed as its receiver. He settled claims against the institution, amounting to $240,000, paying sixty cents on the dollar, and settled up the concern with the least litigation and in the shortest time of any bank that failed since the inauguration of the present banking system. He has been the president of the Commercial bank ever since it started, in June, 1876, and is the president also of the Tiffin Mutual Aid association, and a member of the Tiffin board of education. During the construction of the Baltimore and Ohio and the Mansfield and Cold Water railroads, he took a very active part, as he always did in all public enterprises.

Mr. Noble owes his great success in life to that indomitable industry, integrity and perseverance that have marked his whole life from his boyhood.

WILLIAM H. GIBSON

Was born in Ohio, May 16th, 1822, and soon thereafter his parents moved to Seneca county, in the same year. His paternal grandparents were from Ireland, and his maternal grandparents from Wales. He was reared on a farm on Honey creek, in Eden, and worked with his father, John Gibson, at the carpenter trade. After he had attended the common schools, he attended one year at the Ashland academy. He read law in Tiffin in the office of Rawson & Pennington, and was admitted to the bar in 1845. He was the Whig candidate for attorney general in 1853, but was defeated. He was elected treasurer of state in 1855, and resigned in 1857. He entered the army as colonel of the 49th O. V. I., in 1861, and commanded a brigade and division of the army of the Cumberland, leading his command in forty-two conflicts. He left the army with the rank of brigadier-general, and resumed the practice of the law in Tiffin. He quit the practice in 1872, and applied himself very industriously to railroad enterprises. He bore a very conspicuous part in all the political campaigns ever since the organization of the Republican party. He is an orator of no ordinary calibre, and during the past two years he preached under a license in the M. E. church. When Governor Foster was inaugurated governor of Ohio on the second Monday in January last, General Gibson was appointed adjutant-general of Ohio, which office he holds to this day.

G. B. KEPPEL

Was born May 8th, 1845, in Hopewell township, Seneca county, Ohio. He graduated at Heidelberg college in 1869; was admitted to the bar in 1871, and is now the prosecuting attorney of the county.

NELSON L. BREWER

Was born in Washington county, Maryland, September 17th, 1832; graduated at Heidelberg in 1855; was admitted to the practice in 1858, and immediately located in Tiffin.

JACOB K. HUDDLE (HOTTAL)

Was born October 8th, 1846, in Bloom township, Seneca county, Ohio. He is the seventeenth child of a family of eighteen children. He was admitted to practice law in 1871. In 1873 he edited the *Tiffin Star* with much ability. Upon the failure of this enterprise, he returned to the practice. Tracing back his family record he became satisfied that the family name is Hottal.

JOHN M'CAULEY

Was born in Columbiana county, Ohio, December 10th, 1834. He was educated at the university at Delaware, where he finished his course in 1859. He was admitted to the bar in 1860, when he located in Tiffin. He was elected prosecuting attorney in 1865, and held the office four years. He was elected a member of the late constitutional convention to fill the vacancy created by the death of Dr. O'Connor. In October, 1879, he was elected judge of the court of common pleas for this district.

JACOB BUNN

Was born June 6th, 1847, in Thompson (Seneca county). He graduated at Heidelberg college in 1870, and was admitted to the bar the year following, when he located in Tiffin. He was elected probate judge of Seneca county in the fall of 1878.

FRANK DILDINE

Was born in Tiffin, October 15th, 1849; graduated at the Tiffin high school, and afterwards attended the Ohio Wesleyan University, at Delaware, and graduated from the Heidelberg college in 1869; was admitted to the bar in 1872.

HARRISON NOBLE

Was born in Wayne county, Ohio, on the 28th of January, 1826, and was admitted to the bar in 1849, when he located in Tiffin. He was city solicitor four years, and is now the mayor of the city.

NELSON B. LUTES

Was born in Wyoming county, Pennsylvania, March 1st, 1848; came to Tiffin in 1870, and was admitted to the bar in 1872.

JOHN H. RIDGELY

Was born August 16th, 1845, in Allegheny county, Maryland. He is a graduate of Heidelberg college, and was admitted to practice law in December, 1869.

H. C. KEPPEL

Was born in Hopewell township, March 20th, 1847. He is a graduate of Heidelberg college, and was admitted to practice law in 1872, and is now of the law firm of H. C. & G. B. Kepple; was married at Indianapolis to-day, June 29th, 1880.

J. H. PITTENGER

Was born December 10th, 1828, in Frederick county, Maryland; came to Tiffin with his father's family in 1830; was admitted to practice law in 1850, and for very many years was, and now is, of the law firm of Hall & Pittenger.

RUSH ABBOTT

Was born in Seneca county, Ohio, and was admitted to practice April 12th, 1877, when he located in Tiffin.

NETTIE CRONISE AND FLORENCE CRONISE,

Sisters, and graduates of Heidelberg, natives of Tiffin, some six years ago were admitted to practice law; probably the first ladies in Ohio that entered the legal profession. They are both in the practice now. One is practicing by herself, without a partner, and the other is in partnership with another lawyer.

Among the very many remarkable things already related about Tiffin and Seneca county, the most remarkable of all is the fact, that here in Tiffin, two lawyers married each other, and are now raising two most lovely little daughters about three and four years old. Let any other town in the United States say the like.

PERRY M. ADAMS

Was born December 2, 1850, in Wood county, Ohio, read law in the office of W. P. Noble, was admitted to the bar April 13, 1876, and is now of the firm of Noble & Adams.

UPTON F. CRAMER

Was born in Clinton township, Seneca county, Ohio, January 19, 1842; graduated at Heidelberg college. He was admitted to practice law in 1867. He was elected probate judge three times, and was succeeded by Judge Bunn in 1877.

CHARLES H. CRAMER

Was born in Seneca county, Ohio, August 20, 1847; was admitted to practice in Mansfield, in June, 1875, and located here.

LA FAYETTE L. LANG

Was born April 10, 1851, in Tiffin; attended Heidelberg college and Cleveland commercial institute. He was teller in First National bank, read law in his father's office, and was admitted to practice in 1877, when he became the law partner of his father.

JOHN B. SCHWARTZ

Is the son of Augustus and Littia Schwartz, and was born in Austin, Texas, November 1, 1854. His mother is a Massony, whose father's family were among the early settlers in Hopewell, and came from Belgium. She went with the family of Jesse Stem from here to Texas, where Stem was Indian agent, and where he was killed by some Indians. John B. Schwartz was admitted to the bar in 1879 and located in Tiffin.

W. L. KERSHAW

Was born in New York city in November, 1856; was admitted to practice in Mansfield, Ohio, July 20, 1879, and settled in Tiffin soon thereafter.

H. J. WELLER

Was born January 21, 1856, in Thompson township, in this county, and was admitted to the bar June 2, 1880, at the supreme court in Columbus. He located in Tiffin immediately thereafter.

GERALD E. SULLIVAN

Was born June 20, 1856, at Tiffin, Ohio; was admitted to the bar and located in Tiffin December 12, 1878.

JAMES F. LEAHY,

Was born May 14, 1855, in the county of Kerry, Ireland; was admitted to the bar in Tiffin December 30, 1879, and then located here.

The following are the names of young men who are reading law in Tiffin now, with a view of pursuing the profession, viz: J. Calvin Royer, Walter S. Cramer, John C. Rickenbaugh, Ira E. Strong, Warren F. Noble, Henry J. Weller, James H. Platt, R. B. Reed, David W. Speilman, John W. Leahy, Charles W. Repp, Frank Hess. There is also a young lady reading law—Miss Edith Sams.

After the commencement of this work two members of the bar of Tiffin died very suddenly and unexpectedly. Mr. Alfred Landon died at his residence after a few hours' illness, in a sinking chill, and a few weeks after, near the close of the fall term of the court of common pleas, Mr. George W. Bachman was found dead near his gate, having fallen out of his buggy.

Mr. Landon died Saturday morning, October 4, 1879.

Mr. Bachman died October 21, 1879.

Mr. Landon was a member of the Tiffin bar for twenty-five years and held the offices of prosecuting attorney and mayor of Tiffin.

Mr. Bachman was also mayor of Tiffin, prosecuting attorney and one of the directors of the Seneca County Infirmary. He was a member of the Tiffin bar since 1867.

It is a most remarkable fact that all the lawyers who have died in Seneca county passed away very suddenly, without being sick any length of time. Mr. Seney dropped dead on the floor; Richard Williams died suddenly; Jesse Stem was shot dead in Texas; Joel W. Wilson was not considered seriously ill when he died; Thomas C. Tunison was sick only a day or two; Leander Stem was killed in the battle of Stone River; Afred Landon and George Bachman died as related above, and Luther A. Hall passed away before the brethren knew that he was seriously ill; Mr. Rawson was complaining only a few days before he died; William M. Johnson expected to get well the day before he died, but had been suffering from consumption for years.

JAMES PILLARS

Promised a half dozen times to furnish the writer with a little sketch of himself, to be entered here, and having neglected to do so, I can only say of him that he is a very able jurist, and that since he has served on the common pleas bench ten years, he has returned to the practice in Tiffin.

WILLIAM LANG.

Want of room and want of desire to write my biography will make the story of the writer a very short one.

Mont Jarvis is the end and the highest peak of the Vosges mountains in the Palatinate in Germany. A little south of its foot, and where the Vosges slope away by low hills into the bottom lands of the Rhine, and on its left bank in the Canton of Weimweiler, is the pleasant little town of Sippersfeld. Here I was born on the 14th day of December, 1815. I was the seventh child and the first son of Henry and Catherine Lang.

Father kept me at school until we started for America. It was his intention to prepare me for the profession of school teacher. When we arrived in Tiffin on the 18th of August, 1833, my German education could not be utilized very well, and I entered the cabinet shop of D. H. Phillips, as an apprentice. I worked at the trade seven years, when, in the spring of 1840, I entered the office of Mr. Joshua Seney to read law. Mr. Seney gave the practice no attention, and when Mr. Cowdery located in Tiffin late in the fall of the same year, at the suggestion of Mr. Seney, I entered Mr. Cowdery's office as a student. On the 25th day of July, 1842, I was admitted to the practice at Lower Sandusky, Ohio. Judge E. Lane administered the oath to me. Judge D. Higgins was the chairman of the committee that examined me. Brice J. Bartlett, John C. Spink, Cooper K. Watson, R. P. Buckland and others were members of the committee.

In the fall of 1844 I was elected prosecuting attorney of Seneca county, and re-elected in 1846. In 1851 I was elected the first probate judge of Seneca county, with the highest majority that Seneca county ever cast for any man to office. In the fall of 1854 I was re-nominated by my party and would have been re-elected had it not been for the storm of Know-Nothingism that swept the country like a mad cyclone, in the fall of that year. Seneca gave a majority of 1,400 for the Know-Nothings. In 1859 I was nominated by the Democrats of Seneca county as a candidate for representative to the legislature, with Mr. Morris P. Skinner, Seneca county being entitled to two members that time. Mr. Skinner (Democrat) and Mr. Jones (Republican) were elected. It will interest but very few to relate the causes that led to my defeat. In 1861 I was elected to the senate of Ohio from the counties of Seneca, Crawford and Wyandot, and re-elected in 1863, serving four years and during the war. In 1865 I was nominated by the Democratic party of Ohio as its candidate for lieutenant-governor, on the ticket with General G. W. Morgan for governor. In the fall previous the state went Republican some 60,000 majority. The campaign was a quiet one; there was no hope of a Democratic success, but with all, the Republican majority was reduced one-half. General Morgan and myself made a vigorous campaign, and had but very little local aid, working against hope. In 1869 I was elected treasurer of Seneca county, and re-elected in 1871, serving four years. I was the first mayor of the city of Tiffin, and the first president of the school board of Tiffin, and being a member of the same board now, I take great pride in holding the highest office that the law gives to any man. I have now been at the Tiffin bar longer than any other lawyer connected with it, except it be brother Pennington.

Just in time, and before these sheets go to the printer, I can add the fact, that at the Democratic state convention, held in Cleveland on Thursday, the 22d day of July, 1880, I was nominated by acclamation as the candidate for secretary of state. On my return to Tiffin on the day following, a large party of my friends and neighbors, some five hundred, with a band of music and carriages, met me at the depot in Tiffin and escorted me home. Dr. J. A. Norton announced my nomination to the assembled crowd in front of the court house; W. P. Noble made a speech of welcome in glowing terms, and Republicans and Democrats joined in their hearty congratulations. It was a scene the like of which Tiffin never witnessed before. The ovation was a personal compliment, without distinction of party. I record it here in gratitude as the happiest day of my life. The good opinion of one's neighbors is a price far beyond the emoluments of office.

CHAPTER XXIV.

DRS. DRESBACH, KUHN, FISHER, O'CONNOR—TIFFIN MEDICAL SOCIETY—INDUSTRIES IN TIFFIN—SENECA COUNTY AGRICULTURAL SOCIETY—THE PRESS: MESSRS. LOOMIS, NAYLOR, GROSS—THE SENECA COUNTY INFIRMARY—THE TIFFIN GAS LIGHT COMPANY—AGRICULTURAL WORKS, ETC.—THE SENECA COUNTY PIONEER ASSOCIATION—DER BRUDERBUND—THE PHILHARMONIC SOCIETY—MRS. HARRIET CRAWFORD.

BIOGRAPHICAL SKETCH OF DR. ELY DRESBACH.
[By J. A. McFarland.]

DR. ELY DRESBACH was born in Northumberland county, Pennsylvania, in the year 1802. While he was yet quite young, his parents, David and Catherine Dresbach, removed with him to Pickaway county, Ohio, where they lived to a good old age. As he grew up, young Dresbach was engaged, for some time, in the mercantile business, but this occupation was not to his taste, and at an early age he resolved to qualify himself to enter the medical profession.

Unlike many young men, he was fortunate in choosing the vocation for which nature had eminently fitted him.

He pursued his studies with great assiduity and success in the office, and under the direction of Dr. Luckey, an eminent physician of Circleville. After the usual time, thus spent, he attended a course of lectures, at the Medical college of Ohio.

He then decided on trying his fortune among the pioneers of northwestern Ohio, and finally settled down in Fort Ball; and after a few years he crossed over the river to Tiffin, the seat of justice for the newly organized county of Seneca. His old office in Fort Ball, a small, one-story brick building, is still standing on Sandusky street, a few rods north of McNeal's storeroom. The rooms he occupied as an office, for some years before his death, were on Washington street, where the Commercial bank now stands.

The winter of 1827-8 was passed in Cincinnati, attending a second course of lectures, at the close of which he took the degree of doctor of medicine. Again in his chosen field of labor, his popularity went on increasing, till, at the end of the next decade, it was immense and well merited.

"None knew him but to love him,
None named him but to praise."

And his name is still a household word in many of the old families of this county.

In the practice of medicine and obstetrics the Doctor took rank with the foremost men of his time; in surgery his standing was only fair, as he had no ambition to venture upon the more brilliant operations; these he turned over to such men as Mott and Mussy, who made surgery a specialty.

Dr. Dresbach was of medium height, stoutly built, and a little inclined to corpulency. His brain, though not very large, was active, with a good anterior development. His temperament was sanguine; hair light auburn, eyes blue, nose large and slightly aquiline, neck short, chest and limbs well developed, and his whole appearance that of an elegant gentleman, as he was. In the matter of dress, he was scrupulously careful, always wearing the finest and most fashionable garments. His kind, courteous, graceful demeanor insured him a hearty welcome wherever he went, whether in the sick chamber or the drawing-room.

The Doctor was fond of books, and was well posted in current literature; he was a most agreeable companion, indulging freely in anecdotes and personal reminiscences, and had good conversational powers, though he made no pretentions as a public speaker.

While a general favorite with the ladies, and fond of their society, and, at one time matrimonially engaged, he lived all his days in single blessedness.

He was a lover of the fine arts, and of music especially; and many a leisure half hour was filled with sweet strains from his favorite instrument—the violin; and to his love of music, and to the encouragement he generously gave to resident professors and amateurs, our city is, in some measure, indebted for its present high culture in music.

And now, kind reader, would you have some glimpses to illustrate the dual character of poor human nature; to show, side by side, its good and its bad qualities, in the life under review?

Well—but no matter—'tis enough to say that while the Doctor was not sinless, most of his faults were not of a malignant type, but rather of the kind that are said "to lean to virtue's side."

But whatever they were, a most ungracious task it would be, to dwell upon their unpleasant memory; and the writer must ask to be excused, preferring, as he does, the reversal of the custom indicated in the following lines:

> "The evil that men do, lives after them;
> The good is oft interred with their bones."

The Doctor was a member of the Masonic order. In politics he was a Whig, and took a leading part in every campaign. In 1846 he was the Whig candidate for congress, and, though defeated, had the satisfaction to know that he had run considerably ahead of his ticket. Rodolphus Dickinson was his opponent. David Tod was defeated for governor at the same election.

Vigorous as his constitution naturally was, it had its limit of endurance. Overtasked, mentally and physically, for thirty years, in a malarious climate, it is not surprising that his life was cut short, in his fifty-first year. His end came not suddenly; the way to it was through long suffering, extending over a period of several years.

Gradually declining health induced him to try the effect of a milder climate. The winter of 1851-2 was spent in the south, visiting a brother and making the acquaintance of many of the leading medical men of that region. With the return of the spring, however, there were no signs of returning health; and early in May, he set out for his loved home, stopping a few days in Richmond, to attend the meeting of the American Medical Association.

The last year of his life was one of great suffering. He died April 14, 1853.

The immense multitude that attended his funeral was evidence of the sincere regard and affection of the community for which he had labored so long and faithfully.

DR. HENRY KUHN

Was one of the pioneer physicians in Tiffin, and took a very active part in the development of the town and country.

He was born in Frederick City, Maryland, in 1802, and attended the Frederick college, the oldest institution of western Maryland. He was there so pious and attentive to his studies and so sedate as to have acquired from the teachers and school-mates the soubriquet of "Bishop." After he left the college he read medicine in the office of Dr. Tyler, the leading physician of Frederick City, and finished under Dr. Henry Staley, in Frederick. He graduated with the highest honors from the University of Maryland, at Baltimore, in 1825, and soon thereafter commenced the practice at Woodsboro, in Frederick county, near which place Lewis Baltzell lived. Here he made the acquaintance of Catherine, one of the daughters of Mr. Baltzell, whom he married. Of that union Mrs. William Holt, of Tiffin, and Mrs. Kate Toner, of Canton, Ohio, are the only children living.

The exact time when the Doctor arrived in Tiffin I have not been able to ascertain, but it must have been in 1831. I often heard him say that he helped to cut the first tree in Market street, between Washington and Monroe. He was very popular in his younger days among his schoolmates and acquaintances. His manly personal appearance, his dress and address, his family relationship and their position in society, all added to make the young doctor a distinguished character. He came here into the woods and at once became the compeer of Drs. Dresbach and Carey, with whom he divided the practice among the scattered cabins for many miles around. He was often called to visit the Wyandots, on the Sandusky plains, and became highly esteemed among the chiefs, of whom Sum-mon-de-wat was a special friend, as already mentioned. One time he was called to amputate the leg of a squaw. She sat at the foot of a tree and fanned away the flies with a fox's tail during the operation, without a wince or a groan. Whenever the Wyandots visited Tiffin they would call on the Doctor at his little frame office, on East Market street, and have a chat. The old office is still standing, back of the new jail, but unoccupied.

The father of Dr. Kuhn was for many years the most important and distinguished man in Frederick county. He was the leader of the Republican (Democratic) party for many years (from 1798 to 1824). He had read law but preferred farming. He had 700 acres well stocked with slaves. The abolitionists stole nine of them at one time. Dr. Kuhn brought a slave boy to Tiffin with him. He was a present from some friend. I often heard Dr. Kuhn speak of him but have no knowledge of what became of him. The name of Dr. Kuhn's father was Christian; his mother's maiden name was Elizabeth Browning, daughter of Jeremiah and Cassandra Browning. The old folks, after they were eighty years of age, rode horseback to Steubenville, Ohio, where they bought a farm. The old lady was highly intellectual and one of the most scholarly women in Maryland. They were of English stock. Christian Kuhn was a German, wealthy and popular. He was the first mayor of Frederick City, and frequently a member of the general assembly of Maryland. He traveled to the sessions in his own carriage. He was then a leading spirit in most all leading matters, and for many years held the office of chief judge of the orphans' court of Frederick county.

Dr. Kuhn held his reputation in the esteem of the people and the profession up to his death. Nature seemed to have made him for a physician, but with all his skill he had his weaknesses, too, like many other men. His occasional indulgences in strong drink interfered materially with his practice, while his habitual indifference about his finances kept him poor. He earned money enough in his profession to be one of our wealthiest men, but he seemed to set no value upon it. He would become security for anybody that asked him the favor, and it was no lesson to him when he was compelled to pay. He was warm-hearted and generous, hospitable, sympathetic, benevolent, kind. He could refuse no favor in his power to grant; never learned to say "no." His wife died about 1843. Sometime thereafter he married Miss Maria Pennington, a sister to Robert G. Pennington, of Tiffin. This union was blessed with three children: Robert D. Kuhn, Mrs. Emma Kimball and Louisa, the late Mrs. Fast, of Canton, Ohio. Mrs. Kuhn is still living.

Dr. Kuhn attained to the highest honors in ancient Masonry and often represented the old Sandusky lodge in the Grand Lodge of Ohio. He died at his residence on Clay street, in Tiffin, October 16, 1878.

DR. ROBERT C. J. CAREY

Was a native of Maryland, and located in Fort Ball about the time Dr. Dresbach came here, and the two formed a partnership in the practice.

They had their first office in the small yellow brick, on Sandusky street, still standing. Dr. Carey was considered a very good physician He was very polite, and neat about his person. He died on the 9th day of November, 1836, aged 35 years, 11 months and 20 days.

DR. JAMES FISHER.

The subject of this sketch filled quite a space in public affairs in Tiffin, at an early day, both as a physician and as a man of energy and enterprise.

He was born in Westminster, in Frederick county, Maryland, on the 1st day of January, 1801, and graduated at the Medical University of Maryland, in April, 1823. He commenced practice in Abbottstown and Oxford, Pennsylvania. After practicing a few years, he took a trip through the west and south and returned to Westminster in 1829, when he made the acquaintance of the family of Dr. Thomas Boyer, of Uniontown, Maryland, and especially that of the Doctor's daughter, Elizabeth M. This acquaintance with this daughter ripened into their marriage, which took place in July, 1829. The name of the other daughter was Mary R., who married Mr. Lloyd Norris. Both couple were married on the same day, the Rev. Daniel Zollikoffer solemnizing the marriages.

Dr. Fisher then practiced medicine at the Union Bridge, four miles from Uniontown, in a neighborhood of excellent people. The families of Drs. Boyer and Fisher moved to Tiffin in 1832, where Dr. Boyer died in 1835; and Mrs. Boyer died here in 1847.

Dr. Fisher held the postoffice here, kept a drug store at an early day, practiced medicine, speculated in lands and handled a great deal of money. In 1866 he removed with his family to Springfield, Missouri, where Mrs. Fisher's health declined; they never felt satisfied with the change; but their children were married and settled there and they remained. Mrs. Fisher died September 19, 1878, and was buried in Maple Grove cemetery, having lived in happy wedlock with the Doctor 49 years. She was a splendid lady, highly cultivated, kind and sociable. They have four daughters: Hannah E., wife of Charles A. Wright; Mary E., wife of James Patterson; Laura, wife of Joe M. Steiner, and Pattie D., wife of R. L. McElhany; and one son, Thomas B. Fisher, all living.

Dr. Fisher, at nearly four score, is still enjoying excellent health, but since the death of his wife, feels himself alone in the world.

The family of Dr. Boyer was highly cultured and much esteemed. The same air of old-style Maryland and Virginia aristocracy, mentioned on former occasions, was well marked in this family also, but here, as everywhere, it was always associated with politeness, kindness and broad and generous hospitality.

Among the physicians practicing medicine in Tiffin at this time, Drs. J. A. McFarland (who located here in 1837), J. N. Heckerman, A. B. Hovey, H. B. Martin, E. J. McCollum, and S. S. Bricker are pioneers. There are also in the practice now, Drs. W. Crawford, W. G. Williard, J. T. Livers, J. F. E. Fanning, J. P. Kinnaman, W. H. Hershiser, J. Breidinger, J. Huss, F. H. Lang, W. H. Stover, D. Wells, and Maurice Leahy.

SENECA COUNTY MEDICAL SOCIETY.

This is an auxiliary to the State Medical society, and is governed by the same code of ethics, but has its own constitution and by-laws.

The state society was organized in a parlor of the old Neil house, in Columbus, May 14th, 1846; the first Seneca county society at Dr. E. Dresbach's office in 1852. Dr. McFarland was elected president, and Dr. George Sprague secretary.

The present society was organized in one of the parlors of the Shawhan house, in Tiffin, on the 25th day of September, 1878, with Dr. A. B. Hovey as president, and Dr. A. L. Waugaman as secretary. The society has its regular meetings on the fourth Wednesday of every month.

Of the members of this society some minutes have been collected and are here noticed:

J. U. HECKERMAN

Was born in Chambersburg, Pennsylvania, November 22d, 1825; graduated at Washington college in 1846, and located in Tiffin.

H. B. MARTIN

Was born in Chillicothe, Ohio, November 15th, 1823; graduated at Charity Hospital, Cleveland, Ohio, in 1850.

F. W. SCHWAN

Was born in Lancaster, Pennsylvania, March 3d, 1843; graduated at Rush Medical college, Chicago, in 1867.

E. W. SULLIVAN

Was born in Tiffin, Ohio, March 22d, 1856; graduated at the medical department of the Wooster university in 1878.

E. J. M'COLLUM

Was born June 10th, 1826, in Richland county, Ohio; graduated at the

Jefferson Medical college, Philadelphia, in March, 1853, and soon thereafter located in Tiffin.

H. B. GIBBON

Was born March 12th, 1852, at Big Prairie, Wayne county, Ohio; graduated at the Cincinnati College of Medicine and Surgery in June, 1877, and located in Seneca county in July the same year.

J. B. BLAND

Was born in Muskingum county July 22d, 1840; graduated at Starling Medical college, Columbus, and located at Benton, Crawford county, in 1869.

L. E. ROBINSON

graduated at Rush Medical college, Chicago, in 1873, and settled in Republic in 1876.

BENJAMIN S. STOVER

Was born June 13th, 1856, at Brooklyn, Cuyahoga county, Ohio; graduated at Jefferson Medical college in 1878; located in Republic the same year.

W. H. PAUL

Was born in Richland county, Ohio, April 14th, 1848; graduated at Miami Medical college, Cincinnati, Ohio, in 1872; located in Adrian in 1876.

DR. ARIEL B. HOVEY.

Was born in Albany township, Orleans county, Vermont, February 9th, 1829. When a boy fourteen years of age, he started for Ohio, and entered Oberlin college, where he remained six years, and during this time read medicine with Dr. Homer Johnson, of Oberlin. In 1850 he entered the office of Prof. Ackley, in Cleveland, and graduated in March, 1852, and in the same year located in Tiffin, where he has remained ever since in the successful practice of his profession. While Dr. Hovey is regarded as a very able practitioner, he excels as a surgeon, in which branch his skill and courage have made him eminently successful and greatly celebrated. He is a member of several state societies, as well as of the National Medical society.

MAURICE LEAHY

Was born March 14th, 1853, in the county of Kerry, Ireland; graduated in the medical department of the Wooster university, in Cleveland, Ohio, February 27th, 1878, and located in Tiffin in July, 1878.

JOHN D. O'CONNOR, M. D.

Snow covered the earth; the air was very cold; the sky was overcast with heavy clouds; all nature looked gloomy and dreary, and so did the senate chamber of Ohio, when, at ten o'clock in the morning of the first Monday in January, A. D., 1862, the senate was called to order. The city of Columbus was full of soldiers; regiment after regiment was organized and sent to the front. The sound of martial music rang in the streets day and night, and here met the first legislature of Ohio after the breaking out of the rebellion.

The condition of the country on that morning seemed to combine with nature to cast a gloom and a sadness over the senate. The Hon. Benjamin Stanton, president of the senate, took his seat; the members were sworn and seated, and the saddest countenance in that body was that of Senator John D. O'Connor, of Monroe. He was then about forty years of age, about six feet high; he had black hair, brushed back from a high forehead, deeply set dark eyes, a chiseled face; a black beard covered his mouth and chin. Heavy black eyebrows gave powerful expression to the white of his eyes, making his countenance wonderfully striking. He was lean of flesh. The paleness of his face and his entire "make up" were calculated to arrest the attention, if not excite the sympathy, of the most careless observer. Add to this a prudent reserve, close observation, quiet demeanor and polished manners, and you have a fair picture of Dr. O'Connor on that morning.

Party spirit ran high during the war, and the few members of that body who were elected by Democratic constituencies, were treated with indifference, for their votes were not necessary to carry any measure; yet that senate contained many distinguished gentlemen from all parts of the state, some of whom became noted in other high positions which they filled.

Dr. O'Connor and the writer belonged to that small number, and as misery loves company, and for higher reasons, it was not long until mutual respect warmed into mutual friendship that grew brighter as time rolled on, and lasted for life.

Dr. O'Connor's father was an Irishman who had served under Wellington in Spain, and after he was transferred with a portion of the British army to Canada, he ran away with some of his comrades, came to the United States, and settled in Woodsfield, Monroe county, Ohio, in 1817 or 1818. Here he was married to Rebecca Corothers, and elected to the office of county recorder, which office he held for thirty years.

Here in Woodsfield, John D. was born, September 24th, 1822, and here he received such education as the schools of the settlement afforded and the private instructions of Mr. Franklin Gale were able to confer. He entered the office of Dr. Dillon, where he read medicine, and afterwards located at Clarington, a little hamlet situate on the banks of the Ohio, in Monroe county, where Sunfish creek enters the river. To the boatmen of the river the place is best known by the name of "Sunfish."

There, in 1845, he was married to Ruth C. Neff, and soon built up a large and extensive practice. He attended a course of lectures in the Miami Medical college, and graduated from it in 1858. Here he had the benefit of the instructions of the elder Mussey, Murphy, Dawson, Davis and other distinguished men in the profession.

In 1861 he was elected to the senate of Ohio from Guernsey, Monroe and a part of Noble, and re-elected in 1863. After he had served out his second term as senator, in the summer of 1865, the writer visited him at Clarington, and made the acquaintance of his interesting family, consisting of Mrs. O'Connor, four beautiful young daughters, and a little son. The doctor's practice extended along the river bank and over the rough hills and mountains of Monroe, where he had nearly worn out his life in the pursuit of his profession. The children needed education, and there was no good school nearer than Wheeling, twenty-five miles away. I suggested to him the propriety of selling out and removing to Seneca county, which I described as it was, and pictured to him the situation of the Tiffin schools, its society, health, market, topography, etc.

A visit from the doctor and Mrs. O'Connor was enough to prove all I said, and in 1866 the doctor bought the old Biggs farm, on the Melmore road, a short distance south of Tiffin, where he lived until shortly before he died.

Here at Tiffin he stepped at once into the front rank of his profession, where he was highly esteemed, and became so popular among the people that they elected him the delegate from this county to the constitutional convention.

The condition of his health scarcely warranted the task this position required, but to prove his gratitude to the people who elected him, he served the session of the convention in Columbus, and attended the adjourned session in Cincinnati the following winter. The only answer he gave his friends who tried to persuade him not to go to Cincinnati, was that he would rather wear out than rust out, and preferred to die at his post. And he did die at his post, worn out. Nothing but his iron will kept him up for months.

Ordinary men would have succumbed to disease long before; but with all his will power, Dr. O'Connor gradually wasted away, when on Saturday, the 21st day of February, 1874, at nine o'clock P. M., "tired like a child in the arms of its nurse, he fell asleep," as Judge Okey expressed it in his eulogy of the doctor in the convention.

During his short association with the members of the convention he won the love and esteem of them all, and on the morning when the committee who had been appointed to prepare suitable resolutions expressive of the sense of the convention on his death, were about to report, several gentlemen made remarks attesting their love and esteem for the doctor, full of fine feeling and warm appreciation of the good man he was. Judge Okey, Messrs. Voris, Albright, Neil, Cook and others spoke very eloquently. It is to be regretted that space will not permit a reproduction of those eulogies here.

His body was brought to Tiffin by a committee appointed by the convention, on the 24th of February, and kept at the house of the writer in Tiffin, from whence, on the next day, it was taken to the First Methodist Protestant church, where the Rev. J. C. Ogle delivered a very appropriate sermon from Rev. 14: 13v., to a large concourse of friends. He was buried at the new cemetery, near Tiffin, under the beautiful and impressive ritual of the F. & A. M.

Mrs. O'Connor is still living; the girls are all happily married. D. O'Connor, his son, is attending school.

Dr. O'Connor was an excellent physician, possessed of a finely cu-l tured mind; he was a true friend, a devoted patriot, a christian gentleman and an honest man.

THE TIFFIN GAS LIGHT COMPANY

Was organized in 1856 as a joint stock company, under the statute of Ohio. The enterprise was originated by Edward Gwyn, of Springfield, Ohio, who came to Tiffin in that year, and induced several of our citizens here to aid him. The capital stock was $30,000, of one thousand two hundred shares, each twenty-five dollars. Mr. Gwyn subscribed all the stock except about fifty shares, which were taken by others.

The city council of Tiffin granted to the company and its successors and assigns forever, the use of the streets, alleys and public grounds in Tiffin, to lay pipe and all other appliances to distribute and carry gas throughout the city.

The works are built on the old tannery lot near Rocky Creek, on Perry street.

The company contracted with Mr. Gwyn to build the works for the stock he had subscribed and $10,000, to be secured by mortgage on the works, and Mr. Gwyn was virtually the owner of the whole, as the fifty shares were subscribed more as a donation than for profit, and were soon transferred to him.

The original works were small, having only two miles of pipe laid in the streets, having fifty street lamps, and charging $4.50 per 1,000 cubic feet, $3 per year for rent of meter, and $25 per year for street lamps. In 1860 Mr. Gwyn sold the works to his brother, John Gwyn, who continued to be the owner until 1870. Between 1860 and 1870 less than one-half mile of pipes were laid, and the old prices maintained. In 1870 John Gwyn sold out to George E. Seney and John T. Huss. On the death of Huss in 1875, Judge Seney became and still is the owner. Within the past ten years the works have been greatly enlarged and improved. All that now exists of the purchase from Gwyn is the old building and about one mile of pipe; all else is new.

The capital stock now is $100,000; gas $2.50 per 1,000 cubic feet, and no rent charged for the use of meters, with a prospect further to decrease the price of gas as the number of consumers increase. There are now about ten miles of gas pipe in the streets, and one hundred and seventy-four street lamps. It requires two men and a horse to light and extinguish the lamps, who must travel twenty-four miles to do the work. The works consume from 1,200 to 1,500 tons of the best Youghiogheny gas coal, yearly. Five men and two horses are employed at the works. The annual production of gas is from five to six millions of feet.

Judge George E. Seney is president, and John M. Bate secretary and superintendent.

THE OHIO STOVE WORKS.

Amongst the various industries of the city may be mentioned the Ohio Stove works, a joint stock company, whose works are located near the Baltimore and Ohio depot. The company is now well organized and in successful operation.

THE TIFFIN AGRICULTURAL WORKS

Is a joint stock company. The works are located at the corner of Water and Minerva streets, where they cover an area of about four acres. They have a capital stock of about $100,000, and the institution is under the control of efficient officers, and is in a flourishing condition.

THE TIFFIN WOOLEN MILLS

Are also in successful operation, now employing about seventy hands.

THE TIFFIN CHURN FACTORY,

Organized by A. C. Baldwin & Co., is doing a good business; it prosecuted its work steadily during the late severe long panic, proving that the institution is in able hands.

LOOMIS AND NYMAN'S FOUNDRY,

Located near the bridge on Market street, started when, in 1847, they bought the old foundry then conducted by Jesse Wolf. They afterwards bought the property where Van Nest's carriage factory stood, and erected valuable buildings on the premises. The firm is now composed of John D. Loomis, Philetus Nyman and George Loomis. They employ about 28 hands and turn out work annually to the value of $50,000.

THE TIFFIN MANUFACTURING COMPANY

Is also a joint stock company, doing a great deal of work, and in successful operation on Melmore street.

THE TIFFIN WATER WORKS

Were accepted by the council of the city in the fall of 1879. There are about 14 miles of water pipes in the city. The city pays rent for hydrants.

There are now in Tiffin 26 grocery stores, 6 dry goods stores, 5 clothing stores, 8 boot and shoe stores, 1 carpet store, 6 millinery and fancy stores, 5 jewelry stores, 4 drug stores, 4 fruit, confectionery and bakery stores, 3 hardware stores, 4 stove and tin stores, 2 hat and and cap stores, 2 china and crockery stores, 2 book and stationery stores, 3 furniture stores, 3 photograph rooms, 5 harness shops, 2 marble dealers, 4 cigar manufacturers, 6 printing establishments, 7 barber shops, 8 meat markets, 5 blacksmith shops, 6 carriage and wagon works, 2 breweries, 3 wholesale liquor stores, 3 music stores, 6 hotels, 5 boarding houses, 1 plumbing and gas-fitting store, 2 pump shops, about 50 saloons, 2 bent works factories, 2 sash, door and blind factories, 1 foundry, 1 stove factory, 1 woolen mill, 1 churn factory, 2 shoe factories, the gas works, agricultural works and water works.

There also three building loan associations in the city.

THE PUBLIC LIBRARY

Is a new creation and fitting up a fine room in the market house building. It was incorporated in March, 1880, and the following named persons are the officers of the institution, viz:

President—R. W. Shawhan.
Vice-Presidents—Mrs. W. P. Noble, Mrs. John D. Loomis.
Secretary—C. H. Cramer.
Treasurer—J. W. Chamberlain.
Trustees—W. P. Noble, Francis Wagner, George G. Harriman, Miss Flora Cronise, Mrs. Laura B. Sneath, Mrs. Laura G. Bunn.

There will be a public opening of the library on the 12th of May, 1880.

One thousand, six hundred volumes of books are already collected.

There are also two bent works in the city. One on West Market street, owned by F. Smith, and the other on Water street, carried on by the Fishbaugh Brothers. Both are doing successful business.

There are also a number of brickyards in full operation, and a drain tile factory, carried on by John Heilman.

Tiffin has also two flouring mills; one at the north end of the iron bridge, on Washington street, and the other on Mill street; the former runs by steam and the latter by water power; both in daily operation.

Unable to give the exact amount I feel it safe to say that more than five millions of dollars are invested in the various industries in Tiffin.

SENECA COUNTY AGRICULTURAL SOCIETY.

The pioneer legislatures of Ohio comprehended their missions fully and passed laws for the promotion of agriculture, for the protection of stock, to open roads to market, etc., etc. And the manner in which Seneca county threw off her mantle of "native wild " and prepared the way for civilized life, proves the high order of the intelligence of her pioneer farmers. First a cabin, then roads, then meeting-houses and school-houses, then mills, and one improvement after another.

On the 7th of June, 1833, the following notice was published in the *Seneca Patriot:*

TO THE CITIZENS OF SENECA COUNTY—Notice is hereby given that a meeting will be held at the Court House, in the town of Tiffin, (they had no court house), in the county of Seneca, on the 28th day of June inst., for the purpose of organizing an agricultural society, to be entitled the Seneca County Agricultural Society, in pursuance of an act of the legislature, passed February 25, 1833. By order of the Board of Commissioners.

DAVID E. OWEN,
Clerk for the Commissioners.

Nothing was done under this notice, however, for very many reasons, the strongest of which was the fact that the people had nothing to exhibit; fancy stock in horses, cattle, sheep, hogs, poultry, etc., had not been introduced here as yet, and there would have been " no show."

It was not long, however, until the subject was agitated again, and now another notice was published as follows:

GOD SPEED THE PLOUGH.

In conformity with the act entitled, "An act to authorize and encourage the establishment of agricultural societies in the several counties in this state," passed March 12, 1839, notice is hereby given that there will be a meeting held at the court house in Tiffin, on Saturday, the 1st day of January next, for the purpose of organizing, etc. G. J. KEEN,
Auditor S. C.
TIFFIN, December, 1841.

The meeting was held at the M. E. church. John Terry, Samuel Waggoner, Abel Rawson, A. Ingraham, W. Toll, Evan Dorsey, Louis Baltzell, Lloyd Norris, Jacob S. Jennings, R. G. Pennington, Andrew Moore, George Stoner, J. W. Wilson and others took active part.

Samuel Waggoner was elected president; A. Ingraham, vice-president; Evan Dorsey, recording secretary; R. G. Pennington, corresponding secretary; Lloyd Norris, treasurer; Terry, Moore and Stoner, executive committee. A constitution was adopted. Thus the society was put on foot and has flourished ever since. Its county fairs are amongst the best in the state. It owns about twenty-five acres of land near College Hill, between North Greenfield and Portland roads, well provided with halls, race track and stalls. Its present officers are: N L. Brewer, president; Jacob Rickenbaugh, vice-president; H. J. Weller, secretary; John M. Kaull, treasurer. There are eighteen managers, one from each township, two from the city and one from the county at large.

The vast majority of the most successful business men in Tiffin are those who commenced the world with very little capital, or none at all, and I take pride to record the fact, that the leading characters in all branches of industry here, are self-made men.

Some have already been named, and a few more only will now be noticed.

MR. JOHN D. LOOMIS

Was born November 3, 1811, in Osego county, New York and was raised in Cayuga county, same state. He came to Ohio in 1839 and located in New Haven where he remained five years, and then removed to Licking county, Ohio, where he remained two years, and in 1847 removed to Tiffin, Ohio, where he has remained ever since. The firm, of which he has been the head ever since its location, has not only constantly increased since its location here, but has never been under the necessity of borrowing a dollar.

MR. JOHN M. NAYLOR

Was born at Wooster, Ohio, on the 9th of December, 1822. When a boy he became a clerk in a store in Wooster, then carried on by Messrs. Jacobs and Kanke. This was in 1834. In 1847 Mr. Naylor, in company with Mr. Harvey Howard, of Wooster, opened a hardware store in Tiffin, which they carried on here until 1851, when Mr. Howard sold his interest, and the store from that time was conducted in the name of Naylor & Pittenger up to 1855. From that time to 1857 Mr. Naylor conducted the business alone, for three years, when he was joined by a brother, W. W. Naylor, and the firm was called Naylor & Bro. This firm was continued to March 4, 1866, when William W. Naylor died, and the immense establishment has ever since been carried on by Mr. Naylor alone.

On the 11th day of December, 1849, Mr. Naylor was married to Cornelia, daughter of Judge Pittenger. In 1857 he built the beautiful villa on Melmore street, where he still resides. The mother of Mr. Naylor was a sister to Judge Musgrave, of Crawford county. An uncle by marriage was Judge Dean, of Wayne county, and my esteemed friend, Judge E. V. Dean, of Ironton, Ohio, is a full cousin of J. M. Naylor.

Mr. Naylor's life is a fine specimen of a self-made, successful career, based upon industry, economy, ability and honesty. Ever busy, late and early, with a friendly word for everybody, it is a matter of perfect wonder where he ever found time to make himself master of history, civil government and universal geography.

HENRY GROSS.

In the outset of this enterprise, the writer intended to say as little as possible about the living, but to recall the past and present it to the reader in its true light. Having unavoidably touched a few of the living, it would wrong the harmony of the work did I not also mention another distinguished Tiffinite, who, by his genius and skill, has won for himself a national reputation.

Seneca county has not been slow in producing men of distinction in almost every department of life. Our farmers are celebrated for having made Seneca county the first "wheat county" in Ohio; our mechanics are equal, at least, to the best of them; our lawyers and doctors are men of note; the nation found a president as near to Seneca county as possible; we have furnished the state with two state treasurers, one governor, one lieutenant-governor and came within 29,000 votes of furnishing another; we have sent four of our citizens to congress and three colonels to the war, with a fair prospect of sending another; the United States sent one of our citizens to represent her in China, and Pere Hyacinthe married one of our fair daughters.

Henry Gross is the second son of Henry Gross, sen., mentioned in a former chapter. He was born July 21, 1813. When a boy he made himself busy in his father's gun shop and learned the use of tools. As he grew up he formed a great taste for music and the fine arts, and while he acquired and mastered the gunsmith trade, became also an inventor. He secured a patent for a breech-loading rifle, and, in company with Mr. Ed. Gwynn, started a factory. In this, as in almost all his business undertakings, he allowed himself to be over-reached and proved to his friend that he was more of a genius than a financier. He secured many patents on ingenious steel and iron works, time-locks on safes, etc. While he was in the employ of the "Hall Safe and Lock Co.," in Cincinnati, for many years, he was sent for from very many places in the United States to open safes that by some accident had become fastened and nobody found to open them. Mr. Gross traveled many thousand miles on missions of that nature, and never failed in any case. He often astounded the by-standers in opening safes in a few minutes when others had worked for days. It is safe to say that there is not a safe made anywhere that Mr. Gross cannot open in a very short time without knowing anything about the combinations. Were it not for his high order of character and strict integrity, he would certainly be a dangerous man to run at large.

Of his latest and best invention, the papers are full of praise, and a copy of an article that appeared in the *Southern Merchant* of November, 1879, is here added to show how Mr. Gross' genius is appreciated by other people, and not to have it said that William Lang runs wild with his love for old Seneca and his friends.

But here is the article:

In our occupation as journalists, recording the current events of the times—the affairs of governments and political movements, the evil doings of the criminal classes, the gyrations of society, the theatrical stellar attractions, the condition of the great manufacturing interests, the prospects of the growing crops, and the excitement in the great commercial marts, and the educational, religious, and æsthetical interests, it sometimes becomes our duty as well as pleasure to sing the praises of the great geniuses and thinkers who overcome the obstacles of nature and utilize her forces for the good, comfort and happiness of mankind—the men who have a keen appreciation of the disadvantages under which sorrowing humanity toil, and strive to attain happiness, and put forth their best energies to dissipate them.

As one of this illustrious band we take pleasure in classing Mr. Henry Gross, of Cincinnati, Ohio, with whom we had a delightful and instructive interview, learning of his achievements in the various branches of the mechanic arts to which he has turned his attention and thoughts. His name is familiar to almost every banker throughout the country as a skilled expert and the inventor of the finest time and permutation locks extant, and they will no doubt be pleased to learn that he has again come to their aid, promising them still further protection from the hands of lawlessness.

We have neither time nor space to record all the incidents of his eventful career, devoted as it has been to many fields of inventive research, but we wish to speak somewhat limitedly of his later achievements in the construction of devices for the preservation of accumulated wealth, the reward of industry, from the natural and human enemies which beset the possessor— we mean his improvements in the construction of those trusty safeguards of the merchant and banker, the fire and burglar-proof safes and vaults, and the locks and bolt-work thereof.

Mr. Gross has had the most intimate and varied experience in the construction of safes and locks during the past ten years, and as an expert has been invariably successful in exposing the weaknesses of safes put upon the market by their makers with the false claims to security. As the result of this rich and varied experience, we are not therefore surprised that Mr. Gross has apparently reached the goal of excellence in this particular art, and we will take pleasure in speaking somewhat in detail of his various improvements.

First and foremost he exhibits a burglar-proof safe for bankers' use, the door of which is guarded when closed by the most simple and compact bolt work, so constructed that it presents a resistive strength to fracture equal to five times that of any system of train bolts now in use, and this bolt work, with the locks to guard it, is operated by a massive, invulnerable welded steel and iron disc, hung upon inner and outer bearings so truly and perfectly that it can be revolved like a top under the slightest pressure, while it is secured so strongly and closely in a corresponding opening in the body of the door that it would require tons of pressure or shock to remove it. The more immediate cause that developed the necessity of this new departure in safe construction lay in certain discoveries made by Mr. Gross in the course of his expert occupation of opening safes whose locks had become deranged or the combinations lost by carelessness.

He found by experimental test that the various spindles or arbors in common use, by means of which the locks and bolt work were manipulated, could be successfully assailed, so that he seldom consumed more than two hours, and usually about half that time or less, in utterly destroying them and entering the safe. Feeling that such safes could not be conscientiously recommended to the public as burglar-proof, he devised the above described improvement, which entirely does away with the use of spindles or arbors, and with this disc arrangement the safe has then nothing passing through it, and the door and walls are solid alike. Mr. Gross stakes his professional reputation on the merits of this invention, which only requires to be seen to be appreciated ; its simplicity is apparent to everyone, and the practical man can readily see that the inventor has simply taken advantage of the best construction to secure maximum strength in the materials used.

The locks employed to secure this safe are the result of much study, and are most admirably adapted to the purpose. The time movement and permutation tumblers are closely connected within a space of two inches square, and perform all the functions of the ordinary bulky time and combination locks of ten times the size, while possessing new features of convenience and security that will be readily appreciated by users. Mr. Gross also finally presents a fire-proof safe, of excellent design and calculated per maximum efficiency in the protection of its contents from fire.

All the inventions of Henry Gross, from his first "time lock," show the master's hand of genius, and now that he has practically demonstrated the excellence and invulnerability of the two last efforts of his skill, it is sincerely to be hoped that bankers, county treasurers, and those who use safes generally, will look at the merits of his make before they buy the productions of mendacious manufacturers, whose main merits consist in the liberal use of printer's ink.

If Mr. Gross' executive and financial abilities were equal to his genius, he would have been a millionaire long since.

THE PRESS.

The various newspaper enterprises that were established in Tiffin from time to time, the incidents connected with them, the political views they advocated, the questions that agitated the public mind from time to time, and the greater or lesser lights that figured on the affirmative and negative sides of these questions, the results obtained by the elections and all that and more, would make a very interesting book, and it is hoped some Tiffinite will some day take up the subject and write up a volume.

A short history of these establishments in Tiffin, without comment, is all that is intended here.

The first newspaper published in the county was the *Seneca Patriot*, E. Brown, editor and proprietor. The little hand press upon which it was printed was procured from Mr. J. P. McArdle, who claimed for it that it was the first printing press brought to Ohio.

The first number was issued August 4th, 1832. Its motto was, "Constitutional Rights, Republican Institutions, and Union Forever."

The paper came out as circumstances would permit. Sometimes the editor was out of paper; sometimes out of ink. Public patronage was not very good, and the notices and work from the county officials formed the principal part of his support. The greatest trouble of all, however, was the triangular fight between the political parties. The *Patriot* was the only paper in the county, and Mr. Brown undertook to accommodate them all, and secure custom from each. He proposed, therefore, to devote a certain space of each paper to articles suitable to the ideas of each party, and headed them "Clay politics," "Jackson·

politics," "Wirt politics." For awhile he abstained from taking any part and remained neutral, but the Whigs blamed him with partiality, sent in one communication after another, and he bore up with wonderful courage for a while. Finally the thing got so pressing, and the anti-Masons so boisterous, that Mr. Brown lost all power of endurance, and finally, on the 27th of October, 1832, he came out in an editorial to declare his true position. He could stand it no longer. He complained of men of the three parties who were so unreasonable as to claim more than their share of the paper, and being refused, threatened to injure the paper, etc. He finally concluded by saying : "Should we be compelled to haul down our tri-colored flag, or to be more explicit, we shall undoubtedly hoist true American colors, and if we are driven from our position we shall assuredly declare for Andrew Jackson and the Democratic party."

Now the Whigs withdrew their patronage; Ebert and Mercer came out in an open card and refused to support the paper because it was no longer neutral. Brown had gone over to the Jackson men.

In the next issue the editor says: "From what has already transpired we are convinced we can never give satisfaction while we pursue the course first prescribed. Party feeling is so much excited in this place, that jealousies will arise, and unpleasant measures will be taken, however just our cause may be."

That settled it. Mr. Elisha Brown sometime after took sick and died at Cincinnati. His son, J. H. Brown, carried on the paper for a short time thereafter, and then sold the press and material to Mr. Alonzo Rawson.

Before proceeding further in the history of the press, let us record such evidence as can be secured to preserve the history of this old press, which is certainly very remarkable. It was brought to Washington, Pennsylvania, by a Mr. Colerick, prior to the year 1800, from some place on the Atlantic coast. It was removed from Washington to Wellsburg, Virginia, about the year 1820, by J. P. McArdle, who was a very polite and intelligent Scotchman, and lived with his family for a long time in Republic, where one of his sons, Ed. McArdle, still resides. Mr. J. P. McArdle moved this press to Mount Vernon, Ohio, where he published the *Register* in 1816, and the above date of 1820 must be erroneous. From Mount Vernon the press was removed to Clinton, and from there in 1827 to Norwalk. Here it became the property of the Messrs. Browns, who took it to Sandusky City and brought it from there to Tiffin in 1832.

The *Seneca Advertiser*, speaking of this old press one time, said:

"It must be acknowledged that this venerable press, in the service of half a century, has earned at least the reputation of a faithful 'herald of a noisy world.' It has no doubt emblazoned to the world the achievements of many an eminent statesman, and probably chronicled as they occurred the stirring events which gave our government its national existence. Commencing its tour of pilgrimage upon the Atlantic coast, it has wound its way to the fancied 'far west.' It is indeed a relic of other days. He who would compare, at this day, that sturdy lever with the vast improvements made upon its like, since its first days, would behold one of the most astonishing and remarkable evidences of human skill ever developed in any branch of scientific or mechanical invention."

If this be the first press (and it undoubtedly was) that crossed the Alleganies, it should become the property of the west, and here be preserved to attest the improvements in the "art preservative of arts."

Mr. Alonzo Rawson, who bought the press, issued the first number of the *Independent Chronicle and Seneca Advertiser* on the 26th of April, 1834. Making his bow to the people he said he would be independent in politics, and advocate measures, not men. He soon, however, leaned over to the Whigs very strongly, and the leading Democrats put their heads together to buy Rawson out.

Mr. Josiah F. Reed purchased the office from Mr. Rawson, and issued the first number of the *Tiffin Gazette and Seneca Advertiser* in the last week in November, 1835, as the organ of the Democracy.

During a large portion of the year 1836, it seems that there was no paper published in Lower Sandusky, for nearly or all the official notices from Sandusky county during that time were published in the *Gazette* here.

In the latter part of February, 1838, Luther A. Hall, who was one of the principal leaders of the Whigs of Seneca county, bought the whole concern of Mr. Reed, and immediately handed it over to Mr. Joseph Howard, who was one of the early lawyers here, and the second clerk of the common pleas court, a Whig, of course. Mr. Howard kept the name of the *Gazette* for his paper, but dropped the *Advertiser*. In his inaugural he says that he must have the support of all people who want a newspaper, and throws himself upon the Whig party especially. Mr. Howard, after one or two issues, sold the concern to Samuel A. Griswold, who issued his first number on the 7th day of April, 1838, and conducted it as the organ of the Whigs until the fall of 1842, when it was discontinued. Mr. Griswold is at present the editor of the *Lancaster* (Ohio) *Gazette*, which has been under his charge for many years.

What has become of the old press? Now came on the ides of the ever memorable campaign of 1840, and the Democrats without a newspaper! "Willenskraft Wege schafft," says an old German proverb. Money was raised, a new press and type purchased, and the *Van Burenite* saw the light of day; "Cronise and others, editors and proprietors." The "others" were Joshua Seney and Gabriel J. Keen. In the fall of 1841 the *Van Burenite* was discontinued, and in the following spring Mr. John G. Breslin purchased the concern and issued *The Seneca Advertiser*. The first number was published on the 6th of May, 1842. Mr. Breslin conducted the *Advertiser* until 1854, when it was leased to John Flaugher, who continued it about one year, and was succeeded by W. W. Armstrong, now of the *Cleveland Plaindealer*, until the year 1857, when Mr. Armstrong purchased the concern and became its proprietor, as well as its editor. He continued the paper until the spring of 1863, when he rented the office to Messrs. Beilharz & Myers to take charge of the office of secretary of state, to which he was elected in October, 1862. About one year thereafter Mr. Beilharz withdrew, and J. M. Myers had charge of the office alone, and has edited the paper ever since, with his acknowledged ability. The office has been vastly enlarged and improved, and the Myers Brothers have lately abandoned steam power and substituted water power to run their presses. In the line of politics the office has made no change since the first issue of the *Van Burenite*, now forty long years.

The inaugural address of the *Van Burenite* was written by Joshua Seney, Esq , and a copy is preserved in the appendix to this book, which see.

In the summer of 1848 my esteemed old friend, John G. Breslin, was a candidate for member of the house of representatives of Ohio. The leaders of the Democratic party undertook to publish a German Democratic newspaper in the office of the *Advertiser*, and thereby aid in rallying the German citizens in support of the Democratic party.

In conformity with this plan an address was issued and circulated among the Democrats of the county to raise funds, of which the following is a copy.

To— ———

The undersigned, Democratic central committee of Seneca county, desire to secure the publication of a German Democratic paper in Tiffin for the campaign. and, if properly sustained, design making it a permanent issue. Of the success of this enterprise we entertain no doubt, if we can secure sufficient means to purchase the necessary type, etc. We have made arrangements to secure the use of the press, etc., of the *Seneca Advertiser* office, and it now remains only for us to raise the amount necessary to enable us to procure the above articles.

The expense of sustaining the paper, etc., after its commencement, will be borne here by our friends in subscriptions. Our desire in addressing you is, to solicit such aid as you may deem proper to extend, to enable us to commence the publication. And we assure you that such aid as you may afford will be gratefully received, and faithfully applied to the purpose intended, and the furtherance of democratic principles in northwestern Ohio.

The necessity of a German Democratic paper in this section of the State— located, too, in the banner district of Ohio—will be apparent to you, when we state that there are in this (Seneca) county about eight hundred German Democratic voters—at least twenty-five hundred in this congressional district—and doubtless from fifteen to twenty thousand in northwestern Ohio— among whom we can number some of the most unyielding Democrats in the State—yet are comparatively destitute of the means of acquiring political information.

If successful in commencing this publication, we feel assured hundreds, if not thousands, can be rallied to the polls, and many induced to a speedier naturalization, who have heretofore felt indifferent as to the importance of acquiring the rights of citizens, and the glorious privileges of an American freeman—and thus swell, by thousands, the Democratic vote of Ohio.

For such amount as may be contributed by yourself, and other friends in your place, we will, of course, furnish the proper number of papers, weekly, in remuneration. Will you exert yourself actively among the friends of the cause, and advise us as soon as possible of your success, etc.?

JOEL W. WILSON.
RICHARD WILLIAMS.
WILLIAM LANG.
JOHN G. BRESLIN.
Democratic Central Committee.

TIFFIN, February 4, 1848.

This call was answered by funds sufficient to purchase a lot of type for a German paper, and the first copy of the *Seneca Adler* made its appearance about the latter part of April, 1848, and appeared weekly for just six months; William Lang was the editor, and John G. Breslin the publisher. At the end of this time, Mr. Breslin was elected a member of the general assembly, and getting ready to go to Columbus, had nobody to look after the *Adler* in the office, and the writer found other and more profitable employment. The *Adler* was the first German paper published in Seneca county. The next German newspaper published here was the *Unsere Flagge*, J. M. Zahm, editor and proprietor; and the third, *Die Tiffin Presse*, George Homann, editor and proprietor; both of which shall be noticed again.

On the 18th of November, 1845, the first number of the *Whig Standard* was issued by George L. Wharton, editor.

The following is the conclusion of the editor's " salutatory," viz :

" We shall enter our protest against the Locofoco party and labor ardently for the preservation of those principles bequeathed to us by the patriots of the revolution—the principles of the Whig party—a party whose origin was our country's revolution, and whose fidelity and patriotism achieved our independence. Upon this broad platform we shall stand, adhering firmly to liberty, despising anarchy and despotism with an eye single to the interest of our country, feeling assured that upon the integrity of the Whig party, rests our destiny as a nation."

Mr. Wharton conducted the *Standard* until 1848, when he was followed by Abraham Laubach, who continued it only one year, and sold out to Captain McKee, who conducted the paper until 1855, when W. C. Gray became its editor, and changed the name to the *Tiffin Tribune*. He left in 1861, at which time John Robbins purchased it, and continued its publication until 1865, when it again changed hands, passing into the possession of Abraham Kagy, who edited it but a short time, when Messrs. Myers and Miller bought him out, and published the paper until 1868. In November of the year 1868, Messrs. Charles N. Locke and Otis T. Locke purchased the office, and it has ever since been continued under the firm name of Locke & Bro When the Whig party merged over and into the Republican party, the *Tribune* followed the transit, and has ever since been the organ of the Republican party of Seneca county. The paper has a large circulation, and is very ably edited by O. T. Locke, who is still at his post.

In October, 1854, J. M. Zahm, Esq., started a German paper called *Unsere Flagge*, and continued the publication until January, 1867. It supported Democratic principles from an independent standpoint. The office was purchased by Elmer White and Frank Rader in 1868, who commenced the publication of an English paper, independent in politics, called the *Tiffin Star*. In October, 1873, Messrs. J. K. Huddle and Frank Dildine purchased the office, the latter retiring in 1874, after which time the paper was published by Mr. Huddle alone, who turned it into a daily, made a most spicy sheet, and the first daily newspaper Tiffin ever had. It is to be regretted that Mr. Huddle was not sustained with funds, as he should have been, until the office could rely upon its own resources, which it would have done in a short time after it failed.

The *Tiffin Presse*, George Homann, editor and proprietor, made its first appearance on the 6th day of January, 1871; is Democratic in its views; has a large circulation, is generally admired by the German community in the county, and is very ably edited.

The *Evening Herald* was established January 9th, 1877. It is a spicy little daily, well managed; H. C. Kepple, publisher and proprietor; W. H. Kepple, editor.

The *Tiffin Gazette*, Charles L. Zahm, editor and proprietor, issued its first number in April, 1878. It was a weekly neutral family newspaper, well edited, and very clean and neat in its mechanical appearance, decidedly the most readable family paper published in the city; appeared only about one year, when it was suspended for want of proper patronage. Mr. Zahm sold the office some time afterwards to D. J. Statter, Esq., who, as the editor and proprietor of the *Tiffin News*, a weekly family newspaper, issued the first number on April 3, 1880. It is a beautiful and interesting four page sheet.

The circulation of all these weeklies is about 5,000.

In addition to all these newspapers, large quantities of daily papers from Cincinnati, Cleveland, Toledo and Chicago are sold by the newsboys. There are more that 5,000 newspapers and 3,000 periodicals distributed at the Tiffin postoffice every week in addition to the above. What further proof is required to show that Tiffin contains a reading population?

The letters and papers sent by the Tiffin postoffice number over 15,000 per week.

Foreign dailies are sold to the number of 300 or more by the newsboys.

WILLIAM W. ARMSTRONG.

Hitherto, in glancing over the history of the press in Tiffin, very little has been said about two distinguished men connected with it, and who did more than any of their predecessors to elevate the tone of the press and improve the style mentally and mechanically, thus fitting it to the demands of the age and the requirements of a higher order of newspaper literature.

One of these men is the subject of this sketch, and if time and material can be procured before this chapter goes to the printer, there will also be added a short pen-picture of the other.

Mr. Armstrong was born in New Lisbon, Ohio, on the 18th day of March, 1833. He is the youngest son of General John Armstrong, a prominent and influential citizen of Columbiana county. In 1847, on the 27th day of May, when only two months past fourteen years of age, William became an apprentice to the printing business in the office of the *Seneca Advertiser*, at Tiffin, then published by John G. Breslin, Esq., a position he was compelled to take owing to the financial reverses of his father. William was then a small boy, and the writer, being an old friend of Mr. Breslin, and visiting the office of the *Advertiser* very often, well remembers the little fellow sitting at the desk trying penmanship, and looking up into my face with his large blue, sad eye, that seemed to speak of homesickness or loss of friends. Our old citizens too, well remember the boy with his red curls, his friendly face, his polished manners, as he delivered his newspapers every week for a couple of years. It was not long after his arrival here until William had a host of friends among the older classes of our citizens. His sprightliness and ability soon endeared him to his employer, Mr. Breslin, who made him one of his family.

Mr. Armstrong worked at his trade, occasionally contributing to the editorial columns of the *Advertiser*, until 1852. When Mr. Breslin was treasurer of state, he tendered him the office of register of the bank department af the state treasurer's office, which he filled with the satisfaction of the banks and the treasurer for about two years. The life of a clerk was distasteful to young Armstrong, and he returned to Tiffin in 1854, purchased the *Advertiser*, and entered on his majority and editorial career about the same time.

The young writer being an ardent Democrat, the *Advertiser* was conducted as a Democratic organ of the strictest sect, and he being a good business manager and a vigorous writer, soon made his paper a power in northwestern Ohio. In 1857 he was appointed by President Buchanan postmaster at Tiffin, an office which he held until 1861, when he was retired by a Republican successor.

On the 10th of November, 1857, Mr. Armstrong was married to Miss Sarah V., the youngest daughter of Josiah Hedges, Esq. Their union has been blessed with three children, two boys, both now dead, and one daughter, Miss Isabella H., surviving

Mr. Armstrong's position in politics in Seneca county, and his genial nature, made him a strong man in his party in the state, and his strength was manifested in 1862, when, although still but twenty-nine years of age, he was elected secretary of state of Ohio. His determination to make that office one of importance is shown by the fact that under his administration its reports became the most interesting of any of the state departments. He collected election statistics, facts, etc., which made the report much sought after. He served as secretary from 1863 to 1865 during the period of our great civil war, and although an ardent Democrat, was in favor of the maintenance of the union. His name will be found on the commissions of many thousands of officers of the union army from Ohio, who served during the war of the rebellion.

After Mr. Armstrong had served one term of two years, the Republicans returned to power in Ohio and he was again at liberty to return to his favorite pursuit of journalism.

He accordingly, in April, 1865, purchased the material of the lately suspended Cleveland *Plaindealer*, and selling the *Tiffin Advertiser* to the Messrs Myers, he transferred his efforts to the metropolis of northern Ohio, the city of Cleveland.

Owing to the death of J. W. Gray and subsequent unskillful management the *Plaindealer* had been brought into a very unfortunate condition, as was indicated by its suspension.

It is a severe task to revive a dead newspaper, yet Mr. Armstrong not only did that, but in a few years made the *Plaindealer* one of the leading newspapers of the west. A clear, vigorous, ready writer, self-educated and nervy, he naturally took a bold, aggressive course, and neither friends nor enemies had the slightest difficulty in knowing what he meant. He showed himself on all occasions a Democrat of the school of Jackson and Benton, unswerving in favor of state rights, home rule and hard money, and those time-honored principles he was prepared to maintain against all opposition, either by voice or pen, for if Mr. Armstrong had made any efforts he would have taken rank as a very graceful orator and stumper.

In 1868 Mr. Armstrong was elected delegate at large from Ohio to the Democratic national convention, which met at New York, and which nominated Horatio Seymour for president. In 1872 he came within a few votes of securing the nomination for congress in the Seneca—Erie district. In 1873 he removed his family permanently to Cleveland, and settled in a beautiful little home. In 1876 he was chosen by the Democrats of the Cuyahoga district, the second in point of population and wealth in the state, to represent them in the St. Louis Democratic national convention, and again in 1880 the same compliment was paid him by the same district, and he was chosen a delegate to the convention which nominated Hancock and English for president and vice-president. His co-delegates to that convention selected him as the member of the Democratic national executive committee from Ohio. One young printer boy from old Seneca has made himself a reputation as an able and capable politician. In every capacity in life in which he has been tried, he has been found equal to the occasion. A biography in the history of Cuyahoga county says of Mr. Armstrong: "What he is in his office, he is out of it, a man of decided convictions and strong will, always a potent force in the councils of his party and in the community in which he lives." He never has allowed his strong party feelings to control him in his personal and social relations, and he numbers warm friends in all parties. His career is one that has been watched with satisfaction by every resident of Seneca county.

THE "SENECA WHIG."

Tracing the history of the press in Tiffin, I came very near forgetting to record a very strange feature in the history of the old Whig party that affected the old Whigs in Seneca county, and resulted in the establishment of another newspaper called the *Seneca Whig*.

The great question of slavery divided and finally broke down the old Whig party. The Democrats were called pro-slavery men because they could see no constitutional way to get rid of the evil. Many leading men in the Whig party had less constitutional scruples about the question, and organized the "Free Soil party." A host of Democrats joined them; even Martin Van Buren, on whose account, and in whose defense of "Florida war," "gold spoons," "sub-treasury," etc., etc., the Democrats had suffered countless abuse, left them and became the candidate of the "Free Soilers" for the presidency in 1848, with Adams for vice-president. The regular Whigs supported Taylor and Filmore. There was considerable of a stampede from the Democratic party to the "Free Soilers" in some states and just enough to defeat Messrs. Cass and Butler, the candidates of the Democrats. If the course pursued by Mr. Van Buren was the satisfaction of a revenge against Cass, it free-soiled Van-Buren's fame as a statesman and patriot.

A very respectable number of the Whigs of Seneca county leaned over to free-soilism, and Mr. Wharton with his *Standard* supported their cause. This left the old regulars without a paper, and the Clay Whigs said some unpleasant things to Mr. Wharton. Some withdrew their subscriptions and advertisements. In less than a month after Wharton had hoisted the Van Buren banner, a press and type, cases and printers, were brought to Tiffin and the first issue of the *Seneca Whig* saw the light of day on the 29th day of September, A. D. 1848, calling upon the old "faithful and true" to stand firmly by Taylor and Filmore. And they did. Captain J. W. Filler was the editor. He was a very nice looking young man, but a little reckless about running into debt. The paper continued about two years and then became the property of somebody who took it to Findlay.

Four years thereafter the Whigs made their last, grand rally under General Scott and were defeated. Free soilism had assumed proportions.

THE SENECA COUNTY PIONEER ASSOCIATION.

This society should not be overlooked, though it did go into dilapidation by neglect. After much talk and publishing notices in the newspapers of Tiffin, an organization was effected on the 22d of February,

1869, at a meeting held in the city hall of Tiffin in conformity with the call hereto attached. This notice was published only eleven short years ago, and already more than one-half of the signers have passed over the troubled ocean of life; but their names should be preserved.

A PIONEER ASSOCIATION—OLD FOLKS, ATTENTION!

As one after another of the old settlers of Seneca county are leaving us, and their number is continually growing less, we express but a general wish when we call on you, the survivors, whom a kind Providence, has, in his mercy, spared up to this time, to meet with us at the next anniversary of Washington's birthday, February 22, 1869, at 10 o'clock A. M., in the City Hall, in Tiffin, for the purpose of organizing a Pioneer Association.

We desire to preserve among the archives of the association, the names of the old settlers, both male and female, and incidents of frontier life in this county. Let us meet and organize in the morning, adjourn for dinner, and spend the afternoon in social chat, listening to speeches, frontier anecdotes, etc. We would also invite as many of other friends as can make it convenient to be with us; believing that to see the old "bushwhackers" together would afford them pleasure.

Abel Rawson,
Mrs. Ann E. Seney,
G. J. Keen,
J. A. Gibson,
Benjamin Pittenger.
Luther A. Hall,
Mrs. J. A. Pittenger.
J. H. Pittenger,
C. C. Park,
W. H. Gibson,
Dennis F. Cramer,
Andrew Bergderfer,
Mr. Caroline E. Jaeck,
Amos Nichols,
Mrs. Margaret Kroh,
H. A. Buskirk,
G. L. Keating,
Richard Baker,
John Kaga, sen.,
Eden Lease,
W. C. Hedges,
A. Phillips,
H. Kuhn,
Mrs. M. Campbell,
W. H. Keilholtz,
Phillip King,
S. B. Sneath,

Francis Rife,
Andrew Albright,
Phillip Seewald,
A. Keubler,
John Dockweiler,
Jeremiah Williams.
Henry Ebbert,
Samuel Gross,
Elder Lewis Seitz,
Henry St. John,
Levi Davis,
Samuel Herrin,
U. P. Coonrod,
William Toll.
Ezra Derr,
Mrs. Sarah Huss.
Uriah Egbert,
S. S. Hunter,
John Keller,
M. Kirchner,
R. W. Shawhan.
Mrs. G. D. Shawhan.
John W. Eastman.
Samuel Ink,
Mrs. Nancy Kline.
John Guisbert,
Abraham Rine.

Jacob Neikirk,
James Patterson,
W. C. Myers,
Thomas Baltzell,
Wm. Lambertson,
James Pence.
Henry Vandenburgh,
Samuel Kridler,
Mrs. Eleanor Brish,
Mrs. Thomas Lloyd,
Daniel Dildine, sen.,
Thomas Thompson,
Mrs. S. Pennington,
Joseph Bever,
Jacob Price,
Wildman Loomis,
James Goetchis,
Richard Jaqua,
Spencer St. John,
William Lang,
Peter Lantz,
Phillip Wentz,
Samuel Shade,
Dr. A. Benham,
Erastus Jones.

The meeting was called to order by the Rev. John Souder, who

THE PIONEER ASSOCIATION.

called on the Rev. D. C. Howard to open the meeting with prayer. Rev. John Souder was chosen chairman, and W. Lang, secretary; a constitution was adopted and permanent officers elected as follows:

For president, Dr. Henry Kuhn; for vice-president, Philip Seewald; for secretary, William Lang; for treasurer, Lyman White.

Regular meetings were held for several years, which were highly interesting; for many of the old settlers related incidents of pioneer life in Seneca that were both pleasing and instructive. No meetings were held since the death of Dr. Kuhn.

The following is a list of the members, showing the time and place of birth, and time of location of each in this county:

Name.	When and where born.	Time located here.
Mrs. Ann E. Seney	September 13, 1803, Pennsylvania (dead)	November 26, 1831
Mrs. Nancy Ellis	October 14, 1805, Fairfield county, Ohio	Eden, October 1820
Mrs. Margaret Campbell	July 12, 1798, Frederick co., Md. (dead)	Tiffin September 30, 1830
Mrs. Sally Frary	February 4, 1811, Champaign county, O	Fort Seneca, Nov. 19, 1819
Mrs. Elizabeth Snook	March 1, 1813, " "	" " "
Mrs. Sarah Huss	February 27, 1796, Berkley co., Va. (dead)	Tiffin. September, 1825
Mrs. Elizabeth Kridler	January 18, 1798, Allegheny county, Pa.	Tiffin, February, 1831
William Toll	October 11, 1801, Augusta co., Va. (dead)	Tiffin, October 3, 1824
Benjamin Pittenger	January 29, 1798, Frederick county, Md.	Tiffin, December 5, 1825
John Souder	November 26, 1799, Lancaster county, Pa.	Clinton, June 17, 1826
L. A. Hall	August 30, 1813	Tiffin, May 5, 1833
Morris P. Skinner	July 1, 1811, Franklin county, Pa.	London, June, 1833
James M. Stevens	December 31, 1816, Erie county, N. Y.	Eden, November 13, 1827
Daniel Cunningham	March 5, 1804, Baltimore, Md.	Tiffin, July 19, 1834
Samuel Kridler	March 28, 1800, Bedford county, Pa.	Tiffin, November 3, 1823
Jacob Boner	May 2, 1809, Frederick county, Md.	Tiffin, September 19, 1826
Lance L. Todd	January 7, 1806, " " "	Scipio, August, 1828
Christ. C. Park	October 4, 1829, Northumberland co., Pa.	Tiffin, 1830
Mrs. Jane Dewalt	April 5, 1815, " "	Tiffin, April. 1824
Mrs. S. B. Baker	July 11, 1806, Center county, Pa.	Bloom, October 11, 1821
David B. King	January 2, 1809, Butler county, Pa.	Tiffin, May, 1830
Mrs. Ann Eliz. Clark	January 11, 1797, Northumberland co., Pa.	Tiffin, October 12, 1830
Mrs. Polly Stewart	April 6, 1806, Cayuga county, N. Y.	Eden, 1821
George L. Keating	September 8, 1824, Muskingum co., O.	Pleasant, January 13, 1825
James Boyd	January 27, 1805, Center co., Pa. (dead)	Bloom, April 11, 1822
Lewis Baltzell	November 29, 1800, Frederick co., Md.	Tiffin, July, 1829
Abel Rawson	May 11, 1798, Warwick county, Mass.	Tiffin, February 15, 1826
William Lang	December, 14, 1815, Palatinate, Bavaria	Tiffin, August 18, 1833
Lorenzo Abbott	January 18, 1802, Worcester co., Mass.	Pleasant, March, 1822
James Dornan	July 4, 1796, Washington county, Pa.	Tiffin, May 21, 1828
William Raymond	April 27, 1807, Steuben county, N. Y.	Reed, December 1823
R. W. Shawhan	October 19, 1811, Berkley county, Va.	Tiffin, September 10, 1833
Elijah Musgrove	March 4, 1804, Monongahela county, Va.	Scipio, October, 1824
James McEwen	February 14, 1818, Northampton co , Pa.	Clinton, August 6, 1823
Henry Ebert	November 29, 1801, Fayette county Pa.	Tiffin, November 15, 1830
E. G. Bowe	April 5, 1818, Delaware, Ohio	Tiffin, June 7, 1818
Mrs. Maria Rawson	May 16, 1898, Athens, Ohio	Fort Ball, May 4. 1824
Inman Roby	December, 1812, Farquhar county, Va.	Seneca, November, 1832
Levi Keller	September 26, 1806, Fairfield county, O.	Tiffin, September 20, 1820

HISTORY OF SENECA COUNTY.

Name.	When and where born.	Time located here.
James M. Chamberlain	August 26, 1806, Columbiana county, Pa.	Seneca, December, 1852
A. B. McClelland	June 7, 1818, Center county, Pa.	Bloom, November, 1830
Thomas R. Ellis	August 8, 1795, Burlington county, N. J.	Clinton, June, 1828
Fred. Kishler	October 22, 1805, Mifflen county, Pa.	Tiffin, April 20, 1830
Mrs. Elizabeth Kishler	March 26, 1803, Franklin county, Pa.	" " "
Joseph Herrin	July 20, 1810, Columbia county, Pa.	Clinton, August, 1828
Samuel Herrin	August 21, 1812, " "	" " "
John Free	September 1, 1819, Berkley county, Va.	Venice, October 25, 1823
Mrs. Elizabeth Ebert	January 22, 1802, Bucks county, Pa.	Tiffin, November 15, 1831
Mrs. Maria Shawhan	November 15, 1810, Frederick co., Md.	Hopewell, June 28, 1824
Lyman White	November 4, 1814, Oneida county, N. Y.	Reed, spring of 1838
Dr. Henry Kuhn	Oct. 28, 1802, Frederick co., Md. (dead)	Tiffin, August, 1828
Upton R. Flenner	March 12, 1811, " "	Tiffin, May, 1835
Joseph Richards	April 7, 1792, Fayette county Pa.	Clinton, December 10, 1823
Henry Davidson	October 18, 1818, Pickaway county, O.	Seneca, March, 1832
Jacob M. Zahm	November 14, 1808, Palatinate, Bavaria	Thompson, Sept 24, 1832
Hugh Welsh	February 18, 1801, Beaver county, Pa.	Eden, spring of 1819
Miron Sexton	June 1, 1800, Tollard county, Conn.	Huron co., Sept. 20, 1824
Sylvester B. Clark	February 2, 1802, Monroe county, Va.	Tiffin, August 1, 1833
Mrs. Catharine F. Souder	May 22, 1825, Jefferson county, Va.	Hopewell, fall of 1830
Nath. N. Spielman	March 25, 1815, Washington county, Md.	Pleasant, April 20, 1830
John Williams	April 21, 1818, Fairfield county, O.	Clinton, 1821
Enos Cramer	February 24, 1804, Frederick county, Md.	Clinton, 1831
Dewit C. Pittenger	January 24, 1836, Tiffin	
Alma H. Pittenger	October 31, 1844, Steuben county, N. Y.	Eden, ——
Mrs. Margaret Watson	June 25, 1823, Center county, Pa.	Bloom, 1856
Mrs. Elizabeth Dorsey	November 16, 1799, Fayette county, Pa.	Tiffin, 1856
Mrs. Hannah Herin	December 9, 1813, Maryland	Clinton, 1833
Mrs. Mary P. Lang	July 10, 1818, Columbia county, Pa.	Clinton, spring of 1829
Louis Seewald	September 15, 1831, Palatinate, Bavaria	Tiffin, August 18. 1833
James A. Sohn	November 19, 1832, Adams county, Pa.	Tiffin, April 21, 1834
Robert Nichols	December 2, 1827, Berkley county, Va.	Eden, November, 1834
Arthur Morrison	August 8, 1817, Jefferson county, O.	Clinton, March 21, 1828.
Mrs. Jane Dildine	November 29, 1806, Columbia co., Pa.	Clinton, May 10, 1829
James Griffin	April 16, 1796, Berkley county, Va.	Eden, fall of 1831
S. A. Myers	December 4, 1830, Perry county, O.	Seneca, September, 1835
Hezekiah Searles	December 4, 1810, Fairfield county, O.	
Mrs. Eliza A. Searles	July 14, 1817, Northampton county, Pa.	Clinton, 1825
R. M. C. Martin	September 18, 1822, Perry county, O.	Eden, May, 1830
Mrs. Barbara Martin	February 19, 1831, Seneca county, O.	Eden township
Jacob Price	December 18. 1796, Rockingham co, Va.	Eden, 1822
Mrs. Nancy Price	September 14, 1804, Northampton co. Pa.	Venice, September, 1830
Henry H. Schock	November 2, 1800, York co., Pa. (dead)	Eden, 1833
Mrs. Margaret Schock	December 10, 1804, Frederick co., Md.	" "
Mrs. Elizabeth Jaqua	October 2, 1718, Schenectady co., N. Y.	Eden, 1832
John Wax	September 15, 1813, Perry county, O.	Eden, 1835
Mrs. Sarah Wax	March 17, 1811, Franklin county, O.	Eden, 1832
Jacob Hossler	January 28, 1800, Adams county, Pa.	Bloom, 1834
Mrs. Ann Hossler	June 9, 1811, Stark county, O.	" "
Mrs. E. J. Watson	March 9, 1815, Washington county, O.	Eden, 1845
Mrs. Eva Kirshner	September, 1802, Franklin county, Pa.	Eden, 1827
Henry Geiger	March 18, 1812, Baden, Germany	Eden, 1835
Thomas West	September 15, 1801, Brown county, N. Y.	Bloom, 1822
Nancy West	May 15th, 1806, Center county, Pa.	" "
Geo. McLaughlin	October 15, 1798, Juniata county, Pa.	Seneca co., Sept. 22, 1825.
Joseph Miller	March 26, 1807, Cumberland co., Pa.	Seneca co., Sept. 18. 1834.
Archibald Stewart	June 3, 1797, Lycoming county, Pa.	Scipio, 1825
William Davis	January 18, 1819, Perry county, O.	Seneca co., Nov. 12, 1825

It was Thursday evening, November 24, 1853, and eighteen young German citizens of Tiffin met at the hall of Mr. Adams, on East Market street, in Tiffin, and organized a singing society under the direction of Christian Kunold, an old German music teacher:

First tenors—Christian Mueller, Michael Miller, Christian Siegchrist, Louis Zimmer, John Laux.
First bass—Louis Miller, Christian Schneider, John Keirchner, John Merkelbach.
Second tenor—Wilhelm Berger, F. W. Berger, Will Seewald, Simon Stricker, Carl Stadtmiller.
Second bass—Ph. Emich, Francis Ries, Adam Huth, Joseph Yaeger.

After practicing three months, a committee was appointed to draft a constitution which was adopted February 24, 1854, and the society called "Der Bruderbund."

Christian Mueller was elected president, Ph. Emich secretary and William Berger treasurer.

The following persons then also became members, viz: Andrew Waesner, William Speier, Carl Mueller, John Haase, Carl Schindler, W. Wolf, John Schmilt, Michael Welter, William Herold, Francis Adams, John Ries, John Blum, Bernhart Striker.

The number of members soon rose to eighty, but before long it became reduced to about ten active members. A dissolution seemed inevitable, but the perseverance and tenacity peculiar to German life preserved the organization, and the Bruderbund for a long time thereafter was the only German association in Tiffin.

"Die Deutsche Theatergesellskaft" preceded it several years. This was perhaps the first German society organized in Tiffin. It had considerable talent and produced several pieces upon the stage in the old Methodist church on Market street, that were very ably put over the boards.

Let us remember "Feld Hummel's Hochzeitstag." But first of all, the "Deutsche Leseverein," that used to meet at Adam Schickel's, on East Market street, was the pioneer German association in Tiffin, and continued for several years until religious discussions broke it up.

The Sunday evening exercises of the Bruderbund were open to all, and no distinction was made by the association as to a man's politics or his religion.

In 1856 the Bruderbund joined the "North American Saengerbund" and met with its festivals in Cincinnati in 1856, in Detroit in 1857, in Pittsburgh in 1858, in Cleveland in 1859 and in Buffalo in 1860. From this time, and during the war, the "saengerfests" were suspended.

The society lost one member on the battlefield of Gettysburg when Jacob Bise fell.

The first saengerfest after the war, met in Columbus, Ohio, in 1865, the next in Louisville, Kentucky in 1866. It met in Indianapolis in 1867 and in Chicago in 1868. In the two last mentioned the Bruderbund participated by delegates only. At Chicago a resolution was adopted to have bi-annual festivals. The first saengerfest thereafter met in Cincinnati in 1870, when the whole Bruderbund participated. They were with the North Western at St. Louis in 1872 and at Cleveland in 1876.

The Bruderbund then attached itself to the Ohio district and sang at its festival in Columbus in 1878. In 1879 an invitation to meet with the Peninsular Singing Association at Toledo was accepted.

The next Ohio saengerfest will meet at Akron, which the Bruderbund will support.

Mr. Kunold served as director up to 1855, when Charley Boos was elected to succeed him and served until 1857, when George Spies was elected, and who was again succeeded by Mr. Boos, and for the last ten years Mr. Spies has been the director.

Of the first members only three survive, the two Bergers and Mr. Merkelbach. Fourteen honorary members have also died. Since its first organization the society has sung at over one hundred funerals and church and other dedications. During the prevalence of the cholera in Tiffin, when many families had moved away from town and things looked gloomy, the Bruderbund met two or three times a week at the court house yard in the evening and enlivened the stillness of the night with many a beautiful refrain from their choicest pieces. They have now sixty honorary members. The present organization is as follows, viz:

Director—George Spies.
President—George A. Lautermilch.
Secretary—Fred. W. Berger.
Treasurer—William Berger.
First tenors—William Herold, George A. Lautermilch, Charles Weinich, George Lautermilch.
Second tenors—William Berger, F. W. Berger, Pillip Grummel, Nicholas Hoefling.
First bass—John Merkelbach, Jos. Miller, Martin Albrecht, Fritz Eckert.
Second bass—Ph. Pfeiffer, John Dutt, George Homan, Julius Keisling.

THE PHILHARMONIC SOCIETY.

On the evening of the 19th of May, 1876, there met at the house of Mr. Henry Gross, on Sandusky street, a few young men and young ladies to consider the propriety of forming a musical association. The meeting was called to order. Mr. C. H. Miller presided; Miss Jennie Ford was appointed secretary. A committee was appointed to prepare a suitable constitution and report at the next meeting. Professor J. M. Bach, of Sandusky, Miss Mary Ebert (now deceased), Dr. Willard, Mrs. Barnes and Miss Jennie Ford were appointed such committee.

At the adjourned meeting of May 25, 1876, the committee reported and a constitution was adopted. Louis Ulrich was elected president; Mr. Lohr, vice-president; C. H. Miller, secretary; Harry Buskirk, treasurer; Miss Cora Pugh, librarian; Professor J. M. Bach, musical director. Among the active members were L Ulrich, Francis Wagner, Molly, Pauline and Isabella Wagner, Peter Pfeiffer, Harry Gross, Robert Fisher, Homer Bricker, Mary Ebert, Dr. Willard and Michael Scannel.

The first public presentation of the society was a concert at the National Hall, which was followed by many others since. The first opera the society presented was "The Haymakers," by Root; the next was "The Bohemian Girl," by Balfe; then "Martha," by Flotow; then "Lily of Killarney," by Benedicks.

The society have now under rehearsal the "Chimes of Normandy," by Plauquette, which they intend to produce in the coming fall.

The Philharmonic has become one of the institutions of Tiffin, and their productions give strong evidence of their high appreciation of music as an art and of the rapid improvements and achievements they have made under so distinguished a directorship. Every production is a vast improvement upon the preceding one, in both behavior and refinement in execution. Tiffin has every reason to be proud of the Philharmonic. The society would be a credit to any city.

The crowded houses that attend all their productions should also be sufficient proof to the society that they are highly appreciated by our citizens here. Professor Bach is a leader of no ordinary grade.

The present officers are:

President—L. Ulrich.
Vice-President—Otto Reutlinger.
Secretary—Miss Mabel Allen.
Librarian—Peter Pfeiffer.
Treasurer—Francis Wagner.
Director—Professor J. M. Bach.

THE SENECA COUNTY INFIRMARY.

This institution is located in section five, in Eden township, upon a tract of two hundred and forty acres of land on the Melmore road, about two and one-half miles south of Tiffin. The land was bought in 1855, and in 1856 the first buildings were erected. N. N. Speilman had the contract for the brick work, and Myers and Toner the carpenter and joiner work. The work was let in conformity with a notice the county commissioners caused to be published in the *Tiffin Tribune* and *Seneca Advertiser*, on the 30th of January, 1856. David Burns, Isaac Stillwell and James Boyd were the commissioners. The work was accepted September 19, 1856, and orders were drawn for the payment of the same. The first directors of the Infirmary were Andrew Lugenbeel, John Kerr and Daniel Brown, who appointed Harrison McClelland the first superintendent of the Infirmary and farm. Many changes have been made on the farm since, and the farm, as well as the buildings, is in good order under the present superintendent, Mr. Daniel G. Heck, who has had charge of the same six years. The institution has some fifty inmates at this time.

The present board of directors consists of George Haebler, Lewis Spitter and Joseph E. Magers.

The property is worth, at least, $75,000.

MRS. HARRIET CRAWFORD.

The subject of this sketch is certainly one of the most remarkable women that ever lived in Tiffin, or elsewhere.

She was born in Attercliff, England, and when sixteen years of age was married. Her health failing, her physician recommended a sea voyage as the only remedy to restore her health. Her husband, who was a civil engineer, succeeded in finding employment in the East India Company. The young couple sailed for Calcutta, where, after a voyage of six months and seventeen days, they arrived, having landed but once during that time. Shortly after their arrival, the young husband died of cholera, that dreaded monster of the East in those days, and the young widow was left alone in a strange land among strangers.

She became acquainted, some time after, with Dr. William L. Crawford, a young physician in Calcutta, belonging to the British army, and became his wife. They lived at various places in the East Indies some fourteen years, when they moved to the Cape of Good Hope, where they resided some two years. From there they moved to the island of St. Helena, while the great Napoleon was a prisoner there, and then moved back to England. From there they emigrated to Canada, where Dr. Crawford died in 1845.

Mrs. Crawford was the mother of eleven children, eight boys and three girls, who were born on four continents of the globe—some in Asia, some in Africa, some in Europe and some in America.

In 1853 she came to Tiffin from Canada with the family of her son, the present Dr. Crawford, of Tiffin, with whom she lived the rest of her days, spending the evening of her long and eventful life in ease and comfort, and enjoying the respect and veneration of all who knew her.

Her death occurred on the 12th day of September, 1876, from congestion of the lungs.

She reached the high age of eighty-nine years and thirty days. She was the mother of Asiatics, Africans, Europeans and Americans.

CHAPTER XXV.
THE TOLEDO WAR.

AFTER the terrible scourge of Asiatic cholera in 1834, the next subject that aroused public attention in Seneca county, was the question of the northern boundary of Ohio, which became very serious in all its aspects, and threatened to lead to bloodshed between the borderers of Ohio and the territory of Michigan. The subject is nearly lost sight of, and would not be mentioned here because the question in itself had no effect upon Seneca county directly, but when soldiers were called out to protect the citizens of Ohio along the disputed border, it was found that the disputed line was in the 17th division, in which Major-General John Bell, of Lower Sandusky, was the commanding general, and Seneca county was in one of the brigades in that division, and under obligations to furnish her quota of the troops called out by Governor Lucas. It therefore became a matter of interest to Seneca county after all, and especially when about 300 men, " armed and equipped as the law directs," left Tiffin with their baggage and tents in wagons, and provisions for an indefinite time. Colonel Henry C. Brish led these citizen soldiers as their commander, to report to General Bell. John W. Patterson was captain of one company, and John Walker was quartermaster. I remember also that John Adelsberger refused to come to time, and he was arrested and put under guard, but they took him along. Some of the officers were only but partly uniformed; the rest marched into line in citizens clothes.

Henry Gross was "fife major," and here is a copy of his commision:
By the confidence I repose in you, Henry Gross, I appoint you fife major of the 3d regiment. 1st batallion, 17th division of the Ohio militia.
TIFFIN. 22d April, A. D., 1835.
Personally appeared before me the above named H. Gross. taken the necessary oath of the above office. JAMES BOYD,
Colonel 3d regiment. 1st batallion. 17th division.
TIFFIN, 22d April, 1835.

Henry was a good fifer, and so was Jacob M. Ebert (Bro. Ebert) a very good drummer on the Case drum, and he was likewise appointed

THE TOLEDO WAR.   425

drum major. The army left our border, and nothing of any serious nature occurred except one night the Ohio army was aroused from their sleep in the woods and drawn up in line of battle ready to receive the foe " with bloody hands to hospitable graves," (Corwin). Everything was to be conducted quietly; no fire to be made and no loud word of command to be given The music was ordered in front to be ready to march at the signal. Now the drum major's memory as to the rules of war became very vitally refreshed, and he insisted that in time of action the position of the music was in the rear. General Brish knew better, and while the drum major had some wags from the rank and file on his side, the General and the staff officers wanted the music in front. So they had it until the rising sun lit up the woods and proved that there was no enemy in sight. It was a false alarm.

Another ludicrous incident is told of a remarkable chap in Perrysburg who drummed up recruits, marching up and down street while the court was in session. He was a remarkably tall man, and wore a two-story white felt hat, with a narrow brim; but by long use and exposure it had become softened and the crown bulged up so that it was really two-story and an attic. An ordinary tenor drum by his side looked like a boy's drum. He had a strip of paper with the words, " Recruiting for the war," tied around his tall hat. They called him " Big Odle." Another man carried a flag before him, and thus they marched up and down this street, passing the court house every few minutes. Judge Higgins was naturally a little sensative, and bore up with this annoyance as long as he could. Now it got to the boiling point, and the Judge could stand it no longer. He ordered the sheriff to go out and stop that drumming. Odle told the sheriff that he was under orders from Captain Scott to drum for recruits for the war; that in war the military was above the civil authority, and that he would drum until ordered to stop by Captain Scott. The sheriff returned to court and reported accordingly. The Judge's eyes flashed lightning. The sheriff was ordered to arrest Odle and bring him into court forthwith, and also summon Captain Scott. The order was executed in a few minutes, and " Big Ogle " marched up to the bench with his drum and trimmings. He had on an old rifleman's uniform, of green color, and trimmed with black lace. His pants were of domestic cloth, colored with oak bark, and also trimmed with black lace down the legs. Captain Scott explained the drumming, and informed the Judge that Odle was under orders from him, as instructed by Colonel Van Fleet. He said Governor Lucas was at Spafford's Exchange, and had sanctioned this drumming before the court commenced, and that the drumming would be continued until ordered stopped by Colonel Van Fleet or his Excellency.

This was too much for the Judge, and he roared out in stentorian tones: "Mr. Sheriff, take Captain Scott and his music organ to jail, and lock them up. Mr. Prosecuting Attorney, draw up an information against these men for contempt of court, and have the case ready for hearing to-morrow morning."

Jonas Pratt, the sheriff, started with the men to execute the order. Scott and Odle followed willingly until they came to the corner of the building where a path led to the log jail, on the rear of the lot. Here Scott and Odle squared themselves before the sheriff and refused to go further. Scott told the sheriff that in the emergency of war the military was above the civil power, and that if Judge Higgins would undertake to press this thing any further, he would declare martial law, and do with Judge Higgins as General Jackson did with Judge Hall at New Orleans, and have them both arrested.

"That is right; that is right, Captain," said Odle, at the same time doubling up his two hands to about the size of elephant's feet. "That's the way to talk Bully for you, Cap.; stand off, Sheriff." The crowd of bystanders were on the side of war, and the sheriff was strongly impressed with the idea that Judge Higgins' orders could not be executed just then. He retreated up stairs to the court room and reported accordingly.

The Judge never said a word in reply, and continued in the trial of the case on hand as if nothing had happened. Odle slung the drum strap over his neck and continued his march as before, hitting his drum with great force on both ends. After some little time the Judge directed the sheriff to find Captain Scott and ask him to be so good as to take his music to some back street, where it would not disturb the court so much.

The trouble of this northern boundary of Ohio originated with the admission of Ohio into the Union, and was caused by an error in the map that placed the southern bend of Lake Michigan too far south. It vexed the convention that formed the constitution, and Congress in admitting Ohio into the Union. As early as the adoption of the ordinance of July 13th, 1787, providing for a government of the northwestern territory, a provision is made for the northern boundary of states that should thereafter be formed, lying south of a line drawn due east and west from and through the southern bend of Lake Michigan, which east and west line should also be the southern boundary of two states lying north of that line, so that this east and west line finally formed the north line of Ohio, Indiana and Illinois, and the south line of Michigan and Wisconsin.

On the 30th of April, 1802, when Congress passed an act authorizing the people of the territory of Ohio to form a state constitution, they described the northern boundary as follows:

On the north by an east and west line drawn through the southern extreme of Lake Michigan, running east after intersecting the due north line from the mouth of the Great Miami, until it shall intersect Lake Erie, or the territorial line, and thence through Lake Erie to the Pennsylvania line; Provided that Congress shall be at liberty, at any time hereafter, either to attach all the territory lying east of the line to be drawn due north from the mouth of the Miami aforesaid, to the territorial line, and north of an east and west line drawn through the southerly extreme of Lake Michigan, running east, as aforesaid, to Lake Erie, to the aforesaid state, or dispose of it otherwise in conformity to the fifth article of compact between the original states and the people and states to be formed in the territory north of the river Ohio.

When the convention at Chillicothe, on the 29th day of November, 1802, adopted the first constitution for Ohio, they gave the state the northern boundary, as contained in the enabling act with this proviso:

Provided always, and it is hereby fully understood and declared by this convention, that if the southerly bend or extreme of Lake Michigan should extend so far south that a line drawn due east from it should not intersect Lake Erie, or if it should intersect the Lake Erie east of the mouth of the Miami river of the lake, then and in that case, with the assent of congress of the United States, the northern boundary of this state shall be established by and extend to a direct line running from the southern extremity of Lake Michigan to the most northerly cape of the Miami bay, after intersecting the due north line from the mouth of the Great Miami river aforesaid; thence northeast to the territorial line, and by the said territorial line to the Pennsylvania line.

The reader must be patient in looking over the relation of these old "field notes," for he will not understand this boundary question without them.

When congress, on the 19th of February, 1803, admitted Ohio into the Union, nothing was said about the northern boundary. On the 11th of January, 1805, congress created the territory of Michigan, and defined her boundaries as follows:

All that part of Indiana territory which lies north of a line drawn east from the southerly bend of Lake Michigan, and until it shall intersect Lake Erie and east of a line drawn from said southerly bend through the middle of said lake to its northern extremity, and thence due north to the northern extremity of the United States.

Substantially reaffirming the original boundary contained in the act authorizing the territory of Ohio to form a state government.

Michigan then also extended her laws to this, its southern boundary line.

The whole question, therefore, was to ascertain the exact line drawn east through the southern bend of Lake Michigan. To accomplish this the geographical line in north latitude, minutes and seconds, had to be established with positive certainty.

The line the authorities were then talking about was designated on the maps as the "Fulton line," which intersects Lake Erie east of the mouth of the Maumee river, and meets the proviso of the Ohio constitution.

It was then ascertained that this east and west line would not intersect the territorial line between the United States and Canada, but cut across the counties of Cuyahoga, Geauga and Ashtabula. The line, therefore, given by congress to Ohio, was an impossible line, owing to a want of knowledge of the geographical position of Lake Michigan at the time congress passed the enabling act.

When the authorities of Ohio ascertained the uncertainty of the northern boundary, they applied to congress for a survey of the line in conformity with the proviso in the constitution of Ohio.

In 1812 congress passed a resolution directing the commissioner of the general land office, to cause it to be surveyed, but the war with Great Britain and their northwestern savage allies, prevented it, and the line was not run until the year 1817, when one William Harris, under direction from the general land office, ran the line, and it was afterwards known as the "Harris line."

This survey was reported from the general land office to the executive of Ohio, and ratified by the general assembly of Ohio January 29th, 1818.

Applications were then made by Ohio to congress to ratify the Harris line as the northern boundary of Ohio very frequently, but without success, until the events of 1835, so memorable in the conflicts between Ohio and the territory of Michigan.

This disputed territory is valuable for its rich and productive farming lands, and the possession of the harbor on the Maumee river, where the young and flourishing city of Toledo sits in her proud majesty to control things.

This strip of land is five miles wide at the west end, and eight miles at the east end. The line was fixed before any other territory was organized and affected by it.

Toledo had many names. It was then Swan Creek; afterwards Port Lawrence, then Vistule, now Toledo. The early settlers were satisfied to be in the territory of Michigan.

THE TOLEDO WAR.

In 1835 the people, who had settled in the Maumee country, became clamorous for the extension of the Ohio canal from Piqua north, and Toledo was made the point of terminus of the canal. Then the Toledo people saw the point and came to the conclusion that they lived in the wrong state; that it would be to their interest to be Buckeyes. The canal changed their allegiance. Now Governor Lucas was urged to extend the laws of Ohio over this territory in question. On the 23d of February, 1835, the legislature of Ohio passed an act extending the northern boundaries of the counties of wood, Henry and Williams to the Harris line.

The Fulton line was the south line and the Harris line the north line of this disputed tract, and Michigan had hitherto extended her territorial jurisdiction to the Fulton line as the southern boundary of Michigan. Wood county had, however, previously levied taxes up to the Harris line, but the people refused to pay them and that ended it.

The possession of the harbor at the mouth of Swan creek was then made the burning point, and the talk about "legal rights" was the order of the day.

There is no room here for speculation as to what would have been the result had Michigan succeeded. The only object in speaking at length on this subject, now almost forgotten, is to preserve the facts from the tooth of time as long as possible as a point in the history of Ohio, and in which Seneca county took a very active part.

We can read and talk about those scenes and times without getting excited now, but Ohio was then in her boyhood and Michigan growing up to be a "big wolverine" sometime. Stevens T. Mason, the governor of Michigan territory, was a very young man but as spunky as a rat, and felt himself well protected by his guardian, "Uncle Sam," in his territorial jurisdiction.

This law of Ohio, above mentioned, also authorized the governor to appoint three commissioners to re-mark the Harris line. Uri Seely, of Geauga, Jonathan Taylor, of Licking, and John Patterson of Adams, were appointed such commissioners, and April 1, 1835, named for the work to commence. Mr. Mason sent a special message to the legislative council of Michigan apprising them of the act of Ohio and advised proceedings to counteract the same.

On the 12th of February, 1835, the territorial legislature of Michigan passed an act to fine and imprison any person who should undertake to exercise any legal authority in her border, except under the laws of the territory, etc.

Now the people within this disputed territory became alarmed, and they were at a loss to know which of the two jurisdictions they had better belong to. They wrote numerous letters to the governors of both jurisdictions, explaining their dangers and their troubles, etc.

Among the most distinguished men who looked to Governor Mason for help were J. V. D. Sutphen, Coleman J. Kuler, Cyrus Fisher and Samuel Hemmenway, and those that wanted to be Ohioans counted among their number Andrew Palmer, Stephen B. Comstock, Mayor Stickney, Willard Daniels, George McKay and Dr. Naman Goodsell.

Governor Mason wrote to General Brown, who was in command of the third division of the Michigan militia, as follows:

EXECUTIVE OFFICE, DETROIT, March 9, 1835.

SIR: You will herewith receive the copy of a letter just received from Columbus. You will now perceive that a collision between Ohio and Michigan is inevitable, and will therefore be prepared to meet the crisis. The governor of Ohio has just issued a proclamation, but I have neither received it nor been able to learn its tendency. I shall send you such arms as may be necessary for your successful operation without waiting for an order from the secretary of war as soon as Ohio is properly in the field. Till then, I am compelled to await the direction of the war department.

Yours, etc., STEVENS T. MASON.

GENERAL JOS. W. BROWN.

On the 31st of March, Governor Lucas, accompanied by his staff and the boundary commissioners, arrived at Perrysburg on their way to run and re-mark the Harris line, in compliance with the law of the 23d of February previous.

General John Bell, in command of the 17th division Ohio militia, embracing the disputed territory, arrived about the same time with his staff, and mustered into the service some 600 men, fully armed and equipped. On his way to Perrysburg, Governor Lucas, with his staff, stopped all night in Fort Ball, at Smith's hotel. They made a very formidable appearance and when General H. C. Brish met them, there was a show of military etiquette, the like of which Seneca county never experienced before. From here the troops from Seneca followed Governor Lucas and met General Bell at Lower Sandusky, from whence they took the line of march for Perrysburg.

The Ohio army went into camp at Fort Miami. Governor Mason, with General Brown, arrived at Toledo with about 1,200 men at the same time. Governor Mason had his staff with him also. Thus the two armies, ready for the fray, waited for the word, and the country was wild with excitement.

Lewis Cass said well in a letter to Edward Tiffin, under date of

November 1, 1817: "A disputed jurisdiction is one of the greatest evils that can happen to a country."

Governor Lucas had made up his mind to take the risk and send General Bell with his force to Toledo as soon as he could get ready but before they were ready to start, two eminent citizens, Hon. Richard Rusk, of Philadelphia, and Colonel Howard, of Baltimore, arrived from Washington as commissioners from the president of the United States, to use their personal influence to stop all warlike demonstrations. Hon. Elisha Whittlesey, of Ohio, accompanied the commissioners as a voluntary peacemaker. These gentlemen remonstrated with Governor Lucas and reminded him of the fatal consequences that might follow, etc. They urged patience and to wait for a peaceable settlement of the matter by congress.

These commissioners then also visited Governor Brown and urged him to abstain from violence and bloodshed until congress could act in the premises, and finally, on the 7th of April, they submitted to both governors the following proposition, to-wit:

1st. That the Harris line should be run and re-marked pursuant to the act of the last session of the legislature of Ohio, without interruption.

2d. The civil elections, under the laws of Ohio, having taken place throughout the disputed territory, that the people residing upon it should be left to their own government, obeying the one jurisdiction or the other, as they may prefer, without molestation from the authorities of Ohio or Michigan until the close of the next session of congress.

Governor Mason refused to accede to this proposition. Governor Lucas consented and discharged the troops. Governor Mason partially followed suit, and that reluctantly, but kept up preparations for any emergency.

Governor Lucas now thought he could run and re-mark the Harris line without any molestation from the authorities of Michigan, and ordered the commissioners to proceed with the work.

S. Dodge, an engineer on the Ohio canal, had been engaged as surveyor to run the line. He addressed a letter to Samuel Forrer, one of the canal commissioners of Ohio, dated Maumee, April 11, 1835, in which he said, among other things, that Messrs. Rush and Howard had assured them that no resistance should be made to the survey, but that trouble was brewing, and Ohio could not run the line without a strong military force. That it would become necessary to have an extra session of the Ohio legislature to make appropriations, etc. Then he goes on and says:

We shall shart to-morrow for the northwest corner of the state, and the next time you hear from me I shall probably inform you that I am at Monroe, the headquarters of General Brown. General Brown was yesterday at Toledo, at the head of the sheriff's posse of 100 armed men. They came for the purpose of arresting those who had accepted office under the state of Ohio. He informed me that any attempt to run the line would be resisted by the whole force of the territory; that they had 300 men under arms at Monroe and 600 more would soon be there; that they had 1,500 stand of arms taken from the United States arsenal at White Pigeon; that they did not mean to be rode rough shod by Ohio. It was replied that Ohio had not as yet put on her rough shoes, and would not, unless they made it necessary, and that the line would certainly be run. The governor of Ohio started yesterday (8th inst.) for Defiance, and is entirely unprepared to meet the force of Michigan. What course he will pursue I do not know. Our party consists of fifteen or twenty unarmed men, and if we proceed we shall certainly be made prisoners, there not being a sufficient number to prevent surprise. I think the expedition will be delayed. The state of Ohio is affording no protection to the people on the disputed territory, further than through the civil authorities. And those who have accepted office have been obliged to retreat. The governor has power to call out the militia, but has no funds to sustain them. Yours truly, S. DODGE.

President Jackson applied to the attorney general, Benjamin F Butler, of New York, for his opinion in the premises, who replied, saying that the mere running of the line was no cause for hostilities, but that suit might be brought against the commissioners in the courts of the territory.

The commissioners commenced running the line from the northwest corner of the state. General Brown's scouts watched them. When the surveying party got into Lenawee county, the under sheriff, with his posse, appeared on the ground to arrest them, but the commissioners and surveyors escaped and got to free Ohio soil. They reached Perrysburg next day with their clothes badly torn and hungry.

Governor Lucas reported the facts to the president. General Jackson caused a copy of the report to be sent to Governor Mason, with a request to have Mason send his statement also. Thereupon Governor Mason applied to General Brown for information. General Brown, on the 17th of June, 1835, writes from Tecumach to Governor Mason, stating all he did and naming those that had been arrested and refuting the idea that the commissioners had been fired upon.

The news of the breaking up of the surveying party spread through Ohio like wild-fire, and Governor Mason's course was generally condemned.

Governor Lucas finding it impracticable to run the line, called an extra session of the legislature for the 8th of June. That body passed an act "to prevent the forcible abduction of the citizens of Ohio," and to punish the offenders with imprisonment in the penitentiary. Another act was passed creating the new county of Lucas from the north part of Wood county, embracing the disputed territory north of Wood and a portion of the northwest of Sandusky county. It directed a court of common pleas to be held at any convenient house in Toledo on the first Monday of September next.

There was also another act passed at this session, accepting the proposition made by the above named commissioners of the United States; $300,000 were appropriated to carry the law into effect and paying troops, etc. The division commanders were called upon to report the number of troops in each division that would volunteer to sustain the governor in enforcing the laws in the disputed territory. Fifteen out of seventeen divisions in the state reported 10,000 men ready to volunteer, and 2,000 men were estimated that would volunteer in the two divisions that did not report. The Michigan authorities became more violent in their prosecutions of Ohioans Major Stickney, George McKay, Judge Wilson, and many others were arrested and taken to Monroe jail. When Major Stickney was arrested he refused to go. They put him on a horse and held him on it, while a third man led the horse. They tied the Major's legs together under the horse to secure him. In the attempt to arrest T. Stickney, a son of the Major, he took out his pen-knife and stabbed one of the men in the left side, and made his escape.

The stabbing of Wood by T. Stickney was reported to General Jackson, who became very indignant over the affair, and Governor Lucas, anticipating the danger of being put into an unfavorable light at Washington, sent Messrs. N. H. Swayne, William Allen and David T. Disney to Washington, to confer with the president on the subject of the boundary. These gentlemen made a full and fair statement of the whole trouble in writing to the Hon. John Forsyth, secretary of state, July 1st, 1835. The secretary answered on the 3d of July very fully, giving General Jackson's views of the question, and promising to cause an earnest recommendation to be sent to the authorities in Michigan, that no obstructions shall be interposed to the re-marking of the Harris line; that all arrests under the territorial act shall cease until after the meeting of the next congress, and all questions about the disputed lines to be avoided, etc.

Judge Higgins, the president judge of the Maumee judicial circuit, in a letter addressed to Governor Lucas on the 20th of July, expressed great fears of trouble ensuing if he should attempt to hold court in Toledo under the law.

On the 29th of July Governor Lucas wrote to Messrs. Patterson,

Taylor and Seely, the commissioners to re-run the Harris line, informing them of the promise of the president, and advised the commencement of the work on the 1st of September, at a point where they left off. He informed them that he had sent two hundred and twenty-five rifles and sixty-one muskets and equipments to Port Miami, and would send more soon, to protect them in their work; that these arms would be placed under the control of the court, etc.

The authorities of Michigan disregarded all these arrangements, and kept on making arrests. On the 29th of August, Secretary Forsyth wrote to Governor Mason that he was superseded, and that Mr. Charles Shaler, of Pennsylvania, was appointed secretary of the territory of Michigan as his successor, etc.

On the same day Secretary Forsyth also addressed a letter to Governor Lucas, transmitting copies of letters written that day to Governor Mason and Mr. Shaler, expressing a hope that no further attempt would be made by Ohio to exercise jurisdiction in the disputed territory until congress could act on the question, etc.

These letters from Secretary Forsyth had the desired effect. The good sense of Governor Lucas had already shown him the danger of getting into conflict with the United States, who would naturally stand by and protect a territory in its legal rights, and he modified his course very materially.

But the question whether to hold a court in the new county on the 7th of September, was still to be decided. Adjutant-General Samuel C. Andrews was sent by Governor Lucas to Lucas county to consult with the judge and other officers, who directed Colonel Van Fleet to call out his regiment to act as a posse to the sheriff for the protection of the court. Andrew Coffinberry, and old and experienced lawyer, was engaged by the governor to act as an assistant prosecuting attorney. Colonel Van Fleet promptly obeyed the call and ordered his regiment to rendezvous.

Generals Andrews and Bell stopped at a hotel in Toledo, demeaning themselves as private citizens. On Sunday afternoon the sheriff and attendants met at Miami to proceed together the next morning under escort of Colonel Van Fleet's regiment, to hold the court at Toledo. Colonel Van Fleet had 100 men on the ground, which was considered sufficient to disperse any mob that might offer resistance. In the evening one of the Colonel's scouts came in and reported that General Brown had just arrived at Toledo with a large military force to prevent the holding of the court.

The judges were confounded with fear at learning these facts. Judge

Higgins and Count Coffinberry were not present. Consultation lasted a long time. The associate judges hesitated. Some were for giving up and holding no court. Finally it was agreed to leave the matter to Colonel Van Fleet, who had not said a word, but walked up and down the line with sword in hand, in front of his men and within hearing of the judges. The Colonel had his plan arranged. He turned to the judges, and with a determined military look and bearing, exclaimed: "If you are women, go home; if you are men, do your duty as judges of the court; I will do mine. If you leave the matter entirely with me, I will be responsible for your safety, and insure the accomplishment of our object; but if otherwise, I can give you no assurance."

This settled the discussion. The honor and safety of the court, " the peace and dignity of the state of Ohio," were placed in his keeping. The Colonel told his men that he was about to undertake a hazardous expedition, and wanted the services of twenty of the best men of the regiment to go with him, and the balance to remain in camp ready for orders. Those that were willing to go with him were ordered four paces to the front. At the word, thirty advanced, and out of that number twenty were selected. He had only twenty horses. Captain Jones, who was left in command of the camp, was ordered to be prepared to execute any orders he might receive. He told the judges that "the 7th of September commenced immediately after midnight, and the law specified no hour when court should be opened. If we furnish Governor Lucas the record that court was opened according to law, he can show to the world that he has executed the laws of Ohio over the disputed territory. Be prepared to mount your horses to start for Toledo at precisely one o'clock A. M. I will be ready with an escort to protect you."

At the hour named all were in their saddles. Each soldier had a rifle, in addition to his two cavalry pistols. They reached Toledo about three o'clock in the morning, and went to a school house that stood near where Washington street crosses the canal, and opened court in due form of law. Junius Flagg acted as sheriff. The proceedings were hastily written on loose pieces of paper and deposited into the clerk's hat. When the court adjourned all went to the tavern kept by Munson H. Daniels, near where the American House now stands, registered their names, took a drink all around, and while filling their glasses for a second drink, some wag ran in and said a force of wolverines were approaching. They dropped their glasses, sprang on their horses, and hastened away, leaving the bill unpaid. When they arrived on the top of the hill near where the Oliver House now stands, they came to a halt and faced about. It was then discovered that the clerk had lost his hat containing the court journal. It was one of those high, bell-crown hats, then fashionable, and had capacity sufficient to hold a great many papers. Having succeeded in holding the court so well, and then losing the papers, was indeed too provoking, and to have them fall into the hands of the enemy was still worse. They fully believed that they were pursued, yet to lose the papers, was enough to arouse the courage of any soldier. Colonel Van Fleet's courage had not forsaken him. With him to will was to do. He ordered the clerk to dismount, and with two of the guards, to feel his way back carefully in search of the papers, while the balance would keep watch to cover the retreat. He cautioned them to make no noise, and if discovered, to conceal themselves. The hat was found with the papers. The party reported no enemy in sight. The state of Ohio had triumphed, The record was made up from the papers, and signed, " J. H. Jerome, associate judge."

Colonel Van Fleet was so rejoiced at the recovery of the papers that he ordered two salutes to be fired on the spot. The party proceeded to Maumee at leisure, and reached the town a little after daylight.

While the court was in session, Colonel Wing was stationed in town with 100 men to arrest the judges if they should undertake to hold court. Finding that there was no further use for his army, General Brown repaired to Monroe and disbandoned them.

It seems that this Mr. Shaler did not take charge of the office of governor of the Michigan territory, and that John S. Homer became Mason's successor, and was the acting governor with whom Governor Lucas afterwards had a lengthy correspondence, and which resulted in the discontinuance of the prosecutions, except the T. Stickney case, for the stabbing of Wood, the deputy sheriff. Governor Homer made a requisition upon Governor Lucas for him, but Governor Lucas refused to give him up, claiming that the offense had been committed on Ohio soil, and that therefore the courts of Michigan had no jurisdiction over him.

Public sentiment gradually settled down in favor of Ohio, "and peace was again restored to the border." The boundary commissioners resumed the work on the line in November, and finished it without molestation.

At the next session of congress, on the 15th of June, 1836, Michigan was admitted into the Union, with the Harris line for her southern boundary, and the disputed territory was given to Ohio.

Taking into consideration the extensive preparations on both sides for the shedding of fraternal blood over a question that nothing but right and law should have settled, and the other fact that the people in the whole northwest were highly excited over the conflict, and although the scenes have passed away with the excitement and both almost forgotten, it should never be said that the Toledo war was a joke. (See Toledo war by M. V. Way.)

CHAPTER XXVI.

SENECA COUNTY IN THE GENERAL ASSEMBLY—SENECA COUNTY ON THE TAX DUPLICATE—SOLDIERS OF THE REVOLUTIONARY WAR—SOLDIERS OF THE WAR OF 1812—SOLDIERS IN THE WAR WITH MEXICO—INDEPENDENT COMPANIES—OHIO MILITIA.

SENECA COUNTY IN THE GENERAL ASSEMBLY OF OHIO.

THE kind reader, who may be desirous to know how and by whom this county has been represented in both branches of the general assembly of Ohio from the time of its organization hitherto, may save a good deal of time and labor by glancing his eye over a few pages in this chapter.

The time when, and the manner in which the districts, both senatorial and representative, were organized and changed, each including Seneca county, and the time of the election of senators and representatives, and who they were, from 1824 to 1880, a period of 56 years, required patient labor to ascertain, and it is hoped that this part of the present chapter may be appreciated as a reference document in proportion, at least to the work it required to produce it.

Under the old constitution (let it be remembered) senators were elected for two years and representatives for one year. The legislature met annually on the first Monday of December. Under the presen constitution the general assembly is to meet bi-annually and then on the first Monday in January. In spite of this plain provision of the present constitution, there was only one winter during the last thirty years when the legislature did not have a session; and that was the ever memorable year of 1855, when it was discovered that the state treasury was short about three quarters of a million of dollars. In all these years the legislature adjourned to an extra session, in violation of the plain provision of the constitution, under a joint resolution of both houses. In other words: the spirit and plain provision of the constitution is defeated by the construction of the word "adjournment". And this determination to beat down the intention of the constitution of Ohio is a sin of both parties alike. Both are guilty

SENECA COUNTY IN THE GENERAL ASSEMBLY. 439

of the crime and therefore willing to forgive each other. But the good people foot the bill all the same.

Now senators and representatives are each elected for two years. There is no holding over, nor adjournment intended by the new constitution. What further proof is necessary to show its spirit and meaning? However, the people acquiesce in this bi-annual violation of their fundamental law and are willing to pay for it. This is all the politicians want, and are accommodated. But to resume. Below find the years of the elections of senators and representatives, first under the old, and then under the new constitution, the time of their elections and the compositions of the districts in regular order, viz:

SENATORS.

Years.	Counties composing districts.	Who elected.
1824	Delaware Marion Seneca (including Crawford) Sandusky	David H. Beardsley
1826	Delaware Marion Seneca Crawford Sandusky	James Kooken
1828	Huron Sandusky Seneca Wood Hancock	David Campbell
1830	Same counties	Samuel M. Lockwood
1832	Huron Seneca Sandusky	Daniel Tilden
1834	Same counties	Joseph Howard
1836	Same counties	David E. Owen
1838	Seneca Sandusky	William B. Craighill
1840	Seneca Wood Ottawa Sandusky Hancock	John Goodin
1842	Same counties	Moses McAnnelly
1844	Sandusky Seneca Crawford	Amos E. Wood
1846	Sandusky Seneca Wyandot Crawford	Henry Cronise

HISTORY OF SENECA COUNTY.

Years.	Counties composing districts.	Who elected.
1848	Same counties	Joel W. Wilson
1850	Seneca Hancock Wyandot	Michael Brackley

This was the last senatorial election under the old constitution.

REPRESENTATIVES.

Years.	Counties composing districts.	Who elected.
1824	Marion Seneca Sandusky	Jeremiah Everett
1825	Marion Crawford Seneca Sandusky	Josiah Hedges
1826	Same counties	Eber Baker
1827	Same counties	Samuel M. Lockwood.
1828	Sandusky Seneca Wood Hancock	Lockwood re-elected
1829	Same counties	Lockwood re-elected.
1830	Same counties	Josiah Hedges
1831	Same counties	Harvey J. Harmon
1832	Seneca Sandusky	Jeremiah Everett
1833	Same counties	Everett re-elected
1834	Same counties	Jacques Hulburt
1835	June 8. Extra session to consult on Michigan boundary and war.	
1835	Same counties	William B. Craighead
1836	Same counties	Craighead re-elected
1837	Same counties	Samuel Treat
1838	Same counties	John Welsh
1839	Same counties	Welsh re-elected
1840	Seneca Sandusky Wood Hancock Ottawa	Amos E. Wood Moses McAnnelly
1841	Same counties	Amos E. Wood George W. Baird

This legislature broke up in confusion. The Whigs withdrew. See Secretary of State's report, 1875, page 82.

| 1842 | Same counties | Henry C. Brish
George W. Baird |

SENECA COUNTY IN THE GENERAL ASSEMBLY.

Years.	Counties composing districts.	Who elected.
1843	Same counties	William B. Craighead Samuel Waggoner
1844	Seneca	Henry C. Brish
1845	Seneca	Daniel Brown*
1846	Seneca	Warren P. Noble
1847	Seneca	Noble re-elected
1848	Seneca	John G. Breslin (Speaker)
1849	Seneca	Breslin re-elected
1850	Seneca	Jacob Decker

*Elected as a Democrat and voted with the Whigs.

Last election under the old constitution.

The senatorial district under the new constitution has never been changed. It is composed of the counties of Seneca, Crawford and Wyandot.

1851—Joel W. Wilson
1853—Robert Lee
1855—James Lewis (K. N., over W. P. Noble)
1857—Robert McKelley
1859—Thomas J. Orr
1861—William Lang
1863—William Lang
1865—Curtis Berry, Jr.
1867—Curtis Berry, Jr.
1869—Alex. E. Jenner
1871—Alex. E. Jenner
1873—John Seitz
1875—E. T. Stickney
1877—John Seitz
1879—Moses H. Kirby

REPRESENTATIVES

Under the present constitution Seneca is a district by itself.

1851—Jacob Decker
1853—John W. Paine
1855—Joseph Boyer (K. N.)
1859—Morris P. Skinner (D.)
Gideon Jones (R.)
1861—R. R. Titus
1863—R. R. Titus
1865—Isaac Kagy
1867—E. T. Stickney
1869—John Seits
E. T. Stickney
1871—John Seits
1873—James A. Norton
1875—James A. Norton
1877—James A. Norton
1879—Amos Decker

SENECA COUNTY ON THE TAX DUPLICATE.

Land bought from the United States was free from taxes for the term of five years from the date of purchase. The values, therefore, that were put upon the duplicate during that time were upon personal property only, and hence comparatively small. The duplicate swelled in proportion as the five years expired.

The following table gives the amount of taxes paid by Seneca county into the state treasury for ten years, from 1826 to 1835, both included, except the canal tax already mentioned:

Year.	Amount.	Year.	Amount.
1826	$ 62.26.6	1831	$720.26.3
1827	254.49.4	1832	832.63.6
1828	326.32.0	1833	834.79.8
1829	444.44.3	1834	954.80.1
1830	600.05.7	1835	814.13.8

It would be tedious and dry reading to follow the figures of assessment and taxation from year to year, and the reader must be content with short references to show simply how Seneca county swelled in proportions, in both wealth and on the tax duplicate.

In 1836 the value of town lots in Tiffin was $86,499; in Melmore, $5,463; in Republic, $708; in Carolina, $608; in Attica, $1,464.

Clinton township then had six pleasure carriages, valued at $460; Eden one, valued at $50; Hopewell two, valued at $160. There was then no other carriage in the county. Any spring wagon was a pleasure carriage. There were nine of these, valued at $670.

The following table will show the number of acres and their value on the duplicate in 1836, the number of horses, neat cattle and total taxes for all purposes:

Township.	No. of acres.	Valuation.	Horses.	Cattle.	Total tax.
Adams	6,901	$18,872	126	392	$ 403 31.9
Bloom	11,321	34,215	162	382	526 76.5
Clinton	18,776	85,609	372	510	3,082 58.0
Eden	21,757	65,105	313	530	1,134 25.1
Hopewell	11,749	39,670	127	307	639 67.1
Liberty	78,807	20,097	116	328	373 35.3
Loudon	1,842	2,831	59	185	118 25.6
Pleasant	4,898	24,335	122	303	445 17.1
Reed	12,972	30,124	124	397	533 68.4
Seneca	9,475	31,784	179	374	521 88.6
Scipio	17,067	42,953	203	535	985 12.2
Thompson	11,244	25,269	214	515	480 34.0
Venice	4,274	12,277	80	352	264 81.5
Big Spring	492	1,057	95	319	115 41.6
Jackson	1,040	2,203	46	158	82 63.5

Total tax... $9,707 26.4

SENECA COUNTY ON THE TAX DUPLICATE.

The following table shows the same articles for taxation, and the taxes for each township and the towns for 1879:

Township.	No. of acres.	Valuation.	Horses.	Cattle.	Total tax.
Adams	23,146	$ 805,842	725	1,174	$ 14,194 85
Great Springs		131,494	24	17	
Bloom	23,096	733,255	613	1,309	16,405 75
Bloomville		216,489	75	60	
Big Spring	22,807	908,194	736	1,351	9,481 59
Clinton	21,122	1,292,448	648	1,245	1,252 37
Eden	22,762	1,019.168	667	1,525	10,757 83
Hopewell	22,854	1,038,048	712	1,363	12,262 21
Jackson	23,166	763,960	560	1,208	7,648 81
Liberty	22,878	958,638	698	1,668	12,987 27
Loudon	22,422	891,530	679	1,235	10,602 53
Fostoria		1,043.237	253	152	25,248 13
Pleasant	22,460	884,707	544	955	10,937 55
Reed	24,594	804,470	678	1,282	8,889 55
Scipio	22,737	965,868	674	1,154	13,941 68
Republic		185,220	75	56	
Seneca	22,668	981,431	758	1,312	10,615 19
Thompson	23,341	1,079.407	756	1,143	
Venice	25,048	832.460	630	1,764	15,038 52
Attica		170.119	75	45	
Tiffin—1st ward.			102	97	
2d "			81	81	
3d "		2,403.593	101	58	83,087 83
4th "			113	92	
5th "			74	44	

Total tax for 1879...$ 285,375 26

The foregoing values include also the personal property and the values of Big Spring; also Adrian and New Reigel.

The total valuation of the county is $18,500,000. It is presumed that the appraisement now about being made will increase the valuation of the real estate over the appraisement of 1870 about two millions.

Estimated population of 1880, 37,000.

The acres above mentioned, with the above enumeration in 1879, produced one and one-half millions of bushels of wheat. Of this quantity—at a rough guess—one-half million was used for seed and bread, leaving one million of bushels for market, representing so many dollars.

All other surplus products put together make two millions more—three millions surplus farm products, to which may be added one-half million manufacturing products, to be divided among the above population; this would seem to be a fair representation of Seneca county in the busy life of the world.

This would average about $100 to each man, woman and child in the county for one year.

For the population of Seneca county in 1870 and 1880 see chapter forty-four.

SENECA COUNTY IN THE WAR.

This subject would make a book by itself. There is only room here to state facts; commentaries must be left to the reader.

The bones of seven revolutionary soldiers rest in the ground of Seneca county. It is possible that there were others, but record is made here only of those whose death here could be ascertained.

FREDERICK SHAWHAN

Was a native of Kent county, Maryland, but settled in Virginia after the revolutionary struggle was over. He took a very active part in the revolution, having enlisted when he was only seventeen years old. He served under Generals Wayne, Green, Lafayette and Washington. He was at Stony Point, in the battle of Monmouth, at the crossing of the Delaware, and at the battle of Trenton. He moved to Ohio in 1812, and located in Fairfield county. In 1820 he moved to Wayne county, and afterwards came to Seneca county, where he died near Tiffin, August 26th, 1840, in the eightieth year of his age. He is buried in the new cemetery.

JOHN W. KENT

Was another revolutionary soldier, whose history, however, there is nobody able to relate. He lies buried in the cemetery at Bascom. He died November 16th, 1844, aged ninety-nine years, nine months and seven days.

WILLIAM HARRIS,

The gunsmith, has already been mentioned among the early settlers near the old Fort Seneca.

JEDEDIAH HOLMES,

The father of our old pioneer friend, Jedediah Holmes, is buried in the Melmore cemetery.

ELI WRIGHT,

Another old soldier of the revolution, is buried at the cemetery near McCutchenville.

JEREMIAH WILLIAMS,

Of the Maryland continental line, afterwards served under General Marion. He is buried in Pleasant township.

MATSON PETERSON

Died in Scipio township in 1846, at the age of eighty-two years. He was from New Jersey, and is buried at the cemetery near John Hall's.

There were a goodly number of soldiers of the war of 1812 in Seneca county, and the writer regrets his want of success in ascertaining their names. Every effort was made to that end, and the newspapers in Tiffin were kind enough to assist me in calling on the friends and children of the soldiers of the war of 1812 to give me their names and have them recorded in these pages; but it proved a failure and a few only have been collected. One man called on me and wanted to know how much I paid for such information. He went away without giving me any names.

The following are the names of those that were picked up, however:

William Siberal, Pleasant,
Benjamin Turner, Liberty,
Henry Cronise, Tiffin,
Henry St. John, Tiffin,
John Baugher, Tiffin,
Jonathan Chittenden, Scipio,
Reuben Williams, Tiffin,
John Bowerman, Adams.

John Paine came to Adams April 7th, 1829, and died in 1846. He was a volunteer in Captain Barry's company O. M., in 1813, at Circleville, and was at the battle of Ft. Stevenson.

JOHN HETER,

Who located in Thompson in 1830; is still living.

SAMUEL CARSON

Was with General Harrison at Fort Meigs. He died in Venice.

LUDWIG FRIEDLEY

Located and died in Venice. He belonged to a Pennsylvania regiment.

WILLIAM SIBERAL,

Of Pleasant, was shot in the hip at the storming of Erie, and while he was being carried away, was shot again. Yet he lived to a fine old age. He settled in Pleasant in 1828.

JOHN SEARLES

Was drafted in the war of 1812 in Anne Arundel county, on the Chesapeak bay, Maryland, and was in the land service to the close of the war.

JOHN NOEL

Was drafted for the war of 1812, but on account of sickness in his family, was excused from service by paying $12 per month for three months.

DANIEL LAMBERSON

Was drafted in Pennsylvania.

NOAH P. RESSEQUIE

Was the fourth son of a French officer, who served under the great Napoleon. He was a volunteer in the war of 1812; was in the battles of Fort Erie, Fort George and Lundy's Lane, in many other minor engagements, and in numerous incursions into Canada. He was fife major and leader of a band at the execution of James Byrd. He came to Seneca county in 1843, and was buried at Omar in 1855. Mrs. Melinda Lee is his only living daughter.

SOLDIERS FROM SENECA IN THE MEXICAN WAR.

My old friend Louis Beilharz, Esq., of Liberty Center, Henry county, Ohio, was so kind as to furnish me with the names of men who went into the war against Mexico with him in 1847, viz:

Captain—James F. Chapman.
First Lieutenant—John H. Flenner.
Second Lieutenant—Smith D. Baldwin.
Non-commissioned officers:
Second Sergeant—Thomas Little.
Third Sergeant—Louis A. Beilharz.

Privates:

William Boyer,
Russell Smith,
James Goshorn,
Thomas Rosefelt,
John Kennedy,
Martin Leib,
Jacob Hessenauer.
Solomon Smith,
George Rockwell,
George Kelly,
Daniel Kelly,

James Burrows,
William Carney,
Christ. Meyers,
Jacob Wolf,
Martin Smith,
Gottlieb Melcher.
William Smith,
Henry Hoffman,
Nicholas Kirsh,
Edward Daugherty.
Leonard Hoefling,

Benjamin Gee,
Warner Norris,
John Cobert,
William Wells,
George Probasco,
John Morehead,
Nathan Hall,
Joshua Prebble.
Nathan Richards,
Archibald McMullen.
Aloys Rouk (fife major).

And a little dark complexioned German whose name has escaped me. The balance of the company were men from other counties.

THE SENECA BLUES

Were an independent company, very neatly uniformed and well drilled. They organized in 1835. Sorry to say that no roster has been preserved. Henry Ebert was captain, John J. Steiner was orderly. They served out their time under the law, and dispersed soon after the campaign of 1840.

THE OSCEOLAS

Were also an independent company that organized under the leadership of Captain Poorman, in November, 1842. Governor Corwin issued the commissions:

Captain—John Poorman.
First Lieutenant—D. K. Hamilton.
Second Lieutenant—William Dewitt.
First Sergeant—William Lang.

THE WASHINGTON GUARDS. 447

Privates:

James Watson,	S. Griffith,	Aaron Miller,
James R. Cain,	Nicholas Kuntz,	Michael Foncannon,
Bazell Norris,	A. Denzer,	W. D. Foncannon,
A. Taylor,	Daniel Fisher,	Henry Blasius,
William Bogart,	Jacob Bowersox,	M. Kirchner,
Jacob Engler,	Daniel Zeice,	J. M. Kirchner,
—— Kaufman,	John Williams,	John Rosell,
David Smith,	George Dewalt,	David Rosell,
William Bergstresser,	E. J. Wilber,	Paul Von Blon,
William Miller,	Henry Turner,	Philip Von Blon,
John Deaver,	James Wolf,	John Willow,
Daniel Deaver,	George Abbott,	T. Egbert,
John Sheets,	James E. Holtz,	Albert Beilharz,
A. Sohn,	Paul Dewitt,	F. Bernard,
Henry Sohn,	John Deroit,	George Billman,
Jacob Adams,	A. Copenhaver,	John McMeens,
J. Stoner.	Jacob Young.	

THE WASHINGTON GUARDS.

In 1850 a German company was organized here as a rifle company, with the above name. It was considered the best drilled company Seneca county ever produced; neatly uniformed and equipped. For six years it continued to be the favorite of the people. Whenever the company had a public dinner or a ball, or wanted money for some company purpose, it was always well sustained. The following list of its officers and privates is made up from memory. The roll is lost, and perhaps some old comrade will be overlooked.

Captain—William Lang.
First Lieutenant—Valentine Schmidt.
Second Lieutenant—Frederick Harter.
O. S.—William Berger.
First Corporal—Xavier Wehrle.
Second Corporal—Anton Rendler.
Third Corporal—Louis Bang.
Fourth Corporal—Carl Bang.
Flag Bearer—Andrew Denzer.

Privates:

Christopher Snyder,	Ph. Souter,	Joseph Vollmer.
Carl Schuhman,	John Loesser.	C. G. A. Oudit,
Joseph Letterhose.	Ch. Seigchrist,	M. P. Wehrle.
Aloys Rank,	Adam Wagner,	Jos. Christ.
J. M. Kirchner.	John Bossecker,	Jacob Altweis,
J. W. Kirchner.	William Zoeller,	Andrew Irion,
William Armbruster.	Valentine Dinges.	George Denzer.
Henry Schmitt.	J. Muellerweis.	Peter Spelz.

HISTORY OF SENECA COUNTY.

Daniel Labar,
Henry Weisbecker,
Daniel Scheuing,
Jacob Frentzel,
Carl Scheuing,
Ignatz Kirchner.
Fritz Pauli,
Joseph Schmitt,
John Hartman.
Justin Schneider,
Wendel Bur`- art,
Xavier \ ..gner.
John Meyer,
Andrew Bliem,
William Roelle.
J. Ad. Ries.
H. Lemp,

Michael Kirchner,
Carl F. Boos,
Christ. Mueller,
Balthasar Kirchner,
Carl Mutschler,
Ph. Emich,
Jacob Schabacher,
Joseph Kettemeyer,
Dominick Bartel,
Joseph Ranker,
Jacob Zimmer,
Peter Schmittuz,
John Yeutgen,
J. B. Greiveldinger,
John Hessberger,
Louis Seewald,
John Kirchner.

Jacob Gunther,
Moses H. Schwarzenberg,
Joseph Kauffmann,
Lucas Engelfried,
David Leisenring,
Henry Wats,
Franz Keppelmeyer,
John Demuth,
William B. Wolff,
Henry Wolff,
Jacob Foell,
Jacob Huf,
P. Frank Ries.
John Spelz,
—— Chumi.

FORT BALL ARTILLERY

Was the only independent artillery company ever organized in the county. It was well uniformed and well drilled, making a very formidable appearance.

Captain—Truman H. Bagby.
First Lieutenant—D. C. Stoner.
Second Lieutenant—P. H. Reame.
First Sergeant—Amon Rigs.
Second Sergeant—George Hubert.
Third Sergeant—John Gerspacker.
Fourth Sergeant—C. W. Souter.
First Corporal—David Lutner.
Second Corporal—Harman Whiteman.
Third Corporal—W. H. Carlisle.
Fourth Corporal—John Silvers.

Privates:

Samuel Betts.
C. J. Hoot.
Dan. Vollmer.
William Ridenour.
Aaron Ruse.
Melkiah Martin.
P. C. Scheckel.
W. H. Smith.
James Dildine.
John Grady.
Myron H. Forbush.
Edmond Kinney.
M. Hennessy.

Nicholas Liebe,
Fred. Gari,
Henry Keppel,
Leo Liebel.
Ephraim Sohn,
Nicholas Kirch,
Jacob Flaugher, Jr.,
Nicholas Cornely,
James A. Sohn,
Jacob Miller,
David Lebar,
Samuel Shaull,
Felix Beck.

George Strassbaugh,
Gideon Leitner.
George Schwartzmiller,
Pierre Lahr,
Henry Graff.
Joseph Boehler,
Nathan Cadwallader.
Daniel Miller,
Frederick Roller,
John M. B. Carey.
Samuel Downey.
John Millerweis,
John Mackfeld.

OHIO MILITIA.

Levi Keller,	J. H. Leidy,	Michael Lahr,
Andrew Ruch,	Michael Miller,	Samuel Leitner,
Edward Cookerly,	George W. Zeigler,	John Hoefling,
John H. Six,	Nicholas Miller,	George Newbinger,
Daniel Bosler,	Henry Miller,	Robert Gulliver,
William Klinger,	George Schlerret,	Hiram Merchant,
Martin Housman,	Joseph Sanders,	W. B. Merchant,
R. L. Durdy,	George Seifert,	Fred. Rentz,
John Kline,	John Knott,	Francis Wagner,
John A. Young,	William Johnson,	John Courth,
D. H. Dildine,	William Ogle,	W. A. Sweitzer,
Anthony Kuebler,	E. G. Bowe,	Hubert Shorts,
Daniel Youndt,	Fred. Schammel,	Charles Swannager,
J. W. Love,	Michael Fitzpatrick,	Peter Kingseed,
A. Flummerfelt,	Nicholas Bower.	

The company organized on the 10th of March, 1851, and served out its time.

While on the subject of "independent companies," it may be well to remark that since the war of the rebellion two independent companies have been organized in Tiffin, viz:

THE TIFFIN LIGHT GUARDS,

Who have served out their time and disbanded, and the

TIFFIN ZOUAVES,

Who are still in existence. They were both small companies but well drilled.

Otto P. Snyder was the last captain of the Tiffin Light Guards, and Ed. Lepper is the captain of the Zouaves.

OHIO MILITIA.

The system and the laws regulating the militia of Ohio grew out of the condition of things surrounding the settlers when the state of Ohio was in her infancy.

The frontiersman was necessarily a good marksman and the rifle was one of the most indispensible implements of a frontier home. The war of the revolution and the war of 1812 were fought with militia, who have proven valiant and efficient. A standing army was not to be thought of and should not be thought of anywhere. The pioneers embraced the doctrine that "God helps those that help themselves." Self reliance is the main-spring of success at all times and everywhere.

The early statesmen laid down the doctrine that a well regulated militia was the safety of the state. Hence laws were passed for the listing of all able-bodied white male inhabitants by an officer who was called a "lister." The state was divided into districts and divisions, and numbered, with a major-general, and sub-divided into brigades, with a brigadier-general in each. The brigade districts were again sub-divided into regimental districts and company districts. In time of need the militia was easily rendezvoused and each man knew the company, regiment, brigade and division he belonged to. Company muster was held in August and regimental muster in September of each year. On these muster days the officers were elected. The rank and file elected their captains and lieutenants, and these the higher officers and so on. The elections of all commissioned officers were certified up to the governor, who (as now), was the commander-in-chief, and issued the commissions accordingly.

Thus the "army of Ohio" was organized, and it was no small affair to be a captain, major, colonel, or general. Peple took great pride in military affairs and it was considered a mark of honor and distinction to be a military officer and in the line of promotion. There was as much electioneering on those muster days for a captaincy, or to become a colonel as there is now-a-days in the race for an office in civil life.

The muster days were regarded as days of fun and frolic. The hotel keepers and gingerbread shops made the most out of them. The men were ordered out on parade, "uniformed, armed and equipped as the law directs;" but the state furnished no arms and the men had no uniforms. There was no need of a uniform for only two days' drill during the year, and officers being changed so often, refused to uniform on account of the expense. Everybody, therefore, appeared on parade in citizens' clothes and just in such dress as was convenient to each. Some dressed in the best they had and others came just as they left their work. The larger number were in "homespun," colored with bark. It was both convenient and usual to pull the boots over the pants and wear linsey-woolsey wammuses, the corners tied into a knot in front. Some had fur caps on, others straw hats or slouch hats; no two were dressed alike. Standing in line or marching, the men swung their arms, laughed, talked, looked about and generally did as they pleased. If the captain scolded or undertook to be strict in his discipline, they would elect another man next time. Those who had no guns would borrow a piece for the occasion, or use any stick or cornstalk as a substitute for a gun, for there was no time for going through the manual or firing exercises. The captain himself, having no knowledge of military tactics, could give no instructions, and the whole day was spent in marching around, forming line, calling the roll, electing officers, drinking, carousing and fighting. It was customary to have several fights at fisticuffs on every muster day.

In 1842 Dr. Charles Beilhars, a dentist, was elected captain of a Tiffin company, and having no military experience, was very innocent in his new position. After dinner he took charge of his company and marched up and down the street several times and the men got tired of walking so much. The captain had a long, cavalry sword, which he leaned against his right shoulder, and marched at the head of his company in single file. One time the captain and his drummer turned into Market street, marching east, and when he reached the alley east of the court house he looked back, and, to his great surprise, his whole company was gone. They had all "skirmished" and could not be rallied again that day.

A good story is told of a man who had been a standing candidate for captain several years, and finally one morning on a muster day succeeded, by treating all the boys. He bought the out-going captain's *chapeau*, sword and coat, put them on, and at noon recess went home to tell his wife and exhibit himself to her in "war paint." While his wife was busily engaged preparing dinner, the captain employed the time by drilling himself on the porch, giving words of command very strong. There was a trap door in the porch floor leading to the cellar below, and the wife, in her hurry to get dinner, running up and down the cellar stairs, left the trap door open. The captain, full of war, paid no attention to the cellar way. Now he gave the command: "Company, three paces to the rear—march!" and in the execution of the command, he fell into the cellar. His wife heard the racket, ran to his assistance, and helped him up on to the porch again. She brushed him off nicely and consoled him on his lucky escape, having no bones broken and all that, and, when "Richard was himself again," the captain straightened up, looked over his shoulder at his wife, and exclaimed in a loud voice, "Sal, what in h—ll do you know about war?"

When the new constitution was adopted, the legislature made many changes in the militia system of Ohio, and the old "cornstalk muster" was "done away with." The system of the "National Guards" was then inaugurated and is now in vogue.

And is not this idea of "well-regulated militia" the best military system after all? Look at your standing army of idlers and consumers that eat out the substance of the people, and crush out their liberties. Will the world never learn the fact, that the tree of liberty cannot grow in a soil that trembles under the iron heel of the soldier? The history of our own wars has established the fact, that the militia is the best standing army in time of need, and the only standing army that is compatible with a Republican form of government.

452   HISTORY OF SENECA COUNTY.

War seems to be the normal condition of man, anyway, and our people are perfectly imbued with this idea. Our war amongst the states has proven to the world that men can leave their farms, their shops, stores, factories and offices, and in a few short weeks of drilling, make valiant soldiers with an easier mobility, in larger or smaller bodies, than the stiff, garrisoned drones of a standing army, with its endless red tape.

Let those who talk of a strong, centralized, brilliant government, backed and upheld by bayonets, look over the following tables, and if they are Americans, blush:

KINGS AND BAYONETS.

This table shows the daily pay of some of the crowned heads of Europe:

The Czar	$25,000	The Emperor of Germany	$8,000
The Sultan	18,000	The King of Italy	6,400
The Emperor of Austria	10,000	The King of Belgium	1,643

THE ARMIES OF EUROPE ON A PEACE FOOTING.

	Men.		Men.
Russia	447,370	Turkey	130,000
France	446,224	Switzerland	120,077
Germany	418,821	Spain	91,400
Austria	269,577	Belgium	46,333
Great Britain	268,924		
Total			2,506,225

The reserves, the militia and irregular troops are not included in the above numbers. From the *Cincinnati Enquirer* of May 15, 1880, I take the following notice of the proceedings in the German diet:

A Berlin dispatch says: When all the new formations, planned and worked out in their minutest details by the German war ministry, are completed, the total strength of the army will exceed two millions of men.

Germany alone, remember.

The annual appropriations for this consuming host from the exchequers of these states, respectively, run into many millions, thus:

Russia	$127,289,435	Great Britain	$80,259,052
France	110,587,252	Turkey	23,163,295
Germany	81,553,988	Switzerland	2,229,833
Austria	65,850,945	Spain	24,428,384
Italy	34,374,347	Belgium	8,212,247

Making an average of $224 for each man per year.

The average of the daily salary of the president of the United States of America—$138—looks small in comparison, but the annual expense of our standing army of 25,000—$39,000,000—average $1,500 per man for each year. Costly gentlemen, these.

And Europe is the country were bayonets and bibles have been cherished for many centuries. Standing armies crush the masses, from whom they are drawn, to the earth, into poverty, degradation, starvation and rags, and are kept up to cut the throats of their fellow men in christian lands. What a commentary on christian governments. What a lie and burlesque on the beautiful and glorious gospel of Jesus Christ.

CHAPTER XXVII.

SENECA COUNTY IN THE WAR OF THE REBELLION.

THIS is not the place to look for a relation of events that preceded the war of the rebellion, nor for the immediate cause. No opinions shall be expressed on its political aspect; nothing shall be said on the manner in which it was conducted. It is enough to say here, that when Fort Sumpter was fired upon, people were filled with awe, and a sadness inexplicable, pervaded the minds of all thinking, patriotic men. Old Seneca stood by Abraham Lincoln, and more than one thousand five hundred men left the charms and endearments of home and bore their breasts to the storm of war.

The first company that was raised in this county was Co. A, 8th regiment, O. V. I.

Captain—A. H. Winslow. Promoted to major December, 1861.

First Lieutenant—B. F. Ogle. Promoted to captain December, 1861. Resigned December, 1862.

Second Lieutenant—C. W. Barnes. Died from wounds received in the battle of Anteitam September 17, 1862.

Sergeants:

First—A. H. Byers. Discharged for disability.
Second—J. M. Henry. Discharged for disability.
Third—J. C. Kipka. Killed in the battle of Gettysburg, July 3, 1863.
Fourth—J. Weidman.
Fifth—D. J. Goodsell, Jr. Killed in the battle of Gettysburg, July 2. 1863.

Corporals:

First—George Baugher. Discharged for disability.
Second—J. N. Travis. Promoted to 2d lieutenant November 7, 1862.
Third—F. McBride.
Fourth—S. F. Poorman. Transferred to United States hospital.
Fifth—P. J. Hossler.
Sixth—D. Troxell.
Seventh—F. Neely. Discharged for disability.
Eighth—O. McCormack. Died in hospital at Culpepper, October. 1863.

Privates:

L. D. Arnold. Transferred to 6th United States cavalry.

C. A. Adams. Died in hospital at Washington, November, 1862.
N. Backus.
G. Baker.
L. Bang. Discharged for disability.
D. Barnhart, Jr. Discharged for disability.
G. W. Beard. Transferred to invalid corps.
J. H. Beaty. Killed May 12, 1864, in the battle near Spottsylvania.
H. Bloom. Transferred to United States service.
N. J. Brandeberry. Discharged for disability.
J. Brandeberry. Missing; supposed to have deserted.
G. W. Brestel.
H. Breiner.
G. Brown.
J. L. Camp. Discharged for disability from wounds received at Winchester.
J. W. Canary.
F. N. Colwell.
A. D. Colwell.
Philip Diehl.
A. J. Dildine. Killed in the battle of Gettysburg, July 3, 1863.
S. H. Dildine.
M. Dowd. Died in hospital at Grafton, Virginia, September, 1861.
E. A. Fahnestock. Discharged for disability.
J. Fell.
A. Fortney.
J. N. Green.
T. J. Griese. Missing; supposed to have been captured at the battle in the Wilderness.
D. Gross.
H. Harbaugh.
William W. Hathaway. Discharged for disability.
H. Heisserman. Discharged for disability from wounds received December 13, 1862.
J. A. Hoover. Discharged for disability.
Philip Johnson. Discharged for disability.
E. Jones. Died from wounds received at Gettysburg.
J. K. Kershner.
A. R. Kieffer. Discharged for disability.
C. Lampsin, Jr.
H. L. Langdon.
J. R. Lewis.
J. B. Lightcap. Transferred to 6th U. S. cavalry.
M. B. Linn. Died in hospital, at Grafton, Virginia, September, 1861.
J. W. Long.
R. Low.
A. K. Miller.
S. H. Martin. Discharged for disability.
Wm. L. Myers. Discharged for disability.
Wm. Myers. Discharged on account of wounds received at Gettysburg, July 3, 1863.

C. T. Naylor.
Wm. Nuson.
Joseph Nuson.
J. H. Nichols.
A. J. Orme. Transferred to 6th U. S. cavalry.
A. Palmer.
Wm. H. Pockmyer. Discharged for disability from wounds received at Anteitam, September 13, 1862.
J. J. Ranch. Killed in the battle of Gettysburg, July 3, 1863.
Charles Rouch. Died in the hospital at Oakland, September, 1861.
H. H. Ray.
J. Redd. Discharged for disability.
Wm. P. Richardson. Killed at Anteitam, September 17, 1862.
A. Shertzberg. Discharged for disability.
A. Shreiner.
Charles Seewald. Died in hospital at Washington from wounds received at Gettysburg, July 3, 1863.
M. Slart.
S. C. Sloat. Transferred to Invalid corps.
J. Smith.
L. Snover. Appointed commissary sergeant.
J. W. Snyder.
J. H. Sopher.
Charles Sener.
P. Stoner.
Abel Swalley.
J. Teach. Discharged for disability.
H. G. Thurwaechter. Discharged for disability.
N. Watcher.
L. Watcher.
J. Washnich. Killed before Petersburg.
D. G. Watson.
G. W. White. Discharged for disability,
D. Yunker. Killed at Anteitam, September 17, 1862.
W. H. Haas.
S. Z. Beams. Discharged for disability from wounds received while on picket duty at Romney.

This regiment had a bloody history, and covered itself all over with glory.

It enlisted under the first call of the president, between the 16th and 22d days of April, 1861, and all arrived at Camp Taylor, at Cleveland, Ohio, April 29th. The regiment was at Romney, Hanging Rock, Blue Gap, Bloomey Gap, Ceder Creek, Strasburg, Winchester, Front Royal, Malvern Hill, Germantown, Fairfax C. H., South Mountain, Anteitam, Boonsboro, Reedyville, Leesburg, Hulltown, Snicker's Gap, United States Ford, Fredericksburg, Chancellorsville, Gettysburg, Auburn, Bristow,

Robinson's Cross Roads, Locust Grove, Mine Run, Morton's Ford, Wilderness, Spottsylvania C. H., Petersburg, North Anna, Cold Harbor.

The regiment was mustered out the 13th of July, 1864, by Captain Douglass.

I am indebted to my friend Andy Shriner, of Tiffin, for the minutes of company "A," in this regiment.

The 49th, 55th, 101st and 123 regiments O. V. I., were organized in this county, and the names of the officers of each will here be given.

Aside from these organizations, very many men from Seneca county entered the service and joined regiments making up outside of this military district. Some joined Colonel Bousenwein's 58th, forming at Columbus. Captain Philip Faulhaber organized a company, with which he joined Colonel Mungen's 57th. A goodly number of men joined Colonel Buckland's 72d at Fremont. Colonel Louis Zahm's 3d Ohio cavalry was joined by many men from Seneca, and when Colonel Seraphim Myers raised the 107th German regiment, at Cleveland, many joined from here. Some also entered the naval service; so that in every department of the service Seneca county was represented.

THE 49TH O. V. I.

The 49th was organized at Tiffin under special authority from the secretary of war. It started from Camp Noble, near Tiffin (the old fair grounds), to Camp Dennison, the 10th of September, 1861. It was the first organized regiment that entered Kentucky. The boys will always remember Mumfordsville, Pittsburg Landing (where Colonel Gibson commanded the brigade), Corinth, Bridge's Creek, Frankfort, Lawrenceburg, Dog Walk, Nashville, Nolinsville Turnpike, Murfreesboro, Nashville Turnpike, Liberty Gap, Chattanooga, Chickamauga, Orchard Knob, Mission Ridge, Knoxville, Dalton, Resaca, Dallas, Kenesaw Mountain, Chattahoochie River, Atlanta, Jonesboro, Lovejoy Station, Franklin. After a severe march through Texas, it was mustered out at Victoria November 30th, 1865. The whole number in the regiment was 1,552, of whom nineteen were born in Europe. Eight officers were killed in battle, and twenty wounded, six mortally. Of the privates, one hundred and twenty-seven were killed in battle, seventy-one were mortally wounded, sixty-five died from hardship and disease, and seven perished in prisons at Danville and Andersonville; six hundred and sixteen were discharged on account of wounds and sickness.

OFFICERS OF THE 49TH REGIMENT.

Colonels—W. H. Gibson, Joseph R. Bartlett.

LIEUTENANT-COLONELS.
A. M. Blackman,
Levi Drake,
Benj. S. Porter,
Samuel F. Gray,
Luther M. Strong,
Joseph R. Bartlett,
Milton F. Miles.

MAJORS.
Levi Drake,
Benj. S. Porter,
Samuel F. Gray,
Luther M. Strong,
Joseph R. Bartlett,
Milton F. Miles.
J. Kessler,
George W. Pool.

Surgeons—Robert W. Thrift, W. H. Park.
Assistant Surgeons—W. H. Park, H. B. Lung, S. A. Smith, S. H. Spencer.
Chaplains—Erotus H. Bush, George S. Philips.

Captains:

A. Langworthy,
Benj. S. Porter.
Amos Keller,
George W. Culver.
Nathan Callihan,
Joseph R. Bartlett.
Luther M. Strong,
Orrin B. Hayes,
George E. Lovejoy,
James M. Patterson,
Samuel F. Gray,
Jonas Foster.

Lyman W. Mow,
John E. McCormack,
Morris C. Tyler,
John Green,
Hiram Chance,
Daniel Hartsock,
Samuel M. Harper,
John L. Hollopeter,
J. Kessler,
George W. Pool,
Thomas J. Ray.

Shepherd Green,
Theodore C. Pero.
James Ewing,
Jacob Herr,
George S. Crawford.
Dwight R. Cook.
Francis R. Stewart.
Milton F. Miles.
Nathan L. Lutz.
Anthony W. Adams.
Jonathan R. Rapp.

First Lieutenants:

Charles A. Norton.
Samuel F. Gray,
John E. McCormack,
Aaron H. Keller.
Jacob Mosier.
Jonas Foster,
Morris C. Tyler,
Daniel Hartsock,
Hiram Chance,
Alonzo F. Prentice,
William C. Turner,
James W. Davidson,
William Martin.
Moses Abbott.
C. W. Drake.
John Green,
John L. Hollopeter,
John Kessler,
Samuel M. Harper,
Milton F. Miles.

Henry A. Spaythe,
James A. Redman,
Milton Cowgill,
Sheppard Green,
Jacob C. Miller,
Theodore C. Pero,
George W. Pool,
Thomas J. Ray,
James Ewing,
Isaac H. White,
John C. Ramsey,
Jacob Herr,
John Glick,
Silas W. Simons,
Charles Wallace,
George S. Crawford,
Dwight R. Cook,
Francis R. Stewart,
John K. Gibson,

Nathan L. Lutz.
Daniel M. Fultz.
Anthony W. Adams.
Jonathan J. Rapp,
John Vandenburg,
Edwin P. Dana,
Jacob W. Cline.
John J. Fry,
Charles W. England.
George W. Vail,
Ezra P. Phelps,
James F. Harper.
John H. Yarger.
James J. Zint,
Conrad Flaugher,
H. H. Fausey,
Caspar Snyder,
Franklin H. Gibbons,
William Whittacker.

Nearly all the above were second lieutenants and promoted.

Colonel Gibson commanded a brigade, by virtue of his rank, during about two-thirds of his term of service.

He is adjutant general of the state at this writing.

THE 55TH O. V. I.

This regiment went into camp at Norwalk, Ohio, on the 17th day of October, 1861, where it was kept, wasting time, until January 25th, 1862, when it was ordered to Grafton and New Creek, Virginia. At Grafton the regiment suffered severely from measels. At one time over four hundred men were on the sick list. The regiment took part in the following battles, viz: McDowell, or Blue Pasture Mountain, Cross Keys, Slaughter Mountain, Bull Run. The regiment arrived at Chancellorville on the 30th of January, 1863, where it took position in the second brigade. The battle opened about five o'clock in the afternoon, the rebels in strong force upon the right. The national troops were preparing supper, and no scouts had been sent out, hence the attack was a surprise. The first regiment on the extreme right had three hundred and fifty guns stacked, and upon the first fire from the rebels, this regiment fell upon the second, and they not being able to stand the fire, fell back also. The remainder of the brigade also retreated to the left. Regiment after regiment was compelled to fall back, including the 55th. The retreat became general, and was only checked by the darkness of the night. In this engagement the 55th lost one hundred and three men killed, wounded and missing.

This regiment was also present at Gettysburg, where it lost about fifty men, and at Chattanooga. On the 1st of January, 1864, the regiment re-enlisted with three hundred and ninety men, and re-assembled on the 22d of February. It then participated in all the battles of the 20th corps. At the battle of Resaca it lost ninety men, May 15th. It was at Dallas, Cassville, New Hope Church, Marietta and Kenesaw. It was at Atlanta, and at Smith's Farm. The regiment was mustered out at Louisville, Kentucky, on the 11th of July. During its service this regiment enrolled one thousand three hundred and fifty men, of whom seven hundred and fifty were either killed or wounded in battle. Eight officers were killed or died of wounds.

Colonels—J. C. Lee, Charles B. Gambee, Edwin H. Powers.

LIEUTENANT-COLONELS.
George H. Safford,
Charles B. Gambee,
James M. Stevens,
Edwin H. Powers,
Charles P. Wickham.

MAJORS.
John C. Lee,
Daniel F. DeWolf,
Charles B. Gambee,
James M. Stevens,
Rudolphus Robbins,
Charles F. Wickham,
Hartwell Osborn.

Surgeons—J. Kling, Joseph Hebble.
Assistant Surgeons—Henry K. Spooner, J. L. Morris, Joseph Hebble, James C. Myers.
Chaplains—John G. W. Cowles, Alfred Wheeler.

Captains:

Charles B. Gambee,
Augustus M. Bement,
Horatio M. Shipman,
David C. Brown,
Frederick A. Wildman,
James M. Stevens,
R. Robbins,
Ira C. Terry,
Horace Robinson,
Edwin H. Powers,
Benj. F. Eldridge,
Charles P. Wickham,
Henry Miller.

Albert E. Peck,
Frank W. Martin,
Robert Bromley,
Frank J. Souter,
Charles D. Robbins,
Henry W. Persing,
Hartwell Osborn,
F. H. Boalt,
Robert W. Pool,
Francis H. Morse,
Butler Case,
Charles M. Stone,

Charles M. Smith,
Aug. M. Wormley,
Thomas W. Miller,
Henry H. Moore,
John R. Lowe,
Jesse Bowsher,
William S. Wickham,
O. B. Gould,
Russel H. Bever,
Benj. F. Evans,
Joseph H. Gallup,
John H. Boss, Jr.,

First Lieutenants:

Robert G. Pennington,
Benjamin F. Eldridge,
W. D. Sherwood,
Henry W. Persing,
Jacob Thomas,
Charles P. Wickham,
Rudolph Eastman,
Henry Miller,
Albert E. Peck,
Frank W. Martin,
Richard F. Patrick,
Robert Bromley,
Raymond Burr,
Benj. C. Tabor,
Charles D. Robbins,
Frank J. Souter,
F. H. Boalt,
Rob. W. Pool,

Francis C. Morse,
Hartwell Osborn,
Thomas O'Leary,
Butler Case,
Charles M. Smith,
Charles M. Stone,
A. M. Wormley,
Thomas W. Miller,
Charles M. Stillman,
Henry H. Moore,
John R. Lowe,
Jesse Bowsher,
William S. Wickham,
O. B. Gould,
Russel H. Bever,
Ben. F. Evans,
James P. Jones,
Philetus C. Lathrop.

Pliney E. Watson,
Thomas T. Petit,
Adam Cramer,
Joseph H. Gallup,
John H. Boss, Jr.,
Lewis Peck,
Alvin B. Chase,
W. E. Childs,
W. H. Hessinger,
Henry B. Warren,
Frederick Reeser,
James T. Boyd,
John Bellman,
Robert Fewson,
Thomas S. Hossler,
John Burkett,
Henry J. Pelton.

Most of the foregoing were second lieutenants and promoted.

Erie, Huron, Seneca, Crawford and Wyandot were formed into a military district, in which this regiment was organized. It was mustered into the service at Monroeville, on the 30th of August, 1862, while the writer was busily engaged recruiting the 123d regiment, and the 101st occupying Camp Monroeville at the time, was compelled to subsist the troops on the fair grounds near Tiffin.

On the 4th of September the regiment was hurried over the Ohio to Covington, Kentucky, to assist in dispelling the threatened raid of Kirby Smith. The regiment was attached to Robert B. Mitchell's division. It was in the battle at Perryville, on October 8th, and before they had time to learn the manual, but they bore up bravely. It was also at Lancaster, Kentucky, and at Nashville. At Knob Gap fight they captured two bronze field pieces, one of which had on the word "Shiloh." The regiment behaved like old veterans, and deserved great praise.

The 101st was the first regiment to arrive at the battle field of Stone River, and became at once engaged with the enemy's out-posts. It was in the hottest of the fight, changing position six times during the day. The lamented Colonels Stem and Wooster were both killed on the front line on the right of the army, leading on their men to deeds of daring. The regiment remained in the fight to the close of the battle, losing seven officers and two hundred and twelve men killed or wounded. All this work of bravery was executed in less than four months from the time the boys left their farms and workshops to organize the regiment. They were at Liberty Gap, Chattanooga, Chickamauga, where it re-took the national battery from the enemy, fighting over the guns with clubbed muskets. It was at Catoosa Springs and Buzzard's Roost.

The Atlanta campaign kept this poor regiment almost under constant fire. The were at Franklin also, and at Nashville, and were finally mustered out of service at Huntsville, Alabama, June 12, 1865.

It is said that at Franklin, just at nightfall, this regiment was ordered to re-take an angle of the works held by the enemy, which it did with the bayonet, and held the position until eight o'clock P. M., notwithstanding the rebels were almost within bayonet reach during all that time.

The following were the officers:
Colonels—Leander Stem and Isaac M. Kirby.

LIEUTENANT-COLONELS.	MAJORS.
John Trouts,	Moses F. Wooder,
Moses F. Wooster,	Isaac M. Kirby,
John Messer,	Bedan B. McDonald,
Bedan B. McDonald.	Daniel H. Fox,
	John A. Lattimer.

Surgeon—Thomas M. Cook.

Assistant Surgeons—George T. Yingling, Walter Caswell, Henry F. Lacy, H. H. Russell.

Chaplains—Oliver Kennedy, Erastus M. Gravath.

Captains:

Charles C. Calligan,
Thomas C. Fernald,
Bedan B. McDonald,
Henry G. Shelden,
Wm. C. Parsons,
Isaac M. Kirby,
John Messer,
Jesse Shriver,
Newton M. Barnes,
Montgomery Noble,
Franklin Pope,

Lyman Parcher,
Asa R. Hillier,
Daniel H. Fox,
Leonard D. Smith,
John P. Fleming,
Milton F. Ebersole,
Stephen B. Beckwith,
Wm. H. Kelmer,
John A. Lattimer,
Robert D. Lord,
George E. Seney,

Wm. N. Beer,
Benj. F. Bryant,
Henry C. Taggert,
Ira B. Reed,
Horace D. Olds.
John F. Neff,
George W. Hale.
James M. Robert.
Z. C. Butler.

First Lieutenants:

Asa R. Hillier,
J. B. Curtis,
Lyman Parcher,
George E. Seney,
Isaac Anderson,
J. P. Fleming,
Milton F. Ebersole,
Leonard D. Smith,
Stephen B. Beckwith,
Franklin Pope,
Robert G. Ogden,
Robert Lysle,
Robert D. Lord,
Daniel H. Fox,

Jacob Neuhart,
Wm. H. Kelmer,
Wm. N. Beer,
Benj. T. Bryant,
John A. Lattimer,
Henry C. Taggart.
John M. Butler,
Ph. T. Kline,
George W. Hale,
Horace D. Olds,
Charles McGraw.
John F. Neff,
Ira B. Reed,
Alex. C. Hosmer,

James M. Roberts.
Elbert J. Squire.
J. C. Butler,
John G. Petticord.
John S. Milliman.
Wm. P. Myers.
J. C. Smith,
Jasper F. Webster.
Wm. R. Davis.
Orander J. Benham.
Charles Mosfoot.
James R. Homer.
John Shuman,
David Allison.

Second lieutenants were nearly all promoted to first lieutenants, etc.

123D REGIMENT O. V. I.

Most all great men have their peculiarities, and Mr. Robert G. Ingersoll of Illinois, who has made the christian world in America say many unpleasant things of him, because he doesn't want any hell, is in the habit, when driving a nail where a strong point comes in, of saying: "Honor bright; now, be honest." In the little space that shall be devoted to a short record of the 123d O. V. I., I would say, in due deference to those who have written or spoken of this regiment without saying a word as to how it was raised, "honor bright," gentlemen. When you undertake to tell the truth, tell the whole truth. When Mr. Whitelaw Reid got up his "Ohio in the War," he did not know, perhaps, how the regiment was raised, or care but little about the labor it took to raise it, and the injustice that was done to somebody when he said, on page 629, vol. II.: "This regiment was organized at camp Monroeville,"

Having taken a very active part in raising this regiment, and having been assisted and sustained in my work by the military committee of every county in this (then) congressional district, and other good men and women from both political parties, and having succeeded in a most wonderful degree, I have no apology to offer when I speak my feelings on this subject in my own plain way. Having stated facts as they occurred, the reader is left to himself in forming conclusions.

It was the 12th of August, 1862, when, at the solicitation of the military committee of Seneca county, my good old friend, Robert G. Pennington, and the writer went to Columbus to confer with Governor Tod on the propriety of raising another regiment in this district, and to procure his order to that effect. We presented to him the fact that Seneca county was still in arrear in her quota of troops some 600 men; that the draft which was then fast approaching would most likely take some of our citizens who could not well go, and that if a regiment was ordered to be raised under the leadership of the writer, the committee entertained strong hopes of raising men enough to avoid the draft.

The governor said: "Gentlemen, I appreciate your situation, and I have no doubt that all you tell me is true, but I have no authority at this late hour before the draft to order the recruiting of a new regiment. The recruiting must stop and preparations made to enforce the draft." Mr. Pennington undertook to tell the governor who the writer was and what the feelings and hopes of the people were if he were appointed colonel of a new regiment, etc. Governor Tod said many flattering things about his friendship for, and long acquaintance with, the writer, etc., and finally said: "Gentlemen, you go home and write to Secretary of War Staunton, telling him just what you told me, and let your congressman write or telegraph also to that effect. I will myself do so to-night, and urge the order, and as soon as I can obtain it, will telegraph you."

We returned and reported accordingly. Urgent appeals were made to Secretary Staunton for the order.

On the night of the 14th of August, 1862, about midnight, a rap at my door brought me to my feet to let the military committee of Seneca county into the house. Captain John J. Steiner had an order from Governor Tod, authorizing the raising of the 123d regiment, and gave us time to the 22d of the same month inclusive—seven days all told. Instead of returning to bed, we aroused the printer boys belonging to the different printing offices in Tiffin and put them to work printing large handbills and posters, calling upon the people to stop all other work and help in recruiting the regiment, etc. Meetings were held and addressed in various places throughout the district, and companies that had a partial organization were speedily filled up; new ones organized and filled, so that on the evening of the 7th day from the time of receiving the order, the writer was enabled to telegraph to Governor Tod, that the regiment was full, awaiting his orders. We had then the minimum number, and when we finally gathered at Monroeville, we had 1,063 men, and as good men as "ever drew a rammer." During two weeks the writer slept in no bed nor changed clothes until the regiment was full. It required labor and money to accomplish the work. The recruiting service was exhausted and the high premiums had been paid to fill up old regiments, and it looked simply like an impossibility to raise a thousand men under these circumstances without premium or bounty. Yet it succeeded. The loafers and drones of society had all been enlisted. The men that made up the 123d were gentlemen, who left their farms, stores, workshops and factories, and every other path of industry, and joined the regiment without a promise of bounty, and from no other motive than that of a patriotic determination to help preserve the Union and the integrity of these states.

Colonel Stem was ordered to report with his regiment (the 101st) at Monroeville, and for want of a place to rendezvous, the companies of the 123d, from Seneca and Wyandot, were quartered on the old fair grounds, and John Remele, who had a butcher shop, and Dr. Crawford, who owned a bakery, subsisted the men in good style. The citizens furnished quilts, blankets and comforts and camp life commenced in good order.

While the recruiting was proceeding vigorously outside, the men were drilled on the fair ground and on the streets.

Captain F. K. Shawhan filled up his company in Tiffin first, and then we recruited Captain Zimmer's company, made up of Germans. A board shanty was built on the southwest corner of the court house yard and a justice of the peace kept there to administer the oath to the men as fast as they enlisted. The hotels and saloons were kept open all night and the fifers and drummers marched up and down the street until nearly morning. Many of the men were sworn in after midnight.

Here is a copy of one of Captain's Shawhan's handbills:

THE 123D—COLONEL WILLIAM LANG.

" Strike till the last armed foe expires,
Strike for your altars and your fires,
Strike for the green graves of your sires,
God and your native land!"

Authority has been given this military district to raise another regiment, the 123d, to be commanded by Colonel William Lang.

The regiment must be organized and filled by the 22d of August. So all men can see the necessity of lively work. Let every patriot in Seneca county put his shoulder to the wheel!

Seneca county will get credit for all recruits raised within that time, and if our quota is filled by volunteering, the necessity of a draft in our county will be obviated.

Recruiting officers are being appointed. Seven days are given to fill up Seneca companies. Men of Seneca, rally! rally!! rally!!! Awake! Remember that the fortunes of a hundred generations are at stake! Let us show the parricides who would destroy the Republic that she can be as terrible in war as she is gentle in peace.

TIFFIN, OHIO, August 16.

Here is another:

WAR MEETING!

At ————, August —, 1862. Speaking by ————.

Turn out, everybody, and fill up the ranks as volunteers in the 123d regiment. W. Lang, Colonel.

This regiment has just been authorized by Governor Tod to be raised by the 22d of August, then drafting takes place without fail. "Strike till the last." etc.

Recruits wanted to fill up company A, which holds the post of honor in the regiment.

Headquarters at Tiffin, Ohio. F. K. SHAWHAN.

The companies were raised and subsisted as above indicated until Colonel Stem, with the 101st, was ordered to Kentucky, and Colonel Jones, who was the commander of camp Monroeville, telegraphed to the writer to report with the regiment at Monroeville immediately. The order was promptly executed and we entered the camp after taking our supper in town, just at dark. There was nothing to live on in camp. Several boxes of tallow candles and a quantity of blankets were all the 101st had left. The men were assigned to their quarters, the officers of the day were appointed and the camp soon became quiet and orderly. Quartermaster Brown was at his desk, writing, while the writer stretched himself on a pile of blankets for a night's rest.

It was about midnight when a heavy rap was heard at the door of our tent; a Mr. Brown opening the door, a man slipped in and showed him a paper and retired.

Mr. Brown then came to me and told me that this man had the appointment of colonel of the regiment and his name was Wilson. Mr. Wilson used to edit a little Republican paper at Upper Sandusky. On the next morning, taking the early train for Tiffin and arriving there early, the writer received a dispatch about 9 o'clock A. M. from Governor. Tod, in these words: "Mr. Wilson is appointed colonel of the 123d. Will you accept the lieutenant-colonelcy.

D. TOD."

It will interest the reader but very little to know the reason why the office was not accepted, but my answer to the governor is still preserved among the archives of the executive office in Columbus, and it simply says that the kind offer could not be accepted for the respect I bear to the regiment and to his excellency, etc.

Another wrong perpetrated by somebody, worked in this form, viz: Upon our urgent solicitation the Right Rev. Bishop Rappe, of Cleveland, consented to let my highly esteemed and kind friend, the Rev. Father L. Molin, go with the regiment as its chaplain. This fact became known very rapidly, and one speech from Father Molin, in Sandusky City, was sufficient to fill up Captain Rigg's company. Father Molin made every necessary arrangement to go with us, and when Colonel Wilson took charge of the regiment, at Monroeville, Father Molin was left out also with the writer.

I rejoice at the fact, and to this day it is a very great consolation to me to know, that Colonel Wilson took good care of the boys and they became attached to him gradually, but the manner in which he received the appointment is no credit to him nor to those who helped to bring it about. A few words more on the subject and the reader can form an opinion of his own.

There were already three colonels appointed from Tiffin over regiments raised in this district, Gibson, Lee and Stem.

A lawyer in Norwalk, Charles L. Boalt, took great interest to keep Tiffin from having another colonel, and went to Columbus on purpose to carry his point. He there found a little intelligent baboon hanging about the state house and a willing tool to help; and while Boalt succeeded in dissuading Governor Tod from giving the colonelcy to the writer, the other fellow made it count by helping a relative. One thing will not be denied by anybody, and that is this: that while the writer labored hard and faithfully to raise the regiment, and spent his money freely, Colonel Wilson laid around loose about Columbus and simply did nothing for the regiment.

In the winter following Governor Tod, who was one of the most efficient war governors of the north, told the writer that in all his appointments and official acts, he regretted nothing so much as this act to which he had allowed himself to be persuaded by these false friends and designing men.

One other thing will not be denied, and that is this: the leading Republicans who took an active part in helping to raise the regiment, felt the outrage very keenly, and expressed their opinions at the election that followed soon thereafter. They meant what they said in October, 1862. This congressional district went Democratic that fall, and elected the Hon Warren P. Noble to congress.

The regiment was mustered into the service October 16th, 1862, and immediately ordered on the march to Virginia. This same O. M. Brown above spoken of (E. H. Brown), who had been left in charge of stores at Petersburg, on the evacuation of the place by the regiment, put his stores in one of the churches of the town, set fire to it, and burned both church and stores. He was captured by the rebels, but was paroled the next day.

On the 1st of March the regiment was sent up to Winchester, where General Lee, with his whole rebel army, on their way to Pennsylvania, passed through and surrounded the town. On the afternoon of the 13th the regiment had an engagement with General Early's corps, in which it lost in killed and wounded nearly one hundred men. On the next day the national forces were driven into their fortifications, and kept under a severe artillery fire for two hours, and the place was evacuated in the night, leaving the guns spiked. When four miles out on the Martinsburg road, the regiment was captured, and in the attempt to cut their way through, about fifty were killed and wounded. The whole brigade were made prisoners, except Co. D, of the 123d. They were taken to Richmond, where the officers of the 123d were in Libby prison about eleven months. Colonel Wilson was exchanged and sent home. The other officers, after eleven months' confinement in Libby, were removed to Macon and Savannah, Georgia; thence to Charleston, and placed under fire, thence to Columbia. From here several officers made their escape, among whom were George D. Acker, late sheriff of this county, and Thomas W. Boyce. Colonel Wilson, Lieutenant-Colonel Hunter, Captain Chamberlain, now cashier of the National Exchange bank in Tiffin, Lieutenant Schuyler, M. H. Smith, Frank A. Breckenridge, and Charles H. Sowers were exchanged. Captain Charles

H. Riggs, of Sandusky, and formerly a Tiffinite, died in Charleston, South Carolina, September 15th, 1864. Captain W. H. Bender died at Columbia, South Carolina. The privates were exchanged in a few months, and sent to Annapolis, Maryland, and Camp Chase, Ohio. The regiment was finally collected together at Martinsburg. From Cedar Creek it moved under Seigel up the valley. At a sharp fight at New Market, May 15th, it lost twenty-nine killed and wounded.

The regiment was under General Hunter at Port Republic, where, after a short but severe fight, the rebels were whipped and 2,000 prisoners captured. They were also at Lynchburg, from whence they made their flight to Salem. The men suffered very severely on this retreat for want of provisions; some died of starvation. They were also at Snicker's Ferry, where a number of the men were killed. On the 22d of July they had another fight with the rebels at Winchester, where the 123d were driven away, and they retreated across the Potomac into Maryland, at Williamsport. At Berryville they lost twenty-five men killed, wounded and captured. They were again at Winchester, where the rebels were routed. Here the regiment lost five officers and about fifty men. At Strasburg they lost six men. Under the command of General Sheridan, after his ride, they drove the rebels at Cedar Creek and assisted in clearing the Shennandoah valley of the rebels. At Hatcher's Run their loss was quite severe. The whole regiment was captured by the rebel Howe Guards, near High Bridge. They were carried along to Appomattox C. H., where the rebel army surrendered to General Grant, and the prisoners were thus released.

They were mustered out June 12th, 1865, at Camp Chase.

Officers:

Colonel—W. T. Wilson.

LIEUTENANT-COLONELS.
Henry B. Hunter,
Horace Kellogg.

MAJORS.
A. Baldwin Norton.
Horace Kellogg,
John W. Chamberlain.

Surgeons—O. Ferris, William B. Hyatt.

Assistant Surgeons—J. H. Williams, William B. Hyatt, Napoleon B. Brisbine.

Chaplain—Charles G. Ferris.

Captains:

John W. Chamberlain,
Horace Kellogg,
Charles Parmeter,
F. K. Shawhan,
Samuel W. Reid,

Louis Zimmer,
Vill. R. Davis,
David S. Caldwell,
William H. Bender,
Alonzo Robbins,

Edwin H. Brown,
William V. McCracken,
Abner Snyder,
Harvey S. Beverton,
Benj. F. Blair.

123D REGIMENT O. V. I.   469

Curtis Berry, Sr.,   Dwight Kellogg,   M. Hoadley Smith,
Charles H. Riggs,   John F. Randolph, Jr., J. F. Schuyler,
John Newman,   Oswell H. Rosenbaum,   Joshua W. Leonard,
Richard A. Kirkwood.

First Lieutenants:
William V. McCracken,   Abner Snyder,   James B. Pumphrey,
Ed. H. Brown,   Benj. F. Blair,   Elmer E. Husted,
Vill. R. Davis,   Caleb D. Williams,   Charles H. Sowers,
John F. Randolph, Jr.,   Harvey S. Beverton,   Sherman A. Johnson,
Edgar Martin,   James H. Gillian,   George D. Acker,
H. L. McKee,   Josephus E. Schuyler,   Charles M. Keys,
Dwight Kellogg,   M. Hoadley Smith,   David Miller,
Alonzo Robbins,   Frank B. Culver,   Frank A. Breckenridge,
Oswell H. Rosenbaum,   Joshua W. Leonard,   Frederick W. Wickham,
D. S. Caldwell,   Thomas W. Boyce,   George A. Scoby,
William H. Bender,   Mentor W. Willoughby,   James Healer,
Randolph B. Ferris.

Many of the second lieutenants were promoted.

CHAPTER XXVIII.

DR. ROBERT R. McMEENS.

"Majesty of human nature! Shall I seek thee among the masses? You never live but with a few."—*Schiller*.

IN the preceding pages the name of my faithful old friend, Dr. McMeens, has been frequently mentioned, and I would do violence to my own heart and a long, unshaded friendship, did I not devote a separate space amongst these leaves to the memory of a true friend, who, in social life, in the medical profession and on the field of battle, everywhere, was so distinguished for his skill and his many manly traits of character.

The following short record of him will be all the eulogy intended. His widow, one of the most esteemed and distinguished ladies in Sandusky City, has kindly furnished the writer with records, giving the incidents of her husband's closing hours, and they are given here without comment. For a specimen of the Doctor's polished, poetical genius, the reader is referred to the poem entitled, "The Islands of Erie," in the second chapter of this book.

True friendship lives beyond the grave, and fills the soul with hope like the christian longing after eternal life, for—

" In that profound and firm reality
Rests the soul's hope of immortality."

Dr. McMeens was born in Lycoming county, state of Pennsylvania, on the 26th of February, 1820. He graduated from the University of Pennsylvania in the spring of 1841, and soon thereafter settled in Tiffin, Ohio, where he commenced the practice of medicine, and where he soon secured, not only a splendid practice, but also the esteem and confidence of the old doctors and the people generally.

On the 31st of August, 1843, he was married to Ann C., the oldest daughter of John Pittenger, a sketch of whose life has already been recorded.

In the fall of 1846, the Doctor moved to Sandusky City, where he lived to the time of his death and where he was buried. He was of rather small stature, but very active, and took great interest in public affairs. He organized and was captain of the Bay City Guards, one of the finest independent military companies of Sandusky City, and assisted greatly in the organization of the Monumental Association, described in chapter II.

Mrs. McMeens, in sending to me the subjoined papers, said:

SANDUSKY, OHIO, May 9, 1880.

Judge W. Lang:

MY DEAR FRIEND: I am much obliged for your good, kind words, and your interest in my loved one; for, although he has been dead to the world for many years, he lives in our home. I cannot write you as fully as I desire, but will give you some items, and your pen can supply the rest, for you were one of the Doctor's faithful friends, and he was warmly attached to you. I enclose dates, etc., and a published article, written by General W. H. Lytle, of Cincinnati; also a letter from Dr. Shumard to Governor Tod, of our State. These were all published, but I cannot find the papers, so send you the original letter.

Ever truly your friend,
ANN C. McMEENS.

Doctor Shumard's letter to Governor Tod:

MEDICAL DIRECTOR'S OFFICE,
DANVILLE, October 31, 1862.

To His Excellency Governor Tod, Ohio:

SIR: It is with feelings of the deepest regret that I have to announce the death of Surgeon R. R. McMeens, of the 3d regiment Ohio Volunteer Army, which occurred suddenly at Perryville, Kentucky, on the night of the 30th inst.

Surgeon McMeens was among the first to offer his services to his country after the breaking out of the rebellion.

Entering the three months' service as a regimental surgeon, he was immediately after ordered to Camp Dennison, where his gentlemanly deportment and great professional skill soon won for him the esteem and confidence of his brother officers, at whose request he was appointed medical director of the post; all the arduous duties of which office he performed in such a manner as to win for him the warmest commendations of the surgeon general of the state.

From that time until the period of his death, he has continued in active service, filling many important positions in the medical department of the army.

Shortly before the battle of Perryville, he was appointed medical director to the troops under the command of the lamented Jackson, and after having participated actively in the battle, was detailed to assist in taking care of the wounded at Perryville. in which position his kindness of heart, sound judgment, and great professional skill, enabled him to contribute very largely toward the relief of our suffering soldiers.

He has fallen while nobly working at his post; although suffering greatly from disease, he refused to abandon his work, and performed several important surgical operations only a few hours before his death.

In his death the army has lost a kind hearted, faithful and efficient officer; the country a pure patriot, and the medical profession one of its brightest ornaments. I am, sir, respectfully, your obedient servant,

GEORGE G. SHUMARD, M. D.,
Medical Director Danville District.

General W. H. Lytle's letter to the *Cincinnati Commercial:*

THE LATE DR. R. R. McMEENS.

EDITORS COMMERCIAL: The announcement of the sudden death of this distinguished medical officer, at Perryville, will be received with profound sorrow in Ohio. Surgeon McMeens was one of the ranking medical officers in the Ohio line, his commission in the service bearing date April, 1861. He was originally commissioned surgeon in the 3d regiment of Ohio Volunteers. a veteran regiment which did good service in Virginia, and which recently, at Chaplin Heights, side by side with the 10th Ohio, the 15th Kentucky, the 42d and 88th Indiana, and Loomis' battery, constituting the 17th brigade, covered itself all over with glory.

A few days before the battle, Dr. McMeens was appointed acting medical director of the 10th division, commanded by the lamented Jackson, of Kentucky. The writer of this notice met him at Perryville, three days after the fight, apparently in his usual health; but it is quite probable that over-exertion, fatigue and anxiety in his department, had brought on the illness, which so suddenly terminated his career. Surgeon McMeens was a resident of Sandusky City, Ohio, where his professional abilities had secured him an extensive and remunerative practice, while his estimable qualities endeared him to a large circle of attached and appreciative friends. Impelled by a high sense of duty, and the noblest of motives, he exchanged at the very beginning of the rebellion the endearments and comforts of home for the perils and hardships of the tented field. Through the dark ravines. and over rugged mountains of western Virginia under Rosecrans; through Kentucky, Tennessee and northern Alabama under Mitchell and Rouseau; and back again through all the vicissitudes of Buell's last campaign, to where it terminated, in the sanguinary struggle at Chaplin Hights. he discharged with the utmost skill, faithfullness and heroism, his varied and responsible duties. His devoted care and watchfulness; the strict observance which he compelled to the laws of hygiene and police, rendered the camps of his regiment at Huntsville and elsewhere, models in the service.

Officers and men had implicit faith in his professional skill. while his noble, genial and chivalric traits of character, linked all hearts to him inseparably. No soldier. however humble, ever complained of his neglect, nor accused him of sacrificing duty to his personal comfort. The eye of the invalid brightened at his presence, and as he moved through the dreary hospitals, crowded with the ghastly harvests of war, despairing sufferers turned toward him on their pallets and smiled hopefully once more. Beloved and lamented by all who knew him, a brave, whole-souled, gallant gentleman, thus, with "harness on," discharging faithfully the high behests of his profession, died Robert R. McMeens.

Ohio will offer up no nobler sacrifice on our country's altar.

DR. ROBERT R. M'MEENS.

The following are the minutes of the proceedings of a meeting of army surgeons held at Perryville, Kentucky, October 31st, 1862:

DEATH OF SURGEON R. R. McMEENS.

At a meeting of the surgeons of the United States army, held in Perryville, Kentucky, on the 31st day of October, A. D., 1862, Surgeon J. G. Hatchilt, of Kentucky, medical director, was called to the chair, and Surgeon Solomon Davis, of Indiana, was appointed secretary.

The chairman briefly explained the object of the meeting and announced the sudden and unexpected demise of an eminent and distinguished surgeon of the army, Dr. Robert R. McMeens, of Sandusky City, Ohio. Whereupon a committee was appointed to draft suitable resolutions of regret and condolence, consisting of Surgeons T. B. Williams, of Ohio, F. G. Albright, of Pennsylvania, Assistant Surgeon L. T. Fuller, of Wisconsin, Surgeons G. D. Jacques, of Indiana, and J. G. Hatchilt, of Kentucky.

After a short adjournment the committee reported the following, which were unanimously adopted:

WHEREAS, In the order of events and the fortunes of war, an eminent and distinguished medical colleague, Surgeon Robert R. McMeens, of Ohio, has fallen a victim to disease, superinduced by excessive labor and exposure in the discharge of his duty to the wounded soldiers on the field, during the battle of Chaplain Hills and since the battle of Perryville; and

WHEREAS, In his death the public service has sustained a great loss, and science an ardent devotee and surgery one of its brightest ornaments; and

WHEREAS, He has been cut off in the prime of his manhood, and in the midst of his usefulness; universally beloved by all who knew him intimately as one of the most generous and noble-minded men in all relations of private and public life; therefore,

Resolved, That this meeting is deeply impressed with this sad event; that they realize the loss the country has sustained by his untimely death and the sorrow with which his relatives and numerous friends will receive the mournful intelligence; in view of which we tender assurances of our profound regret and heartfelt sympathy.

Resolved further, That we tender to the widow of the deceased our sincere condolence in the melancholy bereavement which she has sustained in the loss of an affectionate and devoted husband. And we pray that in the consolation of the christian religion she may find a solace in her affliction and sorrow.

Resolved, That the proceedings of this meeting be signed by the chairman and secretary and published in the papers at Sandusky City, Columbus, Cincinnati and Louisville, and that a copy be sent to the widow of the deceased.

J. G. HATCHILT, President.

SOLOMON DAVIS, Secretary.

The reader will expect no comments from the writer, and the subject is ended here with the effect the language of the foregoing documents will naturally create and impress upon a noble and patriotic heart.

CHAPTER XXIX.

ADAMS TOWNSHIP.

ADAMS TOWNSHIP—T. 3, N. R. 16 E.

UNDER the treaty of Washington, made on the 28th day of February, A. D., 1831, the Senecas ceded their entire reservation of forty thousand acres to the United States.

By the eighth article of this agreement the United States are bound to sell all this land, deduct from the proceeds certain expenses and six thousand dollars, advanced to the tribe, and to hold the balance of the purchase money until the same shall be demanded by the chiefs, and in the meantime pay them five per cent interest on the same.

The agreement was signed by James B. Gardiner, in behalf of the United States, and by Coonstick, Small Cloud Spicer, Hard Hickory and Captain Good Hunter, in behalf of the Senecas, the Indians making their marks. The witnesses were Henry C. Brish, sub-agent, George Herron, interpreter, W. H. Lewis, Henry Tolan and P. G. Randolph.

In offering the public lands for sale, it was so usual for the presidents in issuing their proclamations to that end, to except the school sections, sixteen, that General Jackson, in his proclamation of November, 1832, putting the Seneca reservation on the market, made the same exception, which was an error, simply because the general government had agreed to sell the whole tract. (See chapter x.)

Section sixteen, in Adams, was, therefore, not sold, and whenever the same shall be sold, the proceeds belong to the Senecas, if any of them still exist.

This was the only section sixteen embraced in the whole reserve in this county, and for want of a school section in Adams, the government granted to this township the west half of section twelve (12). This was done in 1827, and four years before the Senecas sold out. In Pleasant, section sixteen is on the west side of the river, and not in the reserve. The south and east lines   the reserve did not embrace sections sixteen in Clinton and Scipio. For further particulars the reader is referred to the subjoined documents, which explain themselves.

On the 25th of October, 1843, Henry Niles, George Kline and Solomon Drown, trustees of Adams, filed their petition in the court of common pleas of Seneca county, in which they say, that on the 29th of August, 1843, they had posted up nine notices in public places in said township, for a meeting to be held at the late residence of Ebenezer Brown, deceased, on the 30th of September, 1843, at nine o'clock A. M.; that then and there a vote would be taken for the sale of the west half of section twelve, in said township, in pursuance of an act passed March 10th, 1843. The petition says that the meeting was held, and that eighteen persons voted in favor of the sale, that the papers were all legally returned to the auditor, etc. The petition prays for an order to appraise and sell. Thomas R. Ellis, Jacob Souder and Wm. Toll were appointed appraisers. George Heming was the surveyor. The order was issued by C. F. Dreisbach, clerk, and H. C. Russell, deputy clerk. The land was sold for $2,200, and the sale confirmed. (See Chancery Record, vol. 4, p. 421, O. L., vol. 41, p. 142.)

Now if Adams has also sold section sixteen, she has for many years enjoyed an advantage over all the other townships in the county, by the interest of the proceeds of the sale of one-half section of land

It should be remembered here (and there is no room to speak at large on the subject) that the proceeds of the sales of the school sections sixteen, were paid into the treasury of the state, and the interest is paid annually back to the townships respectively, for educating the youth.

On the 30th day of January, 1836, the legislature of Ohio passed an act authorizing the sale of section sixteen, in Adams.

On the 3d day of April, 1837, another act was passed authorizing the auditors of the respective counties to sell the school sections, after a vote was had for that purpose. Under these two laws Levi Davis, then auditor of Seneca county, in the fall of 1839, sold all the lands in section sixteen, in Adams, made deeds for the same, and paid the money into the state treasury.

Thus the matter rested until the session of the legislature of 1845–6, when a joint resolution was passed in these words, viz:

PREAMBLE AND JOINT RESOLUTION

Relative to the confirmation of the title to section sixteen, township 3, N. R. 16 E. Seneca county.

WHEREAS, In the year 1836, section sixteen, in township three, north, in range sixteen east. in Seneca county, pursuant to an act of the general assembly of the state of Ohio, passed January 30th, 1836, was sold as land appropriated by Congress for the use of schools, and full payment has been made by, and deeds executed and delivered to, the purchasers, for the same; and,

WHEREAS, Doubts have been expressed as to the title of the purchasers, and as to the appropriation of the said lands for the use of schools; and,

WHEREAS, In the year 1845, the west half of section twelve, in the same township, pursuant to an act of the general assembly of Ohio, passed March 10th, 1843, was in like manner sold as lands appropriated for school purposes; and,

WHEREAS, It is believed that all the purchasers of both tracts, purchased in the confident belief that they would acquire a good title by such purchase, and gave fair prices for the land so purchased; and,

WHEREAS, It is presumed that the United States will readily comfirm to the inhabitants of such township said section sixteen, and that it was never intended by congress that any larger quantity of land should be appropriated for such township; therefore,

Resolved by the general assembly of the state of Ohio, That our senators and representatives in congress be requested to use their influence to procure the passage of an act of congress, providing for the confirmation of the title of section sixteen, in said township, to those holding the same by grants from the state of Ohio, and also for the payment of the purchase money of the west half of section twelve into the treasury of the United States, according to the terms of the sale thereof.

Resolved, That the governor be requested to forward copies of the above preamble and resolution to our senators and representatives in congress respectively.

ELIAS F. DRAKE.
Speaker of the House of Representatives.

SEABURY FORD,
   Speaker of the Senate.
JANUARY 17. 1846.

It is scarcely necessary to say that the legislature, in passing the foregoing bungling resolution, knew nothing, or cared less, about the treaty of 1831. William Allen and Thomas Corwin were senators from Ohio in congress, and Henry St. John was representative from this district. The subjoined documents will show that the preamble and resolution were received and referred, and the opinion of Benjamin F. Butler, of New York, then attorney general of the United States, obtained.

Mr. Polk was elected president of the United States that fall, and the war with Mexico broke out. The matter slept until some six years ago, when the writer, at the request of some parties interested, caused inquiry to be made concerning the subject, upon which the following correspondence took place:

ADAMS TOWNSHIP. 477

STATE OF OHIO,
AUDITOR OF STATE'S OFFICE,
COLUMBUS, September 15th, 1874.

Auditor of Seneca County, Tiffin, Ohio:

DEAR SIR: Yours of the 14th inst. is at hand. I hand you herewith copies of letters from the Commissioner of the General Land office, dated July 21st, August 10th, and September 2d.

Please bear in mind that the question is, by what authority was the land sold for school purposes? There is no doubt that it was so sold in 1836 and 1837.

It was erroneously excluded from proclamation of sale of the Seneca reservation November 13th, 1831, and sold as school land in 1836. The governor of Ohio was, in 1840, advised that its selection for school purposes was improper, and would not be submitted for the approval of the secretary of the treasury. In 1846, Hon. D. L. Yulee, of the United States senate, in his official capacity, requested information upon the subject. Notwithstanding the question has thus been agitated, it does not appear that during all these years it has been finally disposed of, and I can hardly conceive it possible that the parties interested should be wholly ignorant of what has transpired.

It is proper to add that that part of town 3. R. 16, lying outside the bounds of the reservation, was entitled to a half section of school land, and the west half of section 12 was selected therefor in 1826. I am not aware that any additional selections were ever made for the township, which is entitled to a full section of school land. Respectfully,

JAMES WILLIAMS,
Auditor of State.

STATE OF OHIO,
AUDITOR OF STATE'S OFFICE,
COLUMBUS, September 26th, 1874.

Hon. W. Lang, Tiffin, Ohio:

DEAR SIR: Yours of the 23d inst., in relation to the sale of section 16, T. 3. N. R. 16 E., for school purposes, is at hand. There is no question about the lands having beed sold as school land in 1836 and 1837, paid for in full, and deeds executed therefor by the governor. I can send you certified copies of the same, if desired. I presume, also, that there is no question but what the section should have been sold, with the balance of the reservation, for the benefit of the Indians. That is, it should have been included in the president's proclamation of sale in 1831, for it appears that the subject of title was brought before the general assembly in 1841, and a preamble and resolutions passed requesting our senators and representatives in congress to procure the passage of an act confirming the title to said section, in said township, etc. (See Ohio laws, vol. 44, page 298.)

The question first to be determined is, did congress take any decisive action under the said resolutions? It appears that the chairman of the committee (senate) on private lands, did make this case a matter of inquiry at the General Land office, in February, 1846. It appears, also, that a bill was passed August 8th, 1846, relative to school lands for R. 13 E., T. 1, N. (see United States statutes at large, vol. 9, p. 674.), but from a somewhat careful examination of the United States statutes at large, vol. 9, 1846-51, I do not find any legislation relative to this case. In 1846 William Allen and Thomas Corwin represented this state in the United States senate; Hon. Columbus Delano, secretary of the interior, represented Knox county, and Henry St. John represented Seneca county in the house of representatives. If the latter at that time did not pursue this case to a final issue, it is probable that it now stands precisely as it did in 1846.

If the case remains unsettled, permit me to suggest, that it is properly stated in the preamble and resolutions of January 17, 1846, and a remedy proposed. Such a disposition of it as would give the Indians the same average price per acre as was realized by them from the remainder of the reservation, would be equitable, and I should suppose satisfactory. Truly yours,

JAMES WILLIAMS,
Auditor of State.

DEPARTMENT OF THE INTERIOR,
GENERAL LAND OFFICE,
WASHINGTON, D. C., November 16, 1874.

W. Lang, Esq., Tiffin, Ohio:

SIR: Your letter of the 9th inst. is received, relative to section 16, T. 3, N. R. 16 E., in Seneca county, Ohio, and in reply, I have to state that, by the 8th article of the treaty with the Seneca Indians, dated February 28, 1831, it is stipulated that the land in question should be exposed at public sale, to the highest bidder, and hence the proposition of the present claimants of the land, in said section 16, as stated in your letter, to pay $1.25 per acre therefor, being contrary to the express provisions of the treaty, cannot be entertained by this office. Respectfully,

S. S. BURDETT,
Commissioner.

DEPARTMENT OF THE INTERIOR,
GENERAL LAND OFFICE,
WASHINGTON, D. C., July 21st, 1874.

James Williams, Esq., Auditor State of Ohio:

SIR; In my communication of the 30th ult., you were advised that "the west half of section 12, T. 3, R. 16 E., situated in Seneca county, Ohio, was selected for schools, under the act of May 20th, 1826, in lieu of section 16, then owned by the Seneca Indians; that prior to the cession to the United States by the Seneca Indians (in their treaty of the 28th of February, 1831,) of the lands bordering on this tract, the inhabitants of town 3, N. R. 16 E., selected other tracts for school purposes, in lieu of said section 16, which was then owned by said Indians, among which selections was the west half of section 12: that this selection had been approved by the secretary of the treasury on the 12th of January, 1827, and had never been retroceded to the United States; that section 16, having been ceded by the Indians, it was provided in article 8 of the articles of agreement and convention, made February 28th, 1831, between the Seneca Indians and the United States, that the lands ceded by said Indians should be brought into market and sold for their benefit, and that there was no evidence on file in this office to show that said section sixteen has ever been proclaimed for public sale, according to said article 8."

It now appears, from a further investigation of this matter, that the whole of the lands embraced within the late Seneca reservation, on the Sandusky river, in townships 2, 3 and 4, N. of ranges 15 and 16 East, containing 40,000 acres, were sold in accordance with the president's proclamation, dated November 13, 1831, with the exception of the 16th section, which was excluded erroneously by the said proclamation as land reserved for the use of schools.

In your communication to this office, of the 30th ult., you state that township 3, having a full section 16, the same has been sold for the use of schools therein, and that it is presumed the west half of section 12, referred to, belongs to some other township.

On the 1st of December, 1840, the governor of Ohio was advised by letter from this office that this section 16, by treaty with the Indians, is to be sold for their benefit as other parts of the reserve, and could not, as had been decided by the attorney general of the United States, be set apart for the use of schools, and that under these circumstances, its selection in the present case being considered improper, it was not submitted in the list of school lands for the state of Ohio, for the approval of the secretary of the treasury.

On the 4th of February, 1846, this office received a communication from the Hon. D. L. Yulee, chairman of the committee on private lands, United States senate, enclosing certain resolutions of the general assembly of the state of Ohio, in relation to section sixteen, township 3, N. R., sixteen E., in Seneca county, and requesting to be furnished with such facts in reference to the subjcet as might be useful to the committee, and in reply thereto, dated February 7, 1846, Mr. Yulee was advised that, by treaty stipulations with the Seneca Indians the sixteenth section in question was to be sold for their benefit as other portions of the tract ceded by them, as per treaty of February 28, 1831, and could not, as had been decided by the attorney general, be set apart for the use of schools.

Also that the west half of section twelve, in the same township, had been selected by the inhabitants thereof, in lieu of the sixteenth section prior to the cession to the United States of the latter tract by the Indians, and the selection of said west half of section twelve was approved by the secretary of the treasury January 12, 1827. And also as per article eight of the treaty referred to, all of the lands thereby ceded must be exposed to public sale before they can be entered as otherwise disposed of.

The " articles of agreement and convention " are, in themselves, clear and unambiguous; there is no exception as to the sixteenth section. It would be an infraction of the treaty and unjust to the Indians to admit any claim on the part of the state to any part of the lands embraced in the cession. The doctrine in such cases is stated in the opinion of Mr. Attorney-General Butler, of March 13, 1836, in the matter of the "location of the Choctaw reservation." (Opinions of attorneys general, volume 3, page 56).

The action of this office has heretofore, in similar cases, conformed to the doctrines enunciated in this opinion.

No reason is perceived for any contrary course in this case.

In view of this recitation of facts and authority, it follows, that in the opinion of this office, the action of the state authorities in appropriating and disposing of said section sixteen for school purposes, illegal and conveyed no title to the purchasers, and that said section remains subject to sale under the provisions of the eighth section of said treaty of February 20, 1831.

Respectfully, S. S. BURDETT,
Commissioner.

DEPARTMENT OF THE INTERIOR,
GENERAL LAND OFFICE,
WASHINGTON, D. C., August 10, 1874.

James Williams, Esq., Auditor State of Ohio:

SIR: In the matter relating to section sixteen, township 3, N. R., 16 E., Seneca county, Ohio, and fully treated of in my communication to you of the 21st ultimo, I have to state that a copy of the above communication was laid before the honorable secretary of the interior on the 24th ultimo to obtain his orders in the matter of the sale of said section sixteen.

The secretary, by letter of the 30th ultimo, in reply to the above, concurred in my opinion that said section sixteen was subject to sale under the provisions of the treaty with the Seneca Indians, made February 28, 1831, authorized the tract to be sold accordingly.

In accordance with the above authority, the register and receiver, at Chillicothe, have this day been instructed to proceed in having the above tract brought into market by publication for the period of sixty days in two newspapers having the largest circulation, published nearest to the premises, and at the expiration of the above period, to offer the said section, in legal sub-divisions, to the highest bidder for cash, and not less than $1.25 per acre.

Respectfully, S. S. BURDETT,
Commissioner.

DEPARTMENT OF THE INTERIOR,
GENERAL LAND OFFICE,
WASHINGTON, D. C., September 2, 1874.

James Williams, Esq., Auditor State of Ohio:

SIR: Your letter of 17th ultimo is received, relative to section sixteen, township 3, N. R. 16 E., in Seneca county, Ohio, and in reply thereto, I have to state that on the 31st ultimo, the register and receiver, at Chillicothe, were notified to delay proceedings in the matter of advertising the above section for public sale until further orders.

It is not, however, to be understood that this office has changed or modified the views heretofore expressed relative to the status of said sections, and unless adequate reasons for a prolonged suspension are shown, the order to proceed will, at an early day, be issued.

Very respectfully, S. S. BURDETT,
Commissioner.

STATE OF OHIO,
AUDITOR OF STATE'S OFFICE,
COLUMBUS,............187..

County Auditor:

Please excuse the hasty scrawl enclosed, which is of value only as showing the attitude of the commissioner in the matter. The resolutions of January 17, 1846, referred to in the correspondence, will be found in Ohio Laws, volume XLIV., page 298. One would suppose that the matter would have been adjusted on equitable terms at that date. Possibly this was done.

ADAMS TOWNSHIP.

If not, why was not the land sold for the benefit of the Indians at that date, and an additional half section of land granted the township for school purposes? Respectfully, CHAS. J. WETMORE,
Clerk of Land Department.

The organization of Adams, noticed in chapter x., dates from December 6, 1826. It then included a tier of sections from Thompson, the Indians holding the larger portion on the west. The first township election was held on Monday, Christmas day, 25th of December, 1826, at the house of Samuel Whiteman, when the following ticket was elected:

Clerk—Abraham Rine.
Trustees—Martin Olds, L. T. Butler, Thomas Longwith.
Overseers of the Poor—Charles Shelby, Samuel Whiteman.
Fence Viewers—G. Lee, Samuel Hartsock.
Treasurer—Cyrus Wright.
Supervisors—William Myers, William Mead, Francis Evans.
Constable—Moses Pyatt.

In 1830 it had a population of 830 inhabitants; in 1840, 1,250; in 1870, 1,537. James Crocket, John Kersler, Daniel Rule, Ezra West, James McIntire, John Myers, Nicholas Noel and John Paine were also among the early settlers. In 1880 the population is 1,624.

Adams has a great natural curiosity that has become famous by the "water cure" establishment near Green Springs. It is the spring itself which has become celebrated by the excellent medicinal qualities of its water. The Hedges springs are near the middle of section seven, on lands formerly owned by Josiah Hedges. The Green Springs are just across the line in Sandusky county. The water comes out in large quantities, clear and cold, and the volume is neither increased nor diminished by the change of the seasons. The water from Hedges springs, flowing in a southerly direction, enters Beaver creek, flowing through Adams, entering Pleasant in section twelve and turning northwardly it enters Sandusky county. This creek derived its name from the great number of beavers that were caught along its course.

Mr. Hedges built a mill on this creek in Pleasant, which acquired great popularity from the fact that the dry weather in summer never interfered with its operation. It was patronized by people from many other counties, Wood, Hancock, Crawford and Putnam

On the 26th day of May, 1839, Jacob Stem secured the services of David Reeves and David Risdon, two surveyors, the former from Sandusky county, the latter from Seneca, who surveyed and platted the town of Green Springs, named after the great sulphur springs in the vicinity. The town embraces a part of section five, in Adams, and part of sections thirty-one and thirty-two in township 4, N. R. 16 in Sandusky county.

On the first of January, 1868, a water cure was opened for the reception of patients suffering from diseases of the blood, liver, stomach, kidneys, urinary organs, and all chronic diseases. Many legends are told of the wonderful cures of the water among the Indians, blended of course with their usual superstitions, but time and space will not admit of repeating them, nor is it the intention of the writer to advertise the water cure. Suffice it to say that the cure is well patronized and is a splendid institution. Jacob Stem, Daniel H. Dana and Bishop Adams, with their families, were the first settlers of Green Springs. In 1840 the population of the town was 29, and now numbers some 1,400. It is situated on the Cleveland, Sandusky & Cincinnati railroad; has three Protestant churches and one Roman Catholic church. Daniel H. Dana was the first postmaster of this place.

Another town by the name of Adamsville was surveyed by Thomas Heming, April 30, 1846, Henry Kistter, proprietor. Hedgetown or Sulphur Springs was surveyed and platted in 1833. These towns, together with Lowell, were all failures as towns. Green Springs is now the residence of Judge Hugh Welsh, of whom mention is made elsewhere, and who is one of the oldest inhabitants of Seneca. Mrs. Ingham is the other. Adams is one of the best townships in the county, intellectually, socially and every other way. The soil is rich and the surface rolling.

Mr. Daniel Metzger, of Adams, has furnished the writer with the following interesting communication, viz:

ADAMS, March 22, 1880.
Hon. W. Lang:

DEAR SIR: In compliance with your request, I send you such statements of Adams township as I have at my command. My father, Henry Metzger, was born in Pennsylvania in 1797, and came to Pickaway county in 1812 with his father. He was married in that county to Catherine Wise, whose parents came from Union county, Pennsylvania, and also settled in Pickaway in 1809. In the fall of 1833 moved from Pickaway to this county upon the farm where I now reside, and where he died March 4, 1868. Mother was born in 1794, and if she lives until the 14th day of next August, will be 86 years old. (Right here, and while recording this, May 18,1880, Mr. Metzger informs me that his mother died this morning.) My father entered this land at the land office in Bucyrus. His patent is signed by General Jackson. When we moved onto this farm there was not a tree cut on it, except an occasional one by some Nimrod in the chase. On the direct road from our place to Tiffin, there was but one house until we arrived at Thomas R. Ellis', and that was Uriah Egbert's small cabin. The first time we went to Tiffin we had to cut our way through to the Portland road, near Egbert's. Jacob

Bowerman was another old settler. He came in 1830 from Seneca county, New York. He was born in Pennsylvania and moved to the state of New York when a boy, and married his wife there. Her maiden name was Mary Ritter, who was also a native of Pennsylvania. These old folks lived together as man and wife for 60 years. Bowerman died August 16, 1876, aged 81 years, 6 months and 22 days. His wife died soon after at the age of 78 years, 4 months and 4 days. They lived and died on the farm where they settled 46 years before. John Bowerman, a brother to Jacob, came in 1831. He had served in the war of 1812 in New York. John Petticord came to this township in 1830 from Fairfield county, Ohio. John Paine came about the same time from Pickaway county, Ohio, where he was married to a Miss Lawrence, who is still living and in her 90th year, and does her own housework. Her husband has been dead a number of years. He was a native of New Jersey. John Paine was a soldier in the war of 1812. His widow draws a pension in consequence. William Myers was also one of the first settlers here. He came from Fairfield county, but was born in Virginia. His wife was a Carson and both lived to be very old. There were also four brothers of the Whiteman family among the first settlers here. They came from Pennsylvania. Their names were Samuel, Daniel, Jacob and Abraham. They all lived to a fine old age, but are now all dead.

Quite a number of our young men went to the war against Michigan in 1835. Those that I remember were Samuel Metzger, William Paine, Solomon Hoppes and Adam Spade.

Another old settler lived on the Kilbourne road, northeast of Republic, some four miles. His name was Webb. He kept a small store. He located here about 1823.

There are four creeks flowing through this township. Beaver creek enters the township at the southest corner, running west about two miles, when it turns northwest and takes up the Sulphur Springs and runs north into Sandusky county, and through it to the bay. Sugar creek takes its rise in the north part of Scipio township and enters Adams about one and a-half miles from the southwest corner, and taking a northwesterly course crosses the Portland road, near Daniel Rule's, and from there runs westerly into the Sandusky river. Hog run heads in a small prairie on the farm of Nicholas Noel. It is a short stream and enters the Beaver about one mile south of the centre of Adams. Emerson creek rises in the northwest part of Thompson, and taking up the waters of the famous Royer ditch, runs nearly due west and enters the Beaver one mile north of Adams centre. There was good fishing at the mouths of both these last named creeks in early days.

Hoping these minutes may be of interest to you,

I remain, respectfully, yours,

DANIEL METZGER.

JOHN NOEL

Was born October 15th, 1777. in Adams county, Pennsylvania. He was married to Elizabeth Beamer (who was born in the same state, July 21st, 1780,) on the 15th day of June, 1801. They moved to Ohio in 1822, and located near Massilon, Stark county, and in April, 1830, located in this township, on the farm where their son Nicholas now lives, fifty years ago.

John Noel and his wife were the parents of fifteen children, seven boys and eight girls, of whom four boys and three girls are still living. John Noel died October 29th, 1863, aged eighty-six years and fifteen days. Mrs. Noel died in September, 1847, at the age of sixty seven years, three months and twenty-seven days.

DANIEL RULE.

The sketch of this veteran pioneer is given in his own words, as nearly as possible:

My grandfather was a soldier in the revolutionary war. He returned from the army and died from an abcess in his side, leaving my father, Albert A., his only child. They lived in he southern part of Pennsylvania, where my father was raised, and where he married Elizabeth Tivens. My parents moved to near Liverpool, in Perry county, Pennsylvania, onto a farm. Here I was born, on the banks of the Susquehanna river. They lived here about nineteen years, and when I was about twelve years old, we moved to Columbiana county, Ohio, and settled on a farm near New Lisbon, in 1816. My father had two children by his first wife, and four by his second. My two sisters, Barbara and Catharine, were married ; the former to Luke Stage, and the other, who was married twice, died, and left two daughters and one son, who live in Illinois. Two years after we moved to Columbiana county, we moved to Bloomfield, in Trumbull county, near Warren. My father had bought a farm here and we settled on that. Here, on the 7th day of June, 1821, I was married to Jane, the daughter of farmer Grosscost, in this township of Bloomfield. I have also a brother, Samuel Rule, making four of us children, two boys and two girls. Samuel lives in Illinois now.

In 1824, in the spring, and after my brother Samuel was married, he and his family, with father and mother, moved to Scipio township, in this county, and about six years thereafter they sold out and bought on section thirteen, in Clinton township, where brother Samuel opened a nice farm. Father and mother lived with him until they died, but in a separate house. Father died in 1846, and mother two years thereafter.

When brother Samuel, father and mother left Trumbull county, I was married and could not go with them that spring, but I followed them to this county in the next fall. Here I bought an eighty acre piece in Scipio, at the land office in Bucyrus. It is the land now owned by Philip Miller. I built a cabin here and cleared about forty-five acres. My family were sickly nearly all the time we lived here, and I sold the place to buy land in Adams. My first purchase in Adams was one hundred and seventy-three acres. When I raised my cabin here I had to bring nearly all my help with me from Scipio, there being but very few settlers on the reserve. About one year after I moved here I bought ninety-seven acres from Joseph Culbertson, and soon after eighty acres more from Dr. Stevenson.

Afterwards I bought ninety-three acres more from Mr. R. R. Titus, admin-

istrator of Earl Church, deceased. I let my two sons, Isaac and Byron, have one-half section of this land.

I still remain on the old homestead. My wife died on the second day of December, 1879, aged seventy-seven years, nine months and eighteen days. Since she is gone I feel lost, and as if I were of no account to the world. We had ten children, viz:

Lucy, who is the wife of Jeremiah Egbert; Elizabeth, the widow of Isaac Stillwell; Samuel, who died in 1850, when twenty-four years old; Albert A., who died a few days after Samuel, both of small-pox; Byron, who married Matilda York, of Clyde, Ohio; Matilda, who died when six years old; Mary, wife of David W. Dudrow; Isaac P., who was wounded at the battle of Chickamauga, and died next day; he was lieutenant of Co. I, 101st regiment O. V. I., and leading his company when he received the wound; and Daniel C., who married Eleanor, daughter of Earl Church, whose widow is still living. Our youngest child was still-born. Five of my children are still living. My two sons, Byron and Daniel, are living near me, and doing well, and so are also the daughters I have left.

I knew Small Cloud Spicer well. He was a half breed, tall, slender, well proportioned and good looking. He had sandy hair, but dressed like the other Indians. His wife was a Crow, and a clean, pleasant woman. When I came onto the reserve here the white settlers were but few, James Crocket lived on the Watson farm; Mr. McEwen lived on the McMeens place; 'Squire Rider raised a cabin on the place that Jacob Holtz bought afterwards; Slike Clark lived near the river.

I was born October 28, 1801.

CHAPTER XXX.

BIG SPRING TOWNSHIP.

BIG SPRING TOWNSHIP—T. 1, N. R. 13 E.

THIS township was organized March 6th, 1833, and received its name from the big spring of water in the southwest part of the township. The first election was held April 4, 1833, and the following were the officers chosen, viz:

Trustees—E. Bogart and Richard Reynolds.
Clerk—William Brayton.
Treasurer—Hugh Mulholland.
Fence Viewers—Cornelius Bogart, Andrew Springer and Joshua Watson.
Overseers of the Poor—Elijah Brayton and Charles Henderson.
Constable—Austin Knowlton.

Mr. Knowlton is still living, and while he enjoys good health in his old age, is a very pleasant, congenial gentleman. The others of those officers are all dead, I think.

In 1840 the township had a population of 925; in 1870 there were 2,224; in 1880 it is 2,048. The above named officers and John Peer, Hiram Bogart, Ph. Peer, J. Luzader, the Young family, the Stiles, and others, were among the early settlers.

It will be noticed that the first settlers were American born and no German name is found among them. From 1833 to 1842 a very large number of German and French families came on, and after Mr. Anthony Schindler bought land and located in section twelve, many of his old neighbors from Germany settled round about him. Here he laid out a town and named it after his native town in Germany, New Reigel. The old German settlers were Anthony and Carl Schindler, Joseph Bischof, Joseph, Stephan and Landelin Brosamer, Jacob Kabele, Michael Schon, Nicholas Perl, Nicholas and Francis Eltig, Peter Rinehart, Michael Wolly, Nicholas and Francis Etchen, John Wagner, Ignatz Lehnhart, M. Schlachter, John Moes, Joseph Ries, the Kern family, the Dannenhoeffers, the Schiraks, the Seibenalers, and others.

BIG SPRING TOWNSHIP. 487

Among the French families were the Lafontaines, the Filliatres, the Wernements, F. Collet, J. Mangett, the Gilliaumes, and others. William Tempelman was an original sort of a character.

My esteemed old friend, Theodore M. Frink must not be overlooked and a short sketch of his life will be found below.

Charles Schindler moved upon the land where he now lives in 1835. He bought a cast iron stove from one Jacob Alexy, in Loudon township about three miles north of where he lives. He started with his team and George Wehrle to get the stove, very early one morning, and after the stove was loaded on the wagon, they had a very slow drive with their ox team through the swales. They stalled many times and when they reached the cabin of Mr. Lafontaine, it was pitch dark and they had to stay all night. They reached home near noon next day. Charles Schindler was born in Hechnigen, Baden, in 1805.

The Lawheads, the Bouchers, the Flicks and others were also among the early settlers.

The Germans will soon own the whole township. They have everything their own way now to a very great extent, buying out all their old American neighbors and turning Big Spring into one of the most wealthy and prosperous townships in the county.

Elijah Brayton, in 1825, lived in Crawford county, which then included Wyandot, and soon after moved to this township. In that year, on the 20th of September, he lost a little boy, then about eight years old, in the following manner, viz: The child had followed an older brother and a neighbor, who were looking for cattle that were missing, and the little fellow was sent back to the house. He followed the path that had been pointed out to him and was never heard of again. Upon the return of the others, the alarm was given throughout the neighborhood and everybody turned out, even the Indians, and scoured the country far and wide, but without any clue to the missing boy.

During this search Neal McGaffey, of Fort Ball, the first clerk of the court of common pleas, and some others, camped all night on the spot that was afterwards included in the town of Risdon and which is now in Fostoria.

The town of Springville was surveyed by David Risdon in 1834 for Benjamin and John Jenkins, proprietors. The town never grew much. The spring was once a very powerful one and formed a small lake. The water was very deep, clear and cold. Since the country has been cleared up, the spring has lost much of its former celebrity and would now be noticed no more than any good spring on a farm.

The town of Oregon (now Adrian) was surveyed by R. M. Shoemaker, on the 17th of February, 1844, on sections 35 and 36, on the Mad River & Lake Erie, now the Cleveland, Sandusky & Cincinnati railroad. Erastus H. Cook and D. C. Henderson were the proprietors. Eli Gehr, Adam Vetter, John Gants and Charles Foster were the first settlers here. The town grew up to its present size within a few years after it was laid out, and stood there ever since.

Anthony Schindler, who laid out New Reigel, was a very active, lively and enterprising man. Very soon after the laying out of this town, people settled in and around the town, and put up a log church, which in time gave way to a brick church, and that in its turn to one of the largest and most beautiful Catholic churches in northern Ohio.

The town of New Reigel is now settled up by farmers who have become wealthy, and wish to spend their last days at their ease near the church, and a brotherhood and sisterhood of the 'Society of the Precious Blood," who own very large tracts of land near the town. The sisters officiate as teachers of the youth. Father M. Sales Brunner was the founder of this order, and the first priest in New Reigel. There are about sixty persons in the nunnery at New Reigel at the present time.

The land in Big Spring is very rich, and when the prairie in the southwestern part shall be thoroughly drained, as efforts to that end are now being made, Big Spring will be the rich garden spot of the county.

There is a stony ridge in the southern part of the township.

Among the early settlers should also be mentioned the Boucher families, Peter Lantz, Isaac Dewitt, Frederick Waggoner, Ira Taft, William Blue, Israel Harmas, W. Burgess, Peter Wanner, M. Clark, Louis Schany, William Clark, E. H. Cook, E. Brayton, the Jenkins', Joseph Clapper, John Ellerton, Henry Mulholland and C. Woolford.

JOHN YOUNG

Settled in the woods about half way between Springville and New Reigel, in the spring of 1833. He came from near Canal Dover, where he hired a four horse team to bring him here It took him three weeks to get here, and the few inhabitants of Springville were about one-half whites, and the others Indians. Here Mr. Young met a man whom he once knew in Stark county, by the name of Jacob Gwyer who offered to pilot Young to his land, and said he lived near Springville, and pretended that he had to go home first to get the number of the section; but instead of going he lingered around, and was seen several times peeping into the big wagon, no doubt watching for a chance to get into the big chest. When Mr. Young told him that it was time to get the map, he went away and never returned, but was seen by some hunters sneaking around the camp the following night, dressed in an Indian costume.

On the next day Mr. Young moved out onto his land, where the family was left in the woods, and the teamster returned to Jenkins' to feed Jenkins kept a sort of trading post at the Spring. To get onto the land was no small job. There was no road that way, and the swales were full of water. Night overtook them before the land was reached. They unhitched, cut some wild grass for the horses, and ate and slept in the wagon. Mr. Young's family consisted of himself, his wife and three small boys. His father and his wife's brother came out here with him to see him get started in the woods.

At night the men took turn about in watching. They kept up a large fire, and had a Newfoundland dog with them, who saved their lives, as will soon appear. On the next day they reached the land, about two o'clock, where they hastily unloaded, to give the teamster time to return to Springville to feed his starving horses. The men then put up a very temporary shanty by planting four forks into the ground, upon which poles were laid, and covered with clap-boards in a very rude manner. This "Grand Hotel de Young" answered the purpose about ten days, when the other house was ready to move into.

Just as the family were about to retire on the first night in this shanty, the big dog sprang out into tne darkness, barking very fiercely. He saw a man, and would have taken hold of him had not Mr. Young called him away. Mr. Young thought it was some hunter or friendly Indian that wanted to see the new-comers, but the man walked away, and Mr. Young concluded that it was Gwyer. Mr. Young's horse was let loose, and the cow was driven away that night. This created the fear in Mr. Young's mind that this plan would make the men run after the lost animals next day, and give the villain an opportunity to rob the shanty. There was no money in it, however, for Mr. Young had used it about all to pay for his land. Gwyer some time afterwards confessed the whole plan. The men were on the lookout, and kept themselves well armed.

This Jacob Gwyer was afterwards arrested for murdering a man named Boyd, near Bucyrus. When his arrest took place in Detroit, he confessed the murder and several robberies, for which he had never been blamed; also his attempt to rob Samuel Young. Before the day arrived for the execution, he and three horse-thieves made their escape to Ohio, and Gwyer was re-arrested near Dayton, where his wife lived. While there in prison he cut his throat with a knife.

Samuel Young was born in Washington county, Pennsylvania, August 13th, 1794. He was a cooper by trade. He married Isabella Sutton, November 17th, 1818. He was five feet six inches high, had black hair and deep blue eyes, light complexion short stubby nose, small mouth and chin, and was rather delicate in his features. He spoke some German, and was always very lively in conversation. He was a pleasant and peaceable man and esteemed for his good qualities and christian bearing. He served on juries often and refused several times to serve as a township officer. He died many years ago. Mrs. Young is still living at her home in Adrian. She is now 78 years old and enjoys the love and respect of all her neighbors and especially that of her children and grand-children, who annually gather around her with their smiles and congratulations.

Mr. Young was 63 years old when he died here in 1859.

Mrs. Young was born December 31, 1802, and enjoys very good health for a lady of her age. She is the mother of ten children.

In those early days a large family was a pride and a glory. The sin and crime of avoiding to have a family, are the children of these later* days; sins and crimes that are not punished by law, and against which the church shuts both eyes, but the victims may be counted by the thousands.

What will the world come to when this dreadful crime reaches the masses and religion fails in her mission to save?

THEODORE M. FRINK, ESQ.

Among the few native Americans that live near New Reigel and have not yet sold out to the Germans is Theodore M. Frink, Esq., the subject of this sketch.

He was born in West Springfield, Hamden county, Massachusetts, at a place where Holyoke City now stands, on the south bank of the Connecticut river. When about 17 years old he moved with his father to Northampton. On the 25th of April, 1832 he was married to Miss Sabeah Torry, and in May, 1836, he started with his family for the west. For want of any better conveyance they took a canal boat at West Troy for Buffalo, and from there they came by steamer to Cleveland and then made their way to Ravenna, Portage county, where a brother of his wife then lived. This brother-in-law, Torry, had a son living in Tymochtee, who had come home on a visit. With him Squire Frink came west in October of that year and bought the land where he still resides. This took about all the money he had, and he made his way back to Ravenna, one hundred and fifty miles, on foot. In January following he bought a yoke of oxen, made a sled, put his wife and goods upon it and started for Big Spring. Here he opened a farm, where he is now comfortably situated. During all this time he has enjoyed the respect and esteem of the good people of Big Spring to such an extent that for eight years he served them as a trustee, and as justice of the peace ever since 1848. What better proof can be required of his good report among his neighbors? There is no man living in the township who stands better in the esteem of its citizens than Squire Frink. His good counsel is sought daily and he has saved many litigations by his good advice. His first wife died on the 3d of February, 1855. He was married to his present wife July 3, 1862. The Squire remains among his neighbors as one of the olden school, and as the years increase, the esteem of the people for his white head grows in proportion.

CHAPTER XXXI.

BLOOM TOWNSHIP.

T. 1, N. R. 16 E.

IN the preceding chapters the recurrences to Bloom township and its early settlers were so frequent that very little else seems proper to be said in making up its history. One feature, however, must be admitted by all, viz: that the early settlers here were men of good judgment and great sagacity, when they resolved to drive their stakes for homes. They saw in the near future the grandeur, beauty and agricultural wealth these valleys, in the hands of industry, intelligence and economy, would present to the world Its soil, timbers, building stones, prospects for market, all these and more, were great incentives for the founding of new homes in the forest. A glance at Bloom township now, with its beautiful farms in a high state of cultivation, with large barns, splendid farm houses, fields teeming with rich crops, its pastures enjoyed by excellent stocks of horses, cattle, sheep and hogs; its commodious school houses and churches, etc., give strong proof how well the aim of the pioneer settler was directed when first the tall timbers fell by the woodsman's axe, along Honey creek and Silver creek, running through the township.

Thomas Boyd was one of the earliest settlers here. He came in 1822, and settled on section eleven, where he lived until his death, which occurred November 27th, 1847. Soon after him came also his brother, James Boyd, and his widowed sister, Mrs. Mary Donnell. Mrs. Thomas Baker is a daughter of James Boyd, and is still living. Her father moved to Iowa, where he died. Thomas Boyd had four sons: James, Jesse, Jefferson and Samuel, of whom Jesse is the only one living. He is a wealthy farmer at Springfield, Ohio.

Thomas Boyd was a remarkable man. He was of fair complexion; his hair was thin and white; he had a nervous temperament, and was very active. He was about six feet high, very raw-boned, and a little stoop-shouldered, very careless about his dress, very talkative, and possessed of a great quantity of good sense. He belonged to the Presbyterian church, and was very outspoken on the subject of slavery. While he was a pioneer on the frontier, he was also a pioneer in the then young idea of abolitionism. He made war on both the old parties who could see no constitutional way to get rid of the institution. Nor could the Abolitionists; but with them the system was wrong, and that was enough The task was not so easy with statesmen, however, who regarded the rights and integrity of states as fixed principles in our form of government. The institution fell, as a result of the rebellion, and we are all Abolitionists now. Arms and "higher law" in deadly conflict sometimes accomplish ends that statesmanship tremblingly abandon.

In the same year Joseph Birnside arrived here from Fairfield county, and settled near the mouth of a little run that puts into Honey creek just a little north of Bloomville, but ascertaining soon that the land had been entered by somebody else (Mr. Reber), he moved into Clinton township, and bought the land just east of the new cemetery, where he lived the rest of his days.

In 1823 came also Joseph McClelland and Nehemiah Hadley, who were followed by George Free, Lowell Robinson, John C. Martin and Thomas West, with their families. Mr. Martin and Mrs. West are still living in Bloom. James Boyd settled on section eight, on the left bank of Honey creek. George Free settled on section three, near the "Goose Pond," which was a considerable body of water in a bend of Honey creek. Lowell Robinson settled on section eight. He died in California. Mr. Robinson was one of the associate judges of Seneca county, a large muscular man, and possessed of a good quantity of common sense. He was a good neighbor, and rather popular. His wife was a very small woman, and for some reason or other the two did not live very happily together. One time, while Mr. Robinson was yet associate judge, his wife prosecuted him for assault and battery, and the Judge was bound over to the court of common pleas. He was indicted by the grand jury, and when the case came up for trial, the Judge had to leave the bench, come down to the trial table, and act the part of a prisoner. During the trial of the case the testimony disclosed, among other things, the fact that one morning, while the Judge was down upon his knees before a chair, at prayer, with his head down, Mrs. Robinson put a saddle on his back and jumped up on to it. For this he probably struck her.

Dr. Graves used to tell a good joke on Judge Robinson, sometimes in his company. Judge Robinson had a very large mouth. He came to Dr. Graves one day to have a tooth pulled. He sat down on a chair, and when the Doctor came up to him with his turnkey Judge Robinson opened his mouth very wide, and Dr. Graves said to him, " Never mind, Judge, I prefer standing on the outside."

Thomas West settled on section three also, but soon sold out to David Roop, and moved on to section ten, where he lived many years, and then sold to Jacob Detwiler, when he moved to Bloomville, where recently he died.

Mrs. Donnell bought a piece of land near that of her brother Thomas. Her land had a very fine spring on it, which still bears her name. She sold out and went to Iowa with her brother James.

John Seitz, Isaac Rohrer, Levi Neibel, Lyman Robinson, Jacob Meyer, Rufus Kirshner, Henry Perkey, David Crapo, Truman King, James Wilson, Evan Dorsey, John Newman, Lewis Seitz, John Davis, Mr. Jeffries. Mr. Donald and J. C. Hampton are also honored names among the old pioneers.

Bloom was organized, as already stated, in June, 1824. In 1830 it already had a population of 389. Between 1830 and 1840 came also David Roop, John T. Reed, Simon Koller, Benj Huddle (Hottel), Philip Heilman, David Troxell, Adam Baker, John Fisher, Samuel Gross, Edward Cooley, Henry Andres, James Trail, and Greensberry and Notley Trail, William and Zeliphant Owen, John Valentine, Henry and Samuel Nestly, Jonas Hostler, D. T Lee, George Showman, Geo. King, Samuel Shaffer, Jacob Hossler, the esquire, and James Wilson, the lawyer. The census of 1840 showed a population of 1,168 souls. In 1870 it was 1,492; in 1880 it is 2,162. At this time (1840) the land in the township was nearly, if not quite all, taken up, and the light of day was rapidly let in upon the ground, while the fields increased in number and proportions.

Mr. James Steel, from Pennsylvania, built the first grist mill in the township, on the banks of Silver creek. The Hershbergers turned it into a sawmill sometime after the Koller mill and the Engle mill were put up. The first meeting house in the township was a Presbyterian church, erected in 1834. It was a small frame building. They held meetings in it before it was plastered; all that spring and summer and in the fall of that year, while it was being plastered. By some unknown cause, it took fire and burned down. Then a brick church was built on the same spot, which answered for many years, until finally it was torn down and the brick used in the construction of the brick church in Bloomville. The old church stood northwest of Bloomville, near the cemetery. The Methodists built a church soon after on the land owned

BLOOM TOWNSHIP. 495

by J. W. Stinchcomb, but it was superceded by the stone church down the creek.

The tradition about the two young men naming Silver creek and Honey creek has no historic merit, and is therefore excluded. The name of Bloom is very appropriate.

BLOOMVILLE.

Philip J. Price, Julius Treat and Thomas T. Treat, in the summer of 1837, laid out a town upon the corners of sections nine, ten, fifteen and sixteen, and called it Bloomville. Simon Koller owned the land on the northwest corner, Edward Cooley on the southeast corner, Price and the Treat brothers on the southwest corner, and Edward Owen on the northwest corner. Mr. Cooley built the first house on the town site, which stood where the *Record* printing office now is. The Treat brothers built the next house, which was removed several times, and finally occupied by Thomas Treat as a store and postoffice. The Brown brothers bought out Price and Treat's store and continued it for a while. In 1850 the town contained a dozen buildings. Frederick Zimmerman, Conrad Klachr, William Hathaway, Ch. Keller, Jno. Hunsicker, Wm. Cooley, Dr. George Weeks, Jonathan Kastner, Jacob Estep, and Jacob Breiner, with their families, were the inhabitants. Hathaway and Kuntz were the pioneer shoemakers in the village. Webster had a blacksmith shop on the corner now occupied by the Hossler block. Dr. Weeks succeeded Dr. Bellville, who, with Dr. Peter J. Smith, were the pioneer physicians. Mr. Keller was the first tailor, and Mr. Klachr the first wagon and carriage makers. Soon after John Seitz, Jr., and William Dewitt opened a store on the corner now known by the name of the "burned district." Mr. Dewitt was afterwards elected county recorder, and died while in office. Mr. Seitz represented Seneca in both branches of the legislature. (See chapter XXVI.) Dr. Weeks entered the war against the rebellion, and became surgeon general in the department of Tennessee. Thomas Dysinger opened the first tavern. The Bloom House was built by Benj. Knopp in 1855 or 1856. Among the enterprising citizens who have helped to build up Bloomville, may be mentioned, Benj. Knopp, Henry Dittenhafer, John Hunsicker, E. P. Bliss. Mathias Teach and Henry Briner were the first men that enlisted from Bloomville for the war.

The location of the Mansfield and Coldwater railroad gave Bloomville a "fresh start in the world." Large brick edifices for business and dwelling houses, the general increase in the number of buildings and population, the warehouses and factories, show the healthy increase and prosperity of the town.

On the 4th of July, 1874, the Rev. Robert Lockhart established the first newspaper here, the *Enterprise*. He published the paper about three months, when he turned it over to J. N. Lee, who, after a few weeks, sold it to D. W. Fisher, who issued the first paper January 1st, 1875—the *Bloomville Banner*. The Adams Brothers then became the owners next, and sold to Mr. Kaga, and he again to Mr Fisher, who, after one issue, sold to W. S. Hammaker, and he, after about eight months, stopped the publication, and sold the institution to the present enterprising and able editor of the *Seneca County Record*, O. M. Holcomb, Esq., who is making the *Record* a success.

Bloomville was incorporated by a special act of the legislature in 1871. Jacob Hossler, Esq., was elected its first mayor. Several additions have been made to Bloomville during the ten years last past, by Conrad Klachr, Mrs Melinda Lee, Eli Winters and John Krilly. The oar factory, established in 1874, by J D. Wilsey, was quite an important event in the history of the town.

The Rev. George R. Brown, Universalist, preached here in 1840. Dr. Jones is the pastor of the M. E. Church, and Rev. J. W. Shaw of the Reformed Church.

In 1875 the public schools opened up, under the superintendence of Mr. J. K. Hamilton. The building is a fine two-story edifice, with four rooms, and cost about $7,000.

The grain depot of Einsel & Co. added much to the enterprise of the town.

(NOTE—I am under obligations to my friend Mr. Holcomb, for his kindness in furnishing me with meterial and dates.)

My reverend and esteemed friend, the venerable Elder Lewis Seitz, was so kind as to furnish the writer with a statement of his early recollections of Bloom township, and the reader will find pleasure in its perusal, I am very sure. It is given here as written, without a word of comment. May its moral lesson be heeded and cherished.

RECOLLECTIONS OF PIONEER DAYS IN BLOOM TOWNSHIP.
[By Elder Lewis Seitz.]

In October. 1825, at the age of twenty-three, with my wife and one child, I removed to my present home (on an adjoining farm) in Bloom township. The name of Bloom had been suggested by my brother John just one year before my arrival, and adopted in 1824 at the organization of the township. I came from my native county, Fairfield, into an almost unbroken wilderness of forest trees, with less than a score of settlers in advance of me.

BLOOM TOWNSHIP.

Nearly all who were here before me had settled along the rich valley of Honey creek. For two or three years before mine was reared, cabins had begun to appear in our wilderness. Among their occupants I remember Joseph McClellan, James and Thomas Boyd, the Donalds, George Free, Roswell Munsel, Nehemiah Hadley, John Stroh, Lowell Robinson, my brothers John Seitz and Noah Seitz. J. C. Hampton (who came in 1822 with the Boyds and Donalds, from Ross county,) informs me that he aided in erecting the first cabin put up in the township. This was for my brother Noah, on Silver creek. Hampton made his home for a time with his companions from Ross. Their shelter at first was in a log pen covered with logs split in twain, the under tier being with flat side up, and the top tier covering the cracks with the flat side down. The beds were for the women, on bedsteads, with one post. That is, in one corner of the "pen" two poles were entered in the logs, with the other end in this "post." Baswood bark furnished the "cords." The men slept on the ground, with hickory bark spread down for sheets. Hampton says: "Our first supply of flour was brought by us on horseback from Mansfield, through the woods." I also helped cut out the small timber west and south of Roop's Corners, to make a public road. But to continue with the names of the first settlers: Jacob Rodegeb, Abraham Kagy, John Davis, Edward Sutherland, Christopher Perkey, Bartholomew Stout, John Stinchcomb and Richard Ridgely. Within a very few years after my arrival came also Jacob Webster, the Bixlers, John Pennington, J..T. Reed, John Einsel, Edward Cooley, Samuel Gross, John Valentine, Gain Robinson, Zelaphel Owen, Joshua Watson, Samuel and Henry Nisley, Lewis and Jacob Spitler.

During these early days a wilderness of forest trees covered the earth, and the first need of the settler was to clear away space enough for a cabin, and then it was "root, hog. or die." While I brought from Fairfield county enough flour to last two years, very few of my contemporaries were thus provided. One season, however, usually sufficed the industrious pioneer to clear a small field and grow bread to do. As for meat, everyone had his gun to supply him with wild turkey or venison, which were abundant. Often, too, as we lay upon our pillow at night, were we saluted with the howl of wolves, apparently at our cabin door. Not only did they make night vocal with their cries, but woe to the sheep or young pigs not well guarded. An occasional bear passed through, but I think none made their home in our township. There were some otter about the marsh near Bloomville. A wild cat was shot within one hundred rods of our cabin. Indians often visited us, generally of the Wyandot tribe, who then had their headquarters at Upper Sandusky. A few Senecas, from their reserve below Tiffin, straggled hither occasionally. Our red brother was uniformly friendly, and, as a rule, honest, but a tricky one appeared sometimes. Unlike his white brother of modern times, however, he had not the cheek to attempt a repetition of his trick in the same vicinity. Shamed by that conscience which, as Shakespeare puts it, "makes cowards of us all," his victim seldom saw him again.

Mr. N. Hadley was admitted to be the boss hunter and trapper on Honey creek. Mr. Hadley, at a single hunt, brought down seven deer, six of them by torchlight, and the seventh by sunlight in the morning. So fond was

Hadley of hunting, that, game getting scarce, he had J. C. Hampton to haul his family and goods (mostly steel traps) to the head of canoe navigation on the Scioto, in Hardin county. Here he dug out two large walnut canoes, lashed them side by side, and started for Cairo, on the Mississippi. With one boat wrecked on the raging Scioto, he nevertheless reached Portsmouth with the other, his family walking most of the way. At this point a captain of a steamer bound for Iowa, whither Hadley was going, struck with admiration for a man who would venture his all in a canoe on the Ohio, offered to carry him without charge to his destination. Thus the boss pioneer hunter of Bloom township left Ohio for game in the far west.

An encounter of a Wyandot Indian with a pack of hungry wolves in South Bloom is worth recording. He had tracked a wounded deer some distance in the snow, when suddenly he came upon it surrounded by a pack of wolves, making of it a hasty meal. Intent upon having some of the meat himself, he tried to drive the wolves by shooting one of them. This enraged the rest, and they rushed upon him. Backing against a tree, he kept them at bay with his tomahawk, till hunger overcoming rage, they returned to finish their meal upon the deer. The Indian, convinced that "discretion was the better part of valor," was glad to escape. The pioneer who succeeded best in making a comfortable living, did not make a business of hunting, but chopping and logging and burning was the chief work. Much timber, which to-day would be valuable in market, was burned on the ground. No where could finer poplar, walnut, blue ash and butternut trees be found than in Bloom township.

The first saw mill was built by Roswell Munsel and the Donalds, on Honey creek, near the present Kaler mill. Soon after John Davis built another mill, a mile further down, where my first lumber was made. A few years later Abraham Kagy put up a saw mill, and the Steeles a saw and grist mill on Silver creek. It may be well to remind the reader that in those days our water courses furnished power much more steadily and for a greater part of the year. Through the clearing away of fallen timber and general drainage, our creeks gave short lived spirts of water, and then Steele's grist mill could be heard day and night for more than half the year. My first grinding was done at Hedges' mill, just below Tiffin. When we began to have wheat to sell our nearest public market was at Venice or Portland (Sandusky City.) This was so until the pioneer railroad in Ohio made us a market at Republic.

In those days neighbors were neighbors, indeed. Was a cabin to be "raised," logs to be "rolled," or assistance of any kind needed, a simple notice was enough. A "neighbor" could be found at a much greater distance than now. The whisky of those days was not charged with "killing at forty rods" as now, but the "brown jug" or the "barrel" was found in nearly every home, and it was esteemed an indispensable "mechanical power" at "raisings" and "loggings," etc., etc.

Our public schools were held at first in cabins like our dwellings, with a huge fire place on one side, with a "stick and mud" chimney on the outside. Religious meetings were held in these "school houses," or in the cabins of the settlers. The Presbyterians, Baptists and Methodists were the first to organize societies or churches in Bloom. James Robinson, a Presbyterian clergyman, organized the first church of that name, about the year 1830.

On the 27th of May, 1827, the Baptist church, named "Honey Creek," was organized. The "council" was composed of Elders Thomas Snelson, of Highland county, and Benjamin Caves, of Pickaway, and Deacon John Hite, of Fairfield. In 1830 the undersigned was chosen pastor of this church and has sustained this relation ever since. As will be noticed, ministers in those early days traveled a great way in the pursuit of their calling. But not as now, cosily and swiftly in a railway coach, but invariably on horseback, equipped with "saddle-bags," with Bible, hymn book, a few "dickeys" (a sort of shirt-front with collar attached), and some provisions, perhaps. The messenger of "peace and good will," through the cross of Christ, traveled in all kinds of weather, over all sorts of roads (or no roads through the wilderness). Perhaps such experiences, if presented to many of our clerical brethren to-day, as a part of their labors, would lead to some more congenial calling. But it must be remembered that the privations and trials of pioneer life were shared by all classes, and hence borne the more cheerfully. While we may freely admit that this generation is enjoying much that is good and desirable as the fruit of the labors and purposes of their pioneer fathers and mothers, it is a matter of profound regret that the rugged virtues and beautiful friendships could not have been transmitted with the improved culture, conveniences, comforts and luxuries enjoyed by our children. They are enjoying the material blessings for which their fathers and mothers toiled and dared and suffered. Modern improvements have obviated the necessity for much of the personal effort and deprivation of pioneer life, but when we cease to practice their manly and womanly virtues, all our boasted progress cannot save us from the penalties of violated moral law.

Of all my first neighbors, Abraham Kagy, J. C. Hampton, Mrs. Thomas West and John C. Martin alone remain. The rest have passed to that "bourne from whence no traveler returns." We, too, shall soon pass away, but may He who guides the destinies of men and of nations, bless our children and our country with civil and religious liberty, and every good resulting from the reign of truth and righteousness is the prayer of

Yours truly   LEWIS SEITZ.

WILLIAM DAVIS

Says: I am the oldest son of John Davis, who came to Bloom in November, 1824, and settled on section eight, near Honey creek, one and one-half miles west of Bloomville. We came from Perry county, Ohio, and were thirteen days on the road with two wagons, and drove our cows and hogs before us. We had all the meat, flour and whisky we needed for one year.

On the following fall father went back and also to Zanesville to get mill irons for a saw mill, with which he returned, and in company with Mr. Munsel, put up a saw mill on said section, which was the first saw mill in the township. He also built the first frame house in the township, now occupied by Rev. John Shauts. Our first grinding was done at Hunter's mill, carrying the grain and grist on horseback. Father was an old Methodist from Maryland and helped to build the first church of the township, took an active part in its welfare, and was the steward of it when he died. He died July 14, 1849, in his sixty-third year. Mother died November 4, 1840. There were six children of us, of whom five are still living. Father was a devoted christian and kind to all his neighbors, and especially to the poor. He supplied all those that were needy, and he had plenty to do with.

The Boyds, Robinsons, Valentines, Martins, father, Blackmans, Treats, Donalds, Roops, Coolys, and others were the leading Whigs. The McClellands, Perkeys, Seits, Strohs, Ruchs, Kagys and Joseph Miller were the leading Democrats of the township.

JACOB HOSSLER, ESQ.

Is one of the distinguished citizens in Bloom. He was born January 30, 1806, in Steuben township, Adams county, Pennsylvania, on a farm. When fourteen years old, in 1820, his father moved to Stark county, Ohio. Here, on the 23d of September, Mr. Hossler was married, and in 1834 he moved to Bloom township, where he still resides. For twenty years he ran a saw mill on Stoner creek. He moved right into the woods when he came, and opened up a fine farm. To show how Mr. Hossler stands in the estimation of his neighbors, it is only necessary to say that for thirty years he held the office of justice of the peace and was mayor of Bloomville four years. He is still in the enjoyment of excellent health.

JOHN T. REID

Is also one of the pioneers of Bloom, who have imprinted their individualities upon the township. He was born in Frederick county, Maryland, on the first day of January, 1807. His father died when John was but six years old, and he was taken care of by his uncle, Paul Talbot, who moved to Fairfield county, Ohio, where he was married. There they settled in the woods and young John worked among the farmers and was finally set in to work on a carding machine on Indian creek, in Fairfield county, owned by one David Swasey. From there he came to Bloom in 1828, in the fall, and worked for his uncle, John Valentine, until the following Christmas. The Mohawks, Senecas and Wyandots were then "swarming through the woods." He became well acquainted with all the old settlers here, already named. He returned to Fairfield, and all his earnings in the following spring put together amounted only to the sum of $80, lacking $20, to buy eighty acres at government prices. A friend loaned him the $20 and he started on foot for Delaware, in the fall of 1829, and entered the eighty acres that John Heilman now owns, near Honey creek. He returned to Fairfield and worked eighteen months longer on a farm until he had earned some more money. His uncle, John Valentine, then wrote to him that Mr. Bever had eighty acres, which he would sell, adjoining the other lot. Mr. Reid started on Christmas day and came to Bloom on foot, where he arrived and bought the Bever land on New Year's day, 1831.

Before he left Fairfield county he had taken a school to teach, and there were three weeks to teach before the term closed. He returned, finished his school, came back to Bloom in February, with an axe and a bundle of clothing, which he carried on the axe-handle. He built a cabin in his forest and commenced clearing it. His uncle, William Norris, came from Fairfield county, and lived in the cabin with him awhile, and until his uncle, Norris, bought the land on which Fostoria now stands. On the 25th of April, 1833, Mr. Reid was married to Eliza Boyd Watson. They had four children, of whom three are still living.

Mr. Reid is a tall, slender man, over six feet high, strong and muscular and has always enjoyed good health. He and Mrs. Reid are both members of the Presbyterian church and highly esteemed. Poor as Mr. Reid was when he commenced, his career is a conclusive proof of what industry, honesty and economy will accomplish. He now counts his wealth by many thousands, and lives at his ease.

Mention has already been made of the picnics the younger generation prepare annually about the first of September, in Schoch's woods, to show their gratitude and esteem for their pioneer parents. I desire to refer to the subject again, here, only to say that at one of these, after Father Thompson, the pioneer minister of the gospel, closed his remarks on collecting the sheep that were lost in the woods, Mr. J. C. Hampton was called upon for a speech, in which, among other many interesting things, he described Judge Cornell, and spoke of him as a very excellent character and citizen. He related an affair that took place before some justice of the peace when a fellow got very angry at the justice and threatened to whip him and would do so if he was not a magistrate. The justice told the fellow to go out into the road and he should be relieved of his consciencious scruples. The fellow backed out.

Mr. Hampton also said:

When I came from Ross county in 1822, my uncle, Thomas Boyd, lived in a small cabin. Ten boys of us went there to work for him. We made out to live. Our bed was a very primitive affair. A half dozen of us slept together. During the three months I staid there we had not a bit of bread. The little flour we had they stirred into boiling milk. That constituted the principal meal. We had a fish basket in Honey creek, close by, that furnished us all the fresh fish we wanted.

Sorry that no more of the speech could be preserved.

Dr. Gibson also spoke, relating his boyhood days and scenes of early life on Honey creek. His mother held the chair while her husband was sitting upon it, shaking with the ague His father got nearly crazy every time the fever came on. One time his father was at Sandusky for provisions. It always took a week to get back. The roads were bad and the horses poor. Judge Leath happened to be at Sandusky the same time with a load of water melons to sell. He and the Doctor's father started for home together. On the way the latter became crazy with the fever, and had it not been for the Judge he would never have found his way back. The Doctor also referred to Black Jonathan, who lived with the Mohawks on the Vanmeter place. Jonathan Pointer was half negro and half Indian. He was the interpretor for the preachers and gave the Indians the sermons by piece-meal as best he could, but whenever a subject or a point was a little difficult to transfer or comprehend, he would add: "I don't know, myself, whether that is so, or not."

Dr. Gibson when yet a boy was very attentive upon the sick in the neighborhood, and thus naturally became a doctor. He applied himself to the books, and with hard study and his experience, became a distinguished physician. He was, indeed, a gentleman and a valued friend. He was one of that class of thinkers who take nothing for granted because they cannot help it. We ought to have much charity for such people.

The venerable Noah Seitz must not be forgotten. He came here from Fairfield county and settled on the northwest quarter of section five on the 5th of April, 1822, and it is generally admitted that he was the first settler in Bloom. He sold out soon after to Edward Southerland and moved to Eden. Mrs. Southerland is still living in the third ward of Tiffin, and is known as the widow of Francis Bernard.

Mrs. West, J. C. Martin and Abraham Kagy are among the few pioneers here that are still making "foot-prints in the sands of time."

Who will not remember the tall slender form of Abraham Kagy, Esq., and his beautiful, pleasant home on Silver creek, where, for more than a half century, you were met with a hand of welcome and an open, honest, friendly countenance? These honored land marks of time should ever be cherished by those who will occupy the places so rapidly becoming vacant.

JAMES R. WILSON, ESQ.,

Is the only lawyer in the place. Happy town! He was born in Green county, Pennsylvania, May 19th, 1825. In the fall of 1826, his father moved with the family to Ohio. He was a native of Ireland, and at the time he came to Ohio was a traveling preacher of the M. E. church. He died on his circuit while holding a protracted meeting. The family moved to Bloom township in April, 1834, and settled in the southeast part of the township, when there were but two families in that part, south, and but one house east for three miles. Mr. Wilson had one brother older than he, and also an older sister The sister taught school in the neighborhood when only twelve years old. Mr. Wilson helped to clear up his father's farm, and after his death he opened up a farm for himself. In 1856 he moved to Bloomville. In 1857 he was elected justice of the peace and re-elected. In 1866 he was admitted to practice law, and has ever since been a member of the Tiffin bar.

CHAPTER XXXII.

CLINTON TOWNSHIP.

T. 2, N. R. 15 E.

THE early scenes described in these narratives, and the incidents attending the dawn of Seneca as a county, having clustered around places that are now covered by Tiffin, and involved the names of so many of the early settlers, whose biographies are already recorded, there is scarcely anything further left to say about Clinton township. This chapter will, therefore, necessarily be short It is proper, however, to preserve names of the early pioneers and describe some of those not already talked about.

The location of the land offices in Tiffin tended greatly to give Tiffin a start. It brought many people here from abroad and introduced to them not only our citizens but also the many advantages this county promised for the future. No other county in Ohio, west of the Sandusky river, settled up as fast as Seneca county.

When congress, on the 4th day of May, 1828, granted to Ohio 500,000 acres of land to build the Miami canal, it next became the duty of the legislature to provide for the sale of the land. By an act of February 12, 1829, two land offices were established for the sale of these half million of acres, one of which was located at Tiffin. The land office for the sale of the land in the Delaware land district was located here in April, 1828. Small as Tiffin then was, and far removed from the canal lands to be sold, it should nevertheless be remembered that there was, at that time, no other town between Tiffin and Fort Wayne, in Indiana. The reader will see, therefore, that Tiffin was the principal frontier town in northwestern Ohio at that time and for some time thereafter, notwithstanding the organization of Sandusky county prior to Seneca.

These land offices here, I say, helped very much to bring Tiffin into notice and gave it an air of stability and business enterprise. For several years the hotels were frequented by strangers, who bought land or prospected for locations. The old army road was a sort of thoroughfare for emigrants, many of whom stopped here—in fact, there was no other road in Ohio, west of the Sandusky river. By remembering these things we are enabled to see how this vast northwest must have looked at that time.

Clinton township being so closely identified with Tiffin, and everything that is said of Tiffin and her people meaning Clinton township at the same time, may be the reason why neither Mr. Butterfield, in his history, nor Mr. Stewart, in his "Atlas," had anything to say about Clinton township and her pioneers. But there were some old settlers here, and men, too, of no ordinary grade, who should and shall be mentioned, for many of their names are too dear and valuable to be lost so soon. These pages will preserve them for awhile.

JOHN KELLER,

The father of Levi, Lewis and Joel Keller (the sons are all still living), was an early settler and a man of wonderful industry and perseverance. He took a very active part in all public affairs and became intimately acquainted with the business of the public offices. He filled the office of county commissioner several years, and after he got his mill on the river in running order, there was scarcely a farmer in Seneca county but was acquainted with Uncle Johnny Keller. He was very talkative when he had time, and always ready to give information when required. With his knowledge of farming he combined much mechanical skill, and he was in his place on the farm or in the mill. His practical good sense, his friendly nature and honesty of purpose made Uncle Keller a very popular citizen.

He was born September 17, 1785, in York county, Pennsylvania, near Little York. He was married to Elizabeth Mitsell, in 1804, and soon after moved to Fairfield county, Ohio. At the land sales in Delaware he bought the land the old Keller mill was on, in 1821, and moved on to it in 1828. In 1824 he let out a job of clearing four acres. In the fall of that year he came up with a team and a lot of apple trees, with which he planted an orchard on the four acres. When he came back the following spring, his apple trees were all gone. Somebody had stolen them. This was probably the first orchard planted in the county.

Mrs. Keller died in September, 1857. John Keller died October 9, 1859.

HENRY C. BRISH

Was a man of medium size and weighed about 165 pounds. He was of fair complexion, had regular, manly features, was well proportioned and good looking, more so in citizen's clothes than in uniform. He had deeply set, large hazel eyes. He shaved smooth, except small side whiskers. He had a well balanced nature, a high forehead, and turned bald at middle age. General Brish was a polished gentleman and his home was the gathering place for many of the elite in the then rustic society. He had a kind word for everybody, and soon became popular with all classes of people. The Senecas were his pets and they made Rosewood a stopping place whenever they came up the river. Dr. Cary was a brother to Mrs. Brish. He and Dr. Dresbach made the General's house their home. Whenever they could not be found about town, you would almost be sure to find them at Brish's. Some people thought the General was very high-strung and quick tempered, but they were only those who did not know him intimately, and judged him only from the several knock-downs he was blamed with. The facts are, the General would bear almost any opposition in business or politics as long as his opponent would abstain from reflecting on his honor and calling him names. He struck very quick when that rule was violated, and the size of the opponent or his standing in society made no difference. His relation with the business of the county has been mentioned so often that it is only necessary to say that he was one of the associate judges of the court of common pleas here, and was elected a member of the house of representatives, besides filling many other local offices.

When, on the 28th day of February, 1831, at the treaty of Washington, the Senecas sold their reservation to the United States, as already stated in chapter VIII. (and see also chapter XXIX.), General Brish, who had taken care of the chief to Washington and back to Seneca, was kindly remembered by them. At their own request a section was put into the treaty giving to General Brish a quarter section of land in the reservation. The section reads as follows:

Sec. 11. The chiefs of the Senecas being impressed with gratitude towards Henry C. Brish, then sub-agent, for his private advances of money and provisions and numerous other acts of kindness towards them, as well as extra services in coming with them to Washington, and having expressed a wish that a quarter section of a hundred and sixty acres of land ceded by them should be granted to him in consideration thereof, the same is hereby granted to him and his heirs, to be located under the direction of the president of the United States. (See vol. 7 Laws U. S., p. 350.)

The General selected his section and sold it. He then bought the southwest half of section eighteen in Clinton. General Brish cleared up a part and moved onto it. He called it Rosewood, because Mrs.

Brish raised rose bushes all around the house. Here the General spent the rest of his days.

Henry Colgate Brish was born in Frederick county, Maryland, November 22, 1799. At the age of ten years he became clerk in the register's office of that county, under Captain Steiner, where he remained until he was married, and where he received all the education he had. He was married to Miss Eleanor S. Carey on the 7th December, 1824, by Bishop Jones, of the Episcopal Protestant church.

Mrs. Brish was born July 27, 1805. They left Frederick for Seneca county, and landed here on the 6th of July, 1828, Sunday afternoon. They made the whole distance in a little covered carriage, perhaps one of the first that came to Seneca. The General died at Rosewood in February, 1866.

Mrs. Brish, who is still living says:

I brought my old piano with me, and have it yet. When we came here, we moved into a cabin that Agreen Ingraham had built. It had a puncheon floor, which I covered with carpet that I brought along, and I had some nice china, also, all of which, I think, were the first of the kind in Tiffin, perhaps in the county. Our cabins were all clustered around McNeal's store, and there was the "hub of fashion." David and Elisha Smith, Levi Cresey, Mr. Custar, Mrs. Mounts, Mrs. Kessler, Abel Rawson and Samuel Hoagland all lived between McNeal's and the campbell-back bridge over the railroads. One time we made a ball for the young people from Maryland and they called it the "Maryland ball." The river was high and the girls from the Tiffin side could not get over on the first day, but they came on the second day. We had young folks from Lower Sandusky and from up the river, some sixty in all. We danced two days and three nights. It was the first big ball in the county. David Smith was the fiddler. Mr. Cronise had a cornfield where the public square is in Fort Ball. One night Drs. Carey and Dresbach stole a lot of roasting ears there and brought them to our house to have them cooked. We made a big feast of them.

John Stoner lived immediately north of Rosewood. He was also from Maryland, and raised a number of sons, who became wealthy. I remember George, Christian and Dennis. Dennis is the youngest of them and is still living here. My efforts to procure a better description of this pioneer family and that of the Neikirks, who are now scattered through Scipio, Adams and Clinton, have failed also.

JOHN BEARD

Settled on the northwest quarter of section thirty-four. Leveret Beadley lived near by him on the west. North of the road lived Wm. McEwen, with his wife and twenty-one children. He was the first blacksmith in this neighborhood. Thomas Vanatta came in 1825, and settled on the southwest quarter of section thirty-four, where some of the family still reside. Vanatta bought out a man by the name of Stripe, who moved to Lower Sandusky, where he dealt in fish. He died of cholera in 1834. Joseph Richards came in 1827 or 1829. David E Owen came in 1829, and lived on the Huber farm. The Frees and Herin folks came in 1828. Reuben Williams entered the Coe farm and built the saw mill, which is still in running order, in 1824. Daniel Dildine came in the same year. He built a cabin and planted the apple trees that are still to be seen just north of the new cemetery. Daniel Lamberson entered the southeast quarter of section thirty-four. James Myers came in 1833 or '34. James Wolf used to work for Reuben Williams, and when he had earned $100, Williams bought for him the eighty acres in the southwest corner of section twenty-six, where he afterwards lived and died.

Mr. Beard was born in Northampton county, Pennsylvania, on the 14th of April, 1794. He was married to Hannah Doan in 1817. They had eight children, of whom six are still living. He was about five feet, ten inches high; walked very erect; had black hair and whiskers and blue eyes; he was very talkative and full of jokes and was a good neighbor and strictly honest. He died in 1832, and was buried in the old cemetery in Tiffin.

(I am indebted to his son, Joseph, for the above narrative.)

DANIEL LAMBERSON

Was born December 13, 1783, near Belvedere, New Jersey, and died December 5, 1852. He came and located here in the fall of 1824.

JOHN CRUM.

Mr. Hamilton F. Crum furnished the writer with the following statement concerning this veteran pioneer:

On the 20th of February, 1792, my father, John Crum, was born in Frederick county, in the state of Virginia, and in 1813 he married Barbara Crum (no blood relation). In 1821 he moved to Ohio and settled in Columbus. In 1822 he bought 160 acres of land in Seneca county, three miles north of Tiffin on the Fremont road, and in 1824 he moved upon his land. We lived in a cabin for a while, not far from our land, until we could build a house. Our house had the first shingle roof between Tiffin and Lower Sandusky. We experienced many of the hardships common to new settlements. Father was sick nearly all the first winter. We lived in the woods; our neighbors were scattered, none nearer than a mile, but they were very friendly and social. Our first neighbors were Moses Abbott, Eliphalet Rogers and Captain Sherwood, but others soon came in.

My father was a hard-working man and did all his clearing. I was the oldest boy, but only eight years old when we came, and of course could not help much, but was always with him. Mother died when I was fifteen years old. Sometime afterwards father was married to Margaret Evans, with whom he lived about twenty years, when she died. Afterwards father married Nancy Booth. Father died in Tiffin on the 28th day of February, 1873. His widow died July 8, 1874. HAMILTON F. CRUM.

Mr. Crum was an excellent citizen and took a very active part in public affairs He was county commissioner sometime (see last chapter) and while he was not a fast talker, he was a strong thinker. His judgment was clear and well matured. The writer knew him well.

REV. JOHN SOUDER.

As you go north on the Fremont road and pass through the Stoner farm, the next place to the left was formerly the home of Captain Sherwood mentioned several times already; and here lived the subject of this sketch when the writer first knew him. The old veteran has lived here so long, and his quiet, pure, christian life has exercised so much of moral influence upon this community for more than half a century, that it is really a pleasure to speak of him.

He was born in Lancaster county, Pennsylvania, on the 26th of November, 1799. His father moved to Frederick county, Maryland, in 1810, where he died in August, 1820.

Mr. Souder was married to Elizabeth A., daughter of John Walker, on the 15th of May, 1823. He became a member of the M. E. church in October, 1815, and entered the cause of reform in the Fort Seneca organization, at the Rev. Montgomery's, in 1829 He was ordained to preach in 1845, having been licensed in 1842. Mrs. Souder died on the 11th of November, 1861. On the 5th of November, 1862, he was married to Mrs. Frees. He sold his farm in 1860, and retired to private life in Tiffin, where now, over four score years, he is still in the enjoyment of good health. He furnished the writer with the following statement, which speaks for itself:

INCIDENTS AND EXPERIENCES WITHIN THE KNOWLEDGE AND OBSERVATION OF JOHN SOUDER.

In the fall of 1824 my father-in-law, John Walker, and I, left Frederick county, Maryland, on horseback, for the purpose of exploring the west in our own way. We took the national pike to Wheeling, which at that time was the national highway as far as it was made. We crossed the Ohio river at Wheeling and reached Cincinnati by way of Zanesville and Circleville, a distance of over 500 miles from our home. The settlements through Ohio were sparse and quite new, deadened timber standing everywhere.

There was no market for anything, scarcely. Wheat was worth only thirty-one cents, and corn twelve and one-half cents, other provisions in proportion, but there was no money in circulation. Everything was trade and exchange. We arrived at home in safety, and in spite of the gloomy outlook in Ohio, I resolved to emigrate there, and in May, 1826, I sold out and started for Ohio with a large wagon and four horses. My family then consisted of a wife and one child, about one year old, two single sisters and my brother-in-law, John Walker, who was then yet unmarried. Richard Sneath and his family came with us. That family consisted of Mr. and Mrs. Sneath, two or three small children, Jacob Huss and Henry Zimmerman, who were single men. They also had a large wagon and three horses. Taking us altogether, we were a jolly set for such an excursion.

Nothing occurred worth remembering until we reached a place in the Alleghany mountains called "the Shades of Death." It was a pinery through which our road passed, seven miles across, without a single human habitation. There was a tavern and a blacksmith shop just east of the dense forest. One of my horses lost a shoe just before sundown. He could not travel on the hard pike without being shod. It was about time to put up for the night, but the bad reputation of the tavern made us conclude to press on. While my horse was being shod, Sneath, with his family and the young men, passed on, leaving me with the women and the child behind. This compelled me to travel these seven miles through the dark alone. It was very inconsiderate in Sneath and the others to leave us thus. One or two armed men could have had us at their mercy, for all I had in the world I had with me. Under a kind Providence we passed through in safety. No accident occurred until we crossed the river at Wheeling. Here we were in Ohio. A road leads up a high hill nearly two miles from the river before it reaches the uplands. The national pike here was just in process of construction, and we were often compelled to take side roads that were dangerous at places. My wife became so disgusted with the country that she exclaimed at one time, "Any man that will bring his wife and child to such a country as this, ought to be shot."

The greatest impediment to the prosperity of Ohio was a general want of market. The canal connecting the Ohio river with the lake was laid out, but not constructed. Our first idea was to locate somewhere near its line. At Granville, in Licking county, we found a vacant house, which we rented for the time being, in order that we might explore the country round about. We were not pleased here, and resolved to strike for Tiffin, and see how that country would please us. Mr. Sneath and I came out here on horseback, leaving our families at Granville. We inquired for Fort Ball and found it. We saw a gentleman standing in the road there, and Mr. Sneath, who was given to be mischievious at times, inquired of the man how far it was to Fort Ball. The man said: "You are right in the midst of it." The stranger was Mr. McNeal, the merchant.

George and John Stoner used to be old neighbors of ours in Maryland. We inquired for them and found them. Here we put up for the night. The Sandusky country pleased us better than anything we had seen in Ohio, being a rich, level, limestone country, such as we had been accustomed to. We really did not know how new it was until we moved into it. Tiffin and Fort Ball were then very small beginnings. Mr. Sneath found a large frame building in an unfinished condition (Bradley's Central Hotel afterwards,

Remele's butcher shop now). This was offered for sale, and Mr. Sneath bought it for $400, I think. Somebody showed me the land of Mr. Sherwood. I had almost made up my mind to buy it, but did not at that time, but I liked the country very much.

We returned to Granville to bring our families here, re-loaded our wagons and set sail for Seneca county. We were used to traveling by this time, and we pursued our journey with cheer, especially so since we knew the point of destination. In the night before we reached Upper Sandusky it rained. In the morning the travel was heavy, and I had a bigger load than Mr. Sneath. He and the young men put on ahead and left me behind, just as they did once before. They got clear out of sight. A little beyond Marion the horses, endeavoring to avoid going through a mud hole, crowded a wheel onto a stump, which nearly upset my wagon; both wheels were at least a foot from the ground, but all the horses rushed forward with speed through the mud hole, and the wagon righted up again. My wife and child were alone in the wagon at the time, and an upset there and then might have been a very serious affair.

It was long after night before we reached Upper Sandusky, and there found our friends nicely tucked away in bed at Walker's Hotel. We had not seen them all day.

We had another fearful time before we reached Upper Sandusky. My wife and my sisters had never seen an Indian before, and all they ever heard of them was savage cruelty. As night came on the Indians rode after us on their ponies, yelping and hooping. This frightened the women very much. I was on my saddle horse, and they kept calling to me in an undertone, "drive on, drive on." I had seen them before, and remained quiet. We kept together after leaving Upper Sandusky.

When we reached Love's hill, near Tiffin, the joke turned the other way. Sneath's horses got very smooth, and Love's hill was steep and slippery. Sneath was on his saddle horse and attempted to ascend the hill, but failed, and his saddle horse fell down, the wagon ran back close to the bank of the river, and came very near upsetting into it, but all went on safely, and we kept together to the town.

The best part of the joke came in when Mr. Sneath jumped up after his horse fell and exclaimed that he might have got his leg broken, regardless of the danger of losing the lives of his entire family.

Mr. Sneath moved into his house, and I found an empty cabin in Fort Ball, belonging to Mr. McGaffey. Mr. Spencer was the proprietor of Fort Ball, Mr. McNeal had a small store, Elisha Smith kept tavern, Levi Reasey was a blacksmith. David Smith was a cabinet maker, a justice of the peace and a fiddler. He lived near the river. Dr. Dresbach, lawyers Rawson and Dickinson were here; all single men and the three occupied the same small office together. It was about twelve by fourteen feet, and is still standing on Sandusky street.

Dr. Dresbach's motto was, "Root, hog, or die." Mr. McGaffey was clerk of the court at that time. One time in conversation he predicted that within fifteen years we would have a railroad through the country. When I left Maryland the Baltimore and Ohio company had only thirteen miles of road out of Baltimore.

HISTORY OF SENECA COUNTY.

I bought the Sherwood place containing nearly 440 acres, mostly in section seven, for $1,900, and got possession on the 1st of July, 1826. We arrived in Fort Ball on the 10th of June that year. Mr. Sherwood was not a very successful man in business. He kept a barrel of whisky in his house. Whisky and business never run well together.

Mr. Bowe had a few acres cleared alongside of the Stoner farm.

Wm. Montgomery kept a tavern in a small way on a six-acre lot taken off of a corner of the land I bought. These were all the improvements in that neighborhood.

My neighbors were Mr. Bowe and George and John Stoner, who came in the fall of 1822.

John Stoner lost his life by a simple accident. In the fall of 1826 he shot a squirrel and tried to finish it with the butt of his gun. He slipped and fell on the mzzle of his gun, which injured him internally to such an extent that he died after great suffering, in January, 1827. He was the first person buried in the Stoner graveyard.

John, Jacob and Abraham Crum, three brothers; E. Rogers, John Crum and old Mr. Abbott were also neighbors.

The Rosenbergers, Shaulls, Klines and others were Virginians and had a little settlement west of Wolf creek.

George Puffenberger lived in a cabin some distance west, and John Flack in (now) Liberty, lived the farthest westward of any man I could hear of. I was in company with others in view of a new road and we stopped at Flack's. It seemed very lonesome to live so entirely alone in the forest as Flack did.

Mr. Cornelius Flummerfelt and the Parker brothers came about the time I did.

The Indians were troublesome at times, but never dangerous, except when intoxicated. The Wyandots made their annual trips to Malden to receive presents from the British government for services rendered in the war against the United States. On their way out they bought whisky at Fort Ball and elsewhere, and generally camped in front of our house, where they all got drunk and rested a whole day to sober up. They generally had their whole families with them. They used to come into the house and wanted everthing we had, especially bread. Sometimes they took all the bread we had and my wife had to bake again. They always paid for what they bought, often paying twenty-five cents for a loaf of bread. One time a drunken Indian got angry at my wife and drew his knife on her. He would have used it had it not been for a sober Indian close by. The sober Indians often stayed all night at our house, sleeping by the fire in the same room we slept. We often bought venison and cranberries from them. A camp of drunken Indians and squaws is a most disgusting sight; the papooses strapped on a board sitting against the trees, and the men and women reeling around, the squaws squealing like wild cats. But with all their general degradation, we had some interesting interview with those who had been christianized at camp and other meetings.

Mr. Moler, a very early settler, took up the land where Mr. Maule lived. John Doran, another pioneer, was at the raising of Mr. Hedges' mill on the river, and became crippled for life by the falling of a tree in a storm while raising the mill.

My mother lived with me, after my father's death, until she died in 1840, at the age of 76 years.

DAVID RICKENBAUGH

Was born in Washington county, Maryland, December 9th, 1799. In October, 1827, he moved to Stark county, Ohio, and in September, 1833, to Seneca county, Ohio, locating three and one-half miles east of Tiffin, on the North Greenfield road, where he bought two hundred and forty acres, all woods, except about ten acres that had been cleared by Uriah Egbert, from whom he purchased the land. By industry and good management he became successful in farming, finding market in Sandusky. It was customary in the early days here with farmers, who lived near Tiffin, Melmore or Republic, that when they took a load of produce to Sandusky to bring back a load of goods for the merchants. There were most always some of their goods piled up there awaiting transportation. Mr. Rickenbaugh's personal integrity won the confidence of everybody that knew him, and the merchants gave him orders to bring goods with pleasure.

He was married on the 27th of February, 1822, to Margaret Sprecher, of Washington county, Maryland, who is a sister of the distinguished divine, the Rev. Samuel Sprecher, D. D. and L. L. D , the president of Wittenberg college, at Springfield, Ohio.

This marriage was blessed with two daughters and four sons. Two sons only survive; Samuel living on the old homestead, and Jacob living near Tiffin, Ohio. Mr. Rickenbaugh died April 17th, 1859, at the age of sixty years, highly esteemed for his many traits of manly virtues, and mourned by those who had learned to love and admire him as a good and true man in life.

Mrs. Rickenbaugh still survives, at the advanced age of eighty, spending the evening of her life with her son Samuel, on the old homestead.

DANIEL DILDINE, SR.

The subject of this sketch was an early pioneer of this township. He was born in Northampton county, Pennsylvania, September 24th, 1780. His father died when Daniel was but ten years old. Some years thereafter he commenced the struggle for life single handed and alone by driving a team over the mountains of Pennsylvania, which business he followed for several years. In 1803 he was married, and in 1805 he moved to and located in Fairfield county, Ohio, being among the first settlers of that portion of Ohio, then the frontier. In 1806 he moved to Pickaway, and located upon a tract of land purchased from the government at three dollars per acre. In 1824 he sold this land, moved to this county, and purchased land of the government on Rocky creek, from which the new cemetery is taken, and as already described. It took him seven days to move from Pickaway here. He stopped for a few days with Reuben Williams, on the Coe farm, in the log house still standing there, and until he could build a cabin for himself. He arrived here in April, and his cattle were compelled to subsist on brouse until pasture came on. The poor animals were so used to brouse that when they heard a tree fall they would all run and devour the tender branches with avidity. John Searles, Joseph Foncannon and George Stoner, who lived from three to five miles apart, were about all the persons who had corn to sell, and Mr. Dildine had to buy his corn where he could get it, and for the provisions for his family he had to go to Franklin county and to Mansfield, where he obtained them in exchange for salt and fish, which he took with him. The fish were caught here in great abundance in the creeks, the river and the lake. The salt was shipped from Syracuse; both salt and fish selling in the central counties with a handsome profit.

Mr. Dildine cleared a good portion of his farm, and in 1830 sold it to Thomas Coe. He then bought two hundred and forty acres on the South Greenfield road, about three and a half miles east of Tiffin, where he lived the rest of his days. He retained to his last his mental and very much of his physical powers. He was a man of wonderful endurance; quiet in his nature, kind and generous. He lived to a fine old age, and exchanged the scenes of this life for the realities of a higher order of existence at the ripe age of ninety-one years and three days, on the 27th day of September, 1872.

NICHOLAS GOETSCHIUS

Was a soldier in the war of 1812, under General Harrison. He was born in Montgomery county, New York; moved from there to Franklin county, Ohio, and came to Seneca in 1825, in April. He first located on the North Greenfield road, near Egbert's, and located on the Portland road in 1835, upon the eighty acres he had entered. He was about seventy-eight years old when he died, at one of his son's-in-law in Sandusky county. He had two sons and three daughters.

JAMES GOETSCHIUS,

His oldest son, who came here with his father, lives on the old homestead. He was born September 24th, 1807, in Franklin county, Ohio. His wife, Permelia Smith, came here with Joseph Biggs from Maryland.

When they settled in Clinton there was no house for seven miles east on the North Greenfield road. Samuel Scothorns, in Reed, lived there. There was no road open to town. They had to underbrush a road to Tiffin, and then followed the blazed trees. Hunter's mill was built in 1825.

FREDERICK CRAMER

Was born in Frederick county, Maryland, of German parentage, on the 23d day of September, 1779, and was married about March 25th, 1806, to Catharine Barrack, who died January 17th, 1864, aged eighty-two years, two months and nineteen days.

Mr. Cramer arrived here on the 30th day of September, 1830 (being twenty-one days on the road), and bought the northeast quarter of section sixteen, here in Clinton, on the 1st day of October in that year, and where he resided all the balance of his days. He died on the 8th day of August, 1842, aged sixty-two years, ten months and fifteen days Six of his children died in infancy, and four are still living. Dennis F. Cramer is the oldest son, now living in Tiffin, and the father of a large family. Three of his sons are lawyers, of whom Upton F. held the office of probate judge many years. Father Cramer was not very tall, but corpulent and large. In his dress and general appearance he was the very embodiment of a Quaker, but he was an esteemed member of the German Reformed Church.

JAMES MYERS

Was born in Martinsburg, Berkley county, Virginia, February 23d, 1800. When about two years old, his father emigrated to the state of Ohio, then just admitted into the Union, and settled in the hills of Fairfield county, near where Lancaster now stands. The country around there was almost an unbroken wilderness at that time, there being but a few pioneer settlers, who had to battle with the forest, wild beasts and wild Indians. They were obliged to raise their own living, and raise and make their own homespun garments. James was the oldest of John Myers' family of nine children, and was of necessity compelled to work as soon as he was able to assist in maintaining the family. Their advantages for education were limited, there being no school houses and few scholars, and in fact their necessities did not allow them much time for education, but whatever they did get was mastered by themselves before a great log fire, of nights and stormy days.

In this condition his youth and boyhood was spent, working with his father at the carpenter trade, building their rude houses and barns, until he was twenty-four years of age, when, on January 1st, 1824, he was married to Sarah Gaw, a young woman of Newark, Licking county, Ohio. After marriage he commenced business for himself, and tried his fortune at raising tobacco among the hills of Fairfield county, which business he followed for several years, until his own family began to increase. When it consisted of himself, wife and four children, he began to think he must own some land in order to be able to raise his family properly, but by that time all the tillable land of Fairfield county was already occupied, and his scanty means would not allow him to purchase second handed, so he began looking over the territories of the far west, as it was then called.

Himself and a friend, Isaac Lepurd, (who settled near Attica, in Venice), started out in search of government land, and as the tide of emigration had begun to lead to Seneca county, he and his friend directed their steps thither; I say steps, for they traveled on foot, it being before the days of steamboats and railroads.

In September, 1831, they arrived at a land office, now called Tiffin, which, at that time, was composed of old Fort Ball, and two or three log cabins on the east side of the river. After looking over the country a couple of weeks, they both suited themselves, and entered as much land as their means would allow, and returned home to Fairfield, to collect money enough again to move him and family to his newly acquired possessions.

It was not until in June, 1833, that he left Fairfield county with his family, in a two horse wagon, with all his worldly effects. His family then consisted of his wife and four children, Maria Louise, Martha, George and David, then a babe three months old. They were on the road fifteen days, and traveled a distance of less than a hundred miles, the road most of the way being in the woods, only an Indian trail or a blazed route to guide footmen. They arrived on the 23d of June, and began immediately to make for themselves a home by clearing off a piece of land and building a house, with which they took extra pains to have it large and fine for those days, and which is still standing, the same that is occupied by Conrad and George Gillig as a residence on the old homestead, but for several weeks they slept in their wagon and cooked their meals by a stump-fire.

Four more children were born to them in Seneca county, Ann, James C., Jennie and John. Maria, the eldest, died in the 15th year of her age, and John, the youngest, died the same year, and are buried in the old Rockrun cemetery, they being the only deaths that have occurred in the family. All the rest are well, and give prospect of long lives. They lived upon the old farm forty-four years.

CLINTON TOWNSHIP.   517

In 1875, being old and almost blind, and Aunt Sally, his wife, being unable to attend to her household duties, and having no children at home, he concluded to sell their homestead and spend the balance of their days in ease and comfort. So they sold off all real and personal estate, retaining nothing but a horse and carriage, and moved to the home of the oldest daughter, Martha, living in Henry county, Ohio, where they still reside in peace and happiness, being both well, with prospects of living a good many years yet. They have lived together fifty-six years January 1st, 1880.

"Uncle Jim," as he was familiarly called, was a whole-souled, kind hearted man, always giving to those in need. The beggar was never turned from his door empty. He had a kind look and a pleasant smile for everybody he met. He was a friend to everyone, and all seemed glad to see him and take a friendly shake whenever they met. For the last few years he has so nearly lost his eyesight that he cannot read nor scarcely recognize his friends. This is a great loss to him, as he was a great reader, and few men were better posted than he in matters and things in general; but now he depends entirely upon his friends to read for him, and they are very kind to him, doing all that can be done to make him comfortable.

Samuel Waggoner, Martin Frees, Ezra Baker, William Baker, Jacob Adams, Jacob Souder, old Mr. Olmsted, David Olmsted, Elisha Olmsted, Thomas Vanatta, Asa Crocket, John Wolf, Peter Schuch, Joseph Herin, Samuel Herin, Jacob Frees, William Williams, James Meyers, Peter Frees and others were also old settlers in Clinton, in addition to those already named.

The first patent issued by the United States for any land sold in this county, by an act of congress passed April 24th, 1820, providing for the sale of the public lands (called the new purchase), was for the west half of the southwest quarter of section twenty-three, T. 2, N. R. 15 E., eighty acres, to John Anway. For want of a county here this patent was recorded in the recorder's office at Lower Sandusky.

I found more to say about Clinton township than I first anticipated, but there is history in all of it.

THE SWANDER FAMILY,

Who filled a very conspicuous place in public estimation, one of whom is still living here, and the numerous grandchildren being scattered far and near, deserve particular mention in the history of this township.

Frederick Schwander came from the Canton of Bern, in Switzerland, to the colony of Pennsylvania in 1750, and settled in South Whitehall township, Lehigh county, on a farm that has ever since and up to this time been known as the "Schwander place." He was married here and raised a family. After his death the oldest son, Jacob, became the owner of the farm on which he was born.

A. Mr. Shriver lived some eight miles away, and had living in his house with him as a sort of quasi slave, a beautiful Swiss girl by the name of Barbara Gerster. He bought her at Philadelphia for her fare across the ocean. The reader should remember here, that it was considered not only right and fair to sell the passengers to America who could not pay for their passage, but the act was legalized by statute. They were sold at auction for the least number of months or years a person would buy them for and pay the fare. Families were thus often separated, many of them abused and ill-treated, and by people, too, that soon after this system of slavery was abolished, raised a terrible hue and cry against black slavery. After the shipowners of Boston had become rich in the African slave trade, they all became Abolitionists. But to return to the wedding.

Near Mr. Shriver's was a place called Egypt, for it produced great quantities of grain. Jacob Schwander and the Swiss beauty were lovers. One day they went to Egypt, and the young couple were married by a preacher. After the wedding ceremony was over, the young bride took a seat on Schwander's horse, behind the groom, and they rode back to the farm. After dinner bride and groom took their sickels and went into the harvest field reaping wheat the balance of the day. This was their bridal tour. There were no railroads leading to the fashionable watering places, and there were no "shoddies" in the country at that time.

Life meant work, and the sentence of Adam was the order of the day. This wedding took place in 1775.

When Frederick Schwander came to this country his father and grandfather were still living. Jacob had eight children, five boys and three girls. John Schwander was his oldest son, and was born on the farm where his father was born, and while his father was serving in the revolutionary army, under Washington, on the 21st day of June, 1776, and thirteen days before the Declaration of Independence. John was raised on the same farm, and in the year 1800 was married to Miss Elizabeth Glick, of Lehigh county. The writer heard the old gentleman say that he voted for Jefferson in the same year he was married. John Schwander had thirteen children in this union, seven boys and six girls. The sons are all dead but Edward, who is the youngest son, but the daughters are all living at this writing. The sons were John, James,

Thomas, Joseph, Edward and Stephen (who died when he was fourteen years old on the old farm in Pennsylvania), and another died there also in infancy. The daughters are Hannah, wife of Henry Kunkle, of Lucas county, Ohio; Etelia, widow of Francis Trexler; Sarah, widow of William Burkhalter; Eliza, wife of Edward Knouse; Mary Ann, wife of William Snyder, and Caroline, wife of William Sohn, all living in Seneca county. John died in New Jersey, where he lived, at Newhope. James, Joseph and Thomas died on their farm homes in Clinton township, where they had lived near together on the Mansfield state road.

John Schwander, the father of these children, after his marriage in 1800, rented farms in the neighborhood of the old homestead until 1807, when he moved to Ohio and located in Fairfield county, but becoming dissatisfied with the country, returned to Lehigh county and bought the old homestead. Here his son, Edward, was born, and all of the younger girls; the homestead of their great grandfather, Frederick, a circumstance very rare in America, where people are moving from place to place with a wonderful facility and where the love of home is not a cardinal virtue among the people.

These children of John Schwander dropped the "ch" in the name as they grew up, and attended English schools. Edward was married in Lehigh and moved into Clinton in 1840, where he settled on the northwest quarter of section twenty-seven, and where he still lives, the only male survivor of that once large family. After living here about one year, he lost his wife, and in 1844 he was again married to Hannah, the youngest sister of the writer. In this union eight children were born, of whom six are still living. Hannah died December 4, 1865.

About one year after Edward moved to Clinton, the father sold the old Schwander place in Lehigh and came to Seneca also.

When you go eastward on the South Greenfield road, about two miles from Tiffin, you strike the Morrison state road. Looking north you see a neat little brick house, painted red, standing close to Willow creek and a spring. This house John Schwander built. Here he lived until he died on the 17th of June, 1859. His wife also died here on the 7th of February, 1861, less than two years after his death.

The old gentleman was remarkable in his physical and mental make-up. He was about five feet, six inches high, stout and compactly built; had a fair complexion, large, blue eyes, and a fine head, which became bald as he grew old. He was very pleasant in conversation, and instructive. He spoke very interestingly, relating transactions and affairs in Pennsylvania, his exploits when he drove a big team on the pikes, his knowledge of men and events, and his age put no obstacle in his way of relating laughable anecdotes. He was a gentleman by nature and education; always pleasant, always kind to everybody, and being possessed of a cheerful nature, enabling him to look upon the sunny side of life, no doubt prolonged his days. He and the old lady died highly esteemed in the community, where they spent the evening of their days. This family of Schwanders is the only one by that name known in the United States.

One historic incident in the life of the aboved named Jacob Schwander should not be omitted:

During the administration of the elder Adams, Pennsylvania passed an act taxing the doors and windows of the houses. The law proved exceedingly obnoxious to the people, and on several occasions the collectors were abused. The people in the Lehigh valley had stood by the United Colonies during the revolutionary war, and contributed men and means in support of it. When this new form of stamp-tax was inaugurated, some of them met a collector who came amongst them on horseback, made him get off his horse and told him that they would show him how the stamp-tax operated. One of the men raised the horse's tail and the others pushed the collector's nose to where the crupper makes a crook. For this rough treatment the men were arrested and placed in the jail in Bethlehem, which was then the county seat of Northampton county, and before the county of Lehigh was organized. The imprisonment of the men aroused the indignation of the people of Lehigh valley to such an extent that one time, in open daylight, several hundred men assembled near Bethlehem and marched to the jail. Here they formed two lines in open order when a squad of them demanded the release of the men, and this being refused by the sheriff, the doors of the jail were forced open and the men released. The sheriff called out the militia and a regiment of soldiers camped near Bethlehem, assisting the sheriff in making arrests. The whole country was aroused, and many of the rescuing parties fled into the mountains. Those who were arrested were prosecuted and fined, or acquitted. A warrant was issued also against Jacob Schwander, who was, perhaps, as guilty as any of them, but he escaped the vigilance of the sheriff, his posse and the military by secreting himself in a large stone quarry, not far from his farm—the Schwander place. For three months his wife carried his victuals to him in the night, returning before morning, unobserved. If she had attracted the attention of anyone, even, there was nobody to tell tales out of school. The law had no friends in the Lehigh valley. Schwander escaped unpunished.

JOHN SECRIST

Was born October 27, 1803, in Frederick county, Maryland, and raised as a farmer. He married Margaret Waltman, August 4, 1825, who was born April 23, 1803. They settled in the woods on the farm where Judge Pittenger now lives, on the Melmore road, in October, 1828, and took their share of the frontier joys and hardships with the rest of the settlers.

Mr. Secrist died April 6, 1848. Mrs. Secrist lives with her daughter in Tiffin, Ohio.

MR. CHARLES KELLEY

Was born on the 6th of March, 1798, in Huntington county, Pennsylvania. When he was yet a child, his father moved with his family into Wayne county, Ohio, and settled four miles east of Wooster. In the summer of 1821 he, with seven others, his comrades, started on foot to see the western country. They came to Mansfield and from there they took a road that was called the "McCormack trail," which led through the woods to Tiffin, by way of Caroline. They stayed here one week, and while here they helped to put up a cabin for a man by the name of Armstrong Drennin. Mr. Hedges had made him a present of a lot with the condition that Drennin would build a cabin upon it and move his family into it.

The party wanted to board at Mr. Bowe's, but when Bowe found out that they were going to build a cabin on this side of the river, he got angry and refused to board them. They put up the cabin, however, and boarded themselves. Mr. Kelley was the cook. A man came along with some flour, which they bought, together with some pork. Two Indians took hold and helped them some in getting up the logs, but when dinner was ready they refused to eat with the whites. They stayed apart by themselves, but they would eat all that was brought to them.

The cabin was put up on the lot south of the woolen mill and on the spot where the frame building now stands, on the west side of Washington street, and is occupied by the Yingat family. It was the first cabin erected on the plat of Tiffin. The logs were cut in the woods around one day, and on the next morning the deer were seen browsing on the tops of the trees that were cut down on the lots where the court house now stands.

Mr. Drennin moved into his cabin that fall, and he, his wife and three children died here within a short time of each other. The men who helped to build the cabin were Christ. Witz, Henry Miller, David

Fowler, Mr. Drennin, three others and the two Indians. This cabin was put up before the county seat was located here.

Captain Sherwood lived north of town a piece, and John Welsh about four miles south.

Mr. Welsh acted as our pilot through the woods when we started back. There was no house between New Haven and Fort Ball.

Mr. Kelley is the father of Mrs. Dr. Samuel W. Bricker, in Tiffin, now on a visit to his daughter, and the foregoing statement gives his words as nearly as possible.

WILLIAM M'EWEN.

Mr. James McEwen says:

My father, William McEwen, was born in Berwick, Pennsylvania. He went to Northampton county, Pennsylvania, to learn the trade of a blacksmith, and was married there to Sarah Johnson. We came here in the fall of 1823 and brought with us one half ton of hay, which we made at New Haven. With this hay we kept four horses and two cows all winter. There was plenty of picking in the woods all winter in 1823. Father entered the southwest quarter of section twenty-seven, in Clinton, and put up a cabin there and a blacksmith shop.

Leverett Bradley settled on the southeast quarter of section twenty-eight, right west of us. Asa Crocket built the first barn on that farm.

Cal. Williams lived north of us, on the place where old father Schwander lived and died, on the Morrison road, in section twenty-two. He was an old bachelor, had a dog and cat, and all three took their meals together.

Joseph Herrin's father and mother, with their families, came in 1826; the children were all single then, except Mrs. Hines; the rest were married here.

When the Herrin's folks came they stopped at our house, and we were so crowded some had to sleep in wagons.

My parents had twenty-one children altogether, of whom sixteen were then living. I am the youngest of the family.

Mrs. Rachael Frees was also married. She was a sister of the Herrin boys also.

Thomas Vanatta came two years after and settled where some of his daughters are still living. Peter Schuk lived there once.

The first school house was built on the Bradley place, and Jonas Doan taught it. Another log school house was put up north of the road and opposite the church on Rocky creek.

Hugh Welsh settled on the Richardson farm and lived there when we came. Birnsides were also here before us and lived on section twenty-eight.

We had to go clear to Columbus for flour, and cut our way through the woods. We lived on milk and potatoes for a good while until we could do better. I used to plough with a wooden mold-board and wore buckskin pantaloons.

JACOB HOLTS

Was born in Frederick county, Maryland, June 17, 1786, and was married to Susannah M. Fiege, who was a sister of the father of John Fiege, of Tiffin, Ohio. They moved to this county and arrived in Tiffin on the 28th of April, 1834 and settled on the northwest quarter of section fifteen, in Clinton, where the son, Dennis, still lives.

Mr. Holts was about five feet, eleven inches high, straight and muscular, but not fleshy; he had dark brown hair, a large, dark eye, black, bushy eyebrows and a very expressive countenance. He spoke slow and positive, and while his conversation was pleasant and agreeable, he nevertheless carried an air of personal dignity about him that corresponded well with the general respect he enjoyed in the community. He died December 28, 1859.

PETER MARSH

Was also a Clinton township pioneer. He settled in the northwest quarter of section twenty-seven, about the time the McEwen family came here. He was then a young man but recently married. He, his wife and his wife's sister, who came with them, were all three excellent singers. They all belonged to the Presbyterian church, and were very nice, kind and quiet people. Mr. Marsh used to teach singing school and soon became very popular in the neighborhood. He started a Sabbath school and a prayer meeting in the vicinity and took a great interest in church affairs generally. When the first railroad from Sandusky, by way of Republic, was being built, he took a job of grading a mile, including the fill over Willow creek. The company failed in making payment as it was agreed, and Mr. Marsh broke up, losing nearly all he had. He left and located in Kenton, Ohio, where he recuperated to some extent, and where he and his wife both died.

COLONEL BALL,

After whom the fort and Spencer's town were named, was present at the great Whig celebration, at Fort Meigs, in 1840, where a friend of mine saw him for the last time. He was six feet high, well proportioned: his hair was gray and bushy; he had a florid complexion and wore side whiskers; he had gray eyes, thin lips, heavy jaw, a loud, clear voice, talked scholarly and lived with his family in Richland county at that time. He was a powerful man and walked very erect. Before his hair turned gray it was of auburn color. His entire make-up exhibited great force of character and energy.

Clinton township has an excellent market, is well watered, enjoys the privileges of the city of Tiffin with her schools and otherwise, while the land is in a high state of cultivation and very valuable. Splendid farm houses in all directions indicate the general prosperity of the people.

As already mentioned, the township was organized in June, 1820, and the first election was held on the 15th of June, 1822. The population of Clinton, including Tiffin, in 1840, was 2,195; in 1850 it was 4,330; in 1860 it was 6,041; it increased to 7,174 in 1870, and in 1880 it is 1,701. Tiffin, in 1880, has 7,882 inhabitants, which, added to the township, makes 9,583.

Tiffin proper, in 1840, had 788 souls; in 1850, 2,718; in 1860, 3,992 and in 1870, 5,648.

JOHN DITTO

Was one of the early settlers of Clinton. He came in 1822, and settled in section thirty-one, where he owned eighty acres, and he also owned another eighty in Eden. These lands he entered at the Delaware land office, and immediately thereafter built his cabin in the woods. He was a small man, less than medium size, and compactly built. He was very industrious and honest, a good hunter and interesting talker. He verified his hunting stories by his singular habitual expression of "bei der liebens." There was no meaning to it, but it was intended to fix the story beyond all question of doubt. He spoke German mostly.

Mr. Ditto was born in Northumberland county, Pennsylvania, October 14, 1785. He told the writer that he voted at the first election in Seneca county; he lived and died a Democrat. His wife's name is Elizabeth, who is the daughter of Louis Eckhart. She was born June 13, 1795, and is still living, enjoying good health, on the old homestead, near the Mohawk road. They had eleven children, of whom two are still living, viz: Mrs. DuBois and Mrs. Henry Sheets.

CHAPTER XXXIII.
EDEN TOWNSHIP.

T. 1, N. R. 15 E.

THIS township was organized in 1821, as already stated, and the election of its first officers was also mentioned. When Mr. Butterfield says that it was so named for its remarkable fertility of soil, it is strange that the early records spell the word "Eaton." The township settled up rapidly after the first settlers had located, and there are many good reasons for it. The pioneer settlers were intelligent and good men. Such always make good neighbors. The soil was rich, the timber excellent, and the fine water privileges of old Honey creek inviting. The proximity to the county seat and many other things, induced selections of homes along this stream.

In 1824 it was the most populous township in the county. In 1830 it had 819 inhabitants; in 1840, 1,471; in 1870, 1671, and in 1880, 1,598.

William Fleet is perhaps the largest land owner in the township. Samuel Baker, John L. Downy, John Seitz, Samuel Herrin, A. N. Armstrong, Ed. Wing, C. Y. Brundage, Abr. Brown, H. H. Schoch's heirs, Fred. Borck, Charles Meeker, the Klais', S. M. Ogden, Hez. Searles, Eden Lease and others are among the most successful farmers.

Where the Kilbourn road crosses Honey creek, Colonel Kilbourn in 1824 surveyed and platted a town he called Melmore, already described and sung. Case Brown was the principal proprietor. John C. Jones erected the first dwelling house on the plat. He died here in 1828. Buckley Hutchins, who figured very largely as a man of business, was the first postmaster. In 1830 its population was 130; in 1880 it is perhaps less than 200.

The names of many remarkable personages are identified with this township. The Butterfield family used to live here. One of the sons is the celebrated historian, Consul W. Butterfield. One of the daughters is the present Mrs. Hyacinthe, of Paris, whose husband is a Catholic priest of great distinction, and who, while he was priest at Notre Dame, preached and wrote against celibacy of the priesthood, and to prove the sincerity of his teachings, married a sister of Consul W. Butterfield. She was then in Paris, a correspondent of the *New York Herald* and Madam Demorest's papers, and noted for her great intelligence, gracefulness and beauty. Mr. Anson Burlingame, who has become so distinguished in his mission in China, used to teach school in Eden township. General Gibson was raised on the banks of old Honey creek, in Eden, and while he speaks in glowing colors of her pioneer settlers, there is always a moisture observable in the southwest corner of his eye.

There never was another such man as Philip J. Price, and if room would permit, a description of him would fit here. Eden had a number of local characters of mark. Dr. Selden Graves was a most remarkable man in every way. He was stern in his bearing, honorable in his dealings, a good physician, an excellent neighbor; a man of clear judgment and of wonderful endurance. In every walk of life he was respected and esteemed.

On the 16th day of July, 1836, (Saturday,) the M. E. church was raised in Melmore, and Amroy Butterfield, assisting as one of the hands, was killed by the falling of a piece of timber. He was then father of eight children, Consul W. and Mrs. Hyacinthe among the number.

John Gibson's was the first barn that was raised in the county, and Thomas Baker introduced the first Merino sheep into Seneca, from Steuben county, New York.

Melmore was quite a trading post at one time, and its citizens were possessed of a spirit of enterprise that would have been a credit to any town. When the question of the Mad River and Lake Erie railroad was being agitated, great efforts were made to have the line from Republic through Melmore, by way of Upper Sandusky, to Springfield, and when that failed, Melmore determined to have a railroad for its own use, and to run a line from Melmore to Republic, and to intersect the Mad River road there. Meetings were held in Melmore, Republic and Tiffin; a temporary line was surveyed between the two places; committees were appointed, and books opened for the subscription of stock.

The names attached to the following notice will revive early recollections and help to preserve memories of those days. This notice was published in the *Tiffin Gazette* of May 30th, 1836, and long before a railroad reached Republic:

MELMORE AND REPUBLIC RAILROAD.

Notice is hereby given that the books of the Melmore and Republic railroad company will be opened for the subscription of the stock of said company, at the house of Jacob Buskirk, in Melmore, and at the house of Mr.

Miller, in Republic, and at the house of Calvin Bradley, in Tiffin, on the 4th day of July next, and will be kept open for five days in succession, from 10 o'clock A. M. until 2 o'clock P. M.

Buckley Hutchins,   Thomas J. Baker,   Timothy P. Roberts,
P. J. Price,   William Patterson,   Samuel Waggoner,
Case Brown,   Isaac J. Halsey,   Calvin Bradley,
Micagah Heaton,   William Cornell,   Hamilton McCollister,
Selden Graves.
May 30th, 1836.

The road was never built, because the stock was not taken very fast, but some of these gentlemen entered into the enterprise with great energy.

The old pioneers had their weaknesses also, and were not angels at all. Old Adam was still alive in some of them (as now), and re-generation had not become universal.

Hamilton McCollister was a justice of the peace in Eden, and his neighbor, Mathew Clark, not having the fear of God before his eyes, one Sunday morning looked for his hogs, that got away from him the day before Uncle Mathew's dogs followed him, and 'Squire McCollister saw Clark driving the hogs home. This act was a clear case of Sabbath breaking in the mind of the court, and on the next morning the 'Squire sent the constable and had uncle Mathew arrested. It was a clear case; the court saw it himself, and Mr. Clark was fined. The officers of the law taxed no costs. The insulted law was vindicated, and that was enough. This was on the 13th day of November, 1827. But uncle Mathew felt aggrieved for being arrested, and old Adam got up to law-heat in him, so he goes to Tiffin for redress, and Dickinson & Rawson filed a declaration against McCollister for $3,000 damages for false imprisonment.

The 'Squire employed David Higgins to defend him, and when the case was finally tried to a jury, they gave the plaintiff a verdict of $21.50. At the next trial the jury could not agree. The case at last was taken up to the supreme court, where it was discontinued.

The Rev. Joseph Bever kindly presented to the writer a statement of his early recollections of Eden, as follows:

I am a son of Peter Bever, one of a family of thirteen children; was born in Virginia in 1815. My father moved from Virginia to this county in the fall of 1823, and settled on the banks of Honey creek. The prospects of opening a farm and making a living here in this forest, for so large a family, were not very flattering, for Seneca county at that time was nearly an unbroken wilderness. It had neither roads, bridges, markets, or any other advantage. Persons who never saw this country as it looked fifty-seven years ago, cannot imagine how dense the forest was, and the underbrush that met the eye on every side. If you can imagine a little spot of about an acre, cleared off, and a log cabin standing in the middle, and all around you an unbroken forest, with underbrush and vegetation so dense that you could not see ten feet ahead, especially in the bottoms—then you can form some idea of the wilds of Seneca county in 1823.

We settled about five and a half miles south of Tiffin, and about three miles northwest of Melmore. Both towns were very small villages, then built of log cabins. We had no neighbors nearer than Melmore and Tiffin, except Jacob Price, who lived about one mile south of us, and Ruel Loomis, who lived about the same distance northeast of us, on school section sixteen.

About half way between us and Tiffin was the village of Mohawk Indians, who were quite friendly, and visited us very frequently. Indeed, they became quite troublesome after we had lived here a few years, for they made their friendship a source of annoyance by their constant and persistent begging. They wanted white bread every time they came, and that was very often. Sometimes whole squads came, together with their guns, bows and arrows, then women and children, and wanted white bread for all of them. At begging the Indian seems to have no conscience for either frequency or quantity.

The second year after we came here we cleared a field of bottom land about half a mile down the creek from our house. Between this field and our house was very thick woods, and as I was going to the bottom field one day alone, I espied an Indian coming around a little curve in the path, and supposing he had not discovered me, (and I being a little timid lad of about eleven years,) my first thought was to get out of his way. so I stepped to one side and laid down behind a large oak log, expecting the Indian to pass by without noticing me. But the first thing I knew he looked over the log and exclaimed "Cooh!" and laughed heartily. I was deeply mortified, but my fear was all gone.

A few days after this one of these Indians, Isaac Brandt by name, came to our house with two little axes he had made by a blacksmith in Melmore for his two boys—he said—and asked me to turn the grindstone for him to grind the little axes. I had turned grindstone before to sharpen axes forged out by blacksmiths, and as they were all very thick at the edge, I did not crave the job. I made all sorts of excuses, and told him that my father would whip me for leaving my work and turn the grindstone for him a half day, and all that. Brandt replied: "Tell fodder Indian here; grind axe; had to shove." So I turned for him until he was done. In the meantime he tried to teach me Indian, but I concluded that it cost more than it come to. But to present me with some compensation when the grinding was done he took my hand and shook it very heartily, thanking me for the service.

At that time it was an easy matter to raise grain and vegetables where the land was clear, but the great trouble was to save them. Squirrels, chipmonks and other vermin were so abundant that they would devour a field of corn almost entirely, being surrounded by thick woods and weeds. We used to have dead-falls for every fence corner, and some one of the family had to go around the field with a gun nearly all the time at certain seasons. I remember well that during the warm weather, such was the stench from the carcasses of dead vermin, that it became nearly unbearable.

EDEN TOWNSHIP. 529

Game was plenty in those days, and when meat was wanted it was easily procured by killing some deer, turkey, or other game. Honey creek and the Sandusky river were teeming with fish, some of them of enormous size. When we wanted fish, we took our poles and lines to some eddy in the creek or river and caught fish behind some boulder or log, where they seemed quite tame. Creeping up to them quietly, we often caught them with the hand. In the winter when the ice was thick enough to bear a person, we cut holes in the ice and caught them with snares made of horse hair, tied to a stick. The loop was passed over the head and caught them behind the gills.

We were not annoyed with ravenous animals, except wolves. These, however, were quite numerous for a few years. Sometimes they would run our stock into the barnyard after night, and annoy them until the dogs made their appearance, when they would scamper.

My brother Solomon is still living on an eighty acre lot of father's old farm, and has lived nowhere else since we first settled in this county. Perhaps you cannot find another man in Seneca county who has lived on one farm fifty-seven years. We suffered a great many privations and inconveniences that our people now cannot appreciate. We had no roads, no markets, no churches, no schools, and not much society. We received a *bush*, not a *book* college education. J. BEVER.

VAN MATRE.

The best historic exposition concerning the family of the Van Metre (Van Matre) and the Mohawk reserve in Eden township, the writer has been able to find, is contained in a letter that Judge Pillars, of Tiffin, many years ago, wrote to a relative of this Seneca Van Metre, then living in Cincinnati. The Judge was so kind as to place it at my disposal, and with his permission I copy the whole letter:

TIFFIN, SENECA COUNTY, OHIO,
SUNDAY, December 12th, 1858.

Daniel Van Matre, Esq., Cincinnati, Ohio:

DEAR SIR: We were talking on the 29th ultimo, in Cincinnati, about one John Van Matre (always spelled Van Meter), a brother of yours, or a brother of your father, I don't remember which—being taken by the Indians —a reservation of land being made to him in this county, etc., etc.

The facts connected with his life, etc., are of great historic interest to me, and of course are of the same and still greater interest to you. I will give you my understanding of them, and propose that you shall correct my errors and supply any deficiency.

John Van Matre, or Van Meter, was stolen by the Indians in March, 1778, at the age of about five years, at Greenbriar, near a place now called West Liberty, in the state of Virginia.

The people of the neighborhood, having been frequently alarmed by Indian aggressions, had assembled on that day for the purpose of building a fort to protect themselves. It was a beautiful day in the spring, and two of the elder boys of the Van Matre family were out to a "clearing" to fix up

34

some brands. John, or Johnny, as he was called by the family, accompanied them, while the father went to the fort, and the mother and sister remained at home.

The boys had but just got at their work, when a party of Indians came upon them. The two older ones made their escape, but Johnny was taken. The Indians then went to the house of Van Matre, and set it on fire, having first killed his wife and daughter. Then they fled to the wilderness, carrying with them their captive boy.

He grew up and always lived among the Indians, and partook of their manners, habits, dress, etc., etc. He forgot entirely his native tongue, though he learned it again before he died. He always remembered, however, that his name was Johnny Van Meter.

In after life he was induced to visit some of his relatives, but utterly refused to remain with them, preferring, as he said, the innocent, unrestrained indulgences of the Indian's life, to the arbitrary restraints of civilized society.

He married an Indian woman, by whom he had one child only—a son, whom he called John. His wife's name was Susan Brandt, a name well-known in the state of New York, and in the history of that state, and a relative of the celebrated Joseph Brandt, who, in 1787, completed the translation of St. Mark and other portions of the scriptures and the book of common prayer, into the Mohawk language.

The Mohawks were originally a powerful tribe of Indians, inhabiting the country from the northwestern part of Pennsylvania, north through New York into Canada. Their true name was the Bears. Mohawk being but a corruption of their name for Bear.

The Brandt family was the royal one of the Mohawk nation; the chiefs always coming from that family, either by descent or election, probably the latter.

There is a likeness of one of these Brandts, an Indian chieftain, and it is the noblest head I ever saw

The Mohawk nation gradually wasted away, and finally emigrated west, or at least the central portion of it, and at last settled down in this county, and within two and one-half miles of where Tiffin now stands.

On the 29th of April, 1817, a treaty was held at the foot of the rapids of the Miami of Lake Erie, near Perrysburg, Wood county, Ohio, between Lewis Cass and Duncan McArthur, commissioners of the United States, of the one part, and the sachems, chiefs and warriors of what was then called the Wyandot, Seneca, Delaware, Shawnees, Potawatomie, Ottawa and Chippawa tribes of Indians, when all their lands within the limits of Ohio were ceded to the United States forever.

Now at the above treaty there was not in fact a Seneca Indian present. Instead of the Seneca it was the Mohawk tribe of Indians that participated with the other tribes in that treaty, or at least the remnant and head portion of the tribe.

At this treaty there was reserved by the United States:

"To John Van Meter, who was taken prisoner by the Wyandots, and who has ever since lived amongst them, and has married a Seneca woman, and to his wife and three brothers, Senecas, who now reside on Honey Creek, one

EDEN TOWNSHIP. 531

thousand acres of land, to begin north 45 degrees west, 140 poles, thence and from the beginning, east for quantity."

This John Van Meter was Johnny, the captive boy, and this Seneca woman whom he had married was the last female, and these her three brother, Senecas, were the last males of that great, noble, christian and royal family of Brandt, the ruler of the Mohawk nation of Indians.

They were consequently Mohawks, not Senecas. The names of these three brothers was Thomas, Isaac and Paulus Brandt. Thomas was the chief of the tribe.

The tribe continued to reside upon the above reservation until in 1829, when they joined other Indians and left the country. The place or locality goes to this day by the name of Mohawk, or Mohawktown. It is noted on the map as " Van Meter Reserve."

At the time the Mohawk tribe left here, as above mentioned, it didn't exceed probably twenty-five families.

John Van Meter lived, died and was buried on the reserve, and I am assured that one of our physicians has his skeleton. His death was some years before his tribe moved west.

He was a man of more than ordinary decision of character, of a benevolent disposition, and friendly to the whites. This county commenced to be settled along in 1817, 1818 and 1819. Van Meter was comparatively wealthy, owning large stocks of horses, cattle, etc. These early settlers had to rely much upon his generosity, and it was never in vain that they sought relief at his hands.

He died, leaving his son John, above spoken of, his only heir. A suit was afterwards commenced by some of the " Van Matres " against this son John, Jr., to recover his father's share, one-quarter of the above reserve. This suit was predicated upon the ground that the son John, Jr., was not the heir at law of John Van Meter, for the reason that the latter and his wife, Susan, were never married according to law, and that consequently the plaintiffs were the true heirs.

The son John, Jr., proved, however, that his father and mother were married ; that his father went out and killed some venison, and brought it in, and his mother brought in some corn ; that she then dressed and cooked the venison and corn, and the two parties then ate it together, in the presence of witnesses, and that that was the marriage ceremony among the Mohawk Indians.

The court held the marriage good and valid, and John, Jr., the lawful heir.

John, Jr., and his three uncles, the Brandts, sold out the Van Meter reservation, in 1828, to Mr. Lloyd Norris, who afterwards lived (and died) upon it, for the sum of $2,500.

In 1829 the Mohawk tribe, as I have said, moved west of the Mississippi river. John, Jr., went with them.

The above reservation is upon Honey creek, within two and a half or three miles of this place, and is as good land as there is in the state. There are some very fine springs upon it. Van Meter creek empties into Honey creek in this reserve. Mr. Norris has a fine grist mill upon the former creek, a short distance from its confluence with the latter. (The mill is burnt down.)

I forgot to state how the Indians caught Johnny at Greenbrier, Virginia, which was as follows: His two elder brothers easily cleared the fence, and ran, but Johnny undertook to crawl through a crack of the fence, but got fast. In this situation the Indians caught him.

What tribe of Indians was this? Please correct any and all errors in the foregoing as far as you are able. Truly,

JAMES PILLARS.

The old settlers knew all these old Mohawks, and spoke of their kindness and benevolence with feelings of pleasure.

Esquire Heaton furnished the writer with a statement concerning his father's family, from which the following is extracted:

MICAGAH HEATON

Emigrated from Pennsylvania to Coshocton county in 1817, and entered land in Bedford township. He camped in the woods until he had built a cabin. He had then a wife and two children. Here he laid out the town of New Bedford, which is now about the size of Melmore. He there kept the first hotel and postoffice. In 1829 he moved to Seneca county, and bought a quarter section from Mr. Searles, in Eden township, about three-quarters of a mile south of Melmore, on the Kilbourn road. He traveled from Coshocton to Seneca, about one hundred miles, in a big old-fashioned Pennsylvania four horse wagon, riding the saddle horse. He built two cabins, and commenced clearing land and finding subsistence for his large family of eleven persons. He was a bricklayer by trade, and often compelled to work at jobs to earn money. The sugar-trough was used as a cradle in our house, and mother used to do her baking in a "Dutch-oven." Flax was raised for summer clothing, and manufactured by the family. The spinning was done by hand. Mother carded the wool while my sisters spun it into yarn for cloth. We boys were allowed one pair of shoes per year, which would be worn out during winter. and in the summer we had to combat with the thistles and nettles, which grew very thick. They used to have "log rollings" in the neighborhood. The men would work hard all day and then

"Dance all night,
'Till broad daylight,
And go home with the girls in the morning."

My father was a justice of the peace. General Sea and Mr. Cowdry, the Mormon lawyer, attended court at our house one time.

In the first few years after we settled here, the Indians often stopped at our house with cranberries to sell, and to beg. One day a younger brother and I were playing "horse" in our cabin, when a big Indian came in, armed to his teeth. He set his gun behind the door and walked up to the fire. The "horses," who were down on all fours, took fright at the Indian and ran away to the other cabin. The Indian wanted to stay all night, and father took care of him.

Father lived to see nearly all the old settlers pass to their long homes. He died in the year 1866, at the advanced age of eighty years.

The wilderness, inhabited by prowling savages, had been changed into fruitful fields. The Indians had departed for the far west, and good markets were established at home, for want of which, in former times, the settlers had to go to other towns far away.

There were so many distinguished men among the pioneers of Eden that but a few of them can be noticed here, and of these only those that were best known to the writer, and of whose life information was furnished.

Some of the readers of this book will scarcely realize how discouraging it is to a man when he undertakes to produce a faithful history, and meets with people in his search for information who take no interest in his mission and furnish no information.

There lived in Eden also an old German by the name of Philip Von Blon. He came here with a large family in 1834, and located near Samuel Martin's, on the Negrotown road. He was from Waldmohr, in the Palatinate, and rather a marked character. He was a great reader and a vigorous thinker; a man of good moral character and highly esteemed. He lived to about eighty years of age and died in Tiffin. Mrs. John Fiege, already mentioned, was his oldest daughter. His children have taken no interest in this enterprise, and it is to be regretted that no better sketch can be produced.

SAMUEL S. MARTIN.

Of this distinguished old friend of mine I here insert an obituary notice I found in one of the Tiffin papers, and which is short but a very faithful picture of him:

DEATH OF AN OLD CITIZEN OF SENECA COUNTY.

Samuel S. Martin was born in the town of Mifflin, Mifflin county, Pennsylvania, October 24th, 1795, and died April 10th, 1864, and was therefore sixty-eight years, six months and seventeen days old. His father died when he was quite young, and he was obliged to depend upon his own energies to carry him through the vicissitudes of life. He removed to Ohio in 1812, and in 1821 bought land in Eden township, to which he emigrated in 1829. In common with the early settlers of the county he was subjected to the hardships and privations of a pioneer life. He was a man of good natural endowments, which soon made him prominent in the community; he was twice elected assessor of the county, under the then existing laws, and held the office of justice of the peace for many years in Eden township. He scrutinized every measure propounded to the public with great care, and when his conclusions were reached, he never departed from them. Politically, he was a Democrat, and felt great interest in the success of the great conservative measures of his party. Few men can boast the coolness and serenity of temper which Mr. Martin always exhibited. Affable in his intercourse with men, scrupulously honest in business, moral and high-minded in character, he challenged the esteem of all who knew him, and left this bitter world without an enemy.

Mr. Martin quietly entertained his own views of religion, but upon his dying bed professed a hope in the saving pardon of God, and frequently said that he was going to the realms of endless glory. He has left behind him a record of virtue worthy of our imitation. His disease was chronic asthma.

Is it not singular that in writing up a short history of a township, obituary notices of father and son, both distinguished and good men, and both especial dear friends of the writer, should follow each other so closely in succession? But we all follow each other in close succession, and one has scarcely time to tell the tale of his friend before he is himself called away to realize the scenes of another mission.

ROBERT M'CANDISH MARTIN

Was born in Perry county, Ohio, September 18, 1822, and died April 4, 1879, and was therefore aged fifty-six years, six months and sixteen days. In the spring of 1829 he came here with his father's family, Samuel S. Martin, noticed above, and has resided in Eden township to the time of his death, except only a few years, as hereafter noticed. In his youth he taught school in the winter and labored on his father's farm during the summer and fall until 1846, when he was appointed to the office of county recorder by the county commissioners, to fill the vacancy caused by the resignation of William H. Kessler, who had accepted a clerkship in some department at Washington. In 1847 Mr. Martin was elected to this office and re-elected in 1850, making his aggregate term of service about seven years. His official administration was characterized by a high degree of capacity and singular punctuality at his post of duty. On October 12, 1848, Mr. Martin was married to Barbara Kagy, daughter of Abraham Kagy, Esq., who still resides in Bloom township. Thirteen children resulted from this union, ten of whom, together with their bereaved mother, survive to lament their loss. The funeral cortege which followed the corpse to the burial was the largest ever known in the township, being nearly a mile in length. During his prostrated illness of more than two years, Mr. Martin manifested an almost heroic fortitude, and at the trying end of his earthly race he met the remorseless "King of Terrors" with such calm resignation that seemed to mock his power. The family of of the deceased realized the fact that he must leave them, only a few minutes before the end, and the wildest manifestation of grief prevailing, Mr. Martin essayed to calm their sorrow and counsel them for the future He retained his reason and spoke up to within a minute or two of his death, and thus peacefully and calmly he closed his timely career. To Robert Martin, all who ever knew him record the highest and noblest tribute to his memory. He was an honest and upright man and an exemplary citizen.

The foregoing is taken from an obituary notice, slightly changed; and if there is anything to be added to describe Robert as he looked and walked, let me say that he was about five feet, seven inches in height, well proportioned, had a high and noble forehead, dark eyes, fair complexion, regular, delicate but manly features, and always met you with a smile. His friendship was warm and firm and his notions of honor high and sound. While he was decided in everything he had put through the crucible of his own thoughts, he had great respect for the opinions of others no matter how widely they differed. A man of nobler impulses and warmer friendship than Robert Martin the writer never knew.

Among the enterprising farmers of forty years ago may be remembered also: Richard Baker, George Denison, Thomas Baker, Selden Graves, Sylvanus Arnold, John Baker, James Watson, Jesse Koler, William Watson, David Olmsted, Benjamin Brundage, Daniel W. Eastman, Philip Bretz, John Kagy, Adam Pennington, Hezekiah Searles, John Bretz, Jonah Brown, John Gibson, John Crum, Jacob Price, John Downs, Philip Springer, Jacob Andre, Samuel Kennedy, James Gray, William Ireland, Dr. Bates and John Lamberson. James Stevens, Jacob Buskirk, the Arnolds and others, were among the early settlers of Melmore, also.

JOHN SEARLES

Was born in Anne Arundel county, Maryland, February 20, 1775, on a farm where he was raised. He was drafted to the army in 1812, after he was married and had settled near the town of New Lancaster, Ohio He moved from there in the fall of 1820, with his wife and seven children, to this county and occupied for a while one of the block houses of the old Fort Ball, where he lived in one room with his whole family. Paul Butler, the man who built Spencer's saw mill, occupied another room. Mr. David Risdon boarded with him. Another room was occupied by Mr. Henry Creesy and his family. Creesy was a blacksmith by trade. The pickets were all standing then and the roofs of the block houses were covered with clap-boards. The army road ran along the river bank between the fort and the river. There was just room enough for the road.

The fort had three block houses, one on each corner and one in the middle, all facing the river. Back of the block houses was an open yard, inside the pickets, of about half an acre. There was room enough in the block houses for about two hundred men. Mr. Bowe's tavern was a double cabin and stood in the street north of the iron bridge, and the army road ran along in front of it also. David Smith occupied, for a while, the same room with Mr. Creesy. Rollins lived on the Souder farm, (so-called afterwards).

In the spring of 1821, Mr. Searles helped to open a road from Tiffin to Rocky creek, where the church now stands, and where he had bought 167 acres of land. Here he built a cabin in the woods, and in 1825 he built a frame barn which was probably the first one in the county. Reuben Williams was the boss carpenter. Mr. Searles attached himself to the M. E. church when he was a young man, and up to his death remained a faithful and honored member. After he located here on Rocky creek, his house became a stopping place for all the preachers, and headquarters at nearly all the camp and quarterly meetings. For several years the elections were held at his house. Except Tiffin, Eden township contained the most decided politicians, strong Whigs and strong Democrats, but in their township elections they picked their officers from both parties. Here they voted for men only.

Mrs. Searles' maiden name was Duncan. They were the parents of nine children, five boys and four girls, of whom four sons and two daughters are still living.

The foregoing was gathered from what Mr. Hezekiah Searles related, and he goes on to say: "Our neighbors were the Welches, who had located on the Olmsted farm. Charles Bretz, Mr. Sponable, Cal. Jacqua, the Boyds, father Shelden, Thomas Vannatta, the Sneaths and and others came on soon after.

"One time in the winter we lost a colt. We built a fence around it with a trap lid and caught five wolves. This was before Seneca county was organized, and we took the scalps to Lower Sandusky, where we got $5 a piece for them. The rivers and creeks abounded in good fish and the woods in game. We suffered the deprivations and enjoyed the pleasures peculiar to that sort of life.

"Father died May 14, 1844, and mother October 30, 1871."

There is here in Eden township a sort of counterpart to the old stone fortifications described by Mr. Swigart in Bloom, near Honey creek. This one is near the same creek in the Vannatta section. After you leave the Mohawk road, turning to the right at the corner of the old Wolf farm, crossing the bridge going west, you come across the bottom and approach a hill, where you see a high bluff a little to the left, forming a rounded corner at the northeast point. Upon this bluff there is a circular embankment embracing nearly two acres of land. The embankment is now nearly flat on the top and looks as if at one time it must have been a very substantial parapet. Mr. Randall says he saw oak trees growing upon it two feet in diameter. The Mohawks lived all around over this part of the country and knew no more about it than the present generation of white people.

In a direction of a little east of north from this rampart, and within the range of a rifle, are found very many leaden bullets of various sizes, from grape shot down to 130 to the pound. Some of these have the mark of the twist of a rifle barrel still clearly marked upon them.

Was this parapet once a part of an old fort? Has history ever traced the march of an army along this creek? Was there ever a battle fought in this valley, and if so, by whom? What people built round fortifications? Will somebody explain all this some day?

HUGH WELCH.

For a while, it was a question in the mind of the writer as to which township in the county a sketch of this distinguished pioneer should be attached, because he has now lived in Green Springs some time, but he first located here in Eden, where he drove his stake in the woods near Rocky creek. He has lived longer in Seneca county now than any other man in it. His father was in Washington's army, and so was also his father's neighbor in Huron county, Mr. Seifert. These old revolutionary veterans often talked over their scenes of strife for independence. Both were great admirers of General Washington.

In the month of February, 1819, Thomas and Hugh Welch, sons of the above-named veteran, started from Huron county to find homes in the wilds of Seneca. They camped out the first night and in the morning found themselves near Honey creek. Vegetation had already started to grow, for in the dense forest a certain degree of warmth was retained, and the ground never froze very hard in the winter. They followed down the stream, and somewhere near the late residence of Mr. William Fleet, they came upon a band of Seneca Indians, who were making sugar, and with them they encamped for the night. On their journey down the creek on the next day, they arrived at the Mohawk village, on the Van Meter section, already spoken of. Van Meter made the Welchs welcome at his cabin and directed them to some very eligible land in the neighborhood, which they bought, and turned into homes Here they opened up the first settlement in Eden township. In June following, two other brothers, Martin and John, also came. Thomas died soon after. John became a member of the Ohio legislature from Seneca county. Hugh and Martin moved to

Wyandot county. Martin and John are now also dead, and the Judge is the only survivor of that once large family.

Hugh Welch was the first postmaster in Eden township, and he held the office at his opening, which was afterwards known as the Olmsted and Richardson place. This was the first postoffice in Seneca county east of the river. Mr. Welch was appointed by President Jackson. John McLean was postmaster-general at that time and signed the commission as such. It is dated August 4, 1825. Mr. Welch sold the Olmsted farm and the Richardson place and moved into Wyandot county, where he was appointed one of the associate judges of Crawford county. Wyandot was then a part of Crawford. This commission is dated September 22, 1834, and is signed by Robert Lucas, governor, and M. H. Kirby, secretary of state. He was re-elected associate judge, and his second commission bears date of February 4, 1842, and is signed by Thomas Corwin, governor, and Samuel Galloway, secretary of state. The Judge sold his Wyandot farm and again moved into Seneca county.

He laid out the town of Mexico soon after he moved into Wyandot; helped to build the M. E. church there; donated the lot upon which it was built, and for a long time and until he sold his property near Mexico, was one of its most influential members.

Judge Welch was born in Little Beaver township, Beaver county, Pennsylvania, on the 18th day of February, 1801. His father's name was Felix, and his mother's name was Margaret Barnes, who came from England. His father was a native of the county of Derry, in Ireland. The parents had six sons and four daughters. Hugh was the fifth son.

In 1816 the parents moved with their children to Huron county, Ohio, where they lived until the sons found better homes, in Seneca county. Hugh was married on the 18th day of September, 1823, to Polly, second daughter of John Gibson. They had three children: Eliza, married to William A. Watson; a little son who died at the age of about four years, and Maria, who married Frank McBride, and who has two interesting daughters, nearly young women grown. Judge Welch's brother, Martin, was the first stationed minister at Toledo in the M. E. church. The Judge was well acquainted with all the Mohawk Indians on the Van Meter section, and knew Charline, who was a nephew of the Brandt's, and the bitter, unforgiving foe of the Americans. He carried his hatred to the grave with him. He had the skin of the leg and foot of a child tanned, in which he carried his trinkets. He would not talk to a white man, and died from eating warm bread beyond the Mississippi.

Judge Welch says that there were three brothers of these Brandt's, Thomas, Paulus and Isaac. Isaac was his favorite. They were both of about the same height and age; both full of fun and great wrestlers Van Meter was a generous and noble man, and a great horse fancier.

Charline was about eighty years old when he left with the Mohawks for the west.

Mrs. Welch died June 6th, 1869, at Green Springs She was the first patient at the water cure. From the 8th of October, 1825, hitherto Judge Welch has been a faithful member of the M. E. church.

CHAPTER XXXIV.
HOPEWELL TOWNSHIP.

T. 2, N. R. 14 E.

THIS township was organized on the 7th day of December, 1824, as already stated. The first election was held on Christmas day, the same year, at the house of Joseph Pool. Joseph Rosenberger, John Stover and Nathan Cadwallader were elected as trustees; James Gordon, clerk; John Stoner, treasurer. Robert and John Shippy and John Chaney were also early settlers.

In 1830 the population was 549; in 1840 it had increased to 918, in 1870 it was 1,477, and in 1880 it is 1,635.

Hopewell is also a wealthy township. The soil is very fertile and the drainage is yearly improving it.

On the first of February, 1837, Mr. John Miller laid out the town of Bascom. George W. Gist was the surveyor. It is located on section seventeen. Bascom is a station on the Baltimore & Ohio railroad.

Agreen Ingraham, Jacob S. Jennings, John Sleeper, David Cover, James Mathews, John Baughman, Peter Lonsway, Peter Young, Aaron Ruse, C. Weikert, Thomas Elder, Philip King, Joseph Ogle, Thomas Rickets and others were also among the early settlers here.

The Coldwater railroad had also been constructed through this township, and the iron laid. The project was abandoned and the iron taken up, never to be laid down again (?).

On the 6th day of August, 1836, Samuel Waggoner laid out a town by James Durbin, surveyor, on section sixteen, which he called Hopewell, but no trace of it can be found. It never flourished.

Among the distinguished men who died in Hopewell was Joseph McClelland, one of the old Seneca county pioneers. He was born in Mifflin county, Pennsylvania, August 25, 1787, and was married in Ross county, Ohio, in or near Chillicothe, in the early part of 1815. He moved to Shelby county, Kentucky, in the same year. His wife was Jane Boyd, sister of Thomas Boyd, one of the old county commissioners.

Mr. McClelland moved to Bloom township in 1822 and settled on section three. In 1838 he moved to Silver creek, settling on section nineteen. In 1854 he moved to Hopewell, where he settled on section thirty-five, and there died at the age of seventy-two years, four months and thirteen days.

Mr. McClelland was a stout, active and industrious man, faithful to his promises and prompt in the payment of his debts. He took a deep interest in all public affairs and held the office of county commissioner six years, having been elected in 1842 and in 1845. He lived and died in the enjoyment of the love and respect of all his neighbors and a host of friends.

SAMUEL SMITH

Was born November 8, 1806, in Kent county, Delaware. Soon thereafter his father moved with his family to Ohio and settled near Rushville, in Fairfield county.

When Samuel was about twenty-three years old, he came to Seneca county and entered the west half of the northwest quarter of section twenty-two, in Hopewell. Here he built a cabin and helped to open the road towards Bascom. He worked out among farmers, drove team for Mr. Hedges, and in 1833 he married Elizabeth Zeis, a daughter of a German family that lived in Liberty township After he was married he moved upon his land, where he still resides. His wife died September 11, 1870, the mother of ten children, who are all still living and doing well. Mr. Smith, himself, is still in the enjoyment of good health, physically and mentally.

When he settled here in Hopewell, Mr. Henry Creeger was already living on his farm near Wolf creek.

Samuel Todd, David Betts, David Cover, John Kune, George Shaull, Joseph Ogle and a few others were in the neighborhood.

There were about twenty-five acres cleared on the school section, and Mr. Covel moved onto them in 1834, under a lease of the trustees. There was also a small clearing on the James Mathews farm, now owned by Mr. Neligh. The balance of this neighborhood was all woods.

JOHN MAULE.

One of the old settlers of this township was John Maule, who was born in Chester county, Pennsylvania, October 21, 1793. When but seven years of age his father died in Baltimore of yellow fever. He learned the trade of a blacksmith, and in 1827 he married Elizabeth Derr, sister of our old pioneer friend, Ezra Derr, of Clinton township.

In June, 1830, he arrived here with a party consisting of his wife and two children, his father-in-law, Thomas Derr, his wife's sister, Margaret (who afterwards became the wife of William Baker), and Joseph Heltebrake.

Mr. Maule bought a farm one-half mile north of Tiffin, on the state road, where he also worked at his trade for seven years and then moved one-half mile west onto the farm where the family now live.

While at his trade he did much work for the Indians, shoeing their ponies, etc., and they esteemed him very much. He was well acquainted with Red Jacket, Hard Hickory, George Harriman, the Walkers and Dennis's

His neighbors were Erastus Bowe, John Souder, George Stoner, Henry Rosenberger, David Risdon, Bartholomew Shaull, David Smith, John Rosenberger, Henry and William Brish.

Mr. Maule was six feet two inches tall; his weight was about two hundred pounds. He had but few gray hairs when he died, on the 31st of October, 1866. He was a Quaker, and faithful to his creed; was honest, truthful and quiet. He was the father of six children, four sons and two daughters. Mrs. Maule was born December 14th, 1804, and is still living.

GEORGE SLOSSER

Was born in Washington county, Maryland, in 1770; in 1800 he bought property in Jefferson county, Virginia. He was married to Mary Painter, in Washington county, Maryland, in 1805, and then moved onto his land in Virginia, 133 acres. They had nine children in all, four girls and five boys, who are all living but one. Mr. Slosser moved with his family to Seneca county and located in Hopewell in 1832. Mrs. Slosser died in 1840, aged fifty-three years, and Mr. Slosser died in 1843, aged seventy-three years.

PETER SLOSSER

Is the oldest son of George Slosser, and came out here with his father. He was born July 14th, 1806, and was married to Isabella Mitchell, in Jefferson county, Virginia, March 28th, 1830. He is the father of five living children

Mr. Slosser tells me that one night in March, 1834, a wolf made an attack on his dog, and when Mr. Slosser came up to the combatants, the wolf left the dog and made for Mr. Slosser, who picked up a stick of wood and struck the wolf a heavy blow, which felled him, and was soon dispatched.

In August, the same year, a deer was in his wheat field. Mr. Slosser and his hired man halloed at him, which scared him, and, jumping

HOPEWELL TOWNSHIP.

over the rail fence into a brush heap, he became entangled and was killed.

David Fox, Peter Wagner, Abraham Miller, Jacob Bogart, William Rickets, Samuel Kime, Joseph Ogle, Henry Creeger, Jacob Ruie, Charles Chaney, John Chaney, Robert Shippy, Elias Kime, William Kime and others were neighbors.

JOHN DAWALT

Came to Hopewell in 1833. One time, while he was walking on the road leading from Tiffin to Fostoria, about one-half mile from Bascom, where Mr. Hall now lives, he met a bear on the road, who made for Dawalt. Having neither a gun nor an axe, he defended himself with a hickory cane he had for a walking stick. The bear was very close to him, and Dawalt having no chance to run, it became a fight for life. He belabored the bear with his club in such good style that he came down, and Dawalt killed him. Mrs. Dawalt ran up while the fight was going on, but Dawalt told her to stay away until the danger be over

JOSEPH OGLE.

The road that runs from Tiffin to Fostoria was surveyed along a ridge, and on the highest ground that runs east and west through this township. Along on this ridge and on the banks of the Wolf creeks the first settlements were made. The east branch of Wolf creek runs longitudinal with the river in its general course. Near the southwest corner of section one another branch puts into it from the west. Near the north line of section twenty-three another branch of Wolf creek puts into this east branch

Williard Sprague and Charles and John Chaney had a lease on section sixteen, known as Hopewell Center. These men, with their families, were probably the first settlers in the township. Mr. Peter Schultz now owns the southeast quarter of the section. Joseph Ogle came to Tiffin on the 15th of June, 1824, and very soon thereafter bought from James Aiken the southwest quarter of section twenty-three, which has ever since been known as the Ogle farm. When he landed in Tiffin he rented a cabin from Mr. A. Ingraham, and underbrushed a road to his land on Wolf creek. Mr. Ogle's family was the third family that landed in Tiffin after the organization of this county. George Park, Horton Howard and David Bishop were here. Thomas Loyd also, who was then a single man. Mr. Hedges brought on his family about that time. Eben Mills had about thirty acres cleared on land near Mr. Ogle, which he leased to Ogle on shares. During this year Ogle built a cabin on his land and moved into it in 1826, in April, and cleared a few acres that year. Thomas Ogle, the oldest son of Joseph, says he cut the first tree on the land. It was not much of a tree, and Thomas was not much of a boy then. Mr. Ogle helped to build the first school house in this township. It was put up on the southeast quarter of the school section, some two and one-half miles from the Ogle place. Sprague and Charles Chaney split the pungeon for the floor. Mr. Chenowith and John Chaney built the stick chimney. Abraham Miller and Joseph Ogle put up the desks and benches. These were none of your patent benches, by any means, but were constructed in this manner: Two-inch auger holes were bored into the logs along the sides and sticks driven into them about two feet long. Loose clapboards were laid onto these sticks, and the desk was done. The seats were pungeon benches. Mr. Chenowith was the first schoolmaster in the township, and taught in this school house. Reading, writing and spelling constituted a full course. Mr. Ogle had a son born to him while he lived on the Mills place, and when the family moved into the new cabin, Mrs. Ogle was removed to the house of 'Squire Plane, in Tiffin, with her babe, to remain there until the cabin was dry enough for her to come home in safety. The youngest child, Benj. F. Ogle, was born in the new cabin.

When Mr. Ogle came here, two years before the Hart family, Bartholomew Shaull and John A. Rosenberg lived further down the creek. Nathan Cadwalader lived up the creek, in section thirty-four. The Daughertys were also here then. One of the Daugherty girls was married to George Park, in Tiffin, and another to Samuel Hoaglin.

In the spring of 1825, after Hedges' mill first commenced running, they had a sort of celebration there. Mr Ogle and William Stripe hitched up their ox-teams, and Mr. Hedges' ox-team was also hitched up. The women got into the wagons, the men drove the teams and walked to the mill. Here they had a lunch and a general good time. Some washed themselves in corn-meal, and threw meal into each other's faces. It was fun of that peculiar kind, but nevertheless a celebration.

When Mr. Ogle settled on Wolf creek they lived on corn, which they could get no nearer than Upper Sandusky. He and his son, Thomas, rode horseback to the plains, and bought two bags full of corn, each rider having a bag before him. The trip took two days. Upon their return the corn was taken to Moore's mill, near Lower Sandusky, to be ground into meal, which took two days more. Upon their return from the mill they had three bushels of meal, less the toll. A large family would soon get away with that quantity of meal, especially when it was bread and dinner for them all.

In the fall of 1826 Thomas Brandt and another Indian came into Ogle's cabin and wanted bread. Brandt was drunk and drew a tomahawk to strike Mrs. Ogle, but the other Indian stopped him.

The wolves were very plenty, and one evening while Mrs. Ogle was milking the cows near the cabin, a lot of them came close to her, howling, which scared her very much. One evening as the boys were returning from spelling school, the wolves got after them and followed them to the house.

Mr. Ogle described to the writer the situation of the brush dam and saw mill of Spencer, and the old fort and stockade then still in good condition.

Joseph Ogle was born in Frederick city, Maryland, February 7, 1781. His father was one of the proprietors of the town. He was married October 15, 1809, in Mechanicstown, Frederick county, Maryland. They lived on the old Ogle farm, in Frederick county, a while, when they moved to Hagerstown, where he kept tavern; then returned and bought the Ogle farm, sold it afterwards and came to Seneca county.

When he died in January, 1864, he was eighty-three years and eleven months old.

He cleared 130 acres of land on his farm here, and raised eight children, two having died in childhood.

Mrs. Ogle died in 1876, eighty-seven years old. Six of their children are still living.

CHAPTER XXXV.
JACKSON TOWNSHIP.

T. 3, N. R. 13 E.

THIS township was organized on the 4th day of December, 1832. The first election of township officers took place on the 3d day of April, 1833, at the house of Abraham Rinebolt. Christian Foster, John Stombaugh and Michael Stahl were elected trustees; Henry Hoffman and Abraham Rinebolt, supervisors; Samuel Rinebolt, Andrew Ferrier and Daniel Swope, overseers of the poor; Enoch Trumbo, clerk; Jonas Hampshire and Jacob Hollinger, fence viewers.

In 1840 the population was 586; in 1870 in had increased to 1,131; in 1880 it is 1,394.

Henry Hoffman, in 1827, moved from Perry county, Ohio, and located on the southeast quarter of section thirty-six, the first settler in the township, and his brother-in-law, Abraham Rinebolt, came from the same county in 1828, and located near him.

Enoch Trumbo is the only old settler living. He came in 1833, and located on section twenty-two, where he still resides. He was once county commissioner, and is highly respected for his good sense and honesty.

Jonas Hampshire located on the northwest quarter of section twenty-two in 1833. He used to take a very active part in public affairs, and was a leader in the Democratic ranks. He was a successful farmer, and has accumulated a handsome fortune. He lives in Wood county now.

Michael Stahl came in 1832, and also located on section twenty-two. Daniel Swope came in 1833, also settled on section twenty-one, and is still there, also one of the oldest settlers living. George Stahl came in 1834. James Robertson, the Hollopeters, William Noble (the father of Hon. Warren P. Noble and Harrison Noble, the present mayor of Tiffin), Robert C. Caples, Samuel Yunker, Robert Shippy, Henry Shoutz, Henry F. Johnson, the Long family, Abraham Craun (who is

JACKSON TOWNSHIP.

still living), Joseph English, Thomas Chance, George Stoner and Christian Foster were among the early settlers.

My good old friend, Henry Stahl, was a boy but fourteen years old when he came to the township in 1836. He married Elizabeth, the daughter of John Reinbolt. He is one of the most substantial men of the township and highly respected for his manly virtues and excellent judgment.

John Lambright, Frederick Feble, William Ash and others, were also prominent citizens.

Isaiah Hollopeter laid out the town of Rehoboth on the 7th of December, 1844, but it never flourished.

The location of the L. E. & L. railroad has brought market to this township, and Jackson station is of great convenience to the people. Some parts of Jackson are rolling and gently undulating, but the larger portion was overflown by Wolf creek and exceedingly undesirable on that account. The settlers entered the dry and best parts and the wet portions could find no purchasers for many years. Even so late as the close of the Mexican war, there were lands in Jackson upon which A. Rank, a Mexican soldier, located his land warrant. This was the last piece of public land sold in the county.

These swales hindered the progress of Jackson many years, but finally, by judicious ditching, the surface water is led away, and Jackson will rank among the best townships in the county, there being very little land within its borders, unproductive.

Harrison's creek is one of the tributaries of Wolf creek.

The following is taken from the history of Fostoria and vicinity, by E. W. Thomas, with his kind permission:

In 1832 a large body of Wyandot Indians camped in Jackson township and engaged in their favorite pursuit of hunting game. They killed eleven bears and one hundred and seven deers, besides large quantities of small game. They were remarkably quiet and well disposed towards the whites. They bought potatoes, corn, etc., but in all their transactions were perfectly honest, and if a white family wished to get rid of Indians, they invariably tried to get them in debt, for when they once got an Indian indebted to them he would not call again; but the majority of them could never be induced to go into debt. They would pay up punctually and often bring presents of deer and bear meat.

The first whisky sold in the township was by John P. Gordon. The Indians used to go to his store, then kept in Risdon, and get their fire-water. They would get gloriously fuddled and make the woods resound with their hideous yells. On one occasion, in the fall of 1832, they had been to Gordon's shebang and imbibed freely of fire-water, and getting their bottles filled, they started for their camp, some four miles distant. They had to pass the cabin of Mr. Nestlerode, on what was then known as the island and bears that name to the present time; the same farm now being owned by Mr. Nestlerode, who is a resident of Fostoria. They stopped, as they had been in the habit of doing before, but were drunk. There were some six or seven in the company. When they arrived at Mr. Nestlerode's cabin, they were too drunk to get off their ponies, but Mr. and Mrs. Nestlerode assisted them to dismount. When they entered the cabin, they commenced upsetting chairs, tables and everything that came in their way. They were feeling up for the floor when a general fight ensued between the whole party, except the chief, Thomas Koon, who was sober.

Their scalping knives and tomahawks were brought into use, and the family were frightened; the children treed under the beds. But Mr. Nestlerode, by order of the chief, took the knives, tomahawks and guns from them, and their bottles of fire-water also. But the chief feared trouble when they reached their camp, and probably fearing they might return, asked Mr. Nestlerode to hand each Indian his bottle of fire-water; which was done, and then assisting them on their ponies, they again started for their camp, but had proceeded but a short distance when one of the party became rather top-heavy, and tumbled off. His companions halted, built him a fire, and left him, and proceeded on to their camp. The Indian who had been left, returned to Mr. Nestlerode's the next morning with his clothes badly burned, and when asked what was the matter, replied: "Indian too much drunk; Indian take too much fire-water; Indian sleep close big fire; fire much burn Indian, but white man get Indian drunk, then cheat Indian much."

On the next day each Indian returned alone for his property, that Mr. Nestlerode had taken from him while drunk. Mrs. Nestlerode was very anxious to get rid of them as soon as possible, so when the first Indian came she brought out all the knives, tomahawks and guns, but he only took what belonged to him, and when each one came he could only be induced to take his own property. They all appeared ashamed of what they had done the day before, and like Adam in the garden of Eden, they lay the blame on some other person. "Bad white man; sell Indian fire-water; Indian get much drunk; Indian bad; white man cheat Indian."

CHAPTER XXXVI.

LIBERTY TOWNSHIP.

T. 3, N. R. 14 E.

THIS township was organized on the 5th day of June, 1832. The first election took place April 1st, 1833, when the following persons were elected as township officers, viz

Trustees—John Rosenberger, Evan W. Brook, Jacob Kaine.
Clerk—John Craun.
Constables—Eben Conway and Nicholas Rumbaugh.
Supervisors—Adam Fleck, Isaac Hartsock, James Hudson, Levi Crissey and Joseph S. Conway.

In 1840 the population was 1,084; in 1870 it was 1,668 and in 1880 it is 2,159.

An area of nearly a mile wide and three miles long, in the northeastern part of the township, is one of those stoney ridges that are found very frequently throughout the northwestern portion of Ohio. In some places the limestone rocks cover the ground almost entirely. In other localities, near the ridge, they are strewn less thickly and the land is cultivated. The township generally is free from stone, which makes this spot rather remarkable from a geological standpoint. It is otherwise level but very fertile and undulating in some localities. Large crops are raised here annually. The western branch of Wolf creek passes in a northeasterly direction through Liberty, driving several saw mills. The supply of water is sufficient to run three mills six months in each year.

A town by the name of Middleburgh was surveyed by D. Risdon, on the 8th of September, 1832, and on section nine. The land was formerly owned by Jacob Kessler. The town never flourished.

On the 12th of April, 1838, John Betts, a very enterprising citizen, laid out a town on section three, and called it Bettsville; David Risdon was the surveyor. It is situate near the west branch of Wolf creek and has now over one hundred dwellings, two churches, one saw mill and sash and blind factory and several stores and shops. The large brick steam flouring mill is doing a good business. Since the location of the Toledo, Tiffin & Eastern railroad the business of the town has improved very materially and is constantly on the increase. Fine brick residences have been erected and the town has assumed a very business-like appearance, and the warehouse of Flumerfelt & Titus has greatly added to its trade.

Abraham Ash, guardian of Jacob Ash, on the 9th day of March, 1855, laid out the town of Kansas, near the northwest corner of the township. It is on the line of the Lake Erie & Louisville railroad. It is fourteen miles from Tiffin and thirteen miles from Fremont. The town has one dry goods store and a store of general variety, one grocery and provision store, one cooper shop, one blacksmith shop, one wagon shop, one stove factory, one steam saw mill and one steam grist mill. There are about fifty dwellings, occupied by over two hundred inhabitants.

The soil of the township is rich and very productive.

James Grimes, Jacob Null, Daniel Lynch, the Brickners, Gassman, Lendelbachs, Smiths, Zimmer, Jacob Zeis, the Robertsons, John Michaels, Joseph Cessna, David Brown, Reuben Lott, John Powell, John Baughman, George Feasel, Orrin Betts, Barney Zimmerman and others are among the earliest and most prosperous farmers. Daniel Reinbolt settled here in 1828.

On Saturday morning, the 7th day of August, 1880, a fire broke out in the back end of A. W. Day's building, and destroyed nine rooms in Bettsville, and other property, estimated over $11,000. Mr. Betts, Schubert, John Cook, C. Norton, Joe Massony, George Schuster and John Perong were the principal sufferers.

MRS. RACHAEL K. TURNER.

This lady is one of the veteran pioneers of the county, spending the evening of her long, eventful life in the shades of Liberty township.

She was born in Franklin county, Pennsylvania, on the 4th of July, 1797. In 1817 she came to Perry county, Ohio, where she remained one year with friends and in the following year she went to Fairfield county, where, in January, 1818, she was married to Benjamin Turner. In 1829 they removed to this county and located one mile west of Sandusky street, in Tiffin.

McNeal's store and Smith's tavern were then the principal buildings in town. Their neighbors were the Ogles, Creegers, Cadwalladers, Millers, Jennings, Gordons, Arbogasts, Adelspergers and Graffs. She was well acquainted with Mr McNeal and Mr. Crissey, and knew

Joseph Jenay, the colored cabinet maker. Crissey was the blacksmith.

In the summer of 1830, when the Senecas prepared for their departure to the west, they came to Fort Ball, where they camped out some two or three weeks and made sale of their ponies and other personal property. General Brish and Mr. Hart went with them to the west.

Mrs. Turner also recollects the excitement occasioned by the accidental drowning of Robert Burns and Batholomew Kinney, who attempted to cross the river to the Tiffin side for the purpose of buying a yoke of cattle.

In the year 1834 the Turner family removed to the northeast corner of Liberty township, where she still resides. She says:

When we came to Fort Ball, we bought 19 acres from Smith, the tavern keeper. We paid him $94 in cash and the other $6 he was to take in game, paying 60 cents for a hind-quarter of deer.

To Mr. C. W. Harris my thanks are due for this statement.

CHAPTER XXXVII.

LOUDON TOWNSHIP AND FOSTORIA—THE FOSTERS—MARTIN KINGSEED.

T. 2, N. R. 13 E.

THE commissioners of Seneca county, on the 5th day of March, 1832, organized township 2, N. R. 13, into a legal township, to be known by the name of Loudon. The first election was held at the house of Benjamin Hartley, on the 2d day of April thereafter, and the following named persons were elected to their respective offices, as follows:

Justice of the Peace—Abner Wade.
Clerk—John Tennis.
Trustees—Benjamin Stevens, Peter T. King, John Rickets.
Constable—Samuel Carbaugh.
Supervisor—Benjamin Hartley.
Overseers of the Poor—Abner Wade, Nathan Shippy.
Treasurer—Benjamin Stevens.
Fence Viewers—Nathan Shippy, John Reese, John Shiller.

In 1840 the population of Loudon numbered 763; in 1870 it was 1,400; in 1880 it is 1,277, exclusive of Fostoria.

Besides the officers above named there were also Samuel Bear, Jacob Rumple, Martin Adams, Philip Hennessy, Robert Rainey, Jacob Fruth, George Heming, Peter Ebersole, Henry Sheller, David Young, Conrad Rumple, Jacob Kaiser, John Good, John Reinbolt, Jacob Dillon, Thos. Dillon, the Peter families, Jacob Mergenthaler, the Fishers, and others scattered over the township.

On the 31st of August, 1832, Roswell Crocker caused to be surveyed on section six, of this township, a town that he called Rome. David Risdon was the surveyor. In 1840 it had a population of 80; in 1850 about 300. It is located on the Fort Findlay and Lower Sandusky state road, and upon the Defiance and Tiffin state road, where it crosses with the Bucyrus and Perrysburg road. It is twenty-two miles from Fremont, fourteen and one-half miles from Findlay, fourteen miles from

LOUDON TOWNSHIP. 553

Tiffin, thirty-six miles from Bucyrus, twenty-five miles from Upper Sandusky, and close to the Hancock county line.

A few days after the platting of Rome, on the 6th day of September, 1832, J. Gorsuch caused to be surveyed on section one, T. 2, N. R. 12, in Hancock county, and on section six, in Loudon, another town, which he named after the old surveyor, and called it Risdon.

Mr. Risdon was a distinguished pioneer, and it is to be regretted that some spot in Seneca county could not have been selected to perpetuate his honored name. This town was intended to accomplish this, but failed, as we shall soon see. Mr. Risdon was a surveyor by profession, but otherwise useful in life. He was a tall, slender man, had a bushy head of gray hair, a large blue eye, well proportioned features; stood about six feet high; spoke slow, with a deep, sonorous voice. With his pants in his high top boots, in his Indian hunting shirt, fringed all around, he was the very picture of a pioneer surveyor.

Mr. Risdon, however, did not survey this town alone; he was assisted by William L. Henderson, of Hancock county.

Henry Welch, Jeremiah Mickey and John P. Gordon were the first settlers here.

In 1848 it contained thirty dwellings, one church, one tavern, three stores, one carding machine propelled by steam, one foundry, one tannery, one steam saw-mill, one cabinet shop, one wagon shop, two shoe shops, two saddle shops and three blacksmith shops. In 1850 its population was about 200. It was a post town also, William Thomas being postmaster.

Dr. Marcus Dana and Dr. R. C. Caples were among its inhabitants. The town was platted on the east branch of Portage river.

These two towns of Rome and Risdon, thus adjoining, became rival towns, and it was wise when, in 1854, they became consolidated into one town, and named in honor of one of its most distinguished early settlers—Charles W. Foster, the merchant—and called Fostoria.

The country surrounding Fostoria is rich in agricultural resources, but withal, it is astonishing how this town has sprung up into its present magnificent condition. Fostoria is rapidly becoming the rival of all its neighboring towns. Its large and numerous business blocks, its splendid school buildings and churches, its beautiful and numerous private dwellings, exhibiting both taste and comfort, its railroads and other general improvements, denote a most remarkable degree of business life, and prove the energy, industry and the mental and financial capacity of its citizens. Numerous additions have been made to Fostoria from time to time, so that now the corporate limits embrace nearly all of section six, extend into section seven, into section thirty-one in Jackson township, and into Hancock county, covering about one thousand acres of land.

The manufacturing enterprises are constantly increasing, and Fostoria is decidedly the best railroad center in northwestern Ohio, except Toledo.

The Baltimore & Ohio road, the Lake Erie & Louisville road, the Columbus & Toledo road, and the Ohio Central, formerly called the Atlantic & Lake Erie railroad, pass through Fostoria. The Mansfield, Coldwater & Lake Michigan railroad had been finished to this place also, but for some reason the iron was taken up again and the track abandoned.

The town of Rome was incorporated by an act of the legislature passed February 19th, 1851.

John F. Morse was then speaker of the house of representatives, and Charles C. Converse speaker of the senate.

On the 2d day of September, 1853, a petition was signed by William Braden, Thomas Brian, H. I. Vosburgh, W. Weaver, A. S. Bement, E. F. Robinson, Ch. Bonnell, John O. Albert, Reuben Brian, I. M. Coe, John Wilson, George Gear, Lyman Kittel, Daniel Free, Abr. Metz, Robert Doke, E. Bement, E. W. Thomas, D. D. Miller, H. W. Cole, James Lewis, Umphrey England and John M. Stewart, who appointed William Braden to act in their behalf, directed to the commissioners of Seneca county, praying that the west half of the northwest quarter of section six, in Loudon township, may be attached to Rome. The order was granted on the 2d day of January, 1854, and Rome and Risdon thereby became one town.

Mr. Stewart, in his atlas of Seneca county, speaking of Rome, says the consolidation took place in 1856, and in his biographical sketch of Mr. C. W. Foster, says it took place in 1852. If he had guessed half way between the two dates he would have been nearer right.

The act of incorporation of Rome by the legislature had twenty-nine long sections, and gave the town all sorts of municipal power. The town would have been ruined by taxation had these powers all been exercised.

Joel W. Wilson was then in the senate, and Jacob Decker in the house of representatives.

The early settlers in Loudon were men of great sagacity. They saw in the near future the wealth that this township must necessarily develop from the richness of its soil, being well watered and timbered.

In 1840 the population of the township was 763; in 1850 it was 1,781;

in 1860 it had increased to 2,465; in 1870 it was 3,133, out of which 2,736 were native born; in 1880 it is 1,277, exclusive of Fostoria.

Fostoria proper, in 1870, had a population of 1,733. My old friend Jacob C. Millhime, Esq., who has just finished his work as census enumerator of Fostoria, makes the population of Fostoria for 1880 to number 3,045, exclusive of the portion in Jackson township and Hancock county, which, being added, makes Fostoria proper number 4,111.

CHARLES W. FOSTER.

It is not only a remarkable fact that here in America the best men are the self-made men, but the fact seems to be the result of our peculiar form of government and the fruit of her free institutions. It requires no hereditary title here to become distinguished among men. A goodly share of common sense, good health, proper deportment, industry, energy, integrity, all well combined and backed by a reasonable quantity of will power, have enabled thousands of men in all avenues of human life to outstrip their fellows and reach the goal of both fame and fortune. Our beautiful school system and our higher institutions of learning are truly the pride of our state; but for success in life, an ounce of sound, mother wit is worth more than a pound of book learning. The great contributors to the sciences; the plotting calculators and thinkers and searchers, generally die poor.

The subject of this sketch belongs to that class of men who, when they know that their plans are right, depend upon perseverance for success.

He was born in Brookfield, Worcester county, Massachusetts, on the 21st of November, 1800. His father moved with his family to western New York, then sparsely settled, and located near Rochester, in 1820.

A gentleman by the name of John Crocker moved to Seneca township, in this county of Seneca, in 1824. Two years thereafter, in 1826, Mr. Foster also came to Seneca township to see Mr. Crocker's family, and especially his beautiful daughter, Laura. It seems that there had been some understanding between the young people before Mr. Crocker left New York.

When Mr. Foster arrived here, he found Miss Laura in bad health and took her to the Saratoga Springs, in New York, where she remained some time and was restored to good health. She then visited her uncle, James Richardson, who lived some thirty miles from the springs, and here the young people were married on the 7th of June, 1827. They then came to Seneca and lived with the Crocker family. Here Mr. Foster worked on the farm of his father-in-law two years, when he moved to the Wolf creek, three miles north of Tiffin, where he had 160 acres in section eleven, in Hopewell, and which he afterwards sold to George Shedenhelm, by whose name it is known to this day. It was then all in the woods and required work to clear it and found a home. Mr. Foster had also another eighty-acre lot at that time. He sold all his land, and with the proceeds of these sales, he and his father-in-law, who had more means, opened a stock of goods in a cabin in Rome, on the same spot where the Foster block now stands. This was in 1832. The business of the firm was carried on in the firm name of Foster & Crocker. Ten years thereafter, when the concern had already assumed large proportions, Mr. Crocker withdrew from it, taking away merely the amount he had put in, and leaving Mr. Foster alone in the possession and control of the constantly increasing business. Thus he continued until his son, Charles, had grown up to nearly man's estate, and who, in his youth, developed a remarkable faculty for business. This feature in the nature of young Charles was inherited and then improved by education, experience and practice. It sustained him in his successes when he became ambitious and turned politician, for in the management of a political campaign, from a business standpoint, Governor Foster has no superior anywhere.

In 1848, when his son was about twenty years of age, Mr. Foster took him as a partner in business, and the firm of Foster & Son increased the growing fame of the house which continued thus six years, when another accession was made, and Mr. Olmsted became a partner. It was then Foster, Olmsted & Co., and continues so still as a grain firm. The store proper is conducted in the firm name of Foster & Snyder Brothers.

Mrs. Crocker died in 1850, and John Crocker in 1854. They lie buried in the Fostoria cemetery. Roswell Crocker, a brother of Mrs. C. W. Foster, is still living in Fostoria, as is also his wife, Sarah Ann, who is a daughter of John Cooper, Esq.

Mr. and Mrs. Foster were the parents of five children, of whom their son, Charles, is the only one living.

When Mr. Foster started here in the woods, forty-eight years ago, his and Mr. Crocker's combined capital in trade did not exceed $2,000, and their annual sales not $3,000. The trade was principally barter for skins and furs. The house now has a stock of about $80,000, and their annual sales reach near $150,000. Including the outside business of the firm in wool, grain, lumber, etc., they handle over a million of cash annually.

Mr. Foster's manner of business was of that pleasant and manly

character that won him friends who constantly increased in number. He kept out of litigation and lived up promptly to his contracts. All this tended to secure him the confidence of the community. Any person who was able to secure Mr. Foster's good opinion, could get credit with him, and at times men owed him more money than they were worth. He could have sold out hundreds of them for debts they owed him at the time, had he so willed, and utterly ruined them; very many of them are now among the substantial men in the country.

The house of Foster has contributed largely to every enterprise that was calculated to build up the town and country. Their sagacity, foresight and promptitude in business have not only stamped their own individualities upon the community, but have also inspired others to enterprise and practical business life, so that now, while the Foster house enjoys its great wealth, the community at large is greatly benefited and in about the same proportions to its constant increase in wealth and business.

Mr. Foster, now nearly four score years, is still enjoying the society of his wife and a host of friends. His health is good and he promises fair to become a centennarian. It is a pleasure to see him on the street every day engaged in familiar, friendly conversation, cracking his old jokes and having a kind word for everybody. And it is still more pleasant to notice the kind, friendly and almost filial affection the people of Fostoria, young and old, seem to entertain for him. There is something besides wealth that creates happiness. A man who has nothing but money is poor, indeed.

CHARLES FOSTER

Was born on the old Crocker place, at his grandfather's house, in Seneca township, on the 12th day of April, 1828. In 1854 he was married to Annie, a daugter of Judge Olmsted, of Fremont, Sandusky county, Ohio. Their union was blessed with two daughters, Jessie and Annie. He entered into business with his father when he was but a boy, and is still associated with, and is the new life of, the concern.

In 1870 Mr. Foster was elected a member of the 42d congress, from the 10th district. He was re-elected in 1872. His attack upon the Sanborn contract and his conflict with General Butler in debate, brought him very popularly before the country. He was re-elected in 1874; and again in 1876. He was nominated again in 1878, but the district having been changed and made so overwhelmingly Democratic, that he was defeated. In October, 1879, he was elected governor of the state. If, at the Chicago convention that nominated General Garfield for the presidency, Mr. Blaine had been nominated, Mr. Foster would, undoubtedly, have been nominated for vice-president. The Republican party would thus have put into the field a ticket more formidable than that of Garfield and Arthur, to say the least of it.

It is a fact worth recording that while the city of Tiffin is named after the first governor of Ohio, the city of Fostoria is named after the last governor of Ohio, and a native of old Seneca. Excellent likenesses in fine steel engravings of both these illustrious gentlemen adorn the pages of this book. Let me say, without vanity, that I am proud of the co-incident. The like of this fact will never be written again.

Tiffin is the only county seat in Ohio named after its first governor, and while this history of Seneca county is being written, a native of Seneca and one of its most honored sons is the chief executive of the state; presiding over three millions of freemen, forming a state whose resources for wealth and human happiness are inexhaustible; whose climate is unsurpassible; whose intelligence and system of education are the admiration of the age in which we live.

MARTIN KINGSEED.

Among the distinguished business men of Fostoria is also my esteemed old friend, Martin, the subject of this sketch, and I am only conferring a great pleasure upon myself when writing a short story of his life. We were boys, frequently meeting each other in Germany, and before we had grown up to be men, found ourselves in the woods of Seneca county, where we have fought the battles of life, each his own way, as best we could. Here we have spent the morning, noon-tide and afternoon of our manhood days in friendship and mutual regard that grows warmer as the evening begins to draw long shadows on the wayside.

Martin was about seventeen years old when his father settled in the woods of Seneca in 1834. He took hold of the work necessary to open up a clearing and starting a home in the woods, with a will. Being endowed by nature with a strong, healthy body and a head of his own, he soon made himself useful all around and worked at home until he was 25 years old. After the death of his mother he started to work for Henry St. John, at a saw mill on the river. Here he remained six years in succession. In 1847 he came very near losing his life: a large log was being rolled into the mill; he fell in front of it, when the log rolled onto him from his feet to his breast and back again. He was carried out of the mill, apparently lifeless, by John Kerr and Mr. McAllister, who happened to be near. Mr. Kerr was a Thompsonian physician at that time, and applying his skill, restored his patient in a short time.

This was on the 2d of January, and on the 6th of May following, he was found under another log at 1 o'clock A. M., which laid him up for some time, and the effects of which he feels to this day. He quit the saw mill and looked for lighter work, being now disqualified to do hard work; he assisted in the survey of the railroad from Bellefontaine to Union City for nine months.

On September 17, 1850, he was married to Elmira Emily Noel (who was born June 19, 1826, in Frederick county, Maryland), and located in Tiffin, where he bought a house near the railroad, on Clay street. Here he entered the store of John G. Gross as clerk, selling hardware and studying the laws of trade in that line for six years. Then he traded his property in Tiffin to Mr. Gross for a stock of hardware he then had in Rome, and moved there in October, 1855. His is now the oldest unchanged mercantile establishment in Fostoria.

Martin was born November 19, 1817.

He is the father of eight children, four sons and four daughters, seven of whom are living. Charles Edwin is traveling for Messrs. McIntosh, Good & Co., Cleveland, Ohio. Francis Dorwin is clerk in his father's store. Some of the daughters are keeping house for their father, and the younger children are going to school. Mr. Kingseed lived very happily with his family until on the 7th day of February, 1877, when Mrs. Kingseed died after a short illness of a few days. The oldest daughters are young ladies now and seek to make the life of their honored father as happy as it is in their power to do, but there is that vacant chair, and the absence of that mother's smile, which always cheered the whole household.

During the twenty-five years that Mr. Kingseed has prosecuted his business here, Fostoria has made a great change and made more rapid progress than any other inland town in Ohio.

Michael Noel, the father of Mrs. Kingseed, died April 11, 1870, and Mrs. Noel April 17, 1878.

In conclusion, I wish to add, that no citizen in Fostoria is more generally esteemed than Martin Kingseed.

RESIDENT LAWYERS IN FOSTORIA, BEING MEMBERS OF THE TIFFIN BAR.

JUNIUS V. JONES

Was born January 23, 1823, in Gallia county, Ohio. His father moved with his family to Wood county, Ohio, in 1832, where Junius was raised to manhood. In 1846 he came to Fostoria, where he held the office of justice of the peace fifteen years. He read law and was admitted to practice in 1868 in Tiffin, and opened an office in Fostoria. He was also admitted to practice in the courts of the United States in 1878.

He was married in 1846, and had seven children, six boys and one girl; all living.

It seems that sometimes the muses take possession of the thoughts of the Squire, and in one of these spells the following poetical effusion of an Indian legend on the Maumee was produced. I give it here with friend Jones' note:

FOSTORIA, OHIO, March 4, 1880.

DEAR JUDGE: In reading this week's installment of your History of Seneca County, I found you had got General Wayne to Defiance, where, in fancy, I suggested the theme for my poem, written some years ago, entitled

THE INDIAN MAIDEN.

A LEGEND.
By J. V. Jones.

I.

In days long ago, in the depths of the wild,
   When the woods rang with shouts of the joyous and free,
An Indian maid, with the voice of a child,
   Fondly played on the banks of the pleasant Maumee.

II.

'Twas far in the past, in the long, long ago,
   In the days of her mirth and youthful glee,
This Indian maiden was oft seen to row,
   On the moonlit waters of the pleasant Maumee.

III.

One pale, moonlight night, near the smooth flowing river,
   She stole from her wigwam, with heart light and free,
To meet her dark lover, with arrows and quiver,
   To rove on the banks of the pleasant Maumee.

IV.

Her bark moved in silence on the dark, flowing river,
   In search of her lover so anxious to see;
No thought for a moment that he would deceive her,
   As she stole near the banks of the pleasant Maumee.

V.

But hark! what is that? the pale face is coming;
   She thought of her lover; could she warn him to flee?
But the conflict was sharp, and the camp-fires were burning,
   Where her lover was slain, near the pleasant Maumee.

VI.

Each year, just at autumn, when the green leaves are fading,
   When the soft winds are sighing o'er woodland and lea,
The pale phantom ghost of this Indian maiden,
   Is seen near the banks of the pleasant Maumee.

LOUDON TOWNSHIP.   561

Squire Jones (as he is familiarly called) once said to the writer: "All the schooling I ever had was attending the school taught by the Hon. Warren P. Noble."

WILLIAM J. SCHAUFELBERGER

Was born January 29, 1853, at Fostoria, Ohio; graduated from Heidelberg college in the class of 1875; studied law in the office of Judge Seney; was admitted to the bar in the spring of 1877 and located here in January, 1878.

ALEXANDER BROWN

(Brown & Guernsey) was born in Perry county, Ohio, May 27, 1832; admitted to the bar in 1864, located first at Perrysburg, Wood, county, Ohio, and then in Fostoria in the fall of 1872.

WILLIAM J. RIGBY

(Rigby & Bever) was born at Fairfield county, Ohio, May 22, 1815; was admitted to the bar in 1860; located in Fostoria in 1867 and is at present the mayor of the city.

CHARLES GUERNSEY

(Brown & Guernsey) was born in Wood county, Ohio, January 31, 1858; admitted to the bar July 11, 1879; located at Fostoria immediately thereafter. On the 31st of January, 1880, he was married to Miss Mina G. Brown, of Fostoria.

J. M. BEVER

(Rigby & Bever) was born December 9, 1853, in Eden township, in this county; graduated at Otterbin University of Westerville, Ohio; he was admitted to practice law April 11, 1878, and immediately located in Fostoria. He was married July 10, 1878, to Miss S. J. Rugg.

DAVID H. EVERITT

Was born in Franklin county, Ohio, February 6, 1849; was admitted to the bar in October, 1871; located first in Kenton, Ohio, then in Fostoria in 1874. He was elected justice of the peace in 1878.

JOHN B. BARNES

Was born in Mahoning county, Ohio, June 20, 1846; admitted to the bar May 3, 1870; located first at Letonia, Columbiana county, Ohio, December 1, 1870 and in Fostoria October 18, 1877.

JOHN A. BRADNER

Was born at Niagara Falls, New York, August 13, 1833. He came to Ohio in 1849, and located in Fostoria in 1863. He was admitted to the bar in 1879. During the past twelve years he held the office of justice of the peace.

DAVID HAYS

Was born December 19, 1819, in Beaver couety, Pennsylvania; admitted to the bar in 1860 and located in Fostoria in 1837.

FOSTORIA ACADEMY.

This institution is in charge of the conference of the United Brethren in Christ, in northwestern Ohio. At their conference, held in 1878, the subject of locating an academy somewhere in northwestern Ohio was suggested, and the Rev. Isaac Crouse, a minister of the order, residing in Fostoria, urged the propriety of, and succeeded in having the Academy located at this place, on condition that Fostoria will subscribe and pay $20,000, or furnish suitable buildings and grounds for such purposes to the value of $20,000. The people subscribed the required sum, Governor Foster assuming one-fifth of the whole subscription. Thereupon the conference met and appointed the following boards, viz:

TRUSTEES.

President—Rev. L. Moore.
Vice-President—Rev. D. R. Miller.
Secretary—Rev. Isaac Crouse.
Rev. A. Rose, Rev. A. Powell, Rev. S. J. Harbaugh, Governor Foster, M. Saltzman, J. M. Bever, R. C. Bennett, Jesse Bower and J. G. Oberholtzer.

EXECUTIVE COMMITTEE.

Rev. A. Rose, Captain F. R. Stewart, M Saltzman, J. M. Bever and Jesse Bower.

BUILDING COMMITTEE

Rev. A. Rose, Captain F. R. Stewart, Rev. R. French, N. Saltzman and J. M. Bever.

The architectural design of the academy is very creditable, in fact, beautiful, and a great accession to Fostoria, indeed. The board of trustees, at their late meeting, commended the executive and building committees for their good management and economy.

The school was begun in the fall of 1879, with about sixty students. Pending the completion of the academy building, the executive committee rented the old Union school house, where their school was continued for one year. The next session will open in the academy August 31, 1880, and promises to be well attended.

FACULTY.

Principal—Rev. W. T. Jackson, Ph.D.—Language and Higher Mathematics.
History and English—E. L. Shuey, A. B.
Science and Mathematics—Mrs. L. A. Macklin, B. S.
Principal Commercial Department—Rev. I. Crouse.
Vocal and Instrumental Music—A. W. Kelley, M. A.
Librarian—E. L. Shuey, A. B.

THE UNION SCHOOL BUILDING

Is a beauty in its appearance outside, situated on most eligible and delightful grounds, and the inside arrangement is said to be one of the best of any school house in northern Ohio. The Union schools of Fostoria are under the care of an efficient board of directors and the superintendent is one of the distinguished educators of Ohio.

Number of children enumerated		1,011
" " enrolled		694
" " in average monthly attendance		563
" " in " daily "		489
" " in the Catholic school		70

The school grounds embrace five acres on the north side of High street, and were purchased at a cost of $7,500. The building was put up at an expense of $22,500. The heating apparatus and furniture cost about $5,000—$35,000 in all.

The following gentlemen constitute the present school board:

President—R. C. Caples.
Secretary—Simpson Jones.
Treasurer—John E. Wilkison.
William H. Grapes, A. S. Williams and J. F. Richart.

INSTRUCTORS.

	SALARY.
Superintendent—E. J. Hartley	$1,400
Teacher in High school—C. T. Abbott	600
Assistant teacher in High school—Tina Thomas	342
Teacher in First Primary school—James Hays	405
Assistant teacher in First Primary school—Emma L. May	315
Teacher in Grammar school—A. B. Hays	300

SECOND PRIMARY.

	SALARY.
F. W. Boley	$300
Kate Owen	300
Emma Shaw	300
Mary Gordon	300
Nelly Ballard	300
Mary Clark	300
L. V. Hendershott	300

THE OPERA HOUSE

In Fostoria adds very much to the appearance of the town and helps to give it the air of a young, growing city. It was put up at a cost of $30,000. Its large hall, 66x100 feet, is lit by gas. The lower story is occupied by three splendid stores. The second and third stories form the opera house proper.

Mr. John Andes, the owner and builder, is a native of Seigelbach, near Kaiserslautern, in the Palatinate of Germany, where he was born August 14, 1835. He came to Tiffin in 1852 and established himself in the carriage business in Fostoria, in 1860. In 1862 he was married to Miss Philipina Reis. He is a fair specimen of a self-made man.

OTHER INDUSTRIES OF FOSTORIA.

Dry goods—Foster & Snyder, Weaver & Adams, L. J. Hissong, C. D. Scott & Co., B. F. Fosty.

Clothing—John Wagner, J. F. Ensminger.

Hardware—M. Kingseed, N. Poits & Co.

Stoves and tinware—F. R. Stewart, D. S. Boyd & Co., R. Alcott, Schatzell & Faulhaber.

Groceries and provisions—R. Crocker, N. Burtcher, James Quinn, S. Starn & Son, I. N. Mickey, John Lenhart, S. O. Slosser, G. A. Fall, D. M. Snyder, G. A. Shrey, M. E. Morgan, Wilson Brothers, Wm. Fisher, John Godfrey, Beamish & McCarthy, Weisbaugh & Guernsey, J. G. Strawman.

Bakeries—G. A. Fall, James Quinn, Wm. Fisher.

Drug stores—Eshelman & Harbaugh, Charles Hays & Co., Fritcher & Shaufelberger, Mussetter & Wolfe.

There are also 12 saloons, 3 billiard rooms, 4 meat markets, 2 flouring mills, 2 saw mills, 2 planing mills, 1 spoke factory.

Cunningham & Co. employ 25 men.

The Fostoria Stave and Barrel Co. employ 35 men.

Foundries and machine works—Ports, Manecka & Co., T. B. Jacobs, Doe, Evenbeck & Co.

Wagon and carriage works—B. M. Myers, John Andes, Wm. Merqunthaler, Billyard & Huth, Ernest & Dale, A. T. McDonel, Doke & Ersig.

Fostoria Novelty Works—Tingle & Bower, proprietors.

Cigar manufacturers—F. J. Kinnaman, Fred Schultz.

Restaurants—Lon. Cunningham, F. H. Gibbons, R. Cooper.

Dentists—Dr. C. E. Davis, Howell & O'Brien.

Banks—Foster & Co. (C. W. Foster, C. Foster, J. E. Wilkinson).

Elevators—Foster, Olmsted & Co., Brown, Nichols & Co.

Livery stables—Daniel W. Musser, T. C. Heilman, S. J. Kintz.

Hack lines—R. E. Smith, Doke & Ersig.

Andes Opera House—F. D. Kingseed & Co., lessees; 750 seats; folding opera chairs; size of stage, 30x66 feet.

Liberty Hall—Seats 400.

Stone quarries—Bradner & Williams, D. P. Lloyd.

Fire Department—C. E. Davis, chief engineer.

Fostoria Tile Works—Overholt & Co., proprietors.

Jewelry stores—Smith & Schaufelberger, E. Fisher, M. Mueller, Samuel Ewing.

Boots and shoes—Yunt & Norris, L. J. Hissong, Foster & Snyder, Weaver & Adams, J. O. Albert, T. C. Simmons.

There are also 8 millinery shops, 7 insurance agencies, 6 tailoring establishments, 1 marble works, 1 brass band, 1 company Light Guards, A. M. Dildine, captain.

LOUDON TOWNSHIP. 565

LODGES.

Masonic, Odd Fellows, Knights of Pythias, Knights of Honor, Grand Army of the Republic.

HOTELS.

Hays House—W. H. Grapes, proprietor.
Fostoria House—Jacob Bick, proprietor.
Central Hotel—Monroe Isenhart, proprietor.
American House—Peter Simonis, proprietor.
Hale House—Randall Hale, proprietor.

NEWSPAPERS.

Fostoria Review, Republican—O. J. & J. P. DeWolf, proprietors.
Fostoria Democrat, Democratic—Frank Hays, proprietor.

CHURCHES.

M. E. Church—Rev. S. L. Beiler, pastor.
First Presbyterian—Rev. Joseph A. Hughes, pastor.
St. Wendlinus, Catholic—Rev. M. Arnoldi, pastor.
United Brethren—Rev. E. A. Starkey, pastor.
English Reformed—Rev. L. Casselman, pastor.
German Lutheran—Rev. C. A. J. Cramer, pastor.
Protestant Methodist—Rev. E. H. Scott, pastor.

FOSTORIA LODGE NUMBER 288, FREE AND ACCEPTED MASONS.

First communication July 30th, 1856. Charter members working under dispensation:

C. R. Staley,	Andrew Wiseman,	Nathaniel Taylor,
R. C. Caples,	C. R. Ferris,	J. W. Griffith,
Jas. Lewis,	A. M. Blackman,	J. S. Walding,
O. Welsh,	James L. Mickey,	Wesley Bradford.

Regularly organized under charter No. 288, dated October 23d, 1856, with the following officers:

W. M.—R. C. Caples.
S. W.—Jas. Lewis.
J. W.—O. Welsh.
Treasurer—J. L. Mickey.
Secretary—B. L. Caples.
S. D.—A. M. Blackman.
J. D.—P. D. Caples.
Tyler—Samuel Dale.

The following are the names of the past masters, all of whom are now living, excepting A. M. Blackman:

R. C. Caples,	J. W. Bricker,	George L. Hoege,
R. W. Hale,	C. E. Davis,	W. D. Robbins,
A. M. Blackman.		

The lodge is in a flourishing condition, with a present membership of ninety-eight.

The following is the calendar and list of present officers of the lodge:

CALENDAR.

Stated communications in Masonic Hall on the first and third Mondays in each month, as follows:

January........... 5–19 May.............. 3–17 September......... 6–20
February.......... 2–16 June............. 7–21 October............ 4–18
March............. 1–15 July............. 5–19 November.......... 1–15
April.............. 5–19 August............ 2–16 December.......... 6–20

Installation, 1880, January 5. Election, November 1. Installation, 1881, January 3.

Officers:

W. M.—F. J. Schaufelberger.
S. W.—J. W. Schaufelberger.
J. W.—C. W. Thomas.
Treasurer—S. G. Malony.
Secretary—A. M. Dildine.
S. D.—O. V. Wood.
J. D.—Samuel Dale.
Chaplain—C. E. Davis.
Marshal—J. J. Worman.
Stewards—S. E. Newcomb, S. E. Hale.
Tyler—J. C. Springer.
Finance Committee—W. D. Robbins, J. P. DeWolfe, E. J. Cunningham.
Grievance Committee—J. A. Bradner, G. L. Hoege, F. R. Stewart.

FOSTORIA LODGE NUMBER 86, KNIGHTS OF PYTHIAS.

Instituted June 22d, 1875. Twenty-eight charter members.
First officers:

P. C. and D. D. G. C.—John J. Worman.
C. C.—David Olcutt.
V. C.—C. C. Young.
P.—James M. Chamberlin.
K. of R. and S.—N. P. Robbins.
M. of E.—Wm. Logan.
M. of F.—Simeon Yunt.
M. at A.—George Enos.
I. G.—S. F. Kiser.
O. G.—Peter Urchel.

Present number of members, forty.

Present officers:

D. D. G. C.—J. A. Noble.
P. C.—L. D. Mussetter.
C. C.—Moses Smith.
V. C.—S. F. Kiser.

P.—William H. H. Williams.
K. of R. and S.—Charles E. Ruben.
M. of E.—William D. Robbins.
M. of F.—N. P. Robbins.
M. at A.—Peter Dennis.
I. G.—John True.
O. G.—T. L. Brown.
Trustees—John J. Worman, Alonzo Emerine, Frank Caples.
Meeting nights Tuesday of each week.

FOSTORIA LODGE NUMBER 305, I. O. O. F.

Instituted June 6th, 1856. Number of charter members, five.
Names of officers when instituted:

P. G.—Samuel Gee.
N. G.—D. S. Luce.
V. G.—Simon Bricker.
Recording Secretary—O. Welsh.
Treasurer—Joseph Haines.

Present number of members (July 1st, 1880), 100.
Names of present officers:

P. G.—Jno. Y. Calahan.
N. G.—L. J. Eshelman.
V. G.—D. Gelmore.
Recording Secretary—Daniel Hunsecker.
Per. Secretary—Martin Adams.
Treasurer—John Wagner.

LOUDON ENCAMPMENT NUMBER 167.

Instituted June 16th, 1873. Charter members:

Jacob Newhouse, A. Georgia, G. A. Knight,
J. Wiseman, Samuel Ewing, R. Adams,
S. G. Malony, J. C. Springer, G. H. Reece,
S. E. Hale, W. J. Seiple.

The following officers were then installed:

C. P.—S. E. Hale.
S. W.—S. G. Malony.
H. P.—Samuel Ewing.
J. W.—Robert Adams.
Scribe—J. Newhouse.
Treasurer—J. Wiseman.

Present officers:

C. P.—D. W. Snyder.
S. W.—L. J. Eshelman.
H. P.—Martin Adams.
J. W.————————.

Scribe—G. A. Knight.
Treasurer—John Wagner.

FOSTORIA COUNCIL NUMBER 68, ROYAL ARCANUM.

Instituted March 29th, 1878. Twenty-four charter members. First officers:

Regent—George L. Hoege.
Vice Regent—L. D. Mussetter.
Past Regent—C. E. Davis.
Orator—J. W. Schaufelberger.
Collector—T. M. Garrison.
Secretary—D. R. Stiner.
Chaplain—A. T. McDonel.
Guide—L. G. Williams.
Warden—D. Asire.
Sentry—M. Smith.
Trustees—J. A. Woolf, P. T. Norris, W. H. Bannister.

Present membership, twenty-eight.

Meets the first and third Wednesday evening of each month.

SENECA COUNCIL NUMBER 172, AMERICAN LEGION OF HONOR.

Instituted April 27th, 1880, with twenty-two charter members. Following is a list of officers for present year:

Commander—A. Weaver.
Vice Commander—W. D. Robbins.
Secretary—J. T. Yunt.
Past Commander—R. Alcott.
Collector—T. M. Garrison.
Orator—G. L. Hoege.
Chaplain—S. L. Beiler.
Treasurer—T. S. Green.
Guide—J. J. Breining.
Warden—Daniel Hunsecker.
Sentry—Randall Hale.
Trustees—J. F. Richart, John Noble, John F. Heilman.

Present membership, twenty-three.

Among the German pioneers of Loudon were also

JACOB FRUTH.

He was from Beindersheim, in the Palatinate, and settled here in 1833. He died in 1872, at the age of eighty-two years. He was a man highly esteemed for his good sense and good morals.

CHRISTIAN SCHLEMMER

Was in the army of the great Napoleon. He came to Ohio in 1832, and died here in 1874, at the age of eighty-four years.

ABRAHAM PETER

Was born in 1786; located in Loudon in 1840, and died here at the age of eighty years.

JACOB PETER

Was also over eighty years of age when he died.

JOHN GEORGE FRUTH

Was also one of the principal German settler, and sixty-eight years old when he died.

JACOB MERGENTHALER

Came here from Wurtenberg in 1833, and was high in the seventies when he died.

MELCHIOR HEISSERMAN

Also came in 1833 and lived to be seventy-eight years of age.

CHAPTER XXXVIII.

PLEASANT TOWNSHIP.

T. 3, N. R. 15 E.

SO much has already been said of the scenes and incidents that clustered around Fort Seneca in the beginning of this book, and many of the men and women who then attracted our attention there, that now, when I am about to close and leave the kind reader to his own meditations, there is nothing further to say about this grand old township, than to describe some more of the men who helped to make it what it now is. And there is history in their lives also that is well enough to preserve.

URIAH EGBERT.

The Reverend and Venerable Father Thomas Thompson, who more than fifty years ago preached to the people scattered through these wilds, the gospel of Jesus Christ, and who is still living at his old homestead on the South Greenfield road, sent to the *Tiffin Tribune* the following communication, which was published on the second day of November, 1876. It gives a short sketch of Mr. Uriah Egbert. It reads:

A PIONEER GONE.

Uriah Egbert was born August 8, 1791, in Hunderton county, New Jersey. His parents moved to Pennsylvania when their boy was but three years old. and subsequently, in 1814, moved to Fairfield county, Ohio. Here he was married to Susannah Williams July 6, 1815, and united with the M. E. church under the ministry of the Rev. Michael Ellis, in 1816, and of which church he was an active member and officer for more than fifty years. In 1823 he founded a home in the woods of Seneca county, and his home was the preachers' home and a sanctuary for the Lord's people. He was devout in worship, old school in his views and held his views with tenacity. To us he was always kind, and some of our happiest moments were spent in communication with him and his family. He was a liberal supporter of the cause of God. Our last intercourse with him was to receive $100 for the American Bible Society and $100 for the Missionary Society of the M. E. church as the bequest of his late companion.

He departed this life October 1, 1876, aged eighty-five years, two months and three days.

His funeral was attended by a large concourse of neighbors and friends on the following Sabbath. T. THOMPSON.

(The name of the county I have changed to the proper one. There is no Huntington county in New Jersey).

Mr. Egbert's first settlement in this county was on the North Greenfield road, where Samuel Rickenbaugh now lives. He sold to Mr. David Rickenbaugh and moved to the ridge in this township, where he and his wife spent the rest of their days. The most beautiful feature in the life of father Egbert was his quiet, pious, peaceful disposition. He was, indeed, highly esteemed by everybody that knew him. He was a good manager, and with all his liberality, he accumulated property. Egbert's was one of the best conditioned homes on the road between Tiffin and Sandusky. He donated the land where the Ridge Road cemetery now is, and where he and his wife lie buried.

Mrs. Carl, the youngest daughter of Mr. Egbert, says that one revolutionary soldier, ten soldiers of the war of 1812 and fourteen soldiers of the war of the rebellion are buried there. Col. Williams was a brother-in-law of Mr. Egbert—his wife's brother. He served in the war of the revolution five years and lies buried in Adams township, where he died in 1841.

Mrs. Egbert died May 13, 1875.

PHILIP STAUB

Was born in Adams county, Pennsylvania, July 15, 1786. He was married to Margaret Kuhn on the 2d day of February, 1817. He moved to Seneca county and settled in Pleasant township in 1834. He died January 14, 1876. His wife died January 24, 1874. Both lie buried in St. Joseph cemetery in Tiffin. Mrs. Staub was born March 6, 1794.

Mr. Staub was a volunteer in the Hanover company and stationed at North Point, in Baltimore, under Colonel Miller. He was eighty-nine years and six months old when he died, and Mrs. Staub was seventy-nine years, ten months and eighteen days old when she died. Both lived to a fine old age and were very excellent people and good neighbors.

MRS. CALEB RICE.

The subject of this sketch, who is still living near Castalia, in Sandusky county, with her son, M. B. Rice, Esq., was so kind as to send me, by her son, an interesting statement of early characters she knew in this township, and I copy without comment:

Caleb Rice and Daniel Rice were born respectively in 1788 and 1791 in the town of Clarendon, Vermont.

Benjamin Barney and West Barney were natives of Savoy, Berkshire county, Massachusetts. West was born in 1791 and Benjamin in 1795. They were all living some five miles below Fort Ball when I (Annar Barney) came here in 1819. We came here from Saratoga, N. Y. When we arrived at Lower Sandusky my brothers, West and Benjamin, were in attendance at a trial of some parties for robbing old man Spicer. Some four persons had been arrested but only one was convicted. Spicer was a white man but was raised an Indian. The people liked him much.

The Chapmans, Shippys, Spragues, Cheneys, Harris's, Dumonds, Culver, Anson Gray and John Eaton were here.

We were six weeks on the way from Saratoga here. I came with my father, Benjamin, Barney and brother-in-law Friend Orr and Sedate Paddleford.

My father returned east with the intention of moving his family out here, but he died before he reached his home. Paddleford also went back and never returned.

On the 24th of October, 1820, West Barney and Sophronia Wilson were married by Daniel Rice, who was a justice of the peace. This is the first recorded marriage in Sandusky county.

Daniel Rice and I were married December 14, 1820, at Harrington's tavern in Lower Sandusky. We had seven children. The two oldest were born in Seneca county: Susannah in 1821 and Deborah in 1823.

In 1825 we moved to Townsend township, in Sandusky county, where I still reside, at the age of 86 years. My husband died in 1872, aged 81 years.

Caleb went to Illinois in 1840, where he died in 1849. Barney West died a few years ago in Missouri, I think. Benjamin Barney resides in Pike county, Illinois, with his grand children. His own children are all dead. He is a great talker and very much respected. He tells very many laughable old stories and incidents of olden times. He was a captain in the Black Hawk war and was with Abraham Lincoln in the service.

My husband cleared land where Columbus now stands before he came to Seneca about the time the war closed. He was in a New Jersey regiment in the war of 1812.

CORNELIUS FLUMMERFELT

Was born in New Jersey July 10, 1774, in Sussex county and was raised on a farm. In 1804 he was married to Catharine Christman. On the the 2d of May, 1826, they started for Ohio. It took them four weeks to reach Seneca county.

He bought the west half of the southwest quarter of section sixteen. Daniel Rice had a lease on this land from the commissioners of Sandusky county, which he also bought. Rice had built a cabin and Mr. Flummerfelt moved into that.

Of the first wedlock there is but one child living. There were six children of the second marriage and of whom Mr. D. V. Flummerfelt, of Pleasant township is one.

Cornelius Thurnerfelt.

PLEASANT TOWNSHIP.

Mrs. Flummerfelt died in 1847.

Caleb Rice was a neighbor of Mr. Flummerfelt and was the first white settler in the township. He lived on the school section also. His daughter, Uretta Rice, was the first white child born in the county. Mr. Rice was a very decided Universalist.

Mr. Cornelius Flummerfelt was six feet high, of fair complexion; had blue eyes and was very straight and well proportioned. He was of purely German type, very firm in his convictions, slow of speech and fixed in his habits. He stuck to his old clothes with great tenacity and refused to put on new ones until he was compelled to. He voted for every Democratic candidate for president since Washington, always taking a very active part in politics. He died on the 20th day of August, 1871, at the high age of 97 years, 1 month and 10 days. He was one of the positive men of the country. His word was his bond and to be relied upon. He was highly respected and esteemed wherever he had become known.

BRIDGES IN PLEASANT TOWNSHIP—DEATH OF STACKHOUSE AND FIGGINS.

To give a full history of the bridges in this township would make a little chapter by itself. A few facts connected with the subject can only be attempted here.

In the building of each bridge much feeling among people on both sides of the river was enlisted, and each time more as to the locality than the propriety.

The first bridge built in the township was called the "Clark bridge," because Calvin Clark was one of the county commissioners at that time, and instrumental in the project, living here at that time. The bridge was located at the "Ludwig Ford" (so called). Mr. Ludwig owned the adjoining land, in section nine. The location of the bridge created such opposition against Mr. Clark that he was defeated in the convention following, when he was a candidate for re-nomination. The people south of the location of the bridge, where the travel was much greater, felt wronged by it. The bridge is still there, and of general use. It was built in 1854, at a cost of two thousand dollars.

The opposition to this bridge wanted it located at Pool's mill.

In 1870, while Mr. Thomas W. Watson was county commissioner, another bridge was built across the river, called the "Watson bridge." This bridge was located in section twenty-one. The people living near Fort Seneca and Pool's mill wanted the bridge near the mill, and the same old fight was renewed. Pool's mill is in section twenty. A vigorous attack was made upon the commissioners to change the location, but Mr. Watson held the fort. The result was that Mr. Watson was blamed very severely by those who were in favor of a bridge at Pool's mill. Much bad blood was stirred up at these bridge fights in Pleasant, and there was scarcely a citizen in the township that took no part in the fight.

Mr. Watson's bridge was more of an experiment than a good job. The timbers were left exposed, and the bridge was not anchored well. When the great hurricane swept over the northern part of Seneca county in June, 1875, unroofed some of the houses and other buildings in its track, blew down the M. E. church of Fort Seneca, throwing it flat on the ground, it also blew the Watson bridge into the river in a body, leaving the abutments only.

The people living near Fort Seneca (town), on both sides of the river, now began a fresh agitation for a bridge. (The reader who is a stranger in Seneca county, must distinguish between this town of Fort Seneca and the old fort; they are of the same name, but distinct places, more than two miles apart. There is no town at the old fort at all.) The first petitioners wanted a bridge at the Pool mill—often called Fort Seneca mill. Now new efforts were made to have a superstructure put upon the abutments of the Watson bridge, and the conflict grew warm again. Both parties urged as a strong reason for a bridge the great public demand, and cited a very sad occurrence that took place on the 3d day of April, 1848, when two citizens lost their lives in the river for want of a bridge. On that day James M. Figgins, Joshua Stackhouse, George Shannon and John Watson, who lived on the east side of the river, were in a "dug-out" canoe, endeavoring to cross the river to attend the election that came off on that day at the township house, on the west side of the river. The place was near the present "Flummerfelt bridge," now so called. When they were about the middle of the river, the hat of one of the men blew off, and in the effort to catch it the boat upset, and all the men fell into the river. Shannon and Watson reached the shore in safety, but Figgins and Stackhouse were drowned.

This circumstance, with many other reasons, were urged upon the attention of the commissioners for a new bridge by both parties, and especially by those who wanted a bridge built upon the old abutments. In the height of excitement the commissioners determined to build a new bridge near the Pool mill.

The work is done, and the bridge is an honor to the county commissioners and a credit to the county. The friends of the lower bridge were discouraged, and abandoned all hopes of having the old Watson bridge re-built.

Those that know Mr. D. V. Flummerfelt well and intimately need no explanation about him. To strangers, however, it is sufficient to say that he has inherited from his father a great deal of his looks and personal appearance, but more so his German tenacity and perseverance. While others fell back in despair, Mr. Flummerfelt, in his own familiar, friendly way, attended the sessions of the county commissioners occasionally, and once in a while expressed his regret at the failure of the project in re-building the Watson bridge, and while it seemed to have been given up as a lost cause, Mr. Flummerfelt, in his own quiet way, made inquiry amongst the contractors and ascertained the amount for which a bridge could be built below, and then visited the commissioners, who finally offered to pay Mr Flummerfelt $2,500, if he would put a good superstructure upon the old abutments.

This offer was so low that the commissioners themselves had no idea at first that it would be accepted. Lumber, labor and iron were low in price at that time. Mr. Flummerfelt had made his figures; he accepted the proposition, and the present beautiful Howe-truss, on the old abutments of the Watson bridge, is ample proof of the sagacity and perseverance of Mr. Flummerfelt. He pledged his own responsibility for the payment, furnished some 14,000 feet of oak lumber, iron and paint, that cost him some $500 over and above the appropriation.

Mr. Flummerfelt is that much out of pocket, but Pleasant township is the best bridged township in this county.

The bridge is now called the "Flummerfelt bridge," and very appropriately so. It is a fair monument of perseverance and sagacity.

Mr. D V. Flummerfelt is one of the old settlers here now. He was born in Sussex (now Warren) county, New Jersey, October 13th, 1807. He came to Seneca with his father's family. He married Melinda Littler, of Hardy county, Virginia, on the 12th of October, 1837. This union was blessed with five sons and four daughters, all living but one, who died in infancy. George is married, and lives in Sandusky county, Ohio; Matilda is the wife of M. T. Lutz, and resides in Kansas; Ann M. is the wife of Dennis Deran, and lives in Pleasant. The balance are at home with their parents. It takes both brain and muscle to manage nearly a thousand acres of land successfully.

RASSELAS R. TITUS

Was born in New Milford county, Connecticut, on the 22d of July, 1819. His father's family had previously resided in the state of New York, and removed to Ohio in 1833, when they settled in this township, and where the subject of this sketch has lived ever since.

On the 21st of April, 1844, he married Miss Elvira S. Clark, L. Abbott, Esq., solemnizing the marriage. Their children are four living daughters: Augusta P. is the wife of Francis J. Fry; Colena M. married Lorenzo A. Abbott; Flora married Oliver S. Watson, and Littie married Robert Watson.

Mr. Titus' father died in 1835; his mother lived to a fine old age, and died in 1872, when she was eighty-three years old. R. R. Titus started the world on his own hook, when about twenty years of age, by working among the farmers of Pleasant township, at $11 per month at first; next year he got $12, and the next year $14 per month.

In 1859 he was elected a member of the state board of equalization. In 1861 he was elected a member of the house of representatives of the general assembly of Ohio, and re-elected in 1863, serving during the whole war. He counts his wealth by the thousands, and his drafts are honored in all the banks in the country. He is in California on a visit at this writing.

Vincent Bell, Benjamin Seckman, John Brush, Nathan Littler, John Siberal, John Houseman, the Watsons and others came into Pleasant later.

The Sandusky river courses through the western part of the township in great meanderings of nearly twelve miles along its shores. East of Fort Seneca it takes a due east course more than one mile; then taking a horse shoe bend to the southeast, turns north, running more than one mile along the section line between sections fifteen and sixteen. In section nine it turns due west three-quarters of a mile, and northwest, leaving the large, rich bottom lands of Samuel Ludwig on the right bank. These bottom lands in Pleasant have made, and forever will make this township justly celebrated. The uplands are rich in soil, but the bottoms are inexhaustible in fertility. Mr. G. W. Lutz was among the most successful farmers in this township for some time, and until within the last few years. In 1859 he raised from 126 acres of land, 8,655 bushels of corn and 1,645 bushels of wheat. Estimating the corn at thirty cents and the wheat at one dollar per busnel, makes $4,241.50 on these two articles alone for the year, and averaging over eighty bushels to the acre.

Other farmers have done as well, no doubt, and a trip through the township will convince any one of the wealth and beauty of the Sandusky bottoms in summer time as lovely as " when first the Day God looked upon a field of waving corn."

It is said that James Gordon, one of the pioneer commissioners, suggested the name of Pleasant for this township. He could not very well have called it Richland township, for that would have meant them all. If the county had been called Egypt, it would have been very appropriate, but such names as "Pleasant," "Eden" and "Bloom," are very suggestive and do very well.

On the 14th of January, 1836, Erastus Bowe and Vincent Bell caused to be surved on the corners of sections nineteen and twenty, in this township, a town to which they gave the name of Fort Seneca. Any other name would have been more appropriate. It is calculated to mislead the general inquirer and lead him to suppose that the fort had been at or near this place, when, in fact, it was nearly three miles away. McNutt's or Swope's Corners, either of these designated the same town.

Fort Seneca is situate six and a-half miles north of Tiffin and eleven miles south of Fremont on the Columbus state road, and numbers about 200 inhabitants. A pike running from Tiffin to Fremont through Fort Seneca would afford one of the most beautiful drives in northern Ohio. Why not have one?

Pleasant township was organized on the 6th day of June, 1831, and while the Senecas were still roaming over it. The early settlers have already been named and described. The population of the township in 1870 was, 1,352, which increased only 65 in the ten years following, making it 1,417 in 1880.

37

CHAPTER XXXIX.

REED TOWNSHIP.

T. 2, N. R. 17 E.

IT was very wrong that the county officers of Seneca county ever consented to have the proper name of this township mis-spelled into Reed, and be themselves guilty. The *Read* family, after whom the township was named, were of Scotch descent, and invariably wrote their name with an " a," and so it ought to have been preserved.

Seth Read and George Raymond came from Steuben county, New York, and settled upon section twenty-four, in what now constitutes this township, on the 18th day of January, 1825, and were the first settlers in the township. They entered their lands at the Delaware land office.

They were followed soon after by Edward Cassety and Elijah Read, Tunis Croukite, Thomas Bennett, Samuel Scothorn, Isaac Bennett and others.

The township was organized December 5th, 1826. The first election was held at the house of Seth Read, on New Year's day following.

The face of the land in this township is generally undulating, and the soil very fertile. There are no mill streams within its limits, and the grist and saw mills are run by steam.

In 1830 Reed had a population of 264; in 1840, 1,240, and it is now about 1,501.

At a later period A. C. Baker, Benjamin Sanford, John B. Schuyler, Jacob Cole, William P. White, Henry Ryno, James Harrison, Levi Read, W. H. Croukite, John Clark, John Hoover and others were among the distinguished farmers here.

On the 4th day of January, 1838, John Terry and Catharine Beard caused to be laid out on sections five and six, a town, which they called West Lodi. It was surveyed and platted by James Durbin.

The first postmaster was Lyman White, who for many years has lived on College Hill, in Tiffin, where he lives now at his ease, cultivating grapes and peach trees.

Robert P. Frazer was the first physician who settled in Lodi, and he is still there in the practice of his profession, and highly esteemed.

Reedtown was made up of a few cabins on the Columbus and Sandusky turnpike. It was also called Cook's Gate, because a man by the name of Cook kept the toll-gate on the pike at that place. It was simply wicked to collect toll on a mud road. Some called it Kellytown also, because a man by the name of Kelly kept a store there. Hanford's was another name for the same town, because Hanford's tavern was the best between Attica and Bloomer's.

My dear old friend Dr. B. D. Williams settled here at an early day. The place is now familiarly known as Reedtown. It was laid out by Isaac Catlin.

DR. B. D. WILLIAMS

Was born January 18th, 1812, in Orangeville township, Genesee county, New York. In 1821 his father located with his family in Sherman township, Huron county, a few miles east of Reedtown. Here young Williams grew up, and received his education and read medicine three years with Dr. Moses C Sanders, in Peru township, in Huron county.

In 1835 he settled at Reedtown, and commenced the practice of medicine, and here, in 1836, the writer made his acquaintance, which grew into a friendship that has grown warmer, like wine, that grows better with age.

On the 7th of November, 1835, Dr. Williams was married to Miss Harriet Newel LaBarre, of Sherman township, with whom he lived three years, until she died. On the 13th of June, 1841, he was again married to Louisa L. Ludlow, of Norwich, in' Huron county. This union was blessed with three children, two boys, who are married and settled in life, and one daughter, long since dead. Here the Doctor settled in the practice, and so near his old perceptor as to have the benefit of his counsel and help in extreme cases, and where he also met Dr. Dresbach, of Tiffin, in consultation.

In a letter to me the Doctor says, speaking of his early practice:

Many times I had very severe cases among females, when I would have given my horse, bridle, saddle, pill-bag and all I had on earth to be safely and honorably through with my lady patient. Oh! such anxiety! such suspense!! It did often seem as if my little bark would break and go under. There was no help nearer than twelve to fifteen miles, nights pitch dark and mud knee-deep. But God was with me, and I always came through with my patient all O. K. Without boasting, I can safely say that during my practice here of forty-five years, out of 2,200 parturition cases, I never lost one.

Dr. Williams practiced medicine in Peru two years before he came to Reedtown, making forty-seven years in all in constant practice without losing a day, except the time spent in attending lectures at Willoughby University, at the Cincinnati Medical University, and at the Cleveland and Western Reserve College, where he graduated. The Willoughby became merged into the Starling at Columbus afterwards. He is now the veteran physician in that part of the country, and I will say, without flattery (for I never flatter), that the Doctor is highly esteemed in all the country far and near, for his personal excellencies, both as a physician and citizen.

Dr. Williams was so kind as to send me some of his early recollections of Reed, from which I have collated the following:

Captain Hanford was an early settler here. He was one of your plain, outspoken men, swore a little at times, a little rough, but kind hearted. One day while the Captain, with his dog, were out in the woods, and chased a weasel into a hollow log, and while they were trying to catch it, a Presbyterian preacher from Monroeville, whom the Captain did not know, came through the woods and got off his horse to help catch the weasel. So the preacher took his post at one end of the log to watch, with his riding whip held up to strike. The position did not suit Hanford, and he said to the preacher: "You don't hold your whip right, by ——, my friend, hold it so, and strike quick, for they are the d——t, quickest things you ever saw, b————." Sure enough! The Captain scared the weasel out, and when the preacher struck, he hit the ground about a rod behind the weasel. "There," says Captain Hanford, "I told you so, b————." The preacher then asked where Captain Hanford lived. The Captain gave him the information, and they separated. The preacher stopped at the house, and Mrs. Hanford, who was a Presbyterian, and had not seen a preacher since she had left the "land of steady habits" about three years before, and was very glad to entertain him. After a while the Captain came home and was quite surprised to see the weasel catcher. Captain Hanford said to him: "I guess I must have scared you with my swearing." The preacher said: "Yes, I was frightened a little and greatly surprised to think that a man having such a Christian lady for a wife would indulge in such language." The Captain felt the effect of the rebuke, but entertained the preacher with his usual hospitality.

Thomas Bennett was the first postmaster in this township, and it was then called Read postoffice. Mr. Catlin had this town surveyed, but never had the plat recorded. It was then called "Catlinville." It was also called "Readsburg." Tunis Croukite and Thomas Bennett were both old settlers and members of the Baptist church at what is now called Omar. They had some difficulty, and agreed that they would not be buried in the same cemetery. The church at Omar has a very respectable cemetery. Bennett owned the land in and around the grave yard, and Croukite owned the land across the pike, adjoining. Croukite died first, and was buried on his land some sixty rods east of the grave yard, then Bennett died, and was buried in the grave yard. Now large monuments adorn the graves of both, in sight of each other, as monuments of bad blood in life.

George Raymond, another old settler here, was the father of triplets, boys, which he called Abraham, Isaac and Jacob. The last two live in our town; the former has been dead twenty years.

Mr. Schuyler was also an early settler. His son is the celebrated mathematician at Baldwin University, at Berea, Ohio.

Elijah Read, another good old pioneer, died about five years ago.

Samuel and John Cassaty were both poor when they came here from Steuben county, New York, but by hard labor and economy, had accumulated quite a fortune, until some twelve years ago, robbers relieved them of about $12,000. John has since died.

Williard Whitney, a merchant of our town, closed his business here with a few hundred dollars left, with which he went to Michigan, bought land, got wealthy, and would have been happy, had he not become blind. His wife had to feed him like a child ten years, when he died at eighty-five.

Dr. Amos Witter lost his wife here. He went west, was elected to Congress, and got rich.

Loren Knopp, a merchant, was quite well off. He had the kidney disease. He moved to Attica, where he soon died. He was to have been married soon, so he willed much of his fortune to his affianced.

Dr. I. T. Gilbert became involved, sold out, and went to Bryan, Ohio. There he invested what little means he had in real estate, which advanced rapidly. The small-pox broke out in Bryan, and Dr. Gilbert having had them once, was allowed to take all the small-pox cases, which soon built him up, but he was not allowed to see any other patients during that time. The Doctor got into very comfortable circumstances, and died there at the age of eighty-two years. He formerly lived here.

John Zeppermick had some bad luck here, but after he sold out and moved to Wood county, he accumulated some property. He owns a good little farm, and seems to be happy in praising God.

Captain Hanford died of apoplexy about twenty-five years ago. Edward, the hotel keeper, died of dropsy, the effects of trying to look through the bottom of a tumbler. James Hanford lived a roving life, and finally broke into the Michigan penitentiary at Jackson for ten years.

Jas. Harrison, whom you also knew, died at his son's house, at the old place.

To show you how Reed looked in former times, let me tell you a short incident. I was called one dark night to visit a sick lady. We had to go through the woods, of course, and before we had proceeded far, the messenger and I both became entangled in the top of a tree that had fallen across the road. In the scrabble to get out, I lost my hat. The messenger said it would not do to hunt for it, had no time, was in a hurry, could lose no time, " must bring you in a hurry, Doctor, so come right along." So I went bareheaded. It was warm weather, however, and there was no suffering, but going home next day without my hat made a comical show. They said Dr. Williams must have been tight last night.

The writer heard a good story told of Dr. Williams, which is too good to be lost. Soon after he was married, and before they had gone to housekeeping, his wife had her home at her father's, in Sherman township, still. So one Saturday evening the young Doctor started, rather late, however, to pay a visit to his father-in-law, and surprise the young lady. It was in the fall, and the leaves had covered the road. Night came on, and the road was no longer discernable. The Doctor got out of the saddle and felt around for the road or path, but could not find it. He hitched his horse to a tree and gave the "bush hallo" several times, but nobody responded only the owls. The Doctor came to the conclusion that the troubles of a married life had commenced in dead earnest. After crowing around through the woods for two or three hours, a lady accidentally heard him and answered. She got a man up out of bed, and sent him after the strange voice. The man was afraid that it might be a panther, but found the lost Doctor, and took him to the house. It was the house of a stranger, however, and two miles away from the house of the bride. In the morning the horse was found and cared for, and a new start taken for the father-in-law. He took breakfast with his wife's people, and they all had a good laugh at the Doctor's night's adventure.

Seneca John, who was executed on the reservation, as already related, used to hunt through Reed, and had a wigwam on the knoll where Dr. Williams' house now stands, in 1821–2. His visits continued up to 1830, and he generally brought his whole family with him. At an evening meal, and while a large kettle of hot water was suspended on a pole over the fire, a daughter of Seneca John was lying on the ground before the fire. The pole was nearly burnt through, and broke, spilling the hot water over the child. They wrapped her in a blanket and took her to the house near by, where Dr. Williams attended her. In removing the blanket the flesh of the poor sufferer literally clung to it, leaving her almost a skeleton. Dr. Williams did all in his power to relieve her sufferings, but death assisted him.

After her death William Williams made a sled, to be drawn by hand, and a number of Indian boys and a mournful cortege conveyed the corpse to the Seneca burying ground. Seneca John became a very warm friend to Dr. Williams.

In the summer of 1834 some movers passed through Reedtown, who had a son about sixteen years of age. In the night he was taken sick. It was a clear case of cholera. He died, and was buried before morning, and the mournful parents went on.

There are six very good church edifices in Reed. The township is supplied with excellent school houses and a good corps of teachers.

When the M. E. church organized northern Ohio in 1830 or 1832, they made the Fort Ball circuit extend east to include a part of Huron county. The preacher appointed for this circuit was a very young man by the name of Arza Brown. He had a fine riding horse, with which he swam the creeks and rivers, tying a suit of dry clothes on his shoulders. These he put on before he commenced preaching. His widowed mother lived at Sandusky. He was well liked and welcomed everywhere, and among those also that did not belong to his church. He became a very able preacher. He afterwards lived in Cincinnati, where he died soon after the rebellion, eighty-three years old.

One very happy feature in frontier life was the mutual enjoyment of the society amongst the old and young. It was a common practice in the winter time to visit some neighbor in the evening. A yoke of oxen were hitched to a sled with a box full of straw, that held the family and some neighbors also.

Arrived at the house, the children and women were "thawed out" by the large hickory fire, and after disposing of a meal of roasted pig, corn cake, potatoes, turnips, squash, wild-grapes, honey, etc., the dance commenced, which often lasted until the dawn of day in the east admonished the dancers that the cows, horses, sheep and hogs at home had to be looked after.

At these dances it was often surprising to see the old men and women move over the pungeon floor with the spring and elasticity of youth, and with a grace and gentle mean that would do honor to a ball room of these latter days.

"Buck and Bright" hitched again to the sled—all aboard! Some with cold chicken or cold pork and corncake for a piece on the road; all started for home, all happy in having had a good old time.

In Dr. Williams' father's family there were five boys and two girls. As the children grew up they needed education, and there was no school in the neighborhood. The mother saw the necessity of a teacher, and for want of another, she taught the oldest, and as they became advanced, she compelled them to teach the younger. Every stranger that came into the house was induced to confer some useful knowledge to the family, and thus the children became educated without a school house to go to. As they grew up, they were all qualified to teach school. One of the Doctor's brothers commenced when he was only sixteen years old, and taught school for forty winters in succession. So much for a mother's resolution to have her children educated.

I have drawn very largely on the Doctor's kindness for the above sketches, and for which I feel thankful, but the flattering remarks, though very true, about myself, are omitted for modesty sake.

Esquire T. M. Kelley was so kind as to send me some historic information, from which I extract:

Friend Lang:

My father, Benjamin Kelley (and whom you well knew), was born in New Jersey, June 6th, 1793. He was a soldier in the war of 1812. Mother, Mahitabel Travis, was born April 3d, 1793, in Tioga county, Pennsylvania. They were married August 19th, 1813, in Seneca county, New York, and lived in Steuben county, in that state, until the spring of 1834, when they moved to this township with a family of six boys and two girls, and settled on the east half of the northwest quarter of section one. They bought the land of a Mr. Davis, who had entered it.

There were but a few trees chopped, and the body of a log cabin erected without a roof. The family stayed at Captain Hanford's hotel until father and the older boys cut and split clapboards and hewed pungeon for the floor and doors. Then we moved into the cabin.

The only place mother had to do her cooking was a kind of a fire-place built of cobble stones, between two oak stumps, from about the 20th of April until the 1st of August that year. It took a barrel of flour and a bushel of corn meal every four weeks to feed us all. The bread was baked in a tin reflector between those oak stumps.

On the 12th day of April the cattle could get a good living in the woods. We worked them all day, and at night we put a bell on one of them and let them go. Sometimes the boys would have to hunt a week to find them again, but generally they were in hearing distance.

The first wheat we raised father took to Cold Creek with an ox cart to get it ground. It took nearly a week to make the trip.

My youngest brother was born after we came here, August 16th, 1836, making a family of seven boys and two girls, all now living except the oldest girl.

Mother and the girls carded and spun the wool and flax, wove the cloth, and cut and made our clothes; the tow-linen for summer wear and linsey woolsey for winter wear. They also made bags, towels, table-cloths, sheets and pillow-slips of flax, raised, pulled, rotted and dressed by the family. The youngest sister, Mrs. J. P. Moore, spun flax at Fremont at the celebration of the centennial tea party of Boston harbor.

Mother died May 31st, 1860, at Elmore, Ohio. Father died April 12th, 1863, at Reedtown.

Thomas Bennett was the first postmaster appointed here, but would not serve, whereupon William Knapp was appointed. Knapp was a storekeeper, and sold the store to a Mr. Ackley, who was killed by the falling of a bent in raising a barn for Harrison Cole. John Emery had his leg broken by the same fall. My father framed the barn. Respectfully your friend.

T. M. KELLEY.

The town of Omar never flourished. Reed is altogether a farming township. The soil is rich, and produces great crops, rapidly increasing the wealth of the township. The beautiful school houses in Reed show conclusively that the cause of education is not neglected.

There is a noticeable elevation running north and south through the township, a little east of the center, but not high enough to be called a ridge, yet sufficiently so to make a water-shed.

Attica station, on the Baltimore & Ohio road, is located in this township, on section thirty-five. This railroad crosses and cuts the entire southern tier of sections of this township, except section thirty-one.

CHAPTER XL.
SCIPIO TOWNSHIP.

T. 2, N. R. 16 E.

Nobody will now dispute the fact that the Anways were the first who identified their names with the early settlement of Scipio township. About the time of the land sales at Delaware, William Anway, from Scipio, Cayuga county, New York, settled in the woods upon land that is now embraced within the geographical limits of this township. It is said that when Mr. Anway arrived and located here in 1821, there were two families living upon the school section, who soon moved away.

The late Mr. Laughery, the father of my old friend, James Laughery, was the first man who purchased land in this township, but the first patent recorded for land purchased in the county was that mentioned in the history of Clinton, by a Mr. Anway.

C. T. Westbrook, John Wright, Adam Hance, Abraham Spencer, Isaac Nichols, Mr. Stevens, Mr. Osborn, Timothy P. Roberts, Morrison McMillon, E. H. Brown, Seth F. Foster, Nathan Foster and William B. Mathewson may be mentioned as early settlers.

Mention has already been made of the time and manner of organizing the township, and that it then took in Reed and contained sixteen inhabitants, etc. It was also stated that Mr. Anway named it after his old home in New York. The time and manner of its survey was also mentioned in chapter x.

The petition for the organization was presented to the county commissioners on the 6th of December, 1824. The petition was granted, of course, and an election ordered to be held on the following 25th day of December, 1824—Christmas day. At this election seventeen votes were cast. Of those voting, thirteen received office, leaving but four to make up what is called the "sovereign people," and the other thirteen were their servants. Let us hope that this distinctive feature in our peculiar American institutions may ever so remain; that our public officers shall be regarded as public servants only and never be permitted to become our masters. So mote it be.

At this first election in Scipio William B. Mathewson was elected clerk; John Wright, Seth F. Foster and Jonathan Nichols, trustees; Adam Hance and Joseph Osborn, overseers of the poor; William Stevens and Ezechial Sampson, fence viewers; William Anway, Jr., lister; William Anway, treasurer; Cornelius T. Westbrook and Morrison McMillen, constables; John Anway and E. H. Brown, supervisors.

Both Rocky creek and Willow creek run through Scipio township, yet Mr. Butterfield says in his history, on page 127: "There is not a stream of water in the township."

In 1840 the population of Scipio was 1,556. The township has rapidly increased in wealth since that time, but less so in population. In 1870 it was 1,642; in 1880 it is 1,836.

In 1834 Sidney Smith caused to be surveyed in this township, upon the corners of sections fifteen, sixteen, twenty-one and twenty-two, a town, which he called Republic. The place was known for a long time as Scipio Center. R. M. Shoemaker (now in Cincinnati) was the surveyor.

Adam Hance and John Wright had entered the larger portion of the land upon which the town was laid out, in the year 1822, Hance owning the east and Wright the west part. John Wright built the first dwelling house upon the plat. The town did not improve very rapidly until the prospect of a railroad from Sandusky began to agitate the people, and when in 1841 the railroad did come, Republic became quite a trading place. Stores and wearhouses, shops and factories sprung up as by magic and the town looked like a bee-hive on a large scale. Such was the importance of the place at our time that Melmore became so much excited as to form a joint stock company for the purpose of building a railroad to Republic. (See chapter XXXIII., Eden township).

It has already been incidentally mentioned that when, on the night of the 21st of May, 1841, the court house in Tiffin burnt, efforts were made to remove the county seat to Republic. General Stickney can tell something about that move. He is one of the most enterprising of all the public men in the county of Seneca, and has, in a great measure, stamped his individuality upon Scipio township and the history of Seneca county generally. And while on this subject, let me say of him, that he was born August 31, 1811, in Franklin county, New York. He came to Seneca county on the 4th of July, 1836. On the 11th of October, 1836, he married Emma, daughter of Timothy P. Roberts, Esq., of Scipio township. Their only child is a daughter.

General Stickney has a large farm of about seven hundred acres, one mile east of Republic, where he lives in comfort with plenty around him.

He has been one of the leading men of the Democratic party of the county ever since he came here. He was justice of the peace in Republic, and held the office of postmaster there for sixteen years. He was a member of the convention that formed the present constitution of Ohio. In 1867 he was elected a member of the house of representatives of the Ohio legislature, and was re-elected in 1869; was a member of the Ohio senate in 1875, and last winter was appointed by Governor Foster, a member of the board of directors of the Ohio penitentiary. The General is still vigorous and active. Mrs. Stickney is a lady of refined mind, and both are highly esteemed.

After the new line of the Cincinnati, Sandusky & Cleveland railroad was made straight through from Sandusky to Tiffin, Bellevue, Lodi and Republic were left out in the cold, and the change played mischief with Republic. Business went all to pieces, houses were deserted and the town soon assumed an air of general dilapidation. It remained in that condition until the making of the Baltimore & Ohio railroad, which has infused new life into Republic, and much business is done there now.

A little east of Republic is a large, three-story brick building that was once the Seneca county academy. It was incorporated by an act passed March 4, 1836, and organized February 8, 1844. The capital stock amounted to $3,000, and was divided into 300 shares of $10 each. There were nine trustees. Timothy P. Roberts was the first president. E. T. Stickney was the treasurer; S. W. Shepard, principal. The institution flourished for many years and the name of Schuyler has given it an almost undying fame. It is to be regretted that the academy was ever permitted to fail. It could and should have been saved. It was a credit to Republic and to Seneca county.

TIMOTHY P. ROBERTS.

Mrs. E. T. Stickney was so kind as to furnish me with the following sketch of her honored father, and I take pleasure in copying it here:

Timothy P. Roberts was born at Middletown, Connecticut, June 11, 1784. Two years later his parents moved with their family to Massachusetts and located in Lee, Berkshire county. Timothy lived with his parents at Lee until he arrived at the age of eighteen years, when he was apprenticed to Deacon Stone to learn the trade of a wheelwright. He moved with Deacon Stone and his family to the town of Locke, Cayuga county, New York.

On the 18th of January, 1808, he was inter-married with Rhoda Chadwick, formerly of Lee, Massachusetts, and settled in Scipio, New York. This union was blessed with seven children, three of whom died in infancy. Emma, now the wife of General E. T. Stickney, and Jane, the wife of S. S. Dentler, are all that remain of the family, except grand children.

Mr. Roberts emigrated from Scipio, New York, to Scipio, in Seneca county, Ohio, with his family, in 1825, and entered 160 acres of land, upon one-half of which he resided the balance of his days. The other eighty acres he gave to his oldest son, Ansel C. Roberts.

Mr. Roberts died at the age of 83 years, 7 months and 17 days, on the 28th of January, 1868. Mrs. Rhoda Roberts died at the residence of her daughter, Emma, March 31, 1872, aged 80 years, 1 month and nineteen days.

Mr. Roberts was about five feet, seven inches high, stout and compactly built; he had a large, well balanced head, and a well proportioned, manly countenance. He was of fair complexion, slow of speech, of clear judgment and strong in his decision. He was mentally, physically and morally strong.

When Mr. William Anway came to this township, in 1821, he had eleven children; the oldest was twenty-one years old, and the youngest but two years. He built the first cabin here, with the help of his family and one man—Benjamin Huntley, from Huron county. Mr. Anway and his son cut the first road through the woods to Tiffin, winding along on the highest ground they could find. Anway's cabin stood near the corner of the Marion state road and the South Tiffin road. The spot is now covered by a circle of pines planted there in memory of the first home of the Anway family. The children of William Anway were John, Susan, William, George, Fanny, Austin, Erastus, Hannah, Harrison and Phoebe.

Moses Smith put up a small frame building across the road from Anways, in which he kept a store.

Robert Dutton was the first man that died in this township, and was buried on his farm, which is now owned by Mr. Frank Fox. William Pierce, a colored man, put up and carried on the first blacksmith shop in the township. Mary, the daughter of John Anway, was the first white child born in the township. She is now the wife of Mr. John Wilcox, living in Republic. Her father's was the first marriage in Scipio township. John is still living at this writing.

ARCHIBALD STEWART

Came here from Lycoming county, Pennsylvania, and settled on section twenty-nine, in 1824. He had two children when he came, and on the 29th of August, the same year, his son James W. was born at their new home here, where he still lives, having lived no other place all this time. The old cabin stood about eighty rods from their present dwelling. The Indians used to camp near their cabin, on the east bank of Rocky creek. There was a very old Indian among them, who had large silver rings in his nose. He was in the habit of boasting that he had the tongues of ninety-nine white men, and needed just one more to make one hundred. The Indians often stayed over night at Mr. Stewart's.

Archibald Stewart was born on the 9th of June, 1797, in Lycoming county, Pennsylvania. He was raised on a farm, and married Martha Johnson, who died here. He is about five feet nine inches high, has a peculiar deep, sonorous voice, is well proportioned and well preserved; has large blue eyes, a fine forehead; his heavy head of hair, which was once a dark brown, has become white by the heavy frosts of Scipio township, but he still walks erect, and is as good and interesting in conversation as ever, bidding fair to become a centennarian.

Mr. Isaac B. Witter tells me that in 1827 Jonathan Witter, Sr., moved from Ontario county, New York, into Reed township, near Captain Hanford's and Dr. Gilbert's. The writer knew Mr. Witter very well. Isaac B. has now lived in Scipio over forty years.

Philip and Adam Steinbaugh, Humphrey Bromley, Michael Hendel, John A. Gale, Chancey Rundell, J. H. Drake, Dr. Maynard, William Parker, Sylvester Watson, the Neikirks, A. H. and R. G. Perry and Michael Chamberlain may also be said to belong to the pioneers here.

N. P. COLWELL,

When about twenty years old, emigrated from Madison county, New York, to Thompson township, in this county, where he arrived at his step-father's, Joseph Philo, on the 9th of October, 1831. In 1832 the election was held at Esquire Knight's cabin, a few rods east of John Royers, where Colwell voted for Jackson for president of the United States. He lived in Thompson two years, and then went to Amsden's Corners (Bellevue), where he built a wagon and carriage shop, and carried on the business for five years, when he returned to New York, where he married his wife, and returned here, located in Republic in August, 1838, where he has lived on the same street ever since. Here he built a shop, and carried on the wagon and carriage business until failing health compelled him to quit. The people elected him township clerk, and he opened the first office in the then new town hall, in the spring of 1850. He continued in office for twenty years, until stricken down by paralysis in 1870 He held the office of township clerk eleven years, and was justice of the peace sixteen years; he was mayor of Republic and member of the council all the time; a member of the board of education seventeen years in succession. During these long years

SCIPIO TOWNSHIP.

of official life he transacted a great deal of legal business, settling estates of deceased persons and attending to guardianships. During and since the war he attended to soldiers claims free of charge, and until a license of $10 was required. This he paid for eight years, and his work in that line increased until on the 27th day of December, 1870, he was stricken with paralysis, when for several months he could not write. He recovered sufficiently, however, to attend to notarial and other office business in his room, where he is confined most of the time Nervous rheumatism in his feet and legs interfere with his walking very much, and he goes out only on clear, warm days.

Friend Colwell said to me in a letter, describing the beauties of Thompson in its wild state:

All the land about Flat Rock (i. e., where it has been built since) was a wild prairie. In the spring time large crops of herbage sprang up, and in May and June it was the most beautiful flower garden I ever saw—wild flowers of all forms, shapes and colors, equal to any cultivated flowers, gave a delightful fragrance to all that country. Snow's cabin, north of where Flat Rock now stands, was the only human habitation in all that region. There were large herds of deer roaming over these prairies. They could be seen almost any time of day swinging their antlers as they cropped the herbage. The scenery was wild and grand beyond description, a perfect Garden of Eden, except the apples. When frost killed the vegetation and the grass had become dry, fires swept all over the country and left it bare. The Indians set it on fire for hunting purposes.

LANCE TODD

Was born on the 7th day of January, 1806, in Frederick county, Maryland, the son of Thomas and Mary Todd. They arrived in Fort Ball on the 8th of August, 1828, and the whole family soon thereafter settled in the northwestern part of Scipio township. There were, besides the parents, three brothers and two sisters, and each had a piece of land in that neighborhood.

Nathaniel Norris was married to one of the girls in Maryland, and the other married Lott Norris, after the Todd family came out here.

Lance Todd built a cabin in the woods on his own land and afterwards put up a good, two-story log house, in which he still resides. He was married here to Mary Miller in 1834, and has two children. The whole family is still living, but the parents, brothers and sisters of Mr. Todd are dead.

When the family settled here on section eight, William Scoville lived on the south end of the same section. Evan Dorsey had a house raised on his land also, but nobody lived in it. They had to make a road out from their place every direction they wanted to go. Abraham Smith came into this neighborhood soon after the Todds settled here; also John Hall.

After the reservation came into market, the country settled up very rapidly, and soon the land was all taken up. Then roads were opened, land cleared, and houses put up, so that it began to look like an old country.

Mr. Todd has about seventy-five acres cleared and about thirty-five acres in woods. He helped to open and start six farms in this neighborhood, and still lives on the place where he located, fifty two years ago.

CHAPTER XLI.

SENECA TOWNSHIP.

T. 1, N. R. 14 E.

IN some previous chapter mention was made of the township of Seneca, when first organized, embracing all that part of Seneca county lying west of the Sandusky river. Every township that was organized in this territory afterwards reduced it in size until finally it was confined to its proper geographical limits (See chapter x.)

The first election held in this township was on Monday, the 1st day of June, 1820, while Seneca county was still a part of Sandusky county. At the next annual election the following officers were chosen, viz: West Barney, John Lay and David Risdon, trustees; John Eaton, clerk, (it is said that he named Eden township after himself); Benjamin Barney, treasurer, (he still lives in Pike county, Illinois,); Joseph Keller and Daniel Rice, overseers of the poor; James Montgomery, Erastus Bowe and Joel Chaffin, supervisors; P. Wilson, lister; Asa Pike, appraiser; Thomas Nicholson and Abner Pike, fence viewers; John Boughton and Joel Lee, constables.

At the state election in the fall of the same year the whole number of votes polled in Seneca township, comprising about three-fourths of the whole county, was twenty-six. (See chapter x.)

In 1830 the population had increased to 369; in 1840, to 1,393 (then Seneca proper); in 1870 it numbered 1,580. It did not reach that number in 1880, when it is only 1,537.

The early settlers in the township, as now constituted, were Henry St. John, William McCormick, Alexander Bowland, John Galbreath, Peter Weikert, Joseph Canahan, William Kerr, Caleb Brundage, Daniel Hoffman, John Yambert, David Foght, William Harmon, Jacob Staib, Benjamin Harmon, John Blair, George Heck, Jacob Wolfe, John Waggoner, James Aiken, James Brinkerhoff, John Crocker, Gustavus Reiniger, Jacob Kroh, Amos Nichols, John Withelm and others.

There was also an Indian grant in this township to Catharine Walker,

38

a Wyandot woman, and to John Walker, her son, who was wounded in the service of the United States. It was a section of 640 acres lying mostly within the present limits of Seneca township, and directly west of the Van Meter section. This grant was secured to these Walkers at the treaty of 1817, at the foot of the rapids of the Miami of the Lake. The writer knew the old lady and William Walker, another of her sons, when they kept store at Upper Sandusky. Judge Lugenbeel bought a large part of the section when the Walkers sold it.

On the 15th of April, 1845, Henry F. Kaestner, William Brinkerhoff and John Campbell caused to be surveyed, on section nineteen, a town, to which was given the name of Berwick (Mr. Campbell came from Berwick, in Pennsylvania, and named this new town after that old one. The Berwick in Pennsylvania is also the birthplace of the wife of the writer.) Berwick is a station on the Cincinnati, Sandusky & Cleveland railroad, eight miles from Tiffin, and is the only village in the township.

Seneca is one of the wealthy townships in the county. The soil is rich and under a good state of cultivation. Its citizens are intelligent and enterprising. Their homes exhibit taste and comfort.

Mention should also be made of some other old settlers here, German pioneers that located in Seneca township about the time the writer came to Tiffin: John Dockweiler, Conrad Schmitt, Ignatz Neumeyer, John Houck, George Weisenberger, Michael Wagner, John Feck, Jacob Kappler, Michael Stippich, Conrad Heirholzer and John Wank.

FRANCIS JOSEPH HIRT.

The reader must excuse the space occupied in the mention of this subject. I would rather speak of men—yes, and of good men, than to describe brutes. The event I am about to describe here took place nearly forty years ago, and has almost been forgotten. A "logging" meant the hauling together and piling up of logs to make a clearing, preparatory to the burning of them. When the logs were cut to the proper length to be handled, and everything was ready for the work, the neighbors were invited for a certain day to come to the "logging." Some brought their ox teams, others their axes, and worked hard all day. The neighboring women came to help the housewife getting dinner and supper for the men, and after supper it was very usual to have a dance and a general good time. It was very customary in those days to have plenty of whisky at these loggings, raisings, sheep-washings, harvests, etc., and sometimes a man would take too much.

A Mr. John Feck lived on a piece of forty acres in the southwest quarter of section five, in this township; Francis J. Hirt also lived in the neighborhood. Both were at the logging of somebody else in the neighborhood, whose name has escaped me. This was early in the spring of 1841. The man that had the logging, Hirt, Feck, and perhaps the whole crowd were Germans. After supper a dance was started. Hirt took part in the dance. Feck stood at one side of the room looking on. Hirt had a pocket-knife in his hand, and becoming very boisterous, somebody tried to quiet him, and during the muddle Hirt stabbed Feck in the belly, cutting a terrible gash, letting out his bowels, and from which he died in a short time. Hirt was arrested and placed in the log jail in Tiffin.

He was a man near six feet high, well proportioned, and very muscular. His carriage was very straight. His pale face contrasted very violently with his very black, bushy hair, large black eyebrows, and his dark, flashy, large eye. He had a very low forehead, clenched lips, and heavy lower jaw; thick, short neck, and very long, bony arms. His nose was short and fleshy, and his teeth were regular and beautiful; in fact, his teeth were the only thing beautiful about him. His whole make-up presented the desperado.

On the 25th day of May, 1841, the grand jury presented an indictment in the court against Hirt, for murder in the first degree, and the prosecuting attorney, Mr. Joel W. Wilson, was busily engaged preparing the case for trial. Cowdery and Wilson were law partners at that time, and the witnesses being nearly all Germans, the writer, then reading law in the office, was of some service to the prosecuting attorney in ascertaining what the witnesses could testify.

Immediately after the occurrence, Dr. George W. Sampson, of McCutchenville, was sent for, who arrived while Mr. Feck was still living. He returned the intestines and sewed up the wound, but Feck had already become delirious. Hirt's knife was found with blood on it, behind a big German chest that stood in the room where the dance took place and the murder was committed. It seems that Hirt threw the knife there after he had cut the fatal wound.

The court commenced on the 24th day of May, 1841, a few days after the fire of the court house. The court was held in the M. P. church, on Monroe street, now fixed up for a dwelling house by Mr. F. Marquart, of Tiffin. When the case of the state of Ohio against Francis J. Hirt was called, it was continued for trial to the next term of the court. It will be remembered that at the fire of the court house, the old log jail at the southeast corner of the court house lot, was saved. Hirt was in this jail.

The following named persons were subpœnaed as witnesses for the state and put under their own personal recognizances for their appearances at the next term, each in the sum of $100, viz: John Neumeyer, John Wank, William Kabala, Joseph Keppler, Henry Naeth, John Weng, Joseph Meng, Joseph Smith, Francis Lenhart, Anthony Sanders, Joseph Hummell, Clements Marks, John Baptist Ilchert and Alexander Swartz (Schwartz).

Hirt broke jail and escaped to Canada, where he lived for many years. His wife instituted proceedings in court, by which she became the owner of all the property of her husband, and it was supposed for a while that she would follow him to Canada. She was a very pious lady, and settled in New Reigel, in this county, near her church, where she lived until about two years ago. She had no child, but her mother lived with her. Hirt himself made his way to Iowa City, Iowa, from whence he kept up a regular correspondence with his wife, and finally prevailed upon her to sell her property in New Reigel and meet him in Iowa City. She complied, and taking her old mother with her, met Hirt at Iowa City. The sight of her husband so horrified her that she could not consent to have him live with her, and finally absolutely refused. She had already purchased a house and lot in the suburbs of Iowa City, where she lived with her mother.

One afternoon, when the two ladies were alone in the house, Hirt came, drew a revolver, and shot his wife and then her mother. It is also said that he set the house on fire and hung himself.

Both ladies were killed, however, and the particulars in the closing scene of the horrible life of this monster are not known here. If they can be ascertained before these pages go to the printer, the proper connections will be added.

My old friend John Houck, the merchant, says the murder of John Feck took place after the raising of a log barn, and not after a logging. I write from my own best recollections and those of others that knew of the occurrence at the time.

GUSTAVUS G. REINIGER

Is one of the German pioneers of Seneca county. The history of Seneca township would not be complete without a short sketch of him. He was born in Vayingen, in Wurtemberg, Germany, on the 9th day of April, 1801; attended school at Attersteig, in the black woods (Schwartzwald), and was afterwards placed under the tutorship of Prof. Heller, in Kalb, where he studied the languages. He next spent two years as a student of the Agricultural Academy at Hohheim. After he left the academy he became book-keeper (actuary) in the office of the "Comptroleur of Forests" at Beutelsbach, in Wurtemberg. Here he made the acquaintance of Fraulein Rosalia Durr, and was married to her in 1822. He remained in this office until the spring of 1832, when he moved with his family to America, and settled in the woods of Seneca township, in August of that year, and where he still resides. His oldest son is dead, and two others are in Iowa, one of whom is a distinguished lawyer there.

It is customary in Germany for all officers in the forest departments to wear uniforms of dark green cloth. The early settlers of Tiffin will remember Mr. Reiniger with his green coat buttoned up to his chin with yellow buttons, and his friendly face smoothly shaven, except the familiar goatee, which he wears to this day.

It is no easy task to comprehend and bring up before the mind the full scene in the change, when a man, with his family, leaves the association of friends and the scenes of his earlier days, and exchanges a life of refinement in the classic hills and valleys of Germany for that of an American frontiersman in the forest. And is it not strange to see so many of that class of men and women quietly embrace and enjoy the free and independent life of an American farmer? Such, however, is the nature of our free institutions, that any honest livelihood here is preferable to the gilded wrongs of European oppressions, and a life under them. *The true man* is the American nobleman.

There are three daughters and two sons still living. Mrs. Reiniger died on the 5th of May, 1869.

THE STAIB FAMILY

Were also among the pioneer settlers of Seneca township. My old friend Mr. Jacob Staib prepared a sketch for me in German, from which I abstract the following:

I was born in Grosz-Heppach, in Wurtemberg, Germany. In the year 1833 I came to America, and landed in Tiffin on the 28th of August, in that year. I worked for Mr. Fellnagel awhile, but my first work here was for Mr. Reiniger. I entered the land where we lived so long, and in 1834 I commenced chopping and clearing on the old Staib farm, and built a house, into which I moved on the 1st day of April, 1835, and where I had no other company than my dog. I bought a yoke of oxen, a cow and some chickens. In May John Ellwanger came and worked with me until my father and the family came on. Father was born on the 6th of August, 1779, in Wurtemberg, when it was yet a Duchy. He died March 28th, 1867. My mother, who is still living with me, and whose maiden name was Elizabeth C. Kloepfer, was born also in Wurtemberg, October 8th, 1783. The family arrived here July 9th, 1835. Now we all worked together, but had many troubles to contend with. Provisions became scarce, and we were compelled to grate unripe corn to make bread. I was lucky enough to buy a barrel of flour from a team that came from the south for $7.00. The man sold the balance of the load in Tiffin for twice that sum.

The German grape plants father brought with him began to bear in two years from the time they were planted, and produced delightful fruit, but in 1843 the mildew affected them, and finally destroyed them. We raised pines from seed we brought with us, which became the firstever green trees in the county. We also had the first grafted fruit in the county, cherries, plums. apricots, peaches, etc. We partook of the work and hardships incident to frontier life. The climate was very unfavorable; great storms, heavy frosts, and thawing weather, interchanging rapidly, was very destructive to wheat, and we harvested more cheat than wheat. (What has become of the cheat anyway? Why are not farmers pestered with it now?—WRITER.)

In the spring of 1834 we had frosts from the 12th until the 20th of May. The fruit trees froze, vegetables, the wheat, and even the leaves on the trees in the woods, so that on the 1st of June the woods looked like winter time. The springs were very wet; the summers exceedingly hot and dry. In the summer of 1834 we were pestered greatly with squirrels; the woods were literally filled with them. We could raise nothing within a few rods of the fences. They often destroyed whole fields of wheat and corn. The woods were full of ravenous animals also, that made it almost impossible to raise poultry or hogs for a while.

In 1840 a cow belonging to Martin Spitler died, and the wolves devoured her in two nights. In 1858 I found a nest of young wolves on my farm. about forty rods from the river, in a hollow tree, where we burned them up. The old one made the nights hideous with her howling.

We also had our share of malarious fevers, and at times were not able to wait upon each other. Sometimes we could not take care of our crops, but there is nothing like good neighbors. There were no rich people here then. and therefore we had no thieves ; there was nothing to steal. The greater number of the old pioneers have passed away, and there are but a few of us left who can look back upon those early days, which were, after all, among our most happy times, in spite of all hard work and privations.

In December, 1833, we built a school house. Our district embraced nearly all the township. We all met on the same day, chopped down the trees. hauled the logs together, raised the house and put the clap-boards on before we quit work. Even the floor was laid, the benches put up, the house chinked and daubed. A few days after school was kept in it.

In 1838 Market street, in Tiffin, was cut out from the river to Julius Fellnagel's. on Sandusky street. Mr. Fellnagel had a lease from Mr. Hedges for a piece of land near by, all covered with trees. My brother Louis and I took the job of clearing it. When we cut down a big maple we found at a point three inches from the center a notch that had been cut with a sharp instrument, about three inches wide. The notch was four inches deep and oblique. We counted more than three hundred rings between this wound and the bark. Some forest ranger more than three centuries before injured the tree. It stood between Mr. Eid's residence and the river.

There was a wedding in Seneca township one night. The clay bake oven, near the house of the bride, stood on block. That night it was full of bread, pies, roasted turkey, cakes, and other good things. Boys are boys, they say, but it was a very ugly trick when they carried away the whole bake oven, with its entire contents, and when the ceremony at the house was over, and the supper to be served up, the bake oven was gone.

I don't like to mention any names, but if any one will ask my old friend G. W Aulger, on the McCutchenville road, he may know something about it. Who ever heard of stealing a bake oven?

ELIJAH MUSGRAVE,

Who is still living, was also an early settler in the county. He came to Republic in September, 1824, and worked for Mr. T. Roberts clearing land, and soon earned money enough to buy eighty acres, near Melmore, from Thomas West. He also worked for Frank Baker, Judge Cornell and Major Stephens. He and John Burns took the job of building the first M. E. church in Melmore, in 1833. He voted at the first election held in Scipio township. Adam Hance was elected justice of the peace. Mr. Musgrave has lived for many years on his splendid farm, in section twenty-seven. He was deputy sheriff under David Bishop in 1833. Mr. Musgrave says:

In the spring, when I was 23 years old, I made 6,000 rails. They only paid 25 cents per hundred for rails down in Coshocton, but here I got 50 cents. I was born in Allegheny county, Virginia, March 4, 1804. In 1810 my father moved to Coshocton county, Ohio. When I came here there was no house between New Haven and Republic. I was married to Harriet, daughter of Micajah Heaton, 17th of May, 1833. When the Toledo war broke out, I was captain of a militia company. Dr. Gibson was our surgeon. Ezra Baker had a company also, and there was a company from Findlay, too. We all went to Toledo, but never got under fire. We had a full battalion. Henry C. Brish was our general. Governor Lucas was there. We all came back safe and sound.

Daniel Reis, Philip and Jacob Scheer, Andrew Burgderfer, Jonathan Kirgis and Peter Miller were also early German settlers, and there were also the Arbogasts, Vannests, John Manges, John Kerr, E. Roley, the Koenigsaamens, Caleb Brundage, George Robb, A. Yambright, Henry Hepp, John Adelsperger, Joseph Lye, Joseph Lonsoway and others; also the Davidsons and Blairs, the Spilters and others.

JOHN DOCKWEILER

Came here from Germany in 1833, and bought the northwest quarter of section five, when it was all woods. Here he built his home and raised a large family. He was a very strong man and very decided in his opinion, which often brought him into conflict with others. He was a good neighbor, however, very hospitable, and for many years a sort of a leader in the vicinity He was born in Martinshoehe, now in the Palatinate, Bavaria, Germany, then belonging to France, on the 26th Nivos, year 9 of the French Republic (January 16, 1801).

Mrs. Dockweiler's maiden name was Mary Schirk. She was born January 6, 1805, at Niederset, Alsacea. They were married near Easter, in 1828, in Philadelphia, Pennsylvania.

Mr. Dockweiler died March 7, 1880. His widow is still living.

Christian Scherer, Philip Bauer, Theobald Wagner, Francis Bartz, Frederick Becker, Franz Masson and John Brandt were also early German settlers in this township.

WILLIAM ARNOLD.

Close by Seneca township, where the state road crosses Thorn creek, a little south of McCutchenville, William Arnold and his young wife located in the spring of 1823. They were married in the fall previous, in 1822, in Fredericksburg, Maryland.

William Arnold was born in Fredericksburg, in 1802. Mrs. Arnold, whose maiden name was Noel, and who was a sister of Michael Noel, was also born in Fredericksburg, Maryland.

Michael Noel lived a short distance south of McCutchenville, also, and was a man of good repute as a farmer and citizen. He raised a family of interesting sons and beautiful daughters, two of whom were married to citizens of this county, one being the wife of my good old friend, the distinguished hardware merchant, Martin Kingseed, of Fostoria.

Here at Thorn creek, Mr. Arnold entered a piece of land and put up a cabin. The state road was surveyed close to his house, and this being the only road running north and south, west of the Sandusky river, it was the only thoroughfare for emigrants and others traveling north and south. Forty years ago, new as the country then was, there was more travel on that road than there is now. The Wyandots were then still living on the plains and became great friends of Mr. Arnold and his wife, who had opened at their house a small beer and ginger bread stand; they also sold carbonated mead, of all of which the Indians were fond. Sometimes the Indians would get too much fire-water at McCutchenville, and going home, stop in at Mr. Arnold's, acting ugly. One time an Indian named Spotted Tail wanted more beer, and the stock being exhausted, became very boisterous and drew a tomahawk to strike Mrs. Arnold, who was alone in the house. For want of any other protection, she set her big dog on the Indian, who drove the savage away.

At another time, "Stokey," another Wyandot, became very insulting at the house and Mr. Arnold struck him with the end of his whip handle over the head.

The Indian became very angry, jumped onto his pony and going away, told Mr. Arnold that he would fix him. He was gone but a short time when he returned with six other Indians. Meantime Mr. Arnold prepared himself for an attack, and when the Indians rode up to the door, where they were met at the small end of Arnold's old musket and other persuasives, they desisted from all further attempts to do injury. Big Crow, Round the Lake and Black Snake were also customers at Arnold's beer shop, but were always of good behavior.

Mr. and Mrs. Arnold were very devout Catholics, and being far removed from a church of their faith, experienced the want very much.

After their first child was born and the mother was able to travel, Mr. Arnold left his lone cabin in the woods, hitched up his team and took wife and babe to Lancaster, Ohio, to have it christened. It took a whole week to make the trip. Soon, however, other Catholics settled in the neighborhood, and Mr. Arnold was one of the prime movers in the establishment of the first Catholic church at McCutchenville.

Mr. Arnold was as ingenious as he was industrious. He was always at work at something, and while he opened up a farm with great industry, he was ever busy making tools and implements for household and husbandry.

They raised a large family of children, and Mrs. George Strausbaugh, who furnished the writer much valuable information of early life on Thorn creek, and Mr. Anthony H. Arnold, of Tiffin, are two of them.

The parents have both passed away and so have also Mr. and Mrs Noel. The latter survived them all and died only recently in the enjoyment of comfort and peace.

GEORGE HECK.

The subject of this sketch is now the oldest settler in the township. The writer has not been able to trace any one who settled here before Mr. Heck and is still living. Mr. Aiken was a very respectable pioneer and he died but a few years ago. He came about the same time that Mr. Heck arrived.

The grandfather of Mr. Heck came from Germany. George Heck was born October 5, 1797, near the mouth of Hocking river, in Athens county, Ohio. He grew up on his father's farm there. He married Sarah Grelle, who was a widow with four children. Samuel Grelle, Esq., late county commissioner, is one of them. With her he had ten children, of whom five are still living, the others having died in childhood. The oldest one living is his daughter, Catharine, wife of Harry Fiser; next, Elizabeth, wife of Thomas Bowlin, and Maria, wife of John Strebin, all living in the state of Indiana; Daniel G. Heck, the popular superintendent of the Seneca County Infirmary, and John, the youngest son, who is living near his father on the old homestead. The children all have families and are all doing well.

Soon after the land sales, Mr. Heck's father bought, at the Delaware land office, the southwest front quarter of section twenty-five, in this township, and made a deed for it to his son George. Three years after he was married he moved onto the land here. Mrs. Heck died on the 18th of December, 1840. About one year thereafter, he married Sarah, the sister of John Kerr, Esq., now residing in Tiffin. She dropped dead on the floor in 1875 after living on the old homestead with Mr. Heck thirty-five years At breakfast, on the morning of the day she died, she told Mr. Heck her dream of the previous night. She said she dreamed that their canoe got loose (their house stands near the river), and drifted to the other side of the river; that she walked after it on the top of the water, and as she reached the other shore, she stepped onto a log, and looking back saw her steps on the log.

Mr. Heck says:

I am my father's youngest son. I had one brother and four sisters, and am the only one remaining of my father's family. My parents talked German to each other, but always English to us children, and therefore I never learned the German.

We hired a team and moved up here in the spring of 1823, by the way of Upper Sandusky along the Negrotown road, as it was then called. It was not the present Negrotown road, but a trail by that name that wound through the woods in all directions. Anderson's and Crocker's were all the houses between Mexico and Tiffin, and they were cabins in the woods.

When we arrived here and found our land, we hunted for, and found, a suitable place to locate near the bank of the river in the woods. We unloaded and the team returned. I paid the man $20 to bring us here, and that left me but $5, all told, and here I was with a wife, five children, five dollars, no house, no team, no neighbor and no friend near. I cut four forks, put them into the ground in a square, laid poles across them, made some clap-boards and covered the shed, and here we camped until my brother-in-law, Peter Baum, who had married my wife's sister, helped me cut some logs, which, for want of a team, we carried together and built a cabin. For want of other material to make a floor, I took the bark of large elm trees and spread it on the ground, which answered very well. There was a spring on the bank of the river, near this cabin, and here we lived two years, when I built a better log house and moved into it. There was not a stick cut on this land nor in the woods for miles around. There were neither roads nor bridges. When I was a boy grown up, my father moved with his family to Perry county, where I was married. From there I came here. We had a couple of cows, and after struggling along during that summer, fall and winter as best we could, my father brought to me a yoke of oxen the following spring. This was a sort of God-send and I began to take courage. Some time afterwards I went back to Perry county and brought home a young brood mare I had left there. My father brought me flour twice, which kept us from starving, and some of the other settlers also. When they found out that we had flour, they came for several miles around to borrow some, to be paid back some time in kind. We had good flour, but some who returned flour brought a very inferior article. Foncannons never brought theirs back until two years afterwards, and others never made return at all. Then the clothes I brought with me were worn out, and how to get others I did not know. I killed two large bucks and took the skins to the Mohawk squaws, on the Van Meter section, who tanned them for me. I paid them for it with a few pounds of flour. I cut a pair of pants out of these skins and my wife helped me sew them. For three years I wore these every day, and they were the most serviceable pants I ever had. I got Jacob Price to tan a skin also, out of which we made a pair of pants for Samuel Grelle, but whenever they got wet and dry again, they became as stiff as boards. Price did not understand tanning deer skins as well as the Mohawk squaws.

When James Aiken came here, he was a single man. William Anderson came here also about the time we did, and Aiken married Anderson's daughter. They lived on the Negrotown road. Aiken was a Virginian, but lived at Delaware a short time before he came here. He was here when I came. Anderson's land joined mine on the east.

The first wheat I raised I took to Moore's mill, near Lower Sandusky to get it ground. We all took sick and had a great deal of trouble with the diseases incident to life in the forest.

Soon after my arrival here I became acquainted with Hard Hickory, of the Senecas. He was a very intelligent Indian and spoke English very plainly. He prided himself on his French blood.

They camped near our house, and brought their camp equipage with them in their canoes. One night Hard Hickory and another Indian killed two deers near my house. The Indians fixed a candle over their heads in the canoes, and while the deers were feeding on the tender grass in the river, they would look at the light, while the Indians, sitting in the dark beneath, could row almost up to them and kill them. They put two forks into the ground and a pole across them about four feet up. The meat was cut into pieces, laid on this pole and dried by a fire made beneath. The meat was salted a little before it was dried, and when thus well cured, it was put into a square pack, the skin of the deer wrapped around it and tied with strings of raw hide. A crooked stick was fastened on the back of a pony and a pack of this dried venison, called "jerk," fastened to each end, to be taken home. This drying and packing and cutting up of the meat was all done by a squaw.

One time when Hickory camped here, and before I had a team, I borrowed one of his ponies to go to Tiffin for a half bushel of salt. He was always kind to me. There was also a Taway Indian through here occasionally they called Pumpkin. He was the biggest Indian I ever saw, and the most savage looking. Everybody, even the other Indians were afraid of him. He was fully six feet high, had a glaring look, showed his teeth very much and he must have weighed fully two hundred pounds.

Somewhere down about Cold creek a white man by the name of Snow, had his cabin. One time, in the absence of Snow, Pumpkin came into the house and killed Mrs. Snow. He then cut her open and took out of her womb a full grown babe, stuck it on a stick and roasted it over the fire in the house. The white neighbors gave the alarm and the Senecas caught Pumpkin and brought him to Snow, telling him that he should kill him or do anything else he pleased with him. Mr. Snow, fearing the consequences, let Pumpkin run. Soon after that, Pumpkin stole a corn hoe from my neighbor, Aiken. Aiken told Pumpkin to leave the country and never show his face again. It was not long after that, when Pumpkin got into a fight with a Wyandot and killed him. They made him sit on a log, when some six of them plunged their tomahawks into his brain.

Joseph Foncannon, two of his brothers and his father, settled near the mouth of Honey creek, in Eden. Joseph was married. His wife was a Poorman. Peter Lott, David Foght and Frederick Wagner also came in soon. Peter Baum settled near Mexico. He moved to Missouri afterwards, where he and his wife both died. Baum was never satisfied anywhere.

We raised hemp and flax and spun and wove tow-linen. Many a cold day I chopped in the woods all day in tow-linen pants, my bare feet in shoes full of water and ice. Sometimes the ice packed around my feet so tight that when I came into the house I had to hold them to the fire a while before I could get them off; but I never had my feet frozen. I often had to go to Tiffin on cold days in winter with tow-linen pants on. We lived very fine after we could raise sheep and have the whole family dressed in linsey-woolsey.

One time my father paid us a visit, and when he started back my wife gave him a loaf of bread to take along on the road. He met a man on the road near Upper Sandusky, who was nearly starved. He had not eaten a mouthful of bread for three weeks, and had lived on boiled nettles and milk. He had a little hut near the road.

ANTON KOENIGSAMEN

Was born June 26th, 1796, in Dreyson, in the Palatinate of Bavaria. On the 26th of January, 1816, he was married to Margaret Rauth, of Boerstadt, in the Palatinate also. She was born July 28th, 1796. They settled in this town of Boerstadt, where he followed the trade of a cabinet maker, until he moved with his family, then embracing six children, to America. He landed in New York in the fore part of October, 1832, after a short voyage of thirty-two days, and soon after located in Hamburg, Berks county, Pennsylvania, working at his trade

My old friend Martin Kingseed was noticed under the head of Fostoria, in chapter XXXVII. He was the oldest son of the family, and was born November 19th, 1817. The other five were Catharine, Peter,

Christian, Magdalena and Margaret. From Berks county Mr. Koenigsamen, in April, 1833, moved to Pine Grove, in Schuylkill county, Pennsylvania, where he located on a farm and undertook farming. The mountains and the stony fields were not congenial to him, and in 1834 he sold out and came to Ohio by wagons.

After a journey of six weeks he reached Tiffin, on the 18th of June, 1834. Here he stayed a few weeks, and bought ninety-four acres of land six miles south of Tiffin, on the Sandusky river, in section fourteen.

Here he opened up a farm, the land being all in the woods. He had but few neighbors. William Hitt joined on the east of him, Richard Connor on the north, Benjamin Peck on the west, and the Sandusky river on the south. Across the river lived Alex. Bowland and William McCormack.

Starting here in the woods he experienced all the hardships of foreigners who had no practical knowledge of clearing land, for this was a peculiarly American science. Farmers in Europe are not compelled to remove the forest in order to make a farm. The first year is generally the hardest, because while you are not able to raise anything, you are compelled to buy all you need, and live out of pocket. So with Mr. Koenigsamen, but the next year he had cleared ten acres and began to raise provisions. Mr. Koenigsamen speaks very feelingly of the kindness of his old neighbors in assisting him with everything needful until he got a better start in the world. The readiness and willingness with which neighbors would come to a raising or logging has frequently been mentioned. So here. Help was never refused. Now the opening grew larger, and grain was being raised in abundance. Everything prospered, and the family were happy until, on the 19th of May, 1842, Mrs. Koenigsamen died, a few days after giving birth to her tenth child. The babe died six weeks thereafter.

Five years later, in 1847, Mr. Koenigsamen was again married, to Catharine Bauer, of this township, with whom he had three children, Joseph, Emelia and Catharine.

On the 26th day of October, 1862, his second wife also died. The elder daughters then took charge of the household, and the youngest, Emelia, is now the matron of the homestead.

For several years past his oldest son, Martin, has been in the habit of arranging surprise parties at the old homestead upon the anniversary of the old gentleman's birthday, when all the children would meet there, with their wives, husbands and children, and have a good time all around. They had another big time there again this year, when they celebrated his eighty-fourth birthday, showing him all honor and filial affection possible, and gladdening the evening of his life with renewed assurances of their love and devotion.

Mr. Koenigsamen is still in the enjoyment of good health, and rather robust for his age. He enjoys his old pipe and a good joke as much as ever, and promises fair to so continue for many years yet to come. His son Anthony lives with him, and has charge of the farm.

CHAPTER XLII.

THOMPSON TOWNSHIP.

T. 3, N. R. 17 E.

THE name of this good old township is especially dear to the writer, for among its best men and prominent citizens many years ago, he counted many true and devoted friends. Its early settlement and organization, etc.. have already been mentioned, and it remains only to refer to several subjects not previously touched upon.

The first township election was held on the 6th day of May, 1820, at the house of Joseph Parmenter.

Among the first settlers in the township were William and Nathan Whitney, Joseph Parmenter, H. Purdy, David Underhill, James Whitmore, James Underhill, Eli Whitney, Jasper Underhill, Benjamin Clark, Solomon Dimick, Benjamin Murray and A H. Twiss, most of whom the writer well knew. They are all dead but Jasper Whitney, of whom mention will be made hereafter.

There were several squatters upon the openings in Thompson, who, owing to the scarcity of water at that time, left the country.

In 1830 the population of the township was 362; in 1840 it was 1,404, and has increased to about 1,900 now.

The face of the country is beautifully undulating and the soil remarkably rich and fertile. The very many improvements all over the township, the large barns, splendid farm houses and excellent stock, indicate comfort and wealth, industry, economy and intelligence. The German element predominates very largely, both in the old Pennsylvania and the European stock. There is a large settlement of German Catholics in the southeastern portion of the township, where they have a splendid church and a nunnery, under the auspices of the Precious Blood Society, mentioned in the chapter on Big Spring township. These German Catholics were among the first settlers in that part of the township and had organized a society as early as 1832-3. Among those early pioneers I will mention Anthony Krupp, John Host, Michael

Reinhart, John Glassner, Anthony Zahm, George Zahm, J. M. Zahm, Franz Hen, David Umlor, Peters Schoendorf and John Gerhartstein.

Among the prominent men of later years may be mentioned Jacob and John Bunn, Samuel Stewart, Jacob and Peter Karn, John Royer, John Decker, Daniel Close, M. Good, John Heter, Peter Dewalt, and others; also the Schochs, the Douglas's the Manleys, the Purdys, the Murrays, the Bloomers, John Hobbes, Elder Jackson and others.

The soil in Thompson, as elsewhere in the county, is drift, resting upon a sub-stratum of loose, shaley limestone, which is full of fissures, forming numerous sink-holes, which are found all over the township. A little stream called Sink creek runs into one of these, where it disappears. Many years ago a saw mill was erected upon this stream, with sufficient water to run it about three months in the year. There is a similar creek with a small saw mill a little west of this. Whenever there is a heavy or continuous rain, these sink-holes overflow, doing a good deal of damage sometimes.

The greatest natural curiosity in Thompson is its celebrated cave. The entrance to the cave is near the south end of the east half of the northwest quarter of section one, on the land once owned by Mason Kinney, one and one-half miles from Bellevue, and three-quarters of a mile from Flat Rock. The discovery of the cave is generally attributed to George and Henry Hasson. It was probably first discovered by Lyman and Asa Strong. It was known as early as the year 1815 by the settlers on the Fire land, and visited frequently by the hunters for the purpose of killing rattle snakes, which were found here in great numbers, and which gave the name of Rattle Snake's Den to the cave. The mouth of the cave is six feet long and three feet wide. Upon examining the land in the immediate vicinity, it appears that about five acres, from some unknown cause, have sunk several feet. Some have conjectured that the limestone rock once rested upon a bed of soap-stone, which being washed away in course of time, left a cavity that swallowed up the whole mass above. There is no doubt but that sometime in the world's history a great convulsion has racked the substratum here, for as you descend the cavity, you find the rocks on one side in a horizontal position, while on the other side they incline to angle of 45°.

Upon entering the cave a natural passage leads downwards, gradually in a northeasterly direction. At a depth of about thirty feet, the light from above is obstructed, below which, darkness forever reigns, unless driven away by the torch of the curious explorer, who examines wonders of this gloomy place. After a descent of about forty feet, you enter a large cavern, and here, as the eye surveys the lofty ceiling and penetrates the recesses all around, the mind is peculiarly impressed with the awful grandeur and magnificence of the scene. Proceeding onward, water is observed dripping from the rocks above, which is found, upon examination, to be impregnated with sulphur and not disagreeable to the taste. Beneath are discovered the tracks of harmless animals that roam about in places inaccessible to man; while overhead bats are seen suspended from the rocks, apparently lifeless, but when brought to the sun, they soon recover, and immediately direct their course to the cave.

After a descent of nearly two hundred feet, the passage is interrupted by a stream of pure cold water, which is very pleasant to the taste, and has a slow current to the northward. This stream rises during the wettest season of the year about eighty feet, and again recedes upon the recurrence of dry weather. In 1844, a year remarkable for rains, the water rose in the cave 170 feet, and within thirty feet of the surface of the earth. When at its minimum height, the stream presents only a few feet of surface, but its bottom has never been reached.

This cave is certainly an object of interest to all who admire the works of nature or delight in subterranean wonders, and were the rocks excavated around the mouth, so as to render the ingress less tedious, it would doubtless be visited by thousands.

I have taken the foregoing description of the cave from Butterfield, and copy also a communication signed " W." to the *Sandusky Clarion* of August 17, 1844. It is so intimately connected with the subject that the reader will peruse it with interest:

MESSRS. EDITORS: I have seen going the rounds of the papers, as a " singular phenomena," the flowing of the water from a well about eleven miles from this place.

Singular, I think it is not, and new I know it not to be. Neither as represented did it commence " all at once to flow," for it was known to rise many days before it commenced to overflow, and had been daily watched. Some days it rose a little, and some days it fell a little, until the last violent rain, when it commenced running over.

But perhaps you will better understand the subject if I give you the result of my observations, and what I have learned concerning the subterranean waters of that region, for the last quarter of a century.

Cold creek, probably the principal outlet of the water, rises in Margaretta township about three and a half miles from Sandusky bay (and at an elevation of fifty feet above Lake Erie), into which it flows in a northerly direction, and in that distance supplies the water for four large flouring mills.

The spring that the creek flows from was originally about an acre in extent, but by damming it close to the head, the course of the water was changed under ground, so as to divert a part of it, which again bursts out at about two hundred rods distant, from a great depth in the earth, forming a hole about ten feet across, which was afterwards partially surrounded by a circular dam, with the intention of forcing the water back to the old creek; but as the water would not run up hill, the dam was extended and a canal dug, uniting the springs in one level. The new spring is now about 100 feet across, bowl-shaped and from 40 to 60 feet deep, with the water so clear that a person looking from a boat on its surface, can see small objects floating at the bottom, and seem themselves to be floating in the air.

These springs rise less than two miles from the Fire lands, which is also our county line, west, within which distance another rises, called the Rockwell spring, which flows west into Sandusky county, and supplies water to a saw mill.

The water that supplies these springs is supposed to come from the extensive swamps and marshes that lie from 25 to 30 miles in a southern direction, and about five miles north of the dividing ridge that separates the waters flowing into the Ohio river and those flowing into Lake Erie at this point, and at rather a gradual elevation of about 400 feet above the level of the lake.

From Cold creek to these swamps, there is strong evidence of large quantities of water running under the surface of the earth. The first is about fifty rods from the head of the creek, where the breaking out of a few stones at the bottom of a small ledge, exposed a large and deep stream of water, constantly running, the bottom of which cannot be reached at twenty feet in a slanting direction, and the surface can be seen ten feet wide. At another place, some two miles south, water can always be obtained by sinking a bottle from 40 to 60 feet in the crevices of the rock. Then, again, about five miles south of Cold creek, is a dishing prairie, of from one to two hundred acres of land, which, after a series of rainy seasons, fills by the water rising from its bottom, through the alluvial soil that forms the surface of the prairie. Then about one mile further south, is a similar prairie, from the south side of which, at about ten feet elevation from its bottom, is the flowing well. The first account of the flowing of this prairie reaches back about twenty-seven years. A man who had settled on the north bank for the purpose of cultivating the lands below, which he found ready for the plow, was in the night alarmed by a loud report and the shaking of the earth, and upon going to the door of his cabin, he heard a sound as of running water. Upon going towards the spot from whence the sound proceeded, he found the water rushing from the surface of the earth with tremendous force, on the south bank of the prairie, in a volume larger than a hogshead, which continued to flow until the prairie was filled, and the water ran off from the northeast side of the basin. After this, the prairie filled several different seasons, through the alluvial soil on its sides and bottom, but not always so as to run over, until about twelve years ago, when the flowing well burst out about 60 rods east of the first one. After it had ceased flowing, a man living near thought to follow the water as it settled down, so as to have a well, it being difficult to find water in this neighborhood. After digging about eighteen feet in a perpendicular direction, the course diverged to the westward, in a descending direction, about as much further; then after removing the rubbish about twenty feet further in a perpendicular direction, it was abandoned at a distance of fifty feet from the surface of the earth. Since that time water could always be found at the bottom in the spring of the year. Eight years ago it overflowed again, since which time there has occasionally been high water in it during a wet season, when it filled the prairie to the extent of about seventy-five acres, floating off the fences and destroying the crops. It lasted about ten days, when it ceased flowing, and ran back, so that the prairie was dry within a week, notwithstanding the bottom of the basin is eight feet below where the water was drained to the well, the water settling away through the soil at the bottom.

While the water was at its highest point at this time, the family upon the farm where the "flowing well" is situated, heard a loud report in the night, which seemed to come from the earth, during a thunder storm. In the morning it was found to have come from the "blowing out" of another hole about three-quarters of a mile in a northwesterly direction, from which the water was flowing in a stream as large as a hogshead. Around all the "blow holes," as they are called, the broken limestone is scattered for many feet, thrown out by the force of the water when it first burst out.

From this spot for ten miles or more, towards the dividing ridge, the face of the country is indented in numerous places, with flowing prairies, and "sink holes," from a few rods to many acres in extent. Many of the "sink holes" are mere bowl-shaped depressions of the surface, occasioned probably during periods of high water, by the wasting away of the earth below, into the cavernous region, through some crevice in the compact limestone, immediately beneath. I am led to this conclusion, from the fact that in some places wells have been dug into the compact limestone, that have furnished water, until some dry season, when it has become low, and in blasting for more, they have broken through into the loose limestone, and lost what they had.

Others of the "sink holes" have openings at the bottom, through which the water rises in a wet season, whilst through the bottom of others the surplus water from the surface of the country runs off.

Advantages have been taken of some of these depressions to form the pond of a saw mill near Bellevue, that runs from two to four months in the spring of the year, carried by water that is accumulated from the draining of a large tract of country above, which after supplying the mill, runs off through a sink hole.

I think if it were not for the sink hole to carry off the water, in many places the country would be full of ponds and swamps rendering it unhealthy. The citizens of Bellevue have been compelled, this season, for the second time, to drain a pond caused by the overflow of a sink-hole.

About two miles, still south of Bellevue, there is an opening into a cavernous limestone, that can be traversed about two hundred feet, at the extremity of which runs a large stream of water, at more than 130 feet from the surface of the earth, and this season the cavern was filled to within from twenty to thirty feet of the surface.

A few miles still further south is a sunken prairie, in the bottom of which stands a black walnut tree that holds a rail cut eighteen inches through amongst its branches, more than twenty feet from the ground, floated there when the water was at that height.

In connection with the above I will mention a circumstance that took place a few years ago in the region of the sink holes: A man well known to myself had a team of three yoke of cattle plowing in the spring. When it commenced raining he stopped his work and turned his cattle loose in the field. The rain proved to be a long storm, lasting several days. When it held up and the cattle were looked after, one of them was missing, and supposed by the owner to have jumped the fence and strayed off, until more than three weeks afterwards the ox was found in the lot, where he had settled down through the soil into a crevice of a rock below, and nothing but his head and shoulders out. He was taken out and lived, with no other injury than the loss of hair from the buried part. Another ox was lost three weeks, and found at the bottom of a sink hole in the woods, the sides of which he had browsed clean.

I will further state that when some parts of the country I have been describing were first settled, they were very much infested with rattlesnakes, which were sometimes found early in the spring in large numbers upon the surface of the earth in their torpid state, driven from the rocks below by the rising of the water, before the sun was sufficiently powerful to warm them into active life.

I have written so much more than I had intended when I commenced that I will finish by adding, that notwithstanding the immense quantity of water in the country above, Cold Creek is never affected by the rising or falling of the water (in Thompson) to the extent of six inches. Yours respectfully,

W.

I have thus copied at length for the purpose of directing the attention of some geologist to the investigation of the subject. The old notion that Cold creek is the outlet of the subterranean stream in Thompson, might as well be abandoned.

Esquire Sherk, of Bellevue, tells me that whenever the water was high in Thompson after a freshet, and running into the sink holes, great quantities of water came out of the ground in the southeast corner of Sandusky county—York township, and in Groton also, in Erie county—and overflowed great tracts of land there, showing that Thompson has a higher altitude than either of the other places named. In 1872 the great "Royer ditch" was constructed, which now carries away all the surface water in its vicinity, and since this time the overflowing in York and Groton has ceased.

On the 1st of January, 1841, Jonas Harshberger, the surveyor, platted a town on sections eleven and twelve, in Thompson. George Schock, Frederick Harpster and Jacob Korner were the proprietors. It is a pleasant little village, but Bellevue absorbed it, and checked its growth. The town was named Lewisville, but the name of its postoffice is Flat Rock, and the name of the town is heard but seldom. The country about the town is rich and beautiful. Two of the proprietors, Harpster and Korner, have gone to their long homes. Mr. Schock is still living.

The Orphans' Home, under the care of the Evangelical church, is situated here, and under the care of its present gentlemanly and intelligent superintendent, the Rev. Mr. Dresbach, will do great good, as it has already established a reputation for itself, to the honor of the church and the county alike.

Thompsontown was surveyed and platted on the corners of sections fourteen and fifteen and twenty-two and twenty-three, on the 14th day of November, 1840. William McCauley, Abraham Sherk and Samuel Sherk were the proprietors. The survey was made in the same month when General Harrison was elected President of the United States. That ended the "hard cider" campaign, but it was no reason why Thompsontown never prospered.

JASPER WHITNEY

Was one of the early settlers in Thompson. He and old father Royer are, perhaps, the only survivors of that class of pioneers. Mr. Royer still resides in Thompson, but Mr. Underhill lives in Wood county as I am informed.

It is said that many years ago Mr. Whitney, while living in Thompson, near Nathan Whitney, was taken sick very suddenly and, after a short illness, died and was laid out on a cooling-board. The neighbors rendered every assistance possible and the doctor assured them all that Mr. Whitney was dead. A coffin was made and brought to the house and preparations made for the burial. Mrs. Whitney could not persuade herself to believe that her husband was dead, and the funeral was put off to an indefinite time. A consultation of physicians was held at the house and no trace of life could be discovered. The doctors, neighbors and all, tried to prevail on Mrs. Whitney to let the funeral take place, but she was unmoved and insisted that her husband was not dead. Some people now began to doubt whether she had her right mind, and matters began to look serious as to her. She cared but little, however, about the gossip of the neighbors, but kept her sleepless watch by the side of her dead husband, occasionally applying restoratives. In the forenoon of the ninth day she discovered signs of life, and in a short time she succeeded in bringing Mr. Whitney to life.

With prompt medical aid and good nursing, he was restored to good, vigorous health in a short time. He heard, while lying in this trance, everything that was said near him, and when he recovered sufficiently to express himself, he said a great many ugly things of those who wanted to bury him alive.

The undertaker refused to take the coffin back, and the family put it up into the loft of the cabin, where for many years thereafter, it was used to keep dried apples in. Several years thereafter the father of Mr. Whitney died and was buried in the same coffin. His name was Gunworth.

Mr. Whitney is still living near, and west of, Woodville, in Wood county, Ohio.

The father of my old friend, Samuel Horner, lived on a farm about one mile east of Flat Rock, which had a little spring on it. All the neighbors came there for water, and kept the spring in bad condition. Mr. Horner thereupon made up his mind to have a well for his own family use, and dug down some six feet, when he came upon a rock. He took a crow-bar and struck the rock, when a stream of water burst up that overflowed the well and formed a constantly running stream. Mr. John Burman lives on the farm now.

CHAPTER XLIII.
VENICE TOWNSHIP.

T. 1, N. R. 17 E.

WHEN, on the 1st day of June, 1829, Ezra Gilbert presented a petition to the county commissioners from the citizens of this township, praying for its organization into a legal township, to be known by its present name, they and he had very small hope that by this time it would be the rich and beautiful township it is. The prayer was granted, and the first election took place on the 13th of June in that year.

The following ticket was then elected, viz :

Township Clerk—Philip E. Bronson.
Trustees—Thomas West, Ezra Gilbert, Moses Smith.
Treasurer—James Halsted.
Overseers of the Poor—Henry Speaker, Elisha Fair.
Fence Viewers—Cornelius Gilmore, Ezra Gilbert.
Constable—Warren Blakesley.

In addition to these officers there were also among the early settlers: Governeur Edwards, John Woollet, David Kemp, Jacob Cook, Andrew Moore, William McPherson, Johnson Ford, Philip Muck, James McKibben. Mr. Ford and Mr. McPherson are living at this writing.

In 1840 Venice had a population of 1,222; in 1870 it had increased to 1,781, and in 1880 to 2,231.

Its soil is excellent, and it is now in the enjoyment of great agricultural wealth. Of late years such farmers as George Ringle, Thomas Bennett, David Ringle, Samuel Shade, James D. Stevens, John McKibben, Henry Meyer, Z. Bretz, the Sourwines, the Labolts, the Steigmeyers and others added greatly towards its development.

Venice has two towns—Attica and Caroline. The former has, to a great extent, absorbed the latter, especially since the Baltimore & Ohio railroad has a station near Attica Both towns are situate on the old Columbus and Sandusky turnpike, which at one time promised to become macadamized, and be a general north and south thoroughfare.

Colonel Kilbourn, who has been often mentioned as one of the pioneer surveyors here, on the 28th day of February, 1828, surveyed and platted Caroline, on sections ten and eleven, and named it after a daughter of Cornelius Gilmore, the first settler in the town and one of the proprietors; Hector Kilbourn and Byron Kilbourn being the others.

Andrew Moore settled in this town in 1830, on the first day of April, and resided there to the time of his death, which occurred on the 6th of August, 1846. (His widow died at this writing.) He was county commissioner one time, and a most excellent citizen. James McKibben located here on the 17th of June, 1830. There were but fifteen families in Venice at that time.

On the 1st day of May, 1833, William Miller and Samuel Miller, two brothers, from Pennsylvania, laid out Attica. David Risdon was the surveyor. The name was derived from the postoffice by that name, which had been located there before the survey of the town. Ezra Gilbert named the postoffice after the town in New York, where he formerly resided. Mr. Gilbert kept the first public house here, and Nathan Merriman kept the first store. In 1836 Attica contained twenty dwellings already, and a population of one hundred. In 1840 it had eighteen more. It is now a very lively country town, and has a fine trade. A lawyer, Mr. Lester Sutton, is located here, and some six physicians. The *Attica Journal* is a very readable weekly newspaper, and very ably edited by my old friend Dr. J. C. Myers. The rich farming community surrounding Attica will always make the town a good trading post. The town has a splendid school house, a healthy situation and a good moral community of intelligent people.

At the centennial 4th of July celebration in Attica (1876) my venerable old friend Mr. Johnson Ford, had read to the assembled multitude an abstract history of this township, which my friend Dr. Myers was so kind as to place at my disposal, and from which I quote. It was ably prepared by his son.

ATTICA, December 29, 1879.

Judge Lang:

DEAR SIR: I send you the history of Venice township and Attica, as prepared for the celebration of the 4th of July, 1876. If you find any matter to help you in your history, I shall feel amply rewarded. My best wishes for your success. J. C. MYERS.

N. B.—It should be mentioned here that the address as delivered was prepared by Mr. H. J. Ford, but I will insist that uncle Johnson Ford furnished much of the material.

VENICE TOWNSHIP. 617

A CENTENNIAL HISTORY OF VENICE TOWNSHIP AND THE VILLAGE OF ATTICA.

Arranged and written by H. J. Ford, and delivered at the celebration in Attica July 4, 1876.

For the names, dates, and all facts pertaining to the earliest record of the then new township of Venice, I am indebted to the two veteran pioneers, Father McPherson and Father Ford, whose heads, whitened by the frosts of more than four score years, are permitted to sit to-day on this platform. (Still living at this writing, May 28th, 1880.)

All honor to them and the other pioneers, to whose perseverance, privations and self-denial we to-day are blessed with a home in as beautiful, productive and wealthy a township as any in the grand old state of Ohio.

Looking over our rich rolling farms, it is hard to realize that only fifty years ago these same fields were an extended and unbroken forest. In the memories of the few whose silvered heads appear among us to-day, those scenes are distinct and real still, while we, the younger generation, must resort to fancy to catch a view.

I wish it were possible to portray the dark forest, the roving Indians, the howling wild beasts, the pioneer hardships met and endured by our fathers, and make the impression go with us through life, so that we might be taught thereby to respect with a proper degree of veneration the gray hairs of the few who remain.

A fact in the history of this township should not be overlooked in reference to the Columbus and Sandusky turnpike. Each alternate section of land was granted by the legislature of the state to a company as an inducement to undertake its construction. Colonel James Kilbourn, of Worthington, Ohio, in 1827, was employed by the company to survey and locate this road. In the same year Cornelius Gilmore built for himself a cabin on the south bank of Honey creek, where the residence of O. J. McPherson now stands, and he was thus the first settler in Venice township. Being a blacksmith by trade, his services were required by customers far and near. Ezra Gilbert settled here in 1829. In August, 1828, Samuel Halsted built a cabin house on the present site of Rininger and Silcox's store. In September of the same year Johnson Ford moved into his cabin, erected where the residence of Dr. Barber now stands. In October, the same year, Thomas West built east of the pike, near Honey creek. In November William McPherson built his house in the center of the township, and in December Elisha Fair settled on the site of L. O. Green's present residence.

In the month of November, 1828, at the instance of Ezra Gilbert, a petition was presented to the commissioners of the county, asking for a road commencing at the township line road, two and one-half miles west of Attica, and running diagonally to the south of east, to intersect the road leading to New Haven, near the Huron county line, three and one-half miles east of Attica. The petition was granted, and David Risdon, the county surveyor, located the road, and immediately Samuel Halsted, Ezra Gilbert and Johnson Ford took their axes, and in six days they underbrushed the whole line, taking their dinners with them, and returning home at night to enjoy their frugal suppers of corn bread and crust coffee. Thus these pioneers, looking ahead to the future, gave us these important cross-roads, which proved the nucleus of our fair village.

Ezra Gilbert, early in the spring of 1829, erected a cabin on the corner where Ford and Strannler's hardware store now stands, and opened a public tavern. Shortly thereafter, Nathan Merriman, from Bucyrus, opened out a small stock of dry goods and groceries in a log building on S. A. Ringle's corner.

On the 19th of March, 1829, Esther, the wife of Johnson Ford, died, leaving her husband alone to his sorrow. A neighbor went to Republic to assist in the preparation of a cherry coffin. At the funeral the remains were placed on a rude sled drawn by oxen. Samuel Halsted drove the team and Ezra Gilbert walked by the side of the lone husband eight miles, to the cemetery in Scipio township. It had been arranged that a funeral discourse should be preached at the house of Ethan Smith, near the place of burial, and the settlers gathered there, but no minister came, and without so much as a Christian prayer, the body was put to rest. The pioneer returned to his lone cabin, and although nearly a half century has passed away, he is with us here to-day.

The second death was a child of Samuel Halsted. Mr. Ford donated an acre in the center of his farm for a burial place, and cleared the same. The remains of a child of Philip Muck was the first interment there and the third death.

During 1829 the following persons settled here: Nathan Merriman, Governeur Edwards, Philip Muck, John Armatage, Jacob Cook, Henry Speaker. Jr., James Willoughby, David Roop, David Kemp, John Woolet, Samuel Woolet, Samuel Croxton and Jollier Billings. Men were also employed on the turnpike.

On the 1st day of June, 1829, this township was a part of Bloom, and the three qualified voters residing here went to the polls of Bloom township to cast their votes for John Quincy Adams, opposing candidate to Andrew Jackson in the autumn of 1828.

On the same day Ezra Gilbert presented a petition to the county commissioners for the organization of this township as originally surveyed. The name was suggested by Johnson Ford, being the name of the township in Cayuga county, N. Y., from whence he came.

It is a fact worthy of note that up to 1840 no township officer made any charge for his services. The postoffice at Caroline was taken away by Gilmore, and the government refused to make other appointments for Caroline. Then the Attica postoffice was established.

From this time forward the settlement of the township and village was rapid. In 1830 or 1831 Jacob Newkirk, from the state of New York, erected the first frame house in the township, on the present site of F. H. Steigmeyer's store. Many of us remember the old Huddleson house. It was removed only six years since, when it was the property of David Ayres.

The first saw-mill in Venice township was erected by Henry Speaker, Sr., about the year 1831, on his farm, between Attica and Caroline. The motive power was a yoke of oxen and an extra steer in a tread-wheel. It was afterwards converted by the owner into a grist mill, with one run of small stone and a carding machine.

VENICE TOWNSHIP.

In 1836 Ebenezer and George Metcalf, with some local aid, erected a steam saw-mill near the present site of the Heabler grist mill, in Attica. In the month of March, 1840, this mill was destroyed by fire, entailing a heavy loss on both the owners and the community.

John and Frederick Steigmeyer were the owners of the next steam sawmill erected on this site. In course of time a grist mill was connected therewith by them, and after a few changes in owners we now have our excellent flouring mill owned by J. Heabler & Bros. Early in our history a steam saw mill and also a grist mill were built at Caroline by Peter Kinnaman, both of which were afterwards swept away by fire.

[NOTE.—In 1857, one morning in the winter, a boy named Ephraim Groves, while standing in front of the boiler warming his feet, was scalded to death by the bursting of the boiler of this mill. He lived a few days after the accident, but never spoke from the time he was hurt.]

After the completion of the school house an invitation was sent to the Rev. Mr. Robinson, a Presbyterian minister living at Melmore, who came and preached to the people, it being the first sermon delivered in the township. After this his services were secured for one year, he preaching every third week on a week day.

In the spring of 1833 a union Sabbath school was organized by Rev. Mr. Patty, an agent of the American Sabbath School Union, and Mr. Martain was chosen superintendent for one year, but he moving away before the expiration of that time, Johnson Ford succeeded him, and his services were retained in that capacity for twenty-five consecutive years, when he resigned on account of defective hearing.

A Presbyterian church was organized in October, 1833, with thirteen members, by Revs. E. Conger and E. Judson, of Huron Presbytery, and John Holmes and J. Ford were ordained elders thereof.

The Episcopal Methodists organized a small class in 1835, and in 1838 the English Lutherans formed a church, and in 1840 or 1841, with the help of the community at large, erected the church now owned by the United Brethren. This house they were unable to finish, and the writer well remembers the rude slab benches without backs, which, for a number of years, furnished the sittings.

This society, failing to pay for their building, were compelled to sell it, and fearing it might be devoted to other uses and the community be deprived of a place for public worship, Johnson Ford shouldered the burden of its purchase, and obtained a clear title thereto. In a short time thereafter it was reseated and improved, and for a number of years the three above mentioned denominations worshiped therein, and in harmony conducted Sabbath school and church services. This is the history of the first religious denominations and church building in our township.

About the year 1840 a one story brick school house was built on the spot where the one in present use now stands. The interior was arranged with desks running along the side walls and seated with slab benches. In the year 1841 the Attica Baptist church was organized with nine members, and on the 2d day of April, 1842. Rev. S. M. Mack became its first regular pastor. In the year 1852 this denomination built its present house of worship. In the winter of 1849 and 1850, as nearly as can be conveniently ascertained, the village of Attica was duly incorporated, and on the 6th day of April, 1850, the first election of city officers was held, resulting as follows :

Mayor—John L. LaMeraux.

Clerk—Samuel Miller.

Councilmen—Samuel Crobaugh, David K. Burg, Benjamin Kelley, John Heckman, John Ringle.

Board of Education—Samuel Miller, M. R. Moltz, John Lay, Ebenezer Metcalf, Orlando Miller, James H. Brisco.

At the first council meeting on the 15th of the same month, S. E. Martin was appointed marshal, and William Rininger treasurer.

Thus was our village launched forth to rank among the small cities of our land.

In the winter of 1853 the buildings then occupying the southeast corner of Main and Tiffin streets were consumed by fire. William Rininger then bought the vacant lot and erected thereon his present storeroom.

Two or three years later a conflagration occurred on the northwest corner of said streets, and the large frame hotel building erected then by William Miller, early in Attica's history, and then owned by H. M. Chandler, was swept away. Chandler then caused to be erected the brick block we see here to-day. Attica has been visited by several smaller fires, of which we have not time to speak.

In the year 1856 or 1857 the school house still in use in our town was built, the contract having been let to Levi Rice, for which he received $1,328.42.

The Universalist society erected their house of worship in the year 1860.

Attica has not been without her sensations, prominent among which are the great fraudulent failures of Higley, Chandler, Schuyler and others in 1856 or 1857, and the discovery of the den of counterfeiters, and the subsequent conviction of one of our citizens for the crime.

Perhaps it would not be out of place, as we draw our history to a close, to give the names of those, and the years in which they served, who have had the honor to serve the village as chief.

John L. LaMeraux served as mayor in 1850; William Miller in 1851; Wm. Rininger in the years 1852, 1853, 1854, 1858, 1860, and 1865; P. Kinnaman in 1855 and 1859; R. H. Blodget in 1856, 1857, part of 1861 and all of 1862; J. R. Buckingham was elected in 1861, but resigning, R. H. Blodget was appointed to fill his place. The record of 1863 and 1864 does not show who served as mayor during those years. William M. Miller was elected in 1866, April 2d, and resigned May 14th, when H. M. Chandler was appointed to fill the unexpired term. Chandler was elected in 1867, and again in 1868, and during the latter year the burden of the purchase of the town hall was imposed upon the people. H. J. Ford served in 1869; J. C. Meyers was elected in 1870 for two years, and re-elected in 1872 for the same time. J. W. Simpson was elected in 1874, but failing health incapacitated him for the service, and his death occurred in the following winter. Our present honorable mayor, James L. Couch, was appointed to act during the unexpired term.

The peoples' voice at the ballot-box a short time since proclaimed James L. Couch mayor for 1876 and 1877.

In conclusion, we have only to add the number of public buildings in township and village, and the population, as nearly as it can be ascertained in this centennial year of our nation and semi-centennial of our township. In the township we have eight churches and thirteen school houses, and a population, including Attica, estimated at 2,300.

Attica, within her corporate limits, contains three churches, one school house, three dry good stores, two hotels, two hardware stores, two tinshops, two drug stores, two provision stores, two furniture stores, one cabinet shop, two undertakers, one clothing store, one marble shop, two harness shops, two blacksmith and carriage shops, two carriage painters, one gunsmith, one flouring mill, sash and blind factory, one foundry and machine shop, one shoe factory, two boot and shoe shops, three millinery stores, one photograph gallery, two cooper shops, one grist mill, one ashery, one carding machine, one confectionery and ice cream room, two billiard and drinking saloons, three village groceries, three tailor shops, one livery stable, one jewelry store, one printing office, one express office, two meat markets, one attorney, four practicing physicians, one dentist, one barber shop, one Odd Fellows lodge, one Masonic lodge, one Grange lodge, one weekly newspaper.

Our village has increased materially in population, and the number of dwellings since the completion of the Baltimore & Ohio railroad and the establishment of a station bearing the name of Attica, which occurred on the 1st of January, 1874.

This centennial year finds us in the midst of prosperity and healthy growth, with a bright business future before us, and our corporate limits extended, giving ample room for those who desire to purchase building lots, and locate among us. We will not attempt to scan the future with prophetic eye and declare what our township and village will be fifty or one hundred years hence, but we may safely say the historian of the second centennial of our nation's life will record as great changes as any we can chronicle to-to-day.

We must not overlook the part our aged mothers took in this war-fare of pioneer life. Side by side they stood with husbands, enduring dangers and privations like heroes, as they really were. Many of them left homes of comfort and even luxury, at the east, to follow the fortunes of the one to whom they had given their heart and hand.

All unused to the solitude of the western forests, and its attendant dangers, they faltered not, but putting their trust in their father's God, and leaning on the strong arm of their husbands, they came, and we to-day have reason to bless their coming.

Let us respect and love them while they live, and when they are gone, may our recollections of them be as swept incense to their memory.

With uncovered head, and bated breath, let us always speak the sacred name of "Mother."

And now, friends and fellow citizens, while we are called upon to-day to review the past and to celebrate the words and deeds of those who, one hundred years ago, declared us a nation of freemen, and whose blood bought the precious boon, let us remember also those who saved our country when rebels sought its life. Some we have laid to rest, and their graves are honored year by year.

Let us cherish the gift of freedom while we live, and transmit it unimpaired to coming generations.

May our love for God and our own kindred alone, take deeper root in our hearts, than our love of country and our country's flag.

On the 4th of March, 1851, an act was passed by the general assembly of Ohio authorizing the establishment of a grammar school in Attica, and which provided for the levying of a tax for that purpose, not to exceed twenty cents on the $100 valuation in the district.

Philip Bollinger, who this day, June 1st, 1880, is ninety-two years old, and perhaps the oldest inhabitant of this township, was born in Homburg, in the Palatinate of Bavaria, and came to this country in 1843. He is healthy and vigorous, and can walk fifteen or twenty miles a day. He is lively and cheerful, and has an excellent memory. He enjoys the comforts of the home of his son, Louis Bollinger, a respected citizen of Venice township.

JOHNSON FORD

Was born in Rensselaer county, New York, June 9th, 1796. His father died when he was but eight years old; his father was poor and had a large family, and consequently the most of the children had to be bound out. Young Johnson was one of them, but fortunately he found a good home, where he remained until he was twenty-one years old, getting all his education while he was yet bound. After he became of age he worked with his brother on a farm they had bought, in the same county, for eight years, when he sold his interest in the farm and married, and immediately removed to Venice township, Seneca county, Ohio, he being the first settler in the township. He entered a quarter section of land, upon a part of which the village of Attica now stands, and built one of the first log cabins, in the year 1828, fifty-two years ago this June, 1880.

He helped to clear off the land and lay out the village of Attica, giving it its name, having come from Attica, New York. For several years he was engaged in clearing up his farm, and assisting in building the Sandusky and Columbus turnpike, which was being built at that time, to develop the resources of the unbroken forest. He cleared the first land, ploughed the first furrow, and raised the first wheat in Venice township. He is in reality the pioneer of this township. His wife died during the first year of his pioneer life from over exertion and exposure, to which her constitution had not been accustomed, and she failed from the trials incident to early life in the woods.

He returned to the state of New York and married again, and returned to his new home, where he has lived to see the forest melt away like the morning dew, and the ground to be cleared from all traces of the old monarchs that formerly stood thickly over the face of the country, the pride of all Americans.

Twelve years ago he sold his farm and retired from active work, and now his means are invested in a large hardware store in Attica, in the firm of Ford and Strandler, a son and son-in-law, from which he derives his support at present.

He has always been an active, hard working, industrious man. He has always been religiously inclined, having united with the Presbyterians in his youth. For twenty-five years he conducted a Sabbath school in Attica, the first and for many years the only one in the township. He raised three children by his second wife—two daughters and a son. One daughter is now living in Great Bend, Kansas.

The wife of James W. Brown is the other daughter.

Young Ford and Brown are partners in the hardware store. Mr. Johnson Ford is wonderfully preserved, having been born June 9th, 1796, which at present, July 22d, 1880, makes him eighty-four years, one month and thirteen days, and from present prospects, he is good for another decade. For the last ten years he has received a second sight, being able at present to read fine print without his glasses, a thing he was unable to do for thirty years.

The following sketches were kindly furnished by Prof. S. McKetrick, of College Hill, Tiffin, Ohio:

History and literature are practically useful only so far, and to such a degree, as they inspire those who read their pages to aspire to the noble example they portray, whether it be in mental discipline or physical execution. History should be nothing but truthful facts, and therein differ from fiction. History is the truth of the past. Fiction is fancy, and belongs neither to time or place. The one is healthful and invigorating, the other weak and debasing.

The page we present here shall be history. We present this page not to relieve memory of its burden, but to recall deeds and their actors, as we all love to do; to live again a few moments with friends of the past; to be enlivened again by their association, though they come but from memory, and from it I draw the most hallowed associations of my life, which were acted in Venice township.

The men who first impressed upon my mind the realities of living, lived and toiled upon its soil. The one who ranks first there was James D. Stevenson. I know little of his early life. He was born in the state of Vermont; served as a soldier in the latter part of the last war with Great Britain. A part of his life was spent as a sailor upon our northern lakes. About the year 1838 he left a wife and five children and came to Ohio. He traveled over the greater part of the state in search of a spot where he might make a home in the new country.

He found, and entered into a contract with, Mr. Zachariah Betts for the farm he owned until 1863. The contract between the parties was that he should chop and clear one hundred acres of land, and for this service he was to receive the full and free title for the one hundred acres which he owned. All in the world he possessed was a strong body and a willing heart. He earned his living by threshing out grain with a flail by the light of a lantern. His board bill was not extravagant, for he told me of many days of hard toil with nothing to eat but batter, baked upon an iron griddle, and maple syrup.

After such hard life for several years, he received the title for his land, and had a few acres cleared and a log house upon it. He then returned and removed his family (who knew nothing of his whereabouts all these years of toil) to their new home in the west.

A few years of such severe toil and the deepest privation and he has changed his forest to a beautiful farm, producing abundance. But in those few years death has visited their circle and taken his wife, and soon after, fire consumes his house and its contents, save himself and children, but soon upon the ashes of that house is built a better one, and his second wife makes cheerful its hearth. Another farm is added to the first, and prosperity smiles on every effort.

About the year 1850 he commenced to shake with the palsy. That strong frame was wrecked. It grew weaker and still less able to battle with the realities it had known so well in life, and fell to its last resting place in Ionia county, Michigan, in the spring of 1865.

In politics my subject was an Abolitionist, a Republican and a true Union man during the dark days of the rebellion.

In religion he was a member of the Baptist church.

The hard circumstances through which he had past made him a close dealer, though in money, weights and measures, strictly honest. He was naturally noble, kind-hearted and true.

MAURICE MOORE

Was born in Germantown, Huntington county, New Jersey, July 15, 1798, and is therefore eighty-two years old. He was raised on a farm, and when twenty-five years of age, he was married and then moved to Harrison county, Ohio, where he located near the county line of Tuscarawas in 1823. Here he lived three years, and being dissatisfied with this hilly country, he left it in the spring of 1834, and packing his household into a covered wagon, he arrived in Venice township with his wife and two children early in June, the same year. Here he immediately entered a quarter section of land in the east part of the township, where he pitched his tent. On the 19th of June he moved into his cabin, and on the following night a heavy thunder storm drove the rain through the clap-boards and the open spaces between the logs, drenching the family in their beds, spoiling their goods and making them wish to be back on the sand lots of New Jersey. On the next morning the woods were a lake. Intercourse with neighbors was completely cut off, and there were none nearer than three miles. During this summer one of the children died of billious fever, then very common among the new settlers. They raised twelve children, six boys and six girls, who, together with grand and great-grand children, number about seventy at present. Among this number are some of the most valued of the citizens of the township and their interests in business affairs are so much interwoven with the progress of the township, that to separate them now from Venice township, would be a great and serious loss to the community.

Mr. Moore and his wife are still in the enjoyment of good health, and promise fair to remain with us many years yet to come.

WILLIAM M'PHERSON.

This venerable pioneer came from the highlands of Scotland, where he was born at Vernesshire, on the 6th day of February, 1793. He is a descendant of the family of William Wallace, who were so justly celebrated for their love of country and liberty, and for their bravery. His family being educated people and of the nobility, young William had the advantage of refinement in education, morals and religion.

Mr. McPherson became dissatisfied with both country and government, despising England's rule, and being of an adventurous turn of mind, at the age of twenty-three years, he followed his inclinations to visit America. In the year 1816, in company with a young friend of about his age, they set sail and arrived at Halifax on the 11th of September of that year. Finding no suitable employment here, they went to Baltimore, where they arrived in October and engaged in the mercantile business, which they conducted several years with success, but Mr. McPherson becoming tired of the confinement of a store, sold out and started for the west with a view of speculating in land. The Indians had sold their reservations and the new purchase had come into market. Mr. McPherson arrived in Tiffin in October, 1828, and by the advice of Abel Rawson and Joseph Howard, the land agents, he followed up Honey creek and selected a tract on the south bank and where the Columbus and Sandusky turnpike was then being built, and purchased it. It contained 800 acres and embraced the present village of Caroline.

Fearing the effects of miasma along the creek, he built his cabin one mile farther south. The cabin, however, was a very large house built of hewed logs, intended for a tavern and was the third house in the township. There was one shanty in Attica and one in Caroline, built by John Gilmore, for the purpose of boarding the hands that worked on the pike. After the turnpike was finished, the company put a tollgate in front of McPherson's hotel and arranged with him to keep it' which he did until the time when it was destroyed by a mob that cleaned out the gates all along the road. The traffic on railroads had now supplanted travel on the public roads and hotel keeping in the country becoming slow business, Mr. McPherson removed to Caroline, and again engaged in the mercantile business. Here he practiced that strict honesty and correctness in dealing that have characterized his whole life. He bought for cash and sold for ready pay only. He was so careful in giving proper measure that it was said of him, "he would bite a grain of coffee in two to balance the scale." He never changed the price of his goods, and sold them as they were marked, often holding them until they were out of fashion.

His old tavern is still standing and was used as a residence in 1879, but Mr. Ph. Schimp, its present owner, has built a fine residence near to it, and the old house is destined to go into decay. It is now used as a shop and tool house. It should be preserved as the first house built in Venice township, being erected in 1828.

After he kept store in Caroline eight years, he sold his stock of goods and moved about five miles further south, to near the edge of Crawford county, where he owned large tracts of land and which he wished to bring into market. He lived here eight years and until he had sold all his land, when he again returned to Caroline and took his old store room.

The Seneca County Academy was then in a prosperous condition, and the children of Mr. McPherson being of such an age that required attention to their education, he moved to Republic and placed them under the tutorship of Professor Aaron Schuyler, whose name has become celebrated among educators since.

He resided in Republic until about 1860, when he again returned to Caroline, where he had built for himself a new house. Here he still resides (July 29, 1880) and will stay until called to go higher. He is quite feeble now, but for a man of 88 years, his mind is still vigorous and clear. He divided his handsome fortune among his children, reserving enough to retire into a warm corner while the shades of evening chill the atmosphere around.

My friend, McKitrick, was so kind as to furnish the author with the following additional statement pertaining to Venice township in relation to the war of the rebellion and matters pertaining to the general charity of the people:

VENICE TOWNSHIP IN THE WAR.

It was half past four o'clock, Friday morning, April 12, 1861, when the first roar of cannon broke the quiet in which our nation had rested many years. We had enjoyed peace and prosperity and were unused to war, and its first sound aroused the nation like an electric shock. Strong men left their quiet homes to join the ranks of war, and every worthy citizen bore a common share in the sacrifices, toils and cares required to preserve the integrity of the Union.

Venice township bore her part manfully, and many of her sons were killed upon the battlefield, died of wounds received in the defence of their country or in rebel prison pens.

And the women of Venice were as patriotic as the men. They started aid societies for the relief of the sick and wounded soldiers, and for that purpose met at the Baptist church in Attica, on the evening of the 22d of October, 1861, when the organization was completed, a constitution adopted, Mrs. Sarah Blodgett elected president, Mrs. Elizabeth Brown secretary and Mrs. Mary Bennett treasurer.

Nearly every family in the community is mentioned in the secretary's report as having contributed something to the society. Great quantities of clothing, provisions, hospital stores, etc., were sent forward from time to time to aid and relieve. The last meeting of the society took place May 29, 1867, when all the money yet remaining on hand, was donated to the order of Good Templars.

The following is an incomplete list of the volunteers from this township for the Union army.

7TH REGIMENT O. V. I.

Stephen Rice, Joshua Creglough (who were both killed at Strassburg, Virginia), Jacob Hines, Lon Jones, Ira Grimes, James Smith, J. Harbaugh.

COMPANY H, 14TH REGIMENT O. V. I.

Sergeant John Brown, Frank Bartholomew (wounded September 19, 1863), Lyman Carpenter, Ambrose C. Croxton, John Goodman, R. J. Jamison, George Metcalf, William H. Miller (who were also wounded on the same day), Henry D. Cain, T. B. Carson, Philip Carothers, W. Deitrich, John Holmes, William Kemp, Maurice Kemp, Henry McDonald, James D. Stevenson, Jonathan S. Philo, George Ringle, Samuel Spencer, Joseph Wheaton and George H. Rice (who was wounded September 1, 1864).

COMPANY B, 49TH REGIMENT O. V. I.

M. B. Todd. V. J. Miller, John Bennington, W. H. Miller, John Todd, Mark Shade, George Bennington, Jehu Weaver, H. B. Courtright, D. M. Miller, James Courtright.

55TH REGIMENT O. V. I.

Otto Hull, Frank Smeltz and Stephen Howland.

66TH REGIMENT O. V. I.

Samuel Croxton, August Tanner (wounded at Kennesaw Mountain, June

19, 1863), Lafayette Parmenter and Henry Ames (wounded at Peach Tree creek and died in consequence in July, 1863).

COMPANY I, 123D REGIMENT O. V. I.

William Bartholomew (wounded at Farmville, Virginia, April 6, 1865), A. W. Hoffman, Joseph Hoffman, Sylvester Ostmer, Joseph Spencer, John Spencer, M. B. Todd, M. W. Mitchner (died from wounds, September 3, 1864), William B. Henry (died from wounds received June 15, 1864, at Winchester, Virginia), J. L. Henry, W. Sheely, Samuel Carpenter, Wright McKibben, John Hillis, David Hillis, James Hillis, Wilson W. English, L. Gibson, Isaac Funk (killed July 18, 1864), Henry Ebersole (killed June 15, 1863, at Winchester Virginia), John Fink, Isaac Seavault, John W. Rogers, John B. Shaffer, David Thompson (wounded June 15, 1863), S. S. Carson, Hugh M. Cory, John H. Carpenter and J. F. Schuyler, lieutenant. This company was discharged at Columbus. Ohio, June 15, 1865.

Moses, John, Jeremiah, Peter and David Cassner were also members of said company.

Quite a number of men served under Captain W. M. Miller in the O. N. G.

Anson and Harvey Bartholomew, F. M. Seed, E. Crow, Joseph Harbaugh, Mr. Shade and W. B. Olds were stationed on Johnson's Island (Sandusky Bay) guarding rebel prisoners.

Samuel Brown, J. Foster, John Huddleson, William Millon (killed in battle), Fred. Thompson and John Thompson served in regiments whose numbers are not known. Many men from Venice also enlisted in other states.

FIRST OHIO HEAVY ARTILLERY.

Clarkson Betts. James Courtright, H. Courtright. S. Grove, Isaac Seppard, Silas McDougal, Alex. McKitrick, W. Shoup and James Pangborn.

In November, 1874, the people of Venice sent to the sufferers by grasshoppers in Kansas. in cash, clothing and provisions, $387.72, all raised in Attica and vicinity. Mrs. Moltz was secretary of the association.

A similar society in the town of Attica and vicinity sent to the sufferers by fire in Chicago. in 1871, $975.99.

J. F. Bunn

Jeremiah Rex

G. B. Keppel

V. J. Zahn

John W. Barrack

Lloyd N. Leese

CHAPTER XLIV.

COUNTY OFFICERS TO 1880 AND CONCLUSION.

OFFICERS OF SENECA COUNTY, NOW IN OFFICE, JULY 1, 1880.

Probate Judge—Jacob F. Bunn.
Clerk of Court of Common Pleas—Jeremiah Rex.
Treasurer—John W. Barrack.
Auditor—Victor J. Zahm.
Sheriff—Lloyd N. Lease.
Recorder—Thomas J. Kintz.
Prosecuting Attorney—G. B. Keppel.
Commissioners—William T. Histe, Solomon Gamby and James H. Fry.
Surveyor—Samuel Nighswander.
Infirmary Directors—George Heabler, Lewis Spitler and Joseph E. Magers.
Superintendent of the Infirmary—Daniel G. Heck.
Coroner—William Smith.

JOHN W. BARRACK

Was born July 28, 1833, in Lycoming county, Pennsylvania. In 1834 his parents moved to Ohio and settled near the base-line in Crawford county. His father's name was John and his mother's maiden name was Jane Dunlap. The father was a carpenter by trade, and when John W. was big enough to learn a trade, he helped his father at his work and became a carpenter. The family lived on a farm and conducted that also at the same time. John W. married Miss Catharine Shoemaker on the 17th of June, 1857. They had nine children, of whom six are living. Mr. Barrack was elected treasurer of this county in 1877 and re-elected in 1879.

JEREMIAH REX

Is a son of William Rex and Susan Sloss. He was born in Stark county, Ohio, on the 9th day of October, 1844. His father located with his family in Seneca county soon thereafter.

Jeremiah was married to Miss Laura J. A. Barrack on the 25th of October, 1865. This union was blessed with seven children, of whom five are living. Mr. Rex served in nearly all the offices of Seneca township for a number of years, and was elected clerk of the court of common pleas, in October, 1875, and re-elected in 1878. Every trust reposed in his hands was filled with promptness and fidelity.

LLOYD N. LEASE

Was born at the Van Meter section, in Eden township, Seneca county, on the 2d day of April, 1838. His father, Otho Lease, came from Harford county, Maryland. His mother's maiden name was Belinda Street. Lloyd lived with his father on the farm until he grew up to man's estate. He then kept a livery stable in Tiffin for about twelve years, when he bought the old Evan Dorsey farm of 350 acres, in Scipio township. Here he remained two years, when he sold his farm and again moved to Tiffin in 1876. In 1878 he was elected sheriff. On the 11th day of March, 1859, he was married to Miss Maria L. Kridler, a daughter of Samuel Kridler. They have but one child living, a son, growing up to be a young man.

Mr. Lease has a passionate fondness for harness and always has a fine horse. He used to deal in horses, and in 1873, when he took a lot of horses to Boston, he met with an accident at a collision in Westfield, Massachusetts, that crushed his left leg and crippled him for life.

VICTOR J. ZAHM

Was born in Tolford, Huron county, Ohio, March 7, 1837. His parents, J. M. Zahm and Henrietta E. Lang, came to America in 1832 and 1833 respectively, and were married in Tiffin in May, 1836. In 1838 they left Tolford, going to Buffalo, New York, where they remained until the year 1846, when they returned to Tiffin.

Victor attended the public schools part of the time, alternately assisting his father, who engaged in mercantile pursuits. At the age of 15 years he entered the *Advertiser* office in Tiffin, as an apprentice to the printing business, which business he followed with success until the fall of 1875.

In October, 1861, he was appointed first lieutenant in the 3d Ohio cavalry, and assigned to duty as adjutant of the 6th battalion of said regiment, and camping and drilling with the regiment, followed it through its various duties until September, 1862, when, owing to reorganization of the cavalry service, the position held by him being abolished, he was honorably discharged the service and returned home.

Upon his return, he resumed his former vocation, and in 1868, became the publisher of the *Unsery Flagge*, a German paper, published in Tiffin by his father, which, however, meeting with poor encouragement, he suspended at the expiration of the year, and then devoted his whole time and attention to job printing, working up a considerable business.

In 1870, being offered an opportunity to purchase an interest in the *Ohio Eagle*, published in Lancaster, Ohio, he sold his job printing establishment, purchased an interest in that paper and assumed control, but his health failing soon thereafter, he was compelled to dispose of his interest, and return to Tiffin. In 1872 he again ventured in the printing business, this time in Toledo, where he remained several years, and again failing in health, he was obliged to relinquish his pursuits at printing.

In February, 1875, he was married in Tiffin to Janet C. Lamberson, daughter of William Lamberson and Mary A., his wife

In January, 1876, he was employed as clerk in the auditor's office and soon after appointed deputy In the summer of 1876 he received the nomination by the Democracy of the county as their candidate for auditor and was duly elected. In the fall of 1878 he was re-elected for the term of three years, the legislature having, in the meantime, fixed the term of the office at three years, instead of two, as formerly.

The office of auditor of Seneca county has ever been characterized by marked ability of the officers, but it is doubtful whether any of his predecessors have shed more credit upon it than the present incumbent.

For personal descriptions of Judge Bunn and G. B. Keppel, Esq., prosecuting attorney, the reader is referred to the chapters on "Bench and Bar," numbers 22 and 23.

POPULATION OF SENECA COUNTY IN 1880.

The census enumerators of Seneca county have made their returns to the clerk's office just in time to record the population of Seneca county for 1880 into this chapter.

The following is clipped from the *Seneca Advertiser* of July 15, 1880:

CENSUS RETURNS.

At last the census enumerators have completed their work, and we are now able to give the population of the county by townships, as below, and with them the population of 1870; also the loss and gain made during the past ten years:

HISTORY OF SENECA COUNTY.

	1870.	1880.	Loss.	Gain.
Adams	1,537	1,624		7
Bloom	1,492	2,162		670
Big Spring	2,084	2,048	36	
Clinton	1,526	1,701		75
Eden	1,483	1,598		115
Hopewell	1,370	1,635		265
Jackson	1,131	1,394		263
Liberty	1,668	2,159		491
Loudon	1,400	1,277	127	
Fostoria	1,733	3,045		1,312
Pleasant	1,352	1,417		65
Reed	1,334	1,501		167
Seneca	1,583	1,537	46	
Scipio	1,635	1,836		201
Thompson	2,070	1,900	170	
Venice	1,781	2,231		
Tiffin—First Ward	3,275	1,330		
Second Ward	2,373	1,538		
Third Ward		1,997		2,234
Fourth Ward		1,378		
Fifth Ward		1,639		
Total	30,827	36,947	379	6,395

POPULATION OF TOWNS, VILLAGES, ETC.

	1870.	1880.
Greenspring		746
Bloomville		689
New Reigel	236	368
Adrian	257	214
Alvada		63
Bettsville		518
Kansas		204
Berwick	188	169
Republic	481	715
Attica	375	663
Fostoria	1,743	3,578

POPULATION OF TIFFIN, 7,882.

The revised figures give Tiffin a population of 7,882, as follows, by wards:

First Ward	1,330
Second Ward	1,538
Third Ward	1,997
Fourth Ward	1,378
Fifth Ward	1,639
Total	7,882

OFFICERS OF SENECA COUNTY.

It will be noticed that Seneca county has made the handsome increase of 6,120 during the past decade, of which our city is to be credited with about thirty-six per cent. The towns seem to have made the most gains, and, in fact, all of the increase. Over one-half of the population of the county is in the towns. The population of our county since its formation has been as follows: 1830, 5,159; 1840, 18,123; 1850, 27,104; 1860, 30,868; 1870, 30,827; 1880, 36,947. Tiffin had a population of 2,663 in 1850; 3,974 in 1860; 5,648 in 1870, and 7,882 in 1880.

This shows a healthy and steady growth, of which the citizens of the county may well be proud."

Township.	Name of Enumerator.
Adams	Christian Hoeltzel
Big Spring	James V. Magers
Bloom	Oscar M. Holcomb
Clinton	Virgil D. Lamberson
Eden	H. C. Pitman
Hopewell	John Corrigan
Jackson	Hugh W. A. Boyd
Liberty	J. D. Reese
Loudon	George D. Acker
Fostoria Precinct	J. C. Millbine
Pleasant	J. H. Davidson
Reed	James Ford
Scipio	William Bogart
Seneca	Rolla W. Brown
Thompson	James A. Feese
Venice	David Sanford
Tiffin—First Ward	Henry J. Weller
Second Ward	John B. Schwartz
Third Ward	Albert Beilharz
Fourth Ward	Ephriam Messer
Fifth Ward	Frank H. Lang

P. S.—To Fostoria should be added 158 persons in Jackson township and 375 in Hancock county—4,111 in all.

OFFICERS OF SENECA COUNTY TO JULY, 1880.

PROBATE JUDGES.

William Lang was elected in 1851.
John K. Hord was elected in 1854.
T. H. Bagby was elected in 1857, and re-elected in 1860.
W. M. Johnson was elected in 1863, and re-elected in 1866 and 1869.
U. F. Cramer was elected in 1872, and re-elected in 1875.
Jacob F. Bunn was elected in 1878.

COUNTY CLERKS.

Neil McGaffey was appointed in 1824.
Joseph Howard was appointed in 1830.

Luther A. Hall was appointed in 1834.
C. F. Dresbach was appointed in 1840.
Henry Ebbert was appointed in 1846.
Philip Speilman was elected in 1851, and re-elected in 1854.
George S. Christlip was elected in 1857, and re-elected in 1860.
William M. Dildine was elected in 1863, and re-elected in 1866.
Jacob C. Millhime was elected in 1869, and re-elected in 1872.
Jeremiah Rex was elected in 1875, and re-elected in 1878.

COUNTY AUDITORS.

David Smith was elected in 1824, and served by re-election until 1832.
David E. Owen was elected in 1832, and re-elected in 1834.
Levi Davis was elected in 1836, and re-elected in 1838.
G. J. Keen was elected in 1840, and re-elected in 1842.
F. W. Green was elected in 1844, and re-elected in 1846 and 1848.
Richard Williams was elected in 1850.
John J. Steiner was elected in 1852.
James M. Stevens was elected in 1854, and re-elected in 1856.
E. G. Bowe was elected in 1858.
Isaac Kagy was elected in 1860, and re-elected in 1862.
John F. Heilman was elected in 1864, and re-elected in 1866.
Walter F. Burns was elected in 1868.
Gus. A. Allen was elected in 1870.
Levi D. Kagy was elected in 1872, and re-elected in 1874.
Victor J. Zahm was elected in 1876, and re-elected in 1878.

COUNTY TREASURERS.

Milton McNeal was appointed in 1824, and elected in 1826.
Agreen Ingraham was elected in 1827.
Jacob Plane was elected in 1828, and re-elected in 1829 and 1831.
John Goodin was elected in 1833, and re-elected in 1835 and 1837.
Joshua Seney was elected in 1839, and re-elected in 1841.
Richard Williams was elected in 1843, and re-elected in 1845.
George Knupp was elected in 1847, and re-elected in 1849.
George H. Heming was elected in 1852, and re-elected in 1854.
Thomas Heming was elected in 1856, and re-elected in 1858.
Samuel Herin was elected in 1860, and re-elected in 1862.
Silas W. Shaw was elected in 1864.
Jacob M. Zahm was elected in 1866, and re-elected in 1868.
William Lang was elected in 1870, and re-elected in 1872.
Francis Wagner was elected in 1874, and re-elected in 1876.
John W. Barrack was elected in 1878, and re-elected in 1879.

It should be remembered that under the new constitution, the treasurer is elected at the October election and his term of office commences in September following. The above figures. therefore, show the years when the term of service commenced, not the year really when the treasurer was elected. Mr. Barrack was re-elected in October, 1879, and his second term of office will not commence until next September.

PROSECUTING ATTORNEYS.

Rudolphus Dickinson was appointed in 1824.
Abel Rawson was appointed in 1826.
Sidney Smith was appointed in 1833.
Selah Chapin was elected in 1835.
John J. Steiner was elected in 1837.
Joel W. Wilson was elected in 1840, and re-elected in 1842.
William Lang was elected in 1844, and re-elected in 1846.
W. P. Noble was elected in 1848, and re-elected in 1850.
W. M. Johnson was elected in 1851, and re-elected in 1853.
L. A. Hall was elected in 1855.
R. L. Griffith was elected in 1857, and re-elected in 1859.
A. Laudon, was elected in 1861, and re-elected in 1863.
John McCauley was elected in 1865, and re-elected in 1867.
Frank Baker was elected in 1869, and re-elected in 1871.
George W. Bachman was elected in 1873, and re-elected in 1875.
G. B. Keppel was elected in 1877, and re-elected in 1879.

SHERIFFS.

Agreen Ingraham was elected in 1824, and re-elected in 1826.
William Patterson was elected in 1828.
David Bishop was elected in 1830, and re-elected in 1832.
Joel Stone was elected in 1834, and re-elected in 1836.
Levi Keller was elected in 1838, and re-elected in 1840.
Uriah P. Coonrad was elected in 1842, and re-elected in 1844.
Eden Lease was elected in 1846, and re-elected in 1848.
Stephen M. Ogden was elected in 1850, and re-elected in 1852.
E. C. Wells (K. N.) was elected in 1854.
Jesse Wurick was elected in 1856, and re-elected in 1858.
Levi Wurick was elected in 1860.
Edward Childs was elected in 1862, and re-elected in 1864.
Peter P. Myers was elected in 1866, and re-elected in 1868.
John Werley was elected in 1870, and re-elected in 1872.
George D. Acker was elected in 1874, and re-elected in 1876.
Lloyd N. Lease was elected in 1878.

RECORDERS.

Neal McGaffey was appointed in 1824.
Abel Rawson was appointed in 1828, and elected in 1836.
William H. Kessler was elected in 1839, and re-elected in 1842 and 1845.
Robert C. Martin was elected in 1847, and re-elected in 1850.
William Kline was elected in 1853, and re-elected in 1856.
Albert Beilharz was elected in 1859, and re-elected in 1862.
James T. Martin was elected in 1865, and re-elected in 1868.
William DeWitt was elected in 1871, and re-elected in 1874.
Thomas J. Kintz was appointed in 1874, elected in 1875, and re-elected in 1878.

COUNTY COMMISSIONERS.

Name.	Year Elected.	Name.	Year Elected.
Thomas Boyd	1824	David Burns	1850
Benjamin Whitmore	1824	Samuel Saul	1851
Doctor Dunn	1824	Calvin Clark	1852
Thomas Boyd	1825	David Burns	1853
Timothy P. Roberts	1826	Isaac Stillwell	1854
James Gordon	1826	James Boyd	1855
Case Brown	1827	Enoch Trumbo	1856
James Gordon	1828	Henry Opt	1857
Timothy P. Roberts	1829	Robert Byrne	1858
Case Brown	1830	Michael Beard	1859
David Risdon	1831	Henry Opt	1860
John Keller	1832	Robert Byrne	1861
John Crum, one year	1833	Peter Ebersole	1862
Marcus Y. Graff, two years	1833	Samuel Grelle	1863
John Seitz, three years	1833	Thomas W. Watson	1864
Lorenzo Abbott	1834	Peter Ebersole	1865
Benjamin Whitmore	1835	Samuel Grelle	1866
John Seitz	1836	H. B. Rakestraw	1867
Lorenzo Abbott	1837	J. E. Magers	1868
John Terry	1838	S. M. Ogden	1869
Andrew Moore	1839	H. B. Rakestraw	1870
George Stoner	1840	J. E. Magers	1871
John Terry	1841	S. M. Ogden	1872
Joseph McClelland	1842	Robert McClelland	1873
Morris P. Skinner	1843	Solomon Gambee	1874
Jacob Decker	1844	Nathaniel G. Hayward	1875
Joseph McClelland	1845	Robert McClelland	1876
Morris P. Skinner	1846	Solomon Gambee	1877
Jacob Decker	1847	William T. Histe	1878
Samuel Saul	1848	James H. Fry	1879
Barney Zimmerman	1849		

SURVEYORS.

David Risdon was appointed in 1824, reappointed from time to time and served until 1836.

James Durbin was appointed in 1837.

Jonas Harshbager was elected in 1839.

Thomas Heming was eletced in 1842, and re-elected in 1845.

— Schuyler was elected in 1847, and re-elected in 1850.

George Holts was elected in 1853.

George Heming was elected in 1856, and re-elected in 1859.

Dennis Maloy was elected in 1862, and re-elected in 1871.

Patrick H. Ryan was elected in 1871, and re-elected in 1874.

Samuel Nighswander was elected in 1877.

CORONERS.

By the laws of Ohio, the office of a coroner is a sinecure, and the officer performs the office of a sheriff only when the sheriff dies, or is himself made defendant in a suit. At the death, removal or resignation of a sheriff, then the coroner discharges the duties of that officer and becomes sheriff, *ex-officio*, a thing that never came to pass in this county.

Christopher Stone was appointed in 1824, and elected in 1826.
William Toll was elected in 1828, and re-elected in 1830.
George Flack was elected in 1832.
Eli Norris was elected in 1834.
Levi Keller was elected in 1836.
Henry McCartney was elected in 1838.
Daniel Brown was elected in 1840.
George H. Shaw was elected in 1842, and re-elected in 1844.
Samuel Herrin was elected in 1846, and re-elected for many years in succession.
Sylvester B. Clark was elected in 1866, and re-elected until 1872.
James Van Fleet was elected in 1872.
Charles Mutschler was appointed in 1873.
George Willow was elected in 1873, and re-elected in 1875.
William Smith was elected in 1877, and re-elected in 1879.

ASSESSORS.

David Risdon was elected in 1827, and re-elected in 1829.
John Wright was elected in 1831.
Reuben Williams was elected in 1833.
John Webb was elected in 1835.
John W. Eastman was elected in 1836.
Robert Holley was elected in 1837.
Samuel S. Martin was elected in 1838.
Benjamin Carpenter was elected in 1840.

ASSOCIATE JUDGES.

These officers were elected by the legislature for seven years, as already stated in the chapters on "Bench and Bar." Of all these, Judge Benjamin Pittenger is the only survivor.

William Cornell, Jaques Hulburt and Mathew Clark were elected in 1824.

Agreen Ingraham, Benjamin Pittenger and Selden Graves were elected in 1831.

Henry C. Brish, Andrew Lugenbeel and Lowell Robinson were elected in 1838.

Andrew Lugenbeel, William Toll and Henry Ebert were elected in 1845.
Thomas Lloyd was also elected to fill a vacancy.

The constitution of 1850 removed the office.

It may be well to say, here, that the office of county assessor expired about 1840, when a law was passed creating the office of township assessors. The county assessor, in early days, had no more work to perform than a township assessor has now. It should be remembered, also, that the land bought at the government land offices was exempt from taxation for five years from the date of the sale. At the expiration of these five years, the land was put upon the duplicate. To do this correctly, was the principal work of the county assessors.

CONCLUSION.

In conformity with the plan I had laid out in the beginning of this work, as to the manner and order of introducing subjects, where to begin and where to stop, I am admonished that this is a very good place to close. I have described a great number of old settlers of Seneca county, and I am fully aware of the fact that very many distinguished men and women of the old pioneers have not been mentioned and were overlooked. I had very little aid in that line.

Nearly all my pen-pictures of persons are from my best recollections. The editors of the newspapers of Tiffin were so kind as to call upon the people of Seneca county during last fall and winter very frequently, to furnish me with such material as might aid in this enterprise. A few have responded Others saw proper to ignore the call. It would have been a very easy task to have told me of some worthy ancestor, who drove his stake in these Seneca woods for a home, and where he came from, what family he had, who his neighbors were, when he died and how he had lived.

I described those I could remember. If others have not been noticed, will you just be so kind as to blame yourself? My purpose was history more than biography, and I picked out such characters as connected history with their lives. In writing of these, it was a pleasure, and like living again with friends I loved, and whose memory I am still left to cherish.

Now, dear reader, you and I are about to part. If the perusal of the preceding pages has instructed, amused or entertained you, it is well. If I have failed to warm up in your heart a feeling of love or veneration for your worthy ancestors, who selected the woods of Seneca county to build homes for themselves and their children; if a glance over Seneca's past and the efforts and struggles of the frontier settler to redeem and build up this heaven-blessed country, will not wake up in the bosom of the living generation, the love and gratitude so nobly earned and so highly due your ancestors, I shall regret that I have failed in my mission, and will hope that I may never find it out.

Oh! that we had the capacity to comprehend the toils, sufferings and hardships, the deprivations and distresses these pioneers of the new civilization endured, in rescuing this land from the grasp of the British lion and his savage ally through two bloody wars; could we but recall the manly strife, the fortitude, the patriotic devotion to country and cause that inspired those men to actions and deeds of noble daring and doing, how much more than we do, would we revere their memories and carry, within our bosoms, hearts more grateful for all we enjoy.

Let me, in conclusion, quote the language of Dr. C. G. Comyges, of Cincinnati, in closing a short biography of Governor Tiffin.

Scattered here and there in our primitive settlement, a few venerable men and women are found, the remnants of a glorious race and an heroic age. The wild solitude of nature, the wild animals they hunted, the savage men who disputed their settlements, the companions of their joys and sorrows, are all gone, and they appear like strangers from a distant land. What Ohio is to-day in her majestic strength; what are her extensive and various benevolent institutions; what is her superb system of education; what is the sublime patriotism that rallied her sons to the dread conflict, growing brighter and stronger to the end, giving the great names that shine brightest in the dark splendor of war; what she is in conspicuous statesmanship, and in the vastness of her material forces and moral power, comes from the noble race of pioneers thus passing away.

Crown their deeds with praise; crown their memory with gratitude; let their hardihood, labors, self-denials and deep piety excite their descendants and those who occupy the fields of their conquests, to emulate their courage, their toil and their public virtue.

A people, to be truly free, must be both virtuous and intelligent.

APPENDIX.

NO. I.

THE EARTHQUAKE—THE GREAT HURRICANE—THE JERKS—THE MORMONS VAN BURENITE SALUTATORY—THE OLD STATE HOUSE.

OCCURRENCES of great importance at the time, but seldom, if ever, mentioned in these days, are recorded here for several reasons : First of all, to add to the general interest of this enterprise, and secondly, to preserve, as much as possible, records of events that at one time or other attracted the attention of the entire country, and defied the power of science to account for some of these wonderful manifestations.

A quantity of other matter is added here for the convenience of the student of history, and for ready references to the subject embraced ; some of these are statistical, and others are historical in their nature. These are hoped will prove a benefit as well as a pleasure to the reader, though, in fact, forming in themselves no part of the history of Seneca county.

PHYSICAL AND MENTAL PHENOMENA.

THE GREAT EARTHQUAKE.

On the 15th day of December, 1811, the first great shock of an earthquake occurred, that shook the whole majestic valley of the Mississippi to the center, and made the Allegheny mountains tremble beneath its gigantic throes. Its convulsions agitated even the waves of the Atlantic ocean. The subterranean forces which produced such results must have been of inconceivable magnitude.

The region on the west bank of the Mississippi and in the southern part of the state of Missouri seems to have been the center of the most violent shocks. They were repeated at intervals of two or three months. These shocks, in their terrible upheavings of the earth, equal any phenomena of the kind of which history gives any record. The country was very thinly settled, and there were but few educated men in the whole region who could philosophically note the phenomena which were witnessed. Fortunately, most of the houses were very frail, being built of logs. Such structures would sway to and fro with the surgings of the earth, but they were not easily thrown down. Vast tracts of land were precipitated into the turbid, foaming current of the Mississippi. The graveyard at New Madrid was at one swoop torn away, and with all its mouldering dead, swept down the stream.

Most of the houses in New Madrid were destroyed. Large regions of forest, miles in extent, suddenly sank out of sight, while the waters rushed in forming, upon the spot, almost fathomless lakes. Other lakes were drained, leaving only vast basins of mud, where, apparently for centuries, in the solitudes of the forest, the waves had rolled.

The whole wilderness of territory extending from the mouth of the Ohio, three hundred miles, to the St. Francis, was so convulsed as to create lakes and islands, ravines and marshes, whose numbers never can be fully known. Some of the effects produced were very difficult to account for. Large trees were split through the heart of the tough wood. The trees were inclined in every direction, and were lodged in every angle towards the earth or the horizon. The undulations of the earth resembled the surges of a tempest-tossed ocean, the billows ever increasing in magnitude. At the greatest elevation these earth billows would burst open, and water, sand and coal would be ejected as high as the loftiest trees. Some of the chasms thus created were very deep.

Wide districts were covered by a shower of small white sand, like the ground after a snow storm. This spread of desolation rendered the region around quite uninhabitable for a long time. Other immense tracts were flooded with water from a few inches to a few feet deep. As the water subsided a coating of barren sand was left behind.

Indeed, it must have been a scene of horror in these deep forests, and in the gloom of the darkest night, and by wading in the water to the middle to fly from those concussions, which were occurring every few hours, with a noise equally terrible to beasts and birds and to man. The birds themselves lost all power and disposition to fly, and retreated to the bosoms of men—their fellow sufferers—in this general convulsion. A few persons sank in these chasms, and were providentially extricated. A number perished who sank with their boats in the Mississippi. A bursting of the earth just below the village of New Madrid arrested the mighty Mississippi in its course, and caused a reflux of its waters, by which, in a little time, a great number of boats were swept by the ascending current into the mouth of the bayou, carried out and left upon the dry earth when the accumulating waters of the river had again cleared the current.

The following is from "The Great West." "There were a number of severe shocks, but the two series of concussions were particularly terrible, far more so than the rest. The shocks were clearly distinguished into two classes— those in which the motion was horizontal, and those in which it was perpendicular. The latter were attended with explosions, and the terrible mixture of noises that preceded and accompanied the earthquakes in a louder degree, but were by no means so desolating and destructive as the other. The houses crumbled, the trees weaved together, the ground sunk, while ever and anon vivid flashes of lightning, gleaming through the troubled clouds of night, rendered the darkness doubly horrible. After the severest shocks, a dense, black cloud of vapor overshadowed the land, through which no struggling sunbeam found its way to cheer the heart of man. The sulphurated gases that were discharged during the shocks tainted the air with their noxious effluvia, and so impregnated the water of the river for one hundred and fifty miles as to render it unfit for use.

In the intervals of the earthquake there was one evening, and that a brilliant and cloudless one, in which the western sky was a continued glare of repeated peals of subterranean thunder, seeming to proceed, as the flashes did, from below the horizon. The night, which was so conspicuous for subterranean thunder, was the same period in which the fatal earthquakes at Caracas, in South America, occurred, and it is supposed that these flashes and those events were part of the same scene.

One result from these terrible phenomena was very obvious. The people in this region had been noted for their profligacy and impiety. In the midst of these scenes of terror, all, Catholics and Protestants, the prayerful and the profane, became one religion, and partook of one feeling. Two hundred people, speaking English, French and Spanish, crowded together, their faces pale, the mothers embracing their children. As soon as the omen which preceded the earthquake became visible, as soon as the air became a little obscured, as soon as a certain mist arose from the east, all in their different languages and forms, but all deeply in earnest, betook themselves to the voice of prayer. The cattle, much terrified, crowded about the people, seeking to demand protection or community of danger.

The general impulse, when the shocks commenced, was to run. And yet, when they were at the severest points of their motion, the people were thrown upon the ground at almost every step. A French gentleman told me that in escaping from his house, the largest in the village, he found that he had left an infant behind, and he attempted to mount up the raised piazza to recover the child, and was thrown down a dozen times in succession. The venerable lady in whose dwelling we lodged, was extricated from the ruins of her house, having lost everything that appertained to her establishment which could be broken or destroyed. The people at the Little Prairie who suffered most, had their settlement, which consisted of a hundred families, and which was located in a rich and fertile bottom, broken up. When I passed it and stopped to contemplate the traces of the catastrophe, which remained after several years, the crevices, where the earth had burst, were sufficiently manifest, and the whole region was covered with sand to the depth of two or three feet. The surface was red with oxydized pyrites of iron, and the sand.blows, as they were called, were abundantly mixed with this kind of earth and with pieces of pit coal. But two families remained of the whole settlement. The object seems to have been in the first paroxysms of alarm, to escape to the hills. The depth of water that soon covered the surface precluded escape.

The people, without exception, were unlettered backwoodsmen, of the class least addicted to reasoning. And yet it is remarkable how ingeniously and conclusively they reasoned, from apprehension sharpened by fear. They observed that the chasms in the earth were in the direction from southwest to northeast, and they were of an extent to swallow up not only men, but houses, down deep into the pit. And these chasms occurred frequently, within intervals of half a mile. They felled the tallest trees at right angles to the chasm, and stationed themselves upon the felled trees. Meantime

APPENDIX.   643

their cattle and harvests, both there and at New Madrid, principally perished.

The people no longer dared to dwell in houses. They passed that winter and the succeeding one in bark booths and camps, like those of the Indians, of so light a texture as not to expose the inhabitants to danger in case of their being thrown down. Such numbers of laden boats were wrecked above the Mississippi and the lading driven into the eddy at the mouth of the bayou at the village, which makes the harbor, that the people were amply provided with provisions of every kind. Flour, beef, pork, bacon, butter, cheese, apples, in short everything that is carried down the river, was in such abundance as scarcely to be matters of sale. Many of the boats that came safely into the bayou were disposed of by the affrighted owners for a trifle, for the shocks continued daily, and the owners deeming the country below sunk, were glad to return to the upper country as fast as possible. In effect, a great many islands were sunk, new ones raised, and the bed of the river very much changed in every respect.

After the earthquake had moderated in violence, the country exhibited a melancholy aspect of chasms, of sand covering the earth, of trees thrown down or lying at an angle of forty-five degrees, a split in the middle. The Little Prairie settlement was broken up. The Great Prairie settlement, one of the most flourishing before, on the west bank of the Mississippi, was much diminished. New Madrid dwindled into insignificance and decay, the people trembling in their miserable hovels at the distant and melancholy rumbling of the approaching shocks.

The general government passed an act allowing the inhabitants of the country to locate the same quantity of land that they possessed here in any part of the territory where the lands were not yet covered by any claim. These claims passed into the hands of speculators, and were never of any substantial value to the possessor. When I resided there, this district, formerly so level, rich and beautiful, had the most melancholy of all aspects of decay. The tokens of former cultivation and habitancy were now mementos of desolation and desertion. Large and beautiful orchards were left uninclosed, homes were deserted, and deep chasms in the earth were obvious at frequent intervals. Such was the face of the country, although the people had for years become so accustomed to frequent and small shocks, which did no essential injury, that the lands were gradually rising again in value, and New Madrid was slowly rebuilding with frail buildings adapted to the apprehensions of the people."

THE GREAT HURRICANE.

Another very wonderful phenomenon that occurred a few years after the great earthquake is also worthy of special record.

On the 18th of May, 1825, and after quite a number of new-comers had settled in Seneca, there occurred one of the most violent tornadoes of which history gives any account. It has usually been called the "Burlington storm," because its greatest severity was experienced in that township. It commenced between one and two o'clock in the afternoon in Delaware county, upon the upper waters of the Scioto, and in the very heart of the state. It seemed for a time to sweep the surface of the earth with indescribable fury. It then apparently rose in the air, rushing along above the tops of the highest trees. Soon it descended with increased violence, and tore its destructive way through Licking, Knox and Coshocton counties. Its general course was a little north of east.

The force and violence of the wind, which accompanied this tempest, have probably never been equalled in a northern latitude. Gigantic forests were instantly uprooted, and enormous trees were hurled like feathers through the air. Some were carried several miles. There was no strength of trunk or root which for a single instant could withstand the assault. Cows, oxen, and horses were lifted bodily from the ground and carried to the distance of one or two hundred rods. There was a creek, flooded with recent rains, over which the tornado passed. The gale so emptied it of its flood that in a few minutes there was only a small, trickling stream to be seen in its bed.

There had been so much rain that the roads were very muddy, and the fields were like sponges saturated with water. The tornado seemed to dispel every particle of moisture, and both roads and fields were left dry and almost dusty. The track of the tornado through Licking county was about two-thirds of a mile in breadth, gradually increasing as the blast advanced. The air was so filled with trees, buildings, and every kind of debris, whirled as high af the clouds, that the spectacles resembled immense birds pressing along in hurried flight.

The very ground trembled beneath the gigantic tread of this terrific storm. Many persons who were at a distance of more than a mile from the track of the tornado, testified that they distinctly felt the earth to vibrate beneath their feet. Those who experienced the fury of the tempest state that the roar of the wind, the darkened sky, the trembling of the earth, the crash of falling timbers, and the air filled with trees, fragments of houses and cattle, presented a spectacle awful in the extreme.

The cloud from which this terrific power seemed to emerge, was black as midnight. It was thought by some careful observers that it rushed along at the rate of about a mile a minute. It sometimes seemed to sink low to the ground, and again to rise some distance above the surface. Tremendous as was the velocity of the storm, sweeping in one continuous course, it is remarkable that no one could tell from the fallen timber in which direction the wind had blown, for the trees were spread in every way.

There were well authenticated incidents which seem almost incredible. An iron chain about four feet long, and of the size of a common plow chain, was lifted from the ground and hurled through the air with almost the velocity of a shot from a gun, for the distance of half a mile, and was there lodged in the topmost branches of a maple tree. A large ox was carried eighty rods and was then so buried beneath a mass of fallen trees that it required several hours' chopping to extricate the animal, which, strange to say, was not materially injured. From the same field with the ox, a cow was carried forty rods and was lodged in the thick branch of a tree. The tree was blown down, and the cow was killed. An ox cart was carried through the air forty rods, and was then dashed to the ground with such violence as to break the axle and to entirely demolish one of the wheels.

Colonel Wright had a house strongly built of heavy logs. His son was standing in the doorway when the gale struck him, and hurled him across

APPENDIX. 645

the room with such violence as to kill him instantly. The house was torn to pieces. A coat, which was hanging up in the same house, was found six months afterward in Coshocton county, more than forty miles from the demolished building. It was taken back to Colonel Wright's, and was clearly identified. Many light articles such as shingles, books and pieces of furniture were carried twenty and thirty miles. A little girl, Sarah Robb, twelve years of age, was taken from her father's house, lifted several feet from the earth, and carried more than an eighth of a mile, when she was gently deposited upon the ground, unharmed as the gale left her. Fortunately, the tornado passed over a wilderness region very sparcely settled, and but three lives were lost.

THE JERKS.

Having thus alluded to remarkable physical phenomena, we ought not pass in silence a mental phenomenon, totally inexplicable upon any known principles of intellectual philosophy, and yet thoroughly attested by competent witnesses.

The Rev. Joseph Badger was the first missionary on the western reserve. He graduated at Yale college about the year 1785, and was the highly esteemed pastor of the Congregational church in Blanford, Massachusetts, for fourteen years. He was a man of enterprising spirit as well as fervent piety, and became deeply interested in the religious welfare of the Indians in northern Ohio. Aided by a missionary society, he visited the country, and was so well satisfied that a field of usefulness was opened before him there, that he returned for his family and took up his residence among the Wyandots of Upper Sandusky, extending his labors to the tribes on the Maumee.

His work amongst the Indians and the scattered inhabitants of the reserve, was very arduous, but interesting and valuable. He was appointed by Governor Meigs, chaplain in the northern army as war broke out with England. He was in Fort Meigs during the memorable seige of 1813, and was afterwards attached to General Harrison's command. Mr. Badger had a high reputation for sound judgment, energy of character and superior intellectual endowments. He died in 1846, at the age of eighty-nine.

Quite a powerful revival of religion commenced under his preaching in the towns of Austinburgh, Morgan and Harpersfield, where, at that time (1803), he was alternately preaching. The revival was attended by a strange bodily agitation called the jerks. We find in " The Historical Collections of Ohio " a very graphic account of this strange occurrence.

It was familiarly called jerks, and the first recorded instance of its occurrence was at a sacrament in East Tennessee, when several hundred of both sexes were seized with this strange and involuntary contortion. The subject was instantaneously seized with spasms or convulsions in every muscle, nerve and tendon. His head was thrown backward and forward and from side to side with inconceivable rapidity. So swift was the motion that the features could no more be discerned than the spokes of a wheel can be seen when revolving with the greatest velocity. No man could voluntarily accomplish the movement. Great fears were often awakened lest the neck should be dislocated.

The whole body was often similarly affected, and the individual was driven, notwithstanding all his efforts to prevent it, in the church over pews and benches, and in the open air over stones and the trunks of fallen trees, so that his escape from bruised and mangled limbs seemed almost miraculous. It was of no avail to attempt to hold or restrain one thus affected. The paroxysm continued until it gradually exhausted itself. Moreover, all were impressed with the conviction that there was something supernatural in these convulsions and that it was opposing the spirit of God to attempt, by violence to resist them.

These spasmodic convulsions commenced with a simple jerking of the fore-arm, from the elbow to the hand, violent, and as ungoverned by the will as what is called the shaking palsy would be. The jerks were very sudden, following each other at short intervals. Gradually and resistlessly they extended through the arms to the muscles of the neck. the legs and all other parts of the body. The convulsions of the neck were the more frightful to behold. The bosom heaved, the features were greatly distorted and so violent were the spasms that it seemed impossible but that the neck must be broken. When the hair was long, as was frequently the case with these backwoodsmen, it was often thrown backward and forward with such velocity that it would actually snap like a whip-lash. We are not informed whether the victim suffered pain under these circumstances or not.

An eye-witness gives the following graphic description of the inexplicable phenomena: "Nothing in nature could better represent this strange and unaccountable operation than for me to goad another alternately on one side with a piece of red hot iron. The exercise commonly began in the head, which would fly backward and forward and from side to side with a quick jolt, which the person would naturally labor to suppress, but in vain; and the more any one labored to stay himself and be sober, the more he staggered and the more his twitches increased. He must necessarily go as he was inclined, whether with a violent dash on the ground and bounce from place to place like a foot-ball, or hop around with head, limbs and trunk twitching and jolting in every direction, as if they must inevitably fly asunder. And how such could escape without injury, was no small wonder amongst spectators.

"By these strange operations the human frame was commonly so transformed and disfigured as to lose every trace of its natural appearance. Sometimes the head would be twitched right and left to a half round, with such velocity that no feature could be discovered, but the face appeared as much behind as before; and in the quick, progressive jerk, it would seem as if the person was transmuted into some other species of creature.

"Head-dresses were of little account among the female jerkers. Even handkerchiefs, bound tight round the head, would be flirted off almost with the first twitch, and the hair put into the utmost confusion. This was a very great inconvenience, to redress which, the generality were shorn, though contrary to their confessions of faith. Such as were seized with jerks, were wrested at once, not only from their own government, but that of every one else, so that it was dangerous to attempt confining them or touching them in any manner, to whatever danger they were exposed. Yet few were hurt, except it were such as rebelled against the operation through

APPENDIX. 647

wilful and deliberate enmity, and refused to comply with the injunctions which it came to enforce.

"All who witnessed this unaccountable movement, agree in the declaration that the convulsions were not only involuntary, but resistless. Stout, burly, wicked men, would come to the meetings to scorn and to revile. Suddenly the paroxysms would seize them, and they would be whirled about and tossed in every direction, though cursing at every jerk. Travelers passing by, and who, from curiosity, looked in upon the religious meetings, would be thus seized. These facts are apparently as well authenticated as any facts can be from human testimony. There is no philosophy which can explain them. The faithful historian can only give them record, and leave them there."—[Abbott's Ohio, 683.

THE MORMONS.

A short history of the Mormons is added to these pages here; not because Seneca county has in any wise been connected with them, but because a distinguished character, who was once identified with the order, was for several years a respected citizen of Tiffin. A man, also, who now holds a high position among the Mormons at Salt Lake City, is a native of Tiffin.

Mormonism is about to undergo a great change. Public sentiment is opposed to it. The Mormons have but this alternative, viz: either to abandon polygamy, or remove beyond the boundaries of the United States, as they did once before. While, therefore, the sect is in this transitory condition, a sketch of their past history may be found of interest to the reader:

MORMONISM.

New England fanaticism always found a large field of familiar spirits on the western reserve, and the jerks were followed by a movement for a new religion in Ashtabula county.

Mr. Solomon Spaulding moved to Conneaut in 1809. He preached sometimes, but with very little success. He was regarded as a worthy man, however, and having turned his attention to the mercantile business for a while, he also failed in that. Some people at that time advocated the idea, that the American Indians were the lost tribe of Israel. Spaulding being a man of eccentric tastes and habits, and of considerable antiquarian lore, became quite interested in the subject of the origin of our country's aborigines.

Conneaut was rich in monuments, mounds and fortifications of a past race; and as the past was buried entirely in obscurity, he undertook to write an imaginary narrative of the wanderings of the lost tribes. The book was intended as a historical romance, written in the style of the Bible, and founded upon the supposition that the American Indians were descendants of the Jews. Mr. Spaulding's brother, John, visited him while he was writing the book, which he entitled, "Manuscript Found." John writes:

"It gave a detailed account of the journey of the Jews from Jerusalem, by land and sea, till they arrived in America. They afterwards had quarrels and contentions, and separated into two distinct nations. Cruel and bloody wars ensued, in which great multitudes were slain. They buried their dead in large heaps, which caused the mounds so common in this country. Their arts, sciences and civilization were brought into view, in order to account for all the curious antiquities found in various parts of North and South America."

Mr. John Spaulding testifies that the Mormon Bible, so called, is essentially this book. Mr. Henry Lake, of Conneaut, also corroborates this testimony in the following emphatic words:

"I left the state of New York late in the year 1810, and arrived at Conneaut the 1st of January following. Soon after my arrival, I formed a copartnership with Solomon Spaulding for the purpose of rebuilding a forge, which he had commenced a year or two before. He very frequently read to me a manuscript which he was writing, which he entitled the "Manuscript Found," and which he represented as being found in this town. I spent many hours in hearing him read said writings, and became well acquainted with their contents. He wished me to assist him in getting his productions printed, alleging that a book of that kind would meet with a rapid sale. I designed doing so, but the forge not meeting our anticipations, we failed in business, when I declined having anything to do with the publication of the book.

"This book represented the American Indians as the descendants of the lost tribes; gave an account of their leaving Jerusalem, their contentions and wars, which were many and great. One time when he was reading to me the tragic account of Laban, I pointed out to him what I considered an inconsistency, which he promised to correct. But by referring to the Book of Mormon, I find to my surprise, that it stands there just as he read it to me then. Some months ago I borrowed the Mormon Bible, put it into my pocket, carried it home and thought no more about it.

"About a week after, my wife found the book in my coat pocket as it hung up, and commenced reading it aloud, as I lay upon the bed. She had read but a few minutes till I was astonished to find the same passages in it that Spaulding had read to me more than twenty years before from the "Manucript Found." Since then I have more fully examined the Mormon Bible, and have no hesitancy in saying that the historical part of it is principally. if not wholly, taken from the "Manuscript Found." I well recollect telling Mr. Spaulding that the so frequent use of the words: 'And it came to pass,' rendered it ridiculous. Spaulding left here in 1812, and I furnished him means to carry him to Pittsburgh, where he said he would get the book printed and pay me. I heard nothing more from him."

The testimony of six other witnesses, is equally clear on this point. Spaulding was vain of his writings and was continually reading them to his neighbors. It is much easier to write such a book than to get any one to publish it. It is not known what use he made of the manuscript. He remained in Pittsburgh two or three years and died in Amity in 1816.

Several years afterwards, when this manuscript, with sundry additions and alterations, appeared as the Mormon Bible, Spaulding's widow testified that it was her impression that her husband took the manuscript to the publishing house of Messrs. Patterson & Lambdin, but that she did not know that it was ever returned. Lambdin died. The establishment was broken up. Patterson had no recollection of the manuscript.

About the year 1823, a man by the name of Sidney Rigdon came to Pittsburgh. He was a very eccentric character, with an unbalanced mind and somewhat of a mono-maniac on the Bible. He had been a wandering preacher without any ecclesiastical affiliation. He became very intimate with Lambdin and was often in the office where the manuscripts were kept. He quit preaching for three years to study the Bible. He was fond of disputations and was a sort of religious Ishmaelite. Here in Lambdin's office Rigdon found Spaulding's manuscript and read it with great interest. His crazy mind absorbed it all. He copied the whole thing and claimed the authorship in himself.

In his wanderings, he made the acquaintance of another singular man, named Joe Smith, who professed to possess the art of divination, by which were revealed to him treasures hidden in the ground. Smith was at that time digging for money on the banks of the Susquehanna. He is represented by those opposed to his pretentions as a man of low associates, averse to all regular industry, very voluble in speech, having great self confidence, and with unusual power of duping others. He had some seer-stones, by which he could look into futurity as well as into the bowels of the earth.

Smith dodged around the country, from place to place, sometimes attending revival meetings, praying and exhorting with great exhuberance of words. It was hard to tell whether Joe was a hypocrite or a fanatic, or a mixture of both. Smith and Rigdon just suited for company. These monomaniacs took the "Manuscript Found" for their guide, and originated Mormonism. No doubt they felt themselves guided by the Holy Ghost to form a new religion. Smith was cunning and versatile and had the seer-stone, in which the illiterate had faith. Sidney was a printer and a preacher, full of words and full of Spaulding's manuscript. Smith had brass and self-confidence that knew no blush. He took the lead.

Writes Mr. Ferris : " A portion of mankind have been looking for the last days for the past eighteen hundred years, and at the period in question were ready to run into Millerism or any other " ism," where their notions could be accommodated in this respect. A prophet, therefore, who could super-add to the discovery of the golden Bible a proclamation of a speedy destruction of all mundane things, a power of attorney for the restoration of an authorized priesthood and the gathering of the saints, and make a formidable display of miraculous powers, was the most acceptable gift which could be made to popular superstition. Here, then, would seem to have been combined the elements of an atmosphere, which has since branched out and gathered strength, until it has become the most noted instance in modern times of the development and growth of religious fanaticism."

Joe Smith's story is as follows: He says, in the year 1820, as he, in a retired place, was earnestly engaged in prayer, two angels appeared to him. They informed him that God had forgiven all his sins, and that he was the chosen instrument to introduce a new dispensation ; that all the then religious denominations were in error ; that the Indians were the descendants of the lost tribes ; that they had brought with them to this country, inspired writings ; that these writings were safely deposited in a secret place, and that he was selected by God to receive them, and translate them into the English tongue.

There was considerable negotiation before the angel condescended to put the plates into his hands. At length the angel told him where they were to be found. About four miles from Palmyra, New York, there was a small hill or mound. Smith dug down on the left side of the mound and found a large stone box, so carefully sealed that no moisture could enter it. Here the plates were found. Orson Pratt, one of the first converts to Mormonism, and one of its most distinguished advocates, gives the following account of the plates as then found :

"These records were engraved on plates which had the appearance of gold. Each plate was not far from seven by eight inches in width and length, being not quite so thick as common tin. They were filled on both sides with engravings, in Egyptian characters, and were bound together in a volume, as the leaves of a book, and fastened at one edge with three rings running through the whole. This volume was something like six inches in thickness, a part of which was sealed.

"The characters or letters upon the unsealed part were small and beautifully engraved. The whole book exhibited many marks of antiquity in its construction, as well as much skill in the art of engraving. With the record was found a curious instrument, called by the ancients the Urim and Thummin, which consisted of two transparent stones, clear as crystal, set in the two rims of a bow. This was in use in ancient times by persons called seers. It was an instrument, by the use of which, they recived revelations of things distant or of things past or future."

Is it not provoking that a boy who had ever attended a school in Tiffin should embrace such humbug as religion ?

Joe Smith boldly exhibited these apparently golden plates, but no unsanctified hands were permitted to touch them. He also showed a very highly polished marble box, which he said had contained the plates, and which, in that case, must have miraculously retained its lustre for countless centuries. But it had been observed some time before that Joe Smith, his brother, Hiram and another man by the name of McKnight were very busily employed in some secret work, which particularly engrossed their time in the hours of darkness. It was suspected that they were engaged in some counterfeiting operations. According to Joe Smith's account, they were engaged in lonely vigils and in prayer.

It was emphatically true of the new prophet that he had but very little honor in his own country. His peculiar claims excited ridicule and contempt. Mobs beset his house, demanding a sight of the most famous plates. At length the annoyance became so great that he fled from Palmyra and took refuge in the northern part of Pennsylvania, where his father-in-law resided. He secreted his plates for the journey in a barrel of beans. Being quietly housed in his retreat, he commenced, by divine inspiration, translating the Egyptian hieroglyphics. As he scarcely knew how to write himself, he employed a scribe, one Oliver Cowdery. Stationed behind a screen, where Cowdery could not see him, he professed to look through the Urim and Thummim, and thus translated the unknown symbols, sentence by sentence.

The work proceeded very slowly, and month after month passed away while it was in progress. During this time, John the Baptist appeared to them, having been sent by the Apostles Peter, James and John, and or-

APPENDIX. 651

dained first Smith and then Cowdery into the priesthood of Aaron. The family of the prophet's father became converts, and then an individual by the name of Martin Harris. The character of this man's mind may be inferred from the fact that he had been a Quaker, Methodist, Baptist and finally a Presbyterian. Harris had some property and Smith importuned him to furnish funds to publish the book, assuring him that it would produce an entire change in the world and save it from ruin.

Mr. Harris, a simple-minded, well-meaning man, was very anxious to see the wonderful plates, but the prophet avowed that he was not yet holy enough to enjoy that privilege. However, after much importunity, he gave Mr. Harris a transcript of some of the characters on a piece of paper. As Mr. Harris was parting with his money, he evidently felt some solicitude lest he might be deceived, since all around him were speaking contemptuously of the prophetic claim of Joe Smith, and he adopted the wise precaution, probably urged to it by some of his friends, of submitting the paper with the hieroglyphics to Professor Charles Anthon, a distinguished Oriental scholar in New York.

Mr. Howe, in writing a history of Mormonism, subsequently wrote to Professor Anthon, making inquiries upon this subject. He received a reply under date of February 17, 1834, from which we make the following extracts:

"Some years ago a plain, apparently simple-hearted farmer called on me with a note from Dr. Mitchell, requesting me to decipher, if possible, the paper which the farmer would hand me. Upon examining the paper, I soon came to the conclusion that it was all a trick, perhaps a hoax. When I asked the person who brought it, how he obtained the writing, he gave me the following account:

' A gold book, containing a number of plates, fastened together by wires of the same material, had been dug up in the northern part of the state of New York and along with it an enormous pair of spectacles. These spectacles were so large that if any person attempted to look through them, his two eyes would look through one glass only, the spectacles being altogether too large for the human face.' ' Whoever,' he said, ' examined the plates through the glass, was enabled not only to read them, but fully to understand their meaning.'

" Although this knowledge was confined to a young man, who had the trunk containing the book and spectacles in his sole possession. This young man was placed behind the curtain, etc., etc.

" The farmer had been requested to contribute a sum of money towards the publication of the golden book, and that he had intended to sell his farm and give the amount for that purpose.

" On hearing this old story, I changed my opinion about the paper, and instead of viewing it any longer as a hoax, I began to regard it as a scheme to cheat the farmer of his money, and I warned him to look out for rogues.

" The paper was a singular scroll. It contained all kinds of singular characters, Greek and Hebrew letters, crosses and flourishes. Roman letters inverted or placed sideways were ranged and placed in perpendicular columns, etc.

Sometime after, the farmer paid me another visit. He brought with him the 'gold book' in print, and offered it to me for sale. I declined purchasing. I adverted once more to the roguery which, in my opinion, had been practiced upon him and asked him what had become of the gold plates. He informed me that they were in the trunk with the spectacles. I advised him to go to a magistrate and have the trunk examined. He said the curse of God would come on him if he did. On my pressing him, however, to go to a magistrate, he told me he would open the trunk if I would take the curse of God upon myself. I replied that I would do so with the greatest willingness and would incur every risk of that nature, provided I could only extricate him from the grasp of a rogue. He then left me, etc.

"Yours respectfully, CHARLES ANTHON."

Again the community became clamorous to see the plates, and it was revealed to Joe, to show them to three witnesses chosen by the Lord. These were Oliver Cowdery, Martin Harris and David Whitmer, a new convert, who subsequently getting into a quarrel with some of the Mormons, was accused, together with Cowdery, of being connected with a gang of counterfeiters, thieves, liars and blacklegs of the deepest dye, to deceive, cheat and defraud the saints. This tirade of abuse was set on foot, however, only after the Mormons had finished their temple at Nauvoo, and Joe Smith found Cowdery to be very much in his way for the leadership, when he resorted to all manner of violence to drive Cowdery out of his way.

The *Elders' Journal* also spoke of Martin Harris in the following disrespectful terms:

"Martin Harris is so far beneath contempt, that a notice of him would be too great a sacrifice for a gentleman to make."

These were the apostles to testify to the golden plates. Their meagre testimony was as follows:

"An angel of God came down from heaven and brought and laid before our eyes, that we beheld and saw, the plates and the engraving thereon."

No one doubted that Joe had prepared these things, yet he was accepted as a divinely appointed prophet. On the 1st of June, 1830, he organized a band of thirty followers at Fayette, Ontario county, Pennsylvania, but these saints were held in such slight repute where they were known, that their leader concluded to remove them to Kirtland, Ohio. Here they assumed the name of the Latter Day Saints. Three thousand persons gave in their adhesion to Joe Smith. Some of these had wealth. Now it was revealed to Joe that they should build for him a house and give him food and raiment and all he needed, which was done. Joe became rich and established a bank which, he said, could never fail, as it was instituted "by the will of God." But it did fail—and badly.

The losers by the failure of the bank procured process for Joe and Rigdon, who both ran away. For this runaway Joe excused himself afterwards upon Bible grounds: And as Jesus said, when they persecute you in one city, flee to another. Joe said, "these persecutors followed them more than two hundred miles, armed with swords and pistols, seeking their lives."

Thereupon the Mormons moved to Independence, Jackson county, Missouri, where they bought a large tract of land. Converts were multiplied, a newspaper established and a town sprang up as by magic. Soon they numbered twelve hundred.

Ere long the disgust of the people of Missouri was excited against them. People did not wish to live near them, and their presence diminished the value of property in the surrounding country. The Mormons became defiant, raised a large military force and declared that they were a law unto themselves, and set the public authorities at defiance. The governor marshalled a force of four thousand militia to keep order and probably to intimidate the Mormons and actuate them to leave the State. There had already been a conflict, in which eight Missourians were wounded and twenty-five Mormons were killed and thirty wounded. The enraged Mormons burnt the small towns of Gallatin and Millport. They ravaged the country in midwinter, driving the women and children from their homes and laying the farm houses in ashes.

General Clark was in command of the governmental forces, who wrote to the governor: "There is no crime, from treason down to petit larceny, but these people, or a majority of them, have not been guilty of; all, too, under counsel of Joseph Smith, the prophet. They have committed treason, arson, burglary, robbery, larceny and perjury. They have societies formed under the most binding covenants and the most horrid oaths to circumvent the laws and put them at defiance, and to plunder, burn and murder and divide the spoils for the use of the church."

The governor issued an order, which was worded very unfortunately:
"The ringleaders of this rebellion, should be made an example of. If it should become necessary to the public peace, the Mormons should be exterminated, or expelled from the State."

The people of Jackson county offered to buy them out and to have the prices of their property fixed by three commissioners, with one hundred per cent. in addition. They refused to leave. The militia disarmed the Mormons and took about forty prisoners, Joe Smith amongst them. They were compelled to enter into a treaty, by which they agreed to withdraw from the state. Five commissioners were appointed to sell their property, pay their debts and aid them in removing. The state appropriated two thousand dollars for their relief. Still there was much suffering, as, in mid-winter, these numerous families traversed nearly the whole breadth of Missouri, and crossing the Mississippi river, entered the state of Illinois.

The cry of persecution had preceded them, and the people of Illinois received them very kindly. The American people are very prompt in throwing their sympathies on the side of those that are persecuted for opinion's sake.

The Mormons settled down in Hancock county, on the eastern bank of the Mississippi. Here they commenced rearing a new city, which they called Nauvoo. Missionaries of the new faith had been sent abroad in all directions. Converts were multiplied. They flocked to Nauvoo. In a short time they increased to fifteen thousand inhabitants. Smith had a new revelation. The faithful were enjoined to "bring gold and precious materials for the building of a temple for the worship of God, and a house for the dwelling-place of the prophet."

Ere long it was estimated that by the labors of the missionaries in this country and Europe, the Mormons numbered 150,000. Nauvoo assumed a thriving aspect. A military band was organized, consisting of 4,000 men, well armed and disciplined. Joe had another new revelation, not only authorizing the saints to take more than one wife, but enjoining it upon them as a duty to take several maidens to wife, and thus lead them to heaven.

This step shocked quite a number of the simple-minded victims and led them to withdraw, but more were lured to join them by the license, and converts were multiplied faster than ever. Joe was accused of seducing the wife of a Dr. Foster. The injured husband published affidavits, clearly proving the charge. A warrant from a neighboring magistrate was secured for the arrest of the culprit. Joe called out his armed men and drove the sheriff from the city. This caused great excitement and the state militia was called out to enforce the laws. There was every prospect for civil war. The governor came to Nauvoo. Joe knew what was coming, and he and his brother, Hiram, surrendered to the warrant under a pledge of personal safety. They were both taken to the jail at Carthage, where they were held under the charge of treason. Popular excitement and indignation were intense. A guard was placed around the jail to protect the prisoners from an exasperated community. The cry was loud for the destruction of Nauvoo, and the expulsion of all the inhabitants.

At six o'clock on the evening of the 27th of November, 1844, two hundred men in disguise approached the jail, thrust the guard aside, broke open the doors, and shot the two Smiths. Joe's last words were, as the balls pierced his body, " O, Lord, my God."

The governor was deeply aggrieved by this violation of the public faith. He issued a manifesto, in which he said :

" I desire to make a brief statement of the affairs at Carthage, in regard to the Smiths. They have been assassinated in jail; by whom, it is not known, but it will be ascertained. I pledged myself to their safety. Upon this assurance they surrendered themselves as prisoners. The Mormons surrendered the public arms and submitted to that the command of Captain Singleton, of Brown county, deputed for that purpose by me. I had secured a pledge of safety for the Smiths, by the unanimous vote of all the officers and men under their command.*   *   *   *   *   When I had marched about three miles a messenger informed me of the occurrence at Carthage. I hastened on to that place. The guard, it is said, did their duty, but were overpowered."

The news of the death of the prophet created the wildest excitement at Nauvoo. In their organization a man by the name of Brigham Young was president of a band called " the Twelve Apostles." These chose Young as the successor of Joe Smith, and to be the head of the church. Sidney Rigdon rebelled, demanding the position for himself. Brigham arrested him: declared him to be an emissary of the devil, excommunicated him, and "delivered him over to the buffetings of the devil in the name of the Lord."

All was quiet for a while, and the Mormons built a temple one hundred and twenty-eight feet long by eighty-eight feet wide. The *Mormon Times and Seasons* said of it: " Our temple, when finished, will show more wealth, more art, more science, more revelation, more splendor and more God than all the rest of the world."

During the calm outside of Nauvoo, all sorts of rumors were in circulation as the great number of crimes being constantly committed within the city.

A convention was called and a resolution passed that the Mormons must leave. Brigham Young saw that it was useless to resist, and at once made preparations to leave and move beyond the boundaries of the United States into the territory of Mexico. Young displayed great skill in removing 15,000 souls many hundred miles, over an almost pathless wilderness, in the midst of winter, to a new home, yet to be made, many hundred miles away. The first band crossed the Mississippi on the ice in February, 1846.

The Nauvoo *Times and Seasons* said : "To see such a large body of men, women and children compelled, by the inefficiency of the law, to leave a great city in the month of February, for the sake of the enjoyment of pure religion, fills the soul with astonishment and gives the world a sample of fidelity and faith brilliant as the sun, forcible as the tempest, and enduring as eternity."

This journey occupied nearly three months. Colonel Thomas L. Kane, brother of Doctor Elisha Kane, who became so illustrious by his polar tour, witnessed this emigration, and writes of it in the most glowing terms for its strict order, the devotional exercises of the people, their quiet endurance, and he concludes : " Every day closed as every day began, with an invocation of the Divine favor, without which no Mormon seemed to dare to lay himself down to rest. With the first shining of the stars laughter and loud talking were hushed. The neighbor went his way. You heard the last hymn sung, and then the thousand voice murmur of prayer was heard, like bubbling water falling down the hill."

The war with Mexico brought Utah, with Salt Lake City, within the enlarged boundaries of the United States. Brigham Young was a man of undoubted ability and great sagacity, but with an exceedingly coarse and vulgar mind. Upon their arrival at Salt Lake, he issued a proclamation to all the world, from which the following is extracted :

"The kingdom of God consists in correct principles, and it mattereth not what a man's religious faith is, whether he is a Presbyterian, a Methodist, a Baptist, a Latter Day Saint, a Mormon, a Campbellite, a Catholic, an Episcopalian, a Mohammedan, or even a Pagan, or anything else. If he will bow the knee, and with his tongue will confess that Jesus is the Christ, and will support good and wholesome laws for the regulation of society, we hail him as a brother, and will stand by him as he stands by us in these things, for every man's faith is a matter between his own soul and his God alone. But if he shall deny the Jesus, curse God, shall indulge in drunkenness, debauchery and crime, lie, swear, steal, etc., etc., he shall have no place in our midst, etc., etc."

With the flood of emigration into Utah, the enforcement of the laws of the United States over the territory, what will become of Mormonism ?

SALUTATORY

In the first issue of the *Van Burenite*, by Joshua Seney :

" We shall advocate with a becoming zeal, and dignifiedly in manner, the great Democratic Republican principles, as established and taught by Thomas Jefferson. That ours is a government of specified and limited—not general—powers, and ought so to be strictly observed, to attain the ends for which it was established, all must admit.

" The few and venerable patriots, who, when our government dated its existence, were upon the bright summit of glory, and have lived till this late day, are willing to exclaim that our *system* of government has eminently exceeded the most sanguine expectations of those who achieved the glorious victory upon which it was established, and became an object, not only of admiration, but of envy and emulation by all the world.

"It is therefore our duty, rendered imperious by the position we occupy as a nation, to preserve for its character as pure and untarnished as the bright and illustrious spirit of liberty, which dictated its existence among its framers, and still serves as a beacon light to the benighted, and a home for the oppressed of mankind, the object for which the blood of our forefathers and heroes—and labor of our ages have been bestowed to obtain.

"In regard to the present federal administration, we unhesitatingly declare that we will wage against it and its measures an unyielding opposition. We would banish from us all prejudice—cast off all party predilection, and admonish the American people to view the awful and deplorable condition of our country, brought about by the short federal predomination of one year, and ask themselves if this is the 'change' to which they were invited.

"The Democracy, who, in trying times, have been entreated to rally and rescue our government, must appreciate the present as a crisis equally important, and prepare to restore her from the dominion of an unprincipled and reckless political party, who are now plunging her into debt, disgrace and dishonor, regardless of consequences. We shall endeavor to maintain a courteous but decided position in regard to the principles we intend promulgating, and in discussion have a strict observance for the truth of what shall appear in our paper. * * * * * *

"With these remarks we throw ourselves upon the support of our friends in the cause of Democracy, and by an honest, fearless and independent course, we hope to merit the support which they shall be pleased to bestow upon us."

THE OLD STATE HOUSE.

The reader will find no fault with the writer for preserving for him a short history of the old State House, and I am sure he will value the "Dirge on the State House Bell." Governor Chase's speech must not be lost.

Columbus took great pride in this occasion of welcome, and the historic data referred to by Governor Chase are so important, and the "Dirge" so beautiful, that they are attached without further comment:

On the evening of the 6th of January, 1857, there was a superb banquet given at the Capitol by the citizens of Columbus to the members of the legislature, heads of departments, judiciary, citizens and strangers—a mighty throng. Visitors were seen from all parts of the state, male and female, and some besides—a prodigious crowd. In fact almost everybody seemed to be there, and they were welcome.

The "Cleveland Grays," a fine looking company, arrived at one o'clock, and were received by the "State Fencibles," of Columbus, whose guests they were. The two companies, when marching, made a splendid appearance.

During the day, the State House was duly prepared for the great convocation. All chairs and furniture were removed from the halls. The rotunda had been arched, and was handsomely decorated with tri-colored muslin, evergreens, etc., the tables for the feasting being within it, and placed in a semi-curcular form.

At night the whole edifice was brilliantly lighted, including the dome, which was finely illuminated, and showed to great advantage. "The crowd at one time inside the yard," says the *Ohio State Journal*, "must have numbered 4,000, while about 1,000 were outside at the door of the old office of the secretary of state, which was the only open place of entry to the inside of the square."

About nine o'clock a. m., the exercises commenced in the hall of the house of representatives. Prayer was offered and addresses made.

At the conclusion of Mr. Kelly's address, Governor Chase arose and said:

EXTRACT FROM THE ADDRESS OF GOVERNOR CHASE.

"It is made my very agreeable duty to respond, in behalf of the people of the state, to the cordial welcome which you, sir, in behalf of the citizens of Franklin county, have just extended to them.

"It was very fit that the citizens of the county—within whose limits the seat of the state government is established—should distinguish the occasion upon which the state capitol is first opened for occupancy, by an invitation to their fellow citizens of other counties, to join with them in their festival of congratulation. The multitudes who now throng these halls, attest the cordial promptitude with which the invitation has been accepted. Only the words of welcome which you have uttered were needed to complete their satisfaction.

"In their name, sir, I thank you. In their name I thank the citizens, whose organ you are; in their name I thank the committee, under whose care this pleasant festival has been provided. I only wish that all the people of the state could be here to participate in it.

"We dismiss, to-night, all memory of party divisions. We forget the things wherein we differ; we remember only the things wherein we agree.

"Over the gates of a city in Scotland once appeared, and perhaps appears now, this inscription, "*Let Glasgow Flourish!*" In the heart of every son and daughter of Ohio, native or adopted, in this city or in the country, at home or abroad, lives and shall live, ever fresh and ever fervent, the warm aspiration, "LET OHIO FLOURISH."

"A century ago, Ohio was a French dominion. French forts—at Sandusky; on the Maumee, then the Miamis; at Erie, then Presqu' Isle; at Pittsburg, then Duquesne—commanded its whole extent, and connected it with the great line of French possessions, extending through the interior, from the mouth of the St. Lawrence to the mouth of the Mississippi. The apparent destiny of Ohio was to French civilization and despotic government.

"But though England, careless of interest or possessions, actually offered to yield to France all the territory west of New York and the Alleghenies, there were Americans who better understood its immediate value and future importance. Conspicuous among these were Washington and Franklin. The former, in 1754, led a military expedition to the banks of the Monongahela; the latter, indefatigable in his endeavors to rouse attention to the importance of extending English colonization beyond the Alleghanies, confidently predicted that the country between the Lakes and the Ohio would 'become, perhaps, in less than another century, a populous and powerful dominion.'

"The efforts of Franklin were partially successful. Nine years later the French dominion had passed away forever. By the treaty of Paris, of 1763, France ceded to Great Britain all her North American possessions east of the Mississippi.

" But the substitute for French civilization proposed by Great Britain was barbarism. Already jealous of the increasing strength of her American colonies, or believing that they would be, commercially, more profitable if confined to the Atlantic slope, she attempted to restrict their westward extension by a Royal Proclamation prohibiting settlements west of the Alleghanies.

"Under the effect of this proclamation Ohio remained a wilderness for twenty years, until, in 1783, another treaty of Paris annihilated British dominion within its limits, and transferred its possession to the American Republic, then first acknowledged as an Independent member of the Community of Nations.

" A new era was now to begin its course. Anglo-Saxon civilization and Republican institutions were now to take the place of savage barbarism. Plans of emigration and settlement were promptly devised and adopted. At the mouth of the Muskingum, between the Miamis, and on the borders of Erie, the noble old pioneers of the west, many of them distinguished officers and soldiers of the revolution, commenced the work of subduing the wilderness. Regular institutions of government were organized under the ordinance of 1787, and that grand career of development and progress, which has so far outstripped anticipation, was fully inaugurated.

" Another twenty years passed away, and Ohio was a state of the American Union. Her first public act recognized the inviolability of personal rights; the sacredness of private obligations; the absolute freedom of conscience, and the indispensable necessity to good government. of religion, morality and knowledge. Upon these stable foundations she has built wisely and prosperously. I need not recite her recent history: you know it well. Nor need I remind you of her great works of improvement. of her liberal provision and organization of education, or of her noble charities. It is enough to say that ' a century ' has passed and the prophetic anticipation of Franklin is more than fulfilled.

" Permit me now to turn from this brief retrospect of our general history to that which forms the special interest of this occasion.

" Forty-five years ago the spot on which we now stand was covered by the primeval forest. The general assembly of 1811-12. ordained the establishment upon it of the seat of government for the state.

" The foundations of the old State House were laid the next year. Three years later it was ready for occupancy, and was actually occupied by the legislature which assembled in December, 1816.

" In that edifice for thirty-five years, the general assembly, invested not only with the whole power of legislation but with the whole power of appointment also, directed the government of the state. The new constitution was adopted in the fall of 1851, and six months later, the old State House, as if unwilling to survive the old constitution, perished by fire.

"Of the stone tablets which were inserted in the wall over each door of entrance, two have been preserved. The inscriptions upon them curiously illustrate the honest manliness and straightforward principles of the pioneers.

"The inscription over the western entrance was this :

"'General good the object of *Legislation*,
perfected by a knowledge of man's wants, and
Nature's abounding means applied by establishing
principles opposed to *Monopoly*.'"—LUDLOW.

"Over the southern and principal entrance, were inscribed several lines by the poet of the Columbiad, perhaps, copied from that very patriotic but most unreadable epic, the sentiments of which will be admitted to be excellent, whatever may be said of the poetry :

"'Equality of Right is Nature's plan,
And following Nature is the march of man.
Based on its rock of right your empire lies,
On walls of wisdom let the fabric rise ;
Preserve your principles ; their force unfold ;
Let nations prove them, and let Kings behold.
EQUALITY, your first firm grounded stand ;
Then FREE ELECTION ; then your FEDERAL BAND :
This holy triad should forever shine,
The great Compendium of all Rights Divine.
Creed of all schools, whence youths by millions draw
Their themes of Right, their decalogues of law ;
Till men shall wonder (in these codes inured)
How wars were made, how tyrants were endured.'"—BARLOW.

"It seems that our sturdy fathers thought that the word 'Federal' was liable to misconception ; for they caused it to be erased by painting over it the word 'Union.' In process of time, however, the paint washed off—what a warning this to politicians !—and the word 'Federal' reappeared, as originally engraved.

"With the OLD STATE HOUSE, and the Old Constitution, terminated an epoch in the history of our state, to which her children will ever look back with patriotic pride. Even now there seem to pass before me the forms of the noble men who made it illustrious. There moves Putnam, honored with the confidence of Washington ; there Harrison, magnanimous in thought and heroic in deeds ; there Worthington, the friend of Jefferson ; there Burnet, wise in legislation and upright in magistracy ; there the honest and unselfish Morrow ; there Vance, faithful to every trust ; there the generous and eloquent Lytle, too early lost ; there the accomplished Hamer, spared by the sword, but felled by disease in a foreign land ; there Morris, the fearless tribune of the people ; there Sherman, exchanging, before life's noon, the ermine for the shroud; there Hitchcock, clear in judgment and inflexible in integrity; and there——but I must break off the enumeration. Time would fail me were I to attempt to name even half of those whose elevation of character, purity of purpose, sagacity in council and vigor in action distinguished that period. Happy shall we be if we prove ourselves worthy successors of such men."

Those who remember the clear and oft admired tones of the old capitol bell, will not regret the insertion of the following appropriate dirge, taken from one of the Columbus papers, as an appendix to this book:

[For the Elevator.]

DIRGE OF THE STATE HOUSE BELL.

BY J. M. D.

Columbus, farewell! no more shall you hear,
My voice so familiar for many a year—
Those musical sounds which you recognized well,
As the clear-sounding tones of your State House Bell.

Ere the red man had gone, I was mounted on high,
When the wide-spreading forest which greeted mine eye,
Gave forth from its thickets the panther's wild yell,
As he heard the strange sounds of your State House Bell.

Unaccompanied, unanswered, I sounded alone,
And mingled my chime with its echo's deep tone;
Till spire after spire, rising round me, did swell
Their response, to the sound of your State House Bell.

I called you together to make yourselves laws,
And daily my voice was for every good cause;
When aught of importance or strange was to tell,
You were summoned full soon by your State House Bell.

As a sentinel, placed on the watch-tower's height,
Columbus, I've watched thee by day and by night—
Though slumb'ring unconscious, when danger befell,
You were roused by the clang of your State House Bell.

But while I watched o'er you, the Fire King came.
And enveloped my tower in his mantle of flame;
Yet, true to my calling, my funeral knell
Was tolled, on that night, by your State House Bell.

Your sons of the Engine and Hose, ever brave,
And prompt at my call, quickly hastened to save;
But alas! their best efforts were fruitless to quell
The flames that rose over your State House Bell.

When my Cupola trembled, I strove but to sound
One peal of farewell to your thousands around ;
But you lost, as 'midst timbers and cinders I fell,
The last smothered tone of your State House Bell.

COLUMBUS, February 10, 1852.

APPENDIX.

NO. 2.

THE TIFFIN PAPERS—JOURNAL OF THE CONSTITUTIONAL CONVENTION—FIRST MESSAGE OF THE FIRST GOVERNOR TO THE FIRST GENERAL ASSEMBLY OF OHIO—MESSAGE OF 1803—MESSAGE CONCERNING THE ARREST OF THE BURR—BLANNERHASSET EXPEDITION—TIFFIN IN THE UNITED STATES SENATE—ELECTION OF SPEAKER OF HOUSE OF REPRESENTATIVES OF OHIO.

THE TIFFIN PAPERS.

THE following records, papers and documents pertaining to the life and public services of Governor Tiffin, were collected with great care. They are so full of historic data and record so many interesting events, that, while the careless reader may treat them lightly, the author feels sure that the thinker and lover of history will value them highly, and for his especial benefit has called them the "Tiffin Papers."

THE FIRST CONSTITUTION OF OHIO.

In July, 1787, the congress of the United States, acting under the provisions of the "Articles of Confederation," enacted the widely known "Ordinance of 1787," for the government of the territory of the United States lying to the northwest of the Ohio; and this may be said to have been the first movement towards the establishment of civil government within that vast region.

For the purpose of carrying that ordinance into effect and of organizing a territorial government, on the 5th of October, 1787, congress appointed General Arthur St. Clair governor and Winthrop Sargent secretary of the territory; and a few days thereafter, Samuel Holden Parsons, John Armstrong and James Mitchell Varnum were appointed its judges.

During the summer of 1788, without respecting the opinions prevailing at that time, when the states, as such, were supposed to possess more dignity and more political rights than belonged or could possibly belong to an unorganized community, even when acting under supposed Federal authority, the governor and two of the judges of the territory assembled at Marietta, and commenced what they conceived to be their duty of legislating for the residents of the territory, but their enactments were disallowed by congress, because they had been framed without warrant in law by those who possessed no power to enact a law.

APPENDIX.

The organization of a new administration under President Washington was followed soon after by a re-organization of the government of the northwestern territory, General St. Clair and Messrs. Sargent and Parsons having been re-appointed, and Messrs. Symmes and Turner called to the bench as judges.

In July, 1790, the secretary, then acting as governor, with Judges Symmes and Turner, met at Vincennes, and repeated the folly of the previous government by enacting other laws for the government of the inhabitants of the territory, none of which, however, were approved by the congress, because they had been enacted as original laws, and had not been adopted from the existing codes of states under the provision of the "Ordinance of 1787," which was the organic law of the territory.

In the summer of 1795 a code of laws was adopted unanimously from the codes of the several states, and in 1799, under the provision of the ordinance, and the territory, having five thousand white male inhabitants, the first general assembly of the territory was convened at Cincinnati.

In 1800 the territory was divided, and soon after, measures were taken to organize a state in the eastern portion of it, not, however, without so strong an opposition, both in the general assembly and in various parts of the territory, that the overthrow of the scheme would have been complete and emphatic, had those who promoted it, for their own purposes, submitted the proposition either to the territorial assembly or to the body of the inhabitants. An act was crowded through the congress, however, notwithstanding the general opposition which was known to exist both in the assembly and amongst the people, " to enable the people of the eastern division of the territory, northwest of the river Ohio, to form a constitution and state government, and for the admission of such state into the Union, on an equal footing with the original states, and for other purposes;" and on the 1st of November of that year, the convention which that act assumed to authorize met at Chillicothe and framed and enacted the first constitution, all of which was done in defiance of the known will of those it was designed to govern, and was thrust upon them by force, without their consent, in order that those who plotted it might be spared from the shame, which its inevitable and contemptuous rejection by "the people" would have brought upon them.

Edward Tiffin was the member from Ross and the speaker of that assembly.

The "Journal" of that convention has been considered one of the rarest, as it is one of the most interesting tracts connected with the history of the west ; and there is but one copy of it, and that is in the state library at Columbus, Ohio. It is a thin octavo of forty-eight pages, shabbily printed, and bears the following title :

" Journal of the convention of the territory of the United States, northwest of the Ohio, begun and held at Chillicothe, on Monday, the first day of November, A. D. 1802, and of the independence of the United States the twenty-seventh. Published by authority, Columbus: George Nash, state printer, 1827."

" In order that it may become better known, and as the first of a series of papers illustrative of the constitutional history of the several states, we reproduce this very important western document, complete, and we assure ourselves that our readers will be glad to see it."—[Editor Historical Magazine:

JOURNAL OF THE CONVENTION.

Begun and held at the town of Chillicothe, in the county of Ross and territory aforesaid, on the first Monday in November (being the first day thereof) in the year of our Lord, one thousand, eight hundred and two, and of the independence of the United States of America, the twenty-seventh.

On which day, being the time and place appointed for the meeting of the convention for the purpose of forming a constitution and state government, by the act of congress entitled : "An act to enable the people of the eastern division of the territory, northwest of the river Ohio, to form a constitution and state government and for the admission of such state into the Union on an equal footing with the original states, and for other purposes," the following members appeared, who produced certificates of their having been duly chosen to serve in the convention, and having severally taken the oath of fidelity to the United States and also an oath faithfully to discharge the duties of their office, took their seats, to wit: (See the names of the members as signed to the constitution).

On motion, the convention proceeded to the choice of a president *pro tem.* when William Goforth, Esq., was chosen and took the chair.

On motion, the convention proceeded to the choice of a secretary *pro tem.* whereupon Mr. William McFarland was chosen and proceeded to the duties of his office.

On motion,

Resolved, That a standing committee of privileges and elections, to consist of five members, be chosen by ballot, whose duty it shall be to examine and report upon the credentials of the members returned to serve in the convention, and to take into consideration all such matters as shall or may be referred to them, touching returns and elections. and to report their proceedings, with their opinions thereon, to the convention.

And a committee was appointed of Messrs. Worthington, Darlinton, Smith, Milligan and Huntington.

On motion, the convention proceeded by ballot to the choice of a doorkeeper, to serve during the pleasure of the convention, and upon examining the ballots, a majority of the votes was found in favor of Adam Betz.

On motion, ordered that a committee of three be appointed to prepare and report rules for the regulation and government of the convention, and that Messrs. Reily, Milligan and Worthington be the said committee.

And then the convention adjourned until to-morrow morning at 10 o'clock.

Tuesday, November 2d, 1802.

Several other members appeared, who severally produced certificates of their having been chosen as members of the convention, and having taken the oath of fidelity to the United States and also an oath faithfully to discharge the duties of their office, took their seats.

Mr. Worthington, from the committee of privileges and elections, to whom was referred the several returns of elections of members to serve in the convention, made a report, which he delivered in at the secretary's table, where the same was read in the words following, to wit:

APPENDIX. 665

"The committee of privileges and elections, to whom was referred the certificates of the election of the following members: (named in the "Journal") having carefully examined the same, find them regular and agreeably to a law of the territory, entitled: 'An act to ascertain the number of free male inhabitants, of the age of twenty-one, in the territory of the United States, northwest of the river Ohio, and to regulate the elections of the representatives for the same, and that the members aforesaid, from the certificates to us referred, appear duly elected.'

The said report was again read and on the question thereupon, agreed by the convention.

On motion,

Resolved, That the convention proceed by ballot to the choice of a president.

The convention accordingly proceeded to choose their president, and upon examination of the ballots, it was found that Edward Tiffin, Esq., was duly chosen, who accordingly took the seat in the chair and delivered the following address:

"GENTLEMEN: I beg you to be assured that I duly appreciate the honor you have conferred in selecting me to preside over your deliberations on this important occasion. The duties of the chair will, I presume, be pleasing and easy, for, from the known characters of the gentlemen who compose the convention, there can be no doubt but that the utmost propriety and decorum will be observed, without the aid of interference from the chair. Whatever rules you may adopt for the government of the convention shall be strictly observed, and in every decision which may be required from the chair, the utmost impartiality shall be evinced."

On motion,

Resolved, That the convention proceed by ballot to the choice of a secretary, and upon examining the ballots, it was found that Thomas Scott, Esq., was duly chosen, who thereupon took the oath of fidelity to the United States and also an oath faithfully to discharge the duties of his office.

On motion,

Resolved, That the convention proceed by ballot to the choice of an assistant secretary, and upon examining the ballots a majority of the votes of the whole number was found in favor of Mr. William McFarland, who thereupon took the oath of fidelity to the United States and also an oath faithfully to discharge the duties of his office.

Convention adjourned until to-morrow.

Wednesday, November 3d, 1802.

Another member, to wit: from the county of Hamilton, John Mitchell, who appeared, produced certificate of his having been duly chosen as a member in the convention, and having taken the oath of fidelity to the United States and also an oath faithfully to discharge the duties of his office, took his seat.

Mr. Reily, from the committee appointed to prepare and report rules for the regulation and government of the convention, made a report, which was received and read, whereupon,

Resolved, That the same be established as the standing rules and orders of the convention. Then follow the standing rules.

On motion, leave was given to lay before the convention a resolution on the subject of forming a constitution and state government, which resolution was received and read the first time.

On motion, the said resolution was read the second time, whereupon,

Resolved, That the convention will immediately resolve itself into a committee of the whole on said resolution.

The convention accordingly resolved itself into the said committee, Mr. Goforth in the chair, and after some time spent therein, Mr. President resumed the chair, and Mr. Goforth reported that the committee had, according to order, had the said resolution under consideration, and made no amendments thereto.

The said resolution was then amended at the secretary's table, and read the third time, and on the question that the convention do agree to the same, in the words following, to-wit:

WHEREAS, congress did by the law, entitled "an act to enable the people of the eastern division of the territory northwest of the river Ohio, to form a constitution and state government, and for the admission of said state into the Union, on an equal footing with the original states, and for other purposes, (provided that the members of the convention thus duly elected, agreeably to the act aforesaid, when met, shall first determine by a majority of the whole number elected, whether it be or be not expedient, at this time, to form a constitution and state government for the people within the said territory;) therefore,

Resolved, That it is the opinion of this convention that it is expedient at this time to form a constitution and state government.

It was resolved in the affirmative—yeas, 32; nays, 1.

The yeas and nays being demanded, the vote in the negative was Mr. Cutter.

"Sec. 7.—No negro or mulatto shall ever be eligible to any office, civil or military, or give their oath in any court of justice against a white person, be subject to do military duty or pay a poll tax in this state; provided always, and it is fully understood and declared, that all negroes and mulattos now in, or who may hereafter reside in this state, shall be entitled to all the privileges of citizens of this state, not excepted by the constitution."

And on the question thereupon it was resolved in the affirmative—yeas, 19; nays, 16.

Ayes—Messrs. Abrams, Baldwin, Blair, Byrd, Caldwell, Carpenter, Donalson, Grubb, Humphrey, Kirker, McIntire, Massie, Milligan, Smith, Morrow, Tiffin, Woods and Worthington.

Nays—Messrs. Abbot, Brown, Cutter, Dunlavy, Gatch, Gilman, Goforth, Huntington, Kitchel, Paul, Putnam, Reily, Sargent, Updegraph, Wills and Wilson.

On motion the fourth article of the constitution designating the qualification of electors, was taken up and read the third time, in order for its final passage.

A motion was made to amend the said article by striking out after the word "elector" in the seventh line of the first section the words following:

"Provided, that all male negroes and mulattos, now residing in this territory, shall, at the age of twenty-one years, be entitled to the right of suffrage,

APPENDIX. 667

if they shall within one year make a record of their citizenship with the clerk of the county in which they may reside; and, provided also, that they have paid or are charged with a state or county tax."

Resolved in the affirmative—yeas, 17; nays, 17. The convention being equally divided, and Mr. President declaring himself with the yeas.

Sec. 19.—The legislature of this state shall not allow the following officers of government greater annual salaries than as follows, until the year 1808, to wit:

The governor not more than one thousand dollars; the judges of the supreme court not more than one thousand dollars each; the secretary not more than five hundred dollars; the auditor of public accounts not more than seven hundred and fifty dollars; the treasurer not more than four hundred and fifty dollars; no member of the legislature shall receive more than two dollars per day during his attendance on the legislature, nor more for every twenty-five miles' travel in going to and returning from the general assembly.

It was resolved in the affirmative—yeas, 21; nays, 13.

November 27, 1802.

Mr. Goforth, from the committee appointed to prepare an address to the president of the United States, and both branches of the federal legislature, expressive of the high sense the convention entertain of the cheerful and philanthropic manner in which they made provision for the admission of this state into the Union; and expressive of the approbation of the present administration of the general government, made a report, which was received and read the first time.

On motion the said report was read the second time, and agreed to by the convention in the words following:

To the President and both Houses of Congress of the United States:

The convention of the state of Ohio, duly appreciating the importance of a free and independent state government, and impressed with sentiments of gratitude to the congress of the United States for the prompt and decisive measures taken at their last session to enable the people of the northwestern territory to emerge from their colonial government and to assume a rank among the sister states, beg leave to take the earliest opportunity of announcing to you the important event; on this occasion the convention cannot help expressing their unequivocal approbation of the measures pursued by the present administration of the general government and both houses of congress, in diminishing the public burdens, cultivating peace with all nations, and promoting the happiness and prosperity of our country.

Resolved, That the president of the convention do enclose to the president of the United States, to the president of the senate and to the speaker of the house of representatives of the United States the foregoing address.

On motion resolved, that the constitution be ratified by the convention, and thereby the following members ratified and subscribed their names to the constitution, to wit: EDWARD TIFFIN,

President and representative from the county of Ross.

From Adams county—Joseph Darlinton, Israel Donalson and Thomas Kirker.

From Belmont county—James Caldwell, Elijah Woods.

From Clermont county—Philip Gatch, James Sargent.
From Fairfield county—Henry Abrams, Emanuel Carpenter.
From Hamilton county—John W. Browne, Charles William Byrd, Francis Dunlavy, William Goforth, John Kitchel, Jeremiah Morrow, John Paul, John Reiley, John Smith, John Wilson.
From Jefferson county—Rudolph Bair, George Humphrey, John Milligan, Nathan Updegraph, Bazabel Wills.
From Ross county—Michael Baldwin, James Grubb, Nathaniel Massie, Thomas Worthington.
From Trumbull county—David Abbot, Samuel Huntington.
From Washington county—Ephraim Cutter, Benjamin Ives Gilman, John McIntire, Rufus Putnam.
William Creighton, Jr., secretary of state; salary, $500.

THE FIRST MESSAGE OF THE FIRST GOVERNOR OF OHIO TO THE FIRST GENERAL ASSEMBLY OF OHIO.

To the General Assembly of the State of Ohio:

GENTLEMEN OF THE SENATE AND OF THE HOUSE OF REPRESENTATIVES: We now exhibit another sovereign, free and independent state, organized northwest of the Ohio, which is about to be added to the confederate government, emphatically styled " the world's best hope ;" many of our citizens have looked forward to that period, and not without reason, when they should become a free people, and I sincerely congratulate you and them, that they have now an entire legislature of their own choice, assembled under a constitution sacred to liberty ; a constitution which rests upon equal rights and displays a pure representative system, a constitution whereby the rulers are derivable from, and amenable to the people; a constitution calculated to excite in all our citizens a patriotic zeal, by giving each individual an opportunity, by merit, of being called upon to participate in the government, that all may strive habitually to feel and distinctly understand its first principles.

The period wherein we commence our national existence is peculiarly auspicious; the government of the United States respected abroad, strong in the confidence of its citizens at home, and by a wise and prudent policy in lopping off all extraneous excrescences from the body politic, requires less fiscal exactions to preserve it in its pristine health and constitutional vigor ; the good effects resulting therefrom to us, in our first essay towards self-government are evident; and it is a pleasing reflection that the sons of Ohio, conscious of the tender solicitude and lively interest manifested for the happiness and welfare of every portion of the American people as well, are fast progressing with their fellow citizens in the other states towards a union of sentiment and affection.

DEMAND FOR A FREE PASSAGE TO THE SEA.

The recent embarrassments to our infant commerce, occasioned by the irregularities at New Orleans, we have every reason to believe, will soon be removed by the prompt and efficacious measures taken by the president of the United States, and which has been aided by the minister of his Catholic Majesty, and from the embassy, which has been wisely adopted, we may further hope that our situation will be bettered, by placing our commerce on a footing not liable to similar interruptions in future. If, however, the just and natural expectations of government should be frustrated, we are consoled by the lively sensibility excited in the general government, and in every part of the Union, for the situation of their western brethren, and although every friend to humanity may have to regret the dernier resort, yet it is as much impossible to prevent the Mississippi from discharging its vast contents, swelled with the numerous navigable rivers with which it is nourished, into the bosom of the ocean, as to prevent, at the call of government, of whose magnanimity I have no doubt, those brave and intrepid citizens who are everywhere settled on their banks and fertile plains from asserting their natural, and acquired rights, and forcing with the stream the fruits of their industry to every part of the world.

In giving to the general assembly information of the state of the government and recommending to their consideration such measures as may be deemed expedient, a wide field of action must necessarily be opened, and discover the important duties devolving on the first legislature; the foundation of the government is laid; to you, gentlemen, it is committed to raise the superstructure, and carry in a great measure into effect the national will.

It will, no doubt, afford you much consolation, on receiving from the proper officers, a statement of our finances, in discovering that the present revenue, if wholly reserved for state purposes, is adequate to all the necessary exigencies of government, and that by a true economy, devoid of parsimony, the public faith and credit may be maintained without any additional augmentation in consequence of that change which has taken place.

The constitution having assigned to the legislature the appointment of all the principal officers in the government, that instrument will consequently pass in review, and in due time occupy the serious attention of both houses. Under the constitution of the United States, you will also have to select two of our citizens to represent the state in the senate of the United States for six years, and to provide by law for the election of one member of the house of representatives.

The laws levying a tax on land, the principal source from whence the revenue has proceeded, expiring of themselves, you will discover the necessity of taking that subject under consideration; and as experience has pointed out the defects which have heretofore existed, you will be hereby aided in devising a system of taxation which shall operate equally on all, and be incapable of misconstruction in favor of any, who either from design or neglect, may fail to comply with the just and necessary requisition of government. It may also be proper to add, that under existing laws, great neglect has been manifested by those who have alienated their lands in making the proper transfers on the books of taxation; that considerable locations have been made by individuals in the United States military tract, in the Virginia military tract, and at some of the United States offices, and which having never been entered for taxation, to provide for bringing all lands under the law, which are subject thereto, and to prevent embarrassments in the collections in the future, are amongst the several objects which will naturally present themselves to your minds when deliberating upon this subject. The return of the special agent sent by the convention to Congress, instructed with certain propositions, is daily expected, and which, if acceded to by them, will affect this subject. As soon as official information is received it shall be immediately communicated.

The constitution having made an entire change in the judiciary system necessary, it will be proper to direct your particular attention to the third article of that instrument upon this subject. To erect and establish courts with common law and chancery powers, with civil and criminal jurisdiction, at whose bar, life, reputation, property and everything dear to freemen may be at stake, as well as to fill the benches with proper characters to pronounce the law, and to provide for an impartial selection of juries, are of such vast importance in every well regulated government as to require the utmost deliberation and caution. Under the same article it will be necessary to provide by law for the election of a competent number of justices of the peace in each township, in the several counties; and it may be an object worthy your enquiry, whether it would not be economical and judicious to establish each county into a court to manage its internal concerns and regulate its general police.

Within one year after the meeting of the first legislature it is required that an enumeration of all the white male inhabitants above twenty-one years of age shall be made; it will therefore be necessary to provide by law for the accomplishment of that object, in order that a due apportionment of senators and representatives may be assigned to each county or district.

A well regulated and disciplined malitia, being justly considered in every republic as its safeguard for protection and defense, I cannot but recommend to your consideration a review of the existing laws relative thereto. The first, passed in the year 1799, is a good system, but as it was adapted to the state of the district, when the Indiana and northwestern territory was one, and much injured by a subsequent act, passed in the year 1801, which repealed that part relative to the appointment of general officers, and which the constitution now recognizes, it is suggestive whether it would not be best to revive the former law, with such alterations as will make it applicable to our present situation, aided with such other improvements as you may find it susceptible of, as well as to provide for the election of its officers.

The season of the year in which you were necessarily convened to carry the government into operation, being inconvenient to many of you, will doubtless excite a wish to curtail the present session, and devote your immediate attention to such objects as are most pressing, and more especially as there is reason to believe you will be much importuned with business of a local nature, from different parts of the state; otherwise it would have been advisable to have taken a review of all the present existing laws, many of which were adopted in the first and enacted under the second grade of the territorial governments, requires much revision; one, however, adopted at an early period, "regulating marriages," whereby the governor is exclusively authorized to grant marriage licenses, and which has been justly complained of, will, I hope, now be expunged from our code, and one better adapted to the object of its institution, and more congenial to the spirit of the government, enacted in its stead.

When we consider the present prosperous situation of the United States, and contemplate our own present and future prospects, situate as we are, in a country where nature has been lavish of her favors to every part; where our soil, climate, and navigable waters present to the mind of observation and contemplation the most pleasing view and prospects of the future greatness and importance of this part of the American empire, we have much reason to render the sincere homage of grateful hearts to that Being who has so highly favored us, and every inducement for the exercise in improving these means now within our reach towards the happiness and prosperity of our country.

"Religion, morality and knowledge are necessary to all good governments," says the excellent constitution under which you are convened, and to this great truth we must all subscribe. The liberal grants of land made by the United States for the purposes of erecting and endowing universities and other seminaries of learning, and for the support of religion, are advantages in these respects superior to those which, perhaps, any other new country can boast of; to improve those means with advantage towards the noble ends for which they were given; to preserve the public faith unimpeached; to practice economy in all public expenditures; to impose no taxes upon our citizens for state or county purposes but what are really necessary for their honest wants; to cultivate peace and harmony with our Indian neighbors, and to exemplify both in our public acts and private life. Every disposition towards discountenancing idleness and dissipation, and by encouraging industry, frugality, temperance and every moral virtue are objects of such importance to our rising republic, that they cannot fail, if attended to, of producing the best effects in forming for us a national character, which may be the admiration of all. On my part, gentlemen, you may rest assured it shall be no less my honest pride than it is made my constitutional duty, cordially to co-operate with you in every measure your united wisdom and experience may devise for the public good. EDWARD TIFFIN.
CHILLICOTHE, March 5, 1803.

GOVERNOR TIFFIN'S SECOND MESSAGE.

To the General Assembly of the State of Ohio:

GENTLEMEN OF THE SENATE AND OF THE HOUSE OF REPRESENTATIVES: We have met together to consider the situation of our political society, and under circumstances the most auspicious, both as it respects our exterior and interior relations, and sufficient to excite in all our hearts the most sincere effusion of gratitude to that Being in whose hands are the destinies of nations and of man.

THE PURCHASE OF LOUISIANA.

At the close of the last session of the general assembly, our fellow citizens were anxiously concerned at the prohibition of an invaluable acquired right which was unjustly withheld by the officers of the Spanish government at the port of New Orleans, and which threatened to annihilate the commerce and becloud the best prospects of this and the neighboring western states; yet, anxiously concerned as they were, and conscious of the great injury they belabored under, they sustained it with a fortitude and prudence which has done them honor—wisely confiding in the general government, to whom alone it belonged to have the evil remedied, and to provide against similar events in future; and herein we have an additional inducement for that confidence which the legislature expressed at their last session in the executive of the United States, and in the measures which were pursuing to accomplish those objects, and which have succeeded beyond our most sanguine expectations.

The right of depositing the produce of exportation of all that extensive, fertile country, whose waters are tributary to the Mississippi, either at New Orleans or anywhere else on the banks of the river near its mouth, although a great object, yet, would have been held at best, but a precarious tenure, while both sides were subject to a foreign government, but by a wise and magnanimous policy, war, ever to be deprecated, with all its inconceivable attendant horrors, has been averted, and expenses to support that war, which might have been incalculable, and could not fail to have been heavily felt, are rendered unnecessary, whilst by a friendly negotiation, and in the most just and honorable way, the city and island of New Orleans, with the whole of Louisiana, are added to the American empire, an acquisition incalculable to the United States, whether considered as a territory, rich in natural resources, as a means of securing the uncontrolled and peaceable navigation of the Mississippi, by possessing its key, or as a great and increasing source of national revenue.

In our own state we have this year been favored with abudant crops, less visited by affliction than heretofore, and strengthened with a greatly increased and still increasing population. We have exhibited the pleasing spectacle of a free people, assuming the right of self-government, purely elective in all its branches, and conducting those elections and organizing that government with a temper, moderation and caution becoming a people capable of enjoying those political and religious liberties, which are their inherent rights.

The present state of the militia calls aloud for your particular attention. When the government was first organized a return to the militia was required of the then adjutant-general, who was directed by the 12th section of the "act establishing and regulating the militia," to make a return to the commander-in-chief annually. His answer to that request showed that the militia law had been neglected, and that not a single regiment in the state was either officered or organized, believing that our safety and freedom depends on this class of our fellow citizens, and finding that the only proper safeguard for protection and defence was in this lamentable situation, it was thought expedient, as the existing militia laws from the change of government which had taken place, were not applicable to our present situation, to issue general orders, requiring the senior officers who were in commission in such county, to hold elections agreeably to the constitution, to fill the vacancies in their regiments and make report to the adjutant-general, that the militia might be placed on as respectable footing as existing circumstances would permit. These orders were attended to by some of the commandants with a zeal and activity highly honorable to them, and a few regiments have been completely officered and disciplined, with light companies annexed to them. A return of the effective force, a communication from the president of the United States on this subject, a requisition from the general government to assemble with the least possible delay, and hold in readiness five hundred of the militia, including officers, to compose a regiment, to march to take possession of the lately ceded country of Louisiana, should the officers of the Spanish government either refuse or delay to give it up, agreeably to treaty, with the measures taken to raise this force, and other documents relative thereto, is hereunto annexed. See exhibit No. 1, and from which you will discover the necessity of taking into early consideration an institution on which every free state should place its greatest reliance for repelling aggressions from without, for maintaining order and good government within its own borders, and which tends to keep alive that spirit which effected our independence and gave the United States a name amongst the nations of the earth.

The laws laying a tax on lands will, I hope, this session undergo a revisal and the remedies which time and experience have pointed out, be applied, particularly, it is suggested, whether it would not be advisable to have all the lands of resident proprietors listed anew, provision made from the several officers a list of all lands which have been located or acquired by individuals, and which are subject to, but have never been entered for, taxation. The public weal also requires that a more expeditious and certain way of obliging delinquent collectors to account for and pay into the treasury their respective balances due the state, should be devised ; and it will further be a proper subject for your inquiry, whether it is not necessary that the revenue arising from this source should be wholly reserved for state purposes.

The act regulating the public salt works, etc., etc., etc.

EDWARD TIFFIN.

CHILLICOTHE, December 5, 1803.

MESSAGE ON THE BURR-BLENNERHASSET EXPEDITION.

The speaker laid before the senate the following written message from his excellency the governor of this state, viz:

To the General Assembly of the State of Ohio :

I now communicate to the representatives of the people such operations as have taken place, under the act passed this session, to prevent certain acts hostile to the peace and tranquility of the United States, within the jurisdiction of this state, that they may be fully possessed of what has already occurred and is still in transit.

Immediately upon receiving the law, after its passage, I dispatched an express to Marietta, with orders to arrest the flotilla on the Muskingum river and the agents engaged in its preparations, and to make due inquiry after such proof as would lead to their conviction, as also to prevent any armaments proceeding that might be descending the Ohio, if possible.

The execution of the operation at Marietta was entrusted to Judge Meigs and Major-General Buell. I also dispatched orders to Cincinnati to plant one or more pieces of artillery on the banks of the Ohio, to keep patroles up the river at proper distances, in order to give notice, in due time, of the approach of the boats, either singly or in numbers, and to call out a sufficient force to be able to meet 300 men, the number I expected might probably be with Blennerhasset's and Comfort Tyler's flotillas, if they should effect a junction ; and lest they might attempt to pass in detachments of one boat at a time, not to suffer a single boat to pass without an arrest and examination. The execution of these operations was entrusted to Generals Gano and Findley and Judge Nimms. I have also given authority to Jacob Wilson, Esq., of Steubenville, to act, if occasion offers for his interposition, in that quarter, and it gives me great pleasure to inform you that I last night received a communication from Judge Meigs, of Marietta, announcing the complete success of the operations intrusted to him and General Buell, and whose patriotic efforts entitle them both to my warmest thanks.

It is suspected notice was conveyed to Blennerhasset's island of the passage of the law, and the preparations making here to carry it into immediate effect; for it appears that on the night of the 9th instant, Comfort Tyler passed Marietta with a number (not yet ascertained) of fast rowing boats, with men armed indiscriminately with muskets, pistols and cutlasses, and anchored at the island, and immediately sent an express after Blennerhasset, who was hurrying on his flotilla; that upon discovering the movements of our militia, they fled full speed to the island, which was guarded at night by sentinels and lighted lanterns at proper distances, and none suffered to pass except by countersign or watch-word. Spies were also placed at Marietta to give notice of the movements there. In the meantime, General Buell, by direction of Judge Meigs, with a detachment of militia, proceeded up the Muskingum river in the night, and arrested ten of the batteaux as they were descending the river to join Tyler's forces; they were so hurried that four more of the batteaux were not got ready to embark and would also be seized, which is, I believe, the whole of the Muskingum flotilla. There were near 100 barrels of provisions seized on board, and which, I expect, he also seized with the same remaining batteaux; these batteaux are each forty feet long; wide and covered and calculated to carry one company of men. It is believed notice was immediately given to the island of this seizure, for in about three hours afterwards, on the same night, Blennerhasset and Tyler made their escape from the island, and have pushed, it is said, through Kentucky. Colonel Phelps, of Virginia, with a few mounted men, is in pursuit of them.

I expect Tyler's boats will descend the Ohio, to meet him and Blennerhasset at some point low down on that river, and I have no doubt but that General Gano will render a good account of them as they attempt to pass Cincinnati.

I also received last night a communication from the secretary of war of the United States, by direction of the government, requiring me, without delay, to raise 150 or 200 volunteer militia, to be formed in companies with one field officer, one captain, two subalterns and 70 men, commissioned officers, privates and musicians to each company, in the pay of the United States, and direct them to march to Marietta, with orders to seize the Muskingum flotilla, and prevent it from being removed until further orders from the president. But finding that this service was in part effected, I have ventured, from the necessity of the case, to vary in some degree from these instructions, and which, I hope, will meet the approval of the general government and also of yours. I sent on orders last night to Marietta to raise one company of volunteers, to be composed of one major, one captain, two subalterns and sixty men, commissioned officers, privates and musicians,

APPENDIX. 675

which I have thought sufficient to guard and keep safe the flotilla and stores already arrested. I have also dispatched an express to Cincinnati, with orders to raise two companies as above, each, as I thought the most force wanted there, to relieve the militia previously ordered out, and to secure Comfort Tyler's flotilla while descending the Ohio, if it was not already done. I have no doubt that these three companies will be instantly under arms, and that this hitherto mysterious enterprise will be completely frustrated, and the intended evil levelled at the peace and tranquility of the United States will fall with all its weight on its projectors.

EDWARD TIFFIN.

CHILLICOTHE, December 5, 1806.

President Jefferson, in a message to congress, dated January 22, 1807, on this subject, amongst other things, said:

"Our confidential agent, who had been diligently employed in investigating the conspiracy, had acquired sufficient information to open himself to the governor of the state of Ohio and apply for the immediate exertion of the authority and power of the state to crush the combination. Governor Tiffin and the legislature, with a promptitude, an energy and patriotic zeal, which entitle them to a distinguished place in the affections of their sister states, effected the seizure of all the boats, provisions and other preparations within their reach, and thus gave a first blow, materially disabling the enterprise in its outset."

GOVERNOR TIFFIN ELECTED TO THE UNITED STATES SENATE.

January 1, 1807.

The two houses then proceeded in like manner to the choice of a senator to represent this state in the congress of the United States for the term of six years, from and after the 4th day of March next, in the room of Thomas Worthington, whose term of office then expires, and the ballots being collected and counted, showed the following result:

CANDIDATE.	VOTES.
Edward Tiffin	25
Philemon Bucher	12
John Bigger	2
Return J. Meigs, Jr	2
Tom Tuff	1
Thomas Konkey	1

Edward Tiffin having a majority of the whole number of votes given, was thereupon declared by the speakers of both houses duly elected.

December, 1809.

During the recess, Mr. Tiffin resigned his seat in the senate of the United States.

GOVERNOR TIFFIN IN THE SENATE OF THE UNITED STATES.

The first session of the tenth congress commenced October 26, 1807.

Mr. John Adams presented the credentials of Hon. Edward Tiffin, who took the oath and was seated.

The president communicated to the senate a letter from the governor of the Indian territory, together with certain resolutions of the territorial legislature, on the expediency of suspending the sixth article of the compact contained in the ordinance passed July 13, 1787, concerning the admission of slaves; also a remonstrance against the same from citizens of Clark county, which was read and ordered to be referred to Messrs. Franklin, Kitchill and Tiffin to consider and report thereon. Upon the report of the committee, the senate resolved that it is not expedient to so suspend.

On the 27th of November, 1807, the following resolution was passed in the senate:

Resolved, That a committee be appointed to inquire whether it be compatible with the honor and privileges of the house that John Smith, a senator from Ohio, against whom bills of indictment were found in the circuit court of Virginia, held at Richmond in August last, for treason and misdemeanor, should be permitted any longer to have a seat therein; and that the committee do inquire into all the facts regarding the conduct of Mr. Smith as an alleged associate of Aaron Burr, and report the same to the senate.

During the discussion, Mr. Tiffin, by permission, read in his place a letter from Mr. Smith, as follows:

"WASHINGTON, November 27, 1807.

"DEAR SIR: Just having heard that a motion is pending in the senate to appoint a committee to inquire into certain charges exhibited against me at Richmond by the late grand jury, I beg you, sir, to assure the senate in my name, that nothing will afford me more pleasure than to have a public investigation of the said charges and an opportunity to vindicate my innocence, and I beg you from your seat to make this statement.

"I am, dear sir, respectfully yours, etc.,

"JOHN SMITH.

"HON. MR. TIFFIN."

Smith was not expelled, however.

In a letter to the author on this subject somebody remarked: "In the case of John Smith, I think there were not quite enough votes to insure his expulsion and Pa., I believe, voted against him. D. M. T."

Amongst the numerous measures that Mr. Tiffin supported with his influence and his vote were the following, viz:

A bill for the preservation of peace and maintainance of the authority of the United States in the ports, harbors and waters under their jurisdiction.

A bill extending the rights of suffrage in the Mississippi territory.

A bill authorizing the president of the United States, under certain conditions, to suspend the operation of the act laying an embargo on all ships and vessels in the ports and harbors of the United States.

An act making provision for arming and equipping the whole body of the militia of the United States.

An act to authorize the president of the United States to cause to be prepared for service the frigates and other armed vessels of the United States.

January 19, 1809.

Mr. Tiffin presented sundry petitions from purchasers of public lands in the state of Ohio, stating, "that from the various incidents to which new settlers are liable, and more especially from the great uncertainty of com-

APPENDIX.   677

manding cash for produce at the present time, they will not be able to make up the final payments for their lands at the time they will respectively become due," and praying that congress will so modify the present land laws as will guard them from the embarrassments and ruin they otherwise apprehend may fall upon them. The petitions were referred to Messrs. Tiffin, Gregg and Bradley, to consider and report thereon.

February 14, 1809.

The senate resumed the consideration of the motion made on the 8th instant: "That the several laws laying an embargo on all ships and vessels in the ports and harbors of the United States be repealed on the 4th day of March next, except as to Great Britain and France and their dependencies; and that provision be made by law for prohibiting all commercial intercourse with those nations and their dependencies and the importation of any article into the United States, the growth, produce, or manufacture of either of said nations, or of the dominions of either of them."

On motion of Mr. Bayard to strike out the following words: "Except as to Great Britain and France and their dependencies," etc., it was determined in the negative. Mr. Tiffin voted no. On the question to agree to the original motion—ayes 22, nays 3, Mr. Tiffin voted aye.

February 28, 1809.

The Senate proceeded to consider the amendments of the house of representatives entitled: "An act to inderdict the commercial intercourse between the United States and Great Britain and France and their dependencies, and for other purposes."

On the question to agree to the amendment of section 11, as follows: strike out the words, "and to cause to be issued, under suitable pledges and precautions, letters of marque and reprisal against the nation thereafter continuing in enforcing its unlawful edicts against the commerce of the United States," it was carried.

Mr. Tiffin voted in the affirmative. Ayes 17, Nays 14.

This was in 1809. The war spirit already kindled, broke out into a flame three years later.

After Mr. Tiffin resigned his seat in the United States senate,he was elected a member of the house of representatives of the Ohio legislature, from Ross county, in 1809.

FIRST BALLOT FOR SPEAKER.

Edward Tiffin...20
James Richard..15
Mathias Corwin... 4
Abraham Shepherd... 2
Othneil Looker.. 1
George Jackson.. 1
Samuel Dunlap... 1

Neither of the persons having a majority of the whole number present, the house proceeded to a second ballot, which resulted as follows:

Tiffin... 24
Richard...19
Shepherd... 1
Looker... 1

Mr. Tiffin having received a majority of all the votes of the members present, was declared by the clerk to be duly elected speaker.

The general assembly begun and held at the town of Zanesville, on Monday the 3d day of December, 1810, being the first session of the ninth general assembly of Ohio.

Members from Ross—Edward Tiffin, Abraham Claypool, James Manary, Henry Brush and William Creighton, Jr.

Mr. Tiffin was again elected speaker.

APPENDIX.

NO. 3.

THE END—CENTENNIAL ORATION AND CELEBRATION OF FOURTH OF JULY 1876, IN TIFFIN.

(From the Tiffin Tribune of July 6th, 1876.)

ONLY AND ORIGINAL CENTENNIAL!
HOW WE CELEBRATED IT!
NOISE, DISPLAY, PATRIOTISM, ETC., ETC.
THE FOURTH IN TIFFIN.

OUR PEOPLE certainly acquitted themselves patriotically on the Fourth of July, 1876. Early Monday afternoon the work of decoration began, and by night nearly all the business houses and many private residences were finely decorated. There was a supply of flags large enough to satisfy the most enthusiastic lover of the Stars and Stripes. The decoration of some of our business places was worthy of mention, but our space will not permit.

At twelve o'clock Tuesday morning, the Centennial Fourth was inaugurated with the ringing of bells, the shrieks of whistles, the firing of guns, pistols, etc. Taking it altogether, it was the most enthusiastic noise ever listened to, and probably fully as patriotic.

The Fourth proper was inaugurated by a National salute by Captain Spier's battery at five o'clock A. M.

The day did not open auspiciously. It was rainy until nearly ten o'clock, which fact delayed carrying out the programme as arranged. Notwithstanding the bad weather, the people began to gather at an early hour, and by nine o'clock an immense crowd were present to take part in the grand occasion. Every one seemed to feel that he had a part in the celebration, and the greatest good feeling prevailed.

The procession was formed at as early hour as possible. The appearance made by it was very fine and far beyond all expectation. It was formed in the following order:

FIRST DIVISION—CAPTAIN F. K. SHAWHAN COMMANDING

Marshal C. Mutchler, and Tiffin Police.
Tiffin Light Guards.
Harmonia Band.
St. John's Benevolent Society.
President, Orator, and Mayor.
Reader and Chaplains.
Vice-Presidents.
Decoration Wagon.
Centennial Choir.

SECOND DIVISION—MAJOR W. W. MYERS COMMANDING.

St. Patrick's T. A. & B. Band and Association.
Fort Ball Cadets.
Tiffin Fire Department.

THIRD DIVISION—CAPTAIN A. W. SNYDER COMMANDING.

Boos' Band.
Independent Zouaves.
Turners.
Bruderbund.
Druids of Humbolt Grove.
Knights of Pythias.
Knights of Hurrah.
C. Mueller's Brewery Wagons.
Theil & Gassner's Stone-Quarry Wagon.
Citizens in Carriages.

The procession paraded through the most important streets, after which the people gathered at the court house yard to listen to the other exercises. Mayor Bachman introduced the president of the day, R. W. Shawhan, who made the following brief and very appropriate remarks:

FELLOW CITIZENS: The pleasant duty now devolves upon me of calling this large assemblage to order; and in doing so I may be permitted to state that we have come together to celebrate and commemorate one of the greatest of all historical events. Go back through all the traditional and historic ages of the past, from Adam to Moses, and then down to the ushering in of our Christian era, one thousand eight hundred and seventy-six years ago—saving and excepting that mysterious birth at Bethlehem—the birth of our nation by the Declaration of Independence, one hundred years ago to-day, was the grandest event ever enacted on the face of the globe. And now with fervent thanks to God for all who have lived to witness and to celebrate this Centennial anniversary, and thanking you all for the honor conferred upon your presiding officer, we will now proceed with the exercises of the day."

Mr. Shawhan's remarks were followed by a patriotic song by the centennial choir, which was executed in a highly creditable manner. Rev. G. A. Hughes then made a most fervent prayer, which was followed by the reading of the Declaration of Independence by D. C. Tunison, who delivered it in a clear, strong voice, and in a most impressive manner. At its close the bells of the city were rung, and the bands played a patriotic piece. The choir sang again, when Mr. Shawhan said: "I now have the pleasure of introducing to you our worthy citizen and ripe scholar, Judge Wm. Lang, who will now address you." Judge Lang came forward and spoke as follows:

MR. PRESIDENT, LADIES AND GENTLEMEN: One hundred years have come and gone; a century has flown off into the ocean of time, with all its epochs for weal or woe to the human race, since the old bell at Independence Hall, in Philadelphia, called together a small band of patriots, who had assembled to represent the people of thirteen colonies under the government of Great Britain, to consult together as to the best mode for the redress of the grievances the people of the Colonies were then suffering. The result of their deliberations was that declaration of principles just read in your hearing; a production that brightens with age and glows with a fire of patriotism that shines forth and points out to the oppressed of all nations the pathway to justice, independence and equality. It is like the leaven that leaventh the whole loaf. It has aroused the pride and patriotism of intelligent men everywhere, and to-day thrones that claimed their power by the grace of God' exist simply by the permission of the people. Man has learned to know his rights, and knowing, will maintain them. England, Germany and Italy have removed many oppressions and compelled their governments to rule in conformity with the will of the people. Spain struggled, but failed for a season, while France enjoys a new life under a republican form of government of their own, having nobody to rule over them by the "Grace of God." Even Herzegovinia, in her might of abject despotism, has caught a ray of the light that burst forth on that day, and she struggles like a hero for independence.

The days of inspiration did not close with the end of Holy Writ, and I mean no sacrilege when I say that every holy, noble, generous thought, motive or action, is *inspiration*, and proves the better part of man, the spark of the deity that is within us, and I claim the right for myself to believe that the work of those great and good men on that day, the fruit of their deliberations in the form of the declaration of those principles of human rights, with the glorious results of a century gone, was the work of inspiration in which God's holy purpose seems manifest. Now while we meet and have just cause to rejoice, every heart should give thanks to Almighty God for the blessings we have enjoyed as a people under the sun of freedom, and pledge anew our lives, our fortunes, and our sacred honor that we will, for ourselves and our posterity, preserve and maintain that same form of government in its purity so vouchsafed to us by those noble men of 1776.

Time will not permit me here to give you anything like even a synopsis of the achievements of these one hundred years. Permit me only to say that the thirteen colonies have increased to thirty-eight prosperous states; the three millions of inhabitants that struck for freedom have increased to 44,-000,000, enjoying the same, spreading from ocean to ocean, and from the lakes to the gulf; that the ship of state during this period breasted the storms of two terrible wars with foreign powers, and a most lamentable fraternal one, and safely sailed home into the harbor of the constitution, and came out of the fire as those youths did out of the fiery furnace, without even the smell of smoke upon their garments.

The form of government is all-important when man claims his natural rights. Perhaps the best interpretation that can be given to the word freedom is "that form of government where man is left free to do as he pleases, except where the rights of his neighbor and public safety need restraint." (Blackstone.) Now if that be freedom, the form of government must be shaped to meet all its demands. Nothing but a republic with democratic institutions can secure that degree of liberty. And I desire here to be strictly understood that I shall use the words " Democracy " and "Republicanism " in no party sense, for both terms are synonymous, mean and express the same thing. "Demos" (people) and " Kratos " (government,) put together make "Democracy," which is the people's government, or a "Republic," and " Republicanism " in its best sense is nothing more than an attachment to a republican form of government. If Alexander Pope had lived in the present age and observed the spread of the principles, expressed in the Declaration of Independence—man everywhere claiming his rights—had noticed the progress of events; the demands of humanity and human rights throwing their storm-waves against thrones that are simply permitted to exist while they reel and totter before they fall—he would not now say again:

"For forms of government let fools contest,
Whatever's best administered is best."

It is not true. A bad form of government cannot be well administered. You can enjoy no right as a free man under a despotism. Talk about free speech. free press. freedom to worship God in accordance with the dictates of your own conscience, where the crude will of a Czar is the supreme law of the land. The form of government is all-important for the preservation of human rights in their purity. What a spectacle to the patriot, the organization and form of the government of these states! Thirty-eight free and independent states. each with its own Republican form of government. making up in its municipal organization a free and independent government of its own, surrendering for unity only such of its natural rights as are absolutely indispensable for the purposes of the general government, and reserving all other rights "to the state and the people." This principle kept intact and cherished and loved as the fathers did, will forever protect and defend the constitution in its purity, make succession and centralization both alike impossibilities. Such a form of government requires for its perpetuation and perpetuity a people who are both intelligent and virtuous intelligently moral. People well educated in letters and figures, but vicious, are no more capable to preserve and maintain a Republic than a people merely moral but abjectly ignorant. Intelligence, embellished by all the virtues of religion and morality, alone qualifies man for the rich boon of freedom. And if this Republic shall ever suffer the fate of Republics that have flourished in time past and are no more, it will be because the people shall. by corruption. luxury and vice, make themselves unfit for the enjoyment of it.

As a man wears clothes that fit him. so does a nation wear just such a form of government as it is capable of maintaining. Now, if we claim to have, and glory in the possession of, the best form of government ever conceived by man, a government just grown out of its childhood to manhood. triumphantly preserving its integrity through a thousand trying ordeals in its history, how necessary and indispensable, that we, to preserve it, should also be inspired with a just appreciation of the responsibility resting upon us.

Judge Marshall, in the Virginia convention of 1788, said : " What are the favorite maxims of Democracy ? A strict observance of justice and public faith, and a steady adherence to virtue. These, sir, are the principles of good government." (Elliot's Debates, vol. III., p. 77). This form of government is best because its standard of moral requisition is the highest. It claims for man a universality of interest, liberty and justice. It is christianity with its mountain beacons and guides. It is the standard of Deity based in the eternal principles of truth, passing through and rising above the clouds of ignorance into the region of infinite wisdom. The great objects of knowledge and moral culture of the people are among its most prominent provisions. Practical religion and religious freedom are the sunshine of its growth and glory. To say that an ignorant and immoral people are capable of self-government, is to say that government may be administered without knowledge and without justice. I am speaking of the inhabitants of the United States as a people, not as a nation.

Whether we possess the attributes of a nation, or whether our general government be a national government, I have neither the time nor inclination to discuss. Enough for me to know and believe that the ends of knowledge, freedom and happiness can be promoted by a proper appreciation and preservation of the form of government we have, and to which we, eith er by virtue of birth or adoption, all owe allegiance ; and who for himself will not say :

" In youth it sheltered me,
And I'll protect it now."

Having been born and raised under a bad form of government, and having made the government of these free states mine by free choice, I can but feel the thrill that this occasion sends through my being while I may not be able to express the emotions that prompt a renewal of the vow of allegiance given in my early manhood. And I will not try. From every city, town and hamlet of our land, shouts and rejoicings rend the air at the close of a century since the " Declaration of American Independence " first saw the light of day. The young shout and cheer with sounds of glee and hilarity the middle-aged man feels a just pride in the discharge of ever duty pertaining to a citizen, and due and owing to the state. The aged pioneer joins the throng with a heart full of gratitude and praise to the Giver of all good, for the preservation of a government he perhaps helped to protect with his treasure and his blood. These emotions are proper and patriotic and holy. None but a slave could to-day feel indifferent, and there are none to be found within our borders, thank God.

The beginning of our government does not date from the 4th of July, 1776, but from the adoption by the states of the constitution in 1788. So as a government we are not 100 years old, but as a people. For the declaration of independence at once and forever separated the allegiance of the colonies and opened fully the war of the revolution. The end of seven long and bloody years of war made England acknowledge, while our people rejoice in, our independence. How fortunate for human rights and freedom that at that epoch, when we were weak and exhausted, when it would have been easy for some military chieftain to have grasped the reins of power and to have established here a monarchy—that with Washington and his compeers, not a man was to be found who would do and dare. Man, prone to love of power as he his, did you ever think of it, my friends, how little it would have required to have lost all that was won by the blood of the revolution? Does it not seem that the hand of Providence was in all this? The spirit that opened the war seemed to close it, and commence the Republic. The spirit that appealed to God for the rectitude of their conduct, moved the men in power, when the war was over, to return their swords and lay them upon the altar of their country.

History never produced such a spectacle since the world began.

And how they shouted and sang of the liberty they had thus achieved:

> "In a chariot of light from the regions of day,
> The Goddess of Liberty came ;
> Ten thousand celestials directed the way,
> And hither conducted the dame.
> A fair budding branch from the gardens above,
> Where millions and millions agree,
> She brought in her hand as a pledge of her love,
> A plant she named Liberty Tree.
>
> This glorious exotic struck deep in the ground,
> Like a native, it flourished and bore ;
> The fame of its fruit drew the nations around
> To seek out its peaceable shore.
> Regardless of name or distinction, they came—
> For freemen, like brothers, agree—
> With one spirit endued they one friendship pursued,
> And their temple was Liberty Tree."

They sang of Columbia thus:

> "Columbia, Columbia, to glory arise,
> The queen of the world and the child of the skies,
> Thy genius commands thee, with raptures behold,
> While ages on ages thy splendor unfold ;
> Thy reign is the last and the noblest of time,
> Most fruitful thy soil, most inviting thy clime.
> Let crimes of the east ne'er crimson thy name,
> Be freedom, and science and virtue thy fame."

The French revolution produced a despot—the American revolution, liberty and free states. Liberty fails when sovereigns become tyrants. The American citizen is the sovereign of the land and makes and enforces his own laws. So long as wisdom and humanity shall be his guide and counsel, he cannot fail of success.

If time would permit, I should be glad to indulge in a few passing remarks on many of the events that have characterized our history as a people hitherto, but I must abstain while I will invite your attention to things and surroundings at home. Let me speak to you a little while on the rise and pro-

APPENDIX. 685

gress of our own immediate neighborhood—of Seneca county, her history, her resources, and her people.

As the triumphs of liberty constitute the way-marks of the world, they have guided and directed the pioneers in opening and developing the resources of this vast country to labor, to commerce, to knowledge and to greatness. The pioneers of Seneca county found here a vast unbroken wilderness, run over by savages and wild animals hunting their prey. The silence of the forest broken only by the crack of the Indian's rifle, and the nights made hideous by the howlings of the wolf and the panther. The woodman's axe brought the first sound of the approach of civilization. West of the Sandusky river was an almost unbroken swale, but the eastern and some portions of the southern parts of the county offered localities better adapted for settlements and homes, and these were selected as the first homesteads in this county. The western portion was taken up much later.

Seneca was formed from old Indian territory, April 1st, 1820, organized April 1st, 1824, and named after a tribe of Indians who had a reservation a short distance north of Tiffin, near the river, and north of the farm owned by the late John Keller. The county was formerly a part of Sandusky county. It extends eighteen miles north and south, and thirty miles east and west, with the base line on the 41st parallel.

There were two general surveys made by the authority of the United States in northern Ohio. The first one established the base line, counties and townships of the "Western Reserve," so called, the fire-lands, etc. It started on the west line of Pennsylvania, running west, and ended at the southwest corner of Huron county. The second survey started at the east line of Indiana, and ended at the southeast corner of Seneca, making the south line of Seneca the base line. This survey made townships and ranges. The townships in Seneca number one, two and three, and the ranges run from 13 east to 17 and 18 east inclusive, making each township contain thirty-six square miles, being six miles square; each section—thirty-six in number—one mile square and containing six hundred and forty acres. Fort Seneca was also named after the Indians, and was situated on the left bank of the Sandusky river, near the village of Fort Seneca, six miles north of Tiffin, and about eleven miles south of Ft. Stephenson, afterwards Lower Sandusky, now Fremont, where the Republican party of the United States, in their deliberations at Cincinnati. have lately, for the choice of a proper person for the presidency, found our distinguished neighbor, Gov. Hayes. General Harrison's troops occupied Ft. Seneca at the time the British and the Indians made an attack on Ft. Stephenson, on the 2d day of August, 1813. General Harrison, while at Ft. Seneca, narrowly escaped being murdered by an Indian.

The circumstances are highly interesting, but I have no time to relate them. Let me refer you to the memoirs of General Harrison for particulars.

The Senecas, of the Sandusky. so called, owned and occupied 40,000 acres of choice land on the east side of the Sandusky river, being mostly in this and part of Sandusky county. Thirty thousand acres of this was granted to them on the 29th of September, 1817, at the treaty held at the foot of the Maumee rapids, Hon. Lewis Cass and Hon. Duncan McArthur being the United States commissioners. The other 10,000 acres, lying south of the other, was granted by the same commissioners at the treaty of St. Mary, on the 17th of September, the following year. On the 28th of February, 1831, these Indians ceded their lands to the general government and agreed to remove southwest of Missouri, on the Neosho river.

At that time their principal chiefs were Coonstick, Small-Cloud, Spicer (whom our esteemed friend, Dr. H. Kuhn, of this city, well knew, as well as some of the others), Seneca Steel, Hard Hickory, Tall Chief and Good Hunter.

General Henry C. Brish, now deceased, was the sub-agent of this band, which numbered about 400 souls at that time, and were considered to be a remnant of the Logans. I remember well in several conversations I had with the General about these Indians, in each of which the General expressed his surprise why they were called *Senecas*, as he said he never found a Seneca amongst them. He said they were Cayugas—who were Mingoes; that they had amongst them some Oneidas, Mohawks, Onondagas, Tuscarawas and Wyandots. They believed in witchcraft, and while here executed one of their best men for that crime. Time will not permit me to give the narrative of the execution.

If you had been present at a meeting of the "Seneca County Pioneer Association," about two years ago, and listened to the address of our esteemed friend, Isaac I. Dumond, near Ft. Seneca, you would have heard an interesting narrative of the annual dog dance and feast of these Indians.

While speaking about the Indians, let me say to you that a question of title to a portion of these lands is still pending and undisposed of. I mention this fact only as a matter of history.

It is very doubtful whether any remnant of that tribe sees this day. The greater probability is, that they have all fallen to the law that seems to rule the general destiny of the race. All we have of them is their name, their lands and their short history. The *new purchase*, so called, included the lands of the Seneca Indians. In 1820 and 1821 the other lands of the "new purchase" were laid off into townships and sections, but the Seneca Reservation was not surveyed until 1832. Speaking of the new purchase, I desire to record an incident in connection with it, too important to be lost. My venerable friend, Isaac I. Dumond, of Pleasant township, built a house near the left bank of the Sandusky river, northeast of Ft. Seneca, in 1820, (a cabin rather,) which is still fit for human habitation and occupied by a family, while Mr. Dumond lives close by in more comfortable quarters.

A few tracts of these lands were sold when the land office first opened at Delaware, at the government price, $1.25 per acre. The greater portion of our county was entered at the same price, after the sale and about the time the land office was removed to Bucyrus, and later still to Tiffin, when Mr. David E. Owen held the office of receiver at this place. The government received nothing but specie for the land. The receiver was provided with a strong iron chest, in which the books and money were to be kept. The chest was about twenty inches wide and twenty deep, and about two feet long. I remember on several occasions when Mr. Owen was about to make his quarterly report at Columbus, Ohio, that quite a number of men were requisite to move the chest from the house into the wagon. The late Daniel Dildine was the teamster generally, who hauled the coin to Columbus Mr.

Owen had his office in the frame building belonging to Esq. Keen, on the north side of East Market street, near the stone bridge. It generally took from three to four days, with a good team of horses, to haul the little iron monster to Columbus. Without any guard or other protection the two men started, and winding their way alone through the forest, found Upper Sandusky, Little Sandusky, Marion, Waldo and Delaware, their stopping places. I remember hearing father Owen relate his troubles with the chest at one time at Waldo, I think. Night overtook them when they got there, and the cabin hotel was full of people. As a general thing, they would back the wagon up to the door and take the chest into the house. But Mr. Owen did not like the looks of the men about the premises, so he concluded to leave the chest, with its contents of about $50,000, in the wagon and cover it with straw. They did so and went to bed. It rained all night, and when they got up in the morning they found everything all right.

It was fortunate for Seneca county that her lands did not fall into the hands of speculators. The men who entered and located, did so for the purpose of acquiring homes, and the purchases were made in conformity with the pile of gold and silver. These piles were usually very limited, and although but fifty dollars would buy forty acres, many of the new-comers did n't have the fifty dollars. All the most valuable lands were soon taken up, however, and when the war with Mexico was over and our soldiers had land warrants to locate, several tracts were still found in Liberty township and taken up by these warrants. Those were the last of the entries and the time for cheap lands in Seneca county has long since passed away, never to return.

The early settlers here came from Maryland, Virginia, New York, Pennsylvania, New Jersey, etc., Germany and Ireland, and made up as completely a mixed population as you see them, or their descendants, to this day. Differing in language, habits and customs, and almost everything pertaining to civilized life, a more generous, kind, hospitable, frugal, industrious people never lived anywhere. Whether mutual poverty and dependence made them so "wondrous kind" I will not stop to decide, but it is enough to say that the latch-string was always out. The inmates of the cabin were ready to divide the best they had with the hungry stranger. No night was too dark or stormy, no swale too wide or deep, when distress or sickness called for help. When a man wanted a cabin raised or needed help, a simple notice was sufficient to make the neighbors all around leave their own work and go, often as far as four or five miles. And go they would and did without asking about the man's religion or politics, nor upon what part of God's green earth he was born, work all day faithfully without price or reward other than that such kindness, if needed, should be returned. I sometimes wished that the primitive life in Seneca had continued all along. Now in these days when you need material help to secure a home, who will volunteer and stand by you until you have one? Now ask a man to help you work one day and when evening comes he wants his pay. Those days are gone, and the men and women that brought here and established the first landmarks of civilization, are fast passing away with many of their primitive virtues that characterized their lives in those days. That generous and open-hearted hospitality of the pioneers has given way to the struggle after the mighty dollar. Even the tales of the trials, difficulties and hardships, the deprivations and sufferings of the early settlers, when told and repeated to the present generation, are received with doubts or indifference. Yet will I venture to call to mind the life in the cabin with some of its incidents as I saw it. There were but few of my German countrymen in Seneca when, in the summer of 1833, I came to this place with my father's family. The large number by far came and located afterward, and as you pass through the county now, and observe a vast "Dutch barn," with many well cultivated fields round about, and a stately mansion with orchard, gardens and everything denoting and speaking of the comforts of life, you ask who lives there? and perhaps you will be told, that that gray-headed venerable looking old man sitting on yonder porch, "smoking his pipe of clay," entered forty acres of land when he first came from Germany, for which he paid fifty dollars, all the money he had, and perhaps a part of that was borrowed from a friend. Right back of where his brick house now is he built for himself a small cabin and made a little opening round about it for a garden, a little truck path for corn and potatoes. He was young then, and his young wife assisted him in his hard work, all she could, to fix up their home in the forest as best they could under the circumstances. Now their money was all gone. More was needed to get a cow, some hogs, tools, a wago oxen, etc., and without which no further progress upon the forest could be made. The chances to earn money in the neighborhood were very bad. Nobody had any to pay with as a general thing, and the few that had could hire a laborer very cheap. At $5 and $6 a month it took a long time to buy those necessaries, and to live and not die of despondency under such circumstances took more moral courage than we, in these degenerate days, possess. The endurance and self-denial of the men and women of those days is beyond the power of a pen to describe. Imagine, now, that cabin, miles away from any neighbor, with only a very crooked road, marked by blazed trees, leading to it; dark forests all around and a small opening made by the little clearing to see God's blue sky.

The nearest public work where money could be earned was the Dayton & Michigan canal, 100 miles away. Here necessity compelled him to leave his wife and little ones and work on the canal all summer, returning home in the fall, when public work was stopped, and thus economizing with his earnings, improved the condition of his family, from time to time, until the clearing had enlarged enough to produce the support of life, and perhaps something for market.

Did you ever think, my friends, how those pioneer women must have felt to be thus left alone in the wild forest, for weeks and months, all summer and fall, with their little ones, and nobody to see to and protect them? You ladies, who live in the lap of luxury and refinement, enjoying the products of nature and art, did you ever think how those noble pioneer mothers lived through those weary years of hardship? The only way that can be accounted for is, they put their trust in God. But to return. After several summers' work on the canal, and having a team of oxen, the little clearing became larger, and the comforts of life gradually increased. Other families settling closer by, all hands joined to open out a road to some mill or market. The oldest of the children grew up large enough to be of some help at the

APPENDIX.   689

house, or to chop. They all worked, young and old, and the little entry of forty acres increased in size to a quarter section, all paid for, with all these fine improvements you see all around. No one asked a favor of him in vain. Ever ready and willing to help where he could, he has the love and respect of the entire neighborhood, while he enjoys, in his declining years, the fruit of a well spent life.

This little picture hits but few now. The larger number have long since gone to their long home. Don't despise the little cabin that you may yet see remaining as you glide along your nice roads in your easy pheaton. It was once the home of love and happiness. Little feet danced cheerily over that puncheon floor, and the great log fire in that chimney cheered the inmates on many a long winter evening, and witnessed the baking of corn bread on the back of an old shovel many years. The hominy block was as indispensable as the rifle. Their meat was game, and their bread of corn meal was made upon a plan as rural as the corn was reduced to meal. How do you suppose, now, that having neither a horse nor an ox to take a little corn away off to some mill to get it ground, the family got meal to make bread with? Take an old shovel or a piece of sheet iron, punch it full of holes; then take an ear of dry corn and roll it over it, like over a grater, and meal is produced slowly but surely, and then—corn-dodgers, Johnny cake, hoe cake or pone. Hunger may be a good cook, but your fine pastry never tasted nicer than the corn bread made by the pioneer mothers.

Ladies, how would you now like to get up a dinner for a large family without a cooking stove, or any other of the modern conveniences in housekeeping, over a big log fire, with nothing but a long-handled skillit, Dutch oven, and iron kettle? It would puzzle you some, I think. Yet it was a long time after the first settlers came here before anybody saw a cooking stove.

Settlers from the eastern states, who had a little money and talked English, fared better; stayed at home and worked their way through. Those that I have described were my countrymen, and the Irish settlers, who took up the land west of the Sandusky river, and settled in the Wolf creek.

I would be pleased to give you some of the incidents of early life in our good old county and short sketches of the lives of the men and women who first located in each township, but must abstain.

I would like to mention the names of the first settlers of each township. I have collected many of them, but for fear that I might miss some of them I will not name any. Amongst them was one soldier of the revolution and many that were in the war of 1812.

So rapid was the increase of population that from the time those lands were first brought into market and up to 1830, Seneca contained 5,157 souls, including Tiffin, about one-half of the present population of this city. The influx of emigration in the next ten years was so great that in 1840 we had a population of 18,139. It seems like a dream of fancy that in the short life of one man a county like ours should be turned from a howling forest to the state of improvement, of wealth and refinement that Seneca now presents. Vast fields in a good state of cultivation, fine residences all over the county, mills, factories, railroads, school houses and churches, printing presses and newspapers, postoffices and telegraphs, and everything that nature and art can contribute to elevate our people higher and still higher in the scale of humanity, and I feel justified when I say that on the score of wealth, health, morals and intelligence, old Seneca has no superior amongst her neighbors.

Let me say a few words about Tiffin. Josiah Hedges laid out Tiffin proper in 1821. Fort Ball had already been located by Mr. Spencer. The postoffice was over there and some of the most influential of the early settlers lived in Fort Ball. The troubles between the rival proprietors of these villages were at times very severe, but ended in the purchase by Mr. Hedges of the entire plat of Fort Ball, and the location of the court house on the Tiffin side of the river. Fort Ball was named after Lieutenant-Colonel James V. Ball, the commander of a squadron of cavalry under General Harrison. Tiffin was named after Edward Tiffin, who was the first governor of Ohio after her organization as a state, and a particular personal and political friend of Mr. Hedges. Your humble servant had the honor of being the last mayor of the old town of Tiffin and the first mayor of the city of Tiffin upon the union of the two villages. Let me remind you of the old sycamore that stood on the right bank of the river now in Mechanicsburg. The boundary line of the city, as then organized, ran through the sycamore southwardly. Forty-three years ago a couple of exiled German boys formed a closer acquaintance and friendship under that tree—one that lasted for life. When the city council entrusted the description of the boundaries of the new city to me, I described that tree as a land-mark. The tree and one of those boys have long since passed away. The residence of Dr. Hovey, in the second ward, covers a part of the ground where the old fort stood.

In 1840 the population of the several villages in Seneca was as follows:

Attica...148
Bascom.. 34
Bettsville... 23
Bloomville.. 13
Caroline.. 27
Fort Ball..129
Fort Seneca.. 52
Green Springs.. 29
Lodi... 30
Melmore..127
Risdon... 39
Rome... 80
Republic...161
Springville.. 35
Sulphur Springs.. 29

Time will not permit me to give you anything like a statistical statement of the resources of the county. Allow me only to say that Seneca in the scale of wealth, population, etc., is an average county amongst the eighty-eight counties of the state.

In 1870 she had a population of 30,823. In 1875 she harvested the crop of 54,000 acres of wheat. In 1876 she pays $244,000 taxes. Her public buildings may not be of the best, but her schools and other institutions of learning are not surpassed in any county around her. She is one in only eighteen counties in the state that is not in debt. Her people commit less crime compared

APPENDIX. 691

with her population than any other county in the state. We have no paupers running at large. In all departments of life, her citizens who have acquired honorable distinction are self-made men. She enumerates 12,000 children entitled to the benefits of the common schools, and pays $79,000 per year for their education. The personal and real property of the county for taxable purposes increased from about $6,000,000 in 1850 to nearly $18,000,000 in 1874. In 1826 her taxes did not exceed $300.

But I must close, and in so doing let me rehearse a short ode on the Fourth of July, by an unknown author. It is so very much in harmony with the spirit of this festive occasion :

> " To the sages who spoke, to the heroes who bled,
> To the day and the deed strike the harp-string of glory ;
> Let the song of the ransom'd remember the deed,
> And the tongue of the eloquent hallow the story.
>   O'er the bones of the bold,
>   Be that story long told.
> And on Fame's golden tablet their triumphs unfurled,
> Who on freedom's green hills freedom's banner unfurl'd,
> And the beacon fires raised that gave light to the world.
>
> 'Twas for us and our children to conquer or die,
> Undaunted they stood, when the war storm burst o'er them ;
> Each blade drew a thunderbolt down from the sky,
> Till the foeman turned pale and lay withered before them.
>   Then from Liberty's band
>   Went a shout through the land,
> As the rainbow of peace their fair heritage spanned,
> Where the banner of freedom in pride was unfurl'd,
> And the beacon fire rose that gave light to the world.
>
> They are gone—mighty men ! and they sleep in their fame ;
> Shall we ever forget them ? Oh, never ! no, never !
> Let our sons learn from us to embalm each great name,
> And the anthem send down " Independence forever !"
>   Wake, wake heart and tongue,
>   Keep the theme ever young ;
> Let their deeds through the long line of ages be sung,
> When on freedom's green hills freedom's banner unfurl'd,
> And the beacon fire raised that gave light to the world."

At the close of the oration Rev. W. A. Samson fervently addressed the Throne of Grace, after which the choir sang the doxology, the audience joining. The benediction by Rev. Mr. Samson closed the exercises, which had been very interesting and impressive, and had stamped themselves indelibly upon the memories of all present. The balance of the day was spent in the usual manner.

The celebration was a success in every particular, and redounded to the credit of the different committees and officers having it in charge.

At night, on the public square, the display of fire-works took place. Everything passed off satisfactorily, and it was a good ending of a memorable occasion.

ERRATA.

Page 5—7th line from top read Captain "Bagby."
" 141—12th line from top read "John Keller."
" 243—10th line from bottom read "Grummel."
" 367—10th line from foot read "Q. M. General."
" 377—5th line from top read "tussuc" for "tissue."
" 387—3d line from top read "Winweiler."
" 412—6th line from top read "Stalter."
" 419—11th line from bottom read "Feldkuemmels hochzeitstag."
" 424—Last line read "base drum."
" 432—10th line from bottom read "Tecumseh."
" 450—12th line from top read "people."
" 474—Bottom line read "of" after the word "lines."
" 499—3d line from bottom read "Shants."
" 506—15th line from bottom read "chiefs."
" 506—2d line from bottom read "southwest quarter."
" 507—22d line from top read "camel-back bridge."
" 511—10th line from bottom read "Levi Creasey."
" 521—8th line from bottom read "Yingst family."
" 564—8th line from top read "N. Ports & Co."
" 614—6th line from top read "Mrs. Whitney."
" 635—In "sheriffs" read "Weirick" for "Wurick."

FULLNAME INDEX

----, Adam 527 Aunt Molly 377
Edward 581 Jim 101 Maria
125 Richard 451 Sal 451 Torry
490
ABBOT, David 668 Mr 666
ABBOTT, 73 110 647 C T 563
Colena M 576 E T 334 Frank
93 117 George 447 Jeanette
128 Jonathan 117 L 576
Lorenzo 92 109 116 128 178
326 417 636 Lorenzo A 576
Melissa 117 Moses 458 508
Mr 48 512 Robert 109 Rush
384
ABRAMS, Henry 668 Mr 666
ACADEMY, Fostoria 562
ACKER, George D 467 469 633
635
ACKLEY, Mr 584 Prof 395
ADAMS, 249 317-319 385 415
496 520 564 Anthony W 458
Bishop 482 C A 455 Francis
419 J Q 204 Jacob 447 517
John 202 675 John Quincy
618 L 347 Martin 552 567 567
Mr 207 419 Perry M 323 384
Robert 567 Township 169 474
ADELSBERGER, John 424
ADELSPERGER, 550 John 599
AGRICULTURAL, Society 401
Works 399
AGUE, 214
AHERN, Father 290
AIKEN, 604 James 543 593 603

AIKEN (cont)
Mr 601
ALBERT, Barbara 251 J J 51 J O
564 John O 554
ALBRECHT, Andrew 251 278
Martin 420
ALBRIGHT, Andrew 299 416 F G
473 Mr 398
ALCOTT, R 564 568
ALEXY, Jacob 487
ALLBRIGHT, 259
ALLEN, Gus A 634 Mabel 421 Mr
245 Mrs 259 S C 356 William
433 476 478
ALLIS, Thomas W 362
ALLISON, David 462
ALTWEIS, Jacob 447
AMES, Henry 628
ANCIENT, Order Of Hibernians
349
ANDERSON, 602 Isaac 462 Mrs
299 Sgt 143 William 318 603
ANDES, John 564 Philipina 564
ANDRE, Jacob 535
ANDRES, Henry 494
ANDREW, L 332 Maria 331
ANDREWS, E B 222 Hattie F 129
Rev 129 Samuel C 434
ANGELO, Fr 345
ANTHON, Charles 651-652
ANTOINETTE, Marie 25
ANWAY, Austin 589 Erastus 589
Fanny 589 George 589
Hannah 589 Harrison 589

ANWAY (cont)
  John 150 517 587 589 Mary
  150 589 Phoebe 589 Susan
  589 William 149 165 586-587
  589 William Jr 587
APPENDIX, No 1 639 No 2 662
  No 3 679
ARBOGAST, 550 599
ARMATAGE, John 618
ARMBRUSTER, William 447
ARMSTRONG, A N 525 Capt 27
  Isabella H 413 John 412 662
  Mr 233 413-414 Robert 144-
  145 170 Sarah 239 Sarah V
  413 W W 239 268 409 William
  W 412
ARMY, Roads 89
ARNDT, D 314 J D 346 J M 345
ARNOLD, 535 Anthony H 601 L
  D 454 Mr 601 Sylvanus 338
  535 William 600
ARNOLDI, M 565
ARRIVAL, In Tiffin 247
ARTHUR, 558
ASBURY, 205 Bishop 91 Francis
  204
ASH, Abraham 550 Jacob 550
  William 547
ASHLEY, 18 Lieut 17
ASIRE, D 568
ASSEMBLY, Members Of 438
ATKINS, B G 344-346
ATTICA, 616 Journal 616
ATWATER, 40
AUGHINBAUGH, G W 268
AUGSPURGER, E 331 Eva 300
  Philip J 300 Philipena 300
AULGER, G W 599
AVERY, 259
AYRES, David 618
BACH, J M 421
BACHER, 286 Henry 283
BACHMAN, Casper 284 George
  W 386 635 Mayor 680
BACKLOGS, 193

BACKUS, N 455
BADGER, Joseph 645
BAEBER, T J 285
BAER, H 285
BAGBY, Capt 110 692 T H 633
  Truman H 448
BAGLEY, Capt 51 T H 50 342
BAINES, H K 284
BAIR, H 286 Rudolph 668
  Samuel 286
BAIRD, George W 440
BAKER, 147 A C 578 Adam 284
  494 Eber 440 Emily 129 Ezra
  92 112 144 517 599 Frank 599
  635 Frederick 285 G 455
  Jacob 129 John 535 Josiah P
  323 Margaret 542 Richard 416
  535 S B 417 Samuel 525
  Thomas 162 492 526 535
  Thomas J 527 William 517
  542
BALDWIN, A C 239 330-331 400
  Mary Jane 239 Michael 668
  Mr 666 Smith D 446
BALFE, 421
BALL, 83 Col 44 143 523 Game
  Of 96 James V 690 Jas V 142
  Maj 82
BALLARD, Nelly 563
BALTZELL, Elizabeth 306 Henry
  C 278 Lewis 268 391 417
  Louis 402 Thomas 306 416
BANG, Carl 447 L 315 455 Louis
  447
BANKS, 337
BANNISTER, W H 568
BAPTIST, Church 276
BAR, Festival 379
BARBER, Dr 617 J S 347
BARCLAY, 65 Commodore 47-48
  58 66 Robert 374
BARKDALL, Thomas 276
BARLOW, 659
BARNES, A T 346-347 C W 454
  Flora 333 John B 561

BARNES (cont)
  Margaret 538 Mrs 421
  Newton M 462
BARNEY, 110 128 Ann 93 108
  111 Annar 572 Benjamin 92
  107-109 111 572 593 F T 56
  Marshal 111 Minerva 107-108
  Mr 95 Polly 108 111 Sidney
  109 Sophronia 572 West 108-
  109 111 164 572 593
BARNHART, D Jr 455
BARON, L A 314
BARRACK, Catharine 515 629
  Jane 629 John W 629 634
  Laura J A 629
BARROWS, 333
BARRUS, Sarah 356
BARRY, Capt 445
BARTEL, Dominick 448
BARTELL, 259 312 D 314
BARTHOLOMEW, Anson 628
  Frank 627 Harvey 628
  William 628
BARTLETT, Brice J 387 Joseph R
  458
BARTOE, Gen 13
BARTZ, Francis 600
BATE, John M 399
BATES, Belle 381 Curtis 352 Dr
  535 William L 381
BATLZELL, Catherine 391
BATTLE, Island 11
BAUER, Catharine 605 Philip
  600
BAUGHER, 250 Elizabeth 280
  George 454 John 176-177 181
  320 345 445 William 280
BAUGHMAN, D C 314 John 540
  550
BAUM, Peter 602 604
BAYARD, Mr 677
BEADLEY, Leveret 507
BEAMER, Elizabeth 483
BEAMISH, 564
BEAMS, S Z 456

BEAR, Samuel 552
BEARD, Catharine 578 G W 455
  Hannah 508 John 507 Joseph
  508 Michael 636 Mr 508
BEARDSLEY, David H 439
BEATY, J H 455
BEAUGRAND, John 168
BEAVER, Joseph 287
BECK, David 320 Felix 286 448
  Nathaniel 278
BECKER, Frederick 600
BECKWITH, Stephen B 462
BEECHER, Mr 351
BEER, 355 Judge 353 Thomas
  354 Wm N 462
BEILER, S L 565 568
BEILHARS, Charles 451 J J 92
BEILHARZ, Albert 447 633 635 J
  J 279 283-284 Louis 446 Mr
  409
BELL, Gen 161 431 434 James
  265 John 326 370 424 430
  Vincent 326 345 576-577
BELLMAN, John 460
BELLVILLE, Dr 495
BELMONT, August 54
BEMENT, A S 554 Augustus M
  460 E 554 R R 331
BENCH, And Bar 351
BENDER, W H 468 William H
  468-469
BENEDICKS, 421
BENEDICT, Platt 348
BENHAM, A 416 F D 347 F Don
  342-343 345 Orander J 462
BENNEHOFF, Wm 283
BENNER, 312 George 314
BENNETT, 378 Isaac 578 Mary
  627 R C 562 Thomas 578 580
  584 615
BENNINGTON, George 627 John
  627
BENTLEY, Israel 345
BENTON, 414 H 348
BERCHARD, Sardis 372

BERGDERFER, Andrew 416
BERGER, F W 419 Fred W 420
　Wilhelm 419 William 420 447
BERGSTRESSER, William 447
BERLEKAMP, F 284 R 284
BERNARD, F 447 Francis 174
　502
BERRY, Curtis Jr 441 Curtis Sr
　469
BETTS, Clarkson 628 David 541
　John 549 Mr 550 Orrin 550
　Sameul 448 Zachariah 623
BETZ, Adam 664
BEVER, J 529 J M 561-562
　Joseph 416 527 Mr 501 Peter
　527 Russel H 460 S J 561
　Solomon 529
BEVERTON, Harvey S 468-469
BICK, Jacob 565
BIG, Spring 486 Spring Township
　174
BIGGER, D D 277-278 294 John
　675
BIGGS, Benjamin 260 Capt 17-18
　Joseph 514
BIHN, J L 293-294 Joseph L 292
BILLINGS, Jollier 618
BILLMAN, George 447
BILLYARD, 564
BIRCHARD, Mr 133 Sardis 129
　133
BIRD, Charles Willing 207
BIRNSIDE, Joseph 493
BIRNSIDES, 522
BISCHOF, Joseph 486
BISE, Jacob 420
BISHOP, David 174 180 249 543
　599 635
BISSEL, Judge 364
BISSELL, Daniel 113
BIXLER, 497
BLACK, George W 369
BLACKMAN, 500 A M 458 565
　Harry 149
BLACKMAN'S, Corners 149

BLACKSTRAP, 246
BLAINE, Mr 558
BLAIR, 259 599 Benj F 468-469 J
　A 339 John 593 Mr 666
　William 52 61
BLAKE, James 349
BLAKESLEY, Warren 615
BLAND, J B 395
BLASIUS, 251 Henry 447
BLENNERHASSET, 673-674
BLIEM, Andrew 448
BLISS, E P 495
BLODGET, R H 620
BLODGETT, Sarah 627
BLOOM, 285-286 Andreas 278
　Andrew 251 253 278 Esq 249
　H 455 Township 165 492
BLOOMER, 608
BLOOMVILLE, 495
BLUE, William 488
BLUM, John 419
BOALT, Charles L 466 F H 460
BOEHLER, Joseph 292 448
BOESEL, Charles 262 Charlotte
　262
BOG, Iron 235
BOGART, Cornelius 486 E 486
　Hiram 486 Jacob 543 M V 348
　William 447 633
BOHN, Conrad 284
BOLEY, F W 563
BOLLINGER, Louis 622 Philip
　622
BOLT, 376 Charles L 351
BONER, Betsey 107 Jacob 417
BONNELL, Ch 554
BONNUTH, Peter 349
BOON, Col 26
BOOS, Carl F 448 Charley 420
BOOTH, Nancy 509
BORCK, Fred 525
BORMUTH, John 293
BORNEY, George H 278
BOSLER, Daniel 449
BOSS, John H Jr 460

BOSSECKER, John 447
BOSTON, 324
BOTT, J S 278
BOUCHER, 487-488
BOUGHTON, John 164 593
BOUR, J 259 Romanus R 333
BOURNE, Sylvanus 156-157
BOUSENWEIN, Col 457
BOWE, 246 E G 342-343 417 449 634 Erastus 108 112 114 144 164 542 577 593 Gilford 170 Mr 109-110 128 170 512 521 536
BOWEN, Judge 307 371 Ozias 353
BOWER, 564 Jesse 562 Nicholas 449
BOWERMAN, Jacob 483 John 445 483 Mary 483
BOWERSOX, Jacob 287 447 Susan 287
BOWLAND, Alex 605 Alexander 593
BOWLIN, Elizabeth 602 Thomas 602
BOWMAN, Fred 283 Henry 283 Rudolph 283
BOWSER, Jacob 287 John 287 Mr 288
BOWSHER, Jesse 460
BOYCE, T W 347 Thomas W 264 467 469
BOYD, 489 497 500 536 D S 564 Ensign 32 Hugh W A 633 J 378 J S 278 James 149 417 422 424 492-494 497 636 James T 460 Jane 540 Jefferson 492 Jesse 492 Mary 149 492 Samuel 492 Thomas 149 165-167 492 494 497 501 540 636
BOYER, Dr 149 250 255 Elizabeth 149 250 Elizabeth M 393 Frances Hannah 250 Jacob 253 278 Joseph 441

BOYER (cont)
Mary R 393 Richard 250 Thomas 393 William 446
BOYERS, 263
BRACKLEY, Michael 440
BRADDOCK, 21 138
BRADEN, William 554
BRADFORD, Wesley 565
BRADLEY, 510 Calvin 176 243 246 527 Leverett 165 522 Mr 247 677 S H 342
BRADNER, 564 J A 566 John A 561
BRAINARD, Dr 94
BRANDEBERRY, J 455 N J 455
BRANDEBURY, A 314
BRANDT, 538 Isaac 528 531 539 John 600 Joseph 530 Paulus 531 539 Susan 530 Thomas 117 531 539 545
BRASS, Henry 251
BRAYTON, E 488 Elijah 486-487 William 486
BRECKENRIDGE, Frank A 467 469
BREDOON, Louis 250
BREIDINGER, J 394
BREINER, H 455 Jacob 495
BREINING, J J 568
BRENDLE, Jacob 284
BRESLIN, John G 248 343 409-410 412 441 Louisa 248 Mr 413
BRESNIN, John K 349 Mrs 314
BRESTEL, G W 455
BRETS, 147
BRETZ, Charles 536 David 264 Jacob 149 John 535 Philip 287 535 Z 615
BREWER, 259 N L 268 402 Nelson L 383
BRIAN, Reuben 554 Thomas 554
BRICK, Buildings 244
BRICKER, Homer 421 J W 565 S S 394 Samuel W 522 Simon

BRICKER (cont)
567
BRICKNER, 550 A J 349 Andrew
J 342
BRICKYARDS, 244
BRIDGE, First 173
BRIDGES, 259 In Pleasant 573
BRINER, Henry 495
BRINKERHOFF, James 593
William 594
BRINKERHOOF, Warren E 333
BRINKMAN, H 284
BRINTON, Field-marshal 15
BRISBINE, Napoleon B 468
BRISCO, James H 620
BRISH, Eleanor 416 Eleanor S
507 Gen 120 123 132 136 425
551 H C 250 430 Henry 542
Henry C 74 125 131 137 424
440-441 474 505-506 599 637
686 Henry Colgate 507 Mr
140-141 William 542
BRITTEN, Jacob 283
BROADHEAD, Col 13
BROCK, Gen 39
BROHL, Catharine 334 H 248
Henry 333-334
BROMLEY, H 348 Humphrey
590 Robert 460
BRONSON, Philip E 615 Rev Dr
51
BROOK, Evan W 549
BROOKOVER, Mr 264
BROOKS, Lieut 65 Sidney 54
BROSAMER, Joseph 486
Landelin 486 Stephan 486
BROUGH, John 358
BROUGHTON, 127
BROWN, 147 152-153 495 564
Abr 525 Alexander 561 Arza
583 Case 144 525 527 636
Daniel 336 348 422 441 637
David 550 David C 460 E 318
406 E H 467 586-587
Ebenezer 475 Ed H 469 Edwin

BROWN (cont)
H 468 Elisha 407 Elizabeth
627 Ethan Allen 219 Ezra 144
151 162 210 G 455 G K 344
346-348 Gen 430 432 434
George R 496 Gov 431 J H 318
407 James W 623 John 627
John D 73 Jonah 535 Jos W
430 Mina G 561 Mr 466 666 O
M 467 Quartermaster 465
Rolla W 633 Samuel 628 T L
567
BROWNE, John W 668
BROWNELL, F 276 Thomas 52
54 62
BROWNING, Cassandra 392
Elizabeth 392 Jeremiah 392
BROWSE, 210
BRUDERBUND, Der 419
BRUNDAGE, Benjamin 535 C Y
525 Caleb 593 599
BRUNNER, M Sales 488 Salesius
F 292
BRUSH, Dam Case 208 Henry
678 John 576 Platt 110 357
BRYANT, Benj F 462 Benj T 462
BUCHANAN, James 303
President 413
BUCHER, Philemon 675
BUCKINGHAM, Ebenezer Jr 220
J R 620
BUCKLAND, Col 457 R P 387
Ralph P 326
BUEL, William M 336
BUELL, 472 Gen 674 Maj-gen
673
BUILDING, Stone 234
BULLINGER, Henry 282
BUNDAGE, 147
BUNN, 259 Benjamin 231 Henry
283 Jacob 335 383 608 Jacob
F 333 629 633 Jacob Sr 283
John 608 John Jr 283 John Sr
283 Judge 385 631 Laura G
401

BURDETT, S S 478 480
BURG, David K 620
BURGDERFER, Andrew 599
BURGDOERFFER, Andrew 285
BURGESS, W 488
BURGOIN, 40
BURGOYNE, 201
BURKE, William 349
BURKETT, John 460
BURKHALTER, Sarah 519
    William 519
BURKHART, Wendel 448
BURLINGAME, Anson 526
BURMAN, John 614
BURNE, Robert 285
BURNET, 659 Judge 201
BURNETT, Jacob 351 Judge 52
BURNS, David 422 636 John 599
    Robert 551 Walter F 634
BURR, Aaron 202 676 Raymond
    460
BURROWS, James 446 W 369
BURTCHER, N 564
BUSER, J J 285
BUSH, Erotus H 458
BUSKIRK, Al 309 H A 339 416
    Harry 421 Jacob 526 535
BUTCHER, Shop 245
BUTLER, 15-16 112 259 Atty-gen
    479 Benjamin F 432 476 Gen
    557 J C 462 John M 462 L T
    481 Mr 415 Paul 535 Paul D
    111 Z C 462
BUTTERFIELD, 98 117 132 141
    609 Amroy 526 Consul W 525-
    526 Mr 105-106 158 161 264
    505 587
BYERS, A H 346 348 454
BYRD, Charles William 668
    James 446 Melinda 446 Mr
    666
BYRNE, Belle 333 Robert 636
CABIN, Building 186
CADWALADER, Gen 51 Nathan
    544

CADWALLADER, 550 M D 320
    Moses D 250 Nathan 448 540
CAIN, Henry D 627 James R 447
CALAHAN, Jno Y 567
CALDWELL, D S 469 David S
    468 James 667 Mr 666
CALLIGAN, Charles C 462
CALLIHAN, Nathan 458
CALVIN, John 282
CAMP, A A 51 J A 51-52 J L 455
    John G 51
CAMPBELL, 79 A M 344 Alice M
    381 Allen 277 David 176 439
    John 318 594 M 416 Maj 33
    Margaret 417 Mr 249 263
    William 248 289
CANAHAN, Joseph 593
CANAL, Tax 221 Work On The
    216
CANARY, J W 455
CANDIDATES, 85
CAPEDER, P Anton 292
CAPLES, B L 565 Frank 567
    Jacob 381 P D 565 R C 553
    563 565 Robert C 546
CARBAUGH, Samuel 552
CAREY, Dr 244 391 393 507
    Eleanor S 507 John M B 448
    Judge 382 Robert C J 392 S F
    268
CARL, Mrs 571
CARLISLE, W H 448
CARNAHAN, D F 276
CARNEY, William 446
CAROLINE, 616
CAROTHERS, Philip 627
CARPENTER, Benjamin 637
    Emanuel 668 Jeremiah 371
    John H 628 Lyman 627 Mr
    666 Samuel 628
CARSON, 483 S S 628 Samuel
    445 T B 627
CARTER, Maj 35
CARY, Dr 506
CASE, 112 Butler 460

CASS, 40 83 Gen 84 139 Lewis 38
  51 54-55 67 69 78 140 221 430
  530 685 Mr 415
CASSATY, John 581 Samuel 581
CASSELMAN, A 285-286 L 565
CASSETY, Edward 578
CASSNER, David 628 Jeremiah
  628 John 628 Moses 628 Peter
  628
CASWELL, Walter 462
CAT, Swamps 213
CATHOLIC, Chapel 244
CATLIN, Isaac 579 Mr 580
CAVE, The 608
CAVES, Benjamin 499
CECIL, 259
CENSUS, Of 1880 631
CENTENNIAL, In Attica 617 In
  Tiffin 679
CESSNA, Joseph 550
CHADWICK, Rhoda 588 Thomas
  173
CHAEFFEE, Joseph 172-173
CHAFFIN, Joel 593
CHAMBERLAIN, Capt 467 J W
  339 345-348 401 James M 418
  John W 468 Michael 590 S
  343 Scudder 323 343 Stephen
  51
CHAMBERLIN, James M 566
CHAMBERS, Maj 44
CHAMPLIN, Capt 63-64 Stephen
  52 54 61
CHANCE, Hiram 458 Thomas
  547
CHANDLER, H M 620 Rev 289
  294
CHANEY, 128 Charles 543-544
  John 540 543-544
CHANGE, 240
CHAPIN, Joel 92 109 164 Manly
  359 Mr 366 Selah 352 635
CHAPMAN, 572 B D 342 D Y 344
  346 James F 446 Jeremiah
  109

CHARLIEU, 137
CHASE, Alvin B 460 Gov 52 54
  56 61 656-657 S P 54
CHATHAM, Lord 13
CHENEY, 572
CHENOWITH, Mr 544
CHILDS, Edward 635 Mr 110
  Nancy 110 W E 460
CHILLS, 214
CHITTENDEN, Jonathan 445
  William E 336
CHOLERA, 261
CHRIST, Jos 447
CHRISTLIP, George S 325 634
CHRISTMAN, Catharine 572
CHRISTMAS, C W 160 J W 158
CHUMI, ---- 448
CHURCH, Directory 294 Earl 485
  Eleanor 485 M H 346
CHURCHES, 191 274 283
CHURN, Factory 400
CLAGGETT, 109
CLAPPER, Joseph 488
CLARK, 23 66 147 Ann Eliz 417
  Aurelia 107 Benjamin 607
  Calvin 326 573 636 David 163
  Elisha 210 Elvira S 576 Gen
  26-27 653 George R 84 John
  578 Judge 377 M 488 Mary
  563 Mathew 527 637 Matthew
  167 351 Sarah Ann 358 Slike
  485 Sylvester B 418 637 Uncle
  Billy 378 William 165 378 488
CLARKE, Alexander 73 C 73
CLARY, U 344
CLAY, 317-319 406 Gen 40 Green
  41 Henry 133 255 359
CLAYPOOL, Abraham 678
CLAYPOOLE, James T 337
CLEMENS, William 232
CLEVELAND, Moses 35
CLINE, Jacob W 458
CLINTON, Dewitt 163 219-220
  Township 163 166 504
CLOSE, Daniel 608 Ephraim 283

CLOSE (cont)
  Robert 283
COBERT, John 446
COCHRAN, Harriet 115 Miss 115
COE, 508 514 I M 554 Thomas 514
COFFIN, C 331
COFFINBERRY, 376-377 Andrew 351 434 Count 435 Mr 209 352
COLD, Creek 609
COLE, H W 554 Harrison 584 Jacob 578
COLERICK, Mr 407
COLLET, F 487
COLLETT, Judge 358
COLLIER, Rev Mr 302
COLLINS, L 54 Mr 324 T 314 T T 349
COLTHURST, William 349
COLWELL, 591 A D 455 F N 455 N P 590
COMEGYS, C G 197-198 206 Dr 196 Mrs 197 Mrs Dr 147
COMMISSIONERS, 165
COMSTOCK, Stephen B 430
COMYGES, C G 639
CONCLUSION, 638
CONGER, E 619
CONNEAUT, 34
CONNELL, 120 John P 359
CONNOR, Mr 43 Richard 605
CONRAD, Adam Adolph 278 Rev 279 283 285
CONSTITUTIONAL, Convention 662
CONVERSE, Charles C 554
CONWAY, Eben 549 Joseph S 549
COOK, 579 Dwight B 458 Dwight R 458 E 52 E H 488 Elutherus 50 54 126 Erastus H 488 Henry 284 Jacob 615 618 John 550 M Scott 197 Mr 398 Thomas M 462

COOKE, E 56 Elutherus 52 Henry D 51 Jay 68 Mr 61 Pitt 51
COOKERLY, Edward 449
COOLEY, Edward 494-495 497 J B 96 Wm 495
COOLY, 500
COON, Cooking 211
COONRAD, 250 U P 243 Uriah P 177 318 345 635
COONROD, J A 345 U P 416
COOPER, Ezechiel 91 John 556 R 564 Sarah Ann 556
COPE, Wm P 268
COPENHAVER, A 447 Jacob 301 Mary Ann 301
CORNELL, 147 Judge 501 599 William 166-167 351 527 637
CORNELY, Nicholas 448
CORNWALLIS, 22
COROTHERS, Rebecca 396
CORRELL, Sophia 255
CORRIGAN, John 633
CORWIN, 319 425 Gov 446 Mathias 89 677 Mr 90 Thomas 89 476 478 538
CORY, Hugh M 628
COUCH, James L 620
COUGHLIN, Michael 349
COUNCIL, With Indians 82
COUNTIES, Organized 35
COUNTY, Officers To 1880 633
COURT, House 175 House Burnt 180
COURTH, John 449
COURTRIGHT, A M 115 H 628 H B 627 James 627-628
COVEL, Mr 541
COVER, David 540-541
COWDERY, 595 651 Mr 179 365 387 Mrs 364 Oliver 364 371 650 652
COWDRY, Mr 532 Oliver 330
COWGILL, Milton 458
COWLES, John G W 460

CRAIGHEAD, William B 440-441
CRAIGHILL, William B 439
CRAMER, Adam 460 C A J 565 C
 H 401 Catharine 515
 Catherine 280 Charles H 385
 Dennis F 416 515 Enos 418
 Frederick 280 515 U F 633
 Upton F 385 515 Walter S 386
CRAPO, David 494
CRAUN, Abraham 546 John 549
CRAW, 147 Henry 164
CRAWFORD, 15-19 30 78 317 Col
 13 20 Dr 423 464 Elizabeth
 276 George S 458 Harriet 276
 422 John 17 Township 172 W
 394 William 14 17 21-22
 William J 276 William L 422
CREASEY, Levi 692
CREEGER, 550 Anna Margaret
 248 Eleanor 248 H W 235
 Henry 541 543 Henry W 227
 229 Josephine 248 Louisa 248
 Martha 248 Theresa 248 309
 Uriah 248 Widow 248
CREEKS, The 222
CREESY, Henry 535 Mr 536
CREGLOUGH, Joshua 627
CREIGHTON, William Jr 668
 678
CRESAP, Col 79
CRESEY, Leroy 94 Levi 507
CRISSEY, 551 Levi 109 549 Mr
 550
CROBAUGH, Samuel 620
CROCKER, 557 602 John 555-
 556 593 Laura 555 Mr 556 R
 564 Roswell 552 556
CROCKET, Asa 517 522 James
 481 485
CROCKETT, Benjamin 329 Mr
 330
CROGHAN, 57 84 Col 55 86
 George 43 Maj 44-46 83
CRONISE, 254 263 409 C 347
 Elizabeth 331 Flora 401

CRONISE (cont)
 Florence 384 H G W 342-343
 Henry 243 253 255 265 299
 318 329 439 445 Mr 246 248
 507 Nettie 384 Thomas J 331
CROSSLEY, 324
CROUKITE, Tunis 578 580 W H
 578
CROUSE, Dr 289 E B 290-291
 Eliza 288 Isaac 562 J 287
 Jacob 288 Rev 294
CROW, 108 E 628 R 110
CROWELL, Mr 102 Samuel 98
CROWLEY, John 275
CROXTON, Ambrose C 627
 Samuel 618 627
CRUM, Abraham 512 Barbara
 508 H D 347 Hamilton F 508-
 509 Jacob 512 John 129 176
 508 512 535 636 Margaret 509
 Nancy 509 Robert 322 334
 345-347
CULBERTSON, Joseph 484
CULVER, 572 Benjamin 107-108
 110 126 Frank B 469 George
 W 458 Mr 109 Mrs 113
 Tabitha 107 110 William W
 352
CUNNINGHAM, 313 564 Daniel
 417 E J 566 Lon 564
CUPP, W 343
CURTIS, J B 462
CUSTAR, Mr 507
CUTRIGHT, James 210
CUTTER, Ephraim 668 Mr 666
DALE, 564 Samuel 565-566
DALRYAMPLE, Johnny 263
DALRYMPLE, Mrs 264
DALTON, Mr 23-24
DANA, Daniel H 482 Edwin P
 458 Marcus 553
DANIELS, H 285 Munson H 435
 Willard 430
DANNENHOEFFER, 486
DARLINTON, Joseph 667 Mr 664

DAUGHERTY, 544 Edward 446
DAVIDSON, 599 Henry 418 J H
 633 James W 458 William 278
DAVIS, 37 258-259 397 C D 347
 C E 564-566 568 John 494
 497-499 Levi 177 250 339 416
 475 634 Mr 584 Solomon 473
 Vill R 468-469 William 418
 499 Wm R 462
DAWALT, John 543
DAWSON, 82 397
DAY, A W 550
DEAN, E V 403 Judge 403
DEAVER, Daniel 447 John 447
DECKER, Amos 341 441 Jacob
 441 554 636 John 608
DEER, Hunting 118
DEIS, W 285
DEITRICH, W 627
DELANO, Columbus 478
DEMICK, 147
DEMOREST, Madam 526
DEMUTH, John 448
DENISON, George 535
DENMAN, Mathias 25
DENNIS, 542 Peter 567
DENTLER, Jane 589 S S 589
DENZER, A 447 Andrew 278 322
 447 George 447
DEPEYSTER, 22 Arentz 15
DERAN, Ann M 575 Dennis 575
DEROIT, John 447
DERR, Elizabeth 541 Ezra 280
 416 541 Rosanna 280 Thomas
 280 542
DETTERMAN, George 284 Henry
 232 284 Herman 284 Samuel
 284
DETWILER, Jacob 494
DETWILLER, Jacob 232
DEUBEL, Christian 284
DEUZER, 259
DEWALD, Nicholas 284 Peter
 284 Philip 284
DEWALT, George 447 Jane 417

DEWALT (cont)
 Maj 375 Peter 608
DEWITT, Isaac 488 John C 73
 Paul 369 447 William 446 495
 635
DEWOLF, D F 346 Daniel F 460
 J P 565 O J 565
DEWOLFE, J P 566
DICKINSON, 511 527 Mr 101-
 102 168 Obed 100 134 R 351
 Rodolphus 145 357 390
 Rudolphus 100 133 167 209
 635
DIEHL, Patricia S 13 Philip 455
DILDINE, 250 A J 455 A M 564
 566 D D 339 D H 449 Daniel
 249 416 508 686 Daniel Jr 359
 Daniel Sr 303 306 513 Frank
 383 411 James 448 Jane 418
 Mr 514 S H 455 William M
 634
DILLON, Dr 396 Jacob 552 Thos
 552
DIMICK, Solomon 607
DINGES, Valentine 447
DIRGE, Of The State House Bell
 660
DISNEY, David T 433
DITTENHAFER, Henry 495
DITTO, Elizabeth 524 John 278
 280 524
DOAN, Hannah 508 Jonas 522
DOCKWEILER, John 416 594
 599 Mary 600 Mr 600
DODGE, H H 355 Judge 353 S
 431-432
DOE, 564
DOG, Dance 97
DOKE, 564 Robert 554
DONALD, 497-498 500 Mr 494
DONALDSON, George 329
DONALSON, Israel 667 Mr 666
DONNEL, John C 210 Mary 149
DONNELL, Mary 492 Mrs 494
DORAN, John 512

DORE, John 349
DORNAN, James 417
DORSEY, Elizabeth 418 Evan 340 345 348 402 494 591 630
DOUGHT, Eli 283
DOUGLAS, 608
DOUGLASS, Capt 457
DOWD, M 455
DOWNEY, Samuel 448
DOWNING, 92 111-112
DOWNS, 147 John 535
DOWNY, John L 525
DOYLE, William 210
DRAKE, 30 C W 458 Col 29 Elias F 476 J H 590 Judge 140 Levi 458 Lieut 32 U 141 Urich 140
DREISBACH, C F 475
DRENNIN, Armstrong 521 Mr 522
DRENNON, 146
DRESBACH, C F 634 Catherine 389 Charles F 345 David 389 Dr 117 120 243-244 248 263-264 390-392 506-507 511 579 E 345 394 Eli 357 Ely 145 389 L R 196 Rev Mr 613
DRESSEL, August 350
DRIFT, 233
DRIVER, Isaac 73
DROWN, Solomon 475
DRUIDS, U A O 349
DRUNKENNESS, Cure Of 245
DU, Esel 249
DUBOIS, Mrs 524
DUDLEY, Col 40-41
DUDROW, David W 485 Mary 485
DUFFIELD, D Bethune 67
DUGOUT, 245
DUKE, 109
DUKES, Andrew 117 Gittie 117 John 117 Mr 118 Sophia 117
DUMOND, 92 109 572 Gittie 117 Isaac I 94 117 126-128 686 Mr 98 118 Sophia 117

DUMONT, Mr 127
DUNCAN, 536
DUNLAP, Jane 629 Samuel 677
DUNLAVY, Francis 668 Mr 666
DUNN, Dr 166-168 636
DUNNELL, David 334 S Grace 334
DUNTON, A S 277
DURBIN, James 145 149 540 578 636
DURDY, R L 449
DURKEE, Caroline S 373
DURLEIN, W 265
DURR, Rosalia 597
DUTT, John 420
DUTTON, Robert 150 589
DYER, Elisha 54
DYSINGER, Thomas 495
EARLY, Gen 467
EARTHQUAKE, The 640
EASTMAN, 147 Daniel W 535 John W 416 637 Rudolph 460
EATON, A 318 James 107 John 108-109 572 593 Polly 107-108
EBBERT, Henry 416 634
EBENEZER, Church 291
EBERSOLE, Henry 628 Milton F 462 Peter 552 636
EBERT, 407 Ann 296 Elizabeth 418 George 296 H 249 Henry 244 246 417 446 637 Jacob M 424 Judge 265 Mary 421 Mr 245 Mrs 265
ECKERT, Fritz 420
ECKHART, Elizabeth 524 Louis 524
EDAR, 246
EDEN, Township 525
EDWARDS, Gov 615 618
EGBERT, 514 Jeremiah 485 Lucy 485 Mr 571 Susannah 570 T 447 Uriah 416 482 513 570
EHRENFRIED, John 349 John B 323
EID, Mr 598

EINSEL, 496 John 497 Noah 233
ELDER, John 180 Thomas 540
ELDRIDGE, Benjamin F 460
ELECTION, First County 165
ELECTIONS, In Townships 163
ELLERTON, John 488
ELLIOT, 683 Capt 47
ELLIOTT, 138 Capt 22
ELLIS, Capt 153 Michael 570
   Nancy 417 Thomas R 418 475
   482
ELLMAKER, Amos 318
ELLWANGER, John 597
ELTIG, Francis 486 Nicholas 486
ELWOOD, Thomas 374
EMERINE, Alonzo 567
EMERY, John 584
EMICH, 286 Jacob 181 Ludwig
   285 Ph 344 419 448
EMICK, 250
EMMERSON, Louisa 109
ENGELFRIED, Lucas 448
ENGELMAN, Mr 177
ENGLAND, Charles W 458
   Umphrey 554
ENGLE, 494
ENGLER, Jacob 447
ENGLISH, 414 Joseph 547
   Lutheran Church 287 Wilson
   W 628
ENOS, George 566
ENRICH, N 285
ENSMINGER, J F 564
EPSTEIN, Eph 268
ERB, John 290
ERNEST, 564
ERNST, Charles 343 Jacob 251
   John 243
ERSIG, 564
ESCHER, J J 284-285
ESHELMAN, 564 L J 567
ESHER, J J 268 279
ESTEP, Jacob 495
ETCHEN, Francis 486 Nicholas
   486

EVANS, Benj F 460 Francis 481
   Margaret 509
EVENBECK, 564
EVERETT, Edward 54 Homer
   374 Jeremiah 440
EVERITT, David H 561
EVRARD, Charles 292 Father
   275 290 Rev Father 294
EWALD, John 349
EWING, James 458 Samuel 564
   567
FAHNESTOCK, E A 455
FAIR, Elisha 615 617
FAIRFAX, Lord 21
FALL, G A 564 564
FANNING, J F E 322-323 394
FARGURSON, Elijah 168
FAST, Louisa 392 S A 343
FAULHABER, 564 Philip 457
FAULHAVER, 251
FAUSEY, H H 458
FEASEL, George 550
FEBLE, Frederick 547
FEBLES, F 285
FECK, 595 John 594 596
FEESE, James A 633
FEINDEL, N 285
FELL, J 455
FELLNAGEL, Julius 251 598 Mr
   253 597
FENNEMAN, W H 284-285
FENWICK, Bishop 290
FERGUSON, Mr 230
FERNALD, Thomas C 462
FERRIER, Andrew 546
FERRIS, C R 565 Charles G 468
   Mr 649 O 468 Randolph B 469
FERRY, The 245
FEW, Col 361
FEWSON, Robert 460
FICKS, G 286
FIEGE, 248 286 John 169 310
   523 533 Louisa 310 Mary
   Louisa 310 Susannah M 523
FIESER, Frederick 258

FIFIELD, Mr 133
FIGGINS, James M 574
FILLER, J W 415
FILLIATRE, 487
FILLMORE, Millard 54
FILMORE, 415
FINCH, Madison 341
FINDLEY, 201 319 Gen 674
FINIS, Capt 66
FINK, John 628
FINLEY, 276 James B 73 127
    Robert 127
FIRE, The Great 311
FISBINGH, 313
FISER, Catharine 602 Harry 602
FISHBAUGH, 259 332 401
    George 315
FISHER, 552 Cyrus 430 D W 496
    Daniel 447 Dr 250 E 564
    Elizabeth 149 250 Elizabeth
    M 393 Hannah E 393 James
    149 246 250 260 393 John 494
    Laura 393 Lewis 232 Lyman J
    276 Mary E 393 Pattie D 393
    Robert 421 Thomas B 393 Wm
    564
FITCH, J W 52 Judge 112
FITZGERALDS, William 331
FITZPATRICK, Michael 449
FLACK, A L 342 George 318 637
    J A 344 John 512
FLAGG, Junius 435
FLAHAFF, Mrs 264
FLAT, Rock See Thompson 00
FLAUGHER, Conrad 458 Jacob
    321-322 Jacob Jr 448 John
    409
FLECK, Adam 549 John L 175
FLEET, 147 William 336 525 537
FLEMING, 309 J P 462 John P
    462 William 343
FLEN, Alf D 300 Augusta 300
FLENNER, John H 446 Upton
    246 Upton R 418
FLICK, 487

FLOTOW, 421
FLOYD, Col 26
FLUMMERFELT, 109-110 550 A
    449 Ann M 575 Catharine 572
    Cornelius 512 572-573 D V
    572 575 George 575 Matilda
    575 Melinda 575 Mrs 573
FOELL, Jacob 448
FOGHT, David 593 604 Mr 235
FOLTZ, Jonathan 280 Susanna
    280
FONCANNON, 603 Joseph 280
    514 604 Michael 447 W D 447
    William 210
FORBUSH, Myron H 448
FORD, 618 623 Esther 618
    Father 617 H J 616-617 J H
    620 James 633 Jennie 421
    Johnson 615-619 622-623
    Seabury 476
FOREST, Culture 212
FORRER, Samuel 220 431
FORSYTH, John 433 Sec 434
FORSYTHE, Maj 152
FORT, Ball 142 Ball Artillery 448
    Lawrence 8 Meigs 39
    Recovery 32 Seneca 81
    Stevenson 44
FORTIFICATIONS, Ancient 145
    150
FORTNEY, A 455
FOSTER, 564 Annie 557 C 154
    564 C W 554 556 564 Charles
    381 488 556-557 Charles W
    174 553 555 Christian 546-547
    Dr 654 Gov 383 556 562 588 J
    628 Jessie 557 Jonas 458
    Laura 555 Mr 557-558 Nathan
    586 Sarah Ann 556 Seth F
    586-587
FOSTORIA, Academy 562
    Lawyers 559 Lodges 565
    Schools 563
FOSTY, B F 564
FOWLER, David 522

FOX, Daniel H 461-462 David
543 Frank 589 Frederick 150
George 374 Simon 56
FRALEY, Oscar 344
FRANKENFIELD, 284
FRANKHAUSER, J 290
FRANKLIN, 657-658 Benjamin
122 F E 346 Mr 676
FRARY, Hattie F 129 James R
129 Milton 129 Phineas 109
115 Sally 129 417
FRAZER, Robert P 579
FRECH, F 290-291
FREDERICI, Francis 278
FREE, 508 Daniel 554 George
149 493 497 John 418 Mr 144
Racheael 522
FREES, Jacob 517 Martin 517
Mrs 509 O P 344 Peter 517
FREESE, Jefferson 250
FRELINGHUYSEN, Mr 359
FREMONT, J C 375 John C 309
FRENCH, R 562
FRENTZEL, Jacob 448
FREY, Ph 286
FREYMAN, Laura 332
FRIED, Benjamin 284
FRIEDLEY, Ludwig 445
FRINK, Sabeah 490 Squire 491
Theodore M 487 490
FRITCHER, 564 James 286
FROST, 259 J H 346-347
FRUITCHEY, Andrew 245
FRUITCHY, Andrew 264
FRUTH, Jacob 552 568 John
George 569
FRY, 109 Augusta P 576 Ed 344
Enoch 230 Francis J 576
James H 629 636 John J 458
FULLER, L T 473
FULTZ, Daniel M 458
FUMEMAN, W H 268
FUNDENBURG, Susanna 254
FUNK, Isaac 628
GADDIS, David 14

GALBREATH, John 593
GALE, E 370 Franklin 396 Jesse
166 173 210 John A 590
GALLATIN, Albert 296 360-361
GALLOWAY, Samuel 538
GALLUP, Joseph H 460 William
276 345
GAMBEE, Charles B 460
Solomon 636
GAMBY, Solomon 629
GANGWER, Ch 286
GANO, Gen 674
GANTS, John 488
GARDINER, J B 73 James 137
James B 71 74 474
GARFIELD, 558 Gen 557
GARI, Fred 448
GARLAND, Lieut 66
GARRISON, T M 568
GAS, Light Company 398
GASSMAN, 550
GASSNER, 680
GATCH, Mr 666 Philip 668
GATES, Ralph 130 Sarah 129
GAW, Sarah 516
GEAR, George 554 Julia 264
GEE, Benjamin 446 Samuel 567
GEHR, Eli 488
GEHRING, J D 284
GEIGER, 284 Henry 418
GELMORE, D 567
GENERAL, Muster 449
GEOLOGY, 226
GEORGE, James F 323
GEORGIA, A 567
GEOTHIUS, Nicholas 320
GEPHART, George 370
GERHART, Dr 271-272 E V 268
284-285 Elizabeth 268
Emanuel Vogel 270 Isaac 270
Sarah 270
GERHARTSTEIN, John 608
GERMAN, Ev Church 278 John
283 Reformed Church 279
Settlers 251

GERSPACKER, John 448
GERSTER, Barbara 518
GIBBON, H B 395
GIBBONS, 218 Daniel 289 F H 564 Franklin H 458
GIBBS, Mrs 324
GIBSON, 147 259 Col 24 369 457 459 466 Dr 502 599 Elizabeth 253 Gen 352 383 526 J A 416 John 13 276 382 526 535 538 John K 352 359 374 458 Joseph 253 Julia Ann 307 L 628 Martha 248 Polly 538 W H 330-331 359 416 458 William H 322 336 382 Wm H 248
GIDDINGS, Joshua R 67
GILBERT, Dr 590 Ezra 615-618 Francis 251 I T 581 Nettie 373
GILLIAN, James H 469
GILLIAUME, 487
GILLIG, Conrad 516 George 516
GILMAN, Benjamin Ives 668 Mr 666
GILMORE, Caroline 616 Cornelius 615-617 John 625
GIRLS, Pioneer 192
GIRTY, 19-20 140 George 138 James 22 138 Michael 139 Simon 16 18 138-139 Thomas 138
GIST, 258 George W 160 320 540
GLASGOW, 157 J 157
GLASSNER, John 608
GLENN, 259 Andrew 244
GLICK, Elizabeth 518 John 458 Mrs 313-314
GNOFF, Jacob 347
GODDARD, C B 370 Gen 371
GODFREY, John 564
GOETCHINS, Nicholas 176
GOETCHIS, James 416
GOETSCHIUS, James 514 Nicholas 514 Permelia 514
GOFORTH, Mr 666-667 William

GOFORTH (cont) 664 668
GOIT, Edson 359 Edson B 129
GOLDSMITH, Oliver 352
GOOD, Adam 283 Adam Jr 283 Elizabeth 273 Emanuel 283 George 231 283 J H 267-268 270 283-285 339 Jeremiah H 273 John 552 M 608 Mr 232 559 Philip Augustus 273 R 268 285 Reuben 267 273 Wm 283
GOODIN, 248 250 255 Elizabeth 295 Joel K 295 John 244 256 295 305 318 439 634 Mr 296
GOODMAN, John 627
GOODSELL, 259 D J Jr 454 Naman 430
GOODSON, 333
GORDON, 550 J W 343 James 540 576 636 John P 547 553 Mary 563
GORSUCH, J 553
GOSHORN, James 446
GOULD, O B 460
GRADY, John 448
GRAFF, 258 550 Henry 448 Hez 365 Joseph 255 318 M Y 176 Marcus Y 636 Marquis Y 173 255 Mary Ellen 381 Silas W 381
GRAHAM, 83
GRAMER, C 290
GRAMMES, Peter 323
GRANDON, Thomas 345
GRANT, Gen 468
GRAPES, W H 565 William H 563
GRAVATH, Erastus M 462
GRAVES, Dr 493-494 Selden 526-527 535 637
GRAY, 259 Anson 92 107 109 116 117 572 J W 414 James 177 535 Jane 92 107 Ronaldo A 323 Samuel F 458 W C 411

GREDING, P 268
GREEN, F W 346-347 634
   Frederick W 110 Gen 297 444
   J N 455 John 458 John L 326
   L O 617 Mr 111 Shepherd 458
   T S 568 Widow 110
GREENVILLE, Treaty Of 33
GREGG, Mr 356 677
GREIS, P G 342 P H 343
GREIVELDINGER, J B 448
GRELLE, Samuel 601 603 636
   Sarah 601
GREULICH, Frank 293
GREYEYES, Matthew 73
GRIESE, T J 455
GRIFFIN, James 418
GRIFFITH, J W 565 R L 635 S
   447 Timothy 305
GRIMES, 232 Ira 627 James 550
GRISWOLD, Samuel A 408
GROFF, Marcus Y 359 Marquis Y 169
GROSENBAUGH, L 284 Louis 268
GROSS, 259 Bovard 247 D 455
   Elizabeth 239 252 Harry 421
   Henry 247 403-404 406 420
   424 Henry Sr 404 J G 346-348
   Jane 247 John 252 John G
   239 339 559 Mr 405 Samuel
   247 416 494 497
GROSSCOST, 484 Jane 484
GROVE, S 628
GROVES, Ephraim 619
GRUBB, James 668 Mr 666
GRUBER, Daniel 284 Jacob 284
GRUMMEL, 692 Phillip 420
GUERNSEY, 564 Charles 561
   Mina G 561
GUGGENHEIM, H 343
GUISBERT, John 416
GULLIVER, Robert 449
GUNN, Mrs 34
GUNTHER, Jacob 448
GUNWORTH, 614

GURLEY, E S 276
GUTELIUS, Samuel 271
GWINN, 259
GWYER, Jacob 488
GWYN, Edward 398 John 399 Mr 399
GWYNN, Ed 404 Martha 333
GYWN, Edward 375
HAAS, W H 456
HAASE, John 419
HADE, Fred 286
HADLEY, 498 N 497 Nehemiah 149 493 497
HAEBLER, George 422
HAINES, Joseph 567
HALDERMAN, Fred K 344
HALE, George W 462 Jacob 286
   R W 565 Randall 565 568 S E 566-567
HALL, 259 355 384 Almon 375
   Cynthia A 239 363 Eugenia
   Hargrace 375 J A 344 John
   444 592 Judge 426 L A 346
   370-371 376 417 635 L W 353
   Luther A 110 177 239 276
   358-359 362 386 408 416 634
   Mr 363 543 Nathan 446 W H 345
HALSEY, Isaac J 527
HALSTED, James 615 Samuel 617-618
HAMBURGER, Maximillian 292
HAMER, 659
HAMILTON, D K 446 Gov 138
   Henry 14 J K 496
HAMLIN, 153 Gen 152
HAMMAKER, W S 496
HAMMERLY, Eliza 239
HAMPSHIRE, Jonas 546
HAMPTON, J C 494 497-499 501
HANCE, Adam 586-587 599
HANCOCK, 31 414
HANFORD, 579 Capt 580 584 590 James 581 Mrs 580
HARBAUGH, 564 H 455 Henry

HARBAUGH (cont)
  272 J 627 Joseph 628 S J 562
HARDIN, Col 27-28
HARENPFLUG, G 290
HARGRACE, Lewis Chadwick 374
HARKEY, Adam 283
HARMAR, Gen 27-28
HARMAS, Israel 488
HARMON, Benjamin 593 Harvey J 440 William 593
HARPER, James F 458 Samuel M 458
HARPSTER, 613 Anthony 283 Frederick 612 Wm 166
HARRIMAN, G G 276 George 542 George G 401
HARRINGTON, Israel 162
HARRIS, 16-17 572 Augustus 107 109 Aurelia 107 Betsey 107 C W 551 Capt 70 H L 348 Hettie 107 J A 51 Jane 92 107-108 John 107-108 113 117 Mark A 110 Marshal 108 Martin 651-652 Mary 107 Minerva 107-108 Miss 126 Mr 116 119 Nancy 107-108 Polly 107 Samuel 107-109 Tabitha 107-108 110 William 92 107 110 128 428 444
HARRISON, 57 66 319 659 Gen 30 33-34 38-41 43-46 48 58 61 63 67 81-89 105 109 142-143 145 161 254 265 445 514 613 645 685 690 James 578 Jas 581 William 22 William H 36 Wm Henry 55
HARSBAGER, Jonas 636
HARSHBERGER, Jonas 612
HART, 544 A M 344 Mr 551
HARTER, 259 Frederick 447 Joseph 175
HARTLEY, Benjamin 552 E J 563
HARTMAN, John 448 Mary 333 Reuben 231

HARTNER, P 314
HARTSOCK, Daniel 458 Isaac 549 Jane 268 Samuel 481
HASELTINE, Sen 367
HASSON, George 608 Henry 608
HATCHILT, J G 473
HATHAWAY, William 495 William W 455
HAWS, J H 159
HAYES, Gen 373 Gov 382 685 Orrin B 458 President 129 133 197 R B 372
HAYNES, Ezekiel S 207
HAYS, A B 563 Betsey 107 Charles 564 Cornet 143 David 562 Frank 565 James 563 Jeremiah 117
HAYWARD, 259 Elijah 161 Nathaniel G 636
HEABLER, George 629 J 619
HEALER, James 469
HEALEY, Rev Father 294
HEALY, Father 275 M 290 345
HEATON, Esq 532 Harriet 599 Micagah 527 532 Micajah 599
HEBBLE, Joseph 460
HECK, Catharine 602 Daniel G 422 602 629 Elizabeth 602 George 593 601-602 John 602 Maria 602 Sarah 601-602
HECKERMAN, J N 394 J U 394
HECKMAN, John 620
HEDGE, 258 498 544
HEDGES, 259 Albert 120 Clarinda 239 Cynthia A 239 363 Eliza 239 Elizabeth 239 Harriet 239 James 143 146 237 Josiah 111-112 120 143 145-146 154 168-169 178 196 208-209 237 265 268 280 290 325 329 357-358 362-363 413 440 481 690 Mary Jane 239 Minerva 239 Mr 147 166-167 171 210 238-240 242-243 248 260 275 319-320 328 331 377

HEDGES (cont)
  512 521 541 543 598 Rebecca
  239 Sarah 239 Sarah V 413 W
  C 259 416
HEETER, John 283
HEIDELBERG, College 267
HEILAND, J B 292 Rev Father
  294
HEILMAN, 259 284 Jacob 259
  John 259 401 500 John F 568
  634 Philip 284 494 T C 564
HEINER, Elias 268
HEIRHOLZER, Conrad 594
HEISSERMAN, H 455 Jacob 284
  Melchior 569
HELFFENSTEIN, H 270
HELLER, Prof 596
HELTEBRAKE, Joseph 542
HEMING, George 475 552 636
  George H 346 634 Thomas 482
  634 636
HEMMENWAY, Samuel 430
HEN, Franz 608
HENDEL, Mary 249 Michael 249-
  250 590
HENDERSHOTT, L V 563
HENDERSON, Charles 486 D C
  488 William L 553
HENNESSEY, Philip 244
HENNESSY, M 448 Philip 552
HENRY, 429 J L 628 J M 454
  William B 628
HENSEL, J A 291 294
HENSINGER, C 283 John 283
  John Jr 283
HENZ, 262
HEPP, Henry 599
HERBIG, Lissette 332
HERFORD, Mr 146
HERIN, 508 Hannah 418 Joseph
  517 Samuel 517 634
HERNDON, 218
HEROLD, William 419-420
HERR, Jacob 458
HERRIN, George 74 118 135 137

HERRIN (cont)
  141 Joseph 117 418 522
  Rachael 522 Samuel 416 418
  525 637
HERRON, George 474
HERSHBERGER, 494
HERSHISER, H K 334 W H 394
HERTZER, G F 347
HERZER, Guenther 349
HESS, Frank 386
HESSBERGER, John 448
HESSENAUER, Jacob 446
HESSINGER, W H 460
HETER, John 445 608
HIGBEE, E E 268 281
HIGGINS, Charles 265 D 387
  David 353 527 Judge 132 425-
  426 433 435
HIGLEY, 620
HILL, James W 260
HILLIER, Asa R 462
HILLIS, David 628 James 628
  John 628
HILSINGER, Joseph 284
HIND, Thomas A 207
HINES, Jacob 627 Mrs 522
HIRT, 596 Francis J 595 Francis
  Joseph 594
HISSONG, L J 564
HISTE, Mary 381 Mr 381
  William T 629 636
HITCHCOCK, 660
HITE, John 499
HITT, William 605
HOAGLAND, Mr 259 320 Samuel
  245 507
HOAGLIN, Samuel 544
HOBBES, John 608 Paul 284
HODGE, Daniel 21
HOEFLING, John 449 Leonard
  446 Nicholas 420 Peter 341
HOEGE, G L 566 George L 565
  568
HOETZEL, Christian 633
HOFFERT, Silas 285

HOFFMAN, 261 A W 628
    Charlotte 262 265 Daniel 593
    Frederick 251 262 Fritz 262
    Henry 446 546 John 262-263
    Joseph 628 Mr 263 Mrs 265
HOFMASTER, Jacob 286
HOGG, Thomas 265
HOHMANN, Mr 251
HOLCOMB, O M 496 Oscar M
    633
HOLDERMAN, Fred K 345
HOLDUP, Mr 64
HOLLEY, Robert 637
HOLLINGER, Jacob 546
HOLLOPETER, 324 546 Isaiah
    547 John L 458
HOLMES, 83 Alex 158 Ira 164
    Jedediah 444 John 619 627
    Mr 157
HOLT, Minnie 333 William 264
    391
HOLTS, Dennis 523 George 636
    Jacob 522 Susannah M 523
HOLTZ, 255 Jacob 485 James E
    447
HOMAN, George 420
HOMANN, George 410-411
HOMER, James R 462 John S
    436
HOMINY, Block 189
HONEY, Creek 150
HONSBERGER, 286
HOOT, C J 448
HOOVER, J A 455 John 578
    Joseph 232
HOPEWELL, Township 166 540
HOPKINS, Capt 143
HOPPES, Solomon 483
HORD, John K 633
HORNER, Samuel 614
HORNUNG, Charles 268
HORSE, Race 120
HOSMER, Alex C 462
HOSSLER, Ann 418 Jacob 418
    494 496 500 P J 454 Thomas S

HOSSLER (cont)
    460
HOST, John 607
HOSTLER, Jonas 494
HOTELS, 245
HOTTAL, Jacob K 383
HOTTEL, Benj 494
HOUCK, 259 John 285 293 342
    348 594 596 Philbert 349
HOUGH, 147
HOUSEMAN, John 576
HOUSMAN, Martin 449
HOVEY, A B 339 394 Ariel B 395
    Dr 142 264 690
HOWARD, Col 431 D C 417
    Harvey 403 Horton 110 543
    Joseph 248 304 358-359 373
    408 439 625 633 M 290 Mr
    431 Simeon B 146 319
HOWE, Mr 651
HOWELL, 564 David 289
HOWLAND, Stephen 627
HOYT, James 122
HUBBARD, Clara S 334 Dr 334
    Dwight 333 E B 333 Helen M
    334 Sheldon B 334
HUBBLE, John 262
HUBER, 259 508 M 290
HUBERT, George 448
HUDDLE, 259 Benj 494 J K 411
    Jacob K 383
HUDDLESON, 618 John 628
HUDSON, James 549
HUF, Jacob 448
HUGHES, G A 680 J 278 Joseph
    A 565
HUKILL, 83
HULBURD, Jacques 167
HULBURT, Jacques 351 440
    Jaques 125 637 Judge 129 Mr
    126
HULL, 13 40 58 Gen 89 Otto 627
    William 39
HUMBOLDT, 218
HUMMELL, Joseph 596

HUMPHREY, George 668 Hiram 348 Mr 666
HUNSECKER, Daniel 567-568
HUNSICKER, Jno 495 John 495
HUNT, Hettie 107 John E 168 Mariah 113 Moses 107 Sylvia Ann 113
HUNTER, 259 499 515 Clarinda 239 Gen 468 Henry B 468 Jane 247 Lieut-col 467 Mary Ann 309 Mrs 259 S S 416 Samuel 146 William 239 277
HUNTER'S, Mill 146
HUNTINGTON, Mr 664 666 Samuel 668
HUNTLEY, Benjamin 589
HURLBUT, Jaques 116 Judge 117
HURONS, Legend Of The 76
HURRICANE, The 643
HURSH, C S A 268
HUSS, J 394 J T 259 Jacob 249 510 John T 338 342 382 399 Mr 339 Sarah 416-417
HUSTED, Elmer E 469
HUTCHINS, Buckley 525 527 Dr 333
HUTH, 564 Adam 419
HYACINTHE, Mrs 525-526 Pere 404
HYATT, William B 468
ILCHERT, John Baptist 596
INDIAN, Armstrong Tuguania 128 Bear-skin 73 Bearskin 304 Beaver 87-88 Between The Logs 304 Between-the-logs 39 Big Arms 304 Big Crow 601 Big Kittle Child 305 Big Kittles 140-141 Big River 304 Big Spoon 304 Black Hoof 39 Black Sheep 304 Black Snake 601 Blue Jacket 30 86-88 97 Bob Cherokee 304 Buckongahelas 30 Capt Good Hunter 137 474

INDIAN (cont)
Capt Good-hunter 74 Capt Harris 78 Capt Smith 78 Charlieu 137 Charline 538-539 Charloe 304 Coffeehouse 70 78 Comstock 118 123 127 131 137 Conicogatchie 123 Coon Hawk 304 Coonstick 74 118 123 131-133 474 686 Cracked Hoof 131 Cross The Lake 304 Crow 114-116 118-119 126 141 Curly Eye 133 Curreesaquoh 304 Daenundee 304 Day-on-quot 304 Douwan-tout 304 Droosrousch 304 Fighter 304 Gayamee 304 George Washington 124 Good Hunter 99 103 118 125 133-134 686 Good Spring 119 Gostick 127 Gray Eyes 304 Ground Squirrel 304 Half John 304 Half King 304 Hard Hickory 98-102 118 131-137 474 542 603 686 Hard-hickory 74 Hays 304 Hisson 304 Hondon-yon-wan 304 Isahowmasaw 70 78 Jim Sky 119 John 132 John Baptiste 305 John Hicks 304 Joseph 70 78 128 Katepocomen 16 Kayroo-hoo 304 Kon-ke-pot 136 Kosciusko 30 Little Chief 304 Little Fox 86 Little Turtle 30 32-33 Logan 79 Manoncue 304 Mathias 304 Monture 304 Mudeatoe 304 Nooshutoomohs 304 Old Shawnee 304 Peacock 304 Piankeshaw 23-24 Pomoacan ---- Half-king 15 Porcupine 304 Pumpkin 604 Punch 304 Racer 305 Red Jacket 542 Ree-wan-dee-nuntoohk 304 Roe-nu-nas 72-73 Ron-ton-dee 304 Ronuneay 304 Round Head 39 Round

INDIAN (cont)
  The Lake 601 Running-about
  70 78 Saint Peter 304
  Satrahass 304 Seneca John
  118 123 127 131 133 136 582
  Seneca Joseph 119 Seneca
  Steel 74 118 137 686
  Septemess 304 Shane 123-124
  127 132 136 She-a-wah 73
  Shreaeohhs 304 Small Cloud
  Spicer 474 Small-cloud Spicer
  686 Small-cloud-spicer 74
  Snakehead 304 Solomon 304
  Soocuhquess 304 Soorontooroo
  305 Split-the-logs 304 Spotted
  Tail 600 Squeendehtee 304
  Steel 123 127 131-133 Stokey
  601 Strong Arm----teguania
  117 Sum-mun-de-wat 74
  Summenturoo 305
  Summondewat 304 Tahautohs
  304 Takawmadoaw 70 78 Tall
  Charles 304 Tall Chief 99 101
  104 123 133-134 686 Taress
  304 Tarhee 82 Tauranyehtee
  304 Tawgyou 70 78 Tay-arron-
  tooyea 304 Tay-on-dot-to-hach
  304 Tay-qua-way 304
  Tecumseh 38-41 48-49 69 78
  82 84 692 The Crow 140 The
  Pipe 18-19 The Prophet 38-39
  78 Thomas 304 Tondee 304
  Touromee 304 Tsooshia 304
  Tuquania 125 127 Tutelu 21
  Walk-in-the-water 39 Warpole
  304 Wasp 304 White Crow
  117 305 White Wing 304
  Widow Big Sinew 304 Widow
  Harrahaat 304 Wingenund
  18-19 Wipingstick 45-46 70 78
  Wolf 137 Yandeenoo 304
  Young Cherokee 304
INFIRMARY, 421
INGERSOLL, Robert G 462
INGHAM, Alexander 129 Justin

INGHAM (cont)
  130 Mrs 126 482 Sally 45 91
  123 128-129
INGLE, C F 291
INGRAHAM, A 209 402 543
  Agreen 114 165 167 169-170
  173 345 347 351 507 540 634-
  635 637 Judge 110 Melissa
  117 Mr 117 210
INK, Samuel 416
INSURANCE, Companies 340
IRELAND, William 535
IRION, Andrew 447
IRVINE, Gen 13-14 16 20
ISENHART, Monroe 565
ISLANDS, Of Erie Ode 53
JACKSON, 317-319 355 406 414
  471-472 590 A M 354 Andrew
  161 407 618 Elder 608 Gen
  160 204 207 309 316 426 432-
  433 474 482 George 677
  Hannah 109 128 Judge 353
  President 432 538 Township
  175 546 W T 562
JACOBS, Mr 403 T B 564
JACOMET, J B 292
JACQUA, Cal 536
JACQUES, G D 473
JAECK, Caroline E 416
JAIL, 169 173
JAMES, John H 105 W 286 W W
  284
JAMISON, R J 627
JANAY, Joseph 306
JANEY, Joseph 242
JAQUA, 147 152-153 Col 154
  Elizabeth 151 418 R 318
  Richard 151 416
JAY, John 34
JEFFERSON, 518 659 President
  38 79 198 202 675 Thomas 31
  655
JEFFRIES, Mr 494
JENAY, Joseph 551
JENKINS, 488-489 Benjamin 487

JENKINS (cont)
  John 487
JENNER, Alex E 441
JENNINGS, 258 550 Jacob S 210
  402 540 Milton 277 329
  Samuel 374
JERKS, The 645
JEROME, J H 436
JEWETT, E R 51
JIGGERS, 216
JOHNNY, Cake 188
JOHNSON, 49 114 197 Alfred
  336 359 Charles L 337 Henry
  F 546 Homer 395 John 105
  Martha 590 Philip 455
  President 363 Richard M 48
  Rolla 342-343 Sarah 522
  Sherman A 469 W M 322 633
  635 William 250 449 William
  M 386
JONATHAN, Black 502
JONES, Bishop 507 Capt 435 Col
  465 Dr 496 E 455 Ed 342
  Erastus 416 Gideon 441 J V
  560 James P 460 John C 525
  Junius V 381 559 Lon 627 Mr
  387 Paul 360 Simpson 563
  Squire 561
JUDGES, 351
JUDICIAL, Districts 353
JUDSON, E 619
JURY, First 210
JUSTICE, James 326 Judge 133
KABALA, William 596
KABELE, Jacob 486
KAESTNER, Henry F 594
KAGA, John 416 Mr 496
KAGG, Abraham 149
KAGY, 147 500 Abraham 233 411
  497-499 502 534 Barbara 534
  Isaac 441 634 John 535 Levi D
  634
KAINE, Jacob 549
KAISER, Jacob 552
KALER, 498

KANAGA, R J J 290
KANE, Elisha 655 Thomas L 655
KANKE, Mr 403
KAPPLER, Jacob 594
KARN, Isaac 232 Jacob 608 Peter
  608
KARSHNER, Eli 283
KASTNER, Jonathan 495
KATING, Elder 112 127
KAUFFMANN, Joseph 448
KAUFMAN, ---- 447
KAULL, 259 John M 402
KAUP, 312
KEATING, G L 416 George L 417
KEDLER, Reuben 111
KEELER, 128 Joseph 165
KEELLER, John 141
KEEN, Esq 248 687 G J 346 402
  416 634 Gabriel 359 Gabriel J
  318 409 Mrs 125
KEFAUVER, L H 281 Rev 294
KEIFFER, M 284
KEILHOLTS, W H 330
KEILHOLTZ, W H 416
KEILHOTZ, William H 322
KEILLER, Joseph A 268 Levi Jr
  341
KEIRCHNER, John 419
KEISLING, Julius 420
KELLER, 258 Aaron H 458 Amos
  458 Ch 495 Eli 283 Elizabeth
  505 F F 345 Joel 505 John 164
  416 505 636 685 692 Johnny
  505 Joseph 593 Joseph A 283-
  284 Levi 248 302 417 449 505
  635 637 Lewis 505
KELLEY, A W 562 Alfred 220
  Benjamin 584 620 Charles 521
  D W 283 David 283-284
  Mahitabel 584 Mr 522 T M
  584
KELLOGG, Dwight 469 Horace
  468 Price F 157
KELLY, 579 Daniel 446 George
  446 Mr 657

KELMER, Wm H 462
KEMP, David 615 618 Maurice 627 William 627
KEMPHER, William H 278
KENDALL, H L 314
KENDIG, H S 308
KENDRICK, Eleazer P 207
KENNEDY, J G 346-347 John 446 John G 345 Oliver 462 Samuel 535
KENT, John W 444
KENTFIELD, Smith 210
KENTON, Simon 16 26
KEPPEL, G B 383 629 631 635 H C 384 Henry 448
KEPPELMEYER, Franz 448
KEPPLE, G B 384 H C 411 W H 411
KEPPLER, Joseph 596
KERN, 486
KERR, John 278 422 558 599 602 Sarah 602 William 593
KERSHAW, W L 385
KERSHNER, J K 455
KERSLER, John 481
KESSLER, J 458 Jacob 549 John 458 Mrs 507 William H 250 318 534 635
KETTEMEYER, Joseph 448
KEUBLER, A 416
KEYS, Charles M 469
KIEFFER, A R 455 J B 268 M 268 270 281 286
KILBOURN, Byron 616 Col 148 150 525 616 Hector 616 James 162 617
KILBOURNE, Road 162
KIMBALL, Emma 392
KIME, Elias 543 John 280 Margaret 280 Samuel 543 William 543
KING, David B 417 Geo 494 George 227 John T 345 Peter T 552 Ph B 345 Philip 540 Phillip 416 Rufus 199 Truman

KING (cont) 494 William 345
KINGSEED, Charles Edwin 559 Elmira Emily 559 F D 564 Francis Dorwin 559 M 564 Martin 558-559 600 604 Peter 449
KINKERTER, John 284
KINNAMAN, F J 564 J P 322-323 347 394 P 620 Peter 619
KINNEY, Batholomew 551 Edmond 448 Mason 608 Mr 290 Patrick 244
KINTZ, S J 564 Thomas J 629 635
KIPKA, J C 454
KIRBY, Isaac M 461-462 M H 538 Moses H 304 441
KIRCH, Nicholas 448
KIRCHNER, Balthasar 448 Ignatz 448 J M 447 J W 447 John 448 M 349 416 447 Micael 292 Michael 348 448
KIRCKWOOD, Richard A 469
KIRGIS, Jonathan 599
KIRKER, Mr 666 Thomas 667
KIRRIAN, Earnest 266
KIRSH, Nicholas 446
KIRSHNER, Eva 418 Rufus 494
KISER, S F 566
KISHLER, Elizabeth 295 418 Fred 418 Frederick 318
KISINGER, J H 321 Samuel H 322
KISSABETH, Jacob 284 Philip 284
KISTLER, Monroe 283
KISTTER, Henry 482
KITCHEL, John 668 Mr 666
KITCHEN, Furniture 188
KITCHILL, Mr 676
KITTEL, Lyman 554
KLACHR, Conrad 495-496
KLAHR, 284 J C 283-284
KLAIS, 525

KLAR, J C 283
KLAUER, Paul 266
KLINE, 512 George 475 John 449
  Nancy 416 Ph T 462 William
  635
KLING, J 460
KLINGER, William 449
KLIPPART, J H 222
KLOEPFER, Elizabeth C 597
KNAPP, 132-133 147 219 Mr 49
  Philipena 300 Russel 300
  Samuel 164 William 584
KNAUSE, 286
KNEBLER, Anton 349
KNEPPER, C C 268 C O 333-334
  Jonathan 334 Margaret 334 S
  Grace 334
KNIEST, J B 268
KNIGHT, 378 Dr 17-22 Esq 590
  G A 567-568
KNIGHTS, Of Honor 344 Of
  Pythias 344
KNISELY, 116 Jacob 115 126
KNITZER, John 144
KNOPP, Benj 495 Loren 581
KNOTT, J W 332 James T 278
  John 314 449
KNOUSE, Edward 519 Eliza 519
KNOWLTON, Austin 486
KNUPP, George 250 330 340 343
  634 Valentine 250
KOCH, C G 291 C H 291
KOENIGSAAMEN, 599
KOENIGSAMEN, Anthony 606
  Anton 604 Catharine 604-605
  Christian 605 Emelia 605
  Joseph 605 Magdalena 605
  Margaret 604-605 Martin 604-
  605 Peter 604
KOLB, 251
KOLBER, 284
KOLER, Jesse 535 Simon 284
KOLLER, 147 Simon 494-495
KONKEY, Thomas 675
KOOKEN, James 439

KOON, Thomas 548
KOONS, Leicester M 287
KORNER, 613 Jacob 612
KOUP, Solomon 113
KRAUSS, John M 232
KRAUTZ, Catharine 334
KREADER, Aaron 343
KREMER, 286
KREUSCH, Mathias 292
KRIDLER, Eleanor 248 Elizabeth
  417 Frederick 177 248 Maria
  L 630 Mr 249 Samuel 416-417
  630
KRILLEY, 284
KRILLY, John 496
KRITHE, C F 284
KROH, D 285 Daniel 281 Jacob
  280 318 593 Margaret 416
  Sarah 280
KRUPP, 250 Anthony 607
KUEBLER, Anthony 449 Joseph
  292
KUHN, Caroline C 374 Catherine
  391 Christian 392 Dr 74 243-
  244 248-249 255 306 392
  Elizabeth 392 Emma 392 H
  320 416 686 Henry 345-347
  391 417-418 Jacob 284-285
  314 Joseph L 374 Kate 391
  Louisa 392 M 314 Margaret
  571 Maria 392 Maria P 259
  Robert D 392
KULER, Coleman J 430
KUNE, John 541
KUNES, Joseph 283
KUNIAMAN, J P 346
KUNKLE, H W 286 Hannah 519
  Henry 519
KUNOLD, Christian 419 Mr 420
KUNTZ, 495 N R 347 Nicholas
  447
LABAR, Daniel 448
LABARRE, Harriet Newel 579
LABOLT, 615
LACY, Henry F 462

LAFAYETTE, Gen 297 444
LAFONTAINE, 487
LAHR, Michael 449 Pierre 448
LAIRD, David 278
LAKE, Henry 648
LAMBDIN, 649 Mr 648
LAMBERSON, Daniel 445 508
 Janet C 631 John 535 Mary A
 631 Sharon C 342 Virgil D 633
 William 631
LAMBERTSON, Wm 416
LAMBRIGHT, John 547
LAMERAUX, John L 620
LAMPSIN, C Jr 455
LAND, Districts 158 Lw 159
 Sales 161
LANDON, Afred 386 Alfred 386
LANE, E 359 387 Ebenezer 167
 351 Judge 117 352-353 358
 373 376-378 Martin 116 140
LANG, 251 256 261 263
 Catharine 252 Catherine 387
 Elizabeth 252 F H 394 Frank
 H 633 George Ludwig Henry
 251 Hannah 252 Henrietta
 252 Henrietta E 630 Henry
 141 251-252 255 387 Judge
 616 Lafayette L 385 Louisa
 252 Louisa Christina 251
 Mary P 418 Philipina 252 W
 70 197-198 376 417 471 477-
 478 482 Wilhelm 251 William
 50 278 322 330-331 333 335
 340-341 370 379 386 404 410
 416-417 441 446-447 465 633-
 635 Wm 107 681
LANGDON, H L 455
LANGHAM, 201
LANGLEY, Mr 150
LANGWORTHY, A 458 Dr 140
LANMAN, Jos 54
LANTZ, Peter 416 488
LAPSLEY, J E 277
LATHAM, Allen 198 206
LATHROP, Philetus C 460

LATTA, Judge 354
LATTIMER, John A 461-462
LAUBACH, Abraham 411
LAUDON, A 635
LAUGHERY, James 586
LAUTERMILCH, G A 349 George
 A 350 420
LAUX, John 419
LAW, Students 386
LAWHEAD, 487 J W 341
LAWRENCE, John 381 Judge 354
 Miss 483
LAY, John 164 593 620
LEAHY, James F 385 John W
 386 Maurice 394-395
LEASE, Belinda 630 Eden 325
 340 416 525 635 Lloyd N 629-
 630 635 Maria L 630 Otho 630
LEATH, Judge 502
LEAVITT, Hallie 332
LEBAR, David 448
LEBARON, 312
LEE, A M 268 Charlotte 265 Col
 375 466 D T 494 G 481 Gen
 467 Gov 265 J N 496 Joel 164
 593 John C 460 Melinda 446
 496 Robert 441
LEGISLATURE, Of Territory 36
LEHNHART, Ignatz 486
LEIB, Martin 446
LEIBE, Nicholas 250
LEIDY, J H 449
LEINER, Charles 249
LEISENRING, David 448
LEITNER, Gideon 448 Samuel
 449
LEMP, H 448 Henry 350
LENDELBACH, 550
LENHART, Francis 596 John 564
LEONARD, Henry 269 Joshua W
 469
LEPPER, Ed 449
LEPURD, Isaac 516
LERCH, J 291 J V 268 Jesse 291
LETTERHOSE, Joseph 447

LEWIS, 110 259 Charles 320
   Isaac 283 J R 455 James 441
   554 Jas 565 W H 474
LEYDEY, John 280 Mary 280
LIBERTY, Township 175 548
LIBRARY, Public 400
LIEBE, Nicholas 448
LIEBEL, Leo 448
LIFE, In The Woods 192
LIGHTCAP, J B 455
LINCOLN, Abraham 454 572 Mr
   363 President 89
LINN, M B 455
LINTON, William C 221
LIOENGOOD, J 287
LITTLE, Thomas 446
LITTLER, Melinda 575 Nathan
   576
LIVERS, J T 394
LLOYD, D P 564 Thomas 416 637
LOCKE, Charles N 411 E 318
   Otis T 411
LOCKHART, Robert 496
LOCKWOOD, Samuel M 439-440
LOESEBER, Malachi 283
LOESSER, John 244 447
LOGAN, 80 Col 26 D S 277 Gen
   26 Wm 566
LOGANTOWN, 9
LOHR, Mr 421
LONG, 285 546 J W 455
LONGWITH, Thomas 481
LONSOWAY, Joseph 599
LONSWAY, Peter 540
LOOKER, Othneil 677
LOOKINGLAND, Mary Ann 301
LOOMIS, 248 260 472 Eleanor
   373 G D 259 George 400 John
   D 339 372 400-402 L M 342-
   343 346 Mr 245 Ruel 528
   Wildman 416
LOOS, John 291
LORD, Frederick 359 Robert D
   462
LOTT, James 341 Peter 604

LOTT (cont)
   Reuben 550
LOUDON, Township 174 552
   Township Pioneers 569
LOUIS, XVI 25
LOUISANA, Purchase 671
LOVE, Andrew 250 328 J W 343-
   344 449 James 323 James W
   344
LOVEJOY, George E 458
LOW, R 455
LOWE, John R 460
LOWRIE, Jacob 287 Sarah 287
LOWRY, Lieut 32
LOYD, Thomas 543
LUCAS, 318-319 Gov 305 424-425
   429-434 436 599 Robert 304
   538
LUCE, D S 567
LUCKEY, Dr 389
LUDLOW, 659 Louisa L 579
LUDWIG, Mr 573 Samuel 576
LUGENBEEL, A 245 340 Andrew
   260 306 318 422 637 Elizabeth
   306 Jemimah 307 Judge 302
   307 594 Mrs 307
LUGENBUL, Andrew 248
LUNG, H B 458
LUTES, Nelson B 325 384
LUTNER, David 448
LUTZ, G W 576 Harry 344 M T
   575 Matilda 575 Nathan L
   458
LUZADER, J 486
LYE, Joseph 599
LYNCH, 66 Daniel 550
LYONS, John 349
LYSLE, R 347-348 Robert 278
   462
LYTLE, 659 Gen 204 Rebecca 380
   Robert C 207 W H 471-472
   William 207
M, E Church 274 P Church 289
M'CAULEY, John 383
M'COLLUM, E J 394

M'EWEN, William 522
M'PHERSON, William 625
MACHEBEOUF, J P 290
MACK, S M 619
MACKFELD, John 448
MACKLIN, L A 562
MADISON, Mr 203-204 206
　President 40 84
MAGERS, J E 636 James V 633
　Joseph E 422 629
MAINZ, Andrew 318
MALONY, S G 566-567
MALOY, Dennis 636
MANARY, James 678
MANECKA, 564
MANGES, John 599
MANGETT, J 487
MANLEY, 608
MARCHUP, Rev 283
MARION, Gen 444
MARKS, Clements 596
MARQUARDT, J F 348
MARQUART, F 595
MARSH, Peter 277 523
MARSHALL, Judge 683
MARSONY, John 323
MARTAIN, Mr 619
MARTIN, 500 Barbara 418 534
　Charles 344-348 Edgar 469
　Frank W 460 H B 394 J C 502
　James T 635 John 280 John C
　493 499 Lambert 285 Melkiah
　448 R M C 418 Robert 535
　Robert C 635 Robert
　M'candish 534 S E 620 S H
　455 Sameul S 637 Samuel 533
　Samuel S 318 533-534
　William 458
MASON, 246 436 Alexander 328
　Gov 432 434 Judge 67 M M
　320 Stevens T 429-430
MASSIE, 202 Col 35 Gen 199 Mr
　666 Nathaniel 668
MASSON, Franz 600
MASSONY, Joe 550 Littia 385

MATHERS, James 164 210
MATHEWS, James 540-541
MATHEWSON, William B 586-587
MATSON, 139
MATZ, John 283 Neri 283
MATZENBURG, Louisa
　Christina 251
MATZINGER, J 284
MAULE, Elizabeth 541 John 541
　Mr 512 542 Mrs 542
MAURER, Mr 262
MAURY, Gottlieb 283 Samuel 283
MAY, 376 Emma L 563 John M 351
MAYER, Frederick 268 Louis 271
MAYNARD, Dr 590
MCALLISTER, Mr 558
MCANNELLY, Moses 439-440
MCARDLE, Ed 407 J P 406-407
MCARTHUR, 40 83 87 319
　Duncan 69 78 530 685 Gen 84
　Gov 67 358
MCBRIDE, Frank 538 Maria 538
MCBRIDGE, F 454
MCCARTHY, 564
MCCARTNEY, Henry 637
MCCARTY, Nicholas 221
MCCAULEY, John 341 355 635
　Judge 353 362 William 613
MCCLEARY, T J 295
MCCLELLAN, Joseph 497
MCCLELLAND, 16 500 A B 418
　Harrison 422 Jane 540 John
　14 Joseph 149 493 540 636 Mr
　541 Robert 636
MCCLUER, James W G 277
MCCOLLISTER, Hamilton 527
MCCOLLUM, 259 Dr 264 E J 342 394
MCCOMB, William 298
MCCORMACK, J E 346-347 John
　E 342 458 O 454 William 605
MCCORMICK, William 593

MCCRACKEN, William V 468-469
MCCULLOCH, 170 William 145
MCCUTCHEN, John 277 Joseph 326 347
MCCUTCHEON, Joseph 72-73
MCDONALD, Bedan B 461-462 Henry 627
MCDONEL, A T 564 568
MCDOUGAL, Silas 628
MCELHANY, Pattie D 393 R L 393
MCELVAIN, Andrew 326
MCEWEN, 523 James 417 522 Mr 485 Sarah 522 William 522 Wm 507
MCFARLAND, Dr 245 249 262 J A 339 389 394 Mrs 249 William 664-665
MCFERREN, Ezekiel 277
MCGAFFEY, Mr 511 Neal 166-167 171 351 358 487 635 Neil 373 633
MCGEE, Mr 117
MCGRAW, Charles 462
MCGUIRE, Adget 289
MCILVAIN, Col 116
MCINTIRE, James 481 John 668 Mr 666
MCINTOSH, Laughlin 13 Mr 559
MCKAY, George 430 433
MCKEE, Capt 411 H L 469
MCKELLEY, Robert 326 441
MCKETRICK, S 623
MCKIBBEN, James 615-616 John 615 Wright 628
MCKINLEY, 18
MCKINSTRY, J P 54
MCKITRICK, 626 Alex 628 Samuel 332
MCKNIGHT, 650
MCLAIN, John 277 Mattie 332
MCLAUGHLIN, Geo 418
MCLEAN, Gen 375 John 73 358 538

MCMAHON, James 276 Maj 32
MCMEEN, R R 50 Sophia 287
MCMEENS, 485 Ann C 470-471 Dr 68 John 447 Mrs 68 R R 52-55 307 342 471 Robert R 470 472-473
MCMILLEN, Morrison 587
MCMILLON, Morrison 586
MCMULLEN, Archibald 446
MCNAMEE, Father 290
MCNEAL, 120 314 389 507 550 A 311 314 Maria 360 Milton 114 165 167 169 243 358 360 634 Mr 510-511
MCNEIL, 245
MCNUTT, 92 Alexander 109 128 Daniel 109 128 Mr 109
MCPHERSON, 626 Col 87 Father 617 Mr 625 O J 617 William 615 617
MEAD, Chambers 107 Mary 107 Nancy 107 William 481
MEDICAL, Society 394
MEEHAN, A 314
MEEKER, Charles 525 Mr 161
MEIGS, Gov 90 645 Josiah 204 Judge 673-674 Return J 39 Return J Jr 303 675
MEILE, A M 292
MELCHER, Gottlieb 446
MELMORE, A Poem 148
MENDENHALL, J W 276 294 345
MENG, Joseph 596
MERCER, 407 James 246
MERCHANT, Hiram 449 W B 449
MERGENTHALER, Jacob 552 569
MERGUNTHALER, Wm 564
MERKELBACH, Emma 332 John 419-420
MERRIMAN, Nathan 616 618
MESSAGE, The First 668
MESSER, Ephriam 633 John

MESSER (cont)
461-462
METCALF, Ebenezer 619-620
George 619 627 Judge 354
METZ, Abr 554 Venie 332
METZGER, Catherine 482 D 369
Daniel 482-483 Henry 369 482
Samuel 483
MEXICAN, War 446
MEYER, Henry 615 Jacob 494
John 448 Joseph 350 M Anton
292
MEYERS, 251 Christ 446 J C 620
MIASMA, 214 243
MICHAELS, John 550
MICHENFELDER, J A 292
MICKEY, I N 564 James L 565
Jeremiah 553
MIFFLIN, Thomas 302
MILES, Milton F 458
MILITIA, 449
MILLBINE, J C 633
MILLER, 33 285 550 A K 455
Aaron 447 Abraham 543-544
Anna Margaret 248 C H 421
Col 571 D D 554 D M 627 D R
562 Daniel 448 David 469
Henry 449 460 521 Isaac 284
J W 248 320 342 Jacob 448
Jacob C 458 Jacob W 178 John
285 540 Jos 420 Joseph 418
Louis 419 Mary 591 Michael
419 449 Mr 411 527 Nicholas
449 Orlando 620 Paul 315
Peter 599 Philip 484 Samuel
616 620 Thomas W 460 V J
627 W H 627 W M 628
William 447 616 620 William
H 627
MILLERWEIS, John 448
MILLHIME, Jacob C 555 634
MILLIGAN, John 668 Mr 664 666
MILLIMAN, John S 462
MILLMORE, Mr 89
MILLON, William 628

MILLR, Joseph 500
MILLS, Daniel 109 Eben 543
Ebenezer 109 Isaac A 51 Wm
S 51
MIM, John 146 169
MINER, Isaac 220 Mr 146
MINERVA, Mrs 325
MITCHELL, 472 Dr 651 Isabella
542 John 665 Lenora 332
Robert B 461 Samuel 345
MITCHNER, M W 628
MITOWER, Andrew 283
MITSELL, Elizabeth 505
MOES, John 486
MOESHINGER, J U 350
MOHAWK, Indian 307
MOHR, Thomas 284
MOLER, Mr 512 Rollin 210
MOLIN, L 466
MOLLER, Rollin 165
MOLON, L 292 M 290
MOLTZ, M R 620 Mrs 628
MONEY, Scarcity Of 215
MONNET, Dr 205
MONROE, James 303 Mr 204
President 45 170
MONTCALM, 137
MONTGOMERY, 109 James 45
90 95 109 123 128 164 276 289
593 John 361 Kaziah 90 Mr 46
91-92 118 131 Rev 509 Sally
45 91 123 128 W N 359
William 91 93 128 Wm 512
MONUMENTAL, Association 50
MOORE, 123 544 Andrew 402
615-616 636 Henry H 460 J P
268 584 L 562 Maurice 624
Mr 95 625 R B 277-278 Rev
278 Zopher T 298
MOOREHEAD, Wm G 54
MOREHEAD, John 446
MORGAN, 318 G W 387 M E 564
MORITZ, M A 268
MORMONS, The 647
MORRIS, 659 J L 460 Thomas

MORRIS (cont)
Fitz 345
MORRISON, Arthur 418 Road 162
MORROW, 659 Jeremiah 220 668 Mr 666
MORSE, Francis C 460 Francis H 460 John F 554
MOSFOOT, Charles 462
MOSIER, Jacob 458
MOTT, 355 390 Chester R 326 354 Judge 353
MOUND, Builders 120
MOUNTS, Mrs 507
MOW, Lyman W 458
MUCK, Philip 615 618
MUELLER, C 680 Carl 419 Christ 448 Christian 310 419 M 284-286 564
MUELLERWEIS, J 447
MULHOLLAND, Henry 488 Hugh 486
MUNGEN, Col 457
MUNSEL, Mr 499 Roswell 497-498
MURPHY, 397
MURRAY, 608 Benjamin 607
MUSGRAVE, Elijah 599 Harriet 599 Judge 403
MUSGROVE, Elijah 417
MUSSER, Daniel W 564
MUSSETTER, 564 L D 566 568
MUSSEY, Elder 397
MUSSY, 390
MUTCHLER, Marshal C 680
MUTSCHLER, Carl 448 Charles 637
MYERS, 259 422 Ann 516 B F 332 B M 564 C 285 David 516 George 516 J C 616 J M 409 James 508 515 517 James C 460 516 Jennie 516 John 481 515-516 Maria Louise 516 Martha 516-517 Mr 411 414 P P 328 Peter P 635 Rosa 333 S

MYERS (cont)
A 418 Sally 517 Sarah 516 Seraphim 457 W C 416 W W 680 William 481 483 Wm 455 Wm L 455 Wm P 462
NAETH, Henry 596
NAPOLEON, 422 445 568 The First 251
NASH, George 663
NAU, John 284
NAYLOR, 254 C T 456 Ed 309 J M 309 339 John M 403 W W 339 William W 403
NEELY, F 454
NEFF, John F 462 Ruth C 397
NEGILE, C F 291 William C 290-291
NEIBEL, Levi 494
NEIKIRK, 507 590 D J 341 D M 341 348 Jacob 416 John 341 Jonas 249 Mary 249
NEIL, 394 Mr 398
NELIGH, John 340 Mr 541
NELSON, 58
NESTLERODE, Mr 548
NESTLY, Henry 494 Samuel 494
NEUHART, Jacob 462
NEUMEYER, Ignatz 594 John 596
NEUSCHMIDT, J G 279
NEVERS, John 356
NEVIN, J W 273 John W 271 Rev Dr 272
NEW, Fort Ball 146
NEWBERRY, J S 222
NEWBINGER, George 449
NEWCOMB, S E 566
NEWHOUSE, J 567 Jacob 567
NEWKIRK, Jacob 618
NEWMAN, John 469 494
NIBERGAL, Philip 285
NICHOLS, 114 564 Amos 416 593 Isaac 586 J H 456 Jonathan 587 Robert 418
NICHOLSON, Frances 361

NICHOLSON (cont)
  James 360 Thomas 164 593
NICOLAI, E 291 Fred 345
NIGHSWANDER, Gen 367
  Samuel 629 636
NILES, Henry 475
NIMMS, Judge 674
NISLEY, Henry 497 Samuel 497
NO, Precious Gem Etc 185
NOBLE, 259 Alice M 381 Belle
  381 Birdie M 325 H 347
  Harrison 239 322-325 381 384
  546 Harry H 325 J A 566 John
  381 568 K N 441 Mary 381
  Mary E 381 Mary Ellen 381
  Minerva 239 Montgomery 381
  462 Mr 325 382 Rebecca 380
  W P 342-343 346 385 388 401
  635 Warren F 386 Warren
  Frederick 381 Warren P 324-
  326 333 335 339 359 441 467
  546 561 Warren Perry 380-
  381 Washington 323 William
  380 546
NOEL, Elizabeth 483 Elmira
  Emily 559 John 445 483-484
  Michael 559 600 Mr 601 Mrs
  484 Nicholas 481 483-484
NOLAN, Mrs 243 Samuel 331
NORRIS, 258 564 Bazell 447 Eli
  166 246 265 320 637 John T
  250 Lloyd 250 393 402 531
  Lott 591 Mary R 393
  Nathaniel 591 P T 568
  Warner 446 William 501
NORTON, A Baldwin 468 C 550
  Charles A 458 J A 388 James
  A 441
NUBEL, N 314
NULL, Jacob 550
NUSER, John 308
NUSON, Joseph 456 Wm 456
NYMAN, 260 Mr 245 Philetus
  400
O'BRIEN, 564

O'CONNOR, D 398 Dr 383 398
  John D 395-396 Mrs 398
  Rebecca 396 Ruth C 397
O'FALLON, John 54
O'LEARY, Thomas 460
O'SULLIVAN, M 290
OAKLEY, 140 170
OBERHOLTZER, J G 562
OBERMILLER, F X 292
ODD, Fellows 342
ODLE, 425-426
OFFICERS, County 629
OGDEN, G M 369 Robert G 462 S
  M 339 525 636 Stephen M 635
OGLE, 312 545 550 A 314 B F
  454 Benj F 544 Elizabeth 280
  F 314 J C 398 Joseph 280 540-
  541 543-545 Mrs 545 Thomas
  544 William 449
OKEY, Judge 398
OLCOTT, Charles 351
OLCUTT, David 566
OLD, Man The 194 State House
  The 656
OLDS, Horace D 462 Martin 481
  W B 628
OLENTANGY, 10 17
OLEVIANUS, Casper 282
OLIVER, 435 Robert 207
OLMSTEAD, Jesse S 165
OLMSTED, 536 538 564 Annie
  557 David 517 535 Elisha 517
  Judge 557 Mr 517 556
OMSTED, 147 George 95 Jesse
  95
OPT, Henry 636
ORGANIZING, County 164
  Territory 23
ORME, A J 456
ORPHANS', Home 613
ORR, Friend 572 Polly 108 111
  Thomas J 441 Widow 110
ORTON, Edward 222
OSBORN, Hartwell 460 Joseph
  165 587 Mr 586 Ralph 207

OSCEOLAS, 446
OSTEEN, John G 261
OSTER, Mrs 256
OSTMER, Sylvester 628
OTT, Elizabeth 253
OUDIT, C G A 447
OURAND, T W 342 Thomas 249
OVERHOLT, 564
OWEN, David E 177 248 318 401 439 508 634 686 David Evan 302-303 Edward 495 Evan 302 H W 346-347 Jerusha 303 John 54 Kate 563 Mr 304-306 687 William 494 Zelaphel 497 Zeliphant 494
OYLER, J 342
PACKER, W F 54
PACKET, Lieut 63-64
PADDLEFORD, Sedate 572
PAGE, H N 55
PAINE, John 445 481 483 John W 231 441 William 483
PAINTER, Mary 542
PALMER, A 456 Andrew 430
PANGBORN, James 628
PAPINEAU, Mr 111
PARCHER, Lyman 462
PARISH, 376-377 Frank 351 Mr 209 O 351 378
PARK, C C 346-348 416 Christ C 417 George 165-166 245-246 320 543-544 John 244 260 362 W H 458
PARKER, 117 376 512 Benazah 116 125 Edward 198 Mr 209 William 590
PARKS, C C 344-345
PARMENTER, Joseph 163 607 Lafayette 628
PARMETER, Charles 468
PARSONS, Dr 50 Mr 663 Samuel Holden 662 Usher 52 54-55 62 67 Wm C 462
PATRICK, Richard F 460 Shepherd 125

PATTERSON, 152 J W 322 328 James 393 416 James M 458 John 429 John W 326 424 Mary E 393 Mr 433 648 Peter 207 William 169 527 635
PATTY, Rev Mr 619
PAUL, 83 John 668 Mr 666 W H 395
PAULI, Fritz 448
PAULL, John 265
PEAS, John R 326
PEASE, Calvin 351
PECK, Albert E 460 Benjamin 605 Lewis 460
PEER, John 486 Ph 486
PELAN, James 345-346
PELON, James 277
PELTON, Henry J 460
PENCE, James 416
PENN, Gulielma 374 William 374
PENNINGTON, 147 381-382 388 Adam 535 B 248 342-343 Caroline C 374-375 Edward 374 Eugenia Hargrace 374 Gulielma 374 Isaac 374 John 497 Joseph 374 Josephine 248 Louisa Annette 375 Maria 392 Mr 375 R G 331 336 371 402 Robert G 359 374 392 460 463 S 416 Sarah 374
PERKEY, 500 Christopher 497 Henry 494
PERL, Nicholas 486
PERO, Theodore C 458
PERONG, John 550
PERRY, 41 52 54-55 58-59 64-68 A H 590 Commodore 47-48 50-51 56 62 O H 61 Oliver H 57 R G 590
PERSING, Henry W 460
PETER, 552 Abraham 569 Jacob 569
PETERS, Mrs 199 W J 283 Wm J 283
PETERSON, Matson 444

PETIT, Thomas T 460
PETTICORD, John 483 John G 462
PETTINGER, Benjamin 174 243 John 243
PEW, Cora 333
PFEIFER, Mathias 350
PFEIFFER, Peter 421 Ph 420
PHELPS, Col 674 Ezra P 458
PHILHARMONIC, Society 420
PHILIPS, George S 458
PHILLIPS, A 416 Allison 181 Boss 263 329 D H 387 Daniel H 249 289
PHILO, Jonathan S 627 Joseph 590
PIERCE, William 150 589
PIERSON, Christopher Y 243 W S 54 Wm S 52 54
PIKE, 128 Abner 92 109 112 144 164 593 Asa 164 593 Asel 109 Hiram 109 114 Phineas 109 Samuel 109 Silas 109 117
PILLARS, J P 346 James 355 386 532 James P 321 Judge 353 529
PIONEER, Association 415 Residences 247
PITKIN, W 51
PITMAN, H C 633
PITTENGER, 403 Alma H 418 Ann C 470 Benjamin 255 308-309 416-417 637 Charles W 308 Dewit C 418 J A 416 J H 308 331 339 384 416 John 255 307-309 470 John H 363 Judge 308 403 521 Julia Ann 307 Mary Ann 309 Theresa 309
PITTINGER, Benjamin 245 248 John 245 Theresa 248
PLANE, Jacob 248 320 329 634 Squire 264 544
PLANK, Roads 317
PLANTS, 355 Josiah S 354 Judge

PLANTS (cont) 353
PLATT, James H 386 Susie R 332
PLAUQUETTE, 421
PLEASANT, Township 174 570
POCKMYER, Wm H 456
POINSETT, J R 305
POINTER, Jonathan 502
POITS, N 564
POLITICS, 317
POLK, Mr 476
POLLOCK, J F 278
POOL, 573-574 Cyrus 326 George W 458 Joseph 173 210 540 Rob W 460 Robert W 460
POORMAN, 604 Capt 369 Flora 333 Jessie 332 John 342 446 S F 454
POPE, Alexander 682 Franklin 462
POPPENBURG, Conrad 266
POPULATION, 1880 631
PORK, 117 Peter 116 125
PORTER, Benj S 458 Mary 203
POWELL, A 562 John 550
POWERS, Edwin H 460
PRATT, 147 Jonas 426 Orson 650
PREBBLE, Joshua 446
PRENTICE, Alonzo F 458
PRESBYTERIAN, Church 277
PRESS, The 406
PRICE, Jacob 416 418 528 535 603 Nancy 418 P J 318 527 Philip J 495 526
PROBASCO, George 446
PROCTOR, 40-41 66 82 138 Gen 44-45 48 84
PROTESTANT, Episcopal 276
PUFFENBERGER, George 512
PUGH, Cora 421
PUMPHREY, James B 469
PURCELL, Bishop 290 Father 308 J B 292
PURDY, 147 608 H 607 J 352 378 James 351 376

PUTNAM, 659 Mr 666 Rufus 25 668
PYATT, Moses 481
QUINN, Edmund 290 James 564 Mr 314
RADER, Frank 411
RAGAN, George 250
RAHAUSER, F 283 Frederick 281 283
RAILROADS, 265
RAINEY, Robert 552
RAKESTRAW, H B 636
RAMSBURG, Christian 280 Susanna 280
RAMSEY, John C 458
RANCH, J J 456
RANDALL, Mr 537
RANDOLPH, John F Jr 469 P G 474
RANEY, Judge 373
RANGES, 156
RANK, A 547 Aloys 447
RANKER, Joseph 251 448
RAPP, Jonathan J 458 Jonathan R 458
RAPPE, A 293 Bishop 290 Rev Bishop 466
RAUCH, F A 271 273
RAUKER, Joe 328
RAUTH, Margaret 604
RAWSON, 258 381-382 511 527 A 311 351 Abel 107 117 145 168 177-178 339 356 360 374 402 416-417 507 625 635 Allen A 360 Alonzo 359 407-408 Aurinia H 360 Edward 356 Homer C 360 Lemuel 356 Maria 360 417 Mr 175 244 248 352 357-359 363 378-379 386 Mrs 314 360 Sarah 356 Sarah Ann 358
RAY, H H 456 Thomas J 458
RAYMOND, 276 Abraham 581 George 578 581 Isaac 581 Jacob 581 William 417

READ, Elijah 578 581 Levi 578 Mr 317 Seth 174 578
REAME, P H 448
REASEY, Levi 511
REBELLION, War Of The 452
REBER, Mr 150 493
REDD, J 456 N 342
REDMAN, James A 458
REECE, G H 567
REED, Ira B 462 J T 497 John T 494 Josiah F 408 R B 386 Seth 169 Township 174 578
REEME, E W 346-347
REESE, J D 633 John 552
REESER, Frederick 460
REEVES, David 481
REGIMENTS, Raised 457
REID, 337 Eliza Boyd 501 John T 500 Mr 501 R W 336 346-347 Rufus W 113 336 345 Samuel W 468 Sylvia Ann 113 Whitelaw 462
REIF, 286 John 350
REILEY, John 668
REILY, Mr 664-666
REIN, Rev 279
REINBOLT, Daniel 550 Elizabeth 547 John 547 552
REINHART, Michael 608
REINIGER, Gustavus 593 Gustavus G 596 Mr 597 Rosalia 597
REIS, Daniel 599 Philipina 564
REITER, Daniel 284
REMELE, 511 John 248 464
REMMELE, 259
RENDLER, Anton 447
RENTZ, Fred 449
REPP, Charles W 386
REPRESENTATIVES, 441
RESERVATIONS, Sale Of 160
RESSEQUIE, Noah P 445
RETTIG, George 285
REUTLINGER, Otto 421
REVENUES, Surplus 316

REVOLUTIONARY, Soldiers 444
REX, Jeremiah 629 634 Laura J
　A 629 Mr 630 Susan 629
　William 285 629
REYNOLDS, 139 Joseph 197
　Richard 73 486 W 207
RHODES, Joseph 341
RICE, Ann 93 108 111 Caleb 93
　109 112 126 571-573 Daniel
　93 95 109 111 572 593 David
　108 164 Deborah 572 George
　H 627 Levi 620 M B 571 Mr
　109 Stephen 627 Susannah
　572 Uretta 573
RICHARD, Daniel C 286 James
　677
RICHARDS, Joseph 418 508
　Nathan 446
RICHARDSON, 522 538 James
　555 Joseph 164 Wm P 456
RICHART, J F 563 568
RICHTER, L 284-285
RICKENBAUGH, David 280 287
　513 571 Jacob 402 513 John C
　386 Margaret 513 Mr 288
　Samuel 513 571
RICKETS, John 119 552 Rezin
　119 Thomas 540 William 119
　543
RICKLEY, S S 331
RIDENOUR, William 448
RIDER, Squire 485
RIDGELY, John H 384 Richard
　497
RIES, Balthasar 327 Francis 419
　J Ad 448 John 419 Joseph 486
　Mr 328 P Frank 448
RIFE, Francis 416
RIGBY, William J 561
RIGDON, 652 Sidney 648-649
　654
RIGG, Capt 466
RIGGS, Charles H 468-469
RIGS, Amon 448
RIKER, Ephraim 181

RINE, Abraham 416 481
RINEBOLT, Abraham 546
　Samuel 546
RINEHART, Peter 486
RINGELI, Yacob 292
RINGLE, David 615 George 615
　627 John 620 S A 618
RININGER, 617 William 620
RISDON, David 144 164-165 167
　481 487 535 542 549 552 593
　616-617 636-637 Mr 109 162
　553
RITSMAN, George 287 Mr 288
RITTER, Mary 483
ROBB, George 285 599 Sarah 645
ROBBINS, Alonzo 468-469
　Charles D 460 John 411 N P
　566-567 R 460 Rudolphus 460
　W D 565-566 568 William D
　567
ROBERT, James M 462
ROBERTS, Ansel C 589 Betsey
　107 David 107 Emma 587 589
　James M 462 Jane 589 Rhoda
　588-589 T 599 Timothy B 587
　Timothy P 149 527 586 588
　636
ROBERTSON, 550 James 546
ROBINSON, 500 E F 554 Gain
　497 Horace 460 James 498
　John 277 Judge 494 L E 395
　Lowell 149 493 497 637
　Lyman 494 Mrs 493 Rev Mr
　619
ROBY, Inman 417
ROCKWELL, George 446
RODEGEB, Jacob 497
ROELLE, William 448
ROGERS, E 512 Eliphalet 109
　128 508 Hannah 128 Henry
　109 John W 628
ROHRER, Benoni 341 Isaac 494
ROLEY, E 599
ROLL, Sophia 256
ROLLER, Frederick 51 448

ROLLINS, 109 111 126 Almon 128 Mary 128 William 112
ROOP, 500 David 494 618 Josiah 348 369
ROOT, 421 Abner 347
ROSE, 16 A 562 Leopold 349 Maj 17
ROSECRANS, 472
ROSEFELT, Thomas 446
ROSELL, David 447 John 447
ROSENBAUM, Oswell H 469
ROSENBERG, John A 544 Mr 287
ROSENBERGER, 512 Henry 542 John 542 549 John A 210 Joseph 540
ROSS, Stephen 117
ROTHFUCHS, John 285
ROUCH, Charles 456
ROUK, Aloys 446
ROUSE, Kaziah 90
ROUSEAU, 472
ROWE, George 370
ROYER, Isaac 283 J Calvin 386 Jared 283 John 283 608 John Sr 283 Manam 283 Mr 613 Samuel 283
ROYERS, John 590 Samuel 231
RUBEN, Charles E 566
RUCH, 500 Andrew 449
RUETENICK, Rev 279
RUGG, S J 561
RUIE, Jacob 543
RULE, Albert A 484-485 Barbara 484 Byron 485 Catharine 484 Daniel 481 483-484 Daniel C 485 Eleanor 485 Elizabeth 484-485 Isaac 485 Isaac P 485 Jane 484 Lucy 485 Mary 485 Matilda 485 Samuel 287 484-485
RUMBAUGH, Nicholas 549
RUMLEY, Gen 96 Mr 95
RUMMELL, George 300-301 Jane 300-301 Mary Ann 301 Mr 302
RUMPLE, Conrad 552 Jacob 552
RUNDELL, Chancey 590
RUPE, Rev 294
RUSE, Aaron 448 540
RUSH, Mr 431
RUSK, Richard 431
RUSSELL, H C 475 H H 462 Rebecca 239
RUST, H 268 270 286 Rev 294
RUTENICK, H J 284 J H 268 O U 268
RYAN, Corporal 143 Patrick H 636
RYNO, Henry 578
SAFFORD, George H 460
SAINT, John's B S 348 Joseph's Catholic Church 289 Mary's Catholic Church 289 Patrick's T A Society 345
SAINTCLAIR, 26 30-32 139 Arhur 662 Arthur 25 28 207 Gen 29 663 Gov 36-37 197-198
SAINTJAGO, Rivera 56
SAINTJOHN, Henry 416 445 476 478 558 593 Spencer 416
SALEM, Church 290
SALTZMAN, M 562 N 562
SAMPSON, Ezechial 587 Ezekiel 210 G W 71 73 347 George W 595
SAMS, Edith 386
SAMSEL, 284
SAMSON, W A 691
SANDEL, W B 283 Wm H 283
SANDERS, Anthony 596 J L 280 John L 280 Joseph 449 Moses C 579
SANDERSON, W F 370
SANDS, Sarah 331
SANFORD, Benjamin 578 David 633
SARGENT, James 668 Mr 663 666 Winthrop 662
SAUER, Amelia 332
SAUL, Samuel 636

SAW, Mill 244
SAWYER, Helen M 334 Judge 334 Victoria 333
SCALPS, Invoice Of 121
SCAMMER, J Y 54
SCANNEL, Michael 421
SCHABACHER, Jacob 448
SCHAMMEL, Fred 449
SCHANY, Louis 488
SCHATZELL, 564
SCHAUB, Jacob 285
SCHAUFELBERGER, 564 F J 566 J W 566 568 William J 561
SCHAUL, Michael 210
SCHECKEL, P C 448
SCHEER, Jacob 599 Philip 599
SCHEIB, P 344-345 Philip 349
SCHEIBER, 259
SCHERER, Christian 600 J 285
SCHEUING, Carl 448 Daniel 448
SCHEURERMAN, L F 291
SCHICKEL, Adam 251 419
SCHILLER, 470
SCHIMMES, Benjamin 349
SCHIMP, Ph 626
SCHINDLER, Anthony 486 488 Carl 419 486 Charles 487
SCHIRAK, 486
SCHIRK, Mary 600
SCHLACHTER, M 486
SCHLEMMER, Christian 568
SCHLERRET, George 449
SCHLOSSER, Peter 280
SCHMID, Jacob 284
SCHMIDT, Valentine 310-311 447
SCHMILT, John 419
SCHMITT, Conrad 594 Henry 447 Joseph 448
SCHMITTUZ, Peter 448
SCHNEIDER, 286 Christian 419 Justin 448
SCHNITZ, N 292
SCHOCH, 309 608 George 283 H

SCHOCH (cont)
H 525 Hannah 252 Henry 275 Michael 252
SCHOCK, George 612 Henry H 418 Margaret 418 Mr 613
SCHOENDORF, Peters 608
SCHOENHENZ, Rev Father 290
SCHON, Michael 486
SCHOOLS, Of Tiffin 328
SCHOUHART, 259
SCHRIKEL, Frederick 350
SCHROYER, George 280
SCHUBERT, 259 550 Ludwig 290
SCHUCH, Peter 517
SCHUETZ, Catharine 252
SCHUHMAN, Carl 447
SCHUK, Peter 522
SCHULTZ, Fred 564 Peter 543
SCHUMACHER, 285
SCHUPP, N 291 Rev 294
SCHUSTER, George 550
SCHUYLER, 588 620 ---- 636 Aaron 626 J F 469 628 John B 578 Josephus E 469 Lieut 467 Mr 581
SCHWAN, F W 394
SCHWANDER, 522 Barbara 518 Caroline 519 Edward 518-519 Eliza 519 Elizabeth 518 Etelia 519 Frederick 517-519 Hannah 519 Jacob 518 520 James 518-519 John 518-519 Joseph 519 Mary Ann 519 Sarah 519 Stephen 519 Thomas 519
SCHWARTZ, Alexander 596 Augustus 385 John B 385 633 Littia 385
SCHWARTZMILLER, George 448
SCHWARZENBERG, Moses H 448
SCIPIO, Township 165 586
SCOBY, George A 469
SCOTHORN, Samuel 210 578
SCOTHORNS, Samuel 515

SCOTT, C D 564 Capt 425-426 E
　H 565 Gen 31-33 309 415
　Thomas 207 665 Winfield 54
SCOVILLE, William 591
SEA, 378 Gen 369 371-372 532
　Mr 377 Sidney 366-368 370
SEARLES, 147 E B 346 Eliza A
　418 Hez 525 Hezekiah 418
　535-536 Joel 342 John 163-
　164 445 514 535 William D
　249 330
SEAVAULT, Isaac 628
SECHRIST, John 287 Mr 288
SECKMAN, Benjamin 576
SECRIST, John 521 Margaret
　521
SECTIONS, 157
SEECHRIST, Joseph 343
SEED, F M 628
SEELY, Mr 434 Uri 429
SEEWALD, 251 256 263 Charles
　456 Elizabeth 256 Louis 255-
　256 418 448 Louisa 252
　Ludwig 255 Philip 248 252
　255-256 278 417 Philipina 252
　Phillip 416 Sophia 255-256
　Valentine 248 252 278 Will
　419 William 256
SEGUR, Harriet 115
SEIBENALER, 486
SEIFERT, George 449 Mr 537
SEIGCHRIST, Ch 447
SEIPEL, 286
SEIPLE, W J 567
SEIT, 500
SEITS, John 441 Noah 149
SEITZ, Elder Lewis 416 John 149
　176 178 441 494 496-497 525
　636 John Jr 495 Lewis 494
　496 499 Noah 497 502
SENATORS, 439
SENECA, Blues 446 Township
　163 593
SENER, Charles 456
SENEY, 255 259 355 Ann 296

SENEY (cont)
　Ann E 416-417 Frances 361 G
　E 346 George E 354 362 375
　399 462 Henry 362 Joshua
　248 296 318 330 352 360-362
　375 387 409 634 655 Judge
　353 561 Mr 362 386
SEPPARD, Isaac 628
SEWARD, W H 54
SEXTON, Miron 418
SEYMOUR, Horatio 414
SHADE, Mark 627 Mr 628
　Samuel 315 416 615
SHAFFER, A L 287 John B 628
　Rachael 287 Samuel 494
SHAKES, 213
SHALER, Charles 434 Mr 434
　436
SHAMACHER, Fred 285
SHANNON, 318-319 George 574
　Gov 370 Wilson 370
SHANTS, 692
SHATTNER, George 284
SHAUFELBERGER, 564
SHAULL, 512 Bartholomew 542
　544 George 541 Hiram 267
　281 M 269 Samuel 448
SHAUTS, John 499
SHAW, Emma 563 George H 637
　J W 496 S 285-286 Samuel
　284 Silas W 634
SHAWAN, R W 330
SHAWHAN, 259 338 379 394
　Elvira 299 F K 464-465 468
　680 Frederick 297 444 G D
　416 Josiah 299 Maria 418 Mr
　299 681 R W 113 245 328 336
　339-340 401 416-417 680
　Rezin W 297-298 326 359
SHEDENHELM, George 556
SHEELY, W 628
SHEETS, Henry 524 John 447
SHEFFIELD, George 232
SHELBY, Charles 481
SHELDEN, 536 Henry G 462

SHELDON, 258 T H 342
SHELLER, Henry 552
SHEPARD, S W 588
SHEPHERD, Abraham 677 Col 138
SHERER, Jacob 284
SHERIDAN, Gen 468
SHERK, Abraham 613 Esq 612 Samuel 613
SHERMAN, 659 Charles R 351 John 372
SHERTZBERG, A 456
SHERWOOD, 512 Capt 508-509 522 Jeanette 128 Mary 128 Mr 511 W D 460 William D 114
SHEURERMAN, L F 290
SHILLER, John 552
SHINNERS, Benjamin 323
SHIPMAN, Horatio M 460
SHIPP, Ensign 44
SHIPPEY, 119 Dorcas 109 Nathan 109 Polly 109 Widow 109
SHIPPY, 572 John 540 Nathan 552 Robert 540 543 546 Widow 92
SHIRK, Joseph 232
SHOEMAKER, Catharine 629 R M 359 487 587
SHORT, Col 45
SHORTS, Hubert 449
SHOUP, W 628
SHOUTZ, Henry 546
SHOWMAN, George 494
SHREINER, A 456
SHREY, G A 564
SHRINER, Andy 457
SHRIVER, Ann Marie 287 Elizabeth 287 Frederick W 280 Jesse 462 Mr 518 William 287
SHUBACH, Jacob 285
SHUEY, E L 562
SHUGAN, W 314

SHUMAN, John 462 Simon 286
SHUMARD, Dr 471 George G 472
SIBERAL, John 576 William 445
SIBLEY, Judge 201
SIEGCHRIST, Christian 419
SILAS, Joseph 117
SILCOX, 617
SILVA, L A 50
SILVERS, John 448
SIMMONS, T C 564
SIMONIS, Peter 177 565
SIMONS, Silas W 458
SIMPSON, J W 620
SINGER, 313 F 315 381 Frederick 330 Mary E 381 Mr 312
SINGLETON, Capt 654
SINK, Holes 616
SISTY, Curtis 250
SIVILS, James 342
SIX, John H 449
SKINNER, Morris P 387 417 441 636
SLART, M 456
SLAVERY, 25
SLEEPER, John 540
SLOAT, S C 456
SLOMAN, 259
SLOSS, Susan 629
SLOSSER, George 542 Isabella 542 Mary 542 Peter 542 S O 564
SLOVER, 15 21-23
SMALL, George C 322
SMELTZ, Frank 627
SMITH, 313 430 550-551 564 Abraham 591 Alexander 347 Capt 70 Charles 231 Charles M 460 Daniel 336 David 108-109 114 165 167 170 447 507 511 536 542 634 Edward 374 Elisha 112 357 507 511 Elizabeth 541 Ethan 618 F 401 Hiram 650 654 J 456 J C 462 J S 348 James 344 347

SMITH (cont)
627 Jerusha 303 Joe 264 364
649-652 654 John 668 676
Jonathan 348 Joseph 596 653
Kirby 461 Leonard D 462
Louisa 259 M 568 M H 467 M
Hoadley 469 Martin 446
Moses 150 566 589 615 Mr
356 664 666 Permelia 514
Peter J 495 R E 564 Robert
339 Russell 446 S A 458
Samuel 541 Sidney 352 366-
367 587 635 Solomon 446
Susan 287 W H 448 William
446 629 637
SMOYER, 313
SMYTHE, David 278
SNEATH, 258 263 312 536 A G
298 339-340 Jane 300-301
Laura B 401 Mr 300-301 511
Richard 243 246 299 329 510
S B 339 416
SNELSON, Thomas 499
SNIDER, John 370
SNOOK, Elizabeth 417 Harriet
239 Henry 239
SNOVER, L 456
SNOW, 604
SNYDER, 259 301 328 556 A W
680 Abner 468-469 Augusta
300 Barbara 251 Caspar 458
Christopher 142 251 299-300
327 447 D M 564 D W 567 J
W 456 Jacob 290-291 John
251 299 Mary Ann 519 Mr 302
O P 300 344 Otto P 449
Philipena 300 Simon 287 303
William 519
SOHN, 286 A 447 Caroline 519
Ephraim 448 Henry 447
James A 418 448 John 344
William 519
SOIL, The 225
SOLDIERS, In The War With
Mexico 446 Of The War Of

SOLDIERS (cont)
1812 445
SOLOMON, John 73
SOPHER, J H 456
SOUDER, 259 Catharine F 418
Elizabeth A 509 Francis 251
278 H H 348 Jacob 255 475
517 Jemimah 307 John 114
251 289 416-417 509 542
SOURWINE, 615
SOUTER, C W 448 Frank J 460
Ph 447
SOUTHERLAND, Edward 502
SOWERS, Charles H 467 469
SPADE, Adam 483
SPARKS, J S 369
SPAULDING, 649 John 647-648
Solomon 647-648
SPAYTHE, Henry A 458
SPEAKER, Henry 615 Henry Jr
618 Henry Sr 618
SPEIER, William 419
SPEILMAN, David W 386 N N
346 422 Philip 634
SPELZ, John 448 Peter 447
SPENCER, Abraham 586 Jesse
112 145 168 170 208-209 John
628 Joseph 628 Mr 171 210
511 590 S H 458 Samuel 627
SPICER, 112 116 118 128 141 572
James 108 John 108 Little
Town 108 118 Mr 114 Small
Cloud 108 118 485 Small-
cloud 137 William 108 110-
111 115 126
SPIELMAN, Nath N 418
SPIER, Capt 679
SPIES, George 349 420
SPILTER, 599
SPINDLER, H C 343 346 J C 349
Mrs 256
SPINK, Cyrus 146 James 146
John C 351 387
SPITLER, Jacob 497 Lewis 497
629 Martin 598

734

SPITTER, Lewis 422
SPONABLE, 147 Mr 536
SPOONER, Henry K 460
SPRAGUE, 544 572 C D 278 Ezra 92 109 Francis 92 109 George 394 Willard 92 109 Williard 543
SPRAUS, 285
SPRECHER, Margaret 513 Samuel 513
SPRINGER, Andrew 486 J C 566-567 Philip 535
SQUIRE, Elbert J 462
STACKHOUSE, Joshua 574
STADTMILLER, Carl 419
STAGE, Barbara 484 Luke 484
STAHL, Elizabeth 547 George 546 Henry 547 Jacob 285 Michael 546
STAIB, Elizabeth 256 Elizabeth C 597 Jacob 593 597
STALEY, C R 565 Henry 391 Mrs 249
STALTER, 692
STANLEY, Mrs 110 117 119 Tabitha 107 W B 235
STANTON, Benjamin 396
STARKEY, E A 565
STARKWEATHER, Mayor 67 S 54
STARN, S 564
STATE, Organized 37
STATTER, D J 412
STAUB, Dr 250 John 246 250 Margaret 571 Mrs 250 Philip 571
STAUCH, Rev 282
STAUFER, T F 285
STAUNTON, Sec Of War 463
STECKEL, Clara 286 Francisca 287 H L 344 William 286-287
STEEL, James 494
STEELE, 498 Caroline C 375 W R 375
STEIGMEYER, 615 F H 618

STEIGMEYER (cont)
Frederick 619 John 619
STEINBAUGH, Adam 590 Philip 590
STEINER, Capt 507 Frances Hannah 250 Joe M 393 John J 250 347 352 446 463 634-635 Laura 393
STEINMETZ, Augustus 283
STELTZER, W 349
STEM, Col 464-466 Jacob 176-177 245 481-482 Jesse 374 385-386 Leander 386 461 M E 308
STEPHENS, Maj 599
STEPHENSON, Dr 109 114
STEPLAR, J A 284
STERN, Jacob 306 Jesse 359 Leander 346
STETTER, Henry 283
STEVENS, Benjamin 552 Guy 249 260 J M 249 346-348 James 535 James D 615 James M 148 417 460 634 Mr 586 William 587
STEVENSON, Dr 484 E W 344 James D 623 627
STEWART, A M 161 Archibald 418 589-590 F R 562 564 566 Francis R 458 James W 589 John 73 John M 554 Martha 590 Mr 505 Polly 417 Samuel 286 608
STICKNEY, E T 339 348 360 369 441 588-589 Emma 587 589 Gen 587 Maj 433 Mayor 430 Mrs 588 T 433 436
STILES, 486 Mrs 34
STILLMAN, Charles M 460
STILLWELL, Elizabeth 485 Isaac 422 485 636
STINCHCOMB, J W 495 John 497
STINER, D R 568
STING, C H 250 Charles 323

STIPPICH, Michael 594
STOCKTON, R F 51 Thomas 370
STOKES, Lieut 66
STOLZENBACH, H J 343
STOMBAUGH, John 546
STONE, A P 337 Charles M 460
  Christopher 167 169 637 Dea
  588 Ezra 351 Joel 320 635 W
  F 51
STONER, 114 259 509 Celesta
  332 Christian 280 507 D C
  448 Dennis 507 George 280
  402 507 510 512 514 542 547
  636 Henry 286 J 447 John 507
  510 512 540 P 456
STORES, 243
STOUT, Bartholomew 497
STOVE, Works 399
STOVER, Benjamin S 395 John
  540 W H 394
STRANDLER, 623
STRANNLER, 618
STRASSBAUGH, George 448
STRASSNER, F 284-285
STRAUSBAUGH, George 601
STRAUSS, Stephen 283
STRAWMAN, J G 564
STREBIN, John 602 Maria 602
STREET, Belinda 630
STRICKER, Samuel 342-343
  Simon 419
STRIKER, Bernhart 419
STRIPE, 508 William 544
STROH, 500 John 497
STRONG, Asa 608 Ira E 386
  John 244 Luther M 458
  Lyman 608 Michael 284 Mr
  377
STRYCKER, Simon 245
STUCKY, Philip 284
SUGAR, Making 210
SUGHRO, Kate 333
SULLIVAN, 259 C J M 322 345 E
  W 394 Gerald E 385 Jeremiah
  221 Rev Mr 264

SURVEY, 156
SUTHERLAND, Edward 497
SUTPHEN, J V D 430
SUTTON, Isabella 490 Lester 616
SWALLEY, Abel 456
SWAN, Gustavus 167 370
SWANDER, 286 517 Ed H 341
  Edward 252 Hannah 252
SWANNAGER, Charles 449
SWARTZ, Alexander 596
SWASEY, David 500
SWAYNE, N H 433
SWEITZER, W A 449
SWIGART, George 284 John 339
  Mr 536
SWIMM, Gittie 117
SWOOPE, James A 344
SWOPE, Daniel 546
SYCAMORE, Township 173
SYMMES, John Cleves 25 Mr 663
TABOR, Benj C 460
TAFT, Ira 488
TAGGART, Henry C 462
TAGGERT, Henry C 462
TALBOT, Paul 500
TALIOFERRO, W T 56
TANNER, August 627
TAPPAN, Benj 220 Judge 38
TAUMPLER, Louis 251 Valentine
  251
TAXES, 441
TAYLOR, 63 415 A 447 Bayard
  217 Jonathan 429 Mark 343
  Mr 434 Nathaniel 565
  President 373
TEACH, J 456 Mathias 495
TELEGRAPH, 327
TEMPELMAN, William 487
TENNIS, John 552
TERRY, Ira C 460 John 402 578
  636
THAMES, Battle Of The 48
THAYER, Sarah J 268
THEIL, 680
THEISSEN, Michael 293

THEURER, J G 290-291
THOMAS, C W 566 E W 547 554
  Jacob 460 Tina 563 William
  553
THOMPSON, David 628 Father
  501 Fred 628 Geo W 374 John
  628 T 571 Thomas 276 416
  570 Town 613 Township 607
THORPE, F S 52
THRIFT, Robert W 458
THURWAECHTER, H G 456
TIFFIN, 146 198 201 Additions
  To 242 259 Corporation 320
  Diathea Madison 197 Dr 205
  Edward 36-37 147 197-198
  200 202 207 430 663 665 667
  671 673 675 677-678 690 First
  Plat Of 242 Gov 196-197 199
  203-204 206 639 662 Joseph
  207 Light Guards 449 Mary
  199 203 Mr 666 676 Mrs 206
  Officers Of 322
TILDEN, Daniel 439
TINGLE, 564
TIPPECANOE, 39 49
TITUS, 550 Augusta P 576
  Colena M 576 Elvira S 576
  Flora 576 Littie 576 R R 341
  441 484 576 Rasselas R 575
TIVENS, Elizabeth 484
TOD, David 390 Gov 463-467 471
TODD, 592 Col 54 John 627
  Lance 591 Lance L 417 M B
  627-628 Mary 591 Samuel 541
  Thomas 591
TOLAN, Henry 474
TOLEDO, War The 424
TOLL, W 402 William 416-417
  637 Wm 173 475
TOMB, 259 B 360 Benjamin 276
  326 336 338 359 375
TONER, 422 Kate 391
TOOMB, Mr 120
TOPOGRAPHY, 222
TORRY, Sabeah 490

TOUCEY, Isaac 54-55
TOWNSHIP, Lines 157
TOWNSHIPS, Organized 163
TRAIL, Greensberry 494 James
  494 Notley 494
TRAUB, Louis 50
TRAVIS, J N 454 Mahitabel 584
TREAT, 500 Julius 495 Samuel
  440 Thomas T 495
TREXLER, Etelia 519 Francis
  519
TRIMBLE, Allen 164
TROTHE, Christ 350
TROUTS, John 461
TROWBRIDGE, R E 71
TROXELL, B 314 D 454 David
  494
TRUE, John 567
TRUMBO, Enoch 546 636
TUFF, Tom 675
TULLER, A 359 Elvira 299
TUNISON, D C 342 680 T C 346
  Thomas C 386
TUQUANIA, Louis 123
TURNER, Benjamin 445
  Benjmain 550 Capt 64 Henry
  447 Mr 663 Mrs 551 Rachael
  K 550 William C 458
TWISS, 147 A H 607
TYLER, Comfort 673-675 Dr 391
  Morris C 458
UHLMANN, J B 292-293
ULRICH, 251 L 421 Louis 349
  421
UMLOR, David 608
UMSTED, E 314
UNDERHILL, 147 David 607
  James 607 Jasper 607 Mr 613
UNITED, Brethren Church 287
UPDEGRAPH, Mr 666 Nathan
  668
URCHEL, Peter 566
URSINUS, Zacharias 282
VAIL, George W 458
VALENTINE, 500 John 494 497

VALENTINE (cont)
    500
VALLMER, Paul 349
VANATTA, 508 Thomas 507 517
    522
VANBUREN, 318-319 Martin 86
    415 President 304
VANBURENITE, Salutatory 655
VANCE, 319 659 Gov 265 358
VANDENBURG, John 458
VANDENBURGH, Henry 416
VANESS, 261 Peter 260
VANFLEET, Col 425-426 434-436
    James 637
VANMATRE, 529 Daniel 529
    John 529-530 John Jr 531
    Susan 530
VANMETER, 537 539 John 529
    531 Johnny 532 Susan 531
VANMETRE, 529 Reserve 158
VANNATTA, Thomas 536
VANNEST, 599 Peter 347-348
VANPELT, Frankie 333
VANSE, Joseph 144
VARNUM, James Mitchell 662
VENICE, Township 615
    Township In The War 627
VETTER, Adam 488
VOGEL, Sarah 270
VOLLMER, 251 Dan 448 Joseph
    293 447
VONBLON, 286 Paul 447 Philip
    447 533
VONBLOU, Mary Louisa 310
    Philip 310
VONDENBROECK, John 292
VONLUTENAN, C H G 268
VONLUTERNAU, G 279
VORIS, Mr 398
VOSBURGH, H I 554
WADE, Abner 552 M S 370
WAELFLING, Bathasar 350
WAESNER, Andrew 419
WAGGONER, 258 John 593
    Samuel 336 359 402 441 517

WAGGONER (cont)
    527 540
WAGNER, Adam 447 F J 314
    Frances 401 Francis 114 349
    421 449 634 Frederick 604
    Isabella 421 John 486 564
    567-568 Michael 594 Molly
    421 Pauline 421 Peter 543 T
    285 Theobold 600 Xavier 448
WAHL, Fred 283 Frederick 283
    285
WALDING, J S 565
WALKER, 246 511 542 Catharine
    593 Elizabeth A 509 John 424
    509-510 594 Joseph 114 180
    239 289 345-346 Mrs 259
    Rebecca 239 William 105 594
WALLACE, Charles 458 William
    625
WALSH, T F 345
WALTER, Michael 284
WALTMAN, Margaret 521
WANDER, Mr 279
WANK, John 594 596
WANNER, Peter 488
WAR, Of 1812 39 445 Records
    400 With Mexico 446
WARNER, Benjamin F 99 134
    136 Benjamin Franklin 137
    Kon-ke-pot 136
WARREN, Henry B 460
WASHINGTON, 13 416 474 518
    573 657 659 684 Gen 14 20-21
    31-32 197 297 444 537 George
    94 198 Guards 447 President
    663
WASHINGTON'S, Sympathy 16
WASHNICH, J 456
WATCHER, L 456 N 456
WATER, Works 400
WATERSONS, Daniel 348
WATS, Henry 448
WATSON, 147 250 485 C K 347-
    348 Caroline 373 Caroline S
    373 Charles B 373 Cooper K

WATSON (cont)
372 387 D G 456 E J 418
Eleanor 373 Eliza 538 Eliza
Boyd 501 Flora 576 James 447
535 John 574 Joshua 486 497
Littie 576 Margaret 418 Mr
574 Nettie 373 Oliver 287
Oliver S 576 Pliney E 460
Robert 576 Sylvester 590
Thomas W 573 636 William
535 William A 538
WAUGAMAN, A L 394
WAX, John 418 Sarah 418
WAY, Asa 369 M V 437
WAYNE, 32 69 Anthony 31 Gen
33-34 78 86 297 444 560
WEAVER, 564 A 568 Jehu 627 W
554
WEBB, 483 John 637
WEBSTER, 495 Jacob 497 Jasper
F 462
WEEKS, Dr 495 George 495
WEHRLE, George 487 M P 447
Xavier 447
WEIDMAN, J 454
WEIKERT, C 540 Peter 593
WEINICH, Charles 420
WEIRICK, 259 692 Levi 342
Sheriff 337
WEISBAUGH, 564
WEISBECKER, Henry 448
WEISENBERGER, George 594
WEISGERBER, Rev 279
WELCH, 147 536 Eliza 538 Felix
538 Henry 146 553 Hugh 164
537-538 John 164 537-538
Judge 373 539 Margaret 538
Maria 538 Martin 537-538
Mrs 539 Polly 538 Thomas
164 537
WELL, Flowing 610
WELLER, H J 342 385 402 Henry
J 386 633
WELLS, Col 44 D 394 E C 635
William 33 446

WELSH, Hugh 109 418 482 522
John 440 522 O 565 567
WELTER, Michael 419
WENG, John 596
WENNER, Wm 285
WENTWORTH, John 54
WENTZ, Ph 259 Philip 278
Phillip 416
WERLEY, John 635
WERNEMENT, 487
WERZ, Henry 284 John George
284
WEST, Ezra 481 Mrs 502 Nancy
418 Thomas 418 493-494 499
599 615 617
WESTBROOK, C T 586 Cornelius
T 587
WESTERN, Exchange 247
Reserve 155
WETMORE, Benjamin 165 Chas
J 481 Wm 54
WETZ, 146
WGGONER, Frederick 488
WHALEN, James 349 Thomas J
341
WHARTON, George L 410 Mr
411 415
WHEATON, Joseph 627
WHEELER, Alfred 460
WHIPPLE, John 277 Sgt 152
WHITE, Elmer 411 G W 456
Isaac H 458 Judge 373 Lyman
417-418 578 William P 578
WHITECKER, James 114
WHITELY, 355 Judge 353-354
WHITEMAN, Abraham 483
Daniel 483 Harman 448 Jacob
483 Samuel 169 481 483
WHITICKER, Jas 166
WHITMAN, Benjamin 37
WHITMER, 364 David 652
WHITMORE, Benj 166 Benjamin
167-168 636 James 607
WHITNEY, 147 Eli 607 Jasper
607 613 Mr 614 Mrs 613 692

WHITNEY (cont)
　Nathan 165 607 613 William
　607 Williard 581
WHITTACKER, William 458
WHITTLESEY, Elisha 51 357 431
WICKHAM, Charles F 460
　Charles P 460 Frederick W
　469 William S 460
WILBER, E J 447
WILCOX, John 150 589 Mary 150
　589
WILDISIN, Eliza 288
WILDMAN, Frederick A 460
WILHELM, Adam 177
WILKERSON, 153 Gen 152
WILKINS, Ross 54
WILKINSON, J E 564
WILKISON, John E 563
WILLARD, Caroline 373 Dr 421
　Edwin R 268 G W 268
WILLIAMS, 205 220 258 429 564
　A S 563 B D 579 Cal 522
　Caleb D 469 Celia 332 Col 571
　Dr 174 580-583 Harriet Newel
　579 J H 468 James 477-478
　480 Jeremiah 416 444 John
　418 447 L G 568 Louisa L 579
　Micajah T 219 R 346 Reuben
　173-174 259 445 508 514 536
　637 Rev 276 294 Richard 179
　343 386 410 634 Samuel 201
　207 Susannah 570 T B 473
　William 517 582 William H H
　567
WILLIAMSON, 16 David 14
WILLIARD, G W 286 George W
　273 287 W G 394
WILLOUGHBY, James 618
　Mentor W 469
WILLOW, George 637 John 447
WILLS, Bazabel 668 Mr 666
WILSEE, Elizabeth 151
WILSEY, J D 496
WILSON, 180 564 Col 466-467 J
　W 340 402 Jacob 674 James

WILSON (cont)
　494 James R 502 Joel W 267
　386 410 440-441 554 595 635
　John 554 668 Judge 433 Mr
　93 179 263 341 466 503 666 P
　164 593 P J 344 Pardon 109
　Sophronia 572 Thadeus 345 W
　T 468
WINCHESTER, Gen 40
WIND, Mills 190
WINELAND, W S 344
WING, Col 436 Ed 525
WINSLOW, A H 454
WINTERS, Eli 496
WINTHROP, Edward 348
WINWEILER, 692
WIRT, 318 407 William 318
WISE, Catherine 482
WISEMAN, Andrew 565 J 567
　567
WITCHES, Killing Of 119
WITHELM, John 593
WITTER, Amos 581 Isaac B 590
　Jonathan Sr 590
WITTMER, John 292
WITZ, Christ 521
WOLF, Gen 31 Jacob 446 James
　447 508 Jesse 400 John 517
　Scalps 171 W 419 William 349
WOLFE, 564 Jacob 593
WOLFF, George D 281 Henry 448
　William B 448
WOLLENSLAGEL, Christian 283
　Conrad 283 George 283 John
　283 John Jr 283
WOLLY, Michael 486
WOLSEY, 153
WOOD, 83 433 436 Amos E 439-
　440 Gov 90 Judge 353 O V 566
　Reuben 51 352 371 William
　296
WOODBURY, Levi 304
WOODCHOPPER, The 182
WOODER, Moses F 461
WOODS, Elijah 667 Mr 666

WOOLEN, Mills 399
WOOLET, John 618 Samuel 618
WOOLF, J A 568
WOOLFORD, C 488
WOOLLET, John 615
WOOSTER, Col 461 Judge 382 Moses F 461
WORMAN, John J 566-567
WORMLEY, Aug M 460
WORSTELL, John P 348
WORTHINGTON, 200-202 659 Gov 199 James T 91 157 Mary 199 Mr 203 664 666 Robert 199 Thomas 199 220 668 675
WRIGHT, Charles A 393 Col 644-645 Cyrus 481 Eli 444 Hannah E 393 John 113 586-587 637 Judge 358 Mariah 113 Nathan L 318 Samuel 113 Sylvia Ann 113
WURICK, 692 Jesse 635 Levi 635
WYANDOT, Treaty 71
WYANT, David 283
WYATT, David 230
WYGART, Tunis 232
WYLLYS, Maj 28
YAEGER, Joseph 419
YAMBERT, John 593
YAMBRIGHT, A 599
YARGER, John H 458
YARNELL, Lieut 47
YEAKY, Henry 117 Peter 210
YEUTGEN, John 448
YINGAT, 521
YINGLING, C J 344 George T 462
YINGST, 692
YORK, Matilda 485
YOUNDT, Daniel 449
YOUNG, 486 America 195 Brigham 654-655 C C 566

YOUNG (cont)
David 552 Isabella 490 J M 293 Jacob 447 John 277 488 John A 449 Mr 489 Peter 540 Samuel 489-490 Sarah A 271
YULEE, D L 477 479
YUNG, Charles 350
YUNKER, D 456 Samuel 546
YUNT, 564 J T 568 Simeon 566
ZAHM, Anthony 608 Charles L 411 George 608 Henrietta 252 Henrietta E 630 J M 235 252 410-411 608 630 Jacob M 418 634 Janet C 631 Louis 457 Mr 412 Victor J 629-630 634
ZANE, 15-16
ZARTMAN, Mary 332
ZEICE, Daniel 447
ZEIGLER, 259 George W 449 John 286
ZEIS, Charles 286 Christopher 251 Elizabeth 541 Jacob 550
ZEISBERGER, 35
ZELLER, O C 339
ZEPPERMICK, John 581
ZERBEE, A S 268
ZIEBER, William K 281
ZIGLER, George W 264
ZIMMER, 550 Capt 464 Jacob 349 448 Louis 419 468
ZIMMERMAN, Barney 286 550 636 C 279 F 284 Frederick 495 H 268 Henry 510 Rev 294
ZINSER, J G 290-291
ZINT, James J 458
ZOELLER, William 447
ZOLLIKOFFER, Daniel 393
ZOUAVES, 449
ZUIT, B 343
ZWINGLE, Ulric 282

www.ingramcontent.com/pod-product-compliance
Lightning Source LLC
Chambersburg PA
CBHW071212290426
44108CB00013B/1165